U0498082

图书在版编目（CIP）数据

重塑人文学：中英人文对话（第一辑）/ 王淑英等编.
—北京：商务印书馆，2023
（中英高等教育人文联盟学术集刊）
ISBN 978－7－100－23008－7

Ⅰ.①重… Ⅱ.①王… Ⅲ.①人文科学 — 教学研究
— 高等学校 — 文集 Ⅳ.①C41-53

中国国家版本馆 CIP 数据核字（2023）第175892号

封面题签　刘　石
封底题词　胡显章

重塑人文学
中英人文对话
（第一辑）

王淑英　杨　华　何伟文　李　利　编

商 务 印 书 馆 出 版
（北京王府井大街36号　邮政编码 100710）
商 务 印 书 馆 发 行
上海盛通时代印刷有限公司印刷
ISBN　978－7－100－23008－7

2023年11月第1版　　开本 710×1000　1/16
2023年11月第1次印刷　印张 39¾　插页 22
定价：198.00元

中英高等教育人文联盟学术集刊

总策划简介

颜海平，清华大学清华学堂世文首席教授、清华大学世界文学与文化研究院院长、国务院第七届外国语言文学学科评议组成员、教育部清华大学中外人文交流研究中心主任、中英高等教育人文联盟执行理事会主任兼秘书长。2014—2020年任清华大学外国语言文学系主任。毕业于复旦大学，后于康奈尔大学获得硕士与博士学位；在美执教二十余年，先后任加州大学洛杉矶分校和康奈尔大学终身资深教授。现任康奈尔大学Diacritics学术指导董事会成员、普林斯顿大学出版社中国学术董事会成员。主要著述聚焦跨国族女性主义、跨文化现代主义、批评性世界主义研究，获学术奖项三十余项。代表著述与论文有《中国现代女性作家与中国革命》《互为的转写：生成的现代性》《全球迁徙者的登场》等。任商务印书馆"世界主义与中国经验"（Cosmopolitics）丛书作者与主编。

早年本科期间发表十幕大型历史剧《秦王李世民》，获文化部和全国剧协授予1981—1982年全国优秀剧本一等奖。该剧收入2009年《曹禺剧本奖作品选》。

主编简介

　　王淑英，现为香港中文大学社会学系教授暨敬文书院院长，中英高等教育人文联盟出版委员会主任。曾任香港中文大学协理副校长、亚洲比较教育学会联席主席。毕业于英国利物浦大学，后于美国斯坦福大学取得硕士及博士学位，并曾在美国和日本多所大学任教。曾获颁美国国家教育学院的斯宾塞博士后研究奖励和日本学术振兴会杰出研究员等荣誉。曾获香港研究资助局、英国经济（ESRC）社会研究理事会及香港研究资助局合作研究计划等多项重点资助；2005年度获颁香港中文大学校长模范教学奖。主力研究教育社会学、比较历史社会学及制度主义和组织。

副主编简介

　　杨华，武汉大学历史学院教授，中国教育部人文社科重点研究基地武汉大学中国传统文化研究中心主任，国家社科基金重大项目"中国传统礼仪文化通史研究"首席专家，主要从事先秦秦汉史、中国文化史，尤其是中国古代礼制方面的研究。出版有《先秦礼乐文化》（1997）、《新出简帛与礼制研究》（2007）、《古礼新研》（2012）、《中国礼学研究概览》（2021）、《古礼再研》（2022）等专著，发表论文130多篇。

　　何伟文，上海交通大学教授，从事早期现代英国诗学、现当代英国小说和西方古典文论方面的研究，出版专著《为诗辩护：菲利普·锡德尼的人生和诗学》（2023）、《艾丽丝·默多克小说研究》（2012），译著《艾丽丝·默多克传》（即出）、《华盛顿广场》（2020）、《漂亮冤家》（2014，2016，2017）、《官僚的正义》（2005）等，发表论文《锡德尼之死：一个英国文化偶像的塑造》等。

　　李利，埃克塞特大学应用语言学教授，主要研究教师认知、"应用"会话分析、思维技能和新科技在语言学习中的应用。在国际刊物发表60多部作品，主持了多项国际研究项目，承担业界核心期刊编委和特邀编辑。出版专著 *Language Teacher Cognition*（2020）, *Social Interaction and Teacher Cognition*（2017）, *New Technologies and Language Learning*（2017），编著 *Thinking Skills and Creativity in Second Language Education*（2019）, *The Routledge International Handbook of Research on Teaching Thinking*（2015）等。李利教授也是大学助理副校长，主持人文、艺术与社会科学学部的全球战略及参与。

学术支持

清华大学世界文学与文化研究院

Institute for World Literatures and Cultures, Tsinghua University

联盟学校名单

清华大学
Tsinghua University

北京大学
Peking University

北京外国语大学
Beijing Foreign Studies University

复旦大学
Fudan University

上海外国语大学
Shanghai International Studies University

武汉大学
Wuhan University

香港中文大学
The Chinese University of Hong Kong

埃克塞特大学
University of Exeter

伦敦大学亚非学院
School of Oriental and African Studies,
University of London

伦敦国王学院
King's College London

伦敦大学学院
University College London

拉夫堡大学
Loughborough University

曼彻斯特大学世界和平研究中心
Manchester University Peace Studies
Institute

剑桥李约瑟研究所
Needham Research Institute of Cambridge

牛津大学中国中心
University of Oxford China Centre

雷丁大学世界电影研究中心
Centre for Film Aesthetics and Cultures,
University of Reading

华威大学人文研究中心
Humanities Research Centre, University of
Warwick

2016

———————

上 海

———————

中英大学人文与智库对话

首届中英大学人文对话嘉宾合影

中英高等教育人文联盟倡议发起仪式合影

首届中英大学人文对话嘉宾与学者发言

首届中英大学人文对话学者发言

首届中英大学人文对话代表合影

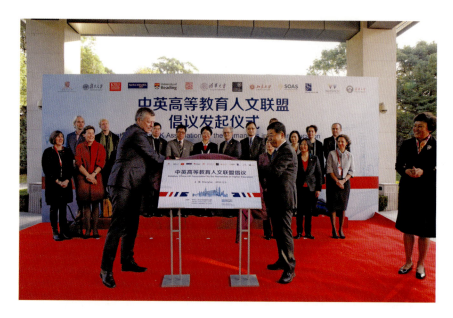

中英高等教育人文联盟倡议揭幕

中英高等教育人文联盟倡议发起仪式签字现场合影

2017

牛 津

交汇：创造历史中的中国与西方
（牛津大学）

第二届中英高等教育人文对话嘉宾发言

第二届中英高等教育人文对话会场

第二届中英高等教育人文对话学者发言

第二届中英高等教育人文对话校长论坛现场

第二届中英高等教育人文对话代表合影

颜海平和田海共同主持联盟执理会工作会议

中英高等教育人文联盟发起倡议

2018

———

香　港

———

中国与人文

（香港中文大学）

第三届中英高等教育人文峰会学者代表发言

第三届中英高等教育人文峰会嘉宾合影

第三届中英高等教育人文峰会圆桌论坛

第三届中英高等教育人文峰会主旨演讲

第三届中英高等教育人文峰会开幕式合影

第三届中英高等教育人文峰会会场

第三届中英高等教育人文峰会开幕式嘉宾合影

2019

——————

北　京

——————

全球性再想象：跨文化人文共同体与
另一种世界主义

（北京大学）

第四届中英高等教育人文联盟峰会嘉宾致辞

第四届中英高等教育人文联盟峰会学者发言

第四届中英高等教育人文联盟峰会主旨演讲嘉宾

中英高等教育人文联盟执理会现场

2019 年 中 英 高 等
2019 China-UK Humani

第四届中英高等教育人文联盟峰会合影

育 人 文 联 盟 峰 会
Alliance Annual Forum
2019. 12. 13

中英高等教育人文联盟首届青年学者论坛代表发言（复旦大学）

中英高等教育人文联盟首届青年学生论坛活动开幕式合影（清华大学）

2020

北京—线上

联盟执行理事会扩大会议
（含资深学者和学术委全体成员）
清华大学并在京盟校线下主场

中英高等教育人文联盟执理会清华大学主会场

中英高等教育人文联盟主席陈旭致开幕词

中英高等教育人文联盟执理会主任兼秘书长颜海平总结联盟工作

清华大学副校长彭刚致闭幕词

中英高等教育人文联盟执理会代表发言

2021

———————

埃克塞特—线上

———————

全球性再想象
（埃克塞特大学）

第五届中英高等教育人文联盟执理会线上和线下代表合影

第五届中英高等教育人文联盟学术论坛

专题 1：在不确定的世界中构建共同体，学者合影

第五届中英高等教育人文联盟学术论坛主旨发言与嘉宾致辞

第五届中英高等教育人文联盟学术论坛

专题 2：跨国身份、流动和旅行，学者合影

第五届中英高等教育人文联盟学术论坛

专题 3：大流行病时期的生物政治学，学者合影

第五届中英高等教育人文联盟学术论坛

专题 4：环境人文与可持续发展，学者合影

2022
————————
上海—线上 / 线下
————————

我们的文化，我们的世界

（复旦大学）

第六届中英高等教育人文联盟学术论坛开幕式嘉宾发言

第六届中英高等教育人文联盟学术论坛主旨演讲发言

第六届中英高等教育人文联盟学术论坛闭幕式嘉宾发言

第六届中英高等教育人文联盟学术论坛与会学者合影

中英高等教育人文联盟发起书

2016年12月6日，上海

当下的经济全球化，作为现代长时段历史中的又一个阶段，改变并且将继续改变着横跨所有国家和地区、为人类所共有的世界的面貌，它包含着人类历史上以前所未有的规模进行的人类和社会生活的再生产。经常有这样一种说法：我们生活在一个超高速发展、超高速转型的科技创新和经济增长的时代，这样一个时代使人的生存历史、心智记忆和人文想象变得无关紧要。而与此同时，越来越不确定的社会归属感，以及各种形式的文化狭隘主义的抬头或推进已经成为了全球性的现象，这一现象要求我们对于给世界带来巨大幅度的财富增长和发展机遇的科技变革与经济成就的文化使用展开思考。在这样的巨变中，以跨文化的知识创新生产和交流交融能力为重心的人文学术和人文教育具有了更为清晰的历史功能和重要意义。无论全球化的科技如何创新、经济财富如何强大，最为重要的是它们对所有人类个体、社群、民族和不同类型的国家在变化中相联、在相联中发展的作用方式。这对于现在和将来，犹如在过去的世界历史上一样，具有重大而全面的后效与影响。

本着这样的认识，清华大学提议成立"中英高等教育人文联盟"，作为不同高校之间在人文学术和人文教育的领域里进行跨文化、跨民族、全球性的对话、探讨和合作的长期机制。

Initiative: China–UK Association for the Humanities in Higher Education

Shanghai, December 6th, 2016

The contemporary era of economic globalization, as another phase of the *longue durée* of modern world history, has been changing and will continue to change the human geographies of the world across all nations and regions, involving no less than a reproduction of humanity and social life itself on an unprecedented scale in human history. It has often been remarked that we live in a time of superfast, hyper-transformative technological innovation and economic growth, when lived histories, the intellectual legacy of human beings and of their humanistic imagination are rendered all but inconsequential. Meanwhile, the deepening sense of social uncertainty and the ground-gaining of cultural parochialism in various forms have become a world-wide phenomenon, urging us to think about the usage and meaningful applications of the technological advances and economic achievements that have brought a dramatic growth of wealth and opportunity to the world. Amidst such sea change, humanities education centered on cross-cultural knowledge production and cultural exchange and transcultural collaboration has taken on ever greater historical significance. Whatever new forms taken by globalized technology, however vast the wealth accumulated, it is the ways in which these are articulated through the formation and reformation of individual human beings, communities, nations and countries of all kinds as well as of their relationships that ultimately matter, and matter tremendously with long-lasting consequence to the present and future, as in the past of world history.

In the spirit of such a recognition, Tsinghua University proposes the initiative of establishing a China–UK Association for the Humanities in Higher Education, as a cross-institutional mechanism for cross-cultural, transnational and global dialogue, exchange, and research collaboration in the humanities and humanistic education.

贺　词

习近平总书记在致清华大学建校105周年贺信中指出："清华大学开创了中西融汇、古今贯通、文理渗透的办学风格。"同年 12 月，由清华大学提议、12所中英核心高校共同倡议发起的国际人文组织"中英高等教育人文联盟"在上海成立，这正是对学校深厚的人文历史底蕴和独具特色的办学风格生动而具体的诠释。

同声相应，同气相求。融合之道，在于交流。作为清华大学2030全球战略中唯一的人文类国际学术组织，"中英高等教育人文联盟"在中英顶尖高校的国际交流与学术合作中发挥了独特而重要的作用，7年以来，来自中英两国顶尖学府的资深专家、青年才俊和莘莘学子以联盟为纽带，在人文学术和人文教育的领域里进行跨文化、跨民族、全球性的探讨合作，取得了丰硕的实质性成果。

《重塑人文学：中英人文对话》作为"中英高等教育人文联盟学术集刊"第一辑，是联盟成立以来学术交流和研究成果的首卷出版，汇集了高质量、原创性的学术著述，凝聚着中英学者的智慧结晶，通过"全球视野""文化比较""文化交汇""历史记忆""方兴未艾"五个栏目，充分展示了如何从跨文化的视角出发，在交流与对话中重塑人文学。

期待本文集成为展示前沿人文研究成果的重要窗口，在促进思想对话、推动文化交流、创新理论方法、培育青年人才等方面发挥新的作用。祝愿"中英高等教育人文联盟"越办越好，为深化中英两国人文交流、构建人文共同体做出更大贡献。

中英高等教育人文联盟主席　杨斌

2023年10月9日于北京

Message of Congratulation

I am delighted that the UK–China Humanities Alliance continues to grow from strength to strength.

The UKCHA is an essential forum for bringing together ideas and perspectives from across our academic communities to help deepen mutual understanding.

This landmark publication featuring contributions from across the UKCHA membership showcases the fruits of our collaboration, and we look forward to continuing to learn and to share through a spirit of positive engagement.

My sincere congratulations to the editorial committee.

Professor Lisa Roberts FRSB FRSA

President and Vice-Chancellor

University of Exeter

前　言

颜海平

    2016年12月6日，在上海举行的中英高级别人文交流机制第四次会议"中英大学人文对话"中，"中英高等教育人文联盟"举行了倡议启动仪式暨首届建盟学者论坛。倡议由清华大学发起，首批倡议高校共12所，分别为清华大学、北京大学、复旦大学、武汉大学、香港中文大学、牛津大学中国中心、剑桥李约瑟研究所、伦敦大学亚非学院、伦敦国王学院、雷丁大学世界电影研究中心、曼彻斯特大学世界和平研究中心、华威大学人文研究中心等。倡议高校和学者认为，在当下的国际语境中，更新中的人文学在增进文化交流和文明互鉴等方面的重要性日益显现；而推动源自不同语言和传承的人文学术和人文教育在对话与合作中发展，是高校的本务。作为中英师生进行跨文化、跨民族、全球性的对话合作机制，"中英高等教育人文联盟"成立执行理事会并通过联盟简章，拟从"中英高等教育人文联盟年度论坛""中英高等教育人文联盟青年学者论坛"和"中英高等教育人文联盟青年人才计划"三个层面推动联盟建设。建盟学者论坛上，提出了"跨学科对话""新人文经典"和"跨文化人文学"的理念。清华大学清华学堂世界文学与文化实验班（简称世文学堂班）首届2015级本科生代表发言，表达了"由阐释世界以叙述中国，以叙述中国而联接世界"的志业方向。

    翌年，第二届联盟2017年度学术论坛暨执行理事会在牛津大学举行。再一年，第三届联盟2018年度学术论坛暨执行理事会在香港中文大学举行；北京外国语大学、上海外国语大学、伦敦大学学院、埃克塞特大学、拉夫堡大学成为盟校新成员；执理会议题包括了听取和通过清华大学本科学生代表展示中英高等教育青年人才计划（China–UK Higher Education Young Talent Alliance，简称HEYTA）学生论坛的设想。主题为"寻人文创新之美，架中英沟通之桥"首届学生论坛于2019年4月在清华大学成功举办。同年9月，青年学者论坛的设想纳入联盟常设论坛"世界地图与世界文化"（World Maps and World Cultures，简称WMWC）系列，与英国社会科学院（British Academy）联合举办了"文学想象中的城市"专题论坛。同年12月，第四届联盟2019年度论坛在北京大学举行。2020年12月，中英高等教育人文联盟执行理事会扩大会议以线上线下相结合的方式在清华大学召开。会议听取了联盟四年工作的总结，秘书处创制的发展即成立以埃克塞特大学为定点的英方工作团队运行情况，中英盟校执行理事分享的参与联盟活动的合作经验与成果，中英学者代表就联盟学术发展提出的议案、议题和实施路径。至此，联盟启动伊始所设目标具体落地：17所中英高校和研究机构双方议事合作模式运行建制完成；年度学术论坛（UKCHA Forum）、"世界地图与世界文化"常设论坛（WMWC Forum）和青年学生论坛（HEYTA Forum）构成从前沿人文研究到基础人文教育三个层面的跨民族对话机制和跨文化学术实践。第五届联盟2021年执行理事会议暨年度大会圆桌论坛由清华大学和埃克塞特大学共同承办，以线上线下融合的方式在清华大学召开；随后由埃克塞特大学承办的年度学术论坛以线上方式举行。第六届联盟2022年度论坛暨执行理事会议由复旦大学承办，以线上线下融合的方式在复旦大学召开。以上所述，记录的是联盟从建盟到加盟的所有各层决策者、部处系科一线工作人员、中英资深著名学者、新锐青年教师、研究生、本科生，由理念认同到相遇推动，在面对不可预测的全球性困难和挑战中持续合作、守望同行的历程。联盟见证的是每一个推动参与者在世界上最可贵的珍宝，即所有人在人世间极为有限的生命时间。如果说2023年9月面世的英文版《翻译研究与中国》（*Translation Studies and China*）[1] 包含的是2022年第

---

[1] Haiping Yan, Haina Jin and Paul Gladston, editors and authors, *Translation Studies and China* (New York / London: Routledge Publishers, September 2023).

七届"世界地图与世界文化"论坛的部分开创性学术成果，本文辑承载的则是联盟从无到有、从零到一历程中踪迹回溯、几脉细流的生命纪念。鲁迅先生曾说大风浪中的人们哪能顾得上书写；联盟出版委员会诸君带着对置身充满尖锐不确定性的时代风浪中，从2016年起在联盟论坛上音容诚恳、明朗对话的中英同行的感怀，持之久远，选编出这首卷早期文辑，并准备续卷出版；而其中诸多学者留存文稿并专做修订在此首发，其中所蕴如何能够言表。很荣幸，与诸君如此共度逝者如斯的巨变七年。

回望历届联盟论坛（2016—2022），173位发言人，28位主持人，20位评议人；这涵盖资深和新锐的221位中英学人，母语和工作语言包括中、英、法、德、南非、南亚和更多的国别与区域的多个语种，专业领域和学术话语有文史哲社及其所属高校机构氛围特性之别；相互之间多数由联盟而相遇以合作。借助首届建盟学者论坛研讨中提出的"跨学科对话""新人文经典"和"跨文化人文学"理念路径，在以各自专业话语、领域框架、民族语种、文明传承为杠杆范畴，又跨出这些范畴一般规定的对话中，相互聆听、以求相识、抵达相联。在现代学科建制分科和学理规定限制下，这意味着对各自所属的不同专业领域和知识体系的某种在延伸中的超越、以超越求延伸的可能，氤氲着跨学科认知边界、跨知识体系常规、跨文化文明既成谱系的活力，指向人文学作为现代知识生产核心范畴的重构与命题增扩更新的可能，开启文化乃至文明观念的跨边界再书写。这是联盟发起书所表达的具体内容。历届承办盟校在主题的选择中贯穿了这一对话驱动和更新探索，2016年"中英大学人文对话"（China-UK Dialogue on the Humanities in Higher Education Forum）、2017年"交汇：创造历史中的中国与西方"（Connections: China and the West in the Making of History）、2018年"中国与人文"（China and the Humanities）；2019—2021"全球性再想象：跨文化人文共同体与另一种世界主义"（Re-imagining the Global: Cross-cultural Communities and Other Cosmopolitans）、2022年"我们的文化，我们的世界"（Our Culture, Our World），以及各主题下设含圆桌在内总数30个分论坛，记录了对话探索中获得的对人文学知识生产状态的三个逐渐清晰的共识：首先，对人文学范畴界定、学理构建和历史探讨长期以欧洲起源的地缘政治等级和语种区隔鸿沟为组织原则，忽视甚或排除中国和包括具体生活中的欧洲在内不可化约之世界经验的局限性的反思。其二，对"人文学"学理基础和"文明论"思考框架再定义的含义和需要，指向一种有别于欧洲式族裔中心主义及其复制变奏、更为多元、更富包容性的对生活世界和人文世界的想象，开启新的人文学地平线（more than humanisms）。其三，旨在推进人类福祉的数十年覆盖世界的科技与经济激变，同时催生了越来越不确定的社会归属感；各种形式的文化本质主义、狭隘主义抬头而成为全球性的现象；所有人类个体、社群、民族和不同类型的国家亟需有效想象在变化中相联、在相联中发展的路径可能、实践方式及包含其中的认知规则、价值坐标的重建；这一切日益指向以跨文化的知识创新生产和交流交融能力为重心的人文学术与人文教育的重要意义和历史功能。要言之，在批判长期主导人文学书写的"中心（西方）—边缘（中国/其他）"（the West vs the Rest）模式及其各种复制版本的基础上，我们需要讲述怎样的人类历史和世界故事？面对在世界范围内涌现的动荡、分歧、挑战与困惑，以言行事的人文书写，如何以对自己所属的专业领域和知识体系在延伸中更新、在超越中提升的具体探索和教研实践，由精专治学而联结和扩展跨学科、跨语种、跨文明的对话时空，坚韧地追问想象世界的方式和讲述世界的诸多可能。这亦是想象和讲述我们每一个的自己。[1]

以上共识在对话中逐渐出现形成，更多的或不同的共识还会出现；变化中的共识蕴含着也生成着当今世界人文学所面对的共性命题，这些命题在本文辑中开始获得表述呈现并可能由此进一步凝练；联盟学者将其中的核心要义概括为"重塑人文学"[2]。联盟第七届2023年度论坛由武汉大学承办，提案早在2020年执行理

---

1 2016—2022年联盟三个系列历届论坛及相关活动的参与专家和师生（含三年线上参与）总计近5000人。

2 感谢联盟出版委员会和联盟学者对此命名的讨论；感谢北京外国语大学张剑教授的最佳版本。

事会扩大会议上获得全体参会成员的支持；主题选择"共同面对：历史回望和未来图景"（Shared Visions: Humanities in Retrospect and Prospect），犹如对这一要义概括的预期和回应。出版委员会和联盟同行有理由期待，这些形成中和生成性的共性命题在后续联盟系列论坛和成果出版中进一步变得更具体、更宽阔；在参与专业领域发展的同时，在中英语境中获得其世界性的延伸、绽放其跨文化的生产性；在联盟学者青年师生不同专长精进的过程中有所作用，甚或逐渐延长变化、助力无限多样的教研成果和思想结晶。联盟出版委员会与商务印书馆上海分馆优异团队通力合作的启动，当逢其时。

　　"重塑人文学"的愿景，内在于人文学者人生志业所处的高等教育的发展愿景。建盟主席陈旭、2022年新任主席杨斌主持下的联盟执行理事会和诸位盟校理事所给予的制度性指导和支持，构成这一当代教育史上首个由中国高校提议、中英盟校共同倡议而诞生的合作平台的决策性建制。2021年联盟执行理事会议暨年度大会圆桌论坛以"全球性大学再想象"，提出了"大学作为一个全球社区"理念。历届联盟论坛中一系列相应命题如"后疫情世界中的大学角色""大学的数字化发展趋势""人文教育如何塑造大学未来""跨语种、跨国界、跨文化学术研究的重要性和大学在文明互鉴中建设国际社会的作用"等论坛，是这一建制的指导、决策和支持性意义在联盟论坛框架中的展开。本辑中北京外国语大学和上海外国语大学在2018年联盟论坛上关于如何面对外文人文教育结构性转变的发言与探讨，和没有能够收入本辑的伦敦国王学院关于科技与人文的发言、香港中文大学关于人文教育与大学未来的发言，都是有代表性的具体案例。2022年12月6日，中英高等教育人文联盟执行理事会工作会议在线上召开。联盟主席杨斌总结道，联盟已经顺利完成初创期的各项目标，为更实质性的开展中英人文对话与创新打下了坚实的基础；联盟将进一步增强包容性、实质性和长期性，以其持续提升的人文出版影响力和国际社会影响力，以其学术科研与人才培养互为延伸的结合，让跨文化人文学术、人文交流和教育教学结出更丰硕的果实。

　　回到2016年的联盟倡议启动仪式。清华世文学堂班首届本科生代表发言，表达了"由阐释世界以叙述中国，以叙述中国而联接世界"的人文学志业方向。迄至2023年6月，世文班已经毕业五届学生；当年发言的两位代表正在国内国外一流高校继续和完成志业之旅。而连续三年线上举行的青年学生论坛，2023年9月以"探索历史脉络，叙述文明交融"为主题回到清华园的第五届欢聚，是青年们阳光灿烂的新出发。作为中英学界一道独特风景、仍在创建中的跨文化传承，第五届学生论坛显示出对语言、文学、文化、科技革命、历史文明的跨文化对话和研究，随着更年轻学人的持续加入，正在以新的活力和想象力绵延。愿这本中英老师们书写和选编的文辑及其系列，有一天由他们接过去、继续出版。愿中英高等教育人文联盟和中英所有同行，青春常在。

2023年9月30日写于清华-锦园

Prologue

Rana Mitter[*]

The 2020s have been a time of immense global turbulence. They also mark the centenary of another time of immense change, the birth of modernism. 1922 is the date often given for this seminal event in the humanities, notably because of the publication of James Joyce's *Ulysses*. It's notable that some of the most important exponents of modernism came from Britain, broadly defined by Joyce himself, Virginia Woolf, and T. S. Eliot.

However, one distinct shift that emerges from the scholarship of the decades since then is the clear sense that modernism was never a movement that simply drew on the western experience. Modernism was defined by terms that came from a much wider range of national and transnational experiences. The greatest cosmopolitan of that era, the Bengali polymath Rabindranath Tagore, was part of a major reorientation of modernism in the Indian context, where it merged with ideas of nationalism and primitivism. China, too, had its modernist moment where the new forms of modernism combined with a new nationalist aesthetic.

This moment from a century ago flags up the value of continued engagement between the UK and China on humanities research. In many areas, the two countries have a shared engagement with the cutting edge of literature, history and philosophy, and there are immense numbers of points of cooperation as well as contrast.

---

[*] Rana Mitter is the former Master of St Cross College, and Professor of the History and Politics of Modern China at Oxford University. He writes extensively on the emergence of nationalism in modern China. His most recent publication is *China's Good War: How World War II Is Shaping a New Nationalism*. Professor Mitter is now ST Lee Chair in US–Asia relations at Harvard Kennedy School.

History is one area of shared experience. The events that tend to dominate the discussion, for understandable reasons, are the Opium Wars and the tragic encounters of the late 19th century. Yet it is also worth recovering other aspects of shared UK–China historical experience. The Second World War period, when China stood together with the United Kingdom, was one period when both sides tended to forget that there was an alliance of interests between the two sides.

Yet beyond the specific events of war and politics, there are wider areas where the history of the two countries bears comparison. In terms of technology and development, the story of the 19th century world was dominated by Britain. In the 20th, the US became dominant. It is too neat, and not accurate, to suggest that China would take the place of either one in the 21st. But there is little doubt that the history of modernity, and not just its cultural expression, is influenced by China today in a way that was not obvious even a few decades ago. Michel Foucault long ago identified the relationship between the powerful state and the surveilled self, and both the western world and China have contributions to make to this new identification of the modern self.

Both China and Britain also have globalization stories to tell. For both, it is a story of diaspora and the entanglement with ideas of economics and empire. For Britain in the 19th and 20th century, the story was one of settlers and governors moving across the globe, with the economic accoutrements of an empire that came with it, and the "empire striking back": that is, the creation of one of the glories of contemporary British culture, the realization that history and literature must be understood a multivocal. Without empire, there would be no Chinua Achebe or Salman Rushdie. With China, the key word is diaspora. That diaspora was subaltern for much of the 19th and 20th century and the voice of that working Chinese community—sailors, merchants, miners—could not be clearly heard. Now, the situation is more complex. A powerful PRC has an ambivalent relationship with its diaspora, and is sometimes reluctant to acknowledge that there is not one "China story" but rather "China stories" in the plural. A Chinese diaspora worker in Africa has their own tales to tell and they come from below, not above. We should look forward to more plural stories from

China as it becomes a more visible global actor.

Both Britain and China have complex relationships between technology and fiction. It was the British writer E. M. Forster, after all, who wrote *The Machine Stops*, one of the first and greatest stories of a world where communication was only through screens, and people lived without ever going outside. The story is a premonition of many things: in our recent memory, the conditions under covid restrictions, but also the growth of surveillance society and the alienation of human beings from one another. In the end, it is the crash of the entire system that forces a reset. In our own era, one of the most exciting voices in science fiction is the Chinese novelist Liu Cixin, who has global reach, but whose vision clearly draws from a range of experiences from within China and beyond, including the Cultural Revolution and the effects of climate change. Both these visions, a century apart, speak to real human concerns: the desire for connection, for individual freedoms, and fear of the consequences that technology can bring.

New media also provide new opportunities for broader engagement with the humanities. Britain has become a major actor in the new world of streaming, where linear television is supplemented and sometimes supplanted by new technologies for watching. Yet at its heart, some very traditional values lie: production values, good sets, and great scripting. It is no accident that Britain is such a central player in the world of streaming services, or has become such a global centre for media training for people from many countries, including China. China, of course, has developed a powerful televisual culture in its own right. In recent years, C-dramas including *Autumn Cicada*, *In the Name of the People* and most recently, *The Knockout* (Kuangbiao) show how sophisticated techniques combined with social commentary, make television drama an important reflection of changes in society. For British viewers who know the hot police anti-corruption series *Line of Duty*, *The Knockout* will seem very familiar. And it's notable that one actor, Jiang Shuying, in one of the biggest series on Chinese TV recently, *Nothing But Thirty*, holds a degree from University of East Anglia in media studies; a great example of UK–China humanities cross-pollination.

The contemporary political era across societies and cultures is marked by a new sense that brassy political certainties do not reflect the complexities and realities of a rapidly-changing world where pandemic, climate change, and confrontational politics have created major uncertainties in the minds of many. This is where the humanities can offer, if not a way out, at least a way forward. Unravelling the complexities of life and power, as it relates to real human lives, is one of the most powerful contributions that the study of the humanities can make.

A century ago, modernism emerged as an answer to the traumas that had been crystallized by the experience of the First World War. And with a century of distance, we can see how important the influence of the global community was. China, Japan, and India were just some of the societies that shaped that modernist moment in literature, drama, visual art, and music. Britain, however, cannot be denied its central part in shaping that agenda. In the early 21st century, the humanities must again provide responses to the crises that assail us. Again, war has reshaped Europe. Climate change demands immense and often jarring human responses. Governments, dismayed by forces beyond their control, seek to control and restrict the stage on which human experience can be understood. In that context, the task of the humanities to respond is more urgent than ever.

/ 目 录 /

全球视野

A Global Perspective

文化比较
Comparing Cultures

文化交汇
Cultural Interplay

历史记忆
Historical Memories

方兴未艾
Looking Forward

全球视野

A Global Perspective

Mutual Arrivals: From Multiculturalism to Transcultural Connection

Haiping Yan[*]

The prolonged global pandemic seems to have come to an end of a kind, with its long-term impact still to be reckoned with, suggesting a critical conjuncture of world history hung in an acute uncertainty. Of the tumultuous scenes occurring throughout the past three years, one stays in my memory with particular fecundity: in late June of 2020, while delivering my graduation speech for the class of 2020 online,[1] I was also concerned about the situation of the class of 2019 graduates, many of whom were studying abroad as waves of the pandemic reached them in Europe and the US. One student asked me if I would like

* Haiping Yan (颜海平) is the Tsinghua Academy Professor of the Class of World Literatures and Cultures (IWLC), and the Founding Director of the Tsinghua Institute for World Literatures and Cultures at Tsinghua University, where she is a faculty member in the department of Foreign Languages and Literatures as well as that of Chinese Language and Literature. She is the Founding Director of the Executive Council and Secretary General of the UK–China Alliance for the Humanities in Higher Education (UKCHA). Formerly a full professor at UCLA and Cornell University respectively, she relocated to Tsinghua and served as the 2014–2020 Chair of its Department of Foreign Languages and Literatures. Her research focuses on comparative studies of literatures, cultural theory and intellectual history of the 19th and 20th centuries with extensive publications on transnational feminism, transcultural modernism and critical cosmopolitanism. Her most recent publications include *Mutual Trans-writings* and *Modern Chinese Women Writers and Generative Modernity*. She is the editor of *Cosmopolitics*, an IWLC series presenting the work of international authors from the Commercial Press of China.

1　This is the 6th graduating class and the last one that I was seeing off as the Chair of the Department of Foreign Languages and Literatures (2016–2020) at Tsinghua University. The experience of this online graduation season with students and faculty gathering together will likely remain as a singular memory for all.

to hold a class meeting, and I immediately agreed. On August 1, these young students, studying in various places, regions or countries and in different language environments, appeared onscreen together. One of them had just returned home from a teaching internship in Tibet. For a moment, it seemed as if a range of temporal and geographical spaces were unified. Yet this unified space-time soon signaled a certain tension among different time-zones and physical locations, and among different languages and cultures. Unlike such meetings periodically held on campus where students gathered and spoke casually on various topics related to academic studies or daily logistics, the conversation was cogent, and the degree of its conciseness was proportional to the degrees of difference with or beyond which, it appeared to me, they seemed to be trying to reach out to one another. "Are you in the student dormitory on campus?" I asked from my home study in Beijing, while looking at a New England style interior background against which a student was looking in the direction of her peers online but not at anyone in particular. She paused, and said gently: "We have moved out of the dormitories. A few friends rent this place together off campus, for the moment." There was a pause. Such pauses recurred during the meeting, indicating time yet also space, as if a period, which is an ellipsis as well, might constitute the instant vibration of an individual life, evoking an echo of multi-layered histories in flux. I watched and listened to each of them, noticing how they tried to connect with each other by passing on their different living experiences, and how they sensed the differences in each "connection" so made, somewhat fluid but palpable. It was an exploration of new ways of arriving at a mutual recognition, however mediated and conditional, and an attempt to hold each other's hands as it were. The topic of the day was "transcultural competence," a pedagogical theme under much discussion in present day Chinese higher education. Afterwards, one of the students emailed me, saying:

When describing the transcultural process, people usually use the imagery of "echo," which refers to the resonance of the information flow from histories and cultures usually taken as other than their own, leaving a slight ripple in the senses of the listener. It can also involve something more, however, a touch upon

4

each other's minds, initiating a critical awareness that moves the minds beyond their comfort zones or toward something like a trans-connection.[1]

The student here referred to the variable ways in which people of different linguistic and cultural formations may connect with each other, as much as how such possible connectives lead to reflections on the linguistic and cultural formations of all parties involved including, in this case, their own "Chinese cultural upbringing" and its significations that are often taken as self-evident.[2] "Transcultural competence" hereby turns from a noun designating a directional capacity into a verb bringing about a process evoking and navigating a fecundity of differential and connective time and space beyond the binary of "one's own" and its "others."[3] Such a dynamic reminds one of the half sentence wish that the British author E. M. Forster once gave to one of his characters, "only connect," with all the challenges implied therein. This phrase, marked by its pause in time or as a space, has haunted the written world since. One may slightly alter this well-known injunction to suggest that "only connect, life happens," as a turning that makes life into a verb of being and becoming, a verb with all its possible ellipsis and uncertainties as much as enabling possibilities.[4] One may read this revised injunction as a utopian statement, but it might well

---

1 Shou Tianyi, "Reflections and Thoughts" (August 1, 2020).

2 The term could be used here in the sense that all students present were Chinese citizens and of Han nationality. The cultural complexity of such a term "Chinese," as I have considered elsewhere, also constitutes a topic of its own and has invited a wide range of exploration. Yan Haiping, "Mutual Transwritings: The Sources of Generative Modernity," in *Translation Studies and China*, eds. by Yan Haiping, Jin Haina, and Paul Gladston (London: Routledge Publishers, 2023).

3 Here the notion of transculturality is predicated upon a modern construct, namely that of a given "national culture." See discussion below. For a further consideration, see Yan Haiping, "Mutual Transwritings: The Sources of Generative Modernity," in *Translation Studies and China*, eds. by Yan Haiping, Jin Haina, and Paul Gladston.

4 E. M. Forster, *Howards End* (New York: Penguin Books, 1992), 148. Forster in fact takes the entire space and time of his novel to deliver a sense of life and beauty coming into being, with the figure of *Howards End* as an embodiment of human "connection" so made therein. Such "connection" is criticized by Fredric Jameson among others as an effect of "providential ideology." See Terry Eagleton, Fredric

be considered a quotidian imperative that provides a certain mental fulcrum for human existence in modern times, including in particular its present moment. Since the social relationships among individuals are neither fixed by a divine order (kings and emperors included) nor confined to a given nation-state, the ways of responding to the question of how to connect—as one of the defining problematics of modern life—are variable in various contexts and variably multi-context contingent.[1] The discussion over the past decades in the fields of the humanities in the US and elsewhere of "World Literature," as part and parcel of the drives for and discourses of "global humanities," is one important example. Through an analysis of several transcultural texts pertinent to this discussion, this essay will begin to explore the topic of "how to connect" across cultural boundaries worldwide. What needs to be briefly explained here is the definition and use of the term "transcultural." Contemporary academics, in China and beyond, have been discussing the idea of "transculturality" for decades. While its premise is what is called "national culture" that has been predicated upon the prevailing category of "nation-state"—as arguably first codified in Europe since the beginning of what has been called modern times[2]—the focus

---

Jameson, Edward Said, *Nationalism, Colonialism and Literature* (Minneapolis: The University of Minnesota Press, 1990), 58.

1 This proposition permeates the entire process of what has been referred to as "secularization in the West," as well as informing the discussion of Chinese literature and society in the modern era in relation to the lifeworlds worldwide. For some of the scholarly works on or related to this topic, see Vincent P. Pecora, *Secularization and Cultural Criticism* (London: Chicago University Press, 2006); Yue Daiyun, *Nirvana and Regeneration* (Beijing: Central Compilation and Publishing House, 2015); Yan Haiping, *Chinese Women Writers and the Feminist Imagination 1907–1948* (London / New York: Routledge Publishers, 2006); "Huweide zhuanxie shi shijie xianglian (Mutural Transwritings)," in *Shehuikexuebao (Social Sciences Today, Weekly)*, Shanghai (September 22, 2022).

2 For some informative discussions on or articulations of such nation-state and its European origins including *The Treaty of Westphalia* from different perspectives or positions, see Antony Negri and Michael Hardt, *Empire* (Cambridge, MA: Harvard University Press, 2001); Henry Kissinger, *World Order* (London: Penguin Books, 2015); Naoki Sakai, *The End of Pax Americana* (Durham: Duke University Press, 2022).

and impetus of transculturality are to go beyond the "social homogeneity, ethnic givenness and cultural boundaries" that such "national culture" implies, implements and coerces,[1] and thus to point to the overlapping, intermingling and connective extensions of differing cultural genealogies.[2] Under this premise, the term "culture" refers to the intellectual tradition, spiritual legacy, and relational way of life understood as being carried by what is essentialized as "the mother tongue" versus "the foreign tongues." In this context, "transculturality" refers to the process by which individuals, or groups of individuals, move beyond their respective "mother tongues" so essentialized and thereby entering into a praxis of dialogical and polylogical encounter that includes two or more languages irreducible to the binary of "the mother tongue" versus its "others" à la "the foreign tongues." What interests us here is the potential of such process to become aware of its own dynamics, and the possible emerging forms of thought and renewal of energies that

---

1 See Fang Weigui, "'Transcultural' Explained," *Literary Studies*, No. 9 (2015), 5–13. "Social homogeneity, given ethnicity, and cultural boundaries" are categories considered to have originated in Europe and to be isomorphic to the modern nation-state. Johann Gottfried Herder proposed the idea of an organic link between people and language, calling for the use of "national languages" to promote the development of national literature. Alexander von Humboldt argued that language is not just a vehicle for expressing thoughts, but itself represents the consciousness and cognitive patterns of the speakers; language determines the worldview (Weltanschauung) of a people and a nation, thus distinguishing different races, ethnicities, societies and nations, and thereby naturalizing the mutual construction of language and literature and the nation-state. Also see Armando Gnisci, "Statement of Transculturation," in *Transcultural Dialogues*, Issue 29, ed. by Yue Daiyun, et al (Beijing: Joint Publishing, 2012), 15–22.

2 A range of productive topics engendered by such transcultural impetus within and beyond the framework of the nation-states and its logic of geopolitics have been embedded throughout the modern history of Chinese humanities. For some recent reflections on and articulations of such practices, see Yue Daiyun and Chen Yueguang, eds., *China's Cultural Orientation in Global Perspectives* (Beijing: Renmin University of China Press, 2018), 274–298. For a few other takes on similar issues from different perspectives, see Ge Zhaoguang, "Three Challenges in Chinese Cultural Studies," and Wang Bo, "Goodwill and Open Space," Keynote Forum at the Third Summit of the China–UK Association for the Humanities in Higher Education (The Chinese University of Hong Kong, December 6–7, 2018).

would thereby transpire.[1] The complex transcultural flux generated by the technological and economic upheavals of recent decades, while not an entire novelty in the chronicles of modern history, has been unprecedented in terms of its scale and speed, and scholars from the humanities have offered a range of understandings of the phenomenon and its continuing variations. The Harvard School of "world literature" that holds optimistic attitudes has been much noted.[2] David Damrosch's (2003; 2008) theoretical argument for "world literature" is an academic statement and a program for practical implementation in curricula design. Martin Puchner, another leading member of such "World Literature," has received much attention from the academic community in China and elsewhere. His work *The Written World* is the printed form of an online general education course on "world literature," the Chinese version of which was published by CITIC Press

---

1 Due to space limitations, the main materials used in this essay are in and of English. Much of Chinese literary studies and the humanities since the 1980s has of course been part and parcel of such transcultural discussion in China and beyond. Institutional innovations including the first admissions of MA students in 1983 in the then new field of comparative literature at Beijing University, Fudan University, Nanjing University, and Heilongjiang University have been groundbreaking. See Yue Daiyun, *An Introductory Course on Comparative Literature* (比较文学简明教程, Beijing: Beijing University Press, 2003), 67. The launching of BA programs in comparative literature and world literature in the departments of Chinese language and literature at all universities across China in the 1990s, followed by gradual establishments of first the MA and then PhD programs therein (thanks to Yang Naiqiao of Fudan University for providing and confirming the information), and some thirty years later the 2017 launching of MA and PhD programs in comparative literature and transcultural studies in the departments of foreign languages and literatures at all universities across China are, respectively, defining moments in the history of the humanities in Chinese higher education. For what has occurred in the field of foreign languages and literatures at Tsinghua University since 2014, see Wang Xiaoshan, "Reshaping Chinese Education in Foreign Languages from the Perspectives of Interdisciplinary Humanities," *21st Century English Language Teaching (ELT) Review* (September 6, 2016); "Reform and Innovation: Foreign Language Education as Central Fields of the Humanities," *21st Century English Language Teaching (ELT) Review* (December 14, 2020).

2 See https://iwl.fas.harvard.edu, the Institute for World Literature, with its academic sessions inaugurated since 2011. David Damrosch, *What Is World Literature* (Princeton: Princeton University Press, 2003); *How to Read World Literature* (Chichester, UK: Wiley-Blackwell, Blackwell Publishing, 2008).

Group in July 2019, titled *The Power of Words*.[1] The 3rd and 4th editions of *The Norton Anthology of World Literature*, edited by Puchner in collaboration with many other scholars specializing in various languages and literatures, were published in 2012 and 2018. Aiming to be inclusive in subject matter and diverse in writing style, the ambition of the Norton Anthology is, of course, not to provide a simple listing of national texts ordered within a hierarchic "family of nations," but rather to bring the texts of literature, written in languages ranging from what has been designated as "ancient" along with the classical and medieval or "pre-national" to "modern" or "national" along with its "post-varieties,"[2] into an interrelated macro-picture, highlighting the historical associations of and interactions among literature of different languages throughout history, as well as the echoes and possible reverberations of important texts and themes in different writings, through which a sense of a world map, world literature and world history transpires.[3] The number of scholars specializing in various languages and literatures who have joined the editing team has significantly surpassed those of the previous editions, ensuring its wide coverage and imbuing it with a sense of contemporaneity, making the 3rd and 4th editions of an "anthology of world literature" appear more justifiably so named than its predecessors.[4]

Echoing David Damrosch and others, Puchner traces the idea of "world literature"

---

1 Martin Puchner, *The Power of Words: How Literature Shapes Human Species, Civilization, and World History* (文字的力量), translated by Chen Fang Dai (Beijing: CITIC Press Group, 2019). References made to this book hereafter are from this edition. For the original English Edition, see *The Written World: The Power of Stories to Shape People, History, Civilization* (New York: Random House, 2017).

2 Such "post-varieties" include "postcolonial Englishes" (in plural) employed, for example, by Wole Soyinka or Ama Ata Aidoo, among others.

3 See report on "Martin Puchner of Harvard University guest lectured at Seminars in World Literatures and Cultures Series" (September 23, 2019).

4 See report on "Opening Ceremony of IWLC Center for Advanced Studies in World Cultures of Tsinghua University and Martin Puncher's Lecture for Tsinghua Forum-IWLC Series Held" (September 11, 2019); https://news.tsinghua.edu.cn/info/1007/53162.htm.

back to Goethe. In September 2019, as a guest lecturer at Tsinghua University,[1] Puchner spoke of how literature emerged around the world four or five thousand years ago as a mental practice, while Goethe's idea of world literature was inspired by his response to a seventeenth-century Chinese novel via its French translation, a response recorded as a conversation between Goethe and his assistant Johann Peter Eckermann on January 31, 1827. Puchner noted that the grand idea of world literature was not born in such metropolises as Paris or Frankfurt. Rather, it was born in the country town where the aging Goethe lived, precisely because Goethe was trying to transcend the spatial limitations of that small town. In the nineteenth-century, as German nationalism flourished, the idea of world literature was born within the contradiction between the idea of the "nation" and the idea of the "world." In the difference between the then prevalent nationalist view of literature in Germany, which was not yet united as one nation-state, and the world literature that Goethe envisioned, Puchner saw an inclusive aspiration or openness. Puchner did not shy away from the broader context of this idea, namely, nineteenth-century European colonial expansion as predicated on the "global dissemination" of "civilizing ideas," and the resulting historical conditions:

> Most colonial powers felt the need to justify their actions by arguing that the European colonists were bringing civilization to other parts of the world. This meant that orientalists who were studying colonial possessions tended to carry with them condescending ideas about the quality of these cultures. (Puchner 2019, 318)

Yet Germany's relative delay in the European colonial competition became the basis for Puchner to separate Goethe from other, presumably more imperialist, thinkers of that time:

---

1   Hosted by the Institute for World Literatures and Cultures (IWLC), this visit was sponsored by some of its programs including Seminars in World Literatures and Cultures Series, University Forum-IWLC Series, and international academic events program of the Department of Foreign Languages and Literature.

Here, Goethe's provincial position in Weimer turned out to be an advantage. His Weimar duchy was not connected to imperialism—none of the many small and medium-sized German states had colonies. This meant that he could indirectly profit from the imperialism of others while being removed from the experience of subjugating foreign cultures and the false feeling of superiority it often induced. (Puchner 2019, 318)

Puchner highlighted Goethe's emphasis on translation and his foresightedness in "regarding the idea of world literature as based on a global literary market propelled by translation" (Puchner 2019, 318). Puchner was hereby dealing with a literary figure in the past, while also indicating, implicitly or at times overtly, how people could or should deal with the drastic changes of the present. Just as Goethe knew that "he had a powerful ally, (namely) the reality of an emerging world market, including literature" for his ideal of world literature (Puchner 2019, 318), [1] we should realize that in our present time, decades of economic globalization have brought about new waves of translations, and the connections made in the business world also exist in the literary worlds of various cultures. The relationship between so-called "national literature" and "world literature" is not as simple as an oppositional one, Puchner commented, while the tensions heightened therein result in a rich productiveness with increasingly important implications, evoking Goethe if not echoing his times (Puchner 2019).[2]

---

1 Also see p. 9, ft. 3, the reading material for the seminar, "103 Puchner, Readers of the World United!"

2 See p. 9, ft. 3. Such a "market reality" is not as evenly distributed or robust as these words seem to suggest, especially in retrospect to our present post-Pandemic conjuncture as a likely prolonged period charged with intricate divisions and sharpening uncertainty. While the given format of book publication (print) has been increasingly weakened in the US as much noted by the publishing industries, at the same time, one may still take the monumental size of the 3rd and 4th editions of *Norton Anthology of World Literature* as an indication of an intensive growth in translation in the publishing markets over the past decades. In the field of Chinese studies, the efforts made by scholars since the 1980s witness as much as partake in such market expansion and market-making. Howard Goldblatt notably has made available in English the works of almost an entire generation of

When I listened to my colleague from afar speaking to Chinese students and teachers about "the world" and "literature," an "echo" evoked memories from years ago.[1] In the early 1990s, when I began my professorial life in the US, one of the main courses in my teaching repertoire was an introductory seminar on comparative literature and theory. I taught (in the demographic terminology of the times) a predominantly Euro-American student body with an active presence of some African-American and Asian-American students, starting, precisely, with a reading and discussion of Goethe's "Weltliteratur" (world literature).[2] I read with my students this renowned 1827 conversation in which Goethe proclaimed that the era of "Weltliteratur" was coming and that "national literature" was

---

contemporary Chinese writers, and decisively contributed to Mo Yan's winning of the Nobel Prize in Literature in 2012. Barbara Cassin's 2004 watershed *Dictionary of Untranslatables*, which has sought to draw attention to the irreducible meanings and histories behind key philosophical terms, as well as many of its resulting critical studies, seems to have registered both the need for translation and the range of challenges involved therein. Routledge's *Translation Studies Reader* of 2000 among others, is one more such example.

1 I should note that, among the predominantly Chinese audience for Puchner's seminar, there was a group of young scholars from the US, namely the IWLC Fellows of Tsinghua-Michigan Society of Fellows, a joint program by the Tsinghua Institute for World Literatures and Cultures and the Michigan Society of Fellows (2016–2023). Having completed their PhD degrees in primarily Anglo-American and European studies at major universities, including UC Berkeley, Harvard, Yale, Chicago, Michigan, Johns Hopkins and others, and selected from a large pool of applicants, their responses to the seminar constituted a range of intellectual variables rich with transcultural implications, a documentation of which invites consideration.

2 I first taught an introduction to comparative literature, and other courses, in the US at Oberlin College in 1992. Most of those students were equipped with either French or German linguistic capability in addition to what is taken as their given language, namely English or an educated (standardized) American English. Yet the often in-articulated sensitivities and memories implicit or embedded in their often elegant and thoughtful English articulation, at the same time, constituted a more nuanced richness or plurality, inviting complex reconsiderations of their shared "mother tongue" and, for that matter, any "mother tongue" as such. I would also note that there was one student from Bangladesh and two from China, whose bilingual presences were critically enabling for the classroom discussion in my memory.

becoming outdated.[1] Goethe's proclamation, on the one hand, registered the technological developments of the time, the rapid formation of the world market, the production of translated literature and travel literature, the accelerated circulation of newspapers and magazines, and the dissemination of various concepts and ideas across national borders;[2] and on the other hand, this same proclamation was an astute response to the so-called "Napoleonic legacy" which constituted the specific European context within which this circulation was received and conceived. Goethe saw that "all nations, jumbled together in the most terrible wars and then restored to themselves, realized that they had observed and absorbed many unfamiliar things," and began to feel "certain previously unknown spiritual needs"; different nations, or more precisely, authors residing in different European nation-states, "should notice and understand each other, and, if they do not wish to love each other, at least learn how to tolerate one another" (Goethe cited in Weisstein 1968).[3] In October 1827, Goethe wrote to his friend Sulpiz Boisseree: "I should also like to observe that what I call Weltliteratur is most likely to come about when the differences prevailing within one nation are reconciled through the views and judgments of other nations" (Goethe cited in Weisstein 1968).[4] The focus here is on cultural Europe, and the European nation-states and their respectively vernacularized national languages and literatures.

In addition, while he advocated world literature with cultural Europe as his focus,

---

1 *Goethe in Conversation* (歌德谈话录), edited by Eckermann, Chinese edition translated by Zhu Guangchen (Beijing: People's Literature Press, 1978), 113. Hereafter reference made to this book is from this edition. For other editions, see *Conversations of Goethe,* by Johann Peter Eckermann, English edition translated by John Oxenford, 1906 (digital production by, 2010), and Johann Peter Eckermann, *Gespräche mit Goethe in den letzten Jahren seines Lebens* (Berlin: Insel Verlag; 4. Juli 1981).

2 A century later, some of the humanities scholars who promote the academic specialties of world literature seem to operate from a similar starting point, focusing their attention primarily on the power of market circulation and less on the social connotations of circulation until that is, the problems embedded therein surface sharply over the past several years.

3 Ulrich Weisstein, *Comparative Literature and Literary Theory*, translated by William Riggan (Bloomington/London: Indiana University Press, 1968), 18–19.

4 Ibid.

Goethe was the driving force for writings in the German national language, and the national language was the very definition and institutional carrier of "national literature" in the process of being so invented. Not surprisingly, Goethe, while finding inspiration in Chinese novels in translation, also believed that the model of world literature could not be located in any region other than ancient Greece, and the ideal of the world appears to be very close to an "expanded German fatherland" based on Greek civilization (Eckermann 1978, 113–114).[1] Being cognizant of such a German-inflected Eurocentric impetus, however, does not mean a total denial of the imaginative strength of Goethe's vision of world literature, which registered an important dimension of social situations and states of mind that have recurred throughout human history. The Great Migrations of successive eras would drive people to exceed, cross over or even transcend established social and cultural boundaries, and initiate a desire or an aspiration if not also a hidden pressure to make and expand connections with varying and varyingly perceived "others." At the same time, the historical knowledge of the modern world, particularly of the twentieth-century and this present one, makes us realize that human "desires" or "aspirations" are inseparable from specific historical conditions and their effects, and that their profoundly multifaceted character always requires reflection, urging us to explore the possibility of establishing "connections" with "others" more concretely, critically and historically, especially attentive to differential and distinctive contexts (as effects of cognitive contextualization) involved in such connectives. The appearance of Goethe's works in the backpacks of German soldiers and officers during the Second World War constitutes a complex phenomenon in world history that cannot be easily written off, as evinced by continuing scholarly endeavors to render it into critical knowledge that expands human cognition and imagination. If we do choose "world literature" as an approach and a vision, it may be crucial to be conscious and reflective of the process of developing the vision and putting the approach into practice; we need to focus on the interplay and results of the interaction of multiple forces at work

---

1   The context of this discussion points to Eckermann, ft. 25.

therein. There will, as before, be deviations or ruptures between designed historical goals and the consequences of specific events irreducible to or despite such or any designs. What has been referred to in the fields of critical historiographies as "unintended consequences" suggests a vital problematic in need of sustained attention, to which I will return later in this essay. Suffice it to say here that, in the current moment of conspicuous and tension-fraught change in literary concepts as well as structural shifts in literary and cultural production, the multifaceted experiences of the past require us to consider specifically how to open up while strengthening a more inclusive, differentiated and productive space for knowledge-making as a cognitive process, extending or broadening humanistic connections in effective ways. It would be fruitful, and imperative, to consider the possibility of making a framework or frameworks distinct from the prevailing paradigm of the modern era that has been taking "Western literature" as the center of gravity in thought, driven by the homogenizing and homogenized world market and prescribed by its apparatuses of codification or assimilation.[1]

In my exchange with Puchner, I explained that the formulation of, and initiative for, the "studies of world literatures and cultures" at the Institute for World Literatures and Cultures (IWLC) and in the Department of Foreign Languages and Literatures at Tsinghua University since the fall of 2014 is descriptive rather than conceptual; it aims to broaden the scope of teaching and research, as well as the space for practice in accordance with the needs, in China, of the studies of languages and humanities of other nations worldwide,[2]

---

1 Of recent critical works on this topic, Amir Mufti's *Forget English: Orientalisms and World Literatures* (Cambridge, MA: Harvard University Press, 2016) is among the more pertinent and noted. One would want to remember, in this context, that "Western literature" does not refer to all literary texts that take place in European and American nation-states, but rather to the limited and solidified genealogy of Occidentalism ("Anglicism" in Mufti's terms) in the field of literature, the kernels of which are the binary opposition of "the canonizing sovereignty" and its effects of extending assimilation to claim "the others." It is worthwhile to keep drawing on the fruitful parts of scholars' discussion on this subject in the past decades.

2 According to a deep-seated sense of the conventional division of the humanities in the context of

allowing teachers and students to actively reflect upon their professional identities often termed as "Chinese experts of foreign languages" in order to be alert to the possible dichotomy at work in the relationship between "Chinese and foreign cultures." In our discussions, we bring together the languages and literatures of different peoples and regions in conversation with the continuous and changing multifaceted Chinese humanistic awareness, and its many-sided genealogies. It is a "descriptive impetus"[1] that gives rise to various concrete dialogues and to an open cognitive mapping of mutual renewal in the fields of languages, literatures and humanistic knowledge productions (please note all the plurals). This description is related to and in one way resonates with the Harvard School's formulation, while its underlying and governing logic does not point to a canonizing, institutionalized and commanding authority on "world literature."[2] Puchner responded that he understood the value of this descriptive proposition. He mentioned that the main purpose of the 3rd edition of the *Norton Anthology* was to increase such openness. First, the

---

American colleges and universities, which shifts over the years but nonetheless endures, literature in English is largely taken as "English literature." Studies of Chinese literature including Chinese literature in English translation, among a range of other non-English and non-European literatures, however, has long been included in "area studies," a convention that constitutes another topic in critical studies of the humanities and its institutional history. See Naoki Sakai, "Theory and Asian humanity: on the question of *humanitas* and *anthropos*," *Postcolonial Studies*, Vol. 13, No. 4 (2010), 441–464.

1   Granted, the "descriptive" and "prescriptive" are often inseparable as a large amount of critical scholarship over the past decades has revealed. Nonetheless, when one allows this "descriptive impetus" to work as a process without foreclosure, it may help as a leverage for articulating much needed imaginative possibilities.

2   In the spring of 2016, Tsinghua University's Department of Foreign Languages and Literatures celebrated its 90th anniversary. The launching of the Institute for World Literatures and Cultures (IWLC) with a year-long international forum series "World Maps and World Cultures" (WMWC) was one of the attempts to put this descriptive formulation into practice involving Chinese, English, French, Japanese and more languages. "WMWC series" has become a standing program of the UK–China Humanities Alliances. See "Afterword by the Editors," in *Translation Studies and China*, eds. by Yan Haiping, Jin Haina, and Paul Gladston.

anthology is intended to be a pedagogical reference for high school and college teachers who teach introductory courses in world literature. In the process of making it, the editors have discovered the interesting phenomenon that the desire for world literature often comes from remote and isolated places rather than elite cosmopolitan metropolises, and that the more remote and less prestigious the local colleges and universities are, the greater the demand for introductory world literature courses. World literature offers those students, who rarely have the opportunity to travel abroad, an opportunity to learn about the world and expand their horizons. Thus, the spirit of the anthology is multiculturalist, encouraging people's openness to more diverse texts. He offered a sketch of some of the notable changes occurring in literature programs in US higher education since World War II. In response to the increasing presence of various European immigrants in American society due to WWII and its aftermath, for example, the literary canon studied in colleges and universities was much expanded but still mainly composed of Western works. As increasing numbers of immigrants and students arrived in the US from all over the world in and since the 1960s, more diverse literary material appeared on course syllabi in humanities programs nationwide, including works from the Middle East, Mexico, and China, giving rise to a more diverse definition of the "classics." Moreover, the form of the "anthology" itself contains a resiliently open and individually variable structure within or against which readers can develop their own choices in making their own worlds of reading and writing, all the more so within this current conjuncture of technological innovation. In our Internet era, many aspects of the Internet offer a kind of "re-curating" space similar to that of an "editorial anthology," in which people can sift, cut, collage, rearrange, and collect texts online, opening up and enriching the range of infinite possibilities for personalized and personalizing "anthologies."[1] Sharing some of the dimensions outlined in Puchner's sketch of such changes, Chinese book reviews are generally positive about the drive for

---

1   See p. 9, ft. 3. "Harvard University's Martin Puchner Guest Lectured at IWLC Seminar on Humanities" (September 17, 2019).

multiculturalism and its noble dreams of inclusiveness as embodied in the Harvard School to which Puchner refers; some see therein an opening for Chinese literature to gain access to European and American book markets and teaching channels, as well as the possibility of inclusion in the category of "world classics," as a result of changes in the way literary history is organized (anthologized), taught and written (Fang 2013; Shen 2019; Li 2020).[1] Among the reviews of Puchner's book that appeared in the US or in the English-speaking context, some take up the perspective that literature is part and parcel of history and daily life, emphasizing the indispensability of the humanities in this era of technological change, in light of which Puchner is seen to have revealed how "foundational texts," emerging from the turbulence of technological change and the mutating modes of writing immanent to such changes, "accrued power and significance over time until they become source codes for entire cultures, telling people where they came from, and how they should live their lives" (Puchner 2019, 10–11; Puchner cited in Chen 2019, 808–810).[2] From this viewpoint, written texts are begotten by authors actively inhabiting turning points in the rise and fall of cultures, civilizations and histories, as much as productively garnering the power of revolutionary technologies; they are a force that maps the patterns of prosperity and decline in and of human worlds, for the betterment of humanities and human species.[3] These multiple, positive insights echo the multicultural perspective that Puchner intends to

---

1 Fang Hanwen, "Chinese Literature that Enters the World Classics," *Guangming Daily* (January 28, 2013). Shen Zuxin, "Martin Puchner's *The Power of Words*: Sketching Paths and Exploring Borders," *Wen Hui Newspaper* (November 4, 2019). Li Junpeng, "The Triumph of Words," *The Paper* (August 11, 2020).

2 Chen Fangdai, "Book Review," *International Comparative Literature*, Vol. 2, No. 4 (2019), 808–810. Cited from Puchner, *The Written World*, xvii.

3 In other words, Puchner traces the effects of the waves of technological revolution throughout human history, reveals the immanent correlation between such technological revolution and the mutation of literature at key particular moments and also over time, and unfolds the interrelationship among technological revolution, literary writing and ways of societal life shaped by writing. He tends to note in that interrelationship an increasingly democratic orientation on a world scale. See p. 9, ft. 3.

articulate with his *Norton Anthology*, and each has its enabling signification for coming to terms with the present sea change worldwide whereby humanities and humanistic knowledge production must endeavor to make and remake humanly enabling and / or empowering connections among different nations, societies, cultures and civilizations otherwise divided by the binary logic of Eurocentric modernity.[1] These echoes, however, do not confront the fact that in the particular case under discussion here, the "multicultural texts," to which the chief editor and the editorial group have devoted so much attention, labor and thought, are carried, circulated and reproduced in one single language, namely, English. Amidst the fluidity of multiculturalism in the United States including Europe over the decades, this concrete but not simple detail reminds us that the contemporary idea and promotion of "World Literature" discussed above, while attempting to embody the finest aspects of multicultural practice, has been unable to deal with the presence and limits of a certain and consequential homogenization indicative of its inherent "Anglicist" and / or "Eurocentric" logos when one takes the term "world" more rigorously, which might result in a range of "unintended consequences" in the actual worldwide contexts, and in need of being recognized, reckoned with and worked through.[2] The critically enabling part of what the humanities achieve, influenced by the so-called "linguistic turn" of the last decades, has taught us that the linguistic limit registered in the anthology under discussion is the presence and limits of language as discourse, and of cultural world orders, geopolitics, circulation mechanisms and / or operative structures of global markets.[3] Some scholars in

---

1   It is here that IWLC's descriptive initiative particularly converges with Puchner's work and its impetus.

2   Aamir Mulfti, mentioned earlier, among others have argued as much or further. See Aamir Mufti, *Forget English!*.

3   The perspective provided by Aamir Mufti and other postcolonial theorists that regards "English as both a literary vernacular and the undisputed language of global capitalism" serves as a notable reference. The decades-long multilingual (English, Chinese, Japanese, and Korean) publishing project of Naoki Sakai and his colleagues at Cornell University, in collaboration with colleagues elsewhere, *Traces* / 印记, is one example of the attempts to overcome such a limit within and from the English speaking context of the US.

19

the US and Europe, most notably Franco Moretti (2013) for a period of time, suggest a turn to "distant reading" as a possible way to deal with, but also perhaps evade, the recurrent conundrum of a sort of imperial vision, even in the process of trying to dismantle that vision.[1] Some others seem to argue for abandoning the idea of "world literature" altogether in order to be free of its co-implication with the "European 19th century" as much as its hidden or overt extensions in "global contexts" today.[2] While neither strategy could or would claim to resolve this conundrum in the age of economic globalization (or de-globalization as its mirror image), both function as acts witnessing its difficult reality and its critical implications. Ongoing debates concerning "global literature" as part and parcel of what is called "Anglicism" in Mufti's (2016) terms or "Anglo-humanities,"[3] along with the arguments to "forget English" (Mufti, 2006), in this sense, are symptomatic of such "presence and limits" as constituting not only a cognitive conundrum, but also a complex historical question inherent in the institutional formations and transformations of knowledge production in what we call the modern world, with all its changing and recurring problems of social, economic, linguistic and cultural, and geopolitical relations.

---

1   Moretti's basic argument is that, given its scale, "world literature" as a subject of study inherently implies an incompetence in terms of language capabilities. One of the ways to deal with this incompetence is to abandon "close reading" in favor of larger units (plot summaries, geographical sites) that are little altered by translation. See Franco Moretti, *Distant Reading* (London: Verso, 2013.)

2   Such arguments, voiced on a range of occasions including academic conferences in a variety of locations including the US, are attentive to the material conditions in humanities education. Limited access to foreign language learning at the secondary school level in the US and recent massive cutting of existent foreign language programs at US universities indicates an Anglo-centrism at work in endless reinventions. The question needs to be furthered as to how to change such a condition. For more attempts to come to terms with different dimensions of such questions, see Natalie Melas, Wai Chee Dimock, and Haun Saussy, among others.

3   "Global humanities-cum-Anglo humanities," a term intended to designate an Anglo-centrism along with its primary linguistic features in some of the advocacies for "global humanities" occurring over the years, has been in use on a variety of academic occasions including, in some relatively earlier instances, the 2010 annual meeting of the Consortium of Humanities Centers and Institutes (CHCI), titled "Who's Global Humanities" (Brown University, June 14–15, 2010).

As noted earlier, the US-based proposition for promoting the idea of "world literature" through a series of academic programs has been in sync with a fluidity of multiculturalism occurring in public discourse, which has also been interconnected with a notable shift in the institutional configuration of humanities in higher education, particularly since the 1990s. When I began teaching in the United States in the early 1990s, I was invited as a junior delegate to a committee on faculty development, and experienced the revision of tenure track humanities positions with such multiculturalism as the guiding principle; such a revision took place in major universities across the United States, amounting to what may be considered as yet one more stage of expansion and innovation in the disciplinary and professorial specialties of the involved fields since the ascendency of US higher education in the post-World War II era, including notably the strengthening of the state public universities in the 1960s. Due to an immensely productive updating (as it were) of the types of scholarship required by faculty positions, at this time, English departments were augmented by, among others, an extensive body of writers and scholars coming from, or specializing in, the studies of former British and other colonies (otherwise known as postcolonial studies and critique). Comparative literature departments began to incorporate languages and traditions other than English, French, and German. Historically meaningful and cognitively consequential, these important changes nonetheless could not deal with the basic logic of the Anglicism / Eurocentric paradigm and its limits. Vincent Pecora (2006, 19),[1] among others, noted that the "openness" of a comparative literature recruitment text was in the end neither so "open" nor free of such basic logic:

... what we are really asking for is someone with a broad grasp of the research traditions that began in the 1950s and originated mainly in France, including

---

1 See Vincent Pecora, "Globalization and Humanism" (Quanqiuhua yu Renwenzhuyi), in *Globalization and the Development of Humanistic Scholarship (Quanqiuhua yu Renwenxueshu de Fazhan)*, eds. by Gao Ruiquan and Yan Haiping (Shanghai: Shanghai Ancient Books Publishing House, 2006), 1–20.

representative figures from Althusser to Žižek and more. These are people who are posited to theoretically deconstruct the Western humanities from within itself.

The ideal applicant would also possess "an in-depth knowledge of one or more non-Western traditions" so as to be able to "see Western philosophy from a non-Western point of view," to "rethink the disciplinary nature and boundaries of comparative literature and to challenge the Eurocentric character of comparative literature" (Pecora 2006, 17–18). Pecora's implicit message is that institutions running such a recruitment text "wanted" an individual who both remained anchored in Western theory or an American-centered idea of theory *and* was completely at home and expert in some non-Western literary traditions to such an extent that that individual could "deconstruct" his or her own institutionally embedded theoretical underpinnings and framework within which this faculty position is situated. And such "wanting of a contradictory mélange of things all gathered in one individual," in his view, is the demonstration of an inherent Eurocentrism, and is in fact impossible to carry out, logically or practically, in the final analysis (Pecora 2006, 17–19). One could shift the angle of observation to suggest that, instead of being bound to the binary between "Western" and "non-Western" as Pecora's phrases somewhat tend to sound, specific case studies of the scholarship required by such recruitment within this cognitive and institutional framework may be productive. It may be helpful in considering, for example, how, specifically, such "wanted impossibility" results not so much in a cognitive act to exceed or move beyond the limits of "Western philosophy," but rather in variable editions of—or variable footnotes to— such "Western philosophy," however self-critically in its nonetheless self-referential and, in some instances, self-centric "deconstruction."[1] Or one can labor with intensified energies to

---

1 The topic is as complex as the discussions it garners multifaceted. Suffice it to say here that such a paradox has been reflectively explored by scholars over the past decades, and remains in need of further discussion. Some of the recent embracement and criticisms of "sino-phone studies" and its paradoxes suggest a relevant case in point.

indeed critique, to variable degrees effectively, the "Eurocentric character" with twice, and more, the accumulated knowledge and inherited or learned resources of one's Anglo-Euro-American peers specializing in the institutional mainstream of academic humanities—in other words, to perform extraordinary surplus intellectual labor for decentering the Eurocentric, while spending a life-long career centered on such a de-centering which keeps the "Eurocentric character" centrally in the view, "critically."[1] Such paradoxical consequences, and many more with all their specific complexities, can be further explored. It is necessary to raise the question about how such "tasks impossible" are variably carried out primarily in the invariable standard language, namely, English as an institutional measurement for cognitive values and an institutional mechanism for validating the cognitively valuable, and how multicultural visions are so enacted as being at the same time inseparable from the "centrality" of such measurement and mechanism comprising the discursive apparatus, star-system of the academia, cultural ordering of the world, shifting deployment of geopolitics, and circulation management of Anglo-centric / Eurocentric global markets.[2] The digital realms of the Internet Age, while enabling individuals to produce

---

1 There have long been what one could further call the "unintelligibles," remotely echoing but distinct from Hannah Arendt's image of the "unclassifiables," whose life and work exceed or transcend the limit of such institutional conditions, of which critical genealogies are yet to be written to witness their unintelligibility and its historical implications in the prevailing chronicles of the modern world and its knowledge production. Much of the work on critical cosmopolitanisms by Bruce Robbins, Leela Gandhi and others inspire more to witness the unintelligibles. See Bruce Robbins eds., *Cosmopolitanisms* (New York: New York University Press, 2017). The decades-long multilingual (English, Chinese, Japanese, Korean) publishing project of Naoki Sakai and his colleagues at Cornell University, in collaboration with colleagues elsewhere, *Traces*/印记, is another example of the effective and powerful attempts to overcome such a limit.

2 Many of these critically productive scholars have been publishing simultaneously in languages other than English (and other than major Western European languages) but the mainstay of their publications is in English as an institutionally regulatory and governing framework. In the light of such regulating logic, the key concern in works such as *Provincializing Europe* can be understood as a cognitive as much as an institutional and ultimately a geopolitical condition of knowledge production. See Dipesh Chakrabarty, *Provincializing Europe: Postcolonial Thought and Historical Difference* (Princeton: Princeton University Press, 2000).

the "infinitely variable anthologies" in which Puchner invests much of his optimism, do not *de facto* resolve or provide a solution to the many paradoxes of such an institutional monolingual character. The center of gravity of the technologically revolutionary digital innovation—that opens as much as commands this realm—is, in the global unification of the network economy, bringing about enormous possibilities laden with recurring problems. Enabling multilingual-cum-multicultural accessibilities (such as *Duolingo*),[1] the realm also gives rise to consequences of potentially abortive implications for the intended propagation of multiculturally inclusive literature and literary and cultural studies: different literary, cultural and civilizational resources can flow parallel to one another as ever morphing and ever expandable individual portfolios, without necessarily generating the need to engage or work through questions such as how their differences implicate specific lives and lifeworlds particularly in and across concrete localities of different time and space zones.[2] The complexity of the situations wherein "different languages and cultures" encounter and relate to each other, and the question and study of how they may connect in the making and remaking of lifeworlds, largely remain unasked or turned irrelevant amidst superfast, hyper-transformative technological upheaval and its capital-driven innovations and growth inscribed with the logic of quantifiable prolificacy and profitability and its recurring aesthetic of mathematical sublimity.[3]

Scholarship that attempts to deal with such issues, thereby turning the question of encounters of or connections between different cultures and cultural differences into a

1 This constitutes another field of research beyond the space of this essay. My thanks to Yumi Selden for drawing my attention to such enabling online programs in language learning as *Duolingo*.

2 The phenomenon of intensive, explosive and ultimately dispersive or dissipating "Fan culture" or simply "fandom," with isolated persons who illusively gather around media images, much studied by young scholars in present day China, is one such example. See Zhang Hanwen and Xie Tingyu, *Kuangbiao yu xiaosan de bianyuan* (*Storm and dissipating margins*, Beijing: Jiuzhou Publishing House, 2023).

3 The increasingly intensified deployment of digitized mechanism and quantifying method to measure the productivity—and value—of the humanities at universities has been a worldwide phenomenon and has long been analyzed as a problem over the past decades. See Alpesh Maisuria, Svenja Helmes, *Life for the Academic in the Neoliberal University* (London / NewYork: Routledge Publishers, 2020).

matter of praxis for the making and remaking of humanity and humanities has, of course, long been available. The question of how "different cultures" relate to each other, and the study of how they might connect, for example, has been an enduring proposition for the making of what has been called "transcultural dialogues (or polylogues)" by scholars around the world including China.[1] A revisit to a range of humanistic scholarship that has long engaged in critical and imaginative examination of such praxis and its complexity can be found in some of the scholarly works in performance studies and in particular the performative methods invented therein to embody English—or any languages—as possibly one vernacular among others and always in search of its dialogical and polylogical connections across various established and naturalized boundaries.[2] Resonating with such works, an increasing range of writings beyond specialized academic terminologies is

---

1 The question of cultural heterogeneity is one of such "differences" that has received sustained attention. Of the notable publications on "encounters of heterogeneous cultures" and their possible transcultural relations by scholars in Europe, China and beyond, see Yue Daiyun and Chen Yueguang, eds., *China's Cultural Orientation in Global Perspective* (Beijing: Renmin University of China Press, 2018). In the US context, reflective treatments of this difficult topic have also been growing, including recently Nan Z. Da, *Intransitive Encounter: Sino–US Literatures and the Limits of Exchange* (New York: Columbia University Press, 2018).

2 The notion of embodiment that keeps human bodies of various shapes and linguistic-cum-cultural inscriptions firmly in view is an important message offered by such scholarship. For earlier works on this subject, see Yan Haiping, "Other Transnationals: An Introductory Essay," in *Other Transnational: Asian Diaspora in Performance*, a special issue of *Modern Drama*, Vol. XLVIII, No. 2 (Summer 2005). Also see works in performance studies by the feminist focus group of the Association for Theatre in Higher Education (ATHE) throughout and since the 1990s, with scholars such as Elin Diamond, Jill Dolan, and (the late) Glenda Dickenson. The recent past online conference for example in July 2020 held by its international branch, International Feminist Theatre Research (IFTR) and its 2023 onsite conference in Accra, Ghana show how such scholarship continues. Such scholarship and the activities in the world of live performance itself, including YoYo Ma's Silk Road initiative of the past two decades and the NY Phil's recent Project 19, and more recently in the Chinese context, the 2023 production of Chekov's *The Seagull* directed by Pu Cunxi at Beijing People's Theatre Company along with a range of innovative theatre, dance and music productions in major cities in China in connection with academic discussions on "transculturality" have been mutual witnesses of what one may call vernacular plurality and its strength.

noteworthy. Due to the limited space here, I would conclude this essay by engaging one example, namely, Pulitzer Prize-winning author Isabel Wilkerson's 2020 article, "America's Enduring Caste System" that re-traces the history of the struggles for racial justice and cultural diversity in the US context. This study re-historicizes, as much as re-contextualizes, the civil rights movement—led by Martin Luther King Jr. of the last century—to recount how the genealogies of the decolonizing movements for independence in the formerly colonized peoples, used to be, have been and can continue to be interconnected in mutually critical, illuminating and possibly transformative ways. Wilkerson (2020) articulates, with specific and quotidian scenes such as King's visit to a high school in Trivandrum whereby his brief dialogue with the enthused and unfamiliar youth there brings an "echo" that "touches" his mind, in an at once disturbing, connective and transformative way, and how such "trans-connection" made with mutual critique and illumination generate multilayered and transcultural impetuses for humanly enabling change across languages, cultures, national histories and civilizations. Such change points towards ever-renewing re-cognitions of the recurring paradoxical problems of modernity inherent in "the continuum of history" as Walter Benjamin puts it, and of the actual moments that open such "continuum" up for mutually transformative interconnections to appear, intelligibly, as a verb, and as a "we" in the making, with the quotidian strength of a vernacular plurality in critical dialogues.[1] Such a "we" constitutes what may be considered the loci of the transcultural art of living humanity and humanities productively at odds with the presence and limits of language as an institutional monolingual framework, and with the coercive logic of geopolitics and its ordering of cultural worlds, as well as with circulation mechanisms and prevalent structures of global markets. One may argue that it is in such art that the actual living and thinking reside and/or can transpire as the quick of life itself. Vernacular plurality in critically enabling dialogues and polylogues, in other words, sustains or even originates the dynamics

---

1   Isabel Wilkerson, "America's Enduring Caste System," *New York Times* (July 1, 2020).

of such living and thinking that have to do with where "we" are from, what "we" might become, and how "we" are becoming, as in the dialogue between Martin Luther King Jr. and the Indian high school teacher and students, recalled and re-narrated by Wilkerson polylogically à la transformatively, in and as a moment of critically reflective awareness in the midst of coming to terms with irreducible differences, thereby generating vital connective re-cognitions.[1]

One would consider that such "living and thinking" in the making of a broadening vision of a "we" beyond the limits of a Eurocentric modernity has been the original intention of the editors of the *Norton Anthology of World Literature*, who revisited how different "foundational texts"[2] such as those discussed in *The Power of Words* have "accrued power and significance over time until they become source codes for entire cultures, telling people where they came from and how they should live their lives" (Puchner 2019, 10–11). In revisiting the enabling aspects of such "power and significance" as these texts have accrued, one would also have to question the ways in which they are deemed enabling, and how the "foundational" value and status of these and any other texts as "source codes for entire cultures" have been made and remade *in relation to one another* in a world hung in a decisive power un-equilibrium as the conditionality of their being so made, *in relation to* the specific and quotidian life scenes of vernacular plurality within each of and among these "foundations" so defined and redefined worldwide, and the ways in which such value and status have been codified *in relation to* "the continuum of history" in this

---

1   Elin Diamond's seminal essay "The Violence of 'We'" has offered a resilient way informed by critical feminist and performance theory for us to come to terms with "differences," transformatively. Elin Diamond, "The Violence of 'We'," in Janelle G. Reinelt and Joseph R. Roach, eds., *Critical Theory and Performance* (Ann Arbor: The University of Michigan Press, 1992), 390–398. A recent article by Laurent Debreuil addresses the issue from a different perspective and political position. Laurent Debreuil, "Nonconforming," *Harper's Magazine* (September 2020).

2   The term "foundational," used by Puchner in his *The Written World*, has been unpacked by critical theorists over the years as a constitutive element of the ready-made ideologies of historical power

human-made world of modernity.[1] To return to my exchange with Puchner: In recent years, the Institute for World Literatures and Cultures (IWLC) and the Department of Foreign Languages and Literatures (DFLL) at Tsinghua University have formulated a new program for the "studies of world literatures and cultures" with the aim of broadening the scope and practical space of teaching and research for the studies of foreign languages and humanities in China, so as to help teachers and students deepen their reflective and dialectical— as much as polylogical—awareness of their work as more than that of "Chinese experts in foreign languages and literatures," thereby becoming more capable of imagining their work as an active relationship always in the process of being made and remade within different and changing languages, cultures and lifeworlds on earth, in ways exceeding the binary logic of an essentialized "mother tongue" and its "others." It is an effort to relate the languages and literatures of the world's different peoples to the Chinese linguistic, literary and cultural traditions in its re-makings with its plurality, and vice versa, to make enabling trans-connectives. The questions of how to deepen one's consciousness of the complexity, richness and fecundity of one's "mother tongue" in relation to different languages, and how "mother tongue" and "foreign" languages—or any mother tongue as one among variable human-made vernaculars of the lifeworlds—are crisscrossing one another as mutually illuminating and enhancing processes, constitute the center of gravity of this descriptive (here means opening) formulation. "Gaining an awareness and reflective

---

apparatuses. With the benefit of insights provided by critical theory, I would also acknowledge Puchner's sense of the adjective that designates a more generalized writing and its significance beyond the paradigm of nineteenth-and twentieth-century novels that has constituted the center of gravity in the studies of modernity as an overriding category for the field of the humanities, and maintain the term here with a qualification that it be taken as dynamic and always in the process of being remade.

1 *The Written World*, as a range of important works coming from Harvard School of World Literature, with its creative spirit that travels into the ancient times and civilizations, is clearly written for the present as future. So is IWLC's initiative, envisioned and implemented at a critical conjuncture of world history with an acutely felt sense of contemporaneity in the making whereby all the pasts and futures of the plural lifeworlds are involved and are at stake.

understanding of one's mother tongue in learning differential languages, and enhancing one's imaginative capability in differential languages while deepening the awareness and understanding of one's mother tongue" may be envisioned and can be understood as mutual arrivals (Yan 2020).[1] And in some moments, tentative or fleeting as they may be, as in the case of the online meeting comprising specifically located parties worldwide with which I began this essay, or in many other scenarios of the quotidian, such an "imaginative" can take place and be embodied, however partially or conditionally, "initiating a critical awareness that moves the minds beyond their comfort zones or toward something like a trans-connection"[2] among not only different languages but also language families. Can we imagine a Goethe of Indo-European formation living in this day and age and, in the conversation among not only different languages but also language families, advocating "world literatures" by appreciating or criticizing texts in Chinese or other languages beyond the Indo-European? Or what if the *Norton Anthology of World Literature* would exist in the form of a multilingual book series such as *TRACES*/印记? At the heart of what we call "hermeneutics," which mainly originated from the "Western tradition," is a method by which to decipher and comprehend the switching of language codes between the world of humans and that of the divine;[3] what state of mind and imaginative power would be nurtured if its focus were to become landed or localized, in and across different places, regions, countries, and continents, thereby generating methods of comprehending and

---

1   Yan Haiping, "On the Need for Transcultural Abilities since Modern Times, in China and the World," *Pengpai News*, Shanghai (July 20, 2020).

2   See p. 3, ft. *.

3   "Hermeneutik comes from Hermes, the name of a messenger in Greek mythology. Hermeneutics is a kind of linguistic transformation, a linguistic shift from one world to another, from the world of God to the world of man, from the world of strange languages to the world of one's own language." *Brecht, Music and Culture: Hanns Eisler in Conversation with Hans Bunge* (布莱希特、音乐和文化, the Chinese edition), translated by Huang Junmei (Xiamen: Xiamen University Press, 2018), 301. *Brecht, Music and Culture: Hanns Eisler in Conversation with Hans Bunge* (English edition), translated by Sabine Berendse and Paul Clements (London / New York: Methuen Drama, 2014); Hans Bunge, Hanns Eisler, *Gespräche mit Hans Bunge: fragen sie mehr über Brecht* (Leipzig: Deutscher Verlag für Musik,1975).

engendering quotidian sharing and concrete transformations across language families, cultures and culturally inscribed civilizations?[1] The multilingual and transcultural makings of connection have not only long been called for but also experienced and practiced by generations of scholars both from China and around the world. Much like literature, such calls and experiences, with all their richness and complexity, constitute an irreducible dimension in and indispensable vision of human reality throughout our modern times. And much like the living human reality inherently and always exceeding the limits of ready-made modes of the modern world and the institutions of its knowledge production, such life experiences and practices provide an invitation for cognitive attempts that may enable knowledge production to be and become a living process, over and again. The continuation of such a vision and its multi-dimensional reality is not sustained and is simply not sustainable by an educational initiative from any one country alone, or by an idea from any one person, be he or she as magnificent as Goethe and his counterparts in different parts of the world. Even if such an initiative happens or can happen at one moment or another, in one place or another, its continuation must rely on social individuals who, having been situated in codified languages, cultures and institutional frameworks of the world modern, reach out to one another across overt and hidden divides or boundaries in concrete transcultural dialogues and polylogues supported by innovative methods of articulations, active networks of producing knowledge, and enduring communities for the humanities, seeking trans-connections, imagined or actual, as processes evocative of and in service of mutual arrivals.

Thus, when Tsinghua University proposed to co-establish with eleven Chinese and

---

1   See Hans-Georg Gadamer, *Truth and Method* (*Wahrheit und Methode*), translated by Donald Marshall (New York: Continuum, 1994). *Truth and Method* (真理与方法, Chinese edition), translated by Hong Handing (Beijing: The Commercial Press, 2007). It may be worth discussing whether or not to develop such a reflection of the many other productive lines of thought in post-World War II European and American academia.

British universities the China–UK Association for the Humanities in Higher Education in 2016, the written initiative was as follows:

The contemporary era of economic globalization, as another phase of the *longue durée* of world history, has been changing and will continue to change the human geographies of the world across all nations and regions, involving no less than a reproduction of humanity and social life itself on an unprecedented scale in human history. It has often been remarked that we live in a time of superfast, hyper-transformative technological innovation and economic growth, when lived histories and the intellectual legacy of human beings have been rendered insignificant. Meanwhile, the deepening sense of uncertainty in social belonging and the ground-gaining of cultural parochialism in various forms have become a world-wide phenomenon, reminding us to think about the usage and meaning of the technological advances and economic achievements that have brought dramatic growth of wealth and opportunities to the world. Amidst such sea change, humanities education centered on transcultural knowledge production and cooperatively sustained creativity has taken on ever greater historical significance. However new the globalized technology becomes, however vast the wealth accumulated, it is the ways in which they are articulated through the formation and transformation of the social individual, human beings, communities, nations and countries, and regions of all kinds as well as of their relationships that ultimately matter, and matter tremendously, bringing long-lasting consequences to the present and future, as they did in the past of world history.

In the spirit of such a recognition, Tsinghua University proposes the initiative of establishing the China–UK Association for the Humanities in Higher Education, as an inter-institutional network for transcultural and global dialogues, dialogic exchanges and research collaborations in the humanities and humanistic education.[1]

"Only connect," and life happens; this can be a vision for life to turn into a verb with all its pauses, ellipses and uncertainties at a particular conjuncture or over time. This can also be a simple description of factual reality breathing in the thick of the everyday, the very impetus of the quotidian, without which humans and the human world at any specific moment or throughout its entire history, could not be, let alone become. Such a verb and its impetus point to the pragmatic fulcrum and *raison d'être* for lives to live, in this humanly made time and space that are always in the process of being remade. And it is the ways through which such a verb happens that invite and demand the most careful consideration, involving high stakes for the welfare of humanity and the humanities as a field of knowledge production, and implicating tremendous consequences, in the present and for the future, as they did in the deep passages of the long past.

(Acknowledgement: An earlier version of this essay in Chinese has appeared in *Journal of Northwestern Polytechnical University (Social Sciences)* Issue 4, 2020. Many thanks to the Journal for permission to incorporate that earlier version in this essay. This article is a revision of the author's speech at the 2021 UKCHA Annual Forum.)

---

1 "Tsinghua Initiates and Eleven Other Universities Jointly Launches China–UK Association for the Humanities in Higher Education," Shanghai (December 6, 2016). "The Initiating of *China–UK Association for the Humanities in Higher Education* in Shanghai," *Education Daily of China* (December 7, 2016). The Association has held its annual forum since.

21世纪中国的世界化逻辑

——以"文明"论为中心

贺桂梅[*]

如何阐释"中国"在21世纪中国知识界发生了可称"范式性"的转型。一种从"文明"论角度展开的中国研究和中国阐释，取代了曾经的诸种中国论述，比如"民族-国家"论、"现代化"论、以社会主义与资本主义冲突为主要内容的"冷战"论等。这里的"文明"，不是一个与"野蛮"相对的形容词，也不是一个大写的普遍价值体，而是一种复数的社会构成体单位。在这种阐释视野中，中国社会被视为"中华文明体"的当代延续，其国家形态区别于西方式民族-国家，其文化认同则需重新深植于古典中国传统的现代延长线上。这一范式的转型起源于20—21世纪之交知识界关于"中国崛起""中国模式""中国经验"等的讨论。阐释者的立场和理论谱系并非一致，有种种复杂的声音交织其中，他们不仅尝试阐释21世纪的中国，也力图阐释全球化时代的世界。

一、"文明-国家"的崛起

以"文明"来勾勒20—21世纪之交的当下世界秩序，始于美国学者亨廷顿（Samuel P. Huntington）的"文明冲突"论。20世纪八九十年代之交，东欧剧

---

[*] 贺桂梅：北京大学中文系教授。主要从事20世纪中国文学史、思想史、女性文学史研究与当代文化批评。

变、苏联解体之后国际理论界迅速出现的两种重要历史叙述，一是福山的"历史终结"论，一是亨廷顿的"文明冲突"论。虽然它们在出现之初都引发了激烈论争，不过，两者的命运却有所不同。不同于"历史终结"论遭到的普遍贬斥，"文明冲突"论固然引起了许多争议，但有意味的是，它迄今仍是极具生命力的一种叙述全球格局的历史叙事形态。这里的关键不在"冲突"，而是用"文明"这样一个范畴来解释今日世界及其构成体，被以不同的方式延续或复制。

亨廷顿将"文明"视为理解冷战之后世界政治格局的新范式，并声称它是取代"冷战"范式的唯一可能："在冷战后的世界中，人民之间最重要的区别不是意识形态的、政治的或经济的，而是文化的区别。"亨廷顿所谓"文明"，主要指"文化"特性，即"用祖先、宗教、语言、历史、价值观、习俗和体制来界定自己"，因此"文明"被视为"一个最广泛的文化实体"。[1]他提出当今世界存在八大文明，"中华文明"与"印度文明""伊斯兰文明""日本文明""东正教文明""西方文明""拉丁美洲文明""非洲文明"并列。在这样一个"多元文明"的世界里，"中华文明"构成了对以美国为中心的"西方文明"的重要挑战。亨廷顿特意凸显了"中华文明"与"儒教文明"的区分，"虽然儒教是中国文明的重要组成部分。但中国文明却不仅是儒教，而且它也超越了作为一个政治实体的中国"，因此他使用"中华"（sinic）来描述"中国和中国以外的东南亚以及其他地方华人群体的共同文化，还有越南和朝鲜的相关文化"。[2]在这样一个文明圈中，中国并不占有特殊位置，由于"4只小老虎中有3只是华人社会"，亨廷顿更强调"华人"这一族群的重要性。

亨廷顿的"文明冲突"论发表之初，即在20世纪90年代的中国知识界引起了极大反响。但在当时，这种论述并没有与重新阐释"中国"直接关联起来。在国际语境中，最早用"文明"来阐释中国的是2010年英国人马丁·雅克（Martin

---

1 ［美］塞缪尔·亨廷顿:《文明的冲突与世界秩序的重建》（修订版），周琪等译，北京: 新华出版社，2009年，第5、21页。

2 ［美］塞缪尔·亨廷顿:《文明的冲突与世界秩序的重建》，第24页。

Jacques）的《当中国统治世界》[1]。他将中国称为"文明国家"，而且声称这种称呼没有任何贬低的含义。继而，张维为在《中国震撼》[2]中，将中国称为"文明型国家"，认为中国糅合了传统"文明国家"与现代"民族-国家"的两种特点，是一个现代却非西方模式的国家。

用"文明"来描述中国的国家特性，直接源自对中国"崛起"的判断和指认，以及在全球化格局中重新认知中国的诉求。汪晖提到，"在1989年之后，中国几乎是当代世界上唯一一个在人口构成和地域范围上大致保持着前20世纪帝国格局的政治共同体"，但是，"在各种有关中国具体问题的讨论中，'何为中国'始终是一个核心的但常常被掩盖了的问题"。[3]正是中国经济的崛起和中国作为一个大国在全球格局中日益重要的地位，使得重新讨论这一问题成为可能，用"文明"来描述中国的国家特性则是回应这一问题的一种重要方式。

事实上，这种论述方式并非始自马丁·雅克或张维为，中国知识界于21世纪之初就已形成类似的叙述，其中影响最大的，一是以甘阳为代表的人文科学学者的"文明-国家"论，另一是以潘维为代表的社会科学学者的"中国模式"论。

甘阳早在2003年就提出，中国应当从"民族-国家"走向"文明-国家"。他借用亨廷顿的相关理论描述，区分了现代化的两个阶段：第一阶段"现代化"被等同于"西方化"，其特征是对自身文明传统的激烈否定和批判；进入第二阶段，则"现代化进程越发达，往往越是表现为'去西方化'和复兴'本己文化'"。21世纪的中国已经进入第二阶段，必须树立一种新观念，"中国的'历史文明'是中国'现代国家'的最大资源"，而非如20世纪主流观念那样，将其视为一种现代化的"障碍"。[4]甘阳认为中国并非联合国上百个国家中的普通

1　[英]马丁·雅克：《当中国统治世界：中国的崛起和西方世界的衰落》，张莉、刘曲译，北京：中信出版社，2010年。

2　张维为：《中国震撼：一个"文明型国家"的崛起》，上海：上海人民出版社，2010年。

3　汪晖：《东西之间的"西藏问题"（外二篇）》，北京：生活·读书·新知三联书店，2014年，第147页。

4　甘阳：《从"民族-国家"走向"文明-国家"》，《21世纪经济报道》2003年12月29日。

一"国"，而应是一个"文明母体"。[1] 中国从古迄今表现出了一些共同特征，即"共同的文化认同""统一的最高主权"和"高度的历史连续性"。甘阳一方面批评西方中心主义的"世界史"范式，认为中国不仅是"非西方文明"，而且"中国在历史上和西方没有任何关系，是完全外在于西方的，西方也完全外在于中国"，所以，用黑格尔那样的"世界史"视野无法理解中国；另一方面强调了中国文明具有的内在同一性与延续性，具体到当下中国，需要完成的是新一轮的传统整合，将现代、当代与古典传统重新融会起来。甘阳由此提出著名的"通三统"说，即"孔夫子的传统、毛泽东的传统、邓小平的传统，是同一个中国历史文明连续统"。[2] 甘阳的这种论述方式和文化立场并不仅是一种个人化表述。通过他主要组织的人文学者群体"中国文化论坛"及其主编的丛书"文化：中国与世界新论"，还包括参与实践的大学"通识教育"等活动，这种中国叙述事实上成了21世纪中国人文知识界极具影响力的声音。

如果说甘阳侧重从历史延续性即纵向的时间轴上理解"中国道路"，那么潘维联合多个社会科学领域的学者而提出的"中国模式"，则更倾向于从共时性角度建立某种关于"中华文明"的模型。如同甘阳以阐释当代中国为其基本问题意识，潘维也是从理解当代中国的历史经验出发，把"中国模式"看作"关于人民共和国60年'成功之路'的理论解释"，而这个模式的基础是"中华文明的延续性"。不仅前后两个30年的当代中国是一个连续展开的过程，而且当代中国与"百年""三千年""五千年"历史也构成了内在的延续关系。"模式"的特征在于结构性要素的稳定性，潘维概括出中国模式的三个子模式，即国民经济、民本政治与社稷体制，而每一子模式又可以分成几种更细微的要素，用以阐释这个模式的共时性特征。他联合社会科学界的诸多学者，从经济学、政治学、社会学

1　甘阳：《"文化：中国与世界"新论·缘起》，《通三统》，北京：生活·读书·新知三联书店，2007年，第1页。

2　甘阳：《三种传统的融会与中华文明复兴》，《21世纪经济报道》2004年12月30日。

以及法律、医疗、乡村治理等不同领域和角度加以阐述[1]，尽管并非所有学者都认可"中国模式"这个提法，但他们阐释中国的共同立场和诉求，是打破西方中心主义范式而从中国自身的历史传统和实践经验出发来解释中国的发展道路。在这样的分析视野中，"中国文明"意味着一种新的阐释平台和研究范式，不再是用西方社科知识来解释中国，也不是用以西方（美国）为模板的现代化范式来规范问题范围，而是打破古／今、中／西乃至社会科学／人文科学的种种区隔，站在中国主体性视野中探询当代中国历史经验的复杂性和丰富性，尤其关注将那些在实践中"行而不知"的经验转化为自觉的理论探讨。可以说，在知识研究范式的层面，"中国模式"作为一种理论范畴的提出，意味着某种明确的反西方化诉求，即从"西方中心"范式、"现代化"范式向"中国学派"[2]的转变。

与理论层面上的"文明-国家"论述相关的，是21世纪以来中国社会普遍出现的"传统文化热"。这里所谓"传统文化"，在宽泛的意义上指涉古典中国不同时期、不同形态的文化，它们有各种各样的称呼，如"中华文明""中国文化""国学""儒学""传统经典"等。对这些文化形态关注、讨论、研究、建构与实践的热情，是新世纪中国一种醒目的文化现象和热潮。这种文化现象同时也是一种政治、经济现象，在国家治理、文化市场运作、社会生活组织和民族心理及精神状态等各个层面都有所表现。[3] 社会实践层面的"传统文化热"与理论层面的"文明-国家"论，构成了彼此塑造的复杂关系。虽然在不同脉络上展开，参与其中的社会力量也纵横交错，难以被统一到某种理论形态中，不过，其共同特征在于：正是在"文明"与"国家"相勾连的视野中，新世纪中国的国家形象、社会组织、文化认同等都发生了某种根本性的改变。这是人们在描述、分析21世纪中国时几乎难以回避的。

---

1 潘维主编：《中国模式：解读人民共和国的60年》，北京：中央编译出版社，2009年；潘维、玛雅主编：《人民共和国六十年与中国模式》，北京：生活·读书·新知三联书店，2010年。

2 吴志攀在为潘维主编的《中国模式：解读人民共和国的60年》所写序言"旧邦新命"中，提出了"中国学派"这一说法（第3页）。

3 相关描述参见贺桂梅：《传统文化热："国家"与"文明"的交互塑造》，《社会科学报》2014年1月9日。

二、"文明"与"中国"

如何从理论上界定"文明"的内涵，并探讨"中国"与"文明"间的独特关系，也构成了21世纪知识界关注的重要问题。

"文明"被视为一个大于"国家"而小于"世界"的人类构成体单位。它的特征一方面在于文明体内部超越时间而存在的某种连续性和稳定性，另一方面则在于其"边界"的模糊性，法国人类学家莫斯（Marcel Mauss）称之为"没有清晰边界的社会现象"[1]。与"民族-国家"所追求的"均质性"和"清晰边界"不同，一个"文明体"能够包容内部的差异性，同时，与他种文明体之间存在着既交融又区隔的复杂关系。由此带来的三个问题，其一是文明体与政治体的关系。比如汪晖提及一个看法，"在欧洲的语境中，国家的边界与文明的边界并不重叠，而中国历史始终存在着一种将文明的边界与政治的边界相互统一起来的努力"[2]，这也是将中国视为"文明-国家"的前提。其二是文明体与"民族-国家"的差别。源发于18世纪西欧的现代民族-国家，其首要特征在于"一个民族一个国家"，以及建立在"国民"与"国家"的直接对应关系上的内部社会均质性。[3]而"文明-国家"及文明体内部则总是包含了多种民族、多个区域的差异，因而呈现出"混杂性"特征。当中国被视为一个由"文明"而非"民族"界定的国家时，其国家特性也发生了变化。其三是文明体间的关系与"世界"想象。亨廷顿的文明理论接近汤因比（Arnold Toynbee）的文明形态学，强调文明体之间的隔绝、对立而非流通、融合的关系，因而构造的是一种"冲突"的世界图景。

这里仅就费孝通、王铭铭与汪晖的相关研究做简单介绍和分析。

---

1 ［法］马塞尔·莫斯、爱弥尔·涂尔干、亨利·于贝尔：《论技术、技艺与文明》，蒙养山人译，北京：世界图书出版公司，2010年，第36页。

2 汪晖：《东西之间的"西藏问题"（外二篇）》，第149页。

3 参见［英］厄内斯特·盖尔纳：《民族与民族主义》，韩红译，北京：中央编译出版社，2002年；［美］本尼迪克特·安德森：《想象的共同体——民族主义的起源与散布》，吴叡人译，上海：上海人民出版社，2005年。

1988年在香港的一次讲座上，费孝通提出了"中华民族的多元一体格局"这一说法，将"中华民族"的形成描述为两个相关联的历史过程：其一是"几千年来的历史过程中形成"的"自在的民族实体"，其二是"近百年来中国和西方列强对抗中出现"的"自觉的民族实体"。"自在的民族实体"并非单质的，而是"许许多多分散孤立存在的民族单位，经过接触、混杂、裂解和融合，同时也有分裂和消亡，形成一个你来我去、我来你去、我中有你、你中有我，而又各具个性的多元统一体"。他同时说，"这也许是世界各地民族形成的共同过程"。也就是说，"民族"并非如民族主义理论描述的那样具有单质性，而总是在"交融"中形成的，中华民族"大混杂、大融合"的历史不过更凸显了这一过程而已。从"自在的民族实体"转化为"一体性"的"自觉的民族实体"，则意味着一个政治性的"国族体"构建过程。[1] 这种描述突破了一般的民族国家理论，而与"文明"论视野中的中国论述关系密切。20世纪90年代后期，为回应亨廷顿的"文明冲突"论，费孝通提出了"文化自觉"说："生活在一定文化中的人对其文化有'自知之明'，明白它的来历、形成过程、所具有的特色和它发展的趋向，不带任何'文化回归'的意思，不是要复旧，同时也不主张'全盘西化'或'坚守传统'。"[2] 王铭铭写道："费孝通先生读了亨廷顿的'文明冲突论'，提出'文化自觉'与之对垒，认为冲突背后有一种秩序，这个秩序也是理想，可以用'各美其美，美人之美，美美与共，和而不同'来理解与期待。"[3] 可以说，在费孝通这里，"文化自觉"的中国诉求与"和而不同"的世界构想是一体两面的，在看似平实的历史性描述中，包含了一些重要的理论设想。

王铭铭承续费孝通的思考，从人类学、社会学和民族学的视野出发，强调"中国"不应被理解为一个"民族体"而应是"文明体"。"民族体"有着将"社

1　费孝通主编：《中华民族多元一体格局》（修订版），北京：中央民族大学出版社，1999年，第3—4页。

2　费孝通：《文化的生与死》，刘豪兴编，上海：上海人民出版社，2009年，第185页。

3　王铭铭：《"中间圈"——费孝通、民族的人类学研究与文明史》，黄平主编：《乡土中国与文化自觉》，北京：生活·读书·新知三联书店，2007年，第61页。

会"与"文化"等同于"国家"的局限,固化了一些实际上是历史地构成的社会单位,因此王铭铭提出"文明人类学",以期形成一种新的宏观研究视野。人类学领域注重传播、交融的"文明"研究,往往采取一种普遍主义的文明观,由于这一理论范畴常与"进步的信念"这种启蒙主义思想相关联,使得强调地方性知识的"二战"后人类学研究者常常避之唯恐不及。不过,王铭铭却认为,放弃"文明"的这一范畴同时也意味着人类学抛弃了与传播论相关联的宏观研究视野。他重新钩沉出20世纪二三十年代法国人类学家莫斯的理论,将"文明"界定为一种"超社会体系",借此分析地方性的"文化"与作为复合体的"文明"之间的互动关联。在体系性的"文明"和结构性的"文化"("社会")之间,王铭铭倡导的"文明人类学"力图打破凝固性的结构主体,特别是社会共同体的民族国家和普遍而单一的世界体系这种二元论。这里的"文明"含义不同于"文明-国家"论的理解。最大的不同在于,它并不将"文明"视为与国家同一的凝固特性,比如"中国模式"那样的"模式",或如张维为归纳的"八大特点",而将之视为"体系性"又不断传播、交流、融合的过程。与之相应的是,被视为"文化"("社会")的那些差异性结构,从来就不是自我生成的,毋宁是"外生的",其独特性总是在"文明"的宏观体系中才能成立。因此他说,"脱离了'超社会体系'研究中的'互为主体'的人文世界观,世界史将是不可能的",对于文明而言,"'融合'同时是历史与价值"。[1]

具体到中国研究,"从历史上看,过去的中国确实是超社会的,它既不同于世界体系,又不同于文化,历史上无疑是一个帝国,一个我们叫做'天下'的东西,但过去这个超社会体系是有价值和伦理定义的,过去的政府处理内外关系,很大程度上依赖某种既非政治经济又非文化的'技巧',这些'技巧'跟莫斯所说的'文明'有些接近,但又不同于他所说的'超社会的宗教'"[2]。如何理解这样一个"超社会体系",是王铭铭重新认知"中国"的基本内容。他提出"三圈

1　王铭铭:《超社会体系——文明与中国》,北京:生活·读书·新知三联书店,2015年,第321、319页。
2　王铭铭:《超社会体系》,第127页。

说"（即汉人核心区、少数民族"混杂区"和国家边界之外的"世界"），以描述中国这一"文明体"的内在世界观。作为一个由圈式结构关系构成的文明体，其中心与边缘的关系并非固定，而存在着圈与圈之间互为主体的可能性。由此，中国既不是民族主义意义上的"国家"，也不是普遍主义意义上的"帝国"或"世界"，而是包含了诸种混杂性族群与区域（"圈"）的"体系"。

汪晖以与王铭铭的"超社会体系"概念对话的形式，提出了一种关于中国的新的界定方式，即"跨体系社会"，并将其实践于对西藏、琉球等"边疆"问题的讨论中。汪晖颠倒了"社会"与"体系"的位置，显示出其中国研究与王铭铭研究的不同侧重点。莫斯/王铭铭的"超社会体系"，是要将"社会"从民族主义知识构造的社会-国家一体中解放出来，将其放在复数文明的体系性关系中加以考察。而汪晖"跨体系社会"概念的重心，则强调中国作为一种具有内在差异性（跨体系）的"社会"即"一体"性面向。他认为任何社会构成体（包括国家、区域、地方、村庄乃至个人）都是"跨体系"的，是在体系性的互动关系中形成的。因此，理解"社会"的前提是其在变动历史关系中形成的"跨体系"性。他由此提出了"区域作为方法"这一基本方法论原则，瞩目于"区域"范畴包含的"独特的混杂性、流动性和整合性"，一方面破解"民族主义的知识框架"，另一方面考察"更广阔的区域内的各政治共同体连接在一起"的历史形态。[1] 比如他在对西藏问题的阐释中，特别强调了"民族区域"作为政治认同单位的建构如何区别于"民族"（自决）与"区域"（自治），从而为当代中国民族和边疆问题提供了独特的阐释思路。[2]

但正如费孝通从"自在"到"自觉"转变的阐释，关键问题在于，诸种多元性结构或体系最终是怎样形成一个统一的政治体，这个"一体"的合法性如何确立呢？汪晖凸显了特定"政治文化"在构造"一体性"认同时的重要性。"多元性"存在于中国多民族、各区域的互动关系中，"一体性"则源自一种超越族群、

1　汪晖:《东西之间的"西藏"问题（外二篇）》，第149—150页。

2　汪晖:《东西之间的"西藏"问题（外二篇）》，第72—96页。

区域身份政治的普遍政治文化的构建。"社会"与"体系"是互动互生的，其关系既是历史性的，也是价值性的（或政治性的）。"历史性"指的是诸如朝贡体系、现代世界体系、殖民体系、王朝中国的政治体制、区域关系、地方性形态等建构与发展的历史过程，"政治性"指的则是特定政治实践与这些历史结构的关系乃是一种自觉建构的产物，总是建立在自觉的政治文化或合法性表述基础上。比如，在论及历代中国王朝的连续性问题时，汪晖如此说道：如果没有用公羊思想特别是"大一统""通三统"和"别内外"等政治文化构想来确立新朝之"正统"的过程，"讨论王朝之间的连续性是完全不可能的"。[1]

这也就是说，"多元一体"之"一体"得以确立的关键在于一种普遍政治原则的确立，"文明"的差异性可以被组织为一种"一体性"的政治共同体，并非一种自然而然的产物，而是自觉的政治化实践的结果。事实上，所谓"文明"的连续性、整合性，既涵盖了制度、宗教、心态、习俗、技艺与技术等层面，更包含了自觉的理论认知和政治化实践。在断裂性的诸历史形态与话语构成之间，缺少"政治化"这个环节，文明的连续性并不会自然生成。

三、"文明"的当代性

在"中国文明"的连续性视野中，"传统"（或"古典"）得到了极大的重视，进而在学科知识形态上形成了一种"古典学"热潮。从当代中国历史经验中追溯出古典"传统"的影响，强调在长时段视野中思考中国文明的当代性，可以说是21世纪中国"文明"论的主要内容。但这一态度和取向与20世纪"反传统"的主流思潮形成了明显的对比，可以说这种对文明当代性的关注显然也是"政治化"的产物。因此需要追问的，一是为什么"传统文化"会在21世纪中国社会成为不同力量的"共识"，并以此来建构中国身份与文化认同呢？二是"传统"的确切

1　汪晖：《亚洲视野：中国历史的叙述》，香港：牛津大学出版社，2010年，第82页。

内涵及其意义应怎样理解，它如何与当代中国发生关联？

就第一个问题而言，"文明"论的兴起确与亨廷顿所谓世界性的"后冷战"处境密切相关。"文明"被视为一种"非政治"或"超越政治"的运作方式，替代了社会主义与资本主义冲突的冷战论述。在"去政治化"的普遍趋势下，"中国文明"这种看似非意识形态的文化身份，更易为人接受。国家形象的建构如此，"新儒家"的兴盛如此，文化市场与文化产业的叙事策略如此，大众社会的认同心理也是如此。

但正因为对"传统的复兴"这一现象缺少足够政治化自觉，传统文化往往成为民族主义意识形态运作的主要场地。对内而言，是通过对"传统"的不断发明和再制造，将国族认同建构为一种基于地缘与血缘、看似"自然"的共同体意识，以强化社会凝聚力，并有效地调解、转移结构性社会矛盾。对外而言，资本主义/社会主义意识形态对抗的失效，使得已然进入全球格局的中国在确立其主体性身份时，可以有效借用的重要资源，主要是前现代帝国的历史与文化传统。在这样的意义上，"全球化"并未能真的"消灭"民族-国家及其身份认同，甚至应该说，民族主义本身便是全球化的副产品。正是全球化格局本身，使得基于国家领土范围内的"文明"传统来重新构造身份认同成为必要的发明，其最大问题在于无法逾越国家（主义）视野。在此，称这一国族体是"民族"还是"文明"，并没有太大差别。这样的问题在将中国视为"文明-国家"的理论阐释，与在现代民族-国家装置内重新发明和构造"传统文化"的热潮中，都同样存在。

霍布斯鲍姆（Eric Hobsbawm）曾将"传统的发明"视为现代社会的普遍现象，不过，21世纪中国的传统文化热却包含着既与之相同又与之相异的因素。就其同而言，这次热潮确是一种现代的发明，它并非一种"复古"行为，而是市场社会、消费时代与全球化语境下对传统的现代性构造。霍布斯鲍姆关于传统的发明阐释的两个要点：其一是"被发明的传统之独特性在于它们与过去的这种连续性大多是人为的"，由此需要将之与实践性的"习俗"区分开来；另一是被发明的传统是一种"形式化和仪式化"的过程，它不同于"实践中的惯例或常规"。[1] 在中国的传统文化热中，情形常常更接近后一种，即"习俗"或"实践中的惯例或常规"。比如"恢复传统节日"并不是无中生有的"发明"，而是原本就一直在民间社会中流传，只是现在以法律形式正式确定为国家法定节日。在许多时候，这些被重新"发现"的传统，更接近"复兴"的含义，其实践性内涵也远大于仪式性含义。"传统文化"在许多人的体认中，是那些一直存在但没有得到承认或理论化的东西，是一种"日用而不知"的形态。

正是从这样一种思考角度出来，在民族主义意识形态之外，也存在着将传统转化为批判性思想资源的可能性。知识界的"文明"论在讨论"传统"问题时，一些具有批判意识的知识人更愿意凸显后一层面的含义。如费孝通所谓"文化自觉"；甘阳所谓"熟知不是真知"，王铭铭所谓"既非政治经济又非文化的'技巧'"等，都包含了超越民族主义和国家主义的思考层面。特别值得一提的是，李零依据地理山川、经典文献、考古材料、制度形态等考察长时段"中国"的稳定性内涵[2]，则更深入地显示出中国文明的延续性并不全然是一种"虚构"。这也是探讨中国"传统"和文明当代性问题时的独特性所在。

不过，对于"传统"如何转化为当代形态，研究者的政治立场和思考方式并不相同。这里仅以甘阳、王铭铭、汪晖为例简要讨论其政治立场的分歧。

甘阳推崇古典政治哲学，特别强调问题的关键乃在"古今之争"。他认为列奥·施特劳斯（Leo Strauss）的不同寻常之处，"在于他坚持必须从西方古典的视野来全面批判审视西方现代性和自由主义"，"在他看来欧洲十七至十八世纪的那场著名的'古今之争'或'古典人与现代人之争'，虽然表面上以'现代人'的全面胜利为结果，但这场争论本身并未真正结束"。[3] 施特劳斯所从事的

1　［英］E. 霍布斯鲍姆、T. 兰格：《传统的发明》，顾杭、庞冠群译，南京：译林出版社，2004年，第2—4页。

2　李零：《我们的经典》，北京：生活·读书·新知三联书店，2014年；《我们的中国》，北京：生活·读书·新知三联书店，2016年。

3　甘阳：《政治哲人施特劳斯：古典保守主义政治哲学的复兴》，香港：牛津大学出版社，2002年，第2页。

这场争战，显然也是甘阳的立场与选择。他回归古典的前提，是对西方现代性危机的诊断，并以立足"古今之争"弥合"中西之争"的方式，将中国古典思想置于与西方古典的同一平台。甘阳据此展开的"通识教育"实践，则强调"精英教育"，将教育理念设定为"教育未来的管理者"。这种思想实践在知识界产生了广泛影响，但其保守主义和精英主义立场如何避免新的西方中心主义，"通三统""文明-国家"等论述如何区别于民族-国家主义仍有可讨论之处。

王铭铭瞩目的，则是以"中国文明"论破除西方式现代民族-国家观念和民族主义知识。他沿用费孝通的说法，称20世纪是"新战国"时代，"这个时代，以民族为单位建立国家，成为一条世界性纲领，但矛盾的是，国与国之间的竞赛，又是这个时代的另一大特征"，"所谓'冷战'、'后社会主义'、'文明冲突'、'全球化'不过是'战国式竞赛'的具体表现"。[1]他提出的"超社会体系"、"三圈说"、"文明"与"天下"是可以互相替换的概念，目的是重构一种新的"世界"观。中国古典社会的结构方式是"'家、国、天下'和'乡民、士绅、皇权'三者之间，相互分阶序交错着，形成不对应的关系体系"，其实践主体则是士大夫阶层，他们构筑的观念体系"规定行为规范并支持这个结构"。近代以来，这种"社会"观念的衰落导致三层结构各丧失了一层，即"天下"观念的缺失和士大夫作为社会中间层的消失，"只剩下家与国或国与家——即我们所理解的'国家'"[2]。但在王铭铭这里，"天下"的世界观和"士"的社会功能如何转换为当代形态，则缺少更明晰的理论构想。

与之相比，汪晖更侧重探寻新的以"人民"为主体的普遍政治的可能性，他对古典和传统的重估也是在这一立场上展开的。在研究现代中国思想如何兴起时他说，需要关注传统中国的"内在视野"，"这不仅仅是用古代解释现代，或用

1　王铭铭：《超越"新战国"：吴文藻、费孝通的中华民族理论》，北京：生活·读书·新知三联书店，2012年，第8页。

2　王铭铭：《经验与心态：历史、世界想象与社会》，桂林：广西师范大学出版社，2007年，第157、163页。

古代解释古代，也不仅是用现代解释古代，而且也是通过对话把这个视野变成我们自身的一个内在反思性的视野"。[1] 在这种反思性视野中，古典与现代处于同等的、"互为主体"的思想平台上，为研究者回应当代问题提供批判性资源。

上述研究者的差异性和深层对话关系，尚需更深入讨论。不过，构成知识界"文明"论述的共识，在于破除进化论的现代性意识形态和"西方中心主义"范式。正是在这样的视野中，中国文明的"过去"得以浮现出来，成为人们探寻未来时的一种重要思想资源。而在如何估价这种重构的"文明"视野在今日中国的"当代性"方面，阐释者的政治立场远非一致。

四、中国与世界：重构批判性的文明史视野

"文明"论提出的，不仅是一种关于"中国"的阐释，同时是一种新的"世界观"，包含了关于中国在全球格局中的位置，以及从中国主体性出发重构世界史的更普遍诉求。很大程度上，这也提出了一种不同于20世纪"现代化"范式而在全球格局中重构中国的新的世界化逻辑。首要的一点在于，这里所谓"文明"范畴的内涵，既不是一个普遍的价值实体，也不是启蒙主义逻辑上与"愚昧"相对的价值体，而是一个社会构成体单位，而"世界"是由复数的多个"文明"所构成。基于这样的界定，"世界"的最大构成单位并非单个的民族-国家，而是由民族-国家构成的文明体，这些为数不多的文明体形构了世界的多元性。而中国，正是这些文明体/世界中的一个文明。当"文明"成为"世界"（"全球"）的实体性单位的时候，"中国"与"世界"关系的理解和想象形态也发生了变化。

"文明"这一范畴，如同"文化"一样，含义极为模糊，将其理论化存在着很大的风险。需要厘清三种不同的文明观：一是普遍主义的文明观，一是民族主义的文明观，再一是介于两者之间的复数的文明观。重构"文明"理论，特别是

1　汪晖：《亚洲视野》，第69页。

不使其为民族-国家主义（或作为其反面的世界主义）所限，需要更广阔的文明史视野。

最早于18世纪法国和英国出现的"文明"概念，是在启蒙主义的视野中，在与"野蛮"相对的"开化"这一意义上使用的。这是文明的基本含义之一，并形成了一种普遍主义的文明论。"它主张存在文明这样一种东西，这种东西与进步的信念相关，仅为少数特权民族或特权集团（也就是人类的'精英'）所拥有"[1]；同时还认为，人类社会最终将统一于一种最高文明，并以此"成为对国族进行世界性的等级排序的手段"[2]。这也使普遍主义的文明论成了殖民主义、帝国主义扩张的意识形态。文明的另一含义等同于"文化"，这是18世纪德意志为对抗法英的普遍主义文明论而发明的一种"特殊主义的文明论"，"文化"的含义等同于"民族"，成为民族主义的具体表征。普遍主义/民族主义的文明论，其实是一体两面，都将文明视为一种单质的价值实体，其特殊性与普遍性同处一个可以互相转化的结构中。

布罗代尔（Fernand Braudel）考证，在1819年前后，出现了一种新的文明论，即复数的文明论。[3] 对于这一历史脉络上的文明范畴，王铭铭做了耐心和深入的关键词梳理。[4] 他回溯了20世二三十年代法国年鉴学派民族学和人类学研究者涂尔干和莫斯，瞩目于他们提出但未受到重视的"复数的文明论"，即人类社会存在多种文明，并且它们都具有同等的主体位置。"文明"作为一种"超社会体系"，既超越了被民族-国家限定的"社会"，具备国际性的流动性，同时也不同于普遍的世界体系，而有其传播、扩散的地理限度。实际上，"复数的文明论"也是法国年鉴学派代表人物的布罗代尔研究的特点。在《文明史纲》中，布罗代尔从地理空间、社会、经济、集体（无）意识等四个方面概括了"文明"的

1　［法］费尔南·布罗代尔：《文明史纲》，肖昶等译，桂林：广西师范大学出版社，2003年，第27页。
2　王铭铭：《人类学讲义稿》，北京：世界图书出版社公司，2011年，第318页。
3　［法］费尔南·布罗代尔：《文明史纲》，第26页。
4　王铭铭：《超社会体系》，第3—70页。

基本特点，并描述了伊斯兰、非洲、远东（中国、印度、日本）等"欧洲以外的文明"和欧洲文明（欧洲、美洲、俄罗斯）的历史演变过程。对"文明"范畴的关注，显示的是布罗代尔的一种新的世界史构想。在被称为"总体的社会学"的观照视野下，布罗代尔对特定文明的存在方式（如地中海文明）、诸文明的传播交流形态（如15—18世纪的物质文明、经济、资本主义）做了典范式研究。这种曾被人概括为"长时段、大范围、跨学科、日常生活"的宏观研究方法，被沃勒斯坦（Immanuel Wallerstein）等学者结合马克思主义理论而发展为现代世界体系研究。

追溯当代文明史研究的形成，20世纪60年代是重要时段。在布罗代尔写作了《文明史纲》（初版于1963年）的年代，一种新的史学形态出现了：麦克尼尔（William McNeill）写作了《世界史》[1]（初版于1967年），斯塔夫里阿诺斯（L. S. Stavrianos）写出了《全球通史》[2]（初版于1970年），而巴勒克拉夫（Geoffrey Barraclough）则确立了不同于"现代史"的"当代史"概念，认为这种"全球的历史观"与19世纪西方中心主义历史观的最大不同在于，它纳入了"欧洲之外的世界"。[3] 就更不用说，阿诺德·汤因比自第一次世界大战期间开始构想，历时30多年终于在1961年出版的巨著《历史研究》。可以说，"文明史"是一种新的"世界史"，突破了欧洲中心主义和黑格尔意义上的世界史的局限。[4] 复数的诸"文明"，它们各自的历史与相互的交往融合，构成了这一"世界"/"全球"历史图景的内容。在同为"地方性知识"这一点上，复数的文明论超越了西方中心主

---

1 ［美］威廉·麦克尼尔：《世界史：从史前到21世纪全球文明的互动》（第四版），施诚、赵婧译，北京：中信出版社，2013年。

2 ［美］L. S. 斯塔夫里阿诺斯：《全球通史》（第七版），吴象婴等译，北京：北京大学出版社，2006年。

3 ［英］杰弗里·巴勒克拉夫：《当代史导论》（初版于1964年），张广勇、张宇宏译，上海：上海社会科学院出版社，1996年。

4 近年也有西方学者对布罗代尔的文明史研究提出批评，认为其未能从根本上超越"西欧中心主义范式"（参见［英］杰克·古迪：《偷窃历史》[2009年英文版]，张正萍译，杭州：浙江大学出版社，2016年）。

义；在强调诸文明体的交流与融合这一点上，复数的文明论超越了民族主义。这使得真正意义上的"世界""全球"理解成为可能。不过，需要区分的是，同为复数的文明观，汤因比的文明形态学和文明比较研究更倾向于将诸文明理解为历史"有机体"式的存在，并偏于文化主义的描述，而布罗代尔等则更突出文明作为一种社会—文化—经济的总体性存在。在这一点上，亨廷顿采纳的，更主要是汤因比式的文化主义文明观。

20世纪60年代出现这种新的史学并非偶然。那是一个欧洲殖民体系瓦解、第三世界崛起、非西方国家成为主权国家、少数族裔与民权运动的解放时代。尽管这仍是一种"西方文明"内部的史学变革，但通过"复数的文明"这一范畴，非西方国家与文明得以确立其主体地位，"世界史"不再是"西方中心的历史"。但是，在殖民主义意识形态延续和冷战历史结构支配下，诸种非西方文明主体很难逾越民族-国家主义与现代中心主义，并将自身的合法性建立在对资本主义/西方主义批判的基础上。很大程度上可以说，冷战历史的终结，也使得这种文明史叙述范式丧失了批判的核心支点。也正是在这一意义上，亨廷顿的"文明冲突论"丧失了文明史研究曾有的批判性，而成为对历史危机的一种表述形态。他一方面立足美国利益将"国家"视为"文明"的真正代理人，同时，则使"文明"变成了一种非历史的范畴。"文明冲突论"不仅无法应对冷战后民族主义、文化复古主义、不同形式的原教旨主义及宗教力量的兴起，它自身就是这种现代性危机的具体表征。比如以"文明"所界定的伊斯兰世界与西方世界的冲突，事实上正是在不言自明的"国家"主体想象基础上强化了"冲突论"的实质，而完全忽略了"文明"自身"没有清晰边界"的融通特性。

对文明范畴与文明史研究的知识谱系考察，可以为从文明论视野展开中国研究提供更可靠的批判支点。复数的"文明"观的出现与20世纪60年代以来的文明史研究实践，都瞩目于破除西方中心主义而从真正"多元"的意义上理解人类历史，但悖谬的是，"反西方中心主义"常常是西方学者与西方学术内部的一种研究和论述。在这一意义上，21世纪的中国学者提出"从中国的视野"或"以中国为本位"[1] 去描述中国和世界历史的变迁，无论如何评价都不为过。而复数的"文明"观，则提供了一种真正"多元世界"的批判性视野。

在现代中国的语境中，"文明"常被视为一种普遍性的价值范畴，而"文化"一词则与民族特性的描述相关。自五四时期开始，"文化"就一直是知识界探讨中国特性的关键词。即便在知识界关于东西方文明的大论争中，人们使用的也主要是"文化"而非"文明"一词。这种思维方式一直延续到20世纪80年代的"新启蒙"思潮中。在如何使用"文明"与"文化"这两个基本范畴的方式背后，实际上隐藏着一种普遍主义的现代化意识形态，其中"中国"与"西方"、"古"与"今"、"传统"与"现代"是一种不言自明的同构关系。这也意味着有关"文明"的理解始终是在民族主义与世界主义的二元对立框架内展开的。21世纪中国知识界的"文明"论，在将中国视为一个"文明体"时，已经提出了一种区别于这一二元框架的不同理解方式，包含了在多元世界图景中理解中国这一特殊文明的复数文明观。但由于对"文明"这一核心范畴的界定与阐释不清楚，文明论述中"国家""文明体""世界"这三者的关系常常是含糊的。

引入复数的"文明"论有助于说明三个重要关系维度。其一是可以同时破除特殊性的"国家主义"与普遍性的帝国/世界主义。作为"没有明晰边界的社会现象"，诸文明体之间存在着"国际间"的流动性。这使得人们有可能在民族主义与普遍主义这两个极端之外来观察特定区域群体之间的交流融合形态。"中国文明"论述若能超越"中国主义"及其变形的"大中华主义"，而关注作为"世界经济体"/"文明体"的中国在复杂地缘政治格局中的交往形态，显然更有助于批判性地理解中国的主体性。其二是可以同时超越复古主义与现代中心主义。文明论所强调的"历史连续性"，可以帮助人们理解长时段视野中的历史关系。但是这种连续关系既是实践性的，也是"解释性"的，所以布罗代尔将"文明史"称为"用过去解释现在""用现在解释过去"这两个双向过程。[2] 这使我们

1　韩毓海:《五百年来谁著史：1500年以来的中国与世界》，北京：九州出版社，2009年，第1页。

2　［法］费尔南·布罗代尔:《论历史》，刘北成、周立红译，北京：北京大学出版社，2008年。

可以从现代中心主义的世界（观）中解放出来，看到前现代的社会与历史，但又并非坠入复古主义，而能够在一种整合性视野中，理解中华文明体的全部历史生存。其三是"文明"这一边界模糊的体系性存在同时也是总体性的。这种"总体性"不同于"整体"，后者是现代国族主义构造的"社会""文化""民族"这样的整一性存在，而"文明"是互相关联而又并非整一的总体性构成体。布罗代尔对之做了非统合性的分层，如物质文明、经济、资本主义。[1] 莫斯则区分了技艺、社会生活团体、制度等可传播性的"文明现象"与缺少传播性的"社会现象"。[2] 王铭铭进一步将其概括为三个层次：宏观方面，可以理解"各种大的文明板块互动的复杂局面"；中观方面，可以"在区域的范围里研究文明互动方式"；微观方面，则可以理解"'生活世界'中的跨文明关系"。[3] 这使得人们可以在多重交互的关系中来理解中国内部与外部不同社会体系的交流融合，而又不凝固于某种边界。

在这种复数"文明"论的前提下重新思考中国，可以成为一种重要的批判性思路。传统中国作为区域性国家形态（帝国）、市场形态（经济）以及独特的世界观体系（文化），不仅可以成为今天重新阐释中国的"活的传统"，也是跳出"现代"之外来思考人类社会的重要资源。这并不是指"回到中华帝国"，而是将其作为一种批判性思想资源吸纳进来，重新构建中国在全球格局中的主体性位置。缺少这样的批判性文明史视野，不仅真正的世界史叙述是不可能的，而且要从民族主义（及其变形的"中华中心主义"）的羁绊中摆脱出来，从世界史高度理解21世纪中国的意义，也是不可能的。

（本文系作者在联盟2017年年度论坛上的发言）

1　［法］费尔南·布罗代尔：《15—18世纪的物质文明、经济和资本主义》，顾良、施康强译，北京：生活·读书·新知三联书店，2002年。

2　［法］马塞尔·莫斯、爱弥尔·涂尔干、亨利·于贝尔：《论技术、技艺与文明》。

3　王铭铭：《超社会体系》，第418—426页。

Writing Style and Cultural Confidence:
The *Sprezzatura* of Sir Philip Sidney's *An Apology for Poetry*

Weiwen He[*]

Sprezzatura was an important concept for Sidney, both as a courtier and as a poet, since his literary career was embedded in the courtly culture in which he lived, and modeled on the careers of earlier "courtly makers." As far as *sprezzatura* is concerned, the approach to *An Apology for Poetry* is largely one of rhetorical theory. Sidney scholars agree that it is a writing style he practiced in the *Apology*, and they give various reasons.[1] Both Myrick (1935) and Dana (1973) hold that *sprezzatura* was practiced because of the code of courtier's good manner.[2] Some other critics discuss Sidney's *sprezzatura* in the context of the current Ciceronianism and Anti-Ciceronianism in his time.[3] None of them go beyond *sprezzatura* as

---

* Weiwen He (何伟文) is Professor of English Literature at Shanghai Jiao Tong University. She has written on the contemporary English novels, the early modern English poetics, and the Greek and Roman poetics.

1 For the discussion concerning the *Apology* as a classic oration, see K. O. Myrick, *Sir Philip Sidney as a Literary Craftsman*, 46–83.

2 K. O. Myrick (1935) argues that it is because of "the urbane nonchalance which seems to treat lightly what must be treated seriously if one is to win distinction." (40) With this M. E. Dana (1973, 320) agrees, and she even applies the *sprezzatura* displayed by the disguised princes in the *Arcadia* to Sidney himself. She argues that the pastoral disguise offers a way in which, even as a young man, Sidney could begin to explore, "with all the courtly grace and nonchalance so characteristic of him, the possibility of heroic narrative. There is a kind of *sprezzatura* in the very conception of the Arcadia. It is the performance of a writer who was content to claim less that he might achieve more."

3 R. Montgomery (1961) claims that *sprezzatura* practiced by Sidney belongs to the plain style advocated by the anti-Ciceronians, and draws to the conclusion that he changed his writing style during the short period he wrote poems. Similarly, W. Trimpi (1962) argues that after his discussion

a writing style. While the approach of rhetorical theory now appears to be old, we may still come away with new findings by adopting its lens. Even in a straightforward explication of the *Apology* via rhetorical theory, there are unsettled questions.[1] Most pointedly, recent criticism all lift Sidney free of a narrowly nationalist context. Stillman (2008), Kuin (2012), and Lockey (2015) all view Sidney as a diplomat and statesman, and Stillman particularly emphasizes the *Apology*'s connections to Philippism's failed attempt to quell the French Wars of Religion and tamp down the tensions that finally erupted in the Thirty Years' War. However, there is something that these current readings miss, which older, close-reading explications have likewise missed, that we ought to be paying attention to. This paper attempts to address and correct this by explicating the *Apology* via close reading, combined with rhetorical theory.

This paper places Sidney and the *Apology* into a nationalist context, and goes beyond the *sprezzatura* as a writing style Sidney practiced in the *Apology*. It argues that the *sprezzatura* was closely related to Sidney's prescription for the illness of English literature. A poet may have a serious purpose in practicing *sprezzatura* with its seemingly reckless and nonchalant mask. George Chapman (1941, 132) commented that he had spent time writing a poem on "so trifling a subject" as Musacus's *Hero and Leander*:

---

concerning the plain style in the *Apology*, Sidney was not able to practice it or keep those principles established earlier, as in his later writings he turned to the ornate style and ornaments. In short, Sidney was unable to reconcile the inter-textual conflicts. Against this view argues N. L. Rudenstine (1967) convincingly that Sidney's critical principles and thought concerning writing style had been well established and matured as earlier as he wrote *Arcadia*.

1   For instance, is the *Apology* unified? How seriously should we take its propositions? For the discussions of these questions, see O. B. Hardison Jr., "The Two Voices of Sidney's Apology for Poetry," 83–99; A. F. Kinney, "Parody and Its Implications in Sydney's Defense of Poesie," 1–19. More recently, there is the question regarding whether the *Apology* should be read allegorically or more as a parable. For the discussion of these questions, see M. Mack, *Sidney's Poetics: Imitating Creation*; R. E. Stillman, *Philip Sidney and the Poetics of Renaissance Cosmopolitanism*.

It goes much against my hand to sign that for a trifling subject, on which more worthiness of soul hath been showed, and weight of divine wit, than can vouchsafe residence in the leaden gravity of any money-monger in whose profession all serious subjects are concluded.

This comment, as A. C. Hamilton (1977) observes, reveals the underlying seriousness of the poet's indifference to his works. The same was true with Sidney. Hidden behind his seeming nonchalance was his serious thought concerning the present and future of English language and literature.[1] At the time of his isolation imposed by Queen Elizabeth I, when he wrote the *Apology*, the Golden Age of English literature was yet to come. The Apollo's Garden in England was rather desolate, and a far distance could be found between the current English poetry and the ideal one, of which Sidney made such an eloquent defense in the main part of the *Apology*. It was his belief that the fault was not with English poetry itself, but with those who abused that noble name. He voluntarily prescribed for the "patient."

Sidney adapted the courtly ideal of *sprezzatura* and *grazia* to new contexts for English poetry. During the pedantic cult of Ciceronianism, many English writers showed no cultural confidence and lost themselves in their servile imitation of the single model Cicero. In the *Apology*, Sidney is out to build up English cultural confidence with a deft demonstration of the capacities of the English language, pointing out its great value and potentiality as a language of literature. While Sidney agreed with Erasmus's thought on imitation, Sidney had a more complex view of the writing styles of English writers. He neither refused the Ciceronian ornate style nor simply advocated the plain style in line with the anti-Ciceronian currents of his age. He was guided in his own choices of style by matters of *Decorum*, which showed primarily respect for one's own subjectivity. *Grazia*, springing from *sprezzatura*, with its emphasis on natural gifts, implies for Sidney the importance of

---

1 Philip Sidney turned to English poetry after being isolated by Queen Elizabeth I. For his purpose, see W. He, *An Apology for Poetry: Philip Sidney's Life and Poetics*, chapter 2.

one's own genuine feeling, wisdom, invention, and tight logical argument. In the *Apology*, a hymn to the powers of invention, Sidney practiced *sprezzatura* to encourage independent development of English literature, making it effective in embodying the English writers' "idea or fore-conceit."

Sprezzatura is "a new word," "una nova parola," used by Baldassare Castiglione in *The Book of the Courtier*. The interlocutors spend much of their time expounding upon the ideal courtier's behavioral performance founded on *sprezzatura*, which is introduced in Book 1, Chapter 26 by Count Ludivico da Canosssa, the speaker assigned to supervise the game of "depicting in words a perfect courtier" (Castiglione 2003, 51).[1] The Count defines the term "*sprezzatura*" as "a certain nonchalance which conceals all artistry and makes whatever one says or does seem uncontrived and effortless." (67) In the words of H. Berger (2002, 296), *sprezzatura* is "an art that hides art, the cultivated ability to display artful artlessness." This is called by him "the *sprezzatura* of nonchalance" (296), though he admits that the name is misleading. Related to this purely aesthetic aspect of *sprezzatura* is its second definitional aspect which appears in Chapter 28. Here, comes "another advantage" of *sprezzatura*:

> For whatever action it accompanies, no matter how trivial it is, it not only reveals the skill of the person doing it but also very often causes it be considered far greater than it really is. (Berger 2002, 70)

W. Rebhorn (1978, 38) paraphrases this aspect of *sprezzatura* as "an art of suggestion, in which the courtier's audience will be induced by the images it confronts to imagine a greater reality existing behind them." It is a *sprezzatura* of conspicuously false modesty. D. Javitch (1983, 23) gives *sprezzatura* a different look by moving it into the political arena and treating it as a strategic response to "the constraints of despotism" in the courtly context

---

1   All subsequent references to this book will be noted parenthetically by page number.

55

of "fierce competition for favors." Berger (2002, 297) observes that this suggests one more definitional aspect of *sprezzatura* as a form of defensive irony: the "ability to disguise what one really desires, feels, thinks and means or intends behind a mask of apparent reticence and nonchalance." In addition, Berger suggests that the performance of *sprezzatura* is "a figuration of power" and "a figuration of anxiety," and it is to be worn as "a velvet glove that exhibits the contours of the handiness it conceals." (298) F. Whigham (1984, 116) understands that perhaps this is used just like "cosmesis," that is, "the use of cosmetic aids to conceal or repair defects." The *sprezzatura* creates in its multifold character a self-fulfilling culture of suspicion within and around its performers.

The above aspects and characters of *sprezzatura* are fundamentally associated with imitation. In *The Book of the Courtier*, all the passages concern how a courtier should imitate his models until the term makes its first appearance. The importance of imitation is made clear by Count Ludivico da Canosssa at the beginning of *The Book of the Courtier*: "Anyone who wants to be a good pupil must not only do things well but must also make a constant effort to imitate." (51) The Count lays stress on imitating many kinds of courtiers, rather than reproducing one master all the time: "It is very profitable for him to observe different kinds of courtiers." (66) In addition, the Count urges the courtier to imitate in a manner like that of bees:

> Just as in the summer fields the bees wing their way among the plants from one flower to the next, so the courtier must *acquire* [rubare] this grace from those who appear to possess it and *take from* [carpendo] each one the quality that seems commendable. (66–67)

It is the manner of a thief, as may be seen clearly in C. Singleton's translation:

> Even as in green meadows the bee flits about among grasses robbing [carpendo] the flowers, so our Courtier must steal [rubare] this grace from those

who seem to him to have it, taking from each the part that seems most worthy of praise. (Castiglione 1959, 32)

In "Castiglione's Verbal Portrait," R. W. Hanning (1983, 134–135) associates this advice with the model of Zeuxis, and claims that it implies "the painter's duty to create an idealized yet mimetic art by imitating only the most nearly perfect models." An ideal courtier should always be ruled and guided by his own good judgment in the process of imitating models of comportment. What he imitates should be something natural or just like nature. The Count concludes, "True art is what does not seem to be art; and the most important thing is to conceal it." (67) If a courtier's nonchalance is affected and inappropriate, it will have exactly the opposite effect of the concealment of art. Affectation is dangerous in all things. "It is said to have been proverbial among certain great painters of the ancient world," the count remarks, "that excessive diligence is harmful; and Protogenes is said to have been censured by Apelles for not knowing when to take his hands from the board." (69) Apelles was in fact blaming Protogenes for finishing his work too thoroughly.

From *sprezzatura* springs *grazia*. In Book 1, about halfway through Chapter 14, when defending the proposition that the ideal courtier should be nobly born, Count Ludivico da Canosssa introduces the term "*grazia*" into the discussion. He says:

Noble birth is like a bright lamp that makes clear and visible both good deeds and bad ... and since their deeds do not possess such noble brilliance, ordinary people lack both this stimulus and the fear of dishonor.... Thus as a general rule, both in arms and in other worthy activities, those who are most distinguished are of noble birth, because Nature has implanted in everything a hidden seed which has a certain way of influencing and passing on its own essential characteristics to all that grows from it, making it similar to itself. (54)

The Count concedes that if aristocrats have no one to give them proper attention, they can "grow wild and never reach maturity." (54) He also concedes that, rather than every aristocrat, certain people "come into the world endowed with *grazia*." (54) He takes Don Ippolito d'Este, Cardinal of Ferrara, as an example. The Cardinal's fortunate birth has influenced his person, his appearance, his words, and all his actions; because of this *grazia*, "he has such charming ways and such a gracious manner." (55) The Count wishes to embed *grazia* securely among qualities guaranteed by noble birth. To those who are not perfectly endowed by nature with this supreme *grazia*, he points out a way for them to improve themselves. "They can," he claims, "through care and effort, polish and to great extent correct their natural defects." (55) So, in addition to noble birth, the Count says:

> I would have the courtier favoured in this respect, too, and receive from Nature not only talent and beauty of countenance and person but also that certain air and *grazia* that makes him immediately pleasing and attractive to all who meet him; and this *grazia* should be an adornment informing and accompanying all his actions, so that he appears clearly worthy of the companionship and favour of the great. (55)

While "care and effort" may help correct their natural defects, *grazia* can only be acquired from nature. As Cesare Gonzaga reminds him in Book 1, Chapter 24, the Count has repeated several times in one evening that the courtier must imbue with *grazia* his movement, his gestures, his way of doing things, and in short, his every action. Cesare adds, "it appears to me that you require this in everything as the seasoning without which all other attributes and good qualities would be almost worthless." (65) So *grazia* is an extra quality added to those more solid properties and conditions that can be acquired by precept. As Cesare reminds the Count again, he has said that as *grazia* is very often "a natural, God-given gift," it is not "in our power to acquire it of ourselves." (65) "*Grazia* is once again assimilated to noble birth," Berger (2002, 304) observes, "as a gift of the fathers and the Father, not something that can be acquired." E. Saccone (1983, 61) distinguishes "the absolute perfection" of those who are "perfectly endowed by nature" from "the imperfection" of those "absolutely ungifted." Berger's reading is similar yet more complex. To reiterate that *grazia* is a grace beyond the reach of art just before the account of *sprezzatura*, Berger (2002, 305) maintains, is "to make deficiency in *grazia* the enabling condition of ideal courtiership." From this comes the difference between the "absolute courtier" and the "ideal courtier." Berger (305) thus argues that "*sprezzatura* is envisaged as the false lookalike that threatens to displace *grazia*." His reason is that:

> The achievement of *sprezzatura* may require him to deny or disparage his nature. In order to internalize the model and enhance himself by art, he may have to evacuate—repress or disown—whatever he finds within himself that doesn't fit the model. (306)

However, in this way, the imitator can only make himself like the model in appearances. It is only the first stage in his imitation. Something innate with him matters.

To reiterate that *grazia* is "a natural, God-given gift" as afore-mentioned, before the account of *sprezzatura*, is to emphasize the importance of something innate with the ideal courtier himself, which distinguishes him from other people. To achieve *sprezzatura*, a courtier must empty himself in the first stage by directing all his attention to his model, and internalize what he imitates. In the second, his own natural genius and instinct play a crucial role in making himself alike to his models in spirit rather than simply in appearances. He is like the Pythian priestess, described by Longinus (1998, 90) in *On the Sublime*, who approaches the tripod, "where there is a rift in the ground which (they say) exhales divine vapor" impregnated by heavenly power. To Longinus, he is even like the young Plato who "had with all his heart and mind struggled with Homer for primacy." (90) The courtier follows his own instinct in due course, and his own nature is fully displayed. Thus, the Count claims that "the highest degree of *grazia* is conferred by simplicity and nonchalance." (86) The real source of grace is the quality of nonchalance, the opposite of affectation. *Grazia* can only be produced with complete ease, and it will vanish if a man takes too much pain to attain it. The only effort that should be encouraged in attaining it, as Rebhorn (1978) remarks, is an effort to conceal the skill on which it is based. The courtier should have and display his ability to handle complicated matters with ease.

With Castiglione's account of *grazia* being in its social sense, Giorgio Vasari further elaborated and applied it to painting, just as Philip Sidney did to English literature decades later. Vasari's art theory most probably came from *The Book of the Courtier*, its crucial feature being the new quality of *grazia*. The term *"grazia"* had been applied to painting before Vasari's time, yet only in the sense vaguely interchangeable with or differing at most in degree from beauty.[1] With Vasari, *grazia* takes on a new function. It is distinguished from, and in contrast with, beauty. Vasari defines beauty as a rational quality dependent on rules, and *grazia* as an indefinable quality dependent on the judgment and therefore on the eyes. He regards delicacy, refinement, and supreme grace as the qualities produced by the perfection of art. If these are lacking, as A. Blunt (1962, 93) argues, "it is not enough for a figure, even if its limbs as a whole are in accordance with the antique and have a certain correct harmony in the proportions." The clearest idea of grace, in the sense used by Vasari, is its connexion with the facility such as rapidity and ease of execution, with which artists finish their work. Vasari boasts in his autobiography that he executes his works "not only with the greatest possible rapidity, but also with incredible facility and without effort." (Vasari 1550, cited in Blunt 1962, 95) He believes that any trace of laboriousness will destroy the grace of a painting and give it the final quality of dryness. It is only after Leonardo da Vinci that the painters achieve that perfect grace, brought about by the disappearance of a certain dryness, hardness, and sharpness left by the excessive study of Piero della Francesca and others.

In Vasari's art theory, both *grazia* and facility derive from a natural gift, which cannot be acquired by pains and study. He believes:

---

1   For instance, Alberti makes the grace and the beauty vaguely interchangeable, and the Neoplatonists of the Quattrocento make a distinction of the same kind as Vasari, but they only apply it to corporal beauty, not to the arts. See A. Blunt, *Artistic Theory in Italy: 1450–1600*.

Very great is the obligation that is owed to Heaven and to Nature by those who bring their works to birth without effort and with a certain grace which others cannot give to their creations either by study or by imitation. (Vasari 1550, cited in Blunt 1962, 96)

It is like the Count's view regarding the *grazia:* it is "a natural, God-given gift." However, it does not mean to say that, in the old problem of the relative importance of art and nature, Vasari denies the value of study and imitation. He blames those artists who do not take the trouble to cultivate their natural talents. As a matter of fact, he approves of careful studies and hard work in one way and disapproves of them in another, and attempts to combine grace with solid draughtsmanship. Taking painting as an example, the artist's hand must be free and skilled, resulting from the study and practice of many years, in his drawing and copying of whatever nature has produced. The artist internalizes all the artistic principles after years of imitation and is totally free of their bondage when he reaches perfect proficiency, and the nature of the artist and of the art becomes one and the same. When the artist comes to execute a particular work, he must act as rapidly as possible without leaving any trace of his effort on the canvas. Throughout the whole process, his own nature plays a crucial role.

With the humanists of the Quattrocento, the painting reached the position of being a learned art, and Vasari's emphasis on the nature of the artist is of no small significance. Blunt (1962, 98) remarks, "With Vasari it was acquiring good manners." While Vasari derived his idea of grace in art from a book of court manners, Philip Sidney similarly attempted to adapt the courtly ideal of *sprezzatura* and *grazia* to English poetry.

When Sidney began his writing in the 1570s, the scene of English literature was rather desolate. From the time of Chaucer, besides his *Troilus and Criseyde*, the *Mirror of Magistrates*, the Earl of Surrey's lyrics, and Edmund Spenser's *Shepherd's Calendar*, Sidney (1965, 133) says in the *Apology* that he remembers "to have seen but few (to speak boldly) printed, that have poetical sinews in them." There were many causes for this deplorable situation for English poetry. Poets of the mid-century faced three major technical problems—forging a poetical language, discovering effective rhythms, and creating new poetical forms—to which they had found various, yet not always entirely satisfactory, solutions.[1] The focus here, of this paper, is on the problem of writing style, including how a poet should develop a level of diction and rhetoric appropriate to the tone and content of their verse. There were two extreme kinds at the time: one was the aureate or ornate style, and the other was the racy, plain one.[2] Both had come into being long before the Elizabethan time. As S. W. May (2011, 551–552) remarks, the "aureate" style featured "unusual words and newly coined Latin derivatives as popularized by the fifteenth-century poet monk John Lydgate"; the plain style was "sprinkled with slang and dialect words developed by the Henrician court poet John Skelton."[3] The Elizabethan poets were rather puzzled as to which of the two was appropriate for any given poem. The style cultivated by the earliest professional Elizabethan poets dominated English verse, which C. S. Lewis (1954, 1) describes as "drab," well into the 1580s. Their emphasis on artifice over substance, or manner over matter, reduced poetry to a rhetorically ornamental art, characteristic of the kind of Ciceronianism Sidney severely criticized.

The emergence and prevalence of Ciceronianism were related to the cultural program of Renaissance humanism. Cicero insists in his rhetorical theory on the union of *sapientia* and *eloquentia*, on the harmonious partnership of words and matter. It has been an ancient commonplace, referred to by Cicero at the beginning of his *De inventione*, that wisdom without eloquence is of little benefit to the state, whereas eloquence without wisdom is

---

1   For an account of these technical problems, see P. Sidney, *The Poems of Sir Philip Sidney*.
2   There is a mid-twentieth century debate concerning these two styles between Yvor Winters and his peers. In which Winters champions the plain style. For starters, see E. Fowler and R. Greene, *The Project of Prose in Early Modern Europe and the New World*.
3   For the discussion of the ornate and high style, see G. Williamson, *The Senecan Amble: A Study in Prose Form from Bacon to Collier*, 11–20.

a great danger. "Of his perfect orator," as A. Vos (1979, 6) observes, "he demands not only skill in speaking, but also a comprehensive knowledge of all important subjects and art." The union of rhetoric and philosophy is the most characteristic of Cicero's vision of culture.[1] His model orator integrates the two. Cicero's program for uniting eloquence and wisdom had universal appeal to Renaissance humanists, and his doctrine found fruitful soil among them. Fundamental to their cultural program was the desire to combine wisdom with eloquence, and philosophy with rhetoric. The intimate connexion between wisdom and eloquence in its relation to life became one of the great principles of Renascence studies. Around the humanists' pious hope for the union clustered the most characteristic features of their program: the demand for a kind of intellectual activity that would find fulfillment in virtuous action; the attack on scholasticism; and the revival of ancient literature itself.[2] However, by the middle of the fifteenth century, the Italian Ciceronians increasingly became preoccupied with Cicero's language. The first step in this direction was the humanists' subordination of philosophy to rhetoric. As J. Seigel (1968, 12–13) argues:

From Petrarch's union of the two arts, in which philosophical standards regarding man's intellectual and moral life retained considerable independence (as they had, with similar inconsistencies, in Cicero's writings), the humanist program evolved by way of Salutati's waverings into Bruni's more confident affirmation of the orator's philosophical perspective and, finally, into Valla's outright demand for the subordination of philosophy to rhetoric. The general direction in which Petrarchan humanism developed into the Quattrocento is hard to mistake: the humanists came to conceive of the combination of wisdom and eloquence in ways which granted increasingly less independence within it to philosophy.

---

1 Cicero's expressions on the union of rhetoric and philosophy are found in the first chapters of *De Inventione* and in *De Oratore* 3.17–90.

2 For a more thorough study of the humanists' hope for the union, see J. E. Seigel, "Ideals of Eloquence and Silence in Petrarch."

Along with this evolution was the humanists' increasing attention to rhetoric. They began to note "the general problems of utterance." They applied the accepted doctrine, which prescribed an imitation of the orators and historians of the great days at Rome, in their attempt to restore a correct Latinity.[1] It is inevitable that Cicero, as a prose stylist, should command the most attention, and he was taken as the chief model for the writers to cultivate a style that both embodied his main principles and met contemporary needs. Imitation was, at this time, interpreted in the most liberal sense, and not confined exclusively to Cicero. While it stood for a revival of classical form and spirit, it was also calculated to produce a style both flexible and spontaneous.[2]

With its long history, it has been a common practice to imitate the model of great ancient writers in writing. As early as Isocrates' time, the importance of example or model for acquiring skill in writing was suggested; and subsequently, at Rome the process of imitation had become generally recognized in both theory and practice.[3] Moreover, Horace set up his creed of classicism in connection with poetry, asserting once and for all the supremacy of classical Greek art, with the classical works by Homer and the Greek tragedians as the models for imitation. In *The Art of Poetry*, Horace (1982, 136) urges the Piso brothers to "study the Greek masterpieces; thumb them day and night." While he encourages them to imitate the best writings of the ancients, borrow their writing skills, and absorb their noble and original subjects, he also advises them to treat a hackneyed theme with originality:

The common quarry will become your own by right, if you do not dally in the cheap and easy round; if you do not, an all too faithful translator, essay to

---

1 See J. W. H. Atkins, *English Literary Criticism: The Renascence*, 8–34. See also: P. O. Kristeller, "Humanism and Scholasticism in the Italian Renaissance," 85–105.

2 For the establishment of a Ciceronian tradition, see J. W. H. Atkins, *English Literary Criticism: The Renascence*, Chapter 2.

3 For the theory in its original form in the writings of Roman critics of 1st-Century, see J. W. H. Atkins, *Literary Criticism in Antiquity: A Sketch of Its Development*, Chapter 1 to 7.

render your author word for word; if you do not—a mere copyist—take a plunge into some narrow pit from which diffidence or the conditions of their work itself forbid you to escape. (Horace 1982, 132)

According to Horace's noble conception of imitation, true imitation is not simply a repetition, but a re-creation. It is "an appeal to antiquity that is to lead finally to originality in expression." (Atkins 1934, 79) However, by the mid-Quattrocento, the concept of imitation had been severely distorted, and the Ciceronian tradition had been degenerating into a pedantic cult that demanded an exclusive imitation of Cicero, with expression strictly limited to the Ciceronian vocabulary, accidence, and syntax. The Renaissance critics of Ciceronianism termed it a disease or malady, and they declared decisively against the servile following of a single model.

To understand the general situation regarding the Ciceronianism and Anti-Ciceronianism in England, in order to understand Sidney's position, we shall focus on Erasmus and Roger Ascham because of their great influences on the English intellectual life of the times. In the opening decades of the sixteenth century, together with John Colet and Juan Luis Vives, Erasmus was "intimately bound up with contemporary English life," whose influences were "definite factors in the intellectual life of the times." (Atkins 1951, 37)[1] H. B. Lathrop (1933, 32) points out:

The New Learning in England was of a character that may be called Erasmian, for though it was clearly apprehended by Colet and Linacre, it was typically embodied and most energetically set forth by Erasmus.

---

1 Erasmus' influence could also be strongly felt in the seventeenth century. See G. D. Dodds, *Exploring Erasmus: The Erasmian Legacy and Religious Change in Early Modern England*; M. P. Gilmore, *The World of Humanism, 1453–1517*.

N. Perry (2005, 370) acutely observes, "Erasmus's vison of a uniquely Christian eloquence was widely disseminated in England by the humanist pedagogy of his friend and admirer, John Colet." When Erasmus published his satirical *Ciceronianus* (1528), the first and greatest critique of Ciceronianism, the afore-mentioned malady had generally not yet spread beyond the Alps. However, by the end of the century, England too had succumbed to Ciceronianism and Senecanism, which were, in Bacon's (1859, 284) words, only instances of "the first distemper of learning, when men study words and not matter."

According to Erasmus (1995), Cicero's rhetoric was out of place in sixteenth-century Christian societies. He maintained that while Cicero's rhetoric had been framed for a society whose legal and political matters were dealt with in the large assemblies, where public and formal modes of eloquence were appropriate, sixteenth-century politics and law were far less public, and the ornate rhetoric and the high style were out of place in serious, devout, unpretentious Christian societies. In one of his letters, he derides "the new sect in employing only terms and phrases which Cicero had used and in not venturing to speak otherwise than Cicero had spoken." (qtd in Atkins 1951, 46) "If Cicero came to life again," he explains, "he himself would laugh at these Ciceronians." (qtd in Atkins 1951, 46) The reason is that "times are changed, our instincts, needs and ideas are not those of Cicero." (Erasmus 1531, cited in Atkins 1951, 46) In his *Ciceronianus*, Erasmus (1995) suggests that the ancient material should be treated in accordance with modern needs, and demands some expression of individuality. His recommendation is that, as Atkins (1951, 47) puts it, "a judicious, but not an exclusive, use should be made of Cicero as a model, and that the spirit, rather than the letter, of his writing should accordingly be studied."

Moreover, in Erasmus's view, the anachronical use of Ciceronian style is related to sin. In *Ciceronianus*, as N. Perry (2005) observes, Erasmus associates the linguistic and historical anachronism of the Ciceronians with sin, particularly with the "fallenness" of all good models from their original purity. He identifies their tendency to conflate the appearance of a thing with its essential reality as idolatry, as they advocated the strict imitation of Cicero as the sole criterion of eloquence. Erasmus (1995, 65) says:

Just as men dishonor St. Benedict by boasting themselves Benedictines when in dress, in title, and in life they approach nearer Sardanapalus than St. Benedict ... and possibly the Christ when they have nothing of him except the title: so men cast a blot on the fame of Cicero who have nothing on their tongues except Cicero and Ciceronians, when none are farther from the eloquence of Cicero than they.

While Erasmus (1995) insists that a true Ciceronian should privilege essence over appearance, he also advocates something "more severe, less theatrical, more masculine" than Cicero's usual manner, as he has a doubt if such theatricality is "appropriate for Christians" who look "rather to living virtuously than to speak ornately and elegantly." (84) "When times and circumstances had changed, even granting that the eloquence of Cicero was useful once," Erasmus asks, "what is its use today?" (84–85) So he prescribes an Attic plain style, which stresses more on the matter than the manner, as an antidote to Ciceronian excesses. It is worthwhile to note that the style recommended by Erasmus is suitable for non-literary writings—such as pamphlets, letters, legal pleas, political orations, etc.—for which the matter seems, not surprisingly, to be more important than the manner.

Like Erasmus, Ascham also showed an absorbing interest in how to cultivate a correct style. In *Of Imitation*, he reminds his readers not only of the teachings of the ancients but also of the varied pronouncements of later Humanists, including Erasmus. However, what he advocates practically contributed to the spread of the "first distemper in England." Ascham defines imitation as a following of the best authors and observes that Cicero, whose writing is an example of successful imitation of several models, had reproduced the varied stylistic excellences of the great writers in the past. He suggests that in eloquence writers follow choicely a few and chiefly someone. Ascham (1950, 18) quotes, with approval, Cheke's statement:

... he that will dwell in these few bookes onelie, first in Gods holie Bible, and than ioyne with it *Tullie* in Latin, *Plato, Aristotle, Xenophon, Isocrates and Demosthenes* in Greke, must nedes proue an excellent man.

However, he holds strongly to the notion that there was an ideal classical period, from which alone Latin models might be safely drawn. He believes that perfection in art endures but for a time, and is followed inevitably by a period of decline and decay. So he maintains that Latin eloquence in its purity lasted for scarcely a hundred years. Among the writings of this period, he concludes that one author alone, namely Cicero, afforded fit models for imitation in prose.[1] In commending Cicero alone as a suitable model for imitation, Ascham shows that he was a pure Ciceronian, much like the way Gabriel Harvey described himself. In his *Ciceronianus*, Harvey (1945, 76–77) writes:

> Why should I tell how great and simon-pure a Ciceronian I was at that time in the choice of every single word, in the composition and structure of sentences, in the discriminating use of cases and tenses, in the symmetry of cut-and-dried phrases, in the shaping of sentence-divisions and clauses, in the careful and elaborated multiplication of all sorts of refinements.

Harvey was, at this time, the kind of man he himself ridicules:

> … a fowler after Ciceronian words, religiously following after him in all the tiniest details, and childishly gathering a few pebbles from Cicero like pebbles on a beach, while trampling under foot the most precious gems of argument and pearls of philosophy. (Harvey 1945, 77)

---

1 For Ascham's views concerning the Ciceronianism, see Roger Ascham, "Of Imitation," 1–45; J. W. H. Atkins, *English Literary Criticism: The Renascence*, 85–96.

Harvey was blind to what was truly valuable in his servile imitation, and Ascham was not better. As C. S. Lewis (1964, 281) observes:

Ascham is a rigid humanist, a professed follower of his contemporary Sturmius, a Ciceronian, and a whole-hearted adherent to the doctrine of Imitation. This does not mean Aristotle's imitation of nature, but that imitation of authors by authors which the dependence of Roman literature upon Greek had elevated into a principle. By Ascham's time it has become imitation of imitation. We are to learn how to copy Tully by studying his methods of copying Demosthenes and then copying them. Ascham's belief in the nutritive value of this feast of husks is astonishing.

In his defense of Ascham against C. S. Lewis's attack, A. Vos (1979, 7) argues that among the English Ciceronians, the concern regarding words springs not from a simple trust in the primacy of words (as it did in slavish apes of Cicero's language), but "from a fuller awareness of the orator's deepest personal allegiances to God, England, and classicism." J. R. Henderson (1995, 226) also observes that the Reformers developed an educational system that was narrowly text-centered, a system "that encouraged not so much original thinking and writing as interpretation and imitation of texts, classical as well as biblical. The result was a new kind of Ciceronianism." Nevertheless, they do not deny the fact that there is a distinctive feature concerning Ascham's concept of imitation that distinguishes it from Horace's.

Ascham's is an imitation of imitation, more of manner than of matter. For him, Tully's method of copying early writers becomes the only model for imitation; and to him, style is coming to be the whole of learning. To use Longinus's terms, it is like the "mechanical" rather than "literary" imitation. Imitators of this kind do not need to use their imagination or make any judgment, and their own creativity and subjectivity have no place in the process of imitation. In the last two decades of the sixteenth century, the ornate style, which derives its authority from the purist imitators of Cicero, was the dominant mode of Elizabethan verse. It is a style of embellishment, overstatement, stately symmetry, and hyperbole. English poetry inevitably became an art of rhetoric ornaments, and the pleasure brought by the poetry came more from rhetoric devices than from dramatic effects.

This was the situation of English poetry that Sidney intended to change. He possessed a sympathetic understanding of the Ramism, a direct rejection of the Ciceronianism newly introduced into England. Though we cannot tell what he learned from Ramus exactly, it is rather clear that Ramus would generally have reinforced his already strong opposition to Ciceronianism.[1] With its preference for words over matters, Ciceronianism would have been one of the many forces urging him to object to excessive ornamentation in verse. "No anti-Ciceronian in his own work and in his influence on his literary associates during 1580s," as Shepherd (1965, 228) observes, "yet by his interest in a controlled and somewhat Ramist rhetoric he was revealed as a conscious opponent of the excesses of the extremists." Since his poems were more widely circulated in manuscripts during Elizabeth's reign than those of any other individual poet, he was likely the formative influence on the development of mature, golden English poetry. (Gavin 2006; Woudhuysen 2009; May 2011)

Sidney was insightful regarding the illness of English literature and the importance of a proper writing style for restoring its health. In his discussion of the illness in the *Apology*, he is mainly concerned with the problem of matter and manner. He points out relentlessly that "for there being two principal parts—matter to be expressed by words and words to express the matter—in neither we use Art or Imitation rightly." (133) By indicating the "infection" among English poets, Sidney makes it clear that his meaning is not to take upon me to teach poets how they should do, but only, finding myself sick among the rest, to show some one or two spots of the common infection grown among the most part of writers. (139–140) Both Myrick (1934, 189) and Montgomery (1961, 64) hold that, by

---

1   For a discussion concerning what Sidney had possibly learned from Ramus, see Neil L. Rudenstine, *Sidney's Poetic Development*; Robert Montgomery, *Symmetry and Sense: The Poetry of Sir Philip Sidney*.

saying "finding myself sick among the rest," Sidney criticizes his own over-decorative style practiced in *Arcadia*; Atkins (1951, 134) takes it to be "a handsome confession and a piece of self-criticism suggested possibly by his experiments in his *Arcadia*." However, Sidney does not really mean to criticize himself. It is his strategy, for the purpose of persuasion, to draw the audience to his side in the defense by a natural inclusion of himself in his own criticism. A similar strategy can also be found at the beginning of the *Apology,* where he regards the audience as the same with himself: "we" are grateful to our "first nurse," while "they," those ungrateful ones, are like the hedgehog or vipers. It is both a form of defensive irony and a gracious act of modesty. They all belong to the afore-mentioned different aspects of *sprezzatura*. By "acknowledging ourselves somewhat awry," Sidney (140) believes, "we may bend to the right use both of matter and manner: whereto our language giveth us great occasion, being indeed capable of any excellent exercising of it."

In Sidney's prescription, for the right use of matter and manner, the first and foremost thing for an English writer is to be confident in his own native language. However, many English writers lacked this cultural confidence. According to Sidney, the illness of English literature had its main symptoms not only among the poets, but also among the prose-printers, scholars, and preachers. They were none other than the Ciceronians, the euphuists, and the diligent imitators of Petrarch's poems. They were busy collecting foreign words. Their works are, as Sidney says, "one time with so many far-fetched words, they may seem monsters, but must seem strangers, to any poor Englishman; another time with coursing of a letter, as if they were bound to follow the method of a dictionary; another time with figures and flowers extremely winter-starved." (138) For the phrase "far-fetched words," we may refer to George Puttenham (1936, 183) in his interpretation of the figure Metalepsis which he calls "the farfet" in *The Art of English Poetry*: "when we had rather fetch a word a great way off than to use one nearer hand to expresses the matter as wel and plainer."[1]

---

1   On Elizabethan attitudes towards exotic borrowings in vocabulary, see R. F. Jones, *The Triumph of the English Language*, 94–141.

This practice of fawning on foreign words was associated with their attitude towards their native tongue. The Renaissance nurtured a profound sense of cultural inferiority, with the achievements of ancient Greece and Rome being viewed as superior to almost everything that contemporary society had achieved. For example, in *Scholemaster*, Ascham (1950, 22) states that:

> ... bicause the prouidence of God hath left vnto vs in no other tong, saue onelie in the *Greke* and *Latin* tong, the trew preceptes, and perfite examples of eloquence, therefore must we seeke in the Authors onelie of those two tonges, the trewe Paterne of Eloquence.

The situation was even worse in England, which had long enjoyed a very low position in the Continent. When commenting on Petrarch's reputation, Boccaccio (1956, 115–116) says that:

> ... his great eminence as a poet has been recognized by—I will not say merely all Italians, for their glory is singular and perennial—but by all France, and Germany, and even that most remote little corner of the world, England; and, I must add, many of the Greeks.

A similar insight may be found in a letter Poggio Bracciolini wrote to his friend Niccolò Niccoli in Florence during his first visit to England in 1418:

> I saw many monasteries, all crammed with new doctors, none of whom you would even have found worth listening to. There were a few volumes of ancient writings, which we have in better versions at home. Nearly all the monasteries of this island have been built within the last four hundred years and that has not been an age which produced either learned men or the books which we seek.

(Niccoli 1418, cited in Greenblatt 2012, 207)

It is not surprising that English had long been looked down upon accordingly by the Europeans as well as the English people. Many English writers in Sidney's time viewed the words from the Continental languages, especially from Italian, as superior to their native ones. During the reign of Queen Elizabeth I, the English language was restricted to a small population on an island far removed from the Mediterranean origins of the Renaissance, and scarcely any Europeans would have deigned to learn it. Most would have thought that English was a barbarous tongue unsuited to poetry. (Buxton, 1963) Some English people held that their mother tongue was a "mingled language" with various deficiencies. As Robinson (1970) observes, they had basically two reasons: firstly, the native vocabulary made clarity or eloquence impossible, and secondly, the grammar and spelling of English were insufficiently standardized. Sidney was repelled by the practice of some poets who borrowed excessively foreign words while ignoring their mother tongue.

Sidney's prescription for the illness was to change the situation. He was confident that the most subtle idea could be expressed beautifully in English. Arthur Golding (1536–1606), completing Sidney's translation of *The Trewenesse of the Christian Religion*, set out in his dedication to Leicester what were most probably Sidney's own principles. He says:

Wherein if any words or phrases shall seeme staunge (as in some places perchaunce they may) I doubt not but your good Lordship will impute it to the rarenesse and profoundnesse of the matters there handled, not accustomed to be treated in our language … Great care hath been taken, by forming and deryuing of fit names and termes, out of the fountaynes of our own tongue, though not altogether most vsuall, yet always conceyuable and easie to be vnderstood. (Golding 1587, cited in Jones 1966, 122)

What is explicitly conveyed in this passage is Sidney's attitude to a foreign language and confidence in the mother tongue. At a time when people generally lacked this confidence, Sidney emphasized the value and function of English, especially in view of its potentiality as a literary medium. He insisted that the Ciceronians should show restraint in their excessive imitation of Cicero.

Compared with those who rejected foreign language rather narrow-mindedly, Sidney fairly acknowledged the actual situation in the 1580s. For instance, to John Cheke, the borrowing of foreign words was damaging to the native tongue, as he wrote in his letter to Thomas Hoby:

> I am of this opinion that our own tung shold be written cleane and pure, unmixt and unmangeled with borrowing of other tunges, wherein if we take not heed bi tijm, ever borrowing and never paying, she shall be fain to keep her house as bankrupt. (Cheke 1557, cited in Jones 1953, 102)

E. K. also complained:

> They patched up the holes with peces and rags of other languages, borrowing here of the French, there of the Italian, every where of the Latine; not weighing how il those tongues accorde with themselues, but much worse with ours: So now they haue made our English tongue a gallimaufray or hodgepodge of al other speches. (E. K. 1950, p. 130)

Sidney was quite different from them. He insisted that great care should be taken to form and derive terms out from native language resources. He sought to improve the English language and to demonstrate its innate capacity for subtle, penetrating, and beautiful expression of ideas.

Nevertheless, Sidney remained rather optimistic concerning the fact that English was a mingled language with many foreign words. English was a language with many foreign elements, yet Sidney maintained that these features only added to its wealth and ease of expression. "For the uttering sweetly and properly the conceits of the mind, which is the end of speech," he claimed, "English has it equally with any other tongue in the world." (140) "It is particularly happy in compositions of two or three words together," added Sidney, "near the Greek, far beyond the Latin." (140) When Latin was still strongly entrenched as the literary medium of scholars, as J. W. H. Atkins (1965, 134) remarks, "this unequivocal pronouncement on the vernacular was without doubt both timely and reassuring." Sidney dedicated a hymn of praise to his mother tongue, which was consistent with the patriotic assurance Richard Tottel (1557) had prefaced his *Miscellany* with some twenty years ago: "Our tong is able in that kind [poetry] to do as praiseworthily as the rest." (Tottel 1557, cited in May 2011, 552)

Apart from assuring the value of the mother tongue, Sidney showed his view on the subjectivity of the English writers. He insisted that they should not simply collect the figures and phrases when imitating the writings of those great writers, but read them for their wisdom and learning. "Truly I could wish, if at least I might be so bold to wish in a thing beyond the reach of my capacity," Sidney claims, "the diligent imitators of Tully and Demosthenes (most worthy to be imitated) did not so much keep Nizolian paper-books of their figures and phrases." (138) By referencing Nizolius, the most notorious of all Ciceronians, Sidney reminds us of Nosoponus, a character in Erasmus' *Ciceronianus* who has made an "alphabetical lexicon" consisting of bona fide Ciceronian words and phrases. Sidney did not conceal his contempt for collecting and copying phrases, a process encouraged by Ascham. Sidney was just like Bulephorus, another character in the same book by Erasmus who insists that a writer should follow the bent of his own nature rather than add to his speech all the beautiful things he has found. It was Sidney's strong conviction that the poets "devour them whole, and make them wholly theirs" (138) in imitating excellent figures and phrases. The "Nizolian paper-books" would restrain this translation, and encourage the step-by-step slavish imitation Horace criticizes severely in *The Art of Poetry*. The imitator of this kind would be like the courtier who is unable to hide his art. The literary works "created" in this way would not have a substantial matter, let alone any originality or sense of personal involvement.

According to Sidney, the subjectivity of the writer was of great importance for the right use of matter and manner. The English Ciceronians followed "words" and neglected "things," and Sidney considered neither himself nor his work to be guilty of the charge. Unlike those who neglected the subject matter when pursuing the words, Sidney cared pre-eminently for the things themselves in his own writings. This was what Hubert Languet urged him to do in a letter written in 1573. "In my opinion, the right way to do it is to read attentively both volumes of Cicero's letters," Languet (2012, 77) wrote, "not only because of the elegance of his Latin, but also because of their very serious content: for nowhere are more clearly explained the causes that plunged the Roman republic to its death." According to Sidney, wisdom and eloquence are more valuable than eloquence alone, and that matter is more important than words; the matter should embody the subjectivity of the poet, namely, his true feelings, thoughts, and invention; and the poet should learn about the substance and style of other poets in the process of imitation, and make them genuinely his own. He asked the poet to accord with his own genius and genuine feeling, and in this way his poem would be like, in Erasmus's words, "a river flowing forth from the fount of your heart." (Erasmus 1995, 123)

The actual condition of the English poetry, Sidney's main concern, was far from it. In the time when Petrarch's love poetry was popular in England, it was not uncommon for the English poets to lose their own subjectivity in their imitation of the foreign model. As Sidney (1965, 137–138) observes in the *Apology*:

But truly many of such writings as come under the banner of unresistible love, if I were a mistress, would never persuade me they were in love; so coldly they apply fiery speeches, as men that had rather read lovers' writings (and so caught up certain swelling phrases which hang together like a man which once told me the wind was at north-west and by south, because he would be sure to name winds enough), than that in truth they feel those passions, which easily (as I think) may be betrayed by that same forcibleness or *energeia* (as the Greeks call it) of the writer.

Here Sidney summed up, as S. W. May (2011, 556) concisely renders it, "the overall shift in aesthetic intent from the mid-century to the 'golden' style." The Ciceronians were not able to make a mistress touched by their own genuine feeling, but only dazzled her with those "fiery speeches" with rhetoric devices for their own sake. Sidney held it the chief fault with the poets. The works produced in this way were of the most debilitating kind of Ciceronianism, with the poets saying something like "the wind was at north-west and by south," broken, illogical, and meaningless. They imitated in the way Ascham (1950) encouraged. In contrast, Sidney himself wrote love poetry designed to move the beloved with an emotionally charged expression of love's passion. Astrophil criticizes in Sonnet 6 the poet whose "song in Jove, and Jove's strange tales, attires," and claims that "I can speak what I feel." (Sidney 2008, 155) Astrophil bluntly criticizes his fellow poets who rely solely on those far-fet helps while ignoring their own genuine feelings as well as lacking confidence in themselves and their own culture, as he says in Sonnet 14:

You that do search for every purling spring

Which from the ribs of old Parnassus flows;

And every flower, not sweet perhaps, which grows

Near thereabouts, into your poesy wring;

You that do dictionary's method bring

Into your rhymes, running in rattling rows;

You that poor Petrarch's long-deceased woes

With new-born sighs and denizened wit do sing:

You take wrong ways, those far-fet helps be such

As do bewray a want of inward touch:

And sure at length stol'n goods do come to light.

But if (both for your love and skill) your name

You seek to nurse at fullest breasts of fame,

Stella behold, and then begin to endite. (Sidney 2008, 158)

Astrophil condemns those poets who do not have their own imaginations and inventions. When they attempt to reproduce the diction, phrasing, and rhythm of Petrarch's, their own "inward touch," most important to a poet, is obliterated. Only when the poets "feel those passions" will their poems have the "*energeia*" in them. According to Aristotle (*Rhetoric*, III) and Scaliger (*Pietices*, III, 26), it is the quality called "*energeia*" that makes concepts or ideas clear in language. In Sidney's use of this term, as Robinson (1970, 81) observes, *energeia* is a conceptual clarity in language, and it can result only from the poet's precise apprehension of his own fore-conceit, a core idea in Sidney's poetics that justifies the poet's position in his little world as parallel to that of God in His world.[1] Sidney proudly claimed that God had given the English people "so good minds," and "hands to write and wits to conceive," and if they were employed, they would have "heavenly fruits." (137) For this reason, he insisted that an English poet should "employ" his own "mind," "hand," and "wit."

As for how to possess the "*energeia*" in a poem, Sidney's emphasis was upon the poet's extraordinary powers of invention and the nature and potency of his proper "matters." Apart from Erasmus's and Harvey's treatment of this topic, Sidney must have been appealed by his own Ramist studies, as revealed by his diagnosis of the English poetry: "Our matter is *quodlibet* indeed, though wrongly performing Ovid's verse, *Quicquid conabor dicere*, *versus erit*: never marshaling it into an assured rank, that almost the readers cannot tell where to find themselves." (133) Sidney's proof for the lack of poetical sinews in English poetry is that if one puts most of the verses into prose, and then ask the meaning, it will be

---

1　It was Sidney who for the first time in the early modern Europe explicitly reintroduced the notion of the literary world as a little world. For more discussion, see R. E. Stillman, "The Scope of Sidney's 'Defence of Poesy': The New Hermeneutic and Early Modern Poetics."

found that "one verse did but beget another, without ordering at the first what should be at the last; which becomes a confused mass of words, with a tingling sound of rhyme, barely accompanied with reason." (133)

It is not difficult to see that the above passage expresses the fruits of Sidney's Ramist studies. Ramus insists upon the primacy of "invention" in persuasive discourse, and his influence must certainly have encouraged Sidney's fondness for tight logical argument for poetry to lead men to "virtuous action." Inspecting Sidney's earliest verse and prose, we find their manifest concern for tight logic and rigorous order of various kinds. This fact remains a convincing testimony to his essential concern with "matter" of his discourse.[1] His logical and rhetorical structures revealed his determination to "marshal" things into an assured "rank." As Rudenstine (1967) points out, the *energeia* is so closely related to one's own thoughts and feelings that all ornaments should be excluded. His allegiance was to his subject matter, to invention, and to the "poetical sinews" of his work while the excessive Ciceronianism would be damaging to it.

Only when writers have their own sense of subjectivity as well as cultural confidence in the native tongue is it possible for them to establish a proper writing style with appropriate use of rhetoric devices suitable to the subject-matter. Sidney's own principles of writing style had been established before he wrote the *Arcadia* poems, and he did not need to change it fundamentally in the Ciceronian controversy. In his early writing career, he was already a poet with a rather complicated writing style and was able to write both in the ornate and in the plain style. In his mature years, he had developed a "mixed" style of his own, giving *sprezzatura* its own special meaning closely related to his view of Ciceronianism. Sidney never objected to rhetorical ornaments per se, but only to the

---

1   For Sidney's fondness for tight logical argument and for the inspection of Sidney's early verse and prose, see R. Tuve, *Elizabethan and Metaphysical Imagery*, 325–410, 319–323. For an analysis of how the tight logical argument works in a poem, see J. E, Curran Jr., "The Pleasing Analysis of *The Faerie Queene.*"

improper use of them. His prescription for the writer was to take a style "fittest to nature," which is the essential meaning of the *grazia*.

Sidney rejected the extreme Ciceronianism of the mid-century, and his anti-Ciceronianism was compatible with the ornament and high rhetoric. As early as 1573 Sidney asked Languet to tell him how he ought to form his own style of writing. To this question, Languet (2012, 77) first gave his remark on the common practice:

> … many believe that it is extremely useful to choose some passage from the letters, and to translate it into another language, then, having put the book away, to translate it back into Latin, and finally to look at the book again and see how close you have come to Cicero's style.

He then asked Sidney to "beware of falling into the school of thought of those who believe that the greatest good lies in the imitation of Cicero, and waste their whole lives on it." (78) To Languet's warning of the danger of Ciceronianism, Sidney (2012, 92) replied:

> Your advice about style I will follow in this manner: first I will translate some letter of Cicero's into French, then it will go from French into English, and then full circle (but not Abondio's) back into Latin.

Though not a diligent imitator of Cicero, Sidney had taken Languet's advice to heart. "I neuer require great study in *Ciceronianisme*," Sidney (2012, 1009) wrote to his brother Robert in 1580, "the chiefe abuse of Oxford, *Qui dum verba sectantur, res ipsas negligent* (Who while they run after words neglect the matter itself). My toyfull Booke I will send with Gods helpe by February." While criticizing the mechanical or extreme use of Ciceronian stylistic devices, this passage combines an expression of anti-Ciceronianism with a reference to the *Arcadia*. Of its ornate style, we may gain an idea from Harvey's advice to his readers:

Gallent Gentlemen, if Homer be not at hand (whome I haue often tearmed the Prince of Poets and the Poet of Princes), you may read his furious Iliads & cunning Odysses in the braue aduentures of Pyrocles and Musidorus [...] Liue euer sweete Booke, the siluer Image of his gentle witt, and the golden Pillar of his noble courage, and euer notify vnto the worlde, that thy Writer was the Secretary of Eloquence, the breath of the Muses, the hoony-bee of the daintiest flowers of Witt and Arte. (Harvey 1950, 264–265)

Harvey's advice shows that Sidney's mode of anti-Ciceronianism is thoroughly compatible with the ornate style of his pastoral-heroic romance and that his anti-Ciceronianism relates to the inappropriate style rather than the rhetoric or high ornaments themselves.

What Sidney condemned was the over-decorative style which led to the illness of English literature. He is most concerned with the exotic imagery and overtly liberal use of similitudes in the *Apology*. It was the common practice of the day that "all herbarists, all stories of beasts, fowls, and fishes are rifled up, that they come in multitudes to wait upon any of our conceits." (139) According to Sidney, this is certainly "as absurd a surfeit to the ears as is possible." (139) This style is characterized by alliteration, antithesis, balance, and, as Shepherd (1965, 230) renders it, "an irresponsible use of material drawn from natural history, in particular from handbooks by Pliny and Erasmus." Typical examples can be found in the writings of the "Euphuists," such as *Euphues* by John Lily and *The Schoole of Abuse* by Stephen Gosson. As Sidney (2008, 154) jeers at in Sonnet 3 of *Astrophil and Stella*, their writings are "with strange similes each line, of herbs or beasts, which Ind or Afri hold." What Sidney strongly objected to was not the similitudes of plants and animals themselves, but the fanatic practices of the Euphuists, with the seeming fineness and ornamentation for its own sake.

Sidney uses oration to reveal the nature of similitudes in the *Apology*, and insists that the "plain sensibleness" and the appropriateness be of supreme importance in choosing a

81

writing style. The similitudes can be indispensable, "to a willing hearer," in expressing the poetic conception; they are superfluous in proving or demonstrating the adequacy of the conception itself:

> For the force of a similitude not being to prove anything to a contrary disputer, but only to explain to a willing hearer; when that is done, the rest is a most tedious prattling, rather over-swaying the memory from the purpose whereto they were applied, than any whit informing the judgment, already either satisfied, or by similitudes not to be satisfied. (Sidney 1965, 139)

Sidney takes the example of two distinguished Roman orators, Marcus Antonius and Lucius Licinus Crassus, one pretending not to know art, the other not to be set by it. One is like the ideal courtier who shows nonchalance, and the other an absolute courtier who follows his own nature, displaying both simplicity and nonchalance which confers the highest degree of *grazia*. They might "win credit of popular ears" by "plaine sensibleness," as "credit is the nearest step to persuasion" and "persuasion is the chief mark of oratory." (139) Sidney's advice is to use those learned arts sparingly, as one does obviously "dance with his own music" if he uses them often, and to pay more attention "to speak curiously than to speak truly." (139) In other words, as the main purpose of oration is to persuade the audience, Sidney agreed with Erasmus that the poet should take the plain style instead of the over-decorative style.

However, for poetry and various other prose, Sidney differed from Erasmus, and his judgment was much more complex. According to Sidney, not all compositions had the same rhetorical purpose as that of prose pamphlets and public orations, and poetry and romance should neither have the plain style of orations nor should they have the over-decorative Ciceronian style. This does not mean to say that he was tired of it, or his objections were to the ornaments themselves, or it was for the sake of plain style that he objected to the excessive use of ornaments. Sidney was against the improper use of rhetorical ornaments rather than the ornaments themselves. For instance, when discussing the lyric, he writes:

I never heard the old song of *Percy and Duglas,* that I found not my heart moved more than with a trumpet; and yet is it sung but by some blind crowder, with no roughter voice than rude style; which, being so evil appareled in the dust and cobwebs of that uncivil age, what would it work, trimmed in the gorgeous eloquence of Pinder? (118)

Sidney invokes Pindar, the exemplar of an ornate style because it would have worked more effectively if it were written in a manner suitable to its heroic matter. What Sidney objects to is the practice of using ornaments for ornaments' sake for expository prose and orations, when the plain style is suitable. When he comes to discuss the deficiencies and the possibilities of the lyrics of his time, Sidney at least theoretically refuses the use of ornaments for their own sake. As he says:

For now they cast sugar and spice upon every dish that is served to the table, like those Indians, not content to wear earrings at the fit and natural place of the ears, but they will thrust jewels through their nose and lips, because they will be sure to be fine.

Tully, when he was to drive out Catiline, as it were with a thunderbolt of eloquence, often used that figure of repetition, *Vivit. Vivit? Imo vero etian in sanatum venit, &.* Indeed, inflamed with a well-grounded rage, he would have his words (as it were) double out of his mouth, and so do that artificially which we see men do in choler naturally. And we, having noted the grace of those words, hale them in sometime to a familiar epistle, when it were too too much collar to be choleric. (138)

Rhetorical ornaments are acceptable, indeed necessary, in their "fit and natural" places.

The sugar, spice, and earrings are all useful when they are served in the right dishes or put in "the fit and natural place." Sidney appreciates Cicero's use of the figure of repetition when he is inflamed with a well-grounded rage, as it expresses his rage naturally. However, if someone who is not enraged by this feeling uses the figure in a place not suitable, simply for the purpose of imitating Cicero, the result would be too affected. This passage explicitly shows that Sidney objected to the inappropriate use of the rhetoric devices unsuitable to the subject-matter, examples of which could often be found in those extreme Ciceronians who, regardless of the nature of their composition, imitated Cicero or Petrarch servilely and mechanically.

Sidney emphasized the rule of decorum and the criterion of "plain sensibleness." Same as that found in Horace's *The Art of Poetry*, the rule of decorum underlies the whole of the *Apology*'s discussion of diction. In fact, Sidney did not give any definite answer as to which style should be chosen, the ornate, the plain, or any other one, but maintained that the styles should be suitable to the genre and the situation and that the judgment should be based on the rule of decorum. He did not banish "*similiter cadences*" for use, but asked the question, "how well store of *similiter cadences* does sound with the gravity of the pulpit." (138) His own choices of style in different writing were guided by the matters of decorum, and he changed his manner to suit his matter. Sidney insisted that the manner should be consistent with the matter, and the poets should necessarily involve a consideration of the decorum of the work at hand. Sidney submitted all writing styles to a common critical standard, with the paramount aim of a "plain sensibleness." In other words, the stylistic restraint was invoked to further the vitality of content. According to Sidney's practice in both the *Apology* and *Astrophil and Stella*, the poet should not show off by using affected eloquence, exotic imagery, and too free a use of similitude. He must tell the truth, and this aim is bound to be inhibited by the abuse of ornament. Therefore, as Montgomery (1961, 72) remarks, "Sidney condemned not only the bad and derivative stylists, but also the entire system of style, represented in prose by the imitators of Cicero and the euphuists."

Sprezzatura is what Sidney encouraged and he himself practiced. Sidney points out in the

Apology with a rare insight, "I have found in divers smally learned courtiers a sounder style than in some professors of learning." (139) Here "professors" includes the afore-mentioned Ciceronians, Euphuists, and the imitators of Petrarch. This is not because the courtiers practiced the plain style. "Of which I can guess no other cause," as Sidney says:

> ... but that the courtier, following that which by practice he findeth fittest to nature, therein (though he know it not) doth according to art, though not by art: where the other, using art to show art, and not to hide art (as in these cases he should do), flieth from nature, and indeed abuseth art. (139)

The courtier writes according to the art fittest to, or according to, his own nature. By comparison, those professors of learning write in an artificial, thus not artistic, way. Sidney implies that, in the two principal precepts characteristic of the ancient doctrines from Aristotle, the rule of art is also the rule of nature, and the rhetorical devices need to be hidden in order to be effective. Here lies the distinction between Sidney and Puttenham. As J. Harington (1950) observes, while the eloquence of Puttenham's courtier poet is artificial yet made to seem natural, that of Sidney's must be acquired empirically and thus can be considered more truly natural. In the art "fittest to nature," his own nature being doubtlessly respected, when the artist can express naturally his own unique feelings, he hides, or rather, is unaware of, the fact that he does according to art. This is the core meaning of *sprezzatura*. Consistent with it was Sidney's own principle in writing: the poet should know his own subject-matter, have his own thoughts and genuine feelings, and his style should reflect this knowledge. Due to a lack of the right sense of subjectivity and cultural confidence, those excess imitators had just the opposite principle.

In conclusion, Sidney not only practiced the *sprezzatura* in the *Apology* as a writing style but also adapted a courtly ideal of *sprezzatura* and *grazia* to new contexts for English poetry. By pointing out some aspects of the common infection amongst most English writers, Sidney provided his prescription. *Sprezzatura* and *grazia*, with their emphasis on the natural gifts, imply the importance of what is innate in a writer. Sidney laid stress on the subjectivity of English writers and their confidence in their own native tongue, pointing out its great value and potentiality as a language of literature. Just as Vasari ensured that painting had a new view of good manner when it reached the position of being a learned art, at the time when English literature was under deplorable circumstances because of the pedantic cult of Ciceronianism, Sidney helped to lead English writers away from servile and pedantic imitations, and toward the proper use of matter and manner. He thus had a formative influence on the development of "golden" English poetry, whose main feature is to allow the manner to serve not itself, but the matter.

(Acknowledgement: This article is a revision of the author's speech at the 2017 UKCHA Annual Forum.)

References

Ascham, R. 1950. "Of Imitation." In *Elizabethan Critical Essays*, Vol. I, edited by G. G. Smith, 1–45. Oxford: Oxford University Press.

Atkins, J. W. H. 1934. *Literary Criticism in Antiquity: A Sketch of Its Development*. Vol. II. Cambridge: Cambridge University Press.

——. 1951. *English Literary Criticism: The Renascence*. London: Methuen & Co. Ltd.

Bacon, F. 1859. *The Works of Francis Bacon*, Vol. III, edited by J. Spedding, R. Ellis, and D. Health, London: Longman.

Berger Jr., H. 2002. "*Sprezzatura* and the Absence of Grace." In *The Book of the Courtier: The Singleton Translation*, edited by D. Javitch, 295–306, New York: W. W. Norton.

Blunt, A. 1962. *Artistic Theory in Italy: 1450–1600*. Oxford: Oxford University Press.

Boccaccio, G. 1956. *Boccaccio on Poetry*. Edited and translated by C. G. Osgood. New York: The Bobbs-Merrill Company.

Buxton, J. 1963. *Elizabethan Taste*. London: Macmillan & Co Ltd.

Castiglione, B. 1959. *The Book of the Courtier*. Translated by C. Singleton. New York: Doubleday.

——. 2003. *The Book of the Courtier*. Translated by G. Bull. London: the Penguin Group.

Chapman, G. 1941. *Poems of George Chapman*. Edited by P. B. Bartlett. New York: Modern Language Association of America.

Curran Jr., J. E. 2023. "The Pleasing Analysis of *The Faerie Queene*." *Studies in Philology* 120 (1): 33–69. Available through: SJTU Library website: library.sjtu.edu.cn. [Accessed 29 March 2023].

Dana, M. E. 1973. "Heroic and Pastoral: Sidney's *Arcadia* as Masquerade." *CL* 25 (4): 308–320.

Dodds, G. D. 2009. *Exploring Erasmus: The Erasmian Legacy and Religious Change in Early Modern England*. Toronto: University of Toronto Press.

"E. K." 1950. "Epistle Dedicatory to *The Shepheards Calender*." In *Elizabethan Critical Essays*, Vol. I, edited by G. Gregory Smith, 127–134. Oxford: Oxford University Press.

Erasmus, D. 1995. "Ciceronianus." In *Controversies Over the Imitation of Cicero in the Renaissance*. Part II. Edited and translated by I. Scott. Mahwah: Taylor & Francis Group: 19–132.

Fowler, E. and Greene, R. 1997. *The Project of Prose in Early Modern Europe and the New World*. Cambridge: Cambridge University Press.

Gavin, A. 2006. *Writing after Sidney: The Literary Response to Sir Philip Sidney 1586–1640*. Oxford: Oxford University Press.

Gilmore, M. P. 1952. *The World of Humanism, 1453–1517*. New York: Harper and Brothers.

Greenblatt, S. 2012. *The Serve: How the Renaissance Began*. London: Vintage.

Hamilton, A. C. 1977. *Sir Philip Sidney: A Study of His Life and Works*. Cambridge: Cambridge University Press.

Hardison Jr. O. B. 1972. "The Two Voices of Sidney's Apology for Poetry." In *English Literary Renaissance* 2 (1): 83–99.

Harington, J. 1950. "A Preface, or rather a Briefe Apologie of Poetrie, prefixed to the translation of *Orlando Furioso*." In *Elizabethan Critical Essays*, Vol. II, edited by G. G. Smith, 194–222. Oxford: Oxford University Press.

Harvey, G. 1945. *Ciceronianus*. Edited by H. Wilson and C. A. Forbes. University of Nebraska Studies in the Humanities, No.4. Lincoln: University of Nebraska. vii and 137.

——. 1950. "From *Pierce's Supererogation*." In *Elizabethan Critical Essays*, Vol. II, edited by G. G. Smith, 245–282. Oxford: Oxford University Press.

He, W. 2023. *An Apology for Poetry: Philip Sidney's Life and Poetics*. Beijing: The Commercial Press.

Henderson, J. R. 1995. "'Vain Affectations': Bacon on Ciceronianism in *The Advancement of Learning*." *English Literary Renaissance* 25 (2): 209–234.

Horace, 1982. "The Art of Poetry." In *Literary Criticism: Plato to Dryden*, edited by Allan H. Gilbert, 125–143. Detroit: Wayne State University Press.

Javitch, D. 1983. "Il Cortegiano and the Constraints of Despotism." In *Castiglione: The Ideal and the Real in Renaissance Culture*, edited by R. W. Hanning and D. Rosand, 17–28. New Haven: Yale University Press.

Jones, R. F. 1953. *The Triumph of the English Language: A Survey of Opinions concerning the Vernacular from the Introduction of Printing to the Restoration*. Stanford: Stanford University Press.

Kinney, A. F. 1972. "Parody and Its Implications in Sydney's Defense of Poesie." *Studies in English Literature, 1500–1900* 12 (1), *The English Renaissance* (Winter): 1–19.

Kristeller, P. O. 1961. "Humanism and Scholasticism in the Italian Renaissance." In *Renaissance Thought and Its Sources*, edited by M. Mooney, 85–105. New York: Columbia University Press.

Kuin, R. 2012. "Sir Philip Sidney and World War Zero: Implications of the Dutch Revolt." *Sidney Journal* 30 (2): 34–55.

Languet, H. 2012. *The Correspondence of Sir Philip Sidney.* Edited by R. Kuin. Oxford: Oxford University Press.

Lathrop, H. B. 1933. *Translations from the Classics into English from Caxton to Chapman, 1477–1620.* Madison: University of Wisconsin Press.

Lewis, C. S. 1954. *English Literature in the Sixteenth Century: Excluding Drama.* Oxford: The Clarendon Press.

Lockey, B. C. 2015. *Early Modern Catholics, Royalists, and Cosmopolitans: English Transnationalism and the Christian Commonwealth.* Surrey: Ashgate Publishing Limited.

Longinus, 1998. "On the Sublime." In *The Critical Tradition: Classic Texts and Contemporary Trends.* Edited by D. H. Richter. Boston: Bedford Books.

Mack, M. 2005. *Sidney's Poetics: Imitating Creation.* Washington, DC: The Catholic University of America Press.

May, S. W. 2011. "Poetry." In *The Elizabethan World*, edited by S. Doran and N. Jones. 550–566. London and New York: Routledge.

Montgomery, R. 1961. *Symmetry and Sense: The Poetry of Sir Philip Sidney.* Austin: University of Texas Press.

Myrick, K. O. 1935. *Sir Philip Sidney as a Literary Craftsman.* Cambridge: Harvard University Press.

Perry, N. 2005. "*Imitatio* and Identity: Thomas Rogers, Philip Sidney, and the Protestant Self." *English Literary Renaissance* 35 (3): 365–406.

Puttenham, G. 1936. *The Arte of English Poesie.* Edited by G. D. Willock and A. Walker. Cambridge: Cambridge University Press.

Rebhorn, W. 1978. *Courtly Performance, Masking and Festivity in Castiglione's "Booke of the Courtier."* Detroit: Wayne State University Press.

Robinson, F. G. 1970. "Notes." In *An Apology for Poetry*, edited by F. G. Robinson, 3–89. Indianapolis: The Bobbs-Merrill Company, Inc.

Rudenstine, N. L. 1967. *Sidney's Poetic Development.* Cambridge: Harvard University Press.

Saccone, Eduardo. 1983. "*Grazia, Sprezzatura, Affectazione* in the *Courtier.*" In *Castignione: The Ideal and the Real in Renaissance Culture*, edited by R. W. Hanning and D. Rosand, 45–68. New Haven: Yale University Press.

Seigel, J. E. 1993. "Ideals of Eloquence and Silence in Petrarch." In *Renaissance Essays* II, edited by W. J. Connell, 1–28. New York: University of Rochester Press.

——. 1968. *Rhetoric and Philosophy in Renaissance Humanism: The Union of Eloquence and Wisdom, Petrarch to Valla.*

Princeton: Princeton University Press.

Shepherd, G. 1965. "Notes." In *An Apology for Poetry or The Defence of Poesy*, edited by G. Shepherd, 143–237. Edinburgh: R. & R. Clark, Ltd.

Sidney, P. 2012. *The Correspondence of Sir Philip Sidney*. Edited by R. Kuin. Oxford: Oxford University Press.

——. 2008. *Sir Philip Sidney: The Major Works, including Astrophil and Stella*. Edited by K. Duncan-Jones. Oxford: Oxford University Press.

——. 1965. *An Apology for Poetry or The Defence of Poesy*. Edited by G. Shepherd. Edinburgh: R. & R. Clark, Ltd.

——. 1962. *The Poems of Sir Philip Sidney*. Edited by W. A. Ringler. Oxford: Oxford University Press.

Stillman, R. E. 2008. *Philip Sidney and the Poetics of Renaissance Cosmopolitanism*. Hampshire: Ashgate Publishing.

——. 2002. "The Scope of Sidney's 'Defence of Poesy': The New Hermeneutic and Early Modern Poetics." *English Literary Renaissance* 32 (3): 355–385.

Trimpi, W. 1962. *Ben Jonson's Poems: A Study of the Plain Style*. Stanford: Stanford University Press.

Tuve, R. 1972. *Elizabethan and Metaphysical Imagery*. Chicago & London: The University of Chicago Press.

Vos, A. 1979. "'Good Matter and Good Utterance': The Character of English Ciceronianism." *Studies in English Literature, 1500–1900* 19 (1): 3–18.

Whigham, F. 1984. *Ambition and Privilege. The Social Tropes of Elizabethan Courtesy Theory*. Berkeley: University of California Press.

Williamson, G. 1951. *The Senecan Amble: A Study in Prose Form from Bacon to Collier*. Chicago: University of Chicago Press.

Woudhuysen, H. R. 1996. *Sir Philip Sidney and the Circulation of Manuscripts, 1558–1640*. Oxford: Oxford University Press.

"Include Me Out": Reading Eileen Chang as a World Literature Author

Carole Hang-fung Hoyan[*]

Introduction

When the notion "world literature" meets Eileen Chang, her image as a literary star in wartime Shanghai and a canonical figure in the Chinese-reading communities undergoes a radical shift. She remains little known in world literature and is even regarded as a case of "failure" in achieving a reputation outside of China. In his plenary lecture for the 2016 IWL (The Institute for World Literature) program at Harvard, "What Isn't World Literature? Problems of Language, Context, and Politics," David Damrosch (2016) quoted the chart "Canonicity by MLA Citation 2006–2015," in which Chang was ranked as a "minor author" for having been quoted 90 times in the MLA Bibliography-indexed articles between 2006 and 2015 in North America, while Lu Xun is ranked as a "major author" having been quoted 247 times during the same period.

If we compare the visibility of Lu and Chang in anthologies on world literature, we will find that Lu appears in *The Routledge Concise History of World Literature* (6 pages; D'haen 2012, 198), *The Routledge Companion to World Literature* (1 page; D'haen, Damrosch, and Kadir 2012, 511), *World Literature: A Reader* (1 page; D'haen, Domínguez, and Thomsen 2012, 366), and *Companion to Comparative Literature, World Literatures, and Comparative Cultural Studies* (9 pages; Tötösy de Zepetnek and Mukherjee 2013, 526)

* HOYAN Hang Fung, Carole (何杏楓) is Professor in the Department of Chinese Language and Literature and Director of Yale-China Chinese Language Center at the Chinese University of Hong Kong. Professor Hoyan's research interests include modern and contemporary Chinese fiction and drama, Eileen Chang studies, Hong Kong literature, world literature and Asian studies.

while Chang remains absent.

Chang's invisibility in world literature is an issue worthy of thought if we consider the similar level of hypercanonicity she has attained as compared with Lu in modern Chinese literature. In his "From Counter-Canon to Hypercanon in a Postcanonical Age: Eileen Chang as Text and Myth," Zhang Yingjin (2011) probes into the issue by measuring Chang against Damrosch's "threefold definition" of world literature, which may be understood as follows:

1. World literature is an elliptical refraction of national literatures;

2. World literature is writing that gains in translation;

3. World literature is not a set canon of texts but a mode of reading: a form of detached engagement with worlds beyond our own place and time. (Damrosch 2003, 281)

In response to the three parts of the definition, Zhang observes that firstly, Chang's self-conscious distance from "national literature" has precluded her from becoming a Chinese "representative" in world literature; secondly, she does not gain in translation, or even in her self-translation in English; and thirdly, Chang may have evaded inclusion in world literature because she has largely failed to inspire "detached engagement" in either English or Chinese (Zhang Yingjin 2011, 628–629). Zhang holds that Damrosch's definition of world literature "does not specifically address the issue of hypercanonicity in Chang." (629)

Zhang subsequently expands his scope of investigation in the article "Mapping Chinese Literature as World Literature" (2015), in which he evaluates the consequences of mapping Chinese literature by the Western view and tests a different set of "technologies of recognition" introduced by Shu-mei Shih in the context of the debate over Chinese versus Sinophone studies. Chang is discussed together with Jing Yong as authors who obtain a "hypercanon" status and exert a global impact without representing a given national literature in the world republic of letters, while Bei Dao, and Mo Yan are discussed as world literature authors who "gain in translation" (Zhang 2015, 7).

Julia Lovell (2010, 207) also juxtaposes Chang's case to others in her "Chinese Literature in the Global Canon: The Quest for Recognition":

> The notable failure of Eileen Chang—an undisputed literary star since the 1940s in Sinophone reading communities, and able to translate her own works into English—to relocate her Chinese literary celebrity into Anglophone reading markets after moving to American in the 1950s is a case in point. Achieving a reputation outside China depends also on a writer's ability to embrace the particularities of a new cultural environment. In the case ... his success has been generated not only by his own talents but also by his endorsement of the national literary values of his adopted country, France.

Instead of a "hypercanon" not receiving her recognition for representing China in world literature, Chang is regarded as a "notable failure" in comparison with success of others in gaining global recognition, due to her inability to embrace a new cultural environment, that is, the United States in her case. The studies of Zhang and Lovell lead us to consider the following questions: How effective is "world literature" as a concept for the analysis of modern Chinese literature? Is it necessary to map China onto "world literature"? What might recent debates on world literature bring to Chinese literary studies and what does Chinese literature have to offer to such debates? Regarding the case of Chang, how may we understand her late years in the United States from a global literary perspective?

This article aims to examine the category of "world literature," together with its applicability and limitations, by re-visiting the case of Eileen Chang as a writer and cultural translator. The issue of reading Eileen Chang in the light of "world literature" may be investigated in two aspects: how Chang or modern Chinese literature is brought to the world, and how the world is brought to Chang or China. The former involves Chang's own efforts in bringing herself to the world, especially to the West, by publishing in English and translating her own Chinese works into English, as well as the efforts of English-writing scholars in introducing her and modern Chinese literature to the West by reviews and anthologies. The latter involves, on the one hand, Chang's role as a playwright writing for a Chinese-speaking readership across national geographic divides and appropriating Hollywood comedies and musicals in her film scripts and, on the other hand, as a cultural translator of English works into Chinese in the global literary context.

This article addresses the above issues as follows: the second section traces Chang's early aspiration to become a world literature author through her English publications and translations during the period 1938–1941. It reads her admiration for (and jealousy of) Lin Yutang in her high school years as a manifestation of her ambition to break into the global literary scene. This section also traces Chang's evolution, from the fifties onwards, into a playwright for a transregional and transnational audience and her appropriation of Western film culture after she moved to Hong Kong and subsequently to the US. To Chang, encountering the world implies both bringing her works and Chinese literature and culture to the world and bringing the world to her works and Chinese literature and culture. This section outlines Chang's engagement with world literature as a lifelong endeavor, so as to pave the way for a discussion of her view on world literature in the next section.

The third section of the article discusses how Chang views world literature through a close reading of the little-known document "Chinese Translation: A Vehicle of Cultural Influence," the transcription of a speech Chang gave in English on several occasions at the State University of New York and the Radcliffe Institute between 1966 and 1969. In this speech given in her forties, Chang shows her concern with Orientalism and with the canonization of world literature through translation, and she holds that it is impossible for the East to meet the West. This section echoes the previous one by revisiting Chang's Lin Yutang dream, as Lin is repeatedly mentioned in the speech, and addresses the issue concerning why Chang could not re-stage Lin's success as a bilingual writer in the world literary scene.

The fourth section addresses the issues of how Chang (fails to) bring(s) herself to the world by publishing in English and how English-writing scholars of modern Chinese literature try to *world* her. It also reflects on the applicability of the category of "world literature" and ponders on the possibility of dialogue between various literary perspectives, including those derived from notions such as Sinophone literature, Chinese diasporic literature, and the *worlding* of literature.

Andrew Jones (1994, 171) once commented that the wall around the "cultural ghetto" of modern Chinese literature on the outskirts of the "global village" was set in place by the very entity that was supposed to tear them down: world literature. The case of Eileen Chang, when read in light of "world literature," seems to provide strong support to Jones's claim. Despite her fame as a hypercanonical writer in modern Chinese literature as mentioned above, Chang encounters great difficulties in her attempts at publishing in the US and the UK. With the recent unearthing and publication of her English novels *The Fall of the Pagoda* (2010), *The Book of Change* (2010), and *The Young Marshall* (2014), we come to a fuller understanding of the discrepancies between her English and Chinese writings. Her exchanges with her friends C. T. Hsia and Stephen Soong actually reveal her intention to cater to the preferences of publishers in order to establish her works in the market.

However, following all the critiques against "world literature," perhaps it is time to envision a way to get along with the notion. This article will employ Shu-mei Shih's term "technologies of recognition" for discussion of the possibility of bringing Chinese literature (in this case Eileen Chang) into the world. The term "technologies of recognition" refers to the mechanisms in the discursive (un)conscious of representation that produces "the West" as the agent of recognition and "the rest" as the object of recognition (Shih, 2004). Shih holds that there are two technologies of recognition, that of academic discourse and that of the literary market.

This article suggests that while Chang did not seem to gain recognition in the West via the literary market, English-writing scholars of modern Chinese literature have somewhat reversed the mechanism of "technologies of recognition" through their efforts of analogizing and in their constant participation in academic discourses as "agent[s] of recognition." Despite the fact that these discourses are never part of the huge Western ideological machine, this article considers the dialectic of rebellion and complicity in the production of the reverse discourse of "World Literature," with a view to opening up new possibilities for the application of the notion.

The Lin Yutang Dream and Chang as Cultural Mediator

Seldom does a Chinese writer manifest his or her desire to become world famous like Eileen Chang. In her biographical essay "Siyu" ["Whispers"], written at the age of twenty-four, Chang (2005, 156) writes of her admiration for the modern Chinese writer Lin Yutang as a mediator between China and the West:

I was full of vast ambitions and expansive plans. After high school, I would go to England to study. There was one period during which I determined that I was going to learn how to make animated movies as a means of introducing Chinese painting to the United States. I want to make an even bigger splash than Lin Yutang. I wanted to wear only the most exquisite and elegant clothing, to roam the world, to have my own house in Shanghai, to live a crisp and unfettered existence.

It is noteworthy that in the above original Chinese text, Chang is directly expressing her wish to be "more famous" than Lin. As a bilingual writer, Lin came to the height of his English-writing success in the 1930s and 1940s, i.e., exactly the time when the young Eileen started her writing career. Lin was the founder of the Chinese journal *Yuzhou feng* (*Cosmic Wind*) and the author of several English better-sellers in America, including *My Country and My People*, an essay collection that explained the cultural differences between China and the West to a foreign audience. Lin was twice nominated for a Nobel Prize in Literature, further reflecting his fame in the Anglophone world. As the most renowned bilingual Anglophone Chinese author of fiction and essays of the first half of the twentieth-century, Lin also harbored a passion for the Chinese language. He was the inventor of the first Chinese typewriter, which transformed and modernized the Chinese written script.[1]

"Whispers" was a Chinese retelling of Chang's earliest English-language essay. The essay was titled "What a Life! What a Girl's Life!" and was published in *Damei wanbao* (*Shanghai Evening Post and Mercury*) in 1938.[2] The fact that the essay was written in English anticipated the "bilingual shuttling in Chang's career" (Wang 2017a, v). Apart from "Whispers," "What a Life!" also left an imprint on other essays of the same period, such as "Tongyan wuji" ["From the Mouth of Babes"]. These essays subsequently form the source text for her English novel, *The Book of Change*, in which *The Fall of the Pagoda* constituted the first part and later became an independent piece. In the process of writing *The Book of Change*, Chang developed its Chinese counterpart, which became the Chinese novel, *Xiao tuanyuan* (*Little Reunion*). While Wang focuses on Chang's aesthetic of rewriting and bilingualism, I would like to return to Chang's ambition as a cultural translator.

In 1939, the year following the publication of "What a Life!", Chang wrote the Chinese essay "Tiancai meng" ["Dream of Genius"] for an essay competition organized by *Xifeng* (*The West Wind Monthly*), for which Lin served as adviser-editor and one of the important contributing writers.[3] As indicated by the motto printed next to the journal title in every

---

1 For a detailed discussion on Lin and his typewriter, see Tsu, *Sound*, 49–111; "Salvaging." For analysis of Lin as an immigrant writer and global figure, see Shen, "Chinese Immigrant." For a bibliography of Lin Yutang's works published in English, see Lin Taiyue's *Lin Yutang Zhuan*, 367–372.

2 "What a Life! What a Girl's Life!" is in itself a rewriting from Chang's Chinese essay "Buxing de ta" ["An Unlucky Girl"], which is her first published work. "An Unlucky Girl" first appeared in *The Phoenix* (Shanghai: St. Mary's Hall, 1932), and was republished in *Lianhe bao* (October 10, 1995). For reviews on this essay, see Chen, "Tiancai."

3 The chief editors of *The West Wind Monthly* were the Huang brothers, Huang Jiade and Huang Jiayin. Huang Jiayin was the translator of the Chinese version of Lin's *The Importance of Living*, which was published in New York in 1937.

issue: "Translating the essence of Western magazines, introducing European and American life and society," *The West Wind Monthly* aimed to introduce Western culture and scientific knowledge through the translation of essays from magazines such as *Reader's Digest*, *New York Times*, *Scientific American*, and *Forum* (*West Wind Monthly* 1940, 35: 501–506, 507–509, 518–520; 1940, 61: 33–36).

Chang manifested her dream of becoming a cultural translator by contributing to the English magazine, *The Twentieth Century*. She published three cultural critiques and six film reviews in English between January and December of 1943 (Chang, "China"; "Chinese Life"; "Demons"; "Mother"; "On the Screen"; "On 'With the Snow'"; "Opium War"; "Still"; "Song"). However, it was not until 1955 that she returned to her creative writings in English. In between these times, she concentrated on the publication of short stories and essays in Chinese and became one of the most famous writers in the Shanghai International Settlement.[1] After the war, Chang went to Hong Kong in 1952 and left for the United States in 1955. During her Hong Kong and US years, Chang earned her living as a translator for the United States Information Agency (USIA) and a playwright for the Hong Kong Motion Picture & General Investment Company Limited (MP & GI).

Recent scholarship on Chang tends to pay closer attention to her transformation from a Shanghai writer to a translator and playwright who envisioned and wrote for a Chinese-speaking readership across national geographic divides (Huang 2016, 128). Chang wrote a total of ten scripts during her eight-year collaboration with MP & GI: until the studio underwent a major reshuffle in 1964, and eight of the scripts were brought to the screen.[2] These scripts displayed a sense of humor that was rarely found in Chang's fiction and essays, and many of them had solid box office successes in Hong Kong. Contrary to the

---

1 For a detailed discussion on Chang's Shanghai-settlement years, see Gunn, *Unwelcome Muse*, 200–231.

2 All of the screenplays Chang wrote for MP & GI were anthologized into a four-volume collection, except for the script of *Dream of the Red Mansion*, which cannot be traced. See Zhang Ailing, *Zhang Ailing dianmou jubenji*; "Eileen Chang: MP & GI Screenplays."

belief that Chang's creativity had already dried up in her US years, her creative energy found an outlet in her script writing and translation. She served as a cultural translator in the transnational film culture by trying her hand at new genres and media. She appropriated Hollywood comedies and musicals in her film scripts and readjusted her textual strategies in response to the demands of the film industry (Liao 2016a; Ng 2008).

Apart from her connection with the transnational film culture, Chang's role as a translator is also important for the discussion of her as a cultural mediator in the global literary context. The term "cultural translator" in this article refers to Chang as a cultural mediator who acts upon the transcultural site.[1] Contrary to the impression that Chang was merely a commissioned translator who worked for the USIA for a living, this article views Chang as an "agent of initiation" by reconsidering her early ambition to introduce China to the West through translation and her writing of cultural critique in English. Her comments on the role as a translator in her speech delivered in the sixties in the United States will also be discussed in this section.

The translation career of Chang started as early as 1941, when she published the abridged translation of Margaret Halsey's *With Malice toward Some* under the title "Nue er nue" ["Sarcasm and Irony"] in *Xishu jinghua Quarterly* (*Essence of Western Books*).[2] Both *Essence of Western Books* and *The West Wind Monthly* belong to the "West Wind Series," and the motto of *Essence of Western Books*, "translating the essence of Western books,

---

1 I am indebted to Peng Hsiao-yen in the use of the term "Cultural Translator," which she uses to refer to the "self-conscious actors who find the intermediary or interstitial space a site for creative transformation." According to Peng, "[A]n artist or writer in cultural translation is more an actor who acts upon the transcultural site than a character who is the site itself. He is not merely a 'receptor / transmitter within that network of communication,' as Taylor puts it, but one who finds 'an agency of initiation' in that network, as Homi Bhabha says in Location of Culture when discussing minority communities." (Peng 191) See also Peng and Rabut, "Introduction," 1.

2 Zhang Ailing, "Nue er nue"; Hasley. For a detailed discussion of the translation of "Sarcasm and Irony," see Hoyan, *"Nue er nue."*

introducing European and American readings," bears a great similarity to that of *The West Wind Monthly*. Eileen Chang (1941, 168) added a prologue before the translation:

Ms. Halsey went to Britain with her husband—her husband went to England to take up a position in Devon as an exchange-professor from the British–American educational institutions—Halsey published her diary with the title "Sarcasm and Irony," in the style of British black humor to reflect the impression of Britain, Switzerland and Norway from the American's point of view. It was very popular.[1]

This translator's note is noteworthy as it indicates the reason why Chang translates Halsey's work—Halsey was also a cultural mediator who traveled with her husband from the US to England and wrote about her observations of England, Switzerland, and Norway. Chang was interested in the dynamics of travel (both in physical mobility and the conceptual exchange in this case) and transculturation.

Considering that Chang's essay "Dream of Genius" and translation "Sarcasm and Irony" were published in two consecutive years, 1940 and 1941, in *The West Wind Monthly* and *Essence of Western Books* respectively, we have a good reason to believe that the choice of translating *With Malice towards Some* was Chang's own. She was in her "Lin Yutang Dream" at that point of her life and crossed paths with "world literature" in the sense that she aspired to become famous in the world by introducing China to the West, by means of translation, writing, and making animated movies. She started her literary career in the direction of a cultural mediator with self-initiation and strong motivation. She also wrote an essay "Lun katung yinghua de qiantu" ["On the Future of the Animated Movies"] at the age of seventeen, in which she held a positive view for the development of animated movies as a cultural vehicle for the dissimilation of knowledge and ideas, including that of

---

1   See "Translator's Note" in Zhang Ailing, "Nue er nue," 168.

science, history, and literature.[1] The following section will further discuss Chang's view on translation as a cultural vehicle through a close reading of the transcription of a speech she once gave.

Translation as a Vehicle of Cultural Influence

In a little-known document, "Chinese Translation: A Vehicle of Cultural Influence," a transcription of Chang's speech given in English on several occasions at the State University of New York and the Radcliffe Institute between 1966 and 1969, Chang openly addressed her concern about Western Orientalism and about the canonization of world literature through translation, holding that it is impossible for the East to meet the West.[2] In the speech, she explicates the complex intersections between translation and society, and attributes the adversity she faces in the US to the West's tendency to exoticize China while dismissing its modernity as inauthentic and unworthy of interest.

Chang's speech starts by showing a concern for the world literary atlas by explicating the complex intersections between translation and society. It traces China's relationship with the world through the years of the late-Qing period, the Republican era, May Fourth, the Japanese Occupation, and the Cultural Revolution, including numerous authors and works from China and the West.

What is noteworthy is that with Chang's endeavors to explain Chinese history and culture for Western audiences, she is at the same time mapping out a world literature atlas in relation to major historical events. In this world literature atlas, though emphasis is placed on the introduction of Western literature to China through translation, she also mentions

---

1 The essay was published in *The Pheonix*, the school magazine of St. Mary Hall in 1937 (Zhang Ailing, *Zhang Ailing wenji*, 8–11).

2 The speech was transcribed with an introduction by Christopher Lee and published in the section "Little Known Documents" in *PMLA*. Chang was staying at the Radcliffe Institute of Independent Study from 1967 to 1969 with a fellowship to work on an English translation of the late-Qing novel, *The Sing-song Girls of Shanghai*.

writers whom she views as important in the world literature atlas. While these writers may not be canonical or hypercanonical, some of them are writers whose artistry Chang admires, such as Maupassant and Maugham, and others are those who highlight the contingency of history, like Rider Haggard.

As present studies have already addressed how Chang maps Maupassant, Maugham, and Marquand into the world atlas by introducing and translating their works,[1] this article will focus on how Chang relates the role of translator as a cultural vehicle to canonization, and how she highlights "the contingency of history" in the case of Rider Haggard, which is closely related to Chang's view on (the impossibility of) world literature.

As indicated by the title of Chang's talk, Chang views translation as a form of cultural mediation that plays a significant role in cross-cultural relations. To her, translation is an important medium of transculturation through which China and other civilizations encounter and generate new forms of knowledge, feeling, and power exchange.[2] In the speech, Chang raises Lin Shu as an example to show the impact of the translator in canonization. She says:

A Chinese critic complained at about the end of the first World War, "Judging from the number of books translated, Rider Haggard must be the greatest Western writer." I don't know if you have heard of him. I myself came across the name Rider Haggard without realizing that he is none other than the great 哈葛德 [Ha Ge'de], master of Western fiction. I've never seen the movie *She*, based on his best-known fantasy, but I've read one of his lesser works in fine Chinese under the title *The Chronicle of the Melancholy City of Haze and Water* … It was translated by Lin Shu. (Chang 2015, 491)

---

1 For a study on Maugham and Chang, see Deppman. For discussion on Chang's appropriation of Marquand's *H. M. Pulham, Esq.* in Chang's *Life of a Half-time Destiny*, see Hoyan, "Hualiyuan."
2 For discussions of translation as a medium of transculturation, see also D. Wang, "Worlding," 19; Peng and Rabut, "Introduction," 1.

Here Chang is highlighting the impact of the translator, in this case Lin Shu, in promoting foreign literature, regarding his choice of work to translate, and his artistry in translating the work. An ordinary writer like Rider Haggard (according to Chang) could be presented as "the greatest Western writer" to the Chinese if he is promoted by translation.

Re-reading the speech in the context of Chang as a translator herself, it is noteworthy that she crossed out a passage in her manuscript, in which she criticizes Americanization and the hegemony of the West:

The May Fourth has set the tone for a rather sterilized view of the West as mentor, and now Hong Kong and Taiwan have perforce become part of the picture of worldwide Americanization, only more so because of their precarious existence—without the disinterested exploratory enthusiasm of the May Fourth. Imagination needs room, it needs distance and an absence of pressure. (Lee, Introduction in Chang 2015, 489)[1]

This passage shows that as a translator working for the USIA, Chang is highly aware of the power struggles between individual and institutional powers involved in transcultural and transnational interactions. In their introduction to *Modern China and the West: Translation and Cultural Mediation*, Peng Hsiao-yen and Isabelle Rabut (2014b, 1) note that "cultural mediators include not only individuals, but also transnational organizations that bring about cross-cultural interactions, and regulating authorities, in the form of both nation-states and ideologies, which dictate what, and even how, to translate." The question Peng and Rabut ask is, in the face of institutional powers, is there room for individuals to exercise their free will, and to what extent are they allowed to do so.

If we consider "cultural translator" as someone who intends to (re)shape certain concepts through the translating act, so as to "negotiate among multifarious institutional powers

---

1   Christopher Lee's "Introduction" to the transcription. See Chang, "Chinese Translation," 489.

that coexist, including traditional and foreign" (Peng and Rabut 2014b, 1), Chang might not be considered a "cultural translator" in the strictest sense, even with her self-initiation in mediating China and the West and her awareness of the power struggle between the institution and the individual. Whether Chang intended to, or tried to, (re)shape certain concepts through the translating act is another question in need of further investigation.[1] I would like to use the term "cultural translator" in a loose sense, to note her critique against Americanization, which parallels her disapproval of Communism, and to take a closer look at Chang's view of translation as a vehicle of cultural influence.

Chang makes four points on the issue of self-censorship in the crossed-out passage quoted above: first, May Fourth has set the tone for a rather sterilized view of the West as mentor; second, Hong Kong and Taiwan follow the May Fourth tradition to regard the West as mentor; third, Hong Kong and Taiwan are doing that not because of May Fourth curiosity but because of their dangerous positions; and fourth, enthusiasm and imagination need room and take place in the absence of political pressure. In fact, Chang's crossing out of the passage may be regarded as an act of self-censorship in support of her last point, which adds a pessimistic touch to her awareness of translation as a cultural vehicle.

---

1 Chang's translation career is a complicated topic for scholars in the history of translation in modern China, especially during the Cold War years. As a translator recruited by the Hong Kong-based *World Today Press*, which was fully supported by the US government, Chang was always discussed in light of notions such as "betrayal," "disloyalty," and "commissioned literature." (Shen, "Betrayal") Chang is one of the most prolific literary translators published by *World Today Press*. She established herself as a Chinese translator of American literature by translating works of the following prominent authors: *The Old Man and the Sea*, *The Yearling*, "The Legend of Sleepy Hollow," and "Hemingway." As observed by Shan Te-hsing, Chang's translation focused on American literature and covered almost every genre in the series, including essay, fiction, poetry, and literary criticism. The authors she translated are also representative, including an earlier canonical writer (Washington Irving); masters of the American Renaissance and Transcendentalists (Emerson and Thoreau); a Nobel Laureate (Hemingway); a Pulitzer Prize winner (Rawling); and contemporary American novel criticism. In other words, the authors Chang translated ranged from eighteenth-century to twentieth-century contemporary literature. Her translation of *The Old Man and the Sea* appeared two years before Hemingway won the Nobel Prize (Shan 110–112).

Towards the end of the speech, Chang (2015, 496–497) revisits the question of whether the East is able to meet the West:

> In this as far as we can go? Can East meet West after all? Even without the political situation the West is in a better position to break that impasse, like Tang China, when China was self-confident enough to take a lot from India and Central Asia without any fear of losing its identity. So far the Western view of China is as set and restricted as the Chinese conception of the West, and in the end a limited view makes for limited interest.

Chang's answer to the question is a pessimistic "no." She also notes in the speech that the West's tendency to exoticize China while dismissing its modernity is inauthentic and unworthy of interest.

Chang's view applies as far as the issue of "world literature" is concerned. As Theo D'haen (2012, 27) observes:

> For most of its history—that is, the history of the term, the concept, and the practice—"world literature" has been an exclusively European, or Euro–American, concern. Only in the last decade or so has the discussion really broadened to voices from beyond Europe and the Americas.

Even with the scope expanded, scholars of modern Chinese literature writing in English have shown little interest in the current debate on world literature, with just a few exceptions including Jing Tsu (2010), Zhang Yingjin (2011, 2015), and Ping-hui Liao (2016a, 2016b). Zhang's "Mapping Chinese Literature as World Literature" (2015) represents an effort to bring China and world literature(s) together by scholars of modern Chinese literature writing in English. Zhang examines two kinds of geopolitics of mapping which comprise two different sets of viewing positions on centers and peripheries: the first one is a European literary tradition with basically France and later Germany as the center; the second set of geopolitics is the new debate on the Chinese versus the Sinophone (Zhang 2016, 3).

Is academic discourse between scholars of various disciplines (comparative literature, Asian Studies, modern Chinese literature, and English literature, etc.) and geographical backgrounds (Western scholars, Chinese scholars writing in English, in North America vs. those in mainland China, Taiwan, and Hong Kong, etc.) possible? Recent research tends to suggest that Chang and other migrant Chinese writers are generally considered from the perspective of either Chinese diasporic literature or Sinophone literature, both of which cover a variety of meanings and critical positions (Shen 2016, 456).

Before returning to this issue in the next section of the article, we shall here return to two questions raised by some recent articles written in Chinese relating to Chang and Lin. The first question is: did Chang drop her admiration for Lin in her later years? Was it that she became so dis-enchanted with Lin that she did not turn to the latter for help with her career as an English-writing author (Yu)? The second question is: why did Chang fail to reproduce Lin's success as an English-writing Chinese author in the Western world (Li and Hu)?

Concerning the first question, we find that Lin was still on Chang's mind in her US years. She mentions Lin three times in the speech on Chinese translation. For the first time, Lin is presented as an authoritative figure granting endorsement and recognition to Gu Hongming:

> Maugham specially went to Chengtu [Chengdu] in the southwest to see Dr. 辜 鴻銘 [Gu Hongming] who studied English and German literature and philosophy in Berlin and Oxford and wrote in English in the style of Carlyle and Matthew Arnold. Lin Yutang thought very highly of his translation of the Confucian classics. (Chang 2015, 493)

What is also noteworthy in this quotation is that Lin is introduced in a discussion about Maugham, one of Chang's favorite authors. Maugham went to see Gu Hongming, and

Chang emphasized Gu's internationality and his transculturality and interdisciplinary training. Gu was recognized by Lin as a translator of Confucian classics.

The second time, Lin is mentioned to juxtapose the Western-oriented leftist literature and the Communist press typified by its "foreign-slanted pedantry and obscurantism." She describes Lin's style as follows: "Lin Yutang's school preferred free translation, typified by the magazine *West Wind*［西風］and the present *Reader's Digest*［讀者文摘］in Chinese." (Chang 2015, 496) The third time, she acclaims Lin's contribution to "old Chinese literature." She says:

> Lin Yutang has done a lot for the casual essay, but it's strongest in poetry and the novel. The poetry has not been as well translated as the Japanese haiku. Some claim it has never really been translated. (Chang 2015, 496)

Here, Chang's remark about the translation of Japanese poetry in contrast to that of the Chinese is remarkable when we consider the fact that politicized assumptions lay at the base of lukewarm interest in modern Chinese literature: during the Cold War, Japan was presented as an ally against Communist China. Japanese literature was translated and viewed as aesthetically humanist, while Chinese literature was at best a source of political (preferably dissident) information on China (Lovell 2010, 201).

Concerning the second question, regarding why Chang could not re-stage Lin's success as a bilingual writer in the world literary scene, Chang hinted at the West's tendency to exoticize China while dismissing its modernity as inauthentic and unworthy of interest. She wrote in a letter to C. T. Hsia on November 21, 1964: "I always have a feeling, for those who like the Orient especially, what they like is exactly what I want to expose."[1] Other Chinese critics suggested that she might have achieved greater success if she had continued to write in English after she published her cultural critiques and film reviews in *The*

---

1   See Hsia, *Zhang Ailing geiwode Xinjian*, 26.

Twentieth Century, or if she had asked Lin, who was more market-oriented and who was also in the United States in the sixties, for help in promoting her *Rice-Sprout Song* instead of turning to Hu Shi (Yu 2009, 147–148; Li 2010, 79).

Before turning to this question in the next section, perhaps it is worthwhile adding the following remarks to round up the story between Chang and Lin. In *Zhang Ailing siyulu* (*Whispers of Eileen Chang*), Soong Yilang (2010, 65) quotes Chang's comment on Lin Yutang as follows:

> I was jealous of Lin Yutang since I was small, because I think he was not up to that [reputation as a good translator], his Chinese is better than his English ... Lin Yutang—always alters the original text as he likes, using one word instead of another does not matter much [to him].

In other words, Chang thinks that Lin's English is not as good as his Chinese. The quotation here offers a glimpse into Chang's private persona—her adoration for the successful bilingual writer in the world literary scene is, nevertheless, not without jealousy.

Another interesting and relevant remark here is Wang Der-wei's linking up of the three literary figures Hu Shi, Lin Yutang, and Chang through their affiliation with Harvard University. Lin was educated at Harvard during the 1910s. Harvard hosted Hu as a visiting professor in 1944, and Eileen Chang as a residential writer (at Radcliffe College) in 1967–1968 (Wang 2017b, 19). The story of Chang, Hu, and Lin shows that travel and migration play an indispensable role in the facilitating of transcultural China and the *worlding* of modern Chinese literature—a topic of the next section of this article.

Worlding Eileen Chang

Chang had always been eager to pursue her way to World Literature. During her years in Hong Kong and the United States, she wrote altogether six novels in English. From 1952 to 1955 in Hong Kong, *The Rice-Sprout Song* (1955) and *Naked Earth* (1957) were written as a part of an anti-Communist literary campaign sponsored by the United States Information Service. *The Rice-Sprout Song* was well received by critics in the United States upon its publication, giving Chang a great encouragement for her attempt at publishing in the Anglophone world. However, the warm reception did not boost the sales of the novel— it disappeared from the market soon after its first printing (D. Wang, Foreword to *Rice-Sprout Song,* xvi–xvii). The second novel, *Naked Earth*, received little attention and was regarded as political propaganda lacking in Chang's personalized artistry. *The Rouge of the North* (1967), which was the output of Chang's project at the McDowell Colony in 1956, was received coldly by both the reviewers and general readers as a mediocre version of its blueprint, Chang's renowned novella, "Jin suoji" ["The Golden Cangue"].[1]

The Young Marshal, the recently unearthed and published English-language novel by Chang, was based on the historical figure Zhang Xueliang. The work served as another example of the difficulties Chang faced in establishing herself as an Anglophone writer. Her letters to Mae Fong Soong and Stephen Soong dated May 6, 1964 and November 11, 1964 suggest that the limited knowledge of modern Chinese history of her potential readers may well be one of the reasons for the adversity Chang faced while publishing in English—both McCarthy of USIA and her publishing manager Rodell had problems with the historical background and the Chinese names (Zhang Ailing 2014, 208). Nonetheless, researchers on Chang provide another perspective: it was her unfamiliarity with a foreign language that hindered her from entering the Anglophone market, where the greatest capital of literary recognition is accumulated. As a result, Chang is barely considered a world literature author due to the difficulties for her to publish directly in English and to gain through (English) translation, either by herself or by other translators.

In her "Global Literature and the Technologies of Recognition," Shu-mei Shih (2004) holds that there are two kinds of technologies of recognition, that of academic discourse

---

1 For the difficulties Chang faced when trying to publish *The Rouge of the North* (originally titled *The Pink Tears*), see Chang's letter to Hsia on September 25, 1963 and Hsia's related annotation (Hsia, 14–17). Also see D. Wang, "Foreword" to *Rouge*, viii–ix.

and that of the literary market. As far as the literary market is concerned, despite strenuous efforts on the part of Chinese critics and Western translators, modern Sinophone literature has for decades struggled to achieve mainstream recognition in the global canon as defined by the publishing markets of the culturally dominant West (Lovell 2010, 201). While it is difficult for Chinese writers to publish directly in English, as in Chang's case, the number of foreign-languages books translated into English and published in the United States has for more than a decade made up approximately 2–3 percent of the publication of new books (Tsu 2010, 95; Lovell 2010, 210).

However, if we consider the technology of academic discourse, we will find academic discourses that supplement and complement one another in their joint efforts to bring modern Chinese literature to the world. Chang's opportunity for publishing in English came posthumously while David Wang read Chang's aesthetics in the light of "remembrance and repetition, transgression and translation" (Wang 1998, xxvii). Ping-hui Liao (2016b) also suggests that Chang's later work in the US years was not a "reminiscence" but an attempt to piece together the fragments of her life in a new home through her multilingual and polyphonic project. Liao positions Chang as a "Sinophone writer" who attempted to reach out to the Anglophone world in spite of a profound sense of being deserted and estranged.

Shih may challenge Liao's suggestion in positioning Chang as a "Sinophone writer" given her hypercanonical status in the Chinese-writing world. If Chang is seldom considered an "Anglophone world literature" author due to her language proficiency and commercial infelicities, is there a possibility of her being considered, in a broader sense, a "world literature author" in Chinese writing?

In reflection of the limitations of the notions such as "Sinophone" and "diasporic literature,"[1] scholars such as David Wang, Jing Tsu and Shen Shuang proposed the term

---

1 As Shih argues for Sinophone literature that highlights both writings produced in overseas Chinese-speaking communities (including Taiwan, Hong Kong, and the Chinese communities in countries such as Malaysia and Singapore) and minority literatures on the Mainland (*Visuality*), Wang proposes to expand its domain form overseas to China proper, which is the source of the Sinophone polemics, and

"global Chinese literature" (Tsu and Wang 2010) and the notion of the *worlding* of modern Chinese literature, which highlight the historical interaction between the production of literatures and moving agents (Tsu and Wang 2010; Shen 2016; Wang 2017b, 457). These discussions not only broaden the scope of modern Chinese literature by going beyond a narrowly defined "China" and the conventional boundaries of Chinese studies as an area studies discipline, but also help to establish Chang as a world author by showcasing her in various controversial discussions.

In *A New Literary History of Modern China*, which is the fourth volume in Harvard University Press's series of national literary histories, David Wang adopts the concept of "worlding" to relink Chinese diasporic literature with world history, so as to answer the questions of how modernity manifests itself in the specific regional context of China, and to what extent the Chinese experience contributes to the global circulation of modernities.[1] What I would like to point out is that Chang is frequently quoted as a prime example to illustrate the themes Wang suggests regarding the "worlding" of literary China that include "architectonics of temporalities" and "dynamics of travel and transculturation," "contestation of wen and mediality" and the move "towards a new literary cartography."[2]

To read Wang's *A New Literary History of Modern China* in the light of Shih's suggestion, we will find this volume that features over 140 Chinese and non-Chinese

---

to account for the "linguistic nativity" within the national territory of China (D. Wang, "Worlding," 24–25).

1 "'Worlding' is a term originally coined by Martin Heidegger (1889–1976). By turning the noun 'world' into an active verb, Heidegger calls attention to the way in which the world is constructed and exists eternally in a constantly shifting state of becoming." (D. Wang, "Worlding," 13)

2 Regarding the first theme, "architectonics of temporalities," Chang is cited as an example as follows: The rediscovery of Eileen Chang "sheds light not only on the sensibilities of the 'Shanghai Modern', " but also on the aesthetics of decadence that anticipated fin-de-siècle postmodernism. (D. Wang, "Worlding," 17) As for the last theme, "towards a new literary cartography," Chang is also cited as an example for modern Chinese writers who shaped the spatial imaginary of the mainland from the vantage points of expatriatism, exile, and diaspora (24). It is also noteworthy that there are two entries for Chang in the volume, including "Eileen Chang in Hong Kong" by Leo Lee and "A Provocation to Literary History" by Shen Shuang.

contributors from throughout the world a "critic's work" demonstrating "workmanship" and joint efforts in relating the "literary arc" of text to the world. As "Worlding" China involves bringing China into the world and the world into China, Wang's conception of "worlding" subtly resonates with the "World Studies 2.0" that Shih proposes in "World Studies and Relational Comparison."[1]

While it is not the aim of this article to synthesize Wang's and Shih's rather divergent viewpoints (as the differences between the two major voices on the Sinophone remain), this article holds that it is the collective effort of these English-writing Chinese scholars that maps Chang into the realm of world literature. When we read Chang as an author of world literature, as this article proposes, we are reading how Chang has been gradually mapped into the realm of world literature through a continuous and incomplete process.[2]

Conclusion: Include Me Out

Returning to the discussion on the status of Chang in world literature, it is worthwhile to note that Chang finally entered "world literature" in 2016. She is included in an anthology titled *Migrancy and Multilingualism in World Literature*, edited by K. Alfons Knauth and Ping-hui Liao—Liao also contributed to the chapter "Sinophone Literature and Global Creolization" and analyzed Chang's case from a post-colonial point of view. While the prestige or value associated with concepts prefaced with "world" or "tans-" may not be indisputable, the *worlding* (or "the coming into the world") of modern Chinese literature will surely enhance its visibility.

---

1 Shih's "World Studies 2.0" refers to a "world literary studies" that "includes both the West and the rest as one world." It takes the world-historical perspectives and uses the method of "relational comparison." ("World Studies," 430–431)

2 *The Oxford Handbook of Modern Chinese Literature* edited by Carlos Rojas and Andrea Bachner represents another joint effort in worlding modern Chinese literature. In this handbook, there are altogether four entries dedicated to Chang (Liao, "Sinophone Literature"; Wang Xiaojue; Sang; Shen, "Where"). See also Nicole Huang's entry "Eileen Chang and Narratives of Cities and Worlds" in *The Columbia Companion to Modern Chinese Literature* edited by Kirk Denton. Chang also appears frequently in *A Companion to Modern Chinese Literature* edited by Zhang Yingjin.

While no cultural history of twentieth-century China would be complete without an account of how the Chang mythology took shape amid wartime turmoil and subsequently evolved and traveled across national and political boundaries in the following decades (Huang 2016), Chang seemed to be the one who was most eager to "de-world" herself, so to speak—that is, to make herself disappear from the world. Not only did she lead a reclusive life in her late years, but she also instructed in her will to have her ashes scattered in a "desolate" place.

In her essay "Include Me Out," first published in *Lianhe bao* (*United Daily News*) on February 26, 1979, Chang quoted this saying of the Polish American film producer Samuel Goldwyn in the following way:

> The supplement of *United Daily News* wanted to start a new column, "The Avenue of Culture." The editor sent me a form to fill out my address and the nature of my job. My particulars were no secret and I liked the title of the column, "The Avenue of Culture" very much.
>
> However, there was me meeting a journalist interviewing the public while strolling along the avenue of culture and window-shopping. The journalist directed the microphone to me—I happened to have met such a reporter on Hollywood Boulevard the day Nixon resigned. I could not help but quote "Include me out." Having written these two paragraphs, could I be exempted from form-filling?

If Chang were asked by the journalist whether she would like to be included in "world literature," one could imagine Chang answering, "include me out."[1] The phrase "include me out" is paradoxical in itself as it may be read in both ways, depending on where the

---

[1] Chang quoted the same phrase "include me out" again in a hand-written letter in 1994, in which she declined the invitation of the Taiwan company *Chunhui yingye gongsi* to film a documentary for her. (Chen, "Include Me Out")

narrating agent stands. If he / she is standing inside, the phrase may mean that he / she would like to be included in the group outside. If he / she is standing outside, he / she may be content with staying where he / she is. But what exactly does it mean to be "included" and yet "counted out"? One possible answer is that Chang would like to be included in world literature, mainly due to her eagerness for fame in her early years and her financial concern in her US years, and at the same time counted out of the literary canon. As argued above, Chang has created her own "world literature atlas," which consists mainly of the middle-brow works such as those by Maugham and Maupassant. In fact, Chang's target journals for publication in the United States were also middle-brow ones, such as the *Saturday Evening Post, Esquire*, and *The New Yorker* (see Hsia 2013). The "world literature atlas" of Chang will constitute a relevant but separated topic for future discussion.

In *Little Union*, Julie wrote about Zhiyong as follows:

> There is no me in his past.
>
> Years pass in solitude.
>
> The backyard remains unfathomable.
>
> The empty room is filled with sunlight,
>
> And it is the ancient sun.
>
> I have to run into it,
>
> Yelling: "I am here
>
> See, I am here."
>
> (Chang cited in Pang 2012, 189)[1]

Julie, in *Little Union*, was yearning for the recognition of Zhiyong. Reading Julie's poem in light of the context of "Eileen Chang meeting world literature," we may visualize

---

1 "她寫了首詩：/他的過去裏沒有我，/寂寂的流年，/深深的庭院，/空房裏曬著太陽，/已經是古代的太陽了。/我要一直跑進去，/大喊「我在這兒，/我在這兒呀！」" (Zhang Ailing, *Xiao tuanyuan* 189–190) Laikwan Pang's translation, see Pang, " 'A Person of Weak Affect'," 189.

Chang yelling in Julie's voice, "I am here / See, I am here." This episode could be read as a reminiscence of the days when Chang was once so eager to make a mark in the world.

This article has sought to examine the notion of "world literature," along with its applicability and limitations, by re-visiting the case of Eileen Chang. It has argued that while reading Chang as a world literature author reveals the limitations of the concept "world literature" in explicating her hypercanonical status, the concept paves a new path for Eileen Chang studies and the studies of modern Chinese Literature in the following way: it bypasses the dichotomy of including versus excluding China in such concepts as "Sinophone" and "Global Chinese literature." Conversations regarding "World Literature" have also pointed out a way of mapping Chinese literature onto the global literary scene by reversing the "technologies of recognition" through anthologizing and critical interventions.

(Acknowledgement: This article was originally published in *Ex-position*, issue 41 (June 1, 2019), 7–32, republished with permission of the journal. My thanks to Mary Wong Shuk-han, Géraldine Fiss, and the anonymous readers of my article for their meticulous comments and suggestions. This article is a revision of the author's speech at the 2019 UKCHA Annual Forum.)

Glossary

Bei Dao	北島
"Buxing de ta"	〈不幸的她〉
Chunhui yingye gongsi	春暉影業公司
Evening Posta and Mercury	《大美晚報》
Gu Hongming	辜鴻銘
Hu Shi	胡適
Huang Jiade	黃嘉德
Huang Jiayin	黃嘉音
Jing Yong	金庸

"Jinsuo ji"	〈金鎖記〉
Lianhe bao	《聯合報》
Lin Yutang	林語堂
"Nue er nue"	〈謔而虐〉
"Lun katung yinghua de qiantu"	〈論卡通映畫的前途〉
Lu Xun	魯迅
Mo Yan	莫言
Reader's Digest	《讀者文摘》
"Siyu"	〈私語〉
The Rouge of the North	《北地胭脂》
"Tiancai meng"	〈天才夢〉
"Tongyan wuji"	〈童言無忌〉
West Wind (*Xifeng*)	《西風》
Xiao tuanyun	《小團圓》
Xishu jinghua Quarterly	
(*Essence of Western Books*)	《西書精華》
Yuzhou feng	《宇宙風》
Zhang Ailing siyulu	《張愛玲私語錄》
Zhang Xueliang	張學良

References

1941. *The West Wind Monthly* (53).

1941. *The West Wind Monthly* (61).

Chang, E. (see also Zhang, Ailing) 2010. *The Book of Change*. Hong Kong: Hong Kong University Press.

——. 1943. "China: Educating the Family." *The Twentieth Century* 5(5): 358.

——. 1943. "Chinese Life and Fashions." *The Twentieth Century* 4(1): 54–61.

——. 1943. "Demons and Fairies." *The Twentieth Century* 5(6): 421–429.

——. 1943. "Mother and Daughter-in-law." *The Twentieth Century* 5(2–3): 202.

——. 1943. "On the Screen: Wife, Vamp, Child." *The Twentieth Century* 4(5): 392.

——. 1943. "On 'With the Show' and 'The Call of Spring'." *The Twentieth Century* 5(4): 278.

——. 1943. "The Opium War." *The Twentieth Century* 4(6): 464.

——. 1943. "'Song of Autumn' and 'Cloud Over the Moon'." *The Twentieth Century* 5(1): 75–76.

——. 1943. "Still Alive." *The Twentieth Century* 4(6): 432–438.

——. 1955. *The Rice-Sprout Song*. New York: Charles Scribner's Sons.

——. 1964. *Naked Earth*. Hong Kong: The Union Press.

——. 1967. *The Rouge of the North*. London: Cassell.

——. 2005. *Written on Water*. Translated from Chinese by A. Jones. New York: Columbia University Press.

——. 2010. *The Fall of the Pagoda*. Hong Kong: Hong Kong University Press.

——. 2015. "Chinese Translation: A Vehicle of Cultural Influence." *PMLA* 130(2): 488–498.

Chen, Z. 1995. "Tiancai de qibu: luetan Zhang Ailing de chunuzuo 'Buxing de ta'" ["The Starting Point of a Genius: A Brief Discussion of Eileen Chang's First Published Works 'An Unlucky Girl'"]. *Lianhe bao*, October 10.

——. 2017. "Bawo baokuo zaiwai" ["Include Me Out"]. *Mingbao*, April 30: 21.

Damrosch, D. 2003. *What Is World Literature?* Princeton: Princeton University Press.

——. 2016. "What Isn't World Literature? Problems of Language, Context, and Politics" [The Plenary Lecture 2016 IWL (The Institute for World Literature) Program, Harvard University]. Available at: https://www.youtube.com/watch?v=jfOuOJ6b-qY. [Accessed December 10, 2018].

——, ed. 2014. *World Literature in Theory*. New York: Wiley-Blackwell.

Denton, K., ed. 2016. *The Columbia Companion to Modern Chinese Literature*. New York: Columbia University Press.

Deppman, H. C. 2001. "Rewriting Colonial Encounters: Eileen Chang and Somerset Maugham." *Jouvert*, [online] 5(2). Available at: https://legacy.chass.ncsu.edu/jouvert/v5i2/hcdepp.htm. [Accessed December 15, 2018].

D'haen, T. 2012. *The Routledge Concise History of World Literature*. New York: Routledge.

D'haen, T., Domínguez, C., and Thomsen, M. R., eds. 2012. *World Literature: A Reader*. London: Routledge.

D'haen, T., Damrosch, D., and Kadir, D., eds. 2012. *The Routledge Companion to World Literature*. London: Routledge.

Gunn, E. 1980. *Unwelcome Muse: Chinese Literature in Shanghai and Peking 1937–1945*. New York: Columbia University Press.

Hasley, M. 1938. *With Malice toward Some*. London: Hamish Hamilton.

Hong Kong Film Archive. 2018. "Eileen Chang: MP & GI Screenplays (in Chinese)." Leisure and Cultural Services Department. Retrieved December 10, 2018.

Hoyan, C. H. F. 2018. "Huali yuanzhong de Ailing nushen: Pulian shenshi, Bansheng yuan he jinnian wutai gaibian tanlun" ["Goddess Eileen in the Vanity Fair: An Investigation of H. M. Pulham Esquire, Half a Lifetime Love and Zuni Icosahedron's Eighteen Springs"]. In *Chongtan Zhang Ailing: Zhangbian, fanyi, yanjiu* [*Re-investigating Eileen Chang:*

On the Adaptation, Translation and Research of Eileen Chang], 103–149. Hong Kong: Zhonghua Book Company.

Hoyan, C. H. F. 1998. "'Nue er nue' xilun: bingtan Zhang Ailing de fanyi yinyuan" ["On Eileen Chang's Translation of Malice Towards Some"]. In *Yuedu Zhang Ailing* [*Reading Eileen Chang*], edited by D. W. Wang, 199–220. Hong Kong: Comparative Literature Department of the Hong Kong University.

Hoyan, C. H. F. 2000. "On the Translation of Eileen Chang's Fiction." *Translation Quarterly* 18–19: 99–136.

Hsia, C. T., ed. 2013. *Zhang Ailing geiwode xinjian* [*Eileen Chang's Letters to Me*]. Taipei: Unitas.

Huang, N. 2016. "Eileen Chang and Narratives of Cities and Worlds." In *The Columbia Companion to Modern Chinese Literature*, edited by K. Denton, 126–128. New York: Columbia University Press.

Jones, A. 1994. "Chinese Literature in the 'World' Literary Economy." *Modern Chinese Literature* 8(1–2): 171–190.

Lau, J. S. M. 2015. *Ailing shuo* [*Eileen Says*]. Hong Kong: Chinese University of Hong Kong Press.

Lee, L. 2017. "Eileen Chang in Hong Kong." In *A New Literary History of Modern China,* edited by D. D. Wang, 478–483. Cambridge, MA: Belknap-Harvard University Press.

Li, J. T. Y. 2010. "Self-Translation / Rewriting: The Female Body in Eileen Chang's 'Jinsuo ji,' The Rouge of the North, Yuannu and 'The Golden Cangue'." *Neohelicon* 37(2): 391–403.

Li, N. 2010. "Zhuyi zuopin zai haiwai chuanbode chengyubai: yi Lin Yutang he Zhang Ailing zuopin duibi weili" ["Overseas Transmission: Success and Failure of Self-translated Works: A Comparison between English Works by Lin Yutang and Eileen Chang"]. *Dongguan ligong xueyuan xuebao* 17(6): 76–80.

Li, P. & Hu, L. 2013. "Chenggong zhilu buke fuzhi: zailun shuangyu zuojia Zhang Ailing he Lin Yutang" ["The Road to Success Cannot Be Reproduced: Re-visiting the Bilingual Writers Eileen Chang and Lin Yutang"]. *Yuwen xuekan* 11: 72–73.

Liao, P. H. 2016a. "Travels in Modern China" In *The Oxford Handbook of Modern Chinese Literature,* edited by C. Rojas and A. Bachner, 39–51. New York: Oxford University Press.

——. 2016b. "Sinophone Literature and Global Creolization." In *Migrancy and Multilingualism in World Literature,* edited by K. A. Knauth and P. H. Liao, 17–34. Zürich: LIT Verlag.

Lin, T. 林太乙. 1993. *Lin Yutang zhuan* [*A Biography of Lin Yutang* 林語堂傳]. Taipei: Lianjing.

—— 林語堂. 1937. *The Importance of Living*. New York: Reynal & Hitchcock.

——.1940. *Leaf in the Storm.* New York: John Day.

——.1939. *Moment in Peking.* New York: John Day.

——.1935. *My Country and My People.* New York: Reynal & Hitchcock.

Louie, K., ed. 2012. *Eileen Chang: Romancing Languages, Cultures and Genres.* Hong Kong: Hong Kong University Press.

Lovell, J. 2010. "Chinese Literature in the Global Canon: The Quest for Recognition." In *Global Chinese Literature,* edited by J. Tsu and D. D. W. Wang, 179–218. Leiden: Brill.

Ng, K. K. K. 2008. "The Screenwriter as Cultural Broker: Travels of Zhang Ailing's Comedy of Love." *Modern Chinese Literature and Culture* 20(2): 131–184.

Pang, L. K. 2012. "'A Person of Weak Affect': Toward an Ethics of Other in Eileen Chang's Little Reunion." In *Eileen Chang: Romancing Languages, Cultures and Genres,* edited by K. Louie, 177–192. Hong Kong: Hong Kong University Press.

Peng, H. Y. 2010. *Dandyism and Transcultural Modernity: The Dandy, the Flaneur, and the Translator in 1930s Shanghai, Tokyo, and Paris.* New York: Routledge.

Peng, H. Y. and Rabut, I., eds. 2014a. *Modern China and the West: Translation and Cultural Mediation.* Leiden: Brill.

——. 2014b. "Introduction." In *Modern China and the West: Translation and Cultural Mediation*, edited by H. Y. Peng, and I. Rabut, 1–11. Leiden: Brill.

Rojas, C. and Bachner, A., eds. 2016. *The Oxford Handbook of Modern Chinese Literature.* New York: Oxford University Press.

Sang, T. L. D. 2016. "Eileen Chang and the Genius Art of Failure." In *The Oxford Handbook of Modern Chinese Literature,* edited by C. Rojas and A. Bachner, 765–778. New York: Oxford University Press.

Shan, T. H. 2007. "Translating American Literature into Chinese in the Cold War Era: The Literary Translation and Cultural Politics of World Today Press." In *Fanyi yu mailuo [Translations and Contexts]*, by Shan Dexing, 109–144. Beijing: Tsinghua University Press.

Shen, S. 2012. "Betrayal, Impersonation, and Bilingualism: Eileen Chang's Self-Translation." In *Eileen Chang: Romancing Languages, Cultures and Genres,* edited by K. Louie, 91–111. Hong Kong: Hong Kong University Press.

——. 2013. "The Chinese Immigrant as a Global Figure in Lin Yutang's Novels." In *Sinophone Studies: A Critical Reader*, edited by S. M. Shih, C. H. Tsai and B. Bernards, 397–408. New York: Columbia University Press.

——. 2016. "Where the 'Trans-Pacific' Meets Chinese Literature." In *The Oxford Handbook of Modern Chinese Literature,* edited by C. Rojas and A. Bachner, 456–473. New York: Oxford University Press.

——. 2017. "A Provocation to Literary History." In *A New Literary History of Modern China,* edited by D. D. Wang, 568–572. Cambridge, MA: Belknap-Harvard University Press.

Shih, S. M. 2004. "Global Literature and the Technologies of Recognition." *PMLA* 111(1): 16–30.

——. 2007. *Visuality and Identity: Sinophone Articulations across the Pacific.* Berkeley: University of California Press.

——. 2015. "World Studies and Relational Comparison." *PMLA* 130(2): 430–438.

Soong, Y. 2010. *Zhang Ailing siyu lu (Whispers of Eileen Chang).* Hong Kong: Crown.

Tötösy de Zepetnek, S. and Mukherjee, T., eds. 2013. *Companion to Comparative Literature, World Literatures, and Comparative Cultural Studies.* New Delhi: Cambridge University Press India.

Tsu, J. 2010. "Getting Ideas about World Literature in China." *Comparative Literature Studies* 47(3): 290–317.

——. 2017. "Salvaging Chinese Script and Designing the Mingkwai Typewriter." In *A New Literary History of Modern China,* edited by D. D. Wang, 573–579. Cambridge, MA: Belknap-Harvard University Press.

——. 2010. *Sound and Script in Chinese Diaspora.* Cambridge: Harvard University Press.

Tsu, J. and Wang, D. D. W., eds. 2010. *Global Chinese Literature.* Leiden: Brill.

——. 2010. "Global Chinese Literature." In *Global Chinese Literature,* edited by J. Tsu, and D. D. W. Wang, 1–14. Leiden: Brill.

Wang, D. D. W. 1998. "Foreword." In E. Chang, *The Rice-Sprout Song*, vii–xxv. Berkeley: University of California Press.

——. 1998. "Foreword." In *The Rouge of the North*, by E. Chang, vii–xxx. Berkeley: University of California Press.

——. 2010. "Introduction." In *The Book of Change,* by E. Chang, v–xxii. Hong Kong: Hong Kong University Press.

——. 2010. "Introduction." In *The Fall of the Pagoda,* by E. Chang, v–xix. Hong Kong: Hong Kong University Press.

——. 2012. "Madame White, The Book of Change, and Eileen Chang: On a Poetics of Involution and Derivation." In *Eileen Chang: Romancing Languages, Cultures and Genres,* edited by K. Louie, 215–241. Hong Kong: Hong Kong University Press.

Wang, D. D., ed. 2017a. *A New Literary History of Modern China.* Cambridge, MA: Belknap-Harvard University Press.

——. 2017b. "Worlding Literary China." In *A New Literary History of Modern China*, edited by D. D. Wang, 1–28. Cambridge, MA: Belknap-Harvard University Press.

Wang, X. 2016. "Borders and Borderlands Narratives in Cold War China." In *The Oxford Handbook of Modern Chinese Literature,* edited by C. Rojas and A. Bachner. New York: Oxford University Press.

Yu, B. 2009. "Zhang Ailing yu Lin Yutang" ["Eileen Chang and Lin Yutang"]. *Xin wenxue shiliao* 2: 145–148.

Zhang, A. 1941. "Nue er nue" ["Sarcasm and irony"]. *Xishu jinghua Quarterly* [*Essence of Western Books*] 6: 168–173.

Zhang, A. [Eileen Chang]. 1991. *Liuyan* [*Gossi*]. Taipei: Huangguan.

Zhang, A. 1992. *Zhang Ailing wenji* [*Collected Works of Eileen Chang*]. Hefei: Anhui wenyi.

——. 2014. *Shaoshuai* [*The Young Marshal*]. Hong Kong: Crown.

——. 2010. *Wangran ji* [*Lingering Regrets*]. Hong Kong: Crown.

——. 2009. *Xiao tuanyun* [*Little Reunion*]. Hong Kong: Crown.

Zhang, Y., ed. 2016. *A Companion to Modern Chinese Literature.* Chichester: Wiley-Blackwell.

——. 2011. "From Counter-Canon to Hypercanon in a Postcanonical Age: Eileen Chang as Text and Myth." *Frontiers of Literary Studies in China* 5(4): 610–632.

——. 2015. "Mapping Chinese Literature as World Literature." *CLCWeb: Comparative Literature and Culture,* [online] 17(1). Available at: https://doi.org/10.7771/1481-4374.2714.

情感劳动与流动的共同体

——论王安忆新世纪以来小说中的移民与家庭

陈湘静*

引　言

王安忆擅长描写市井人物的日常生活，不过，王晓明指出，从2000年的《富萍》开始，王安忆开始有意识地批判"现代化"意识形态，她的视角开始从上海的淮海路、南京路等中心地带转向苏州河、闸北、棚户区等"边缘地带"，并聚焦于保姆、房管处木匠、船工、拾荒者等"边缘人物"。[1]不难发现，这些"边缘人物"的另一种身份便是进城的农村移民。这些移民在现实经济生活中的漂泊不定，恰恰是与王安忆所赞赏的日常生活的"恒常性"相冲突的。对于王安忆小说中的"移民"问题，少有评论者进行探讨。事实上从《富萍》开始，一种关于全球化时代里人的漂移、离散的主题就开始持续贯穿在王安忆的小说中，比如《遍地枭雄》《上种红菱下种藕》《众声喧哗》《匿名》《红豆生南国》等作品。在这些故事中，个体往往从原来的生活世界"脱落"和"逃逸"出来，流落到大千世界中，游历和邂逅形形色色的陌生人。在《富萍》中，无父无母的富萍从乡下

---

* 陈湘静：清华大学外文系教研系列准聘副教授。主要研究方向：比较文学、批评理论、马克思主义、亚洲现代性问题。

[1] 王晓明：《从"淮海路"到"梅家桥"——从王安忆小说创作的转变谈起》，《文学评论》2002年第3期，第13页。

来到上海,跟随着陌生人"奶奶"做保姆,游历和见识上海的各色人群。《遍地枭雄》中,从未离过家的城郊青年韩燕来独自一人在上海开出租车,被劫持后与劫匪共同经历了一段漂泊的生活。在《上种红菱下种藕》中,秧宝宝由于父母在外地打工而离开沈溇老家,寄宿在华舍镇。在《匿名》中,更是充满了各种背井离乡、流落大千世界的形形色色的游民个体。可以说,移民成为王安忆新世纪以来的小说的主要书写对象。

这样一种作家的文学世界的变化或许和新世纪以来的现实世界的变化有一种呼应关系。本来,乡土社会瓦解、个体脱离乡土、进城漂泊,是现代工业社会的普遍特征,但进入新世纪以来,随着产业结构和产业分布的大幅度调整,中国越来越显示出一种后工业主义的显著特征,人口的大规模、跨区域流动成为常态。据统计,至2016年止,中国的人户分离人口已达2.92亿人,占全国总人口21.1%,流动人口已达2.45亿人,占全国总人口的17.7%。[1]其中,农村移民占据显著比重。从1996至2006年,外出农民工数量从0.34亿人增加至1.3亿人。[2]这些没有固定住所、没有固定单位的流动人口,构成了中国社会的一个可观现象。"移民"成为劳动者的主体,而王安忆无疑是在美学上处理了一个非常重要的主题。

我们知道,家庭和日常生活的"恒常性"是王安忆美学的重要构成部分,她对日常生活和情感的理解,都与一种乡土或市井的美学联系起来,是一种类似农人劳作的"种瓜得瓜,种豆得豆"的扎实勤勉的态度。然而,移民社会的高流动性却与这种恒常稳定的日常生活形成了冲突。当全球化的经济使人们离开故土、流散迁徙,当聚散无常成为人际关系的常态,王安忆要如何在一个移民的现实世界中落实她的美学理想?本文打算从王安忆新世纪以来的小说创作入手,探讨王安忆在后现代状况下对移民和家庭的思考。在她的新世纪以来的小说中,家庭和血缘的关系越来越淡漠,而与陌生人的情感联系则越来越强。比如,《乡关处

---

1 国家统计局人口和就业统计司编:《中国人口和就业统计年鉴——2017》,北京:中国统计出版社,2017年,第16页。
2 陈锡文、赵阳、罗丹:《中国农村改革30年回顾与展望》,北京:人民出版社,2008年,第197页。

处》中，月娥与丈夫孩子长年分离，在上海当保姆，却与同住一个屋檐下的上海老人、一只弄堂里拾回来的流浪猫形成了相濡以沫的家人般的关系。《向西，向西，向南》中的陈玉洁，家庭名存实亡，独自在纽约度日，却与偶然邂逅的中餐馆老板娘美棠相依为命。《众声喧哗》中，失去老伴、无人说话的欧伯伯，却与对面小区的年轻保安说起了知心话，两人还和一个来历不明的东北女人结伴。可以说，王安忆以其对现实的敏感细腻的体察，捕捉和把握到了后工业时代下人口离散、家庭难圆的政治经济现实，但她并非对这一政治经济现实进行简单复刻，而是试图以一种独特的逻辑重建人与人之间的关系，在无根无系的移民中间缔造一个"流动的共同体"。

一、全球化时代下家庭的"不可能性"

以"衣食生计"为重要考量，并严格遵循"现实"的逻辑来构建小说情节的王安忆，对于移民家庭难以保持完整的经济生活的现实是有着充分意识的。[1]移民的艰难生活在她的许多小说中都有体现。在《富萍》中，在上海人家帮工做保姆的女人大都是孤身一人。"奶奶"虽然骄傲精明，为自己攒了不少家私，却无法找到真正的感情归宿，只能靠过继和供养远房亲戚的方式，换取养老的保障。吕凤仙虽然有回乡嫁人的机会，却疑心对方要霸占她的锡箔店而最终没有嫁人。而住在富萍隔壁的宁波太太，为了家用而狠下心遣独子到上海学生意，长期母子分离并最终痛失爱子，积攒下的家财背后也有着辛酸的创痛。在《骄傲的皮匠》中，小皮匠与乡下的妻子儿女长期分离，在上海过着清苦寒素的生活，最终无法抵挡对于温暖贴心的日常生活的需求，与弄堂的根娣产生了感情。《乡关处处》中，月娥与家人在一年的大部分时间中分散在天南海北，仅在过年时得以短

---

1 王安忆强调小说的虚构必须建立在现实合理性上，而生计问题是其中不可忽视的重要问题。参见王安忆《小说的当下处境》《小说的创作》，张新颖、金理编：《王安忆研究资料》，天津：天津人民出版社，2009年，第175、198页。

暂团聚。在谋生不易的大城市，金钱和真情似乎始终处于一种对立的关系中，凡是得以立足的移民，似乎都"命硬心硬"，难以保持完整的家庭。对于这些移民来说，情感与物质是分离的，他们"有情无家"，没有足够的经济能力在大城市中扎下根来，只能把家安在乡下，与家人长期分离。

在另一些故事中，移民则是"有家无情"，家庭在经济结构上是完整的，情感却是缺席的。《香港的情与爱》中出身唐人街的老魏，《新加坡人》中的新加坡人，对妻子都没什么感情，家庭更像是纯粹为了谋生而结合的经济单位，"爱情对于他们是奢侈，生存是最要紧的"[1]。正因为家庭的再生产包含着沉重的物质负担，王安忆以"恩"来形容爱情这种沉重性质。[2]在《红豆生南国》中，家庭成为令主人公畏惧的沉重窠臼和桎梏："他很怕近昵！近昵意味受恩，他是个负债累累的人，尽其一身图报都不够用。"[3]出生于福建农村并移民香港的主人公，一路从底层攀升至中产，与家人的情感却在买房还贷、攒养老金等经济事务中磨损殆尽。

移民家庭的难以完整有着深层次的政治经济学原因。克劳德·梅拉苏克斯（Claude Meillassoux）指出，在城市打工的农村移民往往不能像城市居民那样享受完整的福利制度，只能领取计日工资或计件工资，生病、养老、养育后代等费用则由农村的小农家庭经济承担。[4]在这种"农村家内经济"与"城市资本主义经济"并存的结构下，移民无法在城市永久安置并进行家庭的再生产，只能往返于城市的市场经济和小农家庭经济之间。中国当下的城乡二元结构正是这样的机制，由于人多地少，中国不得不以土地作为替代性的社会保障。[5]贺雪峰指出，现阶段中国农村家庭普遍采用青壮年进城务工、妇女老幼在村里务农的代际分工，只有务

---

1 王安忆:《香港的情与爱》,《香港的情与爱（王安忆自选集·第三卷）》,北京:作家出版社,1996年,第520页。

2 王安忆:《香港的情与爱》,第575页。

3 王安忆:《红豆生南国》,《红豆生南国》,北京:人民文学出版社,2017年,第77页。

4 Claude Meillassoux, *Maidens, Meal and Money: Capitalism and the Domestic Community*, tans. by Felicity Edholm, Cambridge: Cambridge University Press, 1981, p. 101.

5 温铁军:《三农问题与世纪反思》,北京:生活·读书·新知三联书店,2005年,第112—113页。

工收入和务农收入加起来才可以维持一个几口之家在农村的正常的再生产并积攒下一定的现金，用以支付嫁娶、盖房、丧葬等大宗费用[1]，"离开务工收入和务农收入中的任何一项，农民都会比较困窘"[2]。换言之，作为一个经济生产单位的小农家庭，是结构性地分裂于城乡之间的。农村移民家庭在政治经济现实上的破碎在许多写底层移民的文学作品中都有所体现。方方的《涂自强的个人悲伤》中，学历平平的涂自强在把母亲接到城里后，因难以维持生计而疲于奔命，并在缺乏社会保障的情况下积劳成疾而死，道出了移民家庭在城里难以进行再生产的现实。陈应松的《野猫湖》中，因丈夫长年在外打工，在情感和身体上长期荒疏的香儿与长期照顾她的庄姐产生了同性之爱，并最终杀了对她来说已经成为陌生人的丈夫，揭示出了移民身体无法"在场"而使家庭难以完整的残酷现实。徐则臣的《跑步穿过中关村》中，我们看到了"非正式经济"和"非正式关系"的两相对照，办假证、卖盗版光盘、做皮肉生意的游民的情感只能落实在同居、嫖娼这些婚姻之外的形式上。贾平凹的《高兴》中，拾破烂的刘高兴虽对发廊妹孟夷纯有真情，却无力阻止她以卖淫的方式挣钱。这些底层小说都是残酷的，甚至是血淋淋的。

然而，王安忆的小说并非对这一政治经济现实的简单复刻。《乡关处处》中，农村保姆月娥的家庭在政治经济学意义上是不完整的，但小说却通过对月娥春节回家后的劳作的描写，传达出其家庭生活的"稳固感"与"恒常感"。有意思的是，王安忆选取了"春节"这一时刻作为描写其家庭生活的切入点。我们知道，一年是农村移民在外漂泊的周期，春节是农村移民得以返乡和家人团聚的时间，也是他们的"家"得以实现完整的唯一时刻。而小说也以一年为周期来结构自身，始于年初月娥进城，终于年末月娥回家，首尾构成一个完整封闭的循环。但这种团圆仅仅是仪式上的，一顿年夜饭，短暂的几天相聚，并不能完成赡养老人、抚育儿女的实质功能。然而王安忆却对月娥在家中劳作的场面给予了详尽的描写，赋予这个仅余形式的"家"以完整感和实在感：

1　贺雪峰：《地权的逻辑：中国农村土地制度向何处去》，北京：中国政法大学出版社，2010年，第229页。
2　贺雪峰：《地权的逻辑》，第36页。

封上坛口，烧一圈蜡，密闭了缝隙。站起身，剥下来的皮扫进簸箕，锅里的饭焦铲下，盛进竹篮，鸡汤熄火。冰箱插上电，打开便亮起灯，向里看看，炒的酱，杀好的鱼，蒸的馒头，从上海带来的一只蛋糕，分生熟冷冻，全归位了，这才关灯上楼。[1]

这样细致而极具物质感的细节描写，明显地有别于对月娥在城里的生活的描写。月娥在城里的时间是被资本主义经济关系所组织的时间，"每日天不亮出门，一个上午转两份人家"，午饭或是在厨房里"找些冷剩热热"，或是"急着吃完撤离饭桌"。[2]对于这样的生活，王安忆仅以流水账式的叙述做交代，但在描写她在农村家里的劳作时，却细致到了每一个动作，仿佛这一年的匆忙遑遽的生活在这一刻慢了下来，仿佛在城里只是"活着"，在农村却是"生活"。张旭东和王斑都曾指出，王安忆对日常生活细节的铺陈是一种本雅明似的、对于人的丰富完整的感性经验的拯救，蕴含着对空洞、扁平的意识形态的抵抗。[3]王晓明认为2000年之后王安忆对日常生活的写作，是对强势而空洞的"现代化"意识形态的抵抗："这是一种重压下的反拨，一种堪称是自觉的对抗，它既是针对身外的恶劣和麻木，也是针对心内的沮丧和悲哀。"[4]换言之，月娥在春节这一刻的劳作是脱离了金钱关系支配的、身心合一的劳动，联系着一个整全的、本真的生活世界。月娥家的"完整"不在于她与五叔的法定婚姻关系或共同的财产，而在于他们共同的劳作——洗衣、生火、铺被窝、剥苋菜。如果说移民的家庭在政治经济学的意义上是不可能完整的，那么王安忆将家庭进行了重新定义，要以一种日常生活的劳作，重建家的"完整性"。

1　王安忆：《乡关处处》，《红豆生南国》，第49页。

2　王安忆：《乡关处处》，《红豆生南国》，第32页。

3　Xudong Zhang, "Shanghai Nostalgia: Postrevolutionary Allegories in Wang Anyi's Literary Production in the 1990s," *Positions: East Asia Cultures Critique*, Vol. 8, No. 2 (2000), pp. 349–387; Ban Wang, "Love at Last Sight: Nostalgia, Commodity, and Temporality in Wang Anyi's Song of Unending Sorrow," *Positions: East Asia Cultures Critique*, Vol. 10, No. 3 (2002), pp. 669–694.

4　王晓明：《从"淮海路"到"梅家桥"》，第14页。

　　在王安忆看来，家庭绝不只是一个单纯的经济共同体，家庭的本质是以日常劳作为中介来铭刻个人情感。理想的家庭与一种前现代农业时代的生活方式类似，需要时间、精力、情感的细水长流的灌注。她说："感情也是有原则的，它和劳动的原则不谋而合。付出的汗水越多，来年的收成越好。"[1]在《香港的情与爱》中，王安忆曾将恋爱比喻为农人似的劳作："就像在地里种庄稼，要犁耕，播种，锄草，施肥，一日一照应，一夜一关护，眼看着它今日发芽，明日长叶，后天再开花。"[2]然而，现代工业社会追求效率、工具至上的导向却侵蚀了感情得以培育的基础："这是个极有效率的世界。当地里的庄稼都在催生素的刺激下飞快地成熟，将自然的规律抛在一边，思想这样人性的产物，便也逃不脱催熟的命运了。思想就像暖房里的蔬菜，缩短了时间。"[3]思想如此，情感同样如此。在这个意义上，家庭的危机来自一种整全的生活意义的丧失，来自感性经验被资本主义时间挤压和剥夺之后异化而空洞的生活状态。

　　当外部的经济压力使得家庭在结构上分裂（如月娥这样的农村打工者），或使得家人关系沦为纯粹的商品关系（如陈玉洁的家庭）时，家庭就变得不再可能。近些年来在中国和日本等国家面临的少子化、结婚率下降、人口出生率下降等问题，从一个侧面说明了不安定的经济状况下家庭越来越难以实现的现实。于是，在王安忆新世纪以来的小说中，我们看到了一种颇有意味的转换，即，日常生活不再存在于家人之间，而是发生于陌生人之间。比如美棠为陈玉洁亲手做的蛋炒饭，比如根娣为小皮匠做的粉丝蛋饺、鱼肚虾仁，比如李老师给秧宝宝编辫子、做鱼圆。在这些小说中，以日常生活为中介，王安忆开启了与陌生人建立情感联系、成为"家人"的可能性。

1　王安忆：《情感的生命——我看散文》，《王安忆研究资料》，第158页。

2　王安忆：《香港的情与爱》，《香港的情与爱（王安忆自选集·第三卷）》，第510页。

3　王安忆：《接近世纪初》，《书屋》1998年第1期，第10页。

二、情感劳动与陌生人的"家人化"

如果将《向西，向西，向南》与《上种红菱下种藕》做对照，我们会发现王安忆提供了一种对缺失的亲情的弥补或替代方式。在前者中，血缘至亲因为缺失了日常劳作而使关系变得疏远；而在后者中，陌生人却能够通过日常劳作发展出家人一般的感情。秧宝宝对陆国慎产生依恋之情，正是因为她做了妈妈通常会做的工作——装米，装水，装菜盒：

> 虽然是不说话，可秧宝宝却时时感觉到陆国慎在场。洗干净、叠好了、端端正正放在她枕头的衣服上，有陆国慎手上的防护霜的气味；饭桌上的几种菜，是陆国慎特有的风格，比如，豇豆也好，茭白也好，茄子也好，南瓜也好，北瓜也好，一律上锅蒸熟，再浇上酱麻油或者腐乳汁；晚饭以后，新闻联播时候，家里人都在，七嘴八舌地说话，其中又多了陆国慎女中音的声音，李老师和闪闪都是有些火暴的，而陆国慎的声音进来，就起了中和的作用，变得均衡了……陆国慎虽然不像闪闪那么活泼有趣，但她却有着一股渗透性的影响力，在她周围，布满着她的空气。[1]

在这里，陆国慎做菜、叠衣服、点蚊香的方式是独特而具有个人化特征的。王安忆对"个人痕迹"和"个人气质"的重视，与本雅明十分相似。在《机械复制时代的艺术作品》中，本雅明指出，一件艺术品之所以不可复制，是因为它诞生于特定的情境中，身上铭刻了当时当地的痕迹，并包含了自身被生产出来的历史。[2]而现代资本主义的机械复制产品和标准化的技术手段使得个人特征、个人

---

1 王安忆：《上种红菱下种藕》，北京：北京联合出版公司，2014年，第124—125页。
2 〔德〕瓦尔特·本雅明：《机械复制时代的艺术作品》，汉娜·阿伦特主编：《启迪：本雅明文选》，张旭东、王斑译，北京：生活·读书·新知三联书店，2008年，第234页。

痕迹趋于消失，随着每一小块土地都被注册登记，住房被编号，"人们在大城市的人群中不留痕迹地消失了"[1]。而在王安忆看来，这种独特的感情和个人气质是包含在个人劳动中、通过劳动而体现出来的。在《小说的情感》中，王安忆曾讲到，一个感情经历坎坷的女人，靠制作梨木梳子度过漫长的岁月，当工厂采取她的技术对梨木梳子进行批量生产时，海外客商却因为梳子毫无特色而退货了。王安忆说："老太太亲手做出的梳子和小工厂成批生产的梳子有怎样的区别呢？老人的梳子里有着她个人的痕迹，这痕迹包含着她情感的过程，这个过程是谁的就是谁的，别人代替不了，这就是个人气质。"[2]同样，现场听音乐会和数码唱片之所以不同，是因为前者包含了"活生生的状态，注入了每时每刻的心情"，而后者则"完全抹去了演奏状态的生动性，我们再也看不见劳动者的痕迹，看不见创作者的激情"。[3]可见，"在场"和"过程"在本雅明和王安忆那里具有重要的意义，过程的不可取代性决定了情感的不可取代性。"家人的陌生化"（陈玉洁的家庭以机械复制劳动取代了家庭劳动）、"陌生人的家人化"（秧宝宝与李老师的雇佣劳动中融入了个人化的情感）正是发生于此。

王安忆发现的这种悖论性的状态，恰恰发生于"情感劳动"（affective labor）的领域。情感劳动是一种以生产或调控人的情绪为目的的劳动，通过与他人的交流和互动而使他人产生出一定的情绪，比如轻松、舒适、满意、兴奋、激情等。[4]保姆的护理工作就是一种典型的情感劳动。[5]有意思的是，秧宝宝与李老师（或陆国慎）实际上是一种类似保姆的雇用关系，但它却沿着家人的逻辑而展开，从而体现出日常劳作对于商品关系的强有力改写。保姆付出的劳动是一种可供购

1 ［德］瓦尔特·本雅明：《发达资本主义时代的抒情诗人》，张旭东、魏文生译，北京：生活·读书·新知三联书店，2007年，第66页。

2 王安忆：《小说的情感》，《王安忆研究资料》，第129页。

3 王安忆：《小说的情感》，《王安忆研究资料》，第130页。

4 Michael Hardt and Antonio Negri, *Multitude: War and Democracy in the Age of Empire*, New York: Penguin Group Inc., 2004, p. 108.

5 Michael Hardt and Antonio Negri, *Empire*, Cambridge, Massachusetts: Harvard University Press, 2000, p. 253.

买的商品。在很长一段时间内，女性在家庭内部的生育和家务劳动的经济价值都得不到承认和偿付，成为一种隐形的无偿劳动。[1] 从20世纪70年代起，在马克思主义女性主义者的推动下，家务劳动的经济价值开始受到重视，家务劳动开始薪酬化。而保姆这一职业在将妇女从家务劳动中解放出来的同时，也将低成本的家务劳动转嫁到了来自较低阶层的妇女身上。但保姆的劳动又与一般的商品不同，它处理的是人的身体和情感，在本质上是一种对人的主体性和社会关系的生产，也即迈克尔·哈特（Michael Hardt）、安东尼奥·奈格里（Antonio Negri）所说的"非物质生产"。[2] 保姆提供的劳动中包含着大量的情感投入，比如在照看小孩的过程中需要投入关注和爱，对雇主的情绪予以及时的照拂、关注和回应。亚莉·鲁塞尔·霍克希尔德（Arlie Russell Hochschild）在其研究情感劳动的开创性著作《被管理的心》中指出，保姆、护工、秘书、空姐、服务员、导游、推销员等服务性行业需要根据不同的客户人群和职业要求，制造或呈现出与特定场合相匹配的情感和情绪[3]，而其中的问题在于，在付出情感劳动时，必须展现出足够的真诚度，在职业性的情感输出中，还有"深层表演"和"浅层表演"的区分，心不在焉或者机械僵硬，都会被视为是不"专业"、不"合格"的服务。因此，这实际上是将人的内在情绪、情感商品化了。[4] 而这种极端异化又被一种政治经济学的不平等所加强，即保姆业被视为一种处于产业链末端的低端劳动，并经常由来自收入和阶层较低的妇女承担，从而催生了菲佣这样的"全球护工产业链"。[5] 在中国，则是由月娥、富萍这样的农村妇女承担。因此，像范雨素这样

---

1 Mariarosa Dalla Costa and Selma James, *The Power of Women and the Subversion of the Community*, London: Falling Wall Press, 1975, p. 33.

2 Hardt and Negri, *Multitude*, p. 109.

3 Arlie Russell Hochschild, *The Managed Heart: Commercialization of Human Feeling*, Berkeley: University of California Press, 2012, p. 11.

4 Hochschild, *The Managed Heart*, pp. 33-34.

5 Sandro Mezzadra and Brett Neilson, *Border as Method: Or, the Multiplication of Labor*, Durham: Duke University Press, 2013, pp. 105-106.

的育儿嫂，为了挣家用，不得不把自己的未成年女儿留在城郊农村，而去照顾别人家的孩子。[1] 2017年杭州蓝色钱江小区发生的保姆纵火案，以及红黄蓝幼儿园的虐童案，都是金钱关系使情感劳动异化加上政治经济学不平等而导致伦理危机的极端例子。

然而在王安忆这里，情感劳动的悖论却向另一个方向转化，情感劳动恢复了其不可化约的独特性，反过来改写了商品的逻辑。在《富萍》《乡关处处》中，保姆往往与雇主有着亲熟的关系，是一个家庭成员般的角色。《富萍》中的"奶奶"掌管东家的开销，指导东家的吃穿起居，很有主见地参与客人的谈话，"看上去，她不像这家的保姆，而像是这家人一个终身未嫁，抑或守寡的姑妈和老嫂子"[2]。月娥在驻沪的台湾人家里做工时，即使语言不通、生活习惯迥异，却在做饭、熨衬衫的过程中自然熟稔而不感觉隔阂，这家人"不把她当乡下人看待，倒不是多么热切，恰恰相反，是平淡的，仿佛在他家已经很久，一个亲戚"[3]。可以说，在这些保姆身上，体现了通过情感劳动、日常生活将商品雇用关系转化为家人和亲情关系的契机。

这种"陌生人的家人化"，体现了生命政治的溢出。从生命政治的角度来看，人的主体性与个人的身体密切相关，受冲动、本能、欲望、情感的左右。保姆的贴身操劳是身体性的，它在日常的、微观的层面上参与着对个体"内在"的欲望、情感、情绪的生产，因而具有改变人的主体性的能量，甚至会越出原有的规定性的秩序（雇用关系或殖民关系）。人类学家安·劳拉·斯托勒（Ann Laura Stoler）在对19世纪荷属印尼的研究中发现，荷兰殖民者在到达东南亚之初，为生活之便，常常将当地土著纳为情妇或家仆，这本是一种等级性的殖民等级关系，但是同在一个屋檐下的长期生活往往滋生出模糊统治者与被统治者界限、扰乱等级秩序的危险——印尼女性往往掌管了一家之内重要的经济事务，荷兰人与

1　参见范雨素：《我是范雨素》，《时代报告》2017年第6期，第94—99页。
2　王安忆：《富萍》，北京：人民文学出版社，2009年，第12页。
3　王安忆：《乡关处处》，《红豆生南国》，第15页。

印尼人发展出亲密关系并生下无法被当局归类的混血孩子，印尼保姆带出来的孩子在穿着打扮、谈吐举止上往往跟随着照顾他们的印尼人而不具备欧洲中产白人家庭的"体面气质"等。[1] 这正是"非物质劳动"在重塑人的主体性、改造社会关系上的强大作用。这让我们想到了王安忆的另一部小说《新加坡人》。新加坡人的前妻本是一个被雇来"替他洗衣，煮饭，收拾屋子"的华人女工，长得并不漂亮，书也读得少，本来两人并无可能婚配，但在照顾饮食起居的共同生活中，产生好感，阴差阳错生了孩子，正体现了日常生活在改造人的主体性上的巨大力量。[2] 王安忆曾说，就算是本无感情的两个人，在处理各种琐屑杂事的共同生活的过程中，也有可能缔造出成功的婚姻。[3] 她的许多小说都体现出这种"共同生活"的力量。《骄傲的皮匠》中，小皮匠远离妻小，过着清苦寒素的生活，却在寄存衣服、热饭热菜的日常往来中，与弄堂的根娣产生了感情。在王安忆看来，"家人"的感情正是发生于这种日常操劳和肌肤接触中，在日积月累中，量变可以引起质变，由陌生人成为亲人。

在现代社会中，人们往往是出于经济和职业的原因而与陌生人打交道，对功利性和有用性的追求往往加剧了本真性意义的虚无与瓦解，但王安忆的小说让我们看到了将商品关系转化为亲情的可能。哪怕与陌生人的关系一开始只是一种雇用关系（月娥和爷爷一家、秧宝宝与李老师、新加坡人与华人女工），亲身参与、共同度过的日常生活却能够改变关系的性质，使非亲非故的陌生人成为亲人。其中，"在场"显示出它的巨大力量，它是使得人与人的感情保持鲜活的重要条件。当家人的身体性的"缺席"使家不再成为家，"在场"的陌生人却可以以"情感劳动"和"日常操劳"为中介成为我们家人一般的存在。由此，孤独脆弱的个体可以在与陌生人的萍水相逢的偶遇中，与非亲非故的陌生人结成"流动的共同体"。

1　Ann Laura Stoler, *Carnal Knowledge and Imperial Power: Race and the Intimate in Colonial Rule*, Berkeley, California: University of California Press, 2002, pp. 48–51.

2　王安忆：《新加坡人》，《王安忆小说选》，北京：人民文学出版社，2009年，第457—458页。

3　王安忆：《用你的矛攻你的盾》，《情感的生命》，北京：中国文联出版社，2008年，第154页。

三、流动的共同体与"乡土人情社会"的重建

在现代社会，人与人的关系被工业经济关系所组织，而这种围绕着交换价值而建立起来的人际关系是空洞的，个人成为商品生产链上可被替代或可被丢弃的一环。而后工业时代的高流动性的经济，则使人与人之间的联系进一步碎片化。这种"名"（与财产秩序关联的个人身份）与"实"（真实的个体情感）的分离，在《匿名》中达到了极致。在里面，写字楼里的租户来了去、去了来，"每时每刻，有多少公司在注销，好比每时每刻发生的失踪人口"[1]。"萧小姐的电话是空号，户口是空挂"，究竟世上有没有这个人都不知道。[2] 杨莹瑛试图寻找丈夫下落而拨打名片上的电话，追踪到的却只是一些疏离的经济关系，这些线索将她带往"物"在世界各地的流向——"四明山的毛竹"、"津巴布韦"、讨债公司——却始终无法带往失踪的人本身。在《新加坡人》里，新加坡人与雅雯有过短暂的邂逅后离开，三个月后再回到上海时，由于员工的频繁流动，在她原来工作的酒店却找不到她了，"这么大个上海，找一个人就像找一枚针。雅雯从此，便从视线中消失"。[3] 在《乡关处处》中，月娥的雇用关系经常在戛然间结束，或是因为台资公司突然撤资，或是因为雇主老病卖房，她不断地与不同的人邂逅和别离，"上海的人就是海里针，手一松就没有了"[4]。

如果说"无常"是资本主义经济的特点，那么人与人之间的羁绊就是乡土社会特有的。如费孝通所说，乡土社会是知根知底的熟人社会，人们遵循着熟习的规则打交道，不像"现代社会是个陌生人组成的社会，各人不知道各人的底细，所以得讲个明白"[5]。乡土社会中不存在一个统摄一切的抽象原则，"亲密的共同生活中各人互相依赖的地方是多方面和长期的，因之在授受之间无法一笔一笔地清

1　王安忆:《匿名》，北京：人民文学出版社，2016年，第91页。

2　王安忆:《匿名》，第50页。

3　王安忆:《新加坡人》，《王安忆小说选》，第442页。

4　王安忆:《乡关处处》，《红豆生南国》，第12页。

5　费孝通:《乡土中国》，北京：北京大学出版社，2018年，第14页。

算往回。亲密社群的团结性就依赖于各分子间都相互的拖欠着未了的人情"[1]。对王安忆来说，"乡土"代表了一种关于人际关系的理想，它代表了人与人之间的一种具体生动的关系，一种稳定的情感羁绊，而这种情感羁绊就成为在流动不居的状态中形成共同体的准备。在《生活的形式》里，她说：

> 我所插队的安徽农村，县里召开基层干部会，是不负责伙食的，那就需要队里自己解决吃饭的问题。……在那里，假如有人病重，要送城里医院治疗，病人要去，病人的丈夫或者妻子自然也要去。父母一走，孩子怎么办？带去。那么猪谁来喂？鸡谁来喂？于是跟去。狗会自己找食，本是不必去的，可因为眷恋家人，便也去了。就这样，医院的院子里都是一家子，一家子，鸡飞狗跳，烟熏火燎，像个野营宿地。可是，有趣味的形式，就是发生于此。[2]

她在《文工团》里描写的正是这样一种乡土式的羁绊关系，对于这个处于社会主义时代尾巴尖上的日暮穷途的集体，王安忆给予了温馨的描绘。在这里，旧戏班子的老艺人、艺术院校毕业的大学生、不得志的政治干部、下放的知识分子，意欲落户的农村青年共同生活在一个院落里，在前途未卜的动荡时代中，相濡以沫，相依为命，"院子里有老有小，有鸡有狗。上班下班，吃喝拉撒，统统一锅端"[3]。"那破败的小院，像老母鸡样，张开了羽毛凋零的翅膀，为他们挡着风雨。"[4]这种羁绊，王安忆形容为"连成一片，唇齿相依"，是"打断骨头连着筋"。[5]

我们可以发现，《上种红菱下种藕》的沈溇、华舍镇，《遍地枭雄》里韩燕来的城郊村庄，都是这样一个充满人情味的乡土社会，但在里面，乡土社会都无

1　费孝通：《乡土中国》，第119页。
2　王安忆：《生活的形式》，《当代作家评论》2005年第1期，第50页。
3　王安忆：《文工团》，《文工团》，上海：上海文艺出版社，2013年，第172页。
4　王安忆：《文工团》，《文工团》，第190页。
5　王安忆：《文工团》，《文工团》，第216页。

可挽回地逝去和瓦解了。在《遍地枭雄》中,上海郊区出生的韩燕来在进入上海这个"原子化"的社会时,感到无比的落寞,他渴望在开出租车的同行身上寻求情感联结,以至于在刚开始上路时竟然死死跟着前面一辆出租车跑,最后,他是在三个劫车的匪徒身上找到了家人般的感情。这四个无根无着的人,在居无定所、亡命天涯的过程中,始终形影相随、不离不弃。这里体现的其实是一种"江湖",这是以一种"同性友爱"(homosociality)的原则组织起来的关系,与家庭、国家这些垂直的隶属性关系不同,它是一种平面的、在个体之间缔结的社会关系,因而是更加自由、更具开放性的,它多见于秘密会社、宗教团体、学术及政治团体之间。[1]"江湖"其实是个陌生人的社会,而"homo-"实际上假设了一种同质性,可被预期的熟悉感,也即"四海之内皆兄弟"。有意思的是,几个劫匪们在路上唱的歌曲,如《难忘今宵》《假如你要认识我》《涛声依旧》等歌曲,唤起的是一种集体主义时代的想象,因此,这四个人的一路同甘共苦,有点像是一种对于业已失落的"集体主义友爱"的召唤和复归。由此,车实际上成了一个"流动的共同体"。对于这种"流动的共同体",王安忆用了一个形象的比喻——藏羚羊群:"它们生活在非常美丽的地方,而且,它们自己也很美丽,没有人能够伤害它们,它们的生存也只需要一点点水和食物,所以,它们就很自由,每天只是跑来跑去,游荡来,游荡去。"[2]而与这一"藏羚羊群"相似的另一个景象则是《匿名》末尾出现的成群结队骑着摩托车的惠安女子。这一景象我们并不陌生。每到春运时节,电视新闻上耳闻目睹的,便是同乡的民工开着摩托车,载着行李、妻小,浩浩荡荡返乡的景象。王安忆的"藏羚羊群"意象很可能正是从这里得到了启发。如果说"游荡来游荡去"是移民不可避免的命运,那么,即使居无定所,他们却始终成群结队,互相陪伴,这正是王安忆心目中对于全球化时代下一个理想"社群"的想象方式。

---

1 Haiyan Lee, *Revolution of the Heart: A Genealogy of Love in China, 1900–1950*, Stanford: Stanford University Press, 2007, pp. 29–30.

2 王安忆:《遍地枭雄》,上海:文汇出版社,2005年,第237页。

这种无根无系的孤独个体在漂泊中结成的"流动的共同体",是对家的替代。她在《匿名》里给出的说法是"在家靠父母,出门靠朋友":

> "出门"这两个字,平时说说没什么要紧的,但在这里,与上半句里"在家"相对,就不是一般的出门了,更可能指的是一去不回,如何的飘零!茫茫人海,哪里是岸?这时候,朋友来了,这就要说到缘了,倘不是前世里修炼,哪里就遇得上。不是根子上发的权,为什么遇到的是他,不是他?这个缘,几抵得上血亲。所以,朋友可说是出门的生命树。两手空空来到外面,指望得上什么人?就是朋友。[1]

类似的"出门"和"飘零"在近年来许多小说中都有体现。余华的《第七天》描写了一群飘零在外、客死他乡、无人安葬的孤魂野鬼。刘震云在《一句顶一万句》中呈现了一个由贩夫走卒、引车卖浆者组成的游民世界,在里面人与人的联结是脆弱的,它或被千山万水阻隔,或是被钩心斗角的算计所损毁。但王安忆却试图为这种"茫茫人海"的虚无提供救赎。王德威注意到,王安忆笔下的蚌埠、文工团、华舍镇,都是一种"中点站"般的存在。[2] 这些"中点站"提供了一个暂时栖息的场所,人们抱团取暖地共同度过一段时光,而后又各奔天涯。王安忆曾谈及蚌埠对于她的意义,即,当"文革"的动荡将生活的常规破坏殆尽时,她却在蚌埠看到了熟悉的日常生活——"蚌埠究竟在以什么吸引着我们?那就是我们所熟悉的,习惯的,深感安全的日常生活,在这里找到了最近的形貌。我们可在其间避身一时,暂忘烦恼。"[3] "我们没想到,经历了所有这一切之后,事情还保持延续。"[4] 同样,王安忆形容"文革"中的文工团是"'圣经'里的方舟,是大动荡

1　王安忆:《匿名》,第261页。
2　王德威:《前青春期的文明小史》,《王安忆研究资料》,第712页。
3　王安忆:《蚌埠》,《中国好小说:王安忆》,北京:中国青年出版社,2013年,第89页。
4　王安忆:《蚌埠》,《中国好小说》,第87页。

里的蔽身之地"[1]。两者都是在世事的动荡中提供了"稳定",在断裂中创造了"延续",可以说,流动的共同体就是在"无常"中创造出"恒常",在"虚无"中创造出"实在",在"漂泊"中创造出"稳定",在大都市中创造出"乡土"。

创造"流动的共同体"方法就是以"乡土人情"去取代"陌生人社会"里的经济关系。王安忆的小说里充满了各式各样的"认亲","认亲"实际上是用已知去预设未知,用熟悉去"驯化"不熟悉。她说:"江湖就是个驯化世界。为什么说'在家靠父母,出门靠朋友',父母是原始血缘,朋友则是驯化的关系。"[2]比如刘教练带杨莹瑛去租房公司查询客户信息,本来是一种经济交往行为,但他与租房中介的打工妹互以"阿妹""阿哥"相称,将其扭转为了"帮朋友找人"的人情关系。《乡关处处》中,月娥把自己照顾的上海老人当成爷爷一般看待,称爷爷的女儿为"大妹妹",称爷爷的小儿子为"小弟弟"。当爷爷女儿嫌月娥照顾不周时,两人将二百块钱掼来掼去,"不像是主雇,倒仿佛一对负气的姊妹,计较赡养父亲,谁付出多,谁付出少"[3]。正因为月娥以一种乡土社会的温情与他人交往,她到哪里都可以随遇而安;处处无亲人,也就是处处有亲人。《匿名》中,养老院的姑子早早失去了丈夫和孩子,但在她看来,"无论病孩子,瘫子,街上拾的老头儿,所长送来的无名无姓人,都跑不了是她的家人,从一条根上发的权,权上再发权,越发越远"[4]。

这种"认亲"可以发生在任意两个个体之间。其缘由可能是偶然的,甚至起于一种说不清道不明的亲切感,比如《匿名》里的智障"二点"对"老新"的错认,比如失忆的"老新"与先天性心脏病患儿之间莫名的投缘,又比如敦睦与狱中高人的邂逅。但这种非理性的"灵感"或"情感"抵御的恰恰是理性、经济的逻辑。野骨的退伍军人、九丈派出所所长、黑社会头子敦睦、九丈养老院、县福

1　王安忆:《文工团》,《文工团》,第203页。

2　王安忆:《匿名》,第330页。

3　王安忆:《乡关处处》,《红豆生南国》,第23页。

4　王安忆:《匿名》,第249页。

利院白化病孩子鹏飞、上海的志愿者，这些背景迥异的个体在现实的经济秩序中本没有交集，却出于对一个走失的上海老人和一个先天性心脏病患儿的情感关切而发生关联，形成了一个奇妙的网络。谢俊认为《匿名》中体现了"一个理想的乌托邦社群"，一个"匿名的细民世界"，"这里，民间的一个宏大事业是以一点一滴的方式展开的，何其艰辛，可是保留着因偶然或侥幸带来的喜悦，因为这个弧度的社会是充满可能的，而且在匿名的大众世界里，每个单体都充满活力，通过力量的集合和协商，他们最终让这个'小天心'进入了国家救助体系，也有了'名'"。[1] 而这些来自不同的阶层、职业、地域的"任意个体"之所以能够在同一时空相遇并产生联结，是全球化时代下高流动性经济的产物。经济全球化使原本被国族、阶层、种族等疆界所区隔的人们，跨疆域流动并杂居一处，桑德罗·梅萨德拉（Sandro Mezzadra）和布瑞特·尼尔森（Brett Neilson）以"劳动的多重分化"（multiplication of labor）和"边界的增殖"（proliferation of border）来形容这种劳动力的混杂和多样性。[2] 而王安忆小说中也常常出现这种"遭遇他者"的"异度空间"，华舍镇、柯桥、九丈老街、腰子弄、铜川路上的水产市场都是聚集着外乡人的地方，但共通的语言"普通话"和共通的情感却把来自不同地域的人们联结了起来。从"乡土人情"出发，王安忆似乎指向了某种天下大同的理想：天下大同就是"乡关处处"。无论在哪里，人与人之间始终可以凭借共通的语言、共通的情感——对贫弱之人的同情、对人的不幸处境的体谅和理解、对同伴的依靠和信赖——结成亲人一般的关系。"这街市就是放大的林窟，放到无限大！集市上的人，不论买卖的哪一方，都是他的乡人。"[3]

显然，这样的流动共同体并不持久。作为一个传统经济单位的家庭尚且经受着分裂的压力，何况是无根无系、萍水相逢的陌生人？王安忆也知道她是以一种

1 谢俊：《匿名的大众：谈谈王安忆新作〈匿名〉中的"真实"与世界》，陈思和、王德威主编：《文学·2016·秋冬卷》，上海：上海文艺出版社，2017年，第69—70页。

2 Mezzadra and Neilson, *Border as Method*, p. 7.

3 王安忆：《匿名》，第156页。

美学的、略带乌托邦色彩的叙述去弥补现实中移民生活的匮乏和破碎，所以这种流动的共同体具有一种瞬间性，提供的是一种美学补偿。秧宝宝在磕磕绊绊中融入李老师一家，与蒋芽儿结下友情，但一年之后又要转学。月娥与爷爷共同居住，彼此适应了生活节奏和生活习惯，但很快又要因为爷爷的生病而另换工作和住处。因此，这种共同体是短暂的，但这并不意味着它是没有意义的。事实上，短暂与长久是相对的。在王安忆新世纪以来的小说中，越来越强调一种存在主义式的体验，"质"超越"量"成为更重要的品质。这种注重"当下"、注重"过程"而不问"结果"，对于移民来说是很现实的选择，物理空间的乡土已经留在了身后，未来在何处安身则无法预期，能把握住的就是"现在"，因此只能好好度过——"无论是过往还是未来的时间都湮灭在混沌中，只有正经历的现在才是具体可感。"[1]王安忆也说过："人生是目的为死亡的行程，所有的意义都在过程，完成人生的一日便是人生消亡的一日。"[2]而这个过程可以用"渡海观音"的"渡"来理解——"'现在'的意义究竟是什么？'现在'的意义就是'度过'。有没有进过庙堂，看见过'渡海观音'？就是那个'渡'字。"[3]茫茫人世，何以为渡？就是与陌生人结成的流动的共同体。王安忆对"过程"的强调实际上是主张以更为通达的态度面对移民的漂泊人生，人生的意义正存在于每一个与陌生人共同度过的"当下"，人们能做的就是珍惜每一次的邂逅，善待每一个遇到的"朋友"，珍惜与陌生人形成的情感联结。

结　语

王安忆新世纪以来的小说，如《上种红菱下种藕》《众声喧哗》《骄傲的皮匠》《新加坡人》《富萍》《遍地枭雄》《匿名》《红豆生南国》等作品中，主人公

1　王安忆:《匿名》，第79页。
2　王安忆:《艺术是一个过程》，《情感的生命》，第201页。
3　王安忆:《遍地枭雄》，第239页。

都过着一种没有家庭的漂泊生活，但他们却在陌生人身上找到了"家"的归属感。一方面，这是对全球化时代下家庭难以为继的政治经济现实的反映，即，人们为生活所迫，在高流动性的经济中四散离徙，只能与陌生人打交道和共同生活。另一方面，她试图以一种"日常生活"和"情感劳动"的逻辑重建人与人之间的关系。"陌生人的家人化"体现在两类题材中，一种是"保姆的故事"，以《上种红菱下种藕》《富萍》《乡关处处》《向西，向西，向南》为代表，在这些作品里，她强调了"在场"和"过程"的重要性，亲身参与、亲身劳作、与他人共同度过的生活，成为缔结情感联系的媒介。另一种是"江湖的故事"，以《遍地枭雄》和《匿名》为代表，在里面，个体彻底脱离了家庭，浪迹天涯、四海为家，但他们却以"认亲"的方式，将"家人"的想象投射在陌生人身上，并为之操劳，从而再造一个"乡土人情社会"。这种在"偶遇"中建立的"流动的共同体"虽然是短暂的，却是一种超越了资本主义经济关系的社会关系，它体现了乡土社会中的互惠互利、互相扶助、暖老温贫的人际关系，甚至是对已经逝去的集体主义的某种挽回和再造。就此而言，王安忆所设想的由迥异的个体组成的"流动的共同体"可以说是对后福特主义时代的"陌生人社会"的一个尝试性的回应和解决方案。

（文章发表于《文学评论》2020年第1期。本文系作者在联盟2021年年度论坛上的发言）

参考文献

［德］瓦尔特·本雅明：《机械复制时代的艺术作品》，汉娜·阿伦特主编：《启迪：本雅明文选》，张旭东、王斑译，北京：生活·读书·新知三联书店，2008年。

［德］瓦尔特·本雅明：《发达资本主义时代的抒情诗人》，张旭东、魏文生译，北京：生活·读书·新知三联书店，2007年。

陈锡文、赵阳、罗丹:《中国农村改革30年回顾与展望》,北京:人民出版社,2008年。

范雨素:《我是范雨素》,《时代报告》2017年第6期,第94—99页。

费孝通:《乡土中国》,北京:北京大学出版社,2018年。

国家统计局人口和就业统计司编:《中国人口和就业统计年鉴——2017》,北京:中国统计出版社,2017年。

贺雪峰:《地权的逻辑:中国农村土地制度向何处去》,北京:中国政法大学出版社,2010年。

王安忆:《蚌埠》,《中国好小说:王安忆》,北京:中国青年出版社,2013年。

王安忆:《遍地枭雄》,上海:文汇出版社,2005年。

王安忆:《富萍》,北京:人民文学出版社,2009年。

王安忆:《红豆生南国》,《红豆生南国》,北京:人民文学出版社,2017年。

王安忆:《接近世纪初》,《书屋》,1998年第1期,第10—12页。

王安忆:《匿名》,北京:人民文学出版社,2016年。

王安忆:《情感的生命——我看散文》,张新颖、金理编:《王安忆研究资料》,天津:天津人民出版社,2009年。

王安忆:《上种红菱下种藕》,北京:北京联合出版公司,2014年。

王安忆:《生活的形式》,《当代作家评论》2005年第1期,第50—52页。

王安忆:《文工团》,《文工团》,上海:上海文艺出版社,2013年。

王安忆:《用你的矛攻你的盾》,《情感的生命》,北京:中国文联出版社,2008年。

王安忆:《香港的情与爱》,《香港的情与爱(王安忆自选集·第三卷)》,北京:作家出版社,1996年。

王安忆:《乡关处处》,《红豆生南国》,北京:人民文学出版社,2017年。

王安忆:《小说的当下处境》《小说的创作》,张新颖、金理编:《王安忆研究资料》,天津:天津人民出版社,
    2009年。

王安忆:《小说的情感》,张新颖、金理编:《王安忆研究资料》,天津:天津人民出版社,2009年。

王安忆:《新加坡人》,《王安忆小说选》,北京:人民文学出版社,2009年。

王安忆:《艺术是一个过程》,《情感的生命》,北京:中国文联出版社,2008年。

王德威:《前青春期的文明小史》,张新颖、金理编:《王安忆研究资料》,天津:天津人民出版社,2009年。

王晓明:《从"淮海路"到"梅家桥"——从王安忆小说创作的转变谈起》,《文学评论》2002年第3期,第5—20页。

温铁军:《三农问题与世纪反思》,北京:生活·读书·新知三联书店,2005年。

谢俊:《匿名的大众:谈谈王安忆新作〈匿名〉中的"真实"与世界》,陈思和、王德威主编:《文学·2016·秋冬
    卷》,上海:上海文艺出版社,2017年,第58—72页。

Costa, Mariarosa Dalla and Selma James. *The Power of Women and the Subversion of the Community*. London: Falling Wall
    Press, 1975.

Hardt, Michael and Antonio Negri. *Empire*. Cambridge, Massachusetts: Harvard University Press, 2000.

Hardt, Michael and Antonio Negri. *Multitude: War and Democracy in the Age of Empire*. New York: Penguin Group Inc., 2004.

Hochschild, Arlie Russell. *The Managed Heart: Commercialization of Human Feeling*. Berkeley: University of California Press, 2012.

Lee, Haiyan. *Revolution of the Heart: A Genealogy of Love in China, 1900–1950*. Stanford: Stanford University Press, 2007.

Meillassoux, Claude. *Maidens, Meal and Money: Capitalism and the Domestic Community*. Cambridge: Cambridge University Press, 1981.

Mezzadra, Sandro and Brett Neilson. *Border as Method: Or, the Multiplication of Labor*. Durham: Duke University Press, 2013.

Stoler, Ann Laura. *Carnal Knowledge and Imperial Power: Race and the Intimate in Colonial Rule*. Berkeley, California: University of California Press, 2002.

Wang, Ban. "Love at Last Sight: Nostalgia, Commodity, and Temporality in Wang Anyi's Song of Unending Sorrow." *Positions: East Asia Cultures Critique*, Vol. 10, No. 3 (2002), pp. 669–694.

Zhang, Xudong. "Shanghai Nostalgia: Postrevolutionary Allegories in Wang Anyi's Literary Production in the 1990s." *Positions: East Asia Cultures Critique*, Vol. 8, No. 2 (2000), pp. 349–387.

Confucian Ethics, Innovation and the Triple Bottom Line: Evidence from Three Chinese Industries

Maya Vachkova, Arsalan Ghouri, Pedro Pablo Cardoso Castro,

Muhammad Shahbaz*

1. Introduction

In the age of globalization and internationalization, the People's Republic of China has risen as one of the most prominent markets in the world. Indeed, the transition from a planned to a market-driven economy revolutionized Chinese social and economic life (Harvey 1999; Xie 2017). Its development has been accompanied by technological innovation as well as sustainability challenges.

The adoption of innovative technologies and the commitment to sustainability in general, come from decisions made within a business. Moreover, sustainability calls for a synergy between economic development and the wider socio-environmental niche where businesses operate. In the age of technology, such synergy is facilitated through the implementation of innovative technologies, which in turn calls for a co-evolution between business ethics, strategy and innovative technologies. The development of East Asian economies is sometimes justified by the influence of Confucian ethics (Chan 2008; Zhang and Zhang 2006). The focus on economic gains, ever so hard to attain under the pressures of free market competition, may naturally sway businesses away from ethical standards. While

---

* Dr Maya Vachkova is a Senior Lecturer in Systems Thinking and Programme Director of the Systems Thinking Practitioner Apprenticeship at the University of Exeter, m.v.vachkova@exeter.ac.uk; Arsalan Mujahid Ghouri, London South Bank University, United Kingdom, arsalan.ghouri@ymail. com; Pedro Pablo Cardoso Castro, University of Cranfield, United Kingdom, P.P.CardosoCastro@ cranfield.ac.uk; Dr Muhammad Shahbaz, Beijing Institute of Technology, China, muhdshahbaz77@ gmail.com.

strategic frameworks like Agenda 2030 (UN 2015) offer a plan for action, they are not prescriptive, but discretionary (Winkler and Williams 2018). Therefore, we endeavored to investigate the pillars of sustainability and the adoption of innovative technologies underpinned by ethical standards, internal to businesses.

This chapter advances several important theoretical and practical contributions. First, this is the first empirical study to review the nexus between the triple bottom line and ethical environment and innovation in the domain of Chinese businesses. Second, we test the businesses size effect on the triple bottom line efforts and innovation. Third, we review sustainable Chinese business practices through a Confucian ethical lens and thus we enhance scholarly understanding of the importance of traditional values to modern-day market relations.

The remainder of this chapter is structured as follows. The next segment discusses prior research in sustainability, as well as a contextualization of our research which will contain an overview of the unique characteristics of Chinese business ethics. The second section will delve into hypotheses development. The third section offers a discussion of our research method, analysis and results. Finally, the fouth section contains a discussion followed by concluding remarks.

2.1. Prior Literature

2.1.1. Sustainability and Innovation

Sustainable development is the process of meeting the present needs of humankind without impinging on the needs of future generations (Brundtland 1987). While the original conceptualization of sustainability does not split the term into categories, sustainable development has been understood as three-dimensional, ergo, development that includes an environmental, a social and an economic dimension. This three-dimensional model has informed definitions of sustainability in scholarship (Fischer et al. 2020; Lozano 2008), international businesses (e.g., CEC 2001, OECD 2000) and textbooks on business ethics and corporate social responsibility (Crane et al. 2008; Rhodes and van Apeldoorn

2010). In business circles, this three-dimensional notion of sustainability is commonly referred to as a triple bottom line (Elkington 2004; Park et al. 2019). The most important recent development of triple bottom line conceptualizations of sustainability is the acknowledgement that all three pillars exist simultaneously, and rather than overlapping, they are nested within each other, which makes their separation impossible and impractical (Marcus et al. 2010; UN 2015).

The People's Republic of China is facing severe environmental problems, as one of the largest energy consumers in the world (Tong et al. 2020). Like many other fast-growing economies, its economic growth comes at the price of high toxic gas emissions (Ali et al. 2017; Heras-Saizarbitoria and Boiral 2019; Liu and Diamond 2005). For instance, China is the largest CO_2 emitter (Ritchie and Roser 2017).

China's growth earned its economy a second place in the global chart (Lewin et al. 2016). To maintain its development, China must overcome pitfalls such as the middle-income trap and environmental degradation. According to Lewin et al. (2016), China could tackle economic obstacles and mediate the harmful effects of its exponential growth through an innovative social transformation. China itself recognized the need to shift towards innovation, as Premier Li Keqiang called for greater scientific and technological innovation, as it is the "golden key" for development (Xinhua 2015). The effort for innovation is generously supported by the government—for instance, the National Innovation System sustains investment in innovation and supports major research institutions to strengthen domestic companies' ability to compete with foreign ventures both within and beyond Chinese borders (Yip and McKern 2016).

The presence of international companies both Asian and Western has stimulated domestic awareness of sustainability and corporate reporting of the triple bottom line (Kolk et al. 2010). Although many still see this as a Western-centric idea (Lehtonen 2004), sustainability as three pillars, has penetrated Chinese business operations both in state-owned and private enterprise (Kolk et al. 2010). Interestingly, the economic model China has pursued after its transition to a market-driven economy has often been characterized as Western. Similarly, sustainability embodied in the SDGs, for example, and triple bottom line initiatives, have also been initiated in the West (Brundtland 1987; Lehtonen 2004). There is ample evidence that in recent years, Chinese industries are striving towards sustainability and their efforts are also supported by the government—for example, programs in rural sustainability have received generous funding (König et al. 2014; Bryan et al. 2018).

2.1.2. Chinese Business Ethics

China is often viewed as a country that struggles to apply ethical standards. Some argue this is due to its transition period and rapid growth, while others claim elements of Chinese ethics are the culprits (Hulpke and Lau 2008). Indeed, to address the latter claim would mean reflection on the meaning of ethics, i.e., the cognitive analytical application of moral principles to complex situations (Wines 2008). It follows that business ethics is the systematic application of moral principles to business dilemmas. The key difference is that within the realm of business ethics, individuals are also bound by business structures that dictate moral reasoning (Key et al. 2019; Wines 2008). Still, businesses and their moral interpretations are also contingent on the wider institutional framework they are nested within which varies depending on the context (Whitcomb et al. 1998). Traditional Chinese culture not only informs the regulations that bound business activities, but they also contribute to the general environment where small, medium and large Chinese businesses operate (Cunningham 2010). To investigate attitudes towards sustainability in Chinese industries, one must also be aware of the specifics of Chinese business ethics. Some comparative management scholars attribute the success of Chinese growth to the recently secularized Confucian ethics that underpin Chinese business operations (Chan 2008; Hoffstede and Bond 1988; Zhang and Zhang 2006).

Confucianism hinges upon the notion of harmony, order and loyalty in personal relationships (Zhang and Zhang 2006). Through the Confucian prism, societies exist through complex networks of harmonious relationships that are governed by rules that ensure social balance (Ip 2009). This balance and stability are due to the recognition that relationships are often unequal, and this inequality need not be a source of oppression; on the contrary—it issues responsibilities for both parties: the dominant side bears the responsibility to protect, while the other side must be loyal and respectful (Whitcomb et al. 1998). Alongside power balance, relationships are defined by virtuous behavior that must be reciprocated throughout the network and also must entail self-improvement and moderation.

Traditionally, Chinese ethics postulated that interpersonal relationships are ruled by social hierarchy (Harvey 1999). The moral rule for "upward" interactions was the loyalty of the subordinate, while "downward" interactions were underpinned by the righteousness of the upper circles who must protect people with less power. In a market exchange situation, although the two parties are considered equal, there is a responsibility for "sincerity" on behalf of the seller (Harvey 1999, 87). The obligation of the seller to protect the interests of their buyer was an extension of righteousness. This model of relationships evolved into contemporary market exchange, where the two principles of sincerity and righteousness serve as fundaments of commercial Chinese ethics. In the context of business, human virtues do not enter into conflict with the pursuit of profit, as long as the interests of the public are taken into account (Chan 2008). Thus, Confucian economic gains are accompanied by "benevolence, righteousness, humanity and the development of one's personality" (Chan 2008, 350). Namely righteousness is enacted in one's responsibility to society (Ip 2009; Su and Littlefield 2001), which coincidentally is also the ethical foundation of many sustainability initiatives, including the Brundtland (1987), The Millennium Development Goals (UN 2000) and Agenda 2030 (UN 2015).

2.2. Hypotheses Development

2.2.1. Sustainability and Innovation

Innovation can be defined as novel ideas that are realized through products, services, processes or business models that have a market value (Yip and McKern 2016). Innovation could be as tangible (products) or intangible (managerial or leadership processes). The roots of innovative behavior of a business can be traced in business climate, spirit and

146

energy which is grounded in deep understanding of the meaning, purpose, significance and value of being innovative and that stands behind the success and competitiveness of a business which is able to develop and realize desirable innovation performance and outputs (Deshpandé et al. 1993). Changes and developments in economic, environmental, and social areas of business operations are accompanied and sometimes even facilitated by technological innovation (Weaver et al. 2017). Sustainable development is reliant on technology and innovation—for example, renewable alternatives to fossil fuels are results of innovative efforts (Juma and Yee-Cheong 2005). Sustainability lies in the interjection and dynamic processes between the often-conflicting agendas of economic and social gains, and environmental conservation (Lehtonen 2004; Poesche 1998).

Social sustainability is the triple bottom line pillar that corresponds with citizen access to healthcare, education and the ability to both contribute and benefit from national economic development (WEF 2012). Studies on China show that the social dimension of sustainability is crucial for business development and success (Lau et al. 2016; Wan and Ng 2018). China's rapid economic development has been accompanied not only by pollution (Liu and Diamond 2005) but also by social inequality (Yang and Greany 2017). As a consequence, social development has been characterized as imbalanced (Zhang et al. 2017). Lack of protection of stakeholders' rights and following the government rules and regulations are some of the more conspicuous manifestations of the ethical issues related to in Chinese economic activities (Strutton 2009; Wright and Schultz 2018).

Fonseca and Lima (2015) contend that there is a high correlation between social sustainability, innovativeness and national competitiveness. On the economic line of sustainability, novel technologies are utilized by businesses for reduced energy, water consumption and for recycling and reuse of materials which saves on resources (Yang et al. 2019; Yin et al. 2019). Such initiatives also contribute to the environmental pillar of sustainability as they dampen negative environmental outputs. Innovation may serve as a vehicle for sustainable transformations (Juma and Yee-Cheong 2005). Additionally, innovation may foster sustainability through the introduction of eco-friendly patterns of consumption and production (Juma 2011) which are also incorporated in the SDGs (UN 2015).

As elaborated earlier, the most popular understanding of sustainability is a three-dimensional model (Lozano 2008; OECD 2000) where every dimension is nested within the other two (Marcus et al. 2010; UN 2015), creating a holistic notion of sustainability. The analytical importance of every dimension depends on the situation where the tripartite model of sustainability is applied, as the model does not attribute more importance to any one of the dimensions. The three-dimensional model of sustainability allows for an analytical abstraction of each pillar and its separate conceptualization (Lehtonen 2004). While we are aware that sustainability is complex and in reality, none of the dimensions exists in isolation, we endeavored to investigate every dimension and its links to innovation. In doing so we also acknowledge that actions within each dimension systemically affect the other two (Marcus et al. 2010). Thus, we propose the following hypotheses that we believe are inextricably connected:

H1a: The economic dimension of sustainability positively relates to innovative behavior.

H1b: The environmental dimension of sustainability positively relates to innovative behavior.

H1c: The social dimension of sustainability positively relates to innovative behavior.

2.2.2. Ethical Environment

Victor and Cullen (1988) discuss the notion of an ethical work climate, which reflects the dominant positions within a given business, regarding what defines ethical behavior. Bobek and Radtke (2007) extend this idea and develop the term "ethical environment," which is a shared perception of moral categories within the business that also informs the actions of individual employees. In a subsequent study, Bobek et al. (2010) investigate the discrepancy between employee and managerial attitudes towards the ethical environment of business. They conclude that executive managers rate the ethical environment as stronger than non-executive staff. In their later work Bobek et al. (2015) discover that leaders have a stronger interest in business ethics as they perceive themselves as serving public interest. Hence, we recruited participants appointed at managerial positions, and we investigated their perception of the ethical climate in their respective businesses and how it relates to innovation. Indeed, sometimes the adoption of novel technologies is divorced from ethical standards and impacts negatively on the dimensions of sustainability (Poesche 1998). Therefore, Stieb (2001) postulates that companies that adopt cutting-edge technologies should also be ready to bear greater responsibility for the potentially harmful effects of businesses on society and the environment. Stieb's (2001) line of argument is that agents with more power such as corporations, should also be held to greater responsibility, conterminous with their elevated status. Considering this, we propose the following hypothesis:

H1d: The ethical environment of firms positively relates to innovative behavior.

2.2.3. Business Size

We measured business size by the number of employees working on a full-time basis at the time of our research (Smith et al. 2005). Thus, in line with previous research, we categorized the sample businesses into two groups in terms of their workforce, i.e., small and medium—those with employees less than 500—and large—those who employ over 500 people (Cunningham 2010; Kirby and Kaiser 2003). Business size has been used as a moderator in numerous studies on Chinese industries. For instance, Zhu et al. (2008) found that medium and large-sized businesses are better equipped with sustainable innovations and thus, implement environmental agendas better than their smaller-sized counterparts. Hence, we advance the following hypotheses:

H2a: Business size moderates the relationship between the economic dimension of sustainability and innovative behavior.

H2b: Business size moderates the relationship between the environmental dimension of sustainability and innovative behavior.

H2c: Business size moderates the relationship between the social dimension of sustainability and their innovative behavior.

H2d: Business size moderates the relationship between the ethical environment of firms and their innovative behavior.

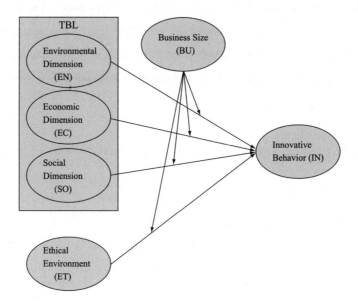

Figure 1: Conceptual model

3. Research Method, Analysis and Results

We tested the proposed model and associated hypotheses in three field studies by utilizing smart PLS 3.0 for data analysis. The studies were conducted in the province of Hubei, famous for its agricultural and automotive industries and for its tourist attractions

(CSP 2018; NEA 2016). We surveyed agricultural, automotive and tourism businesses in studies 1, 2, and 3, respectively. We presented the respondents with a consent form and an information sheet, and ensured they understood the content and the aim of the study. To check the non-response bias for all three studies, we employed the independent t-test method: we compared the first 20 respondents and the last 20 respondents on all variables (i.e., Armstrong and Overton 1977). We believe that conducting three studies on the respective industries would aid a scholarly understanding of the innovative behavior of Chinese businesses in the context of sustainability.

4. Studies

4.1. Study 1

4.1.1. Participants and Design. We collected data from key business decision makers i.e., CEOs, COOs, directors and managers across the agricultural industry in Hubei. We employed online and offline surveys to collect data. We distributed a total of 301 questionnaires: online (209) and offline (92). In the end, 193 responses from 72 businesses were appropriate for further analysis. The 23 incomplete responses were discarded. In terms of demographics, 105 respondents were male and 88 were female, with the average age of all respondents 47.23. In terms of managerial roles, we surveyed 29 CEOs, 27 COOs, 49 directors and 88 managers.

Table 1: Loading, Validity and Reliability of Results

Construct	Item Coding	Loading	Jöreskog's rho (ρc)	AVE
Economic Dimension				
	EC1	0.829	0.833	0.875
	EC2	0.922		
	EC3	0.821		
Environmental Dimension				
	EN1	0.825	0.894	0.715

continued

Construct	Item Coding	Loading	Jöreskog's rho (ρc)	AVE
	EN2	0.857		
	EN3	0.848		
	EN4	0.816		
Social Dimension				
	SO1	0.711	0.891	0.859
	SO2	0.933		
	SO3	0.919		
Ethical Dnvironment				
	ET1	0.893	0.774	0.746
	ET2	0.881		
	ET3	0.888		
	ET4	0.839		
	ET5	0.211		
	ET6	0.844		
	ET7	0.835		
	ET8	0.757		
	ET9	0.794		
	ET10	0.733		
Innovative Behavior				
	IN1	0.901	0.873	0.776
	IN2	0.847		
	IM3	0.804		

Table 2: Descriptive Statistics, Correlation Matrix, and HTMT Results of Underlying Constructs

Construct	Mean	SD	EC	EN	SO	ET	IN	BU
Economic Dimension (EC)	5.43	2.58	0.843	0.323	0.493	0.533	0.557	–
Environmental Dimension (EN)	4.78	2.43	0.543**	0.892	0.322	0.435	0.236	–

continued

Construct	Mean	SD	EC	EN	SO	ET	IN	BU
Social Dimension (SO)	4.91	2.57	0.135*	0.253*	*0.825*	*0.479*	*0.352*	–
Ethical Environment (ET)	4.59	1.59	0.482**	0.469**	0.327*	*0.883*	*0.595*	–
Innovative Behavior (IN)	5.32	2.26	0.594**	0.626***	0.254*	0.463**	*0.843*	–
Business Size (BU)	1.01	1.03	0.035	0.433**	0.032	−0.017	0.544***	–

n=193 respondents

Correlation results=normal text, HTMT results=Italic text

Notes: *=p<.05.   **=p<.01.   ***=p<.001. Two-tailed

4.1.2. Robustness Tests. To deal with the endogeneity issue, we conducted a reverse causality test. In this test, we reversed the temporal order of our independent variable and dependent variable for hypotheses 1, 2, 3, and 4. Table 3 suggested no significant relationships between the two lagged variables of hypotheses 1, 2, 3, and 4. We further checked the multicollinearity concerns (Narayanan and Narasimhan, 2014). The VIF for all of the study variables were below 8.8.

Table 3: Evaluation of the Endogeneity Issue

Variables	EC	EN	SO	ET	*t*-value
IN (H1a)	0.133	–		–	0.93
IN (H1b)	–	0.036	–	–	0.37
IN (H1c)	–	–	0.024	–	0.65
IN (H1d)	–	–	–	0.102	0.98

4.1.3. Analysis and Results. Table 2 hosts the descriptive statistics and correlation results. We used path analysis with the bootstrap option to examine the study's model statistics. Well-performing agricultural businesses were also more involved in innovative behavior than businesses with lower economic performance. Businesses which were focusing on the environment were also more innovative than businesses which were less environmentally considerate. Socially considerate businesses were more innovative than socially less considerate businesses. Those businesses which were more ethical, were also more innovative than their less ethical counterparts.

Large size businesses with good economic performance were also more involved in innovative behavior than small and medium sized agricultural businesses. Large size businesses were more environmentally sensitive and also more innovative than small and medium size businesses. There is no difference between large size businesses and small and medium size businesses with regard to social sustainability. There is no difference between large, small and medium size businesses in terms of their ethicality.

Table 4: Evaluation and Results of the Measurement Model

	Effect	Cohen's f^2	B	Mean	t-value	Value
Normal						
	EC → IN	0.335	0.545	0.567	6.468	
	EN → IN	0.258	0.439	0.442	5.221	
	SO → IN	0.479	0.467	0.471	5.467	
	ET → IN	0.284	0.337	0.340	3.958	
Moderation (large to small medium size)						
	EC → IN	**0.022**	**0.159**	**0.163**	**2.623**	
	EN → IN	**0.104**	**0.242**	**0.247**	**3.225**	
	SO → IN	0.034	0.023	0.025	0.006	
	ET → IN	0.031	0.043	0.047	0.065	
R^2						53.26
Saturated model						
SRMR						0.0712
dULS						1.0061
HI99						1.6732
Estimated model						
SRMR						0.0755

continued

	Effect	Cohen's f²	B	Mean	t-value	Value
dULS						1.3043
HI99						1.7573

*All effects tested on a saturated model.

4.2. Study 2

4.2.1. Participants and Design. In this study, we reached out to CEOs, COOs, directors and managers of the automotive industry in Hubei via online and offline surveys. We distributed 524 (411 online, 113 offline) questionnaires in 249 automotive businesses out of which 191 responses from 85 businesses were suitable for further analysis. The 44 incomplete responses were discarded. In terms of demographics, 88 were female and 103 were male, with an average age of 46.11. In terms of organizational roles, 29 were CEOs, 28 COOs, 47 directors and 85 managers.

Table 5: Loading, Validity and Reliability of Results

Construct	Item Coding	Loading	Jöreskog's rho (ρc)	AVE
Economic Dimension				
	EC1	0.739	0.847	0.863
	EC2	0.848		
	EC3	0.833		
Environmental Dimension				
	EN1	0.916	0.901	0.839
	EN2	0.911		
	EN3	0.895		
	EN4	0.896		
Social Dimension				
	SO1	0.758	0.800	0.783
	SO2	0.739		

continued

Construct	Item Coding	Loading	Jöreskog's rho (ρc)	AVE
	SO3	0.843		
Ethical Environment				
	ET1	0.741	0.805	0.726
	ET2	0.713		
	ET3	0.821		
	ET4	0.844		
	ET5	0.938		
	ET6	0.852		
	ET7	0.833		
	ET8	0.858		
	ET9	0.839		
	ET10	0.791		
Innovative Behavior				
	IN1	0.832	0.812	0.737
	IN2	0.868		
	IN3	0.877		

Table 6: Descriptive Statistics, Correlation Matrix, and HTMT Results of Underlying Constructs

Construct	Mean	SD	EC	EN	SO	ET	IN	BU
Economic Dimension (EC)	5.11	1.75	*0.748*	*0.240*	*0.532*	*0.511*	*0.427*	–
Environmental Dimension (EN)	5.34	2.22	0.428**	*0.662*	*0.368*	*0.378*	*0.242*	–
Social Dimension (SO)	4.88	2.02	0.022	0.284*	*0.732*	*0.574*	*0.357*	–
Ethical Environment (ET)	5.36	1.86	0.322**	0.047	0.429**	*0.755*	*0.427*	–
Innovative Behavior (IN)	5.58	1.47	0.432**	0.346**	0.273*	0.430**	*0.746*	–
Business Size (BU)	1.05	0.98	0.354**	0.045	0.078	−0.045	0.563***	–

n=191 respondents

Correlation results=normal text, HTMT results=Italic text

Notes: *=p<.05.   **=p<.01.   ***=p<.001. Two-tailed. *Robustness tests*

4.2.2. Robustness Tests. For the endogeneity issue, Table 7 suggested no significant relationships between the two lagged variables of hypotheses 1, 2, 3, and 4. Additionally, there is no issue of multicollinearity, as the VIF for all of study variables were below 8.3.

Table 7: Evaluation of Endogeneity Issue

Variables	EC	EN	SO	ET	*t*-value
IN (H1a)	0.127	–		–	1.01
IN (H1b)	–	0.124	–	–	1.03
IN (H1c)	–	–	0.046	–	0.22
IN (Hd)	–	–	–	0.081	0.66

4.2.3. Analysis and Results. Table 6 depicts the descriptive statistics and correlation results. Table 8 illustrates the effect size, path value, mean and *t*-value of normal, moderated relationship with business size, R^2, saturated and estimated model results. Economically sustainable automotive businesses also scored higher on innovative behavior than businesses with lower economic performance. Environmentally friendly businesses were also more innovative than less environmentally considerate businesses. Socially considerate businesses were more innovative than less socially considerate businesses in automotive industry.

Large-sized businesses which were performing economically well, were more involved in innovative behavior than small and medium-sized businesses in the automotive industry. Large-sized businesses that were taking better care of the environment were also more involved in innovative behaviors than small and medium-sized businesses. Large-sized businesses were taking better care of society and were more innovative than small and medium-sized businesses. Large-sized businesses that were more ethical, were also more innovative than small and medium-sized businesses.

Table 8: Evaluation and Results of Measurement Model

	Effect	Cohen's f²	B	Mean	t-value	Value
Normal						
	EC → IN	0.223	0.395	0.397	5.025	
	EN → IN	0.214	0.366	0.369	4.688	
	SO → IN	0.359	0.328	0.333	5.282	
	ET → IN	0.350	0.443	0.448	6.474	
Moderation (large to small medium size)						
	EC → IN	**0.067**	**0.168**	**0.172**	**2.463**	
	EN → IN	**0.132**	**0.175**	**0.180**	**2.658**	
	SO → IN	**0.106**	**0.184**	**0.186**	**2.395**	
	ET → IN	**0.124**	**0.199**	**0.202**	**2.574**	
R^2						46.82
Saturated model						
SRMR						0.0693
dULS						1.3573
HI99						1.9538
Estimated model						
SRMR						0.0711
dULS						1.4368
HI99						2.1774

*All effects tested on a saturated model.

4.3. Study 3

4.3.1. Participants and Design. In the present study, we targeted CEOs, COOs, directors and managers from the tourism industry. We distributed 599 questionnaires (521 online, 78 offline) in 302 tourism businesses. A total of 215 responses from 157 businesses were suitable for further analysis. The 39 incomplete responses were not included in the data. A total of 145 respondents were male and 70 were females, with an average age of 42.37.

A total of 19 CEOs, 46 COOs, 52 directors and 98 managers participated in the survey. Quality checks were performed in accordance with study 1.

Table 9: Loading, Validity and Reliability of Results

Construct	Item Coding	Loading	Jöreskog's rho (ρc)	AVE
Economic Dimension				
	EC1	0.868	0.852	0.796
	EC2	0.844		
	EC3	0.879		
Environmental Dimension				
	EN1	0.868	0.848	0.759
	EN2	0.843		
	EN3	0.885		
	EN4	0.834		
Social Dimension				
	SO1	0.899	0.894	0.831
	SO2	0.877		
	SO3	0.873		
Ethical Environment				
	ET1	0.770	0.847	0.715
	ET2	0.849		
	ET3	0.764		
	ET4	0.880		
	ET5	0.842		
	ET6	0.794		
	ET7	0.936		
	ET8	0.902		
	ET9	0.864		
	ET10	0.841		

continued

Construct	Item Coding	Loading	Jöreskog's rho (ρc)	AVE
Innovative Behavior				
	IN1	0.856	0.863	0.722
	IN2	0.799		
	IN3	0.895		

Table 10: Descriptive Statistics, Correlation Matrix, and HTMT Results of Underlying Constructs

Construct	Mean	SD	EC	EN	SO	ET	IN	BU
Economic Dimension (EC)	4.91	2.11	*0.773*	*0.341*	*0.528*	*0.557*	*0.452*	–
Environmental Dimension (EN)	4.35	2.55	0.125*	*0.753*	*0.448*	*0.463*	*0.546*	–
Social Dimension (SO)	4.59	1.68	0.454**	0.084	*0.837*	*0.462*	*0.473*	–
Ethical Environment (ET)	5.67	1.94	0.623***	0.118*	0.115*	*0.834*	*0.326*	–
Innovative Behavior (IN)	5.24	2.04	0.679***	0.548***	0.495**	0.573**	*0.822*	–
Business Size (BU)	1.18	1.14	0.227*	0.068	0.155*	0.235*	0.313**	–

n=215 respondents

Correlation results=normal text, HTMT results=Italic text

Notes: *=p<.05. **=p<.01. ***=p<.001. Two-tailed.

4.3.2. Robustness Tests. To check the endogeneity issue, Table 11 advised no significant relationships between the two lagged variables of hypotheses 1, 2, 3, and 4. Moreover, VIF of all the study variables below 8.1, suggested no multicollinearity concerns.

Table 11: Evaluation of Endogeneity Issue

Variables	EC	EN	SO	ET	*t*-value
IN (H1a)	0.076	–		–	0.57
IN (H1b)	–	0.095	–	–	0.66
IN (H1c)	–	–	0.044	–	0.58
IN (Hd)	–	–	–	0.087	0.91

4.3.3. Analysis and Results. Table 10 represents the descriptive statistics and correlation results. Those businesses which were performing economically well, were also more involved in innovative behavior than businesses with lower economic performance. Businesses which were focusing on the environment were also more innovative than businesses which were not environmentally considerate. Socially considerate businesses were more innovative than less socially considerate businesses in tourism industry. Those businesses which were more ethical, were also more innovative than their less ethical counterparts. Large-sized tourism industry businesses that were performing economically well, were more innovative behavior than small and medium sized businesses. There is no difference between the large-sized businesses and small and medium-sized businesses with regard to environmental sustainability in the tourism industry. Small and medium-sized businesses were more socially sustainable and innovative than large size businesses from the tourism industry. There is no difference between the large size businesses and small and medium size businesses in terms of their ethicality in the tourism industry. Table 4 also offered appropriate fit indices with $R^2=59.21$.

Table 12: Evaluation and Results of Measurement Model

	Effect	Cohen's f^2	B	Mean	*t*-value	Value
Normal						
	EC → IN	0.291	0.367	0.369	5.464	
	EN → IN	0.226	0.568	0.571	7.043	
	SO → IN	0.316	0.531	0.536	6.347	
	ET → IN	0.158	0.364	0.366	4.368	
Moderation (large to small medium size)						
	EC → IN	**0.128**	**0.127**	**0.131**	**2.552**	
	EN → IN	0.077	0.092	0.096	1.321	
	SO → IN	**0.101**	−0.199	−0.197	−2.792	
	ET → IN	0.028	0.011	0.014	0.002	

continued

	Effect	Cohen's f^2	B	Mean	t-value	Value
R^2						59.26
Saturated model						
SRMR						0.0681
dULS						1.2477
HI99						1.8202
Estimated model						
SRMR						0.0701
dULS						1.3565
HI99						1.9356

*All effects tested on a saturated model.

4.4. Discussion

In the era of globalization, as a result of its transition from planned to market driven economy, which has brought both technological innovation and environmental challenges, China has evidently become an important player in global markets. This is also clear in the commitment China has made to sustainability, which transpires from SME practices investigated by us. Business decisions that inform the adoption of green innovative technologies are an important field of research, as in these decisions, the balance between economic development and wider social and environmental benefits, is being put into evaluation.

Today, China has aligned its policies with international sustainability initiatives and businesses demonstrate increasing awareness of the triple bottom line principles. Despite the international collective efforts toward sustainability in the age of innovation, there is an absence of studies on the impact of the environmental, economic and social facets of sustainability in terms of innovative behavior.

To our knowledge, this is the first research project to explore relationships between ethical environment, innovative behavior and the dimensions of sustainability. Our findings suggest that there is a robust link between ethical environment as perceived by executive staff and innovation. Moreover, the size and industry of the businesses we studied, determined which dimensions of sustainability were most pertinent.

We propose that innovation is a consequence of responsible business practices and an overall high employee morale. To the best of our knowledge, this is the first empirical study which examines the impact business ethics has on innovative behavior. For our investigation, we took into consideration that the ethical environment of Chinese companies would be informed by traditional Chinese values. As our focus is on the business, rather than the end point consumer, employee and other affected stakeholders, the responsibility of protection, carried by the stronger party, is at the core of our hypotheses. This principle was represented by the size of the firms, as we assumed the larger the firms, the more responsible they would be, in congruence with Confucian values. Size is also associated with larger revenue and more capability to invest and develop.

Indeed, the better off firms score higher in the sustainability criteria, meaning that the more revenue a business generates, the more inclined its exec is to invest in innovation and to engage in ethical behavior. Another interesting correlation across all sectors is that those more engaged with environmental sustainability are also more likely to develop innovative capabilities. These general connections, nonetheless, demonstrate there are differences among the sectors investigated. It seems that size matters when looking at different aspects of sustainability across different sectors. The relationships between sustainability pillars, ethics and innovation were almost completely moderated by size, whereby larger businesses were more sustainable and innovative than their small and medium-sized counterparts. In the tourism industry, however, large businesses were less socially sustainable than smaller ones. Businesses which were focusing on the environment, were also more innovative than businesses which were less environmentally considerate. Socially considerate businesses were more innovative than socially less considerate businesses. Those businesses which were more ethical, were also more innovative than their less ethical counterparts. We thus conclude that Confucian values play a role in the ethical behavior of Chinese businesses from the sample industries. This is an important finding, as even though Confucianism is an ancient value system, it still applies to decision making and business behavior nowadays.

This study may aid managers in understanding how the economic dimension, environment dimension, social dimension and ethical environment are linked with innovative behavior related to their respective businesses. As we moderated sustainability with business size, our research illuminates areas of sustainability that are not properly addressed. For example, small and medium sized tourism businesses in China do perform better on the social aspects of the triple bottom line, while larger tourism businesses are more environmental. Since the pillars of sustainability are inextricably connected, such imbalance may jeopardize the overall sustainability of the business, the sector and the area where it operates.

5. Concluding Remarks

The global market has welcomed China as a powerful actor, which has been recognized internationally. The growth of China's capabilities has been accelerated and accompanied by both advanced technologies and sustainability challenges. The economic restructuring that facilitated the Chinese shift from a planned to a market-driven economy is a complex on-going transformation which will continue to offer new avenues for research.

The decision to adopt innovative technologies and prioritize sustainability rests with businesses. To achieve sustainability, businesses must balance economic development with the broader socio-environmental context in which they operate. Implementing innovative technologies facilitates this balance and requires a co-evolution of business ethics, strategy and technology.

Some argue that Confucian ethics have influenced the development of East Asian economies. However, the pursuit of economic gains can sometimes lead businesses to compromise their ethical standards in the face of fierce competition. While frameworks like the Sustainable Development Goals provide a plan for action, they are not mandatory but rather discretionary. Therefore, this study aims to examine how businesses can uphold ethical standards while embracing sustainability and innovative technologies.

In summary, Chinese business ethics are grounded in Confucian principles of harmony, order and loyalty in personal relationships. These principles emphasize the importance of virtuous behavior, reciprocity and self-improvement in establishing and maintaining social balance. Traditionally, this balance was governed by social hierarchy, with upward interactions requiring loyalty from the subordinate, and downward interactions requiring righteousness from the superior. However, in contemporary market exchange, the principles of sincerity and righteousness serve as the foundation of commercial Chinese ethics, guiding the behavior of businesses towards the pursuit of profit while also considering the interests of the public.

Furthermore, the concept of righteousness in Chinese ethics aligns with the ethical foundation of many sustainability initiatives, including the Brundtland Report, The Millennium Development Goals and Agenda 2030. This ethical foundation emphasizes a responsibility to society, which is enacted through benevolence, righteousness, humanity and personal development. In the context of business, this means that human virtues do not have to conflict with the pursuit of profit, as long as the interests of the public are considered. However, the interpretation and implementation of these principles can vary depending on the wider institutional framework in which businesses operate.

It is worth noting that while some scholars attribute the success of Chinese growth to the influence of Confucian ethics, others argue that the transition period and rapid growth have made it challenging to apply ethical standards in practice. Nevertheless, understanding the specifics of Chinese business ethics is crucial for investigating attitudes towards sustainability in Chinese industries. By recognizing the importance of virtuous behavior, reciprocity and social balance in Chinese ethics, businesses can adopt a more sustainable and responsible approach to their operations.

We hope that our work can inspire other researchers to investigate the complex relationship between innovation, organizational ethics and the dimensions of sustainability in other contexts. As innovation is growing in importance and the significance of sustainability dimensions varies among industries, we believe it is an important and promising research field.

Declarations

1. Funding: The study did not receive any funding and is not associated with any grant.
2. Ethical Approval: This article does not contain any studies with animals performed by any of the authors.
· Ethical approval: Ethical approval: If applicable include the following details: (a) Ethical approval granted by Universiti Pendidikan Sultan Idris, Malaysia. (b) All procedures performed in studies involving human participants were in accordance with the ethical standards of the institutional and / or national research committee and with the 1964 Helsinki declaration and its later amendments or comparable ethical standards.
· Informed consent: Informed consent was obtained from all individual participants included in the study.
* Author's contribution: Please include a statement that specifies the contribution of every author in order to promote transparency.
* Conflict of interest: On behalf of all authors the corresponding author, Dr Maya Vachkova states that there is no conflict of interest.
* Data availability statement: The data associated with the study is kept by Dr Ghouri and can be made available upon reasonable request.
** This research did not receive any specific grant from funding agencies in the public, commercial, or not-for-profit sectors.

(Acknowledgement; This article is a revision of the author's speech at the 2021 UKCHA Annual Forum.)

References

Ali, N., Shahzad, et al. 2017. "Currently Used Organophosphate and Brominated Flame Retardants in the Environment of China and Other Developing Countries (2000–2016)." *Environmental Science and Pollution Research* 24(23): 18721–18741.

Armstrong, J. S., and Overton, T. S. 1977. "Estimating Nonresponse Bias in Mail Surveys." *Journal of Marketing Research* 14(3): 396–402.

Bartnik, R., Wilhelm, M., and Fujimoto, T. 2018. "Introduction to Innovation in the East Asian Automotive Industry: Exploring the Interplay between Product Architectures, Firm Strategies, and National Innovation Systems." *Technovation* 70–71: 1–6.

Benavides-Velasco, C. A., Quintana-García, C., and Marchante-Lara, M. 2014. "Total Quality Management, Corporate Social Responsibility and Performance in the Hotel Industry." *International Journal of Hospitality Management* 41: 77–87.

Bobek, D. D., and Radtke, R. 2007. "An Experiential Investigation of the Ethical Environment of Tax Professionals." *Journal of the American Taxation Association* 29(2): 63–84.

Bobek, D. D., Hageman, A. M., and Radtke, R. R. 2015. "The Influence of Roles and Organizational Fit on Accounting Professionals' Perceptions of their Firms' Ethical Environment." *Journal of Business Ethics* 126(1): 125–141.

Bobek, D. D., Hageman, A. M., and Radtke, R. R. 2010. "The Ethical Environment of Tax Professionals: Partner and Non-Partner Perceptions and Experiences." *Journal of Business Ethics* 92(4): 637–654.

Bohnsack, R. 2018. "Local Niches and Firm Responses in Sustainability Transitions: The Case of Low-Emission Vehicles in China." *Technovation* 70: 20–32.

Brundtland, G. 1987. *Our Common Future: The World Commission on Environment and Development.* Oxford: Oxford University Press.

Bryan, B. A., et al. 2018. "China's Response to a National Land-System Sustainability Emergency." *Nature* 559: 193–204.

CEC (Commission of the European Communities). 2001. *A Sustainable Europe for a Better World: A European Union Strategy for Sustainable Development.* Communication from the Commission. Retrieved from https://ec.europa.eu/regional_policy/archive/innovation/pdf/library/strategy_sustdev_en.pdf. [Accessed March 1, 2020].

Chan, G. K. Y. 2008. "The Relevance and Value of Confucianism in Contemporary Business Ethics." *Journal of Business Ethics* 77: 347–360.

Chen, A. S. Y., and Hou, Y. H. 2016. "The Effects of Ethical Leadership, Voice Behavior and Climates for Innovation on Creativity: A Moderated Mediation Examination." *The Leadership Quarterly* 27(1): 1–13.

CSP (China Statistics Press), 2018. *Hubei Statistical Yearbook.* http://cdi.cnki.net/Search/ReportPreview?FileName=N2019010138000193. [Accessed March 11, 2020].

Crane, A., Matten, D., and Moon, J. 2008. *Corporations and Citizenship: Business, Responsibility and Society.* Cambridge: Cambridge University Press.

Cunningham, L. X. 2010. "Managing Human Resources in SMEs in a Transition Economy: Evidence from China." *The International Journal of Human Resource Management* 21(12): 2120–2141.

Deloitte, 2017. "Clean Energy Industry Report 2017." *Deloitte Research Technology, Media & Telecommunications.* Retrieved from: https://www2.deloitte.com/content/dam/Deloitte/cn/Documents/technology-media-telecommunications/deloitte-cn-tmt-clean-tech-industry-report-2017-en-180110.pdf. [Accessed April 10, 2020].

Deshpandé, R., Farley, J. U., and Webster Jr., F. E. 1993. "Corporate Culture, Customer Orientation, and Innovativeness in Japanese Firms: A Quadrad Analysis." *Journal of Marketing* 57(1): 23–37.

Dhanesh, G. S. 2020. "Who Cares about Organizational Purpose and Corporate Social Responsibility, and How can Organizations Adapt? A Hypermodern Perspective." *Business Horizons* 63(4): 585–594.

Elkington, J. 2004. "Enter the Triple Bottom Line." In *The Triple Bottom Line: Does It All Add Up,* edited by A. Henriques and J. Richardson, 1–16. Hearthscan: London.

Fischer, D., Brettel, M., and Mauer, R. 2018. "The Three Dimensions of Sustainability: A Delicate Balancing Act for Entrepreneurs Made More Complex by Stakeholder Expectations." *Journal of Business Ethics* 163: 87–106.

Fonseca, L. M., and Lima, V. M. 2015. "Countries Three Wise Men: Sustainability, Innovation, and Competitiveness." *Journal of Industrial Engineering and Management* 8(4): 1288–1302.

Gao, H., and Zhang, W. 2017. "Employment Nondiscrimination Acts and Corporate Innovation." *Management Science* 63(9): 2982–2999.

Gefen, D., Straub, D. and Boudreau, C. M. 2000. "Structural Equation Modeling and Regression: Guidelines for Research Practice." *Communications of the Association for Information Systems* 4(1): 7. Retrieved from: https://aisel.aisnet.org/cgi/viewcontent.cgi?article=2531&context=cais.

Gimenez, C., Sierra, V., and Rodon, J. 2012. "Sustainable Operations: Their Impact on the Triple Bottom Line." *International Journal of Production Economics* 140(1): 149–159.

Goebel, S., and Weißenberger, B. E. 2017. "The Relationship between Informal Controls, Ethical Work Climates, and Organizational Performance." *Journal of Business Ethics* 141(3): 505–528.

Green, F. 2017. "China's Inside-Out Climate Leadership." East Asia Forum. Retrieved from: https://www.eastasiaforum.org/2017/06/28/chinas-inside-out-climate-leadership/. [Accessed April 12, 2020].

Hall, J., and Vredenburg, H. 2003. "The Challenge of Innovating for Sustainable Development." *MIT Sloan Management Review* 45(1): 61–68.

Harvey, B. 1999. "'Graceful Merchants': A Contemporary View of Chinese Business Ethics." *Journal of Business Ethics* 20(1): 85–92.

Henseler, J., Ringle, C. M., and Sarstedt, M. 2015. "A New Criterion for Assessing Discriminant Validity in Variance-Based Structural Equation Modeling." *Journal of the Academy of Marketing Science* 43(1): 115–135.

Heras-Saizarbitoria, I., and Boiral, O. 2019. "Faking ISO 9001 in China: An Exploratory Study." *Business Horizons* 62(1): 55–64.

Hofstede, G., and Bond, M. H. 1988. "The Confucius Connection: From Cultural Roots to Economic Growth." *Organizational Dynamics* 16(4): 5–21.

Hulpke, J., and Lau, C. 2008. "Business Ethics in China: A Human Resource Management Issue?." *Chinese Economy* 41(3): 58–67.

Hussain, N., Rigoni, U., and Orij, R. P. 2018. "Corporate Governance and Sustainability Performance: Analysis of Triple Bottom Line Performance." *Journal of Business Ethics* 149(2): 411–432.

Ip, P. K. 2009. "Is Confucianism Good for Business Ethics in China?." *Journal of Business Ethics* 88(3): 463–476.

Johnson, M. W., and Suskewicz, J. 2009. "How to Jump-Start the Cleantech Economy." *Harvard Business Review* 87(11): 52–60.

Juma, C. 2011. *The New Harvest: Agriculture Innovation in Africa.* New York: Oxford University Press.

Juma, C., and Yee-Cheong, L. 2005. *Innovation: Applying Knowledge in Development.* London: Earthscan.

Key, T. M., Azab, C., and Clark, T. 2019. "Embedded Ethics: How Complex Systems and Structures Guide Ethical Outcomes." *Business Horizons* 62(3): 327–336.

Klare, M. 2017. "Tomgram: Michael Klare, A 'China first' and 'Russia second' Foreign Policy?." Tomdispatch.com. Retrieved from: http://www.tomdispatch.com/post/176243/tomgram:_michael_klare,_a_. [Accessed April 12, 2020].

Kirby, D. A., and Kaiser, S. 2003. "Joint Ventures as an Internationalisation Strategy for SMEs." *Small Business Economics* 21(3): 229–242.

Kolk, A., Hong, P., and Van Dolen, W. 2010. "Corporate Social Responsibility in China: An Analysis of Domestic and Foreign Retailers' Sustainability Dimensions." *Business Strategy and the Environment* 19(5): 289–303.

König, P., Anand, K., and Heinemann, F. 2014. "Guarantees, Transparency and the Interdependency between Sovereign and Bank Default Risk." *Journal of Banking and Finance* 45: 321–337.

Klug, F. 2013. "How Electric Car Manufacturing Transforms Automotive Supply Chains." In Proceedings of the *EUROMA European Operations Management Association Conference*, at Dublin. Retrieved from: https://www.researchgate.net/profile/Florian_Klug/publication/273131420_How_electric_car_manufacturing_transforms_automotive_supply_chains/links/54f87f5f0cf28d6deca2a81c.pdf. [Accessed April 14, 2020].

Kremer, H., Villamor, I., and Aguinis, H. 2019. "Innovation Leadership: Best-Practice Recommendations for Promoting Employee Creativity, Voice, and Knowledge Sharing." *Business Horizons* 62(1): 65–74.

Lau, C., Lu, Y., and Liang, Q. 2016. "Corporate Social Responsibility in China: A Corporate Governance Approach." *Journal of Business Ethics* 136(1): 73–87.

Lewin, A. Y., Kenney, M., and Murmann, J. P., eds. 2016. *China's Innovation Challenge: Overcoming the Middle-Income Trap.* Cambridge University Press.

Li, C., Wang, H., Miao, H., and Ye, B. 2017. "The Economic and Social Performance of Integrated Photovoltaic and Agricultural Greenhouses Systems: Case Study in China." *Applied Energy* 190: 204–212.

Lowry, P. B., and Gaskin, J. 2014. "Partial Least Squares (PLS) Structural Equation Modelling (SEM) for Building and Testing Behavioral Causal Theory: When to Choose It and How to Use It." *IEEE Transactions on Professional Communication* 57(2): 123–146.

Lozano, R. 2008. "Envisioning Sustainability Three-Dimensionally." *Journal of Cleaner Production* 16(17): 1838–1846.

Marcus, J., Kurucz, E. C., and Colbert, B. A. 2010. "Conceptions of the Business-Society-Nature Interface: Implications for Management Scholarship." *Business and Society* 49(3): 402–438.

Miemczyk, J., and Luzzini, D. 2019. "Achieving Triple Bottom Line Sustainability in Supply Chains." *International Journal of Operations and Production Management* 39(2): 238–259.

Miller-Rushing, A. J., Primack, R. B., Ma, K., and Zhou, Z. Q. 2017. "A Chinese Approach to Protected Areas: A Case Study Comparison with the United States." *Biological Conservation* 210: 101–112.

Moon, J., Orlitzky, M., and Whelan, G. 2010. *Corporate Governance and Business Ethics*. Cheltenham: Edward Elgar Publishing.

Narayanan, S., and Narasimhan, R. 2014. "Governance Choice, Sourcing Relationship Characteristics, and Relationship Performance." *Decision Sciences* 45(4): 717–751.

NEA (Netherland Enterprise Agency). 2016. "Economic Overview of Hubei Province." Retrieved from: https://www.rvo.nl/sites/default/files/2016/08/Economic-overview-Hubei-province-China.pdf. [Accessed March 11, 2020].

OECD (Organisation for Economic Co-Operation and Development). 2000. *Towards Sustainable Development: Indicators to Measure Progress. In Proceedings of the OECD Rome Conference*. Paris. Retrieved from: https://www.oecd.org/site/worldforum/33703694.pdf. [Accessed March 1, 2020].

Park, K. M., Meglio, O., and Schriber, S. 2019. "Building a Global Corporate Social Responsibility Program via Mergers and Acquisitions: A Managerial Framework." *Business Horizons* 62(3): 395–407.

Poesche, J. 1998. "Business Ethics in the Choice of New Technology in the Kraft Pulping Industry." *Journal of Business Ethics* 17(5): 174–489.

Quinn, L., and Baltes, J. 2007. "Leadership and the Triple Bottom Line." *Bringing Sustainability and Corporate Social Responsibility to Life. A Centre for Creative Leadership (CCL) Research Whitepaper*. Retrieved from: https://cclinnovation.org/wp-content/uploads/2020/03/quinn_leadership-and-the-triple-bottom-line.pdf. [Accessed March 17, 2020].

Rastrollo-Horrillo, M. A., and Rivero Díaz, M. 2019. "Destination Social Capital and Innovation in SMEs Tourism Firms: An Empirical Analysis in an Adverse Socio-Economic Context." *Journal of Sustainable Tourism* 27(10): 1572–1590.

Rhodes, M., and van Apeldoorn, B. 2010. "Capital Unbound? The Transformation of European Corporate Governance." In

Corporate Governance and Business Ethics, edited by J. Moon, M. Orlitzky, and G. Whelan, 316–337. An Elgar Research Collection. Cheltenham, UK Northampton, MA, USA.

Ritchie, H., and Roser, M. 2017. "CO_2 and Greenhouse Gas Emissions." *Our World in Data*. Retrieved from: https://ourworldindata.org/co2-and-other-greenhouse-gas-emissions. [Accessed March 2, 2020].

Schot, J., and Geels, F. W. 2008. "Strategic Niche Management and Sustainable Innovation Journeys: Theory, Findings, Research Agenda, and Policy." *Technology Analysis and Strategic Management* 20(5): 537–554.

Sharif, A., Mishra, S., Sinha, A., Jiao, Z., Shahbaz, M., and Afshan, S. 2020. "The Renewable Energy Consumption-Environmental Degradation Nexus in Top-10 Polluted Countries: Fresh Insights from Quantile-On-Quantile Regression Approach." *Renewable Energy* 150: 670–690.

Smith, K. G., Collins, C. J., and Clark, K. D. 2005. "Existing Knowledge, Knowledge Creation Capability, and the Rate of New Product Introduction in High-Technology Firms." *Academy of Management Journal* 48(2): 346–357.

Stieb, J. A. 2001. "Social Responsibility Within and Without Self-Interest: Emergent Technologies and Situations." *Business and Society Review* 106(3): 241–253.

Strutton, D. 2009. "Horseshoes, Global Supply Chains, and an Emerging Chinese Threat: Creating Remedies One Idea at a Time." *Business Horizons* 52(1): 31–43.

Su, C., and Littlefield, J. E. 2001. "Entering Guanxi: A Business Ethical Dilemma in Mainland China?." *Journal of Business Ethics* 33(3): 199–210.

Tong, T., Ortiz, J., Xu, C., and Li, F. 2020. "Economic Growth, Energy Consumption, and Carbon Dioxide Emissions in the E7 Countries: A Bootstrap ARDL Bound Test." *Energy, Sustainability and Society* 10: 20.

UN (United Nations). 2015. *Transforming Our World: The 2030 Agenda for Sustainable Development*. United Nations, New York, NY. Retrieved from: https://sustainabledevelopment.un.org/content/documents/21252030%20Agenda%20for%20Sustainable%20Development%20web.pdf. [Accessed February 19, 2020].

UN. 2000. *United Nations Millennium Development Goals*. New York: United Nations. Retrieved from: www.un.org/millenniumgoals/bkgd.shtml. [Accessed February 21, 2020].

UNCED (United Nations Commission on Sustainable Development). 1992. *Agenda 21*. "United Nations Conference on Environment and Development." Rio de Janeiro, United Nations, New York.

Victor, B., and Cullen, J. B. 1988. "The Organizational Bases of Ethical Work Climates." *Administrative Science Quarterly* 33(1): 101–125.

Wan, L., and Ng, E. 2018. "Evaluation of the Social Dimension of Sustainability in the Built Environment in Poor Rural Areas of China." *Architectural Science Review* 61(5): 319–326.

Wang, L., Wang, Y., and Chen, J. 2019. "Assessment of the Ecological Niche of Photovoltaic Agriculture in China."

Sustainability 11(8): 2268.

Wang, T., et al. 2017. "Integration of Solar Technology to Modern Greenhouse in China: Current Status, Challenges and Prospect." *Renewable and Sustainable Energy Reviews* 70: 1178–1188.

Weaver, P., Jansen, L., Van Grootveld, G., Van Spiegel, E., and Vergragt, P. 2017. *Sustainable Technology Development*. Routledge.

WEF (World Economic Forum). 2012. *The Global Competitiveness Report 2012–2013*. World Economic Forum, Geneva. Switzerland. Retrieved from: http://www3.weforum.org/docs/WEF_GlobalCompetitivenessReport_2012-13.pdf. [Accessed April 10, 2020].

Whitcomb, L. L., Erdener, C. B., and Li, C. 1998. "Business Ethical Values in China and the US." *Journal of Business Ethics* 17(8): 839–852.

Wines, W. A. 2008. "Seven Pillars of Business Ethics: Toward a Comprehensive Framework." *Journal of Business Ethics* 79(4): 483–499.

Winkler, I., and Williams, C., eds. 2018. *The Sustainable Development Goals and Human Rights: A Critical Early Review*. Routledge.

Wright, S. A., and Schultz, A. E. 2018. "The Rising Tide of Artificial Intelligence and Business Automation: Developing an Ethical Framework." *Business Horizons* 61(6): 823–832.

Xie, Q. 2017. "Firm Age, Marketization, and Entry Mode Choices of Emerging Economy Firms: Evidence from Listed Firms in China." *Journal of World Business* 52(3): 372–385.

Xinhua, 2015. "Chinese Premier Stresses Innovation as 'Golden Key' for Development." *China Daily.* Retrieved from: http://www.chinadaily.com.cn/china/2015-07/29/content_21436022.htm. [Accessed April 10, 2020].

Xue, J. 2017. "Photovoltaic Agriculture—New Opportunity for Photovoltaic Applications in China." *Renewable and Sustainable Energy Reviews* 73: 1–9.

Yang, D., Wang, A. X., Zhou, K. Z., and Jiang, W. 2019. "Environmental Strategy, Institutional Force, and Innovation Capability: A Managerial Cognition Perspective." *Journal of Business Ethics* 159(4): 1147–1161.

Yang, Y., and Greaney, T. M. 2017. "Economic Growth and Income Inequality in the Asia-Pacific Region: A Comparative Study of China, Japan, South Korea, and the United States." *Journal of Asian Economics* 48: 6–22.

Yin, J., and Quazi, A. 2018. "Business Ethics in the Greater China Region: Past, Present, and Future Research." *Journal of Business Ethics* 150(3): 815–835.

Yin, W., et al. 2019. "Innovation in Alternate Mulch with Straw and Plastic Management Bolsters Yield and Water Use Efficiency in Wheat-Maize Intercropping in Arid Conditions." *Scientific Reports* 9(1): 1–14.

Yip, G. S., and McKern, B. 2016. *China's Next Strategic Advantage: From Imitation to Innovation*. MIT Press: Cambridge.

Yiu, D. W., Wan, W. P., and Xu, Y. 2019. "Alternative Governance and Corporate Financial Fraud in Transition Economies: Evidence from China." *Journal of Management* 45(7): 2685–2720.

Zeller, R. A., and Carmines, E. G. 1980. *Measurement in the Social Sciences: The Link between Theory and Data*. Cambridge, UK: Cambridge University Press.

Zhang, Y., Yu, C., Bao, J., and Li, X. 2017. "Impact of Temperature on Mortality in Hubei, China: A Multi-County Time Series Analysis." *Scientific Reports* 7(1): 1–9.

Zhu, Q., Sarkis, J., Lai, K. H., and Geng, Y. 2008. "The Role of Organizational Size in the Adoption of Green Supply Chain Management Practices in China." *Corporate Social Responsibility and Environmental Management* 15(6): 322–337.

Zhang, Y., and Zhang, Z. 2006. "Guanxi and Organizational Dynamics in China: A Link between Individual and Organizational Levels." *Journal of Business Ethics* 67(4): 375–392.

文化比较

Comparing Cultures

中国文化研究中的三个难题

葛兆光[*]

在这个论坛中，我想和大家讨论一下有关中国文化研究的三个难题，这也是我觉得比较困惑的问题，这里谈的，只是我的感受，并没有结论。

一

首先是"界定"很难。

过去对于中国文化，有一种泛泛而论的习惯，从晚清民初以来，有关中国文化的论述常常有似是而非、高度概括的习惯，几个抽象的大概念，好像放之四海而皆准。像梁漱溟先生总结中国文化的十四个特点，我念给大家听一听，你们觉得是否能够概括中国文化？第一个"广土众民"，我觉得，这个好像不是文化；第二个"多民族同化融合"，这个好像还有一点意思；第三个"历史长久"，可是，这不是文化特点呀，好像埃及历史更长久；第四个富于和平精神，这就有点儿问题了，难道别的民族就不富于和平精神，只是充满了争强好斗的精神？好像这个不太合适。剩下的，我就不一一讲了。他总结十条，大家听一听这十条是不是真的能概括中华文化特点：自私自利、勤俭、爱讲礼貌、和平文弱、知足自得、守旧、马虎、坚忍和残忍、韧性和弹性，最后一个是圆熟老到。这样的论述

---

* 葛兆光：复旦大学文史研究院及历史学系特聘资深教授。主要研究领域是东亚与中国的宗教、思想和文化史。

似乎不能告诉我们什么是中国文化。

可是，这个习惯成了学界的传统，一百年前，"五四"前后，这种讨论越来越多：什么中国文化是冷的，西方文化是热的，什么印度文化意欲向后，中国文化意欲在中，西洋文化意欲向前。又有的著作说，什么中国文化历史悠久、地大物博，这些就不像是在学术和历史层面上讨论中国文化。直到现在，有些谈论中国文化的著作，用了一些抽象语词概括中国文化，比如独创性、悠久性、统一性、保守性，可是这些"性"，别的民族、别的国家就没有吗？我觉得，这种论述不太像学术界应该使用的方式，我们似乎需要有一些别的概念、理论和方法，否则的话，我们就会在这种似是而非的概念里空谈，无法给读者提供明确和具体的中国文化的内容。

在若干年前，我看到一些书，给我一定的启发，有人谈到中国汉族和非汉人的一些差别，这些差别，在近来一些有关西南中国少数民族历史的书中也提到。他们举了一些很具体的例子，比如，从夫而居的父系家族，有秩序的葬礼和祭祖，习得汉字的能力，使用筷子的饮食习惯，还有农业和定居等等。我们先不管他对不对，但是这提醒我们，必须从"差别"上，清晰地界定一个文化。那么，什么是中国的文化，以及什么是汉族中国的文化呢？我曾经多次提出有关（汉族）中国文化的五个特点，也就是（1）通过汉字思维与表达，（2）家族以及从家庭、家族、家族共同体发展出来的儒家观念，（3）三教合一的信仰世界，（4）阴阳五行的观念、知识和技术，（5）天下观与华夷观。为什么？这里因时间关系不能多说，我要强调的是，不仅因为这几个特点涵盖面很广，而且这些才是（汉族）中国文化特有，或者比较明显，而其他文化没有，或不明显的特征。

使用汉字思维和表达，这是汉族中国历史很长久的传统，非常明显。以前说"汉字文化圈"，包括了东亚好些地方，当然，现在就连日本、韩国、越南也已经不那么依赖汉字了。

家族观念，大家看看费孝通的《乡土中国》就会明白，汉族中国的基础社会就是家庭、家族、家族共同体，而且，儒家思想不是一个抽象体系，而就是从早期中国的这种社会中生长出来的文化。

三教合一，很明显，欧洲也好，日本也好，都没有这种现象，儒释道三教在中国常常是兼容的，儒家治人，佛教治心，道教治身，都臣服于政治权力之下，所以，宗教的绝对性、唯一性也就弱了很多。

阴阳五行，不仅是思想，也衍生出知识、技术和方法，这点大家要注意。

天下观与华夷观，是中国自我认识的定位，也是处理内部和外部关系的观念、思路和原则。

这些应该说都是汉族中国比较特别和明显的文化。我觉得，历史学者必须非常强调界定，论述不能用一些似是而非的概念，但是，界定什么是中国文化，确实非常困难，以上五点，是我初步界定的，也不一定对，大家可以批评。

二

其次是"涵盖"很难。

可是，上面所说（汉族）中国文化的五方面，并不等于就是现在所说的"中国文化"。我非常不喜欢有些人一讲"国学"，似乎就是汉族中国的儒学，甚至只是儒家经典的四书五经之学。显然，刚才我讲的那五条，还是不能涵盖或者等于"中国文化"。为什么？因为现代中国的领土、宗教和族群，远远不止于传统的汉族中国。现代中国是从清王朝、中华民国、中华人民共和国前后相续，逐渐形成的主权国家，谈论这个"中国"的文化，可就没那么简单了。

这一点很麻烦，如果说，前面涉及了什么是"文化"，这里所需要讨论的就是什么是"中国"。汉族代表整个中国吗？汉文化是整个中国文化吗？"多元一体"现在已经一体了吗？中国是五族共和、六族共和还是五十六个民族？不说明什么是"中国"，怎么能说清什么是"中国文化"？经历了几千年历史的波折，尤其是清代奠定了目前的疆域基础和国家格局，中华民国，现在的中国，已经是一个多民族国家。费孝通提出"多元一体"，当然是非常了不起的说法。但我们要注意，"多元"可以肯定，但是不是真的"一体"了？

这里面涉及我们研究中国文化的一个难题，即国家是多民族的、多宗教的、多种风俗的，内部差异性也很大。当你要谈论"中国文化"的时候，你怎样描述中国文化的特征和边界，你说的能否涵盖现在那么复杂的中国的各种文化？当我们不假思索地运用"中国文化"这个概念的时候，我们考虑到了目前"中国"是什么状况吗？

三

再次是"评价"很难。

同样一个"中国文化"，一百多年来，评价中国文化，有两种不同立场。一种人觉得，中国在衰落中，万事不如人，所以要对中国文化有反省和检讨。一种人觉得，中国是文明古国，必然要兴盛，因此要对中国文化有认同和自尊。从追求自强的目的出发，对中国文化进行反省，就看到了抽鸦片、纳妾、裹小脚和精神麻木（胡适、鲁迅）；从寻求自尊的目的出发，对中国文化怀有敬意，就看到社会有序、礼貌文雅、家庭孝顺与爱好和平（梁漱溟、韦政通）。于是，对中国文化的评价会截然相反。其实坦率地说，这两种说法的逻辑是一样的，出于对现状的思索反省过去，有的会寻找缺陷，有的会寻找资源，大多是感觉，都不是学术和历史的研究。

那么，怎样从历史和学术立场评价中国文化？一直到现在也还是很为难的，尊重普遍价值的，和强调中国立场的，似乎仍有分歧。所以我一直建议，我们是否可以接受或者借鉴德国学者伊利亚斯（Norbert Elias）有关"文明"与"文化"的区分，来对中国文化进行评价？按照伊利亚斯《文明的进程》的说法，文化是与生俱来的风俗和习惯，是使不同民族保持不同面貌的东西，是不怎么会变化的东西；文明是一种需要学习得来的，社会群体交往的规则，是使不同人群的差异越来越少的东西，也是不断进步的东西。文化是民族的、特别的，文明是全球的、普遍的。假定我们能这样区分"文化"与"文明"，是不是就可以一方面拥抱文明，一方面保护文化？这样对于中国文化就比较好评价了，就不必畏惧地方性的文化，抵挡不了普遍性的文明。

中国文化，包括世界上所有的地方文化，在欧洲开始的现代文明冲击下，确实受到了一些损伤，但是，文化与文明能不能保持一种协调？刚才我说，文明在很大程度上，是社会规则，是世界秩序，就像篮球有篮球规则，足球有足球规则，没有规则不成方圆，没有规则也不能公平比赛，否则社会或世界就乱了。其实，古代中国的礼制也是一种文明，它强调上下有序，内外有别，它用等级建立秩序，本来它也只是地方性文明，但按照传统中国儒家的看法，它就是放之四海皆准的普世文明，不遵守它就是蛮夷甚至禽兽。但是，这一两百年间西风东渐，它被另一种来自西方的强势文明所取代了，西方文明更强调平等、人权、自由、民主等等交往规则。这是文明的历史性变迁，至少，现在你不能不接受它，适应它。但是，文化呢？世界上各自有各自的文化，就像各有各的口味，各有各的癖好一样，只要不妨碍与其他民族和国家打交道，不妨碍社会交往的公正平等就好。有人经常讲中国文化就是好，这个我不同意，文化没有好坏，有好坏就等于各民族有高低，就等于对不同的族群和人类进行等级区分了，发展下去就会出现种族歧视和文化歧视。现在，世界上对多元文化有质疑，但我个人还是赞成文化多元，以前费孝通讲"各美其美"是有道理的。

作为一个历史学者，我的工作是对中国文化在历史中的形成做学术性的研究，我不愿意凭着情感和本能对中国文化做简单的价值评判。当然，由于国族自尊和认同的需要，有人会把中国文化说得很好，很优秀，这没问题，但是，请记住我刚才讲的，当你把"文化"和"文明"做一个区分，就可以承认不同文化之间没有高低，文化只是族群的特征、族群的习惯、族群的风俗，这是历史形成和积淀的，也是这个民族形成以后，这个民族中的人们与生俱来的传统，就像如影随形在每一个人身上。但是，千万不要因为我们的文化去贬低别人的文化，说自己的文化辉煌，说别人的文化丑陋。

但是，说到文明，文明是有高低之分的，无论是中国的文明还是西方的文明，这都是人类有史以来逐渐摸索出来的伦理、道德、法律等等，用来建立社会秩序和国际秩序的规则，在文明方面，会有文明与野蛮的高低之分。所以，我们应当接受文明，保护文化。可是，因为不能区分文明与文化，把这些混成一团了，这就造成了我们对中国文化评价上的困难。

以上是我的一些想法，请大家指教。

（本文系作者在联盟2018年年度论坛上的发言）

善意与留白

王　博[*]

　　很感谢主办方的邀请，让我有机会来参加本次以"中国与人文"为主题的中英高等教育人文峰会。面对着这个剧烈变化的时代，无论在中国、英国，还是世界的其他地区，人文学面临着深刻的挑战，也迎来一个重要的反思时刻。如何借助于不同文明传统的思想资源，理解当下已经发生、正在发生或将要发生的变化，面向不确定但必须面对的未来，已经成为人类的共同关切。

　　前不久，两个经过基因编辑的生命来到世界，尽管那位科学工作者以"善意"来为自己的行为辩护，仍然无法阻止科学共同体和人文学者等的强烈批评。的确，当人类不再被古老的自然法则支配，可以根据意愿选择生命，或者换一个说法，当一些人可以像定制物品一样定制另外一些人的时候，构成现代人文精神基础的人的理性、尊严、权利、自由、道德意志等将在何处安放？当科学和技术的快速进步让人变得越来越自信之际，我们该如何保存敬畏之心？当知识积累让一些人觉得可以掌握生命和世界秘密的时候，又该如何理解古代哲人一再强调的"无知"的态度呢？严峻的现实和快速抵达的未来已经让人文学者无法逃避他们应该承担的责任。

　　追问人之所以为人者，或者说，让人成为人，是人文学的首要关注。历史上，人类发展出不同的人文精神，在今天仍然具有生命力，并成为理解未来的重要思想资源。以中国为例，儒家和道家开辟了不同的精神传统。儒家人文学的核

*　王博：北京大学哲学系教授。研究领域为中国哲学史、道家、儒家。

心是以"善意"为基础的伦理—政治秩序的构建，道家人文学的核心则是以"留白"为特征的自主—自由生命的追求。重温发生在它们之间的对话，仍然有益于今天的思考。

"善"的观念对于儒家而言是根本性的。从孟子到宋明新儒学，善被认为既扎根于人性，又上通于天道。孟子对于人性善的描述，主要是通过"恻隐之心""羞恶之心""恭敬之心"和"是非之心"展开，它们分别是仁义礼智之端。"四心"之中，作为"仁之端"的"恻隐之心"又居于特殊的地位。这是存在于人和人之间的"人类之爱"的最直接和柔软的呈现，对于属于同类的他人生命的热爱和尊重在此恻隐之心中一览无余，从而成为"仁者爱人"的内在根基。也因此，伤害他人生命和尊严的行为也必将激发"羞恶之心"，这是义的发端。礼建立在仁义的基础之上，通过爱意和敬意的平衡确立起普遍且可遵循的行为规范。智则是根据仁义的原则而来的判断是非和善恶的能力。人之所以为人者，就体现在仁义礼智的实现之中。

在人性善的基础之上，儒家希望建构起一个充满善意和温情的世界。具体而言，善意表现为爱意和敬意。敬意更多地让人们意识到区别，如长幼有序、贵贱有等，包括对于天命、圣贤和鬼神的敬畏；爱意则指向人和人之间、人和物之间亲密的关系。敬意和爱意的结合，形成一个既亲近又差等的一体世界。孟子称之为"亲亲而仁民，仁民而爱物"，后来的宋明新儒学则概括为"仁者以天地万物为一体"，成为儒家最具代表性的观念。对此一体的世界，张载的《西铭》从宇宙论的角度加以论述，乾坤（天地）是人之父母，所有的人都是同胞，而物则是人的伙伴（"乾称父，坤称母""民吾同胞，物吾与也"）。王阳明《大学问》则提供了心学意义上的证明，无论他人、鸟兽、草木，还是一瓦一石，都关联着我们的仁心。从人到物，一体之仁贯通起整个的宇宙。因此，一个儒家意义上的人，就是在差等之序列中，以爱和敬来面对整个世界的人。自我生命的完成，内在地包含着对于他人和世界的责任。其具体表现，则是《论语》所谓"己欲立而立人，己欲达而达人""己所不欲，勿施于人"的忠恕之道，是《中庸》所谓

"成己"和"成物"的结合。爱和敬的善意让儒家充满了伦理的精神，既是成人的基础，也是社会和政治秩序的根基，奠定了中国文化的基本品格。

必须指出，儒家并非没有意识到存在于人经验生命之中的恶的因素，同样属于儒家的荀子甚至突出了人性之恶，主张以人为之善来克服天性之恶。但这也使善既无法获得来自生命内部的支持，也无法获得来自天道的保证，因此缺乏足够的力量。比较而言，性善说的简明之处在于：我们之所以选择善的生活，是因为我们本来就是善的。而善的内涵也相当清楚，即根据仁义的价值，将生命和社会纳入到礼的秩序之中。这正是性善说在后来的新儒家传统中取得主流地位的重要理由。

但是，道家提出了问题。善或者说儒家倡导的善意真的能带来一个更好的世界吗？为了追求善的生命和世界，儒家不得不把善视为人的普遍本质，并希望通过教化的方式塑造人类。与儒家强调"本质"不同，道家更看重"万物"本身。从事比较哲学研究的学者发现了存在主义和道家之间的类似之处，存在先于本质。用道家的语言来说，万物先于任何的命名（"无名，万物之始。"《老子》第一章）。而当我们把目光集中在"存在者"即万物的时候，万物的"无法定义"的一面就得到突显。换言之，万物首先是万物本身，无法简单地用善恶或者美丑等来命名，并且通过这种命名来肯定或否定。电影《鸟人》里的一句名言"A thing is a thing , not what said of that thing"，也许是《老子》第一句话"道可道，非常道；名可名，非常名"最好的翻译。A thing 不是 That thing，因此，当我们更关心万物（a thing）的时候，必须先把善恶等和命名相关的框架放在一边。

根本上无法定义或命名的态度，为万物生长和发展提供了无限的可能性。道家坚持认为，确立起一个"善"的标准，并以之来塑造万物，无疑忽略了万物的差异性和多样性，进而破坏了万物的自主性，在通过"善"肯定一类事物的同时，以"不善"的名义人为地排除或者伤害了其他事物。老子主张"圣人常善救人，故无弃人；常善救物，故无弃物"，"善者吾善之，不善者吾亦善之"，倾向于从万物出发，肯定每一个存在者的合法性，庄子把老子的精神概括为"常宽容于物，而不削于人"（《庄子·天下篇》）。这也就是"道法自然"。"道"是道家认为的万物本原，"法自然"是道对于万物的态度，用王弼的话来说，是"在方而法方，在圆而法圆，于自然无所违也"。《老子》第二章说"天下皆知美之为美，斯恶矣；皆知善之为善，斯不善矣"，一旦我们确立起一个美或者善的标准，必然会导致对于万物的区分。善意随之会转化成恶意，第五十八章"善复为妖"所指即是如此。庄子更叙述了很多善意谋杀的例子，最著名者无疑是"混沌之死"，南海之帝和北海之帝在善意的支配之下，给混沌凿出了七窍，七窍成而混沌死（《庄子·应帝王》）。

在这种思考之下，限制包括"善意"在内的一切人为的力量，尊重他人和世界，就成为道家的精神方向。这就是"留白"。"留白"是从中国艺术传统那里借用来的一个说法，以绘画为例，宋代马远的《寒江独钓图》是留白的典范，一叶扁舟，一个钓者，几笔勾勒出的波纹，留下大片空白的画面，却给人一种波涛浩渺之感。不画之画，"无画处皆成妙境"。美学家宗白华先生说："中国画最重空白处。空白处并非真空，乃灵气往来生命流动之所。且空而后能简，简而练，则理趣横溢，而脱略形迹。"（《艺境》）在哲学上，留白即是认识到"无"或者"虚"的意义。"有之以为利，无之以为用"，"无"就是留白，让"有"更好地展开自己；无为就是留白，让百姓或者万物获得了更大的自主空间；"相忘于江湖"就是留白，与"相濡以沫"的热爱相比，让人处在一种更自在、自得和自由的状态之中。

留白的实质是人和人为的有限性，其认识论基础是根本意义上"无知"的态度。从苏格拉底、康德到老子和庄子，哲学家在意识到知识之伟大的同时，对于知识的有限性也有深刻的体认。苏格拉底一直强调他从德尔菲神庙那里得到的教诲——认识你自己，从而有无知和节制的自觉。康德在为人类知识论证的同时，也通过"自在之物"守护着物的"玄之又玄"，提示知识的界限。《老子》第七十一章说："知不知，尚矣；不知知，病也。圣人不病，以其病病；夫唯病病，是以不病。"知道自己不知道，这本身就是一种知，庄子称之为"无知之知"。

显然，无知并不是对于这个世界一无所知，而是提醒我们知识的限度，以对未知的世界保存敬畏之心，并避免拥有越来越多知识的人类从自信走向自大。无知和随之而来的敬畏让留白获得了更丰富的意义，它是人的有限性的必然体现。

人的创造似乎一直让人自身处在一个两难的境地之中。我们需要权威，又担心权威主宰我们的生活。我们追求自由，追求自我的权利，又担心无法保障社会公正与和谐。我们追求善意，又担心善意泛滥，没有留白的空间。我们需要生命科学的进步，又担心它的无限制发展会永久地改变人性，给人类带来不确定的风险。也许人类永远无法摆脱这种为难的境地，事实上，"无法摆脱"的状态给人文学提供了最好的展开之所，提醒人类在乐观和无奈、自信和有限之间保持平衡，进而在自由与公平、善意和留白之间保持恰当的平衡。

教育也是如此。人类发明了教育，让人成为拥有某种价值观、知识和技能的人，极大地促进了人类发展和社会进步。教育的核心目标是立德树人，北京大学今年夏天承办了第24届世界哲学大会，主题便是"学以成人"（learning to be human）。多元文明传统通过这个大会展开对话，从不同角度呈现对于"成人"的理解。"成人"的不同路径彰显出生命本身的多种可能性，也显示出文化和教育的力量。同样，对于与教育密切相关的"学"，不同的人文精神也形成了不同的认识。孔子说："学而时习之，不亦说乎！"对于儒家来说，"学"是"成人"的必由之路。老子则担心"学"会让生命迷失在某种标准之中，因此提出"绝学无忧"。不同的对于"学"的看法呈现出教育本身的内在矛盾。教育的本意是让我们成为人，成为更好的人，但结果有时候却适得其反。萧伯纳说："我生而聪明，但教育毁了我。"这并非一个随意的调侃，如何理解教育，如何定义人，应该给人填充多少确定的内容，以寻找人类共同生活的基础；又留下多少空白处，为人的自由发展保存空间，也许是一个永恒的问题。意识到这个问题会让我们更加谨慎，也让我们的心灵更加开放。

最后，我想以《周易》的思考作为结束。作为古代中国影响最大的经典之一，《周易》以六十四卦表达对于世界的理解。从乾坤开始，最后是既济和未济。

既济的意思是完成，未济则是没有完成。既济卦的卦象很容易记住，自下而上，六爻以一阳一阴、一阳一阴、一阳一阴的方式展开，给人的感觉是井井有条，头头是道，似乎一切都已经被一个有形之手安排停当。但卦辞中的"初吉终乱"让我们多了一份敬畏。由于变化的神妙莫测，某种看似完成或完美的秩序中却潜藏着未知的危险，并注定要走向未济式的混乱，就像那个被质疑的基因编辑者。"知进而不知退，知存而不知亡，知得而不知丧"让我们陷入"亢龙有悔"的状态。只有意识到自己的局限，无论是知识的还是道德的，承认世界"玄之又玄"的一面，给世界留白，给每一个人留白，人类才能成为"知进退存亡而不失其正者"。

（宋）马远：寒江独钓图

（本文系作者在联盟2018年年度论坛上的发言）

西方诗画关系与莱辛的诗画观

刘 石[*]

作为两个重要的艺术门类，不论中国还是西方，诗与画之间的关系都是各自文艺学史上重要的理论命题。中国的诗画关系不是本文关注的重点，本文所要讨论的问题是，西方文艺学史上的诗画关系究竟是怎样的，应如何看待其中的主要观点，中国学界对西方诗画关系存在哪些误解，这些误解是怎样产生的。西方诗画关系论中最为重要，同时也对中国学界影响最大的著述，是德国18世纪文艺理论家莱辛的《拉奥孔》。我们又该如何认识和评价莱辛在《拉奥孔》中阐述的以诗画分界和诗优画劣为核心的一系列诗画关系学说呢？

西方文艺学史上的诗画关系

梳理西方文艺学史上的诗画关系，需要从西方艺术门类的划分说起。波兰学者符·塔达基维奇（1886—1980）卓有成效的研究告诉我们，西方人从希腊、罗马时期开始就致力于艺术门类的划分工作。早期的人们对艺术的理解与今天差异甚大，比如认为艺术依赖于对规则的认识，无规则、非理性即非艺术，所以产生于灵感的诗不算艺术，几何学、裁缝等技艺反倒算作艺术。艺术中不同门类的地位又各不相同，地位较高的是只需劳心的"自由艺术"，如语法、修辞、逻辑等，雕塑、绘画则由于对体力有所要求而被视作地位低下的"粗俗艺术"。直到

* 刘石：清华大学人文学院教授。研究方向：唐宋文学，中国古典文献学。

文艺复兴时期，"美的艺术"观念渐显，艺术必须从工艺与科学的范围分离渐成趋势，画家、雕塑家、建筑家等艺术家的地位方始得以显著上升，而今日文艺概念的定型，已是迟至18世纪中叶的事情了。[1]

塔氏的研究足以给我们留下这样的印象，艺术门类的划分是西方文艺学的传统，艺术门类的划分中天然地包含着对不同类别的轩轾，就是说，分别艺术门类间的地位高下和功能优劣也是西方文艺学的传统。这种高下优劣之分或受制于时代文化思潮，或基于某些特殊背景甚至个人因素，在今天来看有些仍可成立，有些虽然正确却不具有意义，有些已是不正确甚至荒谬的了。

比如，意大利雕塑家与画家贝尼尼（1598—1680）指出绘画与雕刻的区别是："画可以改正画幅中的错误，但雕刻家不能，因为绘画就是增加，而雕刻则是减缩。"这属于正确但不具意义的比较。而从中得出的结论——"绘画要容易得多，而在雕刻中要臻于完美，则困难得多"[2]——就完全不正确。此前意大利的另一位画家，大名鼎鼎的达·芬奇（1452—1519）也说，"雕塑要求的智巧比绘画少"[3]，惹来他的朋友、雕塑家米开朗基罗（1475—1564）的嗤笑，称"其见解可谓与仆婢相近"[4]。可是米氏又说，"雕刻是绘画的指导，前者是太阳，后者是月亮"[5]，将二者的地位调了个个儿，而其见解与仆婢的距离又何曾比芬奇更远！

不妨说，这些今天看来甚为无谓的争论正反映了西人强为艺术区分高下的普遍好尚，而不同艺术的高下如何区分，考量出的正是对不同艺术的理解能力和认识水平。法国诗人、艺术批评家波德莱尔（1821—1867）认为工业是艺术的死敌，所以摄影不能算作艺术。"如果允许摄影在艺术的某些功能中代替艺术，那

1　［波］塔达基维奇：《西方美学概念史》第1章，褚朔维译，北京：学苑出版社，1990年，第27页。

2　贝尼尼之子关于贝尼尼传记中引及，此据［苏］马祖列维奇：《洛伦索·贝尼尼》，杨德友译，《美术译丛》1980年第3期。

3　［意］达·芬奇：《芬奇论绘画》第1编，戴勉编译，北京：人民美术出版社，1979年，第33页。本文所引芬奇语均见此编。

4　转引自迟轲：《西方美术史话》第5章第3节，北京：中国青年出版社，1983年，第99页。

5　转引自迟轲：《西方美术史话》第5章第3节，第99页。

么，它将凭借着它在群众的愚蠢中找到的天然的盟友而立刻彻底地排挤或腐蚀艺术。"[1] 无独有偶，法国雕塑家罗丹（1840—1917）也说："世间有一种低级的精确，那就是照相和翻模的精确。"[2] 他们表达的是同一个意思，即摄影只有机器在起作用，没有人的作用；只能再现表象与细节，而于反映内心的情感无涉。即使我们考虑到当时摄影艺术的发展水平，也不能不说他们对它的原理与魅力几无所知。在摄影已经成为一门重要艺术的今天，其荒谬就更是显而易见的了。

在西方不同门类艺术的普遍比较中，诗画比较是持续最久、参与最广、内容最丰富、意义最重大的话题。在欧洲美学史上第一篇重要文献《诗学》里，亚里士多德（公元前384—前322）开头就指出诗与画、雕塑等造型艺术的不同，所谓"有一些人，用颜色和姿态来制造形象，摹仿许多事物，而另一些人则用声音来摹仿"[3]。毕辛尼亚人克吕索斯托姆（50—117）也对比诗歌和雕塑的差异："我们（雕塑家——译者原注）塑每一座像的时候都只能塑一个姿态，这个姿态必须是牢固的、经久不变的……但是，诗人却可以把许多姿态包括到他们的诗歌中去，还可以描写人物的运动和休息，行动和言词。"[4] 希腊作家和哲学家卢奇安（125？—192？）则明确表示画优于诗，其理由在今天看来实在难惬心意："希罗多德先生认为视觉更有力量，这是正确的。因为语言有翅膀，'一言既出，驷马难追'。但是视觉的快感是常备的，随时可以吸引观众。所以，可以断言，演讲家要同这间斑斓夺目的华堂争夺锦标，就难乎其难了。"[5] 可就是这样的观点，却遥启了千余年后的达·芬奇。

1 ［法］波德莱尔：《一八五九年的沙龙·现代公众和摄影》，《波德莱尔美学论文选》，郭宏安译，北京：人民文学出版社，1987年，第402页。
2 ［法］罗丹：《罗丹艺术论·遗嘱》，沈琪译，北京：人民美术出版社，1987年，第3页。
3 ［古希腊］亚理斯多德：《诗学》第1章，罗念生译，北京：人民文学出版社，1962年，第4页。
4 ［古罗马］克吕索斯托姆：《谈到对上帝的认识》，转引自鲍桑葵：《美学史》第5章第2节，张今译，北京：商务印书馆，1985年，第145页。
5 ［古希腊］卢奇安：《华堂颂》，《缪灵珠美学译文集》第1卷，章安祺编订，北京：中国人民大学出版社，1998年，第141页。

达·芬奇论证诗不如画的逻辑简单而清晰：第一，"被称为灵魂之窗的眼睛，乃是心灵的要道，心灵依靠它才得以最广泛最宏伟地考察大自然的无穷作品"，所以"视觉比其他感官优越"；第二，"能使最高感官满意的事物价值最高"；第三，"绘画替最高贵的感官——眼睛服务"，"诗人利用了较为低级的听觉"，所以，"断定画胜过诗"。后来又有英国文学家艾迪生（1672—1719）发表过类似的见解："我们一切感觉里最完美、最愉快的是视觉……我所谓'想像或幻想的快乐'，就指由看见的东西所产生的快感：或者是我们眼前确有这些东西，或者是凭绘画、雕像或描写等等在我们心灵上唤起了对这些东西的观念。"[1]这些见解归纳起来就是两点：一是绘画以形似为上，二是绘画因形似而贵。可是，绘画是否就等同于体物存形，描绘是否就是艺术最重要的功用呢？

法国启蒙时期思想家狄德罗（1713—1784）也是诗画异质论者，所不同的是他转而为诗歌争胜。他认为"画家只能画一瞬间的景象；他不能同时画两个时刻的景象，也不能同时画两个动作"[2]，这一观点已与同代人莱辛（1729—1781）相当接近。至于在西方诗画关系论中占有重要地位的莱辛的诗画理论，将在后面专门加以讨论。

进入19世纪，艺术家和理论家仍继续为诗画分界，并在其间分别高下。主张画优于诗者仍不乏其人，法国浪漫主义画家德拉克罗瓦（1798—1863）就是一例。他认为画高于诗的理由也很有趣："观众应该直接面对绘画，这时不要求观众作任何努力——看一眼画就够了！读书就不一样了！书要去买，一页一页地读。先生，你听见没有？"[3]但主张诗高于画的观念明显占据上风。德国美学家黑格尔（1770—1831）虽然认为绘画"可以用外在的东西把内在的东西完全表现出

1　［英］艾迪生：《旁观者》，赵守垠译，《西方文论选》上卷，伍蠡甫主编，上海：上海译文出版社，1979年，第566—567页。

2　［法］狄德罗：《画论》第5章，徐继曾、宋国枢译，《狄德罗美学论文选》，北京：人民文学出版社，1984年，第405页。

3　［法］德拉克罗瓦：《德拉克罗瓦论美术和美术家·论绘画》，平野译，沈阳：辽宁美术出版社，1981年，第311页。

来"[1]，不纯然将绘画视作对自然的再现，但他又自相矛盾地说："绘画也落后于诗和音乐：那就是在抒情方面……只能表现面容和姿势。"[2]他更明确认为诗兼具绘画和音乐的优长，"是把造型艺术和音乐这两个极端，在一个更高的阶段上，在精神内在领域本身里，结合于它本身所形成的统一整体"[3]，最终站到诗歌优越论的行列中去了。

同时，又有英国批评家赫士列特（1778—1830）说："诗歌是比绘画更有诗意的。艺术家或鉴赏家大言不惭地谈到画中有诗，他们显出对诗缺乏知识，对艺术缺乏热情。画呈现事物本身，诗呈现事物的内涵……画表现事件，诗表现事件的进程。"[4]这段话对绘画价值大小、地位高低的评价与上引芬奇的观点正相反对，但体现出的对绘画的理解却是完全一致的，即绘画的功能仅限于对视觉起作用。另一位英国浪漫主义大诗人雪莱（1792—1822）同样说："语言更能直接表现我们内心生活的活动和激情，比颜色、形相、动作更能作多样而细致的配合，更宜于塑造形象，更能服从创造的威力的支配……所以，雕刻家、画家、音乐家等的声誉从来就不能与诗人的声誉媲美。"[5]

再后来的波德莱尔也反对艺术间的融合倾向，他说："今天，每一种艺术都表现出侵犯邻居艺术的欲望，画家把音乐的声音变化引入绘画，雕塑家把色彩引入雕塑，文学家把造型的手段引入文学，而我们今天要谈的一些艺术家则把某种百科全书式的哲学引入造型艺术本身，所有这一切难道是出于一种颓废时期的必然吗？"[6]连生活到20世纪80年代的塔达基维奇也同样持诗画有别论，他说："视觉

1　［德］黑格尔：《美学》第3卷上册第3部分第1章第2节a，朱光潜译，北京：商务印书馆，1981年，第242页。

2　［德］黑格尔：《美学》第3卷上册第3部分第1章第2节c，第290页。

3　［德］黑格尔：《美学》第3卷下册第3部分第3章序论，第4页。

4　［英］赫士列特：《泛论诗歌》，袁可嘉译，《古典文艺理论译丛》第1册，北京：人民文学出版社，1961年，第67—68页。

5　［英］雪莱：《为诗辩护》，缪灵珠译，《古典文艺理论译丛》第1册，第80—81页。

6　［法］波德莱尔：《哲学的艺术》，《波德莱尔美学论文选》，第383页。

艺术表现事物，而诗只是表现符号……这一区别并不是细微末节的，而是艺术原则本身的。"[1]

西方文艺学史上艺术类别相分的传统，归根结底基于西方崇尚分析的哲学思想[2]，它有利于对不同门类艺术规律和特性的探讨，从而促进各门艺术的发展。但贯穿其中的诗画优劣观，不论孰褒孰贬，今天看来均多武断荒唐之论，历史的局限性十分明显。达·芬奇等人以形似论画，其用意本在提高绘画的地位，结果却降低了绘画的价值和意义。黑格尔对绘画在抒情方面落后于诗的批评，也只能体现了他对绘画功能认识的不足。可见，在艺术门类的比较中，对所贬抑的那种艺术一定有不正确的理解，对所推崇的那种艺术，其理解却未必就完全正确。

中国学界对西方诗画关系的认识

朱光潜说："诗和画的关系在西方是一个老问题。"[3]诚然。但这是一个什么样的老问题，就是说，西方文艺学史上对诗画关系的看法怎样呢？由前述可知，艺术类别的划分而不是混同、不同艺术门类间的地位相争而非和平共处是西方文艺学的传统。同理，建立在这个传统之上的西方文艺学史上的诗画关系也不是一致说，而是有别论；不是融合说，而是相分论。

然而，中国学界在讨论这一问题时，却多认为西方诗画关系论中占主导的是诗画一致说。就目力所及，讨论这一问题并得出这一结论的主要依据，就是朱光潜、钱钟书这两段文章中引及的几条材料：

---

1 ［波］塔达基维奇：《西方美学概念史》第3章第12节，第162页。

2 中国文艺学传统中诗画相分的观念远不及西方那么鲜明，毋宁说诗画相通、融合、一律才是主流，这也正是基于中国传统综合的哲学观。活跃于20世纪上半叶的美术史家滕固在《诗书画三种艺术的联带关系》中说："诗书画三种艺术的结合，这种思想在欧洲是不会发生的，在东方也只有在中国可以找到。"（载《中国艺术论丛》，出版地不详：商务印书馆，1938年，第86页）

3 朱光潜：《拉奥孔·译后记》，［德］莱辛：《拉奥孔》，朱光潜译，北京：人民文学出版社，1979年，第216页。

希腊诗人西摩尼德斯所说的"画是一种无声的诗，诗是一种有声的画"，已替诗画一致说奠定了基础。接着拉丁诗人贺拉斯在《诗艺》里所提出的"画如此，诗亦然"，在后来长时期里成为文艺理论家们一句习用的口头禅。在十七、十八世纪新古典主义的影响之下，诗画一致说几乎变成一种天经地义。[1]

嫁名于西塞罗的一部修词学里，论"互换句法"的第四例就是："正如诗是说话的画，画该是静穆的诗。"（西塞罗《修词学》第4卷28章，罗勃本326页）达文齐干脆说画是"嘴巴哑的诗"，而诗是"眼睛瞎的画"。（达文齐《画论》16章，米拉奈西编本12页）[2]

殊不知将西摩尼德斯、贺拉斯、西塞罗、达文齐诸语理解为主张诗画一致是大有问题的，下面逐条予以辨析。

朱氏所引希腊抒情诗人西摩尼德斯（约公元前556—前467）语，所据为莱辛的《拉奥孔·前言》，但莱辛并未交代此语的来历。钱钟书的《中国诗与中国画》亦曾引及，译作"画为不语诗，诗是能言画"[3]，又加注云："艾德门茨《希腊抒情诗》，罗勃本第2册258页。参看哈格斯特勒姆《姐妹艺术》（1958）10又58页。"但这两书显非西氏的原著，也未必是所引语的最早出处，我们一时无法获知此语的上下文，故不能确切理解它的具体含义。罗马统治时期的希腊散文家普鲁塔克（约46—126）曾这样引及西氏此语："诗的艺术是模拟的艺术，和绘画相类。常言道：'诗是有声的画，画是无声的诗。'"[4]普氏所说当然也未必就是西氏的原意，但至少这位时代相对接近的作家的理解是，所谓诗画相类，不过是指二者都是模拟的艺术。

---

1 朱光潜：《拉奥孔·译后记》，[德]莱辛：《拉奥孔》，第216页。

2 钱钟书：《中国诗与中国画》，《七缀集》，上海：上海古籍出版社，1996年，第6页。

3 钱钟书：《中国诗与中国画》，《七缀集》，第6页。

4 [古希腊]普鲁塔克：《青年人应该怎样读诗》，杨绛译，《欧美古典作家论现实主义和浪漫主义（一）》，中国社会科学院外国文学研究所编，北京：中国社会科学出版社，1980年，第56页。

更要紧的是，能否据此认定普氏自己就是诗画相合论者呢？完全不能。他是明确主张诗画相分的人，连莱辛都要借之以壮声势，在"拉奥孔"的书名下赫然引上他的一句话："它们（诗画——引者）在题材和模仿方式上都有区别。"普氏还说过另一段话："绘画绝对与诗歌无涉，诗歌亦与绘画无关，两者之间绝不相得益彰。"[1]这至少说明，讲"诗是有声画，画是无声诗"的人不一定就是诗画一致论者，他完全可能只是站在某个特定的角度将诗画做类比，而不是着眼于诗画作为两种艺术门类的品质的相同或相似。不止于此，这两句话甚至还可以在表达诗画差异的观点时使用，如普氏在另一文中说的那样："西摩尼得斯把绘画称为无声的诗，把诗称为有声的画，因为绘画把事情当时的状况描画出来，文学在这事情完成之后，把这事描叙出来。"[2]一瞬间，一历时，和上举同时人克吕索斯托姆所说的一个姿态和诸多姿态一样，俨然已是一千八百年后莱辛论诗画之别的大辂椎轮。

再看罗马帝国初期诗人贺拉斯（公元前65—公元8）那句话所在的一段："诗歌就像图画：有的要近看才看出它的美，有的要远看；有的放在暗处看最好，有的应放在明处看，不怕鉴赏家锐敏的挑剔；有的只能看一遍，有的百看不厌。"[3]很显然，同普鲁塔克所说的"诗画相类"一样，贺拉斯所说的"诗歌就像图画"（即朱氏所译的"画如此，诗亦然"，又有人译作"诗如画"），也完全是从一个特别角度出发的。硬要说他指的是诗画间的某种一致，那就只能如塔达基维奇所说的意味深长的隽语："贺拉斯在绘画与诗之间所看到的，是一种相当悬殊的近似。"[4]

古罗马共和制末期理论家西塞罗（公元前106—前44）的那句话亦大致如是。

---

1 ［古希腊］普鲁塔克：《即兴演说》第9卷第15章，转引自法国法尔孔奈：《雕刻随想》，《美术译丛》1982年第1期。

2 ［古希腊］普鲁塔克：《雅典人的光荣》，杨绛译，《欧美古典作家论现实主义和浪漫主义（一）》，第56页。

3 ［古罗马］贺拉斯：《诗艺》，杨周翰译，北京：人民文学出版社，1988年，第156页。

4 ［波］塔达基维奇：《西方美学概念史》第3章第9节，第146页。着重号为引者所加。

相关的一段文字是："以互换的形式来表达两个有差异的思想，后者追随前者，尽管在意思上与前者不同，这种手法称作互置，例如：'吃饭是为了活着，但活着不是为了吃饭。'又如：'我不写诗，因为我不能写我希望写的东西，也不希望写我能写的东西。'……又如：'一首诗必须是一幅能说话的画，一幅画必须是一首沉默的诗。'……不能否认，把这些对立的观念并列，并且变换位置，效果是很好的。"[1]可知这里讨论的完全不是诗画关系，而是修辞问题。是否可以说从西塞罗的举例中看见其诗画一律思想的存在呢？从以上两例推之是不能的，从达文齐例来看，同样不能。

达文齐就是达·芬奇，这位文艺复兴时期的大画家也是一位画论家，包括其《画论》在内的相关画学著作早有中译本传世，即前文多所引及的《芬奇论绘画》。"嘴巴哑的诗""眼睛瞎的画"这两句在全书中不止一见："诗画之区别：——'画是哑巴诗，诗是盲人画'。""如果你称绘画为哑巴诗，那么诗也可以叫作瞎子画。试想哪一种创伤更重，是瞎眼还是哑巴？"原来，达·芬奇表面酷似中国古人张舜民、牟巘的两句话[2]，其含义却与之正相反对，不仅表达的是诗画的"区别"而不是一律，还断断争辩于诗画的高下：画比诗更优越！

上面的辨析说明，仅据寻章摘句的字面，便认为诗画一致是西方传统的文艺观，是不一定靠得住的。这些只言片语表达的诗画一致，即所谓都是模拟的艺术、远近明暗看都可以，不仅与中国古人基于审美趣味和艺术功能的同一性而发生的"诗画一律"说是两回事，甚至也与文艺学意义上的"诗画关系"邈不相干！

带着这样的认识，再来看朱光潜下面的一段话，就会发现是有问题的。他说："关于诗和画的关系问题，历来美学家们和文艺批评家们较多地着重诗画的

---

1 ［古罗马］西塞罗：《论公共演讲的理论》第4卷第28章，《西塞罗全集·修辞学》，王晓朝译，北京：人民出版社，2007年，第109页。感谢王教授在译本出版前就将此段文字提供给我。

2 北宋张舜民说："诗是无形画，画是有形诗。"（《跋百之诗画》，《画墁集》卷一，影印文渊阁《四库全书》第1117册，台北：商务印书馆，1986年，第8页）南宋牟巘说："诗乃有声画，画乃无声诗。"（《唐棣诗序》，《牟氏陵阳集》卷十三，《四库全书》第1188册，第117页）

共同点。莱辛在序言中所引的希腊诗人西蒙尼德斯的'画是无声的诗,而诗则是有声的画'一句话,我国宋朝画论家赵孟溁也说过,几乎一字不差。苏东坡称赞王维说:'味摩诘之诗,诗中有画,观摩诘之画,画中有诗。'这是诗画同源说的一个常引用的例证。"[1]按赵孟溁有"画谓之无声诗,乃贤哲寄兴"[2]云云,朱氏所指当即此语。苏东坡那几句说的是诗画一律,与诗画同源无涉,这里姑且不论。这段话最大的问题就在于,仅仅因为字面的相似,便将实质上差异很大的中西两种诗画观混同为一了。"非以其名也,以其取也"(《墨子·贵义》),中国古人循名责实的劝诫值得记取。

近见日人浅见洋二《关于"诗中有画"——中国的诗歌与绘画》一文,开篇即说:"将诗歌与绘画进行比较,力图肯定二者有某种同质性、相似性的论述,西方似乎很早就有了,如西蒙尼底斯的'画是无声诗,诗为有声画'以及贺拉斯的'诗如画'等说法就极具代表性。"[3]日本学者是受了中国学者的影响,还是英雄所见略同,就不得而知了。

《拉奥孔》的诗画分界说和诗优画劣论

西方诗画关系论中居于主导的思想是分不是合,是异不是同,却不能说西方文艺观中不存在诗画相合的思想。文艺复兴以来,达·芬奇等人努力提高绘画的地位,客观上引发了人们对绘画艺术的重视,促进了人们对画与诗共通点的探寻。美国新人文主义学者白璧德(1865—1933)指出:"16世纪中叶到18世纪中叶,人人都用赞许的口吻提及贺拉斯的'诗如画',或西蒙尼得斯的'画是无声诗,诗是有声画'。"[4]塔达基维奇也说:"很少有哪句名言像贺拉斯的这句名言一

---

1 朱光潜:《西方美学史》上卷第10章第2节,北京:人民文学出版社,1979年,第312—313页。

2 参见明朱存理:《珊瑚木难》卷四,《四库全书》第815册,第104页。

3 载《距离与想像——中国诗学的唐宋转型》,上海:上海古籍出版社,2005年,第109页。

4 [美]白璧德:《新拉奥孔》(*The New Laokoon*)第1章,波士顿,纽约,1910年,第3页。引文为引者所译。

样经常为人们所引用，也很少有哪句名言是如此错误地、有违作者原意地为人们所解释。"[1] 错误地、有违原意地解释成什么意思了呢？那就是钱钟书所说的："古罗马诗人霍拉斯的名句：'诗亦犹画'，经后人断章取义，理解作'诗原通画'，仿佛苏轼《书鄢陵王主簿折枝》所谓：'诗画本一律。'"[2]

但很快地，《拉奥孔》出现在18世纪中叶的欧洲，成为西方诗画相分论中最具影响的著述。莱辛虽然在书中称诗画为"姊妹艺术"[3]，可是他眼里的这对姊妹长相迥异，关系也不融洽，她们不是朋友而是敌手，不会合作，只会"竞赛""争胜"[4]。该书的主旨实如同其副题所标示——"论画与诗的界限"，而书中所谓的"一种美的艺术的固有使命只能是不借助于其他艺术而能独自完成的那一种"[5]，则可以视作其分别诗画界限的逻辑基点。

不止于此，这部书的一切论述都旨在说明诗的优越性，为诗画所做的所有分界都指向同一个目标：诗优画劣。

问题是，真的存在只能被某一种艺术表现而绝不能被其他艺术表现的"那一种"东西吗？诗画之间乃至一切艺术之间，真的存在天然的优劣之别，能够让我们去绝对地区分高下吗？从学理出发，《拉奥孔》中的一些观点实在值得商榷。

一、关于诗画分属时空问题

书中所论的诗画界限甚多，其核心是所谓诗画分属时间艺术和空间艺术的问题："物体连同它们的可以眼见的属性是绘画所特有的题材……动作是诗所特有的

---

1 ［波］塔达基维奇：《西方美学概念史》第3章第9节，第146页。

2 钱钟书：《中国诗与中国画》，《七缀集》，第6—7页。虽然如此，有必要再次强调，他们所说的诗画相合与中国传统的"诗画一律"内涵差别极大，不可将二者混为一谈。有关西方"诗如画"概念内涵的演变，可参见伦塞勒·W. 李《诗如画——人文主义的绘画理论》（李本正译，《新美术》1990年第4期、1991年第1期）、格拉汉《诗如画》（诸葛勤译，《新美术》1990年第3期）二文。

3 ［德］莱辛：《拉奥孔》第21章，第119页。

4 ［德］莱辛：《拉奥孔》第22章，第123页。

5 ［德］莱辛：《拉奥孔》附录一丙，第194页。

题材。"[1]"时间上的先后承续属于诗人的领域，而空间则属于画家的领域。"[2]即莱辛认为诗画艺术间判然存在一条鸿沟：画绘物体，诗写动作；画写一瞬，诗写过程；画属空间，诗属时间；彼此不能逾越，也不应逾越。揆诸中西诗画创作的实际，这都只能是一条难以让人信服的虚拟定律，早有人从不同的角度分析其谬误。

与莱辛同时的德人赫尔德（1744—1803）在《批评之林》中指出，莱辛所规定的诗的特征几乎全以荷马为根据，可荷马的诗只表现了诗的一类即史诗的特征，不能成为普遍规律。荷马史诗的灵魂是动作，抒情诗的灵魂是感情，二者大不相同。同时莱辛对绘画的见解也有问题，只有表情、运动和动作才能赋予雕塑家和画家所描塑的对象以生机，不将这些表现出来，雕塑或绘画就没有生命。[3]朱光潜在20世纪中叶也批评其理论与中国文艺实践的龃龉不合，从画来说，莱辛认为画表现时间上的顷刻，势必静止，而中国画讲六法，首推"气韵生动"；莱辛认为画完整模仿自然，表现空间，而中国向来尊重的文人画画意不画物，所写并非实物而是意境，在精神上与诗相近。从诗来说，莱辛根据西方的剧诗和叙事诗认为诗只宜叙述动作，而中国诗向来不重叙事，史诗在中国可以说不存在，戏剧又向来与诗分开。中国诗的传统是擅长景物描写，与莱辛的学说恰相反对，而"一种学说是否精确，要看它能否到处得到事实的印证，能否用来解释一切有关事实而无罅漏"[4]。

1　[德]莱辛:《拉奥孔》第16章，第82—83页。

2　[德]莱辛:《拉奥孔》第18章，第97页。

3　参见[苏]弗里德连杰尔:《论莱辛的〈拉奥孔〉》，杨汉池译，《现代文艺理论译丛》第6辑，北京：人民文学出版社，1964年，第68页。后来的罗丹也认为"没有生命，即没有艺术"，而"动作"是雕塑的"血与气"，参见[法]罗丹:《罗丹艺术论》第4章，傅雷译，北京：中国社会科学出版社，1999年，第63、67页。美国艺术理论家阿恩海姆（1904—2007）则用完形心理学美学理论分析绘画等视觉艺术如何表现运动的问题，参见[美]阿恩海姆:《艺术与视知觉》第9章，滕守尧、朱疆源译，北京：中国社会科学出版社，1984年，第568—608页。

4　朱光潜:《诗论》第7章第4节，上海：上海古籍出版社，2001年，第128页。该书1943年国民图书出版社初版。后来华裔学者叶维廉也有大致相同的分析，参见叶维廉:《"出位之思"：媒体及超媒体的美学》，《中国诗学》，北京：生活·读书·新知三联书店，1992年，第147—152页。

19世纪后期以降，马奈、莫奈、雷诺阿、高更、梵·高、塞尚等印象派、后印象派画家们的笔下更呈现出光影、色彩和笔触的尽情狂欢，呈现出主观感觉的倾心宣泄，物体的空间性和真实感完全不再成为他们作画的出发点和重心。在这些现代派艺术的实践面前，莱辛人为设置的造型艺术的领域局限于空间中的物体的藩篱更只能土崩瓦解了。

二、关于诗画艺术的描绘

与诗画分属时空的见解相关，莱辛又认为"绘画的理想是一种关于物体的理想，而诗的理想却必须是一种关于动作（或情节）的理想"[1]，诗在描绘属于空间的静止的物体上无能为力，也不该染指。他对以描写自然和人物著称的诗歌大加挞伐，称同代人哈勒（1708—1777）《阿尔卑斯山》"洁白的叶透出深绿的条纹，闪耀着五色缤纷的露珠"等诗句"实在表现不出什么，我从每个字里只听到卖气力的诗人，但是看不到那对象本身"[2]。意大利诗人阿里奥斯陀（1474—1533）描写女巫："从面孔正中垂下悬胆似的鼻，神工鬼斧也不能增损毫芒……雪般的颈项，乳般的胸膛，颈项丰润，胸膛宽大饱满……两只胳膊长短合度，不肥不瘦，一双白皙的手看起来窄而微长。"同样被他讽刺成："一个'宽窄合度'的额头，一个'神工鬼斧也不能增损毫芒'的鼻子，一只'窄而微长'的手，这一切普泛的公式能构成什么样的一种形象呢？"[3]

近年来中国学界不时提及的一个话题是，中西文化的进出口存在逆差，不少学者为自己的好东西不为西人所知感到焦急。从莱辛对于描绘体诗的无端指责和彻底否定可以看出，不为所知未必不是一件好事。如果莱辛有机会读到《诗经》，《卫风·硕人》中的"手如柔荑，肤如凝脂"数句难免要惨遭蹂躏；如果莱辛有机会读到宋玉，《登徒子好色赋》中的"增之一分则太长，减之一分则太

1　［德］莱辛:《拉奥孔》附录一乙，第177页。

2　［德］莱辛:《拉奥孔》第17章，第94页。

3　［德］莱辛:《拉奥孔》第20章，第117页。

短，著粉则太白，施朱则太赤。眉如翠羽，肌如白雪，腰如束素，齿如含贝"岂不也要被骂得灰头土脸？

更糟糕的是，就像不能苟同莱辛对诗歌描写物体美的否定一样，莱辛对绘画描写物体美的肯定也难让人接受。他说"只有绘画才能描写物体美"[1]，其实是认为绘画只能描写物体美，所谓"就绘画来说，它的固有使命就是物体美"[2]。这样，绘画的"范围"自然"狭窄"[3]，绘画自然是一种"贫乏"[4]的艺术，绘画自然就劣于诗歌了。这种对绘画艺术的肤廓理解不仅与着眼表现、强调意境、重视抒情写意的中国传统绘画观大相径庭[5]，也与西方人对绘画功能的认识相去甚远。

西人基于艺术起源于模仿这一基本理念，对绘画模仿自然的优势的确自来看重。从柏拉图称画家是"制造外形者"[6]起，强调绘画再现功能的人络绎不绝，甚至有人不恰当地将逼真作为画优于诗的重要理由（如达·芬奇）。

其实不仅西人，以传神为上的中国绘画同样有着重视描绘功能的传统。唐人白居易说："画无常工，以似为工；学无常师，以真为师。"[7]宋人韩琦说："观画之术，唯逼真而已。得真之全者，绝也；得多者，上也；非真即下矣。"[8]因之而视绘画为优的人也可谓屡见不鲜。如元人方回说："文士有数千百言不能尽者，一画手能以数笔尽之。诗人于物象极力模写或不能尽，丹青者流邂逅涂抹，辄出其上。"[9]明人何良俊说："余观古之登山者，皆有游名山记。纵其文笔高妙，善于摩

1 ［德］莱辛:《拉奥孔》第20章，第111页。

2 ［德］莱辛:《拉奥孔》附录一丙，第194页。

3 ［德］莱辛:《拉奥孔》前言，第3页。

4 ［德］莱辛:《拉奥孔》第10章，第62页。

5 中国画学对绘画"摅发人思"功能的阐发，请参见拙文《"诗画一律"的内涵》，《文学遗产》2008年第6期。

6 ［古希腊］柏拉图:《柏拉图文艺对话集·理想国卷十》，朱光潜译，北京：人民文学出版社，1963年，第69页。

7 白居易:《记画》，《白居易集》卷四十三，北京：中华书局，1979年，第937页。

8 韩琦:《题刘御药画册》，《宋诗钞》卷三《安阳集钞》小序引，北京：中华书局，1986年，第99页。通行本《安阳集》未见。

9 何良俊:《钱瓶吴处士善画序》，《桐江续集》卷三十三，文渊阁《四库全书》本。

写，极力形容，处处精到，然于语言文字之间，使人想像，终不得其面目。不若图之缣素，则其山水之幽深，烟云之吞吐，一举目皆在，而吾得以神游其间，顾不胜于文章万万耶?"[1]

但绘画所能传达的岂止是画中物，同样能表现画外意。18世纪以降的西方画论于此发明亦多。法国风景画家柯罗（1796—1872）说："现实是艺术的一部分，只有感情才是艺术的全部。"[2]罗丹说："只满足于形似到乱真，拘泥于无足道的细节表现的画家，将永远不能成为大师。"并宣称："艺术就是感情。"[3]西方现代绘画更将绘画视作表现而不是再现的工具，如法国野兽派画家马蒂斯（1869—1954）表示："我们对于绘画有着更崇高的概念。它是画家体现他的内在感觉的工具。"[4]西班牙画家毕加索（1881—1973）也说："绘画有自身的价值，不在于对事物的如实的描写。"[5]他们的作品对于形似的反叛，已是绘画史上的常识了。

诗画有无区别？答案是肯定的。但只是手段之别、形式之别，若论抒情达意这一本质功能，诗画并无二致！其实何止诗画，一切艺术都是创作者审美情感的物化形态。当代美国学者苏珊·朗格（1895—1982）说得好："假如你继续仔细地和深入地探查各类艺术之间的区别，你就会达到那个从中再也找不到各门艺术之间的区别的纵深层次"，即"一切艺术都是创造出来的表现人类情感的知觉形式"！[6]

三、关于绘画能否表现丑

莱辛认为："诗人可以运用形体的丑。对于画家，丑有什么用途呢？就它作

---

1 何良俊:《四友斋丛说》卷二十八，北京：中华书局，1997年，第257页。中国古人对诗歌描绘功能的
　重视，请参见上举拙文。

2 今东编译:《柯罗、米勒、库尔贝》，天津：天津人民美术出版社，1983年，第26页。

3 ［法］罗丹:《罗丹艺术论·遗嘱》，第4页。

4 ［法］马蒂斯:《论艺术》，《画家笔记》，钱琼平译，桂林：广西师范大学出版社，2002年，第53页。

5 ［德］瓦尔特·赫斯编:《欧洲现代画派画论选·巴勃洛·毕加索》，《宗白华美学文学译文选》，文艺
　美学丛书编辑委员会编，北京：北京大学出版社，1982年，第258页。

6 ［美］苏珊·朗格:《艺术问题》第6讲，北京：中国社会科学出版社，1983年，第74—75页。

为模仿的技能来说，绘画有能力去表现丑；就它作为美的艺术来说，绘画却拒绝表现丑。"[1]这样的判断仍然基于绘画的表现面较诗歌为窄、诗优于画的基本思想，既不适用于古希腊绘画，从更广阔的世界绘画史来看就更乖剌不合。

公元前四世纪的亚里士多德就说"事物本身看上去尽管引起痛感，但惟妙惟肖的图像看上去却能引起我们的快感，例如尸首或最可鄙的动物形象"，并分析快感产生的原因，是人喜爱模仿和佩服画家技巧的天性。[2]同为德国学者，稍晚于莱辛的希尔特（1759—1839）、叔本华（1788—1860）更针对莱辛等人"客观美是古代艺术的原则"的观点提出异议。前者指出，不朽的古希腊绘画"表现了各种各样的姿容，既有最美的，也有最普通的，甚至有最丑的，而表情的再现也总是符合性格和动机。因此，我认为古代艺术的原则不是客观美和表情的柔和，而只是富于个性的意蕴，即特征"[3]。后者则说，古代造型艺术作品中的美"不是用一个，而是用好多带有不同特性的形象来表出的"，"性格方面甚至可以出现为丑"。[4]后来的罗丹对此有更精彩的阐述："自然中认为丑的，往往要比那认为美的更显露出它的'性格'，因为内在真实在愁苦的病容上，在皱蹙秽恶的瘦脸上，在各种畸形与残缺上，比在正常健全的相貌上更加明显地呈现出来。既然只有'性格'的力量才能造成艺术的美，所以常有这样的事：在自然中越是丑的，在艺术中越是美。在艺术中，只是那些没有性格的，就是说毫不显示外部的和内在的真实的作品，才是丑的。"[5]这些见解岂不较莱辛深刻得多！罗丹本人喜欢采用丑陋的模型，正如荷兰画家伦勃朗（1606—1669）喜欢描绘老朽，西班牙画家委拉斯开兹（1599—1660）喜欢表现残废，这类作品以特殊的艺术感染力，

1　[法]莱辛：《拉奥孔》第24章，第135页。

2　[古希腊]亚理斯多德：《诗学》第4章，第11页。活跃于公元1世纪的普鲁塔克观点与此全同，参见　[英]鲍桑葵：《美学史》第5章第2节，第142页。

3　[德]希尔特：《古代造型艺术史前言》，转引自[英]鲍桑葵：《美学史》第9章第2节，第255页。

4　[德]叔本华：《作为意志和表象的世界》第3篇第45节，石冲白译，北京：商务印书馆，1982年，第313页。

5　[法]罗丹：《罗丹艺术论》第2章，第26页。

成就了自己不朽的名声。

在《拉奥孔》第2章中，莱辛以不屑的口吻提到希腊画家庇越库斯勤勉地"专画理发铺，肮脏的工作坊，驴子和蔬菜，好像这类事物在自然中是非常引人入胜的而且是非常希罕的，所以他得到一个'污秽画家'的诨号"。人们常争论美属于主观还是客观，读到这段话的人如果碰巧看见过黄冑的驴、齐白石的大白菜，就一定会感慨美不仅属于主观，也属于特定的文化！张大千画过一幅题为"观物之生"的小品，上有萝卜、白菜数棵。右上角题："偶同子杰莱市见此，索予图之，时希腊爱能小姐在座，大以为奇笔也。"[1]爱能小姐何以视为奇笔，想来就是文化差异的问题。明清之际书法家傅山早说过："宁丑毋媚。"[2]清人郑燮则说："米元章论石，曰瘦、曰绉、曰漏、曰透，可谓尽石之妙矣。东坡又曰：'石文而丑。'一丑字，则石之千态万状，皆从此出。"[3]说莱辛的理论见识在我们的苏轼、傅山、郑板桥之下，不至于委屈他吧！

四、关于绘画艺术的想象

文艺创作和欣赏中想象的重要性，先哲多有发明。黑格尔说："如果谈到本领，最杰出的艺术本领就是想像。"[4]德拉克罗瓦为"想像"下的定义是："对于一个艺术家来说，这是他所应具备的最崇高的品质；对于一个艺术爱好者来说，这一点也同样不可缺少。"[5]苏珊·朗格则说："感性形式和艺术表现力量可以随着人的想像力的丰富而不断地增长。"[6]莱辛对造型艺术欣赏中想象力的作用也并非无所见。他说："凡是我们在艺术作品里发见为美的东西，并不是直接由眼睛，而是由想像力通过眼睛去发见其为美的。"[7]他提出艺术家不能选取情节发展中的顶

1　图见姚梦谷等编纂：《张大千画集》，台北：台湾历史博物馆，1979年，第102页。

2　傅山：《作字示儿孙》，《霜红龛集》卷四，清宣统三年山阳丁宝铨刊本。

3　郑板桥：《郑板桥集·题画·石》，上海：上海古籍出版社，1979年，第163页。

4　[德]黑格尔：《美学》第1卷第3章C·1，第357页。

5　[法]德拉克罗瓦：《德拉克罗瓦日记·1857年1月25日》，李嘉熙译，桂林：广西师范大学出版社，2002年，第447页。

6　[美]苏珊·朗格：《艺术问题》第7讲，第88—89页。

7　[德]莱辛：《拉奥孔》第6章，第41页。

点，因为"到了顶点就到了止境，眼睛就不能朝更远的地方去看，想像就被捆住了翅膀"[1]，正如王朝闻所说，这"不是不善于欣赏艺术者所能提出的"[2]。

问题在于，莱辛不全是以肯定的语气提及这种想象。他将这种想象理解为"欺骗"，说"动物的眼睛要比人的眼睛难受欺骗些；动物只看见他们实在看到的东西，我们人类却被想像所迷惑，所以我们相信看见自己实在没有看到的东西"[3]。他并不因此排斥诗歌创作与欣赏中想象的作用。诗歌中的拉奥孔不妨穿上衣服，因为"对于诗人来说，衣服并不算衣服，它遮掩不住什么，我们的想像总是能透过衣服去看"。可是他却认为雕像中的拉奥孔只能表现为裸体，"假如他（雕塑家——引者）让拉奥孔还带上头巾，表情就会大为削弱"[4]。这表明莱辛认为欣赏雕塑只是眼睛的工作，不需要大脑参与，将想象完全抛弃在造型艺术欣赏之外了。

有了这种误解，对绘画有所谓种种不足的误解也就从而产生了，如前引狄德罗认为绘画只能表现一瞬间，莱辛认为绘画只能描绘空间和物体之类。有意思的是，中国古人持有类似误解的也不在少数，钱钟书在他的名文《读〈拉奥孔〉》中举出过一些，如明人张岱谓王维"泉声咽危石，日色冷青松"的诗句，"'咽'字、'冷'字决难画出"之类。遗憾的是，钱钟书本人对此类见解是完全首肯的，认为它们不仅能为莱辛的观点张目，还可成为莱辛的补充。那就是，画不仅不能表现时间上的承先启后，"像嗅觉（'香'）、触觉（'湿'、'冷'）、听觉（'声咽'、'鸣钟作磬'）的事物，以及不同于悲、喜、怒、愁等有显明表情的内心状态（'思乡'），也都是'难画'、'画不出'的"[5]。

可是，如果我们承认高水平的画家在创作中、高水平的欣赏者在欣赏时能够而且应该运用"想像"这一"最杰出的艺术本领"，画作就可臻于意余于象、画尽意在的境地，欣赏者就可臻于作者不著迹象而观者宛在心目的境地，绘画性就

1 〔德〕莱辛：《拉奥孔》第3章，第19页。
2 王朝闻：《不到顶点》，《王朝闻学术论著自选集》，北京：北京师范大学出版社，1991年，第439页。
3 〔德〕莱辛：《拉奥孔》附录一丙·B·8提纲B，45，第198页。
4 〔德〕莱辛：《拉奥孔》第5章，第39页。
5 钱钟书：《读〈拉奥孔〉》，《七缀集》，第38页。

不等同于描绘性[1]，绘画从根本上讲，就不存在上面所说的这些局限了。蒋寅文中引清嘉道间潘焕龙《卧园诗话》卷二："昔人谓诗中有画，画中有诗，然绘水者不能绘水之声，绘物者不能绘物之影，绘人者不能绘人之情，诗则无不可绘，此所以较绘事为尤妙也。"（道光刊本）不知早于潘氏的康乾间邹一桂早就驳斥过这样的观点："人有言：绘雪者不能绘其清，绘月者不能绘其明，绘花者不能绘其馨，绘人者不能绘其情。以数者虚而不可以形求也。不知实者逼肖，则虚者自出，故画北风图则生凉，画云汉图则生热[2]，画水于壁则夜闻水声。谓为不能者，固不知画者也！"[3]诚哉是言！画能画声[4]，能画语[5]，能画物之动[6]，能画火之性[7]，能画花之香[8]，能画马腹中事[9]，能画人情性笑言之姿[10]，能使欣赏者宛然置身于真实情境[11]，前人固已屡言之矣。

1　蒋寅在《对王维"诗中有画"的质疑》中说："绘画对视觉以外诸觉表达的无能，并不是什么深奥的道理，稍有头脑的人都会理解。"（《文学评论》2000年第4期）这就是将绘画性与描绘性等而同之。

2　唐张彦远记后汉刘褒："曾画云汉图，人见之觉热；又画北风图，人见之觉凉。"（《历代名画记》卷四，北京：人民美术出版社，1983年，第101页）

3　邹一桂《小山画谱》卷下《绘实绘虚》，《画论丛刊》下册，于安澜编，北京：人民美术出版社，1960年，第797页。着重号为引者所加。按宋罗大经《鹤林玉露·丙编卷六》云："绘雪者不能绘其清，绘月者不能绘其明，绘花者不能绘其馨，绘泉者不能绘其声，绘人者不能绘其情。"（北京：人民文学出版社，1983年，第336页）

4　宋米芾称画家范宽："溪出深虚，水若有声。"（《画史》，北京：中华书局，1985年）苏轼称画家李伯时："龙眠独识殷勤处，画出阳关意外声。"（《书林次中所得李伯时归去来、阳关二图后》，《苏轼诗集》卷三十，北京：中华书局，1982年，第1599页）

5　邹一桂《小山画谱》卷下："花如欲语。"（《画论丛刊》本）

6　白居易赞萧悦画竹："萧画枝活叶叶动。"（《画竹歌》，《白居易集》卷十二）

7　宋李廌《德隅斋画品》称唐末张南本画火"笔气焱锐，得火之性"（《画品丛书》本）。

8　苏轼《王伯敭所藏赵昌花四首·黄葵》："君看此花枝，中有风露香。"

9　苏辙《韩干三马》："画出三马腹中事。"（《栾城集》卷十五，上海：上海古籍出版社，1987年）

10　宋郭若虚《图画见闻志》卷五《周昉》载，周昉为赵纵画像，赵夫人称其"得赵郎情性笑言之姿"（北京：人民美术出版社，1983年）。

11　唐方干《卢卓山人画水》："坐久神迷不能决，却疑身在小蓬瀛。"（《全唐诗》卷六百五十一，北京：中华书局，1985年）宋人黄庭坚《题郑防画夹五首》其一："惠崇烟雨归雁，坐我潇湘洞庭。"（《黄庭坚诗集注·山谷诗集注卷七》，北京：中华书局，2003年）

又比如，钱氏在上举文中举出明代画家董其昌的话，以证明画家自己也感到绘画的局限："'水作罗浮磬，山鸣于阗钟'，此太白诗，何必右丞诗中画也？画中欲收钟、磬不可得！"殊不知就是这位董其昌又说过这样一段话："右丞《田园乐》有'萋萋芳草秋绿，落落长松夏寒'，余采其意为此图赠士抑兄。"[1]更早还有宋人郭思列举其父郭熙生前"所诵道古人清篇秀句，有发于佳思而可画者，并思亦尝旁搜广引，先子谓为可用者"[2]，如羊士谔《望女几山》的"心期欲去知何日，惆望回车下野桥"、长孙佐辅《寻山家》的"独访山家歇还涉，茅屋斜连隔松叶"、王维《终南别业》的"行到水穷处，坐看云起时"等。按照钱氏所举各家及其本人的说法，不论是董其昌所画的《田园乐》还是郭思所举各条都难入画。"寒"而且是"夏寒"如何画？"秋"绿的芳草与"夏"日的寒松如何和平共处一幅画中？"惆望"属于"显明表情的内心状态"，可画，可"心期欲去"又如何画呢？"歇还涉"的连续动作，"行到""坐看"的那种禅意又如何画呢！而所有这些，却实不足以成为画家采之入画的障碍，毋宁说，高明的画家宁愿择取这些可以充分激发其灵感、发挥其想象的诗句，将其中的无限意蕴表现于画；所有这些，也不能成为欣赏者欣赏画作的障碍，毋宁说，意蕴越丰厚的画作越能够吸引有艺术鉴赏力的欣赏者，用自己的想象参与创造性的欣赏过程，补充画面没有直接表现的内涵和情节，感受甚至画家自己也未必感受到的一切！顾恺之的"迁想妙得"[3]，苏轼的"古来画士非俗士，妙想实与诗同出"[4]，均是强调想象对画家创作的重要，但对欣赏者一样适用。

一幅画能反映什么，取决于创作者和欣赏者双方的共同作用。创作的能力有限，或欣赏的水平不高，则画不过是一堆线条、墨块或色彩；反之则无不能表现，至少其表现力绝不在诗歌之下！中国古人和西方古人不早说过："天下妙士，

1　董其昌：《画禅室随笔·题自画·松冈远岫为何司理题》，《艺林名著丛刊》本，北京：中国书店，1983年，第55页。

2　郭思：《林泉高致集·画意》，《画论丛刊》上册，第24页。

3　顾恺之：《论画》，《历代名画记》卷五，第116页。

4　苏轼：《次韵吴传正枯木歌》，《苏轼诗集》卷三十六，第1962页。

必有妙眼。渠见妙景，便会将妙手写出来。"[1] "如果你想得到艺术的享受，那你就必须是一个有艺术修养的人。"[2]

结　语

莱辛在《拉奥孔》前言中说，就各类艺术所以能给人带来快感和美的规律进行思考，这样的人就是艺术批评家。无疑，他的这本书就是艺术批评家的工作。他又说，艺术批评家"如果每次把论断运用到个别具体事例上去时，都很小心谨慎，对画和诗都一样公平，那简直是一种奇迹"，我以为这却被他不幸言中了。究其原因，或许在于他自己已经警觉到的，"单从一些一般性的概念出发，去对艺术进行推理，很可能导致一些任意武断的见解，迟早会为艺术作品所推翻"[3]。也可能在于朱光潜所分析的："艺术是变化无穷的，不容易纳到几个很简赅固定的公式里去。莱辛的毛病，像许多批评家一样，就在想勉强找几个很简赅固定的公式来范围艺术。"[4]

但应该指出的是，莱辛的诗画关系理论中并没有完全忽视诗画间的联系。他打比方道："两个善良友好的邻邦，虽然互不容许对方在自己的领域中心采取不适当的自由行动，但是在边界上，在较小的问题上，却可以互相宽容，对仓促中迫于形势的稍微侵犯权利的事件付出和平的赔偿，画和诗的关系也是如此。"[5]俄国学者弗里德连杰尔说："最初，莱辛本来打算把《拉奥孔》写成由三个部分组成的著作。他生前仅仅完成和发表了其中的一个部分。由保存下来的其余部分的草稿里可以明显看出，对于诗和造型艺术之间界限的相对性问题莱辛曾经作过专

1　金圣叹：《杜诗解》卷二《戏题王宰画山水图歌》，上海：上海古籍出版社，1984年，第103页。

2　［德］马克思：《1844年经济学哲学手稿·货币》，北京：人民出版社，1985年，第112页。

3　［德］莱辛：《拉奥孔》第26章，第148页。

4　朱光潜：《诗论》第7章第4节，第130页。

5　［德］莱辛：《拉奥孔》第18章，第98页。

门研究。按照本文作者的想法，这个问题在《拉奥孔》后两部分应该比在第一部分作更多的阐明。"[1]这种推测应当是正确的。

更需要强调的是，我们在看到莱辛诗画理论不足的同时，应充分理解莱辛如此重视诗画分界的文化背景和思想意义。小莱辛20岁的德国最伟大的文学家歌德（1749—1832）曾说："我们要设想自己是青年，才能想像莱辛的《拉奥孔》一书给予我们的影响是怎样，因为这本著作把我们从贫乏的直观的世界摄引到思想的开阔的原野了。"[2]俄国理论家车尔尼雪夫斯基（1828—1889）也说："从亚里斯多德的时期以来，没有一个能够像莱辛那么正确深刻地理解诗的本质。"[3]

《拉奥孔》何以能赢得一代文豪和理论大家如此高的评价呢？那就是另一位俄国理论家杜勃罗留波夫（1836—1861）所分析的："莱辛通过《拉奥孔》而创造了新的诗论，把生活带进诗论之中，并且粉碎了以前在一切美学中占统治地位的那种死气沉沉的形式主义作风……自从《拉奥孔》出现以来，被公认为诗的本质内容的是变动不居的生活，而不是死板板的形式。"[4]也是德人保尔·莱曼所说的："《拉奥孔》的核心是明确划定诗和绘画之间的区别，这个问题对德国文学的发展具有不可估量的实际意义。实际上，在这里涉及了前进还是后退的问题，涉及到最终战胜整个潮流的问题，战胜作为小资产阶级贪图安逸、骄傲自满的表现的描写性的、田园诗般的'绘画式'文学的问题。莱辛提出动作是诗歌的重要因素，提出了诗歌的战斗任务，虽然他没有直说，事实上是把戏剧文学看作为最重要的文学体裁。"[5]就是说，这和它在18世纪德国乃至整个欧洲启蒙运动中的作用

---

1 ［苏］弗里德连杰尔：《论莱辛的〈拉奥孔〉》，杨汉池译，《现代文艺理论译丛》第6辑，第51页。

2 ［德］歌德：《诗与真》第2部第8卷，刘思慕译，北京：人民文学出版社，1999年，第323页。

3 ［俄］车尔尼雪夫斯基：《莱辛，他的时代，他的一生与活动》第5章，《车尔尼雪夫斯基论文学》中卷，辛未艾译，上海：上海译文出版社，1979年，第425页。

4 《杜勃罗留波夫全集》第5卷，莫斯科：苏联国立文学出版社，1941年，第321—322页。此据弗里德连杰尔《论莱辛的〈拉奥孔〉》转引，苏第41页。

5 ［德］莱曼：《〈拉奥孔〉和德国戏剧》，杨德友译，《山西大学学报（哲学社会科学版）》1980年第4期。

是分不开的。

从这一角度讲，如何评价莱辛在欧洲文艺学史以及思想文化史上的贡献都不为过。相形之下，其有关诗画分界的一些偏颇，对绘画艺术的一些偏见，似乎就算不得什么了。

虽然如此，作为一个重要的学术命题，尤其它曾深刻影响了中国学者对诗画关系的看法[1]，其中的一些偏颇、不足以至错误，必须引起我们足够的重视。我们在分析、研究诗画关系，尤其是与西方迥然不同的中国传统诗画关系时，不必也不能一切唯《拉奥孔》的马首是瞻。

（文章发表于《中国社会科学》2008年第6期。本文系作者在联盟2017年年度论坛上的发言）

---

1 比如，钱钟书在《读〈拉奥孔〉》中完全搬用莱辛诗画异质、诗优于画的观点分析中国传统诗画，论证诗歌的无所不能和绘画的种种无能。蒋寅也在《对王维"诗中有画"的质疑》中力驳苏东坡对王维"诗中有画"的定评，理由是："我们不应该忘记莱辛的告诫，'能入画与否不是判定诗的好坏的标准！'"

试论中西文化的语言基础

褚孝泉*

文者纹也，世上的文化都是缀绣在一定的语言底色上的华彩，不同的语言构成了文化的不同素底。如果我们分别观察一下西方文化和华夏文化所得以生长的语言背景，或许可以看到中西文化之间重大差异的一些因缘。

我们可以先探索一下在所谓的轴心时代期间中西两边的语言情况。最近几十年是中国考古大发现的时代，最令人兴奋的莫过于古代简帛文献的出土，目前还在释读中的这些简册，让我们第一次看到了战国秦汉时古人读的书的原貌。这些佚失了两千多年的典籍提供了古代思想的珍贵资料，可以据以改写中国古代思想史，然而这些文本包含的语言信息也很值得我们注意。至今出土的所有这些简帛文献，都用同一种语言写成。[1]对于中国文化传统中的研究者来说，这毫不奇怪，或许觉得是理所当然的。但是如果我们了解一下西方的情况，就会发现这其实是非常独特的文化现象。二十世纪中叶在西方也有类似的出土文献发现。最著名的要算是在约旦河谷中发现的死海古卷和在埃及沙漠中发现的俄克喜林库斯纸草文卷。死海古卷的书写年代大致是在公元前三世纪到公元一世纪，和中国发现的简帛的制作时间大致相当。死海古卷的内容基本上都与希伯来圣经有关，使用的语言文字有希伯来语、阿拉姆语、古希腊语、拉丁语和阿拉伯语等。俄克喜林库斯纸草文卷跨越的时间段更长，从公元前三世纪一直到公元七世纪，其内容也颇为

---

* 褚孝泉：复旦大学外国语言文学学院教授。研究领域：理论语言学、语言学思想史、社会语言学、句法学、符号学等。

1 ［日］横田恭三：《中国古代简牍综览》，张建平译，北京：北京联合出版公司，2017年，第6—9页。

庞杂，除了典籍片段还有法令、书信、税赋记录、契约等，这些纸草纸文卷至今还在拼接释读过程中，学者们在这些古卷中已经读到了古希腊语、古埃及语（包括用古象形文字，通俗文和科普特文书写成的）、拉丁语、阿拉伯语、希伯来语、阿拉姆语、古叙利亚语和巴拉维语等写成的文本。更往上溯，更往中心地带去，我们发现的还是类似的繁复的语言状况。不仅在公元前后几个世纪中，在中东的这个列国势力犬牙交错的边缘地区里所发现的古卷中，我们读到有多种语言写成的文本；在历史的更深处，在上古大帝国的中心，也同样地流行多种语言。公元前十六至前十三世纪兴盛的赫梯帝国显然就是建立在一个并行使用多个语种的文化环境中的。二十世纪在土耳其安卡拉以西地区发掘出来的赫梯帝国的王家图书馆里，我们读到了赫梯语、阿卡德语、胡利安语、卢维语和巴莱语的文本。而对比来看，与此在时间和地位相近的中国商周时代的甲骨文文献却都是以上古汉语这单一语言写成。

在西方文明起源地区发现的这些古文卷中出现了这么多种语言文字，这并不令学者惊奇，因为中东地区一直是个种族杂居的地区，文本中出现多语现象很自然。需要解释的是中国出土的古文本中的语言单一现象，目前我们看到的战国简大都出土自楚国，先秦时代荆楚地区不属于华夏文化的核心地区，其在华夏文化圈的边缘地位，恰与公元前后中东地区在西方文化圈里的空间地位相仿佛。目前发现的汉简涉及的空间范围更加广大，从甘肃武威到江苏仪征，从内蒙古额齐纳汉边塞到广西贵县，纵横数千里都有汉简出土。时间上的间距更是令人瞩目。战国楚简目前一般被认定为写成于公元前四世纪左右，许多汉简的写作年代要晚至西汉末年，三国吴简则晚至东汉末年。这些简册的年代前后跨越五六百年，然而，除了文字形体上有从战国文字到秦统一的小篆到汉隶的变化，就语言本体来说，书写在这些简册上的语言非常恒定和一致，从词汇到句法都确切地属于同一种语言。我们知道，人类语言在空间的扩散和在时间的延续过程中必定会发生变异，导致方言和新的语言的产生，这是历史语言学揭示的规律，没有理由认为汉语能够是个例外。古人早就明白这个道理，《礼记·王制》说到"五方之民，言语不通"。颜之推指出,"夫九州之人,言语不同,生民已来,固常然矣。自春秋标齐音之传,离骚目楚词之经,此盖较明之初也"[1]。比如战国时楚人的语言显然和中原地区的语言相当不同,杨雄的《方言》记录了他观察到的汉语方言的词语差异。除了汉语的方言,当时中国大地上也还有许多非汉语的语言存在,在秦晋燕赵的境内境外都生活着被称为夷狄的族群,他们说的语言当然不是汉语。然而,在我们目前能看到的当时书写成的典籍文书中没有多语的迹象。西方文明摇篮时期的多语状态,在华夏文明的同时期并不存在,我们有的是一种稳固的单语文化氛围。可以说西方文明是绣在一个杂色的语文底版上的,而华夏文明则是演绎在单色的基底上的。

　　中国的古文书所显示的这种单语状态的原因是什么呢?有个技术性的原因不容忽视,那就是文字的影响。文字是人类最伟大的技术发明,而汉字的发明则对华夏文明的产生和发展有着决定性的作用。汉字最突出的特点是它和汉语的紧密关联,可以说汉字是专为汉语设计的,难以转用于书写其他语言。而起源于美索不达米亚的西方文字体系,在做了些调整后就可以适用于书写不同的语言。苏美尔人在公元前三千年发明的楔形文字很快就被借用来书写阿卡德语、伊兰语、赫梯语等许多种中东地区的早期语言,尽管这些语言互相差别非常大,属于不同的语族。公元前十世纪后腓尼基人发明的字母更可以被灵活地用来书写许多不同的语言,例如古希腊语;而罗马人改造后的拉丁字母后来被广泛用来书写世界上大多数的语言。汉字并不具备这种书写的通用性,作为一种书写体系,汉字和汉语之间更有一种特别紧密的契合。汉字早期被用来书写日语、朝鲜语和越南语,然后在我们的这些邻国里,汉字终究被更适合那里的语言的假名、谚文和罗马字母所取代了(日语里当用汉字被限定了数量,并且常常要用假名来注音)。汉字也曾被用来记录蒙古语的《蒙古秘史》,这部书的释读之难,也表明了汉字作为一种文字系统,与其他语系的语言很不相配。可以设想,在先秦汉魏时代,即便中

1　颜之推:《颜氏家训·音辞第十八》,《诸子集成》第八册,北京:中华书局,1954年,第40页。

国周边和内陆有许许多多使用非汉语语言的族群，他们的文化创造很难用汉字摹写下来。蒙古文、藏文、满文等都是相当晚期的发明了，因此在我们看到的简帛上没有汉语以外的语言痕迹。

不过，汉字的特点这个技术性条件无法从根本上解释华夏文明的单语性。毕竟，需要是发明之母，如果汉语以外的语言在中国文化体系里有其地位，合适的书写方式应该会被发明出来的。事实上也确实有这样的发明，如契丹文和西夏文。但是这些异族古文字都慢慢湮没在历史长河中，传承到今天的华夏文化遗产几无例外都是以汉字写成的。这令人设想，非汉族语言在中国早期文明的文本中的缺席自有其更深层的原因。

我们知道，世界上绝大多数的社群事实上都是生活在多语种的环境中的。社会语言学家们早就观察到，在一定的社会文化结构中，总有不同的语言起着不同的作用并被赋予不同的地位。美国社会语言学家弗格森（Ferguson）曾经定义过一个非常有名的概念——"双层语言"（diglossia），指的是人们会在上层社会生活中和下层社会生活中使用两种不同的方言或语言，显然在许多社会里都存在着这种双层语言现象[1]，例如在当代中国，大多数人会在工作单位或其他正式场合说普通话，而在家里或休闲的场合说自己家乡的方言，普通话就是上层语言，方言就是下层语言。在印度和非洲的许多国家里，人们会根据交际对象的不同而转换使用自己的本族语言和地区或国家的通用语，乡村里使用的族群语言就是下层语言而地区或国家的通用语就是上层语言。然而，这个"双层语言"的概念并不能很好地解释中国文化传统中的语言差异现象，我们在中国文化传统中观察到的语言分布状况与弗格森的"双层语言"结构似相近但又很不一样。"双层语言"指向的是社会中的一般语言交际方式，特别是口语交际方式，而我们想说明的是文化特别是精英文化创造和传承中的语言使用状况。华夏文明和西方文明都属于建立在文字记载上的书面文明，因此我们需要区分的不是口语中的上层语言和下层

1　Ferguson, "Diglossia," *Word*, 15, pp. 325–340, reprinted in Dell Hymes ed. *Language in Culture and Society*, New York : Harpers and Row, pp. 429–439.

语言，而是能够以书面形式保存的语言和一般交际语言。前者可以被称为精英文化语言，后者则是即时交流用语。用来写成表达核心思想的典籍——宗教圣书、诏书法令、历史文献、外交文书、诗赋文章等的是精英文化语言；而面对面的言说使用的是一般交流语言，除了偶然被史家用书面语记录下来，随风而逝不留痕迹。当我们说华夏文化具有独特的单语特点，我们并不是说在中华大地上只有一种语言存在，华夏大地上一直有众多语言，这和西方一样，不同之处在于，在我们的文化传统里，除了汉语，没有其他语言被提升到精英文化语言的地位，而在西方传统里一直有多种语言上升到精英文化语言的地位。因此，传统华夏文明的社会语言交替的地位起落不是表现在不同的口头话语的使用上的，而是以书面文化语和日常口语的界限来划分的。中华文明的书面文化语言以汉字为唯一载体，这种书面文化语言在先秦时期形成并固定后，被使用于中华文明所覆盖的广大地区，举凡政治、外交、文学、思想等精英文化领域里的交流，都使用这种统一的书面文化语。汉文之文，在中华文明中起着非常重大的作用，因此也被赋予了至高的象征意义，所谓"文章，经国之大业，不朽之盛事"[1]，"文"不仅构作成今天所说的文学创作，还是整个社会国家得以形成的织体，"文者，礼教治政云尔，其书诸策而传之人大体归然而已"[2]。汉语中"文"这个词的含义很快从指书面文字扩大到指称国家的整个统治意识和制度，甚至超越经验而关涉大道之行，"心生而言立，言立而文明，自然之道也，……道沿圣以垂文，圣因文而明道，旁通而无滞，日用而不匮。易曰：鼓天下之动者，存乎辞，辞之所以能鼓天下者，乃道之文也"[3]。"文"所具有的这个崇高地位并不是偶然的，这与书面语言在中华文明中所起的至上作用密切相关。今天我们能读到的古代文化遗存，毫无例外地都是使用这种唯一的书面文化语写成的；相反，在口头交际时，即使是在庙

---

1 曹丕：《典论》，《魏晋文举要》，高步瀛选注，北京：中华书局，1989年，第16页。

2 王安石：《上人书》，《全宋文》第六十四册，上海：上海辞书出版社；合肥：安徽教育出版社，第167页。

3 刘勰：《增订文心雕龙校注·卷一·原道第一》，北京：中华书局，2012年，第2页。

堂之上，使用方言或带着浓重方言口音说话并不有损于说话者的地位声望。《世说新语》记载的一个逸事颇能表明社会精英对方言的态度，刘惔去见丞相王导，"刘既出，人问见王公云何，刘曰，未见他异，唯闻作吴语"[1]。刘惔语带讥讽，并不是因为王导说了方言，而是由于南渡的北方士族不喜南方吴语。陈寅恪以为，"永嘉南渡之士族，其北方原籍虽各有不同，然大抵操洛阳近傍之方言，似无疑义"，"东晋南朝官吏接士人则用北语，接庶人则用吴语"[2]。据此，我们知道古代中华文明中的社会语言学意义上的高低之分不在于口语方言的差异上，而主要在书面文化语言和一般交际语言之间。上古华夏文明世界范围里没有汉语以外的其他书面文化语言存在，汉语书面文化语言构成了唯一的上层社会文化空间，这导致了中华文明的一个非常独特的语言文化特征，那就是非常恒定而单一的书面语成了社会精英唯一使用和关注的文化载体，而几乎不理会世上还有什么其他语言。北齐人颜之推很明白地阐述了汉语这种书面文化语言对中国社会的重要性所在："自古明王圣帝，犹须勤学。况凡庶乎。此事偏于经史"，"士大夫子弟，数岁以上，莫不被教，多者或至礼传，少者不失诗论"，"自荒乱已来，诸见俘虏。虽百世小人，知读论语孝经者，尚为人师；虽千载冠冕，不晓书记者，莫不耕田养马。以此观之，安可不自勉耶。若常保数百卷书，千载终不为小人也。夫明六经之指，涉百家之书，纵不能增益德行敦厉风俗，犹为一艺，得以自资"[3]。值得我们注意的是，他发这番议论的背景是异族语言盛行的北胡地区，权势人物大都以非汉族语言为母语。然而，即便那里的王公贵族都操胡语，士人们只有精通经典的汉文，才不致沦为小人。士族精英从不觉得异族语言有什么值得注意的价值，汉唐以来，尽管和中原地区有交往的边地民族使用的语言种类并不少，并没有第二位杨雄来描写和记录各地的种种夷语胡话。

中华文明的这种单一语言性深刻地影响了中华文化传统的面貌。每种文化的

---

1 刘义庆：《世说新语笺疏》，北京：中华书局，2011年，第684页。

2 刘义庆：《世说新语笺疏》，第687页。

3 颜之推：《颜氏家训·勉学第八》，《诸子集成》第八册，第13页。

内涵及其发展趋向，在很大程度上取决于承载该文化的阶层所受的教育的内容；接受什么样的教养便会有什么样的知识和精神上的准备，后继创造出的文化产品就会有什么样的特质。因此，对任何文化来说，在其历史中形成的教育体系会对该文化的发展前景规定方向和限定范围，而所有的教育体系都是无例外地围绕着该文化的精英语言而发展起来的。如果要比较中华文明和西方文明的差异，这两种文明传统中的不同教育要求是一个重要的观察点，而其对文化继承者的语言素养的不同要求和规定，则是一个值得探究的题目。

多语教育在西方文化的人文教育体系中一直占据着中心地位，是否懂得和掌握多个语言，一直是西方社会衡量一个人的教养水平的重要标准。在古罗马，无论是共和国时代还是帝国时代，罗马贵族子弟从小就必须学习希腊语。公元一世纪时，昆体良（Quintilian）在他的《雄辩术原理》中建议，每个罗马孩子应该先学讲希腊语，应该学习希腊文法，再学讲拉丁语，他同时指出，罗马人实际上也就是在这样做的。[1] 许多罗马贵族家庭都直接从希腊找来希腊老师教授他们的孩子讲读希腊语，结果罗马有了一大批娴熟于两种语言的贵族人士，被称为"双舌人"（utraque lingua）。基督教在罗马世界的兴起并没有改变这种双语的文化要求。公元四世纪时，有个虔诚的罗马妇女为她女儿的教育征求圣哲罗姆（Saint Jerome）的意见，圣哲罗姆回复说，"让她背熟很多希腊文的诗句，也要教给她拉丁文"[2]。进入漫长的中世纪后，西方教育的基本内容是有名的七艺，加洛林时代确定的前三艺是七艺的基础，即语法、修辞和雄辩术，教的就是拉丁文的语法和修辞，都是有关语言学习的，而对中世纪的文人学士特别是地中海地区以北的日耳曼蛮族后裔来说，拉丁语就是一种外语。整个中世纪的文人学士全是从学习掌握拉丁文开始他们的学业的。懂得读写拉丁文一直都是学识教养的主要内容，而希腊文知识则是更高学养的标志。在查理曼大帝倡导的欧洲第一次文艺复兴时期，蛮族的贵族开始专心学习遗忘已久的古典语言。查理曼大帝请到他的宫

---

1 Quintilian, *Institutio Oratoria*, Book 1.1, Loeb Classical Library, p. 71.

2 Saint Jerome, Letter CVII to Late, http://www.umilta.net/jerome.htm.

廷里来的大学者阿尔昆（Alcuin）给皇帝陛下的群臣各取一个希伯来语或希腊语的名字，以给这些日耳曼贵族一点高等教养的色彩。从那时起一直到十五世纪的文艺复兴，懂得这几种古典语言成了衡量人的修养的标准。超群绝伦的全才如达·芬奇，还被佛罗伦萨的上流社会视为一个学力不够的匠人，理由就是他的希腊文拉丁文不够好。[1]确实，达·芬奇只是自学了一点拉丁文，在他留下的那些著名的笔记中，还有他做的拉丁文动词变位练习，他对希腊文则几乎完全不懂。一个世纪后的莎士比亚也面临同样的批评，本·强生（Ben Johnson）在那篇著名的对开本题诗中慨叹他只懂"一丁点拉丁文，更少的希腊文"（little Latin, less Greek）。这个揭露，后来成了许多人要否定这位威廉·莎士比亚先生的著作权的重要证据之一，他们不相信一个外文不好的人能够写出这些辉煌的文学经典来。到了宗教改革期间，掌握多门古典语言不只是个文人和艺术家的学识教养的问题，马丁·路德认为，懂不懂这些语言直接关联到信仰的坚定和纯洁，在路德的《告德国各市长和地方长官书》中，他写道，"如果我们从这些语言（拉丁语、希腊语和希伯来语）中没有得到其他什么好处，仅仅把这些语言看成是神授予我们崇高而又光荣的礼物，我说，这一仅有的想法就应该是修习这些语言的强大动力和吸引力……因为撒旦清楚地知道，在这些语言繁荣兴起的地方，他的权力很快就会土崩瓦解，不易修复"[2]。近代以来，拉丁文和古希腊文慢慢淡出，但外文还是西方教育的中心目标。哲学家洛克同时还是位教育思想家，提出了理性的教育理念，他在《教育漫话》中告诉他的英国同胞，"一到他（孩子）能说英语的时候，他就应该学习别种语言。如果建议儿童学习的是法语，那是不会引起任何人的疑虑的"[3]。这和两千多年前昆体良要求他的罗马同胞在学习母语拉丁语的同时一定也要学习希腊语的教育理念一模一样。这个重视多种语言能力的教育思想

1　Bronowski and Mazlish, *The Western Intellectual Tradition*, Dorset Press, 1960, p. 11.
2　［美］E. P. 克伯雷选编：《西方教育经典文献》，任钟印译，北京：人民教育出版社，2016年，第292页。
3　John Locke, *Some Thoughts Concerning Education*, Harvard Classics, Vol. 37, p. 120；万卷出版公司，2006年。

在西方一以贯之，并且在中世纪以来的教育制度中得到了不折不扣的实现。十六世纪上半叶法国的波尔多市决定设立一所第一流的学校，聘来的教育家维内校长为学校制定了一个教学纲要，这个纲要非常鲜明地体现了文艺复兴鼎盛时期的欧洲教育内容：6岁或7岁的孩子入学上十个年级，九年级时就要求他们能用法文和拉丁文流畅而快速地阅读和书写；升到四年级时开始学习希腊文一直到毕业。欧洲其他地区的学校提供的教学课目中都有大体相同的语言必修课。[1] 十七世纪时在美国的新英格兰建立起来的哈佛学院的校规和课程设置中表现出了同样的对多语能力的重视，入学哈佛的条件是能即席读懂西塞罗的作品或同类的古典拉丁文作家的作品，以及按古希腊文的名词和动词变化表正确地变格。入学后，四年级的学生每周四学习希腊文，三年级的学生每周五学习希伯来语和东方语言。当时的东方语言指的是中东地区的语言，如迦勒底语和叙利亚语。[2] 由于西方文明里的这个重视外文教育的传统，不仅历来的学者都通多种语文，一般上流社会人士差不多都能运用两种以上的语言，统治了大半个欧洲的神圣罗马帝国的查理五世皇帝能娴熟地说五六种语言。多语能力，当然，是我们定义的多种书面文化语言的能力，一直是西方社会上层精英的基本素养。

反观中国，我们看到的是一种非常不同的文化传统。从周秦时代起，几乎从来没有哪个文人学士词臣权贵因为不擅外文而遭受轻视。在经典的学识素养中，从没有外文这个因素，汉语以外的语言，从不在中国学人的视野之内，无论是先秦贵族必须掌握的"礼、乐、射、御、书、数"这样的技能性的"六艺"，还是孔子教授儒家弟子的《诗》《书》《礼》《乐》《易》《春秋》这六部典籍的"六艺"，都没有汉语以外的语言的课程。汉代的太学以儒学"九经"为教学内容，以后各朝代从国子监到书院到乡学，其教育内容基本不出儒家经典的范围，只有在教授的经典书目上根据科举的要求而有所增减，但是从没有使用汉语以外的语言的教育内容。当然，中国历史上并不是没有教授外族语言文字的学校，蒙古族

1　［美］E. P. 克伯雷选编：《西方教育经典文献》，第252—255页。

2　［美］E. P. 克伯雷选编：《西方教育经典文献》，第350—352页。

统治的元朝设立有教授蒙古文典籍的"蒙古国子监"和教授"亦斯替非文"即波斯文的"回回国子监",明朝设立有教授周边国家语言的"四夷馆",满清设立有为满族子第开办的旗学[1],但是因为作为核心文化制度的科举里没有考察外语的科目,元朝以后出现的这些教授异族语文的学校并没有冲击华夏文化的单语文化基础,对海内文人士子文化素质的养成并无影响。华夏文化教养中异族语言的缺席,其原因并不是汉语的中华文明没有和其他语言发生过接触。毋庸置疑,像世界上任何文明一样,中华文明从来不是在一个单纯的语言环境中衍生演进的,由于在中国的周边和内部一直有着各种不同的汉语以外的语言,汉王朝的统治者同样地有与使用其他语言的族群交流的需要,然而,与这些语言交际的能力被看作一种低级的技能,士族阶层并不觉得这些外族的语言能作为精英阶层的学养的一部分。在《周礼》的等级制度中,"象胥掌蛮夷闽貉戎狄之国使,掌传王之言而谕说焉",孙诒让注曰,"是此官通番国之辞,故以主宾之辞传译通之也"。[2] 也就是说,掌握他族语言是那些专门的胥吏的事,并不是贵族教养的一部分。汉晋以降,周边许多民族都开始有了自己的文字,二十世纪以来面世的西域古卷,特别是敦煌石室里发现的古文本,表明当时在中国的西边流行着相当多的语种文字。不管当时是为了什么样的目的而把这些文书封存在敦煌的这个密室中的,这些于阗文、古藏文、粟特文、西夏文、回鹘文、古突厥文、梵文和希伯来文的文书被收集在一起保存在同一个地方,清楚地表明当时那个地区在语言使用上的繁复多样的状态,无论是意义范畴,使用者群体还是流通地域,这些语言之间并不是分割断裂的,这说明当时汉人懂外族语文应是常态。其实,不仅在古丝路的西域有多种语言的流行,在华夏文明的中心地带,汉族士人中也一直有通异族语言的人。这是因为无论和战,汉族朝廷一直和四周的民族有着密切来往,自然会有互相习得对方语言的。《世说新语》中有个著名故事,"王丞相拜扬州,宾客数百

1　郭齐家:《中国教育史》,北京:人民教育出版社,2015年,第248—410页。
2　孙诒让:《周礼正义》,北京:中华书局,2015年,第3687—3688页。

人并加沾接，人人有说色，……因过胡人前弹指曰，'兰阇，兰阇！'群胡同笑"[1]。这是王导在运用他的外语能力为立足未稳的东晋政权争取人心。"兰阇"，王应麟认为就是梵文的"兰若"，意为静心。除了在交际场合有用胡语的，更有诗文中掺入外文的。也是东晋时，"郝隆为桓公南蛮参军，三月三日会，作诗。不能者，罚酒三升。隆初以不能受罚，既饮，揽笔便作一句云：'娵隅跃清池。'桓公问：'娵隅是何物？'答曰：'蛮名鱼为娵隅。'桓公曰：'作诗何以作蛮语？'隆曰：'千里投公，始得蛮府参军，那得不作蛮语也！'"[2]郝隆是职守所在而会蛮语，而北宋名臣余靖也在出使契丹时学得契丹语，并同样以外语入诗："余襄公靖尝在契丹作胡语诗云，'夜筵没逻臣拜洗，两朝厥荷情幹勒，微臣雅鲁祝君统，圣寿铁摆俱可忒'。没逻言厚盛，拜洗言受赐，厥荷言通好，幹勒言厚重，铁摆言嵩高也。"[3]余靖以契丹语入诗，和王导一样，是对外族人的一个亲善姿态，实际上汉族士人并不把异族语文当作自己文化修养的一部分，桓玄的反应正是表达了这种态度："作诗何以作蛮语？"在汉文史籍中，将周边的语言都概而名之——胡语、夷语、蛮语，从不留意区分其中的差异。今人读到史载某人"通胡语"，我们并不能知道他懂的是粟特语还是突厥语。中国古代史家对异族语言的含混命名，是出于一种根深蒂固的轻视。《吕氏春秋》有云，"善为君者，蛮夷反舌殊俗异习皆服之，德厚也"，高诱注曰："戎狄言语与中国相反，因谓反舌，一说南方有反舌国，舌本在前，末倒向喉，故曰反舌。"[4]对异族语言的如此偏见，当然不会引起汉族的学士文人对汉语以外的语言文字的兴趣，也不会视其为文化语言。东晋北宋的名相重臣学会胡语，完全是出于对付外族的政治需要。当然，在胡汉混杂异族崛起的南北朝时期，懂得外族语言还是会被看作官吏们的一项很有用的能力。比如在北齐时，会国族语言以外的"四夷语"被当作一个值得赞扬的

1　刘义庆：《世说新语笺疏》，第154页。

2　刘义庆：《世说新语笺疏》，第696—697页。

3　葛立方：《韵语阳秋》卷三，《笔记小说大观》第四十二编，台北：新兴书局，1987年，第639页。

4　王利器：《吕氏春秋注疏》第三册，成都：巴蜀书社，2002年，第239页。

长处："代人刘世清，祖拔，魏燕州刺史，……情性甚整，周慎谨密，在孝卿之右，能通四夷语，为当时第一"[1]；"（祖）珽天性聪明，事无难学，凡诸伎艺，莫不措怀，文章之外，又善音律，解四夷语及阴阳占候，医药之术尤是所长"[2]。不仅在汉胡杂处的北朝时期朝廷要任用懂夷语的官员，承平的东汉时镇守南方边陲的官员也觉得懂点异族语言不无益处，"（益州刺史梁国朱）辅上疏曰，……远夷之语，辞意难正，草木异种，鸟兽殊类，有犍为郡掾田恭与之习狎，颇晓其语，臣辄令讯其风俗，译其辞语。今遣从事史李陵与恭护送诣阙，并上其乐诗"[3]。然而，这样的外语能力只属于"文章之外"的偏才薄技，在正统文士看来，虽然比起平原君的食客们的鸡鸣狗盗之术要高，但也相差不远。即便在盛行多种语言的北齐，虽然权贵们多说胡语，汉族士人还是觉得只有汉语才是真正具有文化价值的。《颜氏家训》里的那个著名故事把这个北胡地区里的语言等级表达得非常清楚："齐朝有一士大夫尝谓吾曰，我有一儿，年已十七，颇晓书疏，教其鲜卑语及弹琵琶，稍欲通解，以此伏事公卿，无不宠爱，亦要事也。吾时俯而不答。异哉此人之教子也。若由此自致卿相，亦不欲汝曹为之。"[4]尽管鲜卑语是当朝者的语言，很能学以致用，但汉族士子还是认为这种权贵们所通用的语言并不能成为士人阶层学识教养的一部分，与他们的文化身份无关。这段议论非常清楚地表明了实用的语言技能和精英文化语言并不具有同等的社会价值的。而且，当汉字构成的精英文化语言等同于了华夏文明本身，则汉语与胡语之间的界限就被赋予了夷夏之别的重大政治内涵，说胡语还是说汉语会成为关联到政制本体性质的严重问题。北魏孝文帝政治改革的一个大举动就是"诏不得以北俗之语言于朝廷"[5]，也就是说禁止鲜卑贵族在朝廷上说自己的母语，以去夷入夏。孝文帝很明白，在中国环境里只有汉语汉文才是精英文化语言，因此而有改行汉语汉字的

1　李百药：《北齐书·列传第十二》卷二十，北京：中华书局，1995年，第267页。
2　李百药：《北齐书·列传第三十一》卷三十九，第516页。
3　范晔：《后汉书·南蛮西南夷列传第七十六》，北京：中华书局，1995年，第2855页。
4　颜之推：《颜氏家训·教子第二》，《诸子集成》第八册，第2页。
5　魏收：《魏书·卷七下》，北京：中华书局，1999年，第120页。

必要性。孝文帝要为自己和他的王朝建立的文化身份同时也是他个人的文化选择，他"雅好读书，手不释卷，五经之义，览之便讲，学不师受，探其精奥，史传百家，无不该涉，善谈庄老，尤精释义"[1]。他所读所讲的"五经百家"当然都是汉语的典籍。很显然，选择汉语禁绝胡语，并不只是个便利的考虑。事关夷夏之别，孝文帝的语言政策招致后人纷纷议论。千年之后的王夫之对其持非常严厉的批评态度，因其时代遭际，他将严守夷夏之别看成儒家的生命底线，"而夷夏者，义之尤严者也，五帝、三王，劳其神明，为天分气，为地分理，以绝夷于夏，即以绝禽于人"[2]。胡人孝文帝施行的包括改胡语胡服等的汉化措施，有违于"绝夷于夏"，所以王夫之严词斥责，他认为"涂饰耳目，是为拓跋宏所行之王道而已。……视宏之所为，沐猴而冠，优俳之戏而已矣，……则亦索虏欺人之术也"[3]。王夫之如此议论，或许想到的是明初太祖登基伊始就发布的禁胡语胡服的诏令[4]，朱元璋不准汉人习用胡语，为的是重建汉家文化身份，以语言区别体现夷夏分野，而明清换代之间的北虏满人贵族们大都熟习汉文，颇有抹杀夷夏界限的气象，王夫之专以一个"伪"字来斥责改行汉文的孝文帝拓跋宏，或许是意指当朝。深感于亡国之痛的王夫之将汉胡语言之别看作分别夷夏的标识，这很能代表汉族士人的正统观念。在这个语言意识背景下，我们能理解为何传统士人对学习异族语言那么没兴趣无动力，反观西方，精英文化并不总是限于一种语言，因此很少有以国家权力禁用外族语言的例子，而精英阶层一直以多识外语为荣，因为在西方文化中，一直有着多种精英文化语言，语言之别从来不是文明和野蛮的分界。在华夏文明范围里，外族语言至多只是一种实用技能，而且一旦与夷夏对立相关，夷狄胡语就包含了危险。通晓胡语的技能在国势强盛时固然可为朝廷所用，在面临异族势力进逼时，这样的技能则会被认为是种威胁，帝王们颇不

1　魏收：《魏书·卷七下》，第126页。

2　王夫之：《船山遗书》，北京：中国书店，2016年，第317页。

3　王夫之：《船山遗书》，第372页。

4　谈迁：《国榷·卷三》第一册，北京：中华书局，1958年，第357页。

喜臣下通夷语。安禄山能动摇大唐的天下，其手段之一，竟是他这个胡人懂外语："禄山通夷语，躬自慰抚，皆释俘囚为战士，故其下乐输死。"[1]到了大清，面临前所未见的来自西方的夷人，乾隆皇帝颇感忧虑，为了防范，他将通夷语本身看成了一种需要防范的罪行。乾隆五十八年（1745年），他对上报的"浙江人郭姓从前曾勾结夷商，今已病故，伊子郭杰观略省夷语。已经严加管住一节"，下旨说，"郭姓曾有勾结夷商之事，伊子又能略通夷语，虽现无勾串情弊，然此人留于浙江究不可信，著即派妥员伴送由别路进京备询"[2]。并没有犯任何法规的一个浙江人，就因为懂夷语，被皇帝下令看管起来，并递解进京。道光皇帝时西夷更加咄咄逼人，他对懂夷语的人的处理也就更加峻急，下旨曰："查广东洋行司事谢五即谢治安，为人奸滑，熟习夷语，素与该国夷商交结，前月夷人乘坐肩舆即谢五送给，现拏获收禁，饬该府县严切根究，务得确情，按律定拟具奏。"[3]当与夷人发生争议时，他首先想到的是要查出谁能和夷人通话："至该逆所称定海开行之船先往镇江南京后到天津等语，系向何人说及？内地民人又何以能通晓夷语？均著向宝山县确切询明，附便具奏。"[4]百姓通夷语是皇帝要严查的大问题，让臣民学习夷族的语言显然不是他所能容忍的事。

当然，清朝中后期官家对夷人语言的警惕显示的是这个朝廷面对西洋的不自信，这并不表示中国朝廷上下在历史上始终是排斥或蔑视外族语言的。曾经有一个时代，中国对外族语言持着开放容忍的态度，甚至还热切地学习，有一种语言似有成为华夏第二种精英文化语言的机会，那就是在大唐时期印度的梵文在中国佛教徒中的流行。大唐高僧们为学习梵文花的功夫，几乎不亚于古罗马贵族对希腊语的那种热心追求。玄奘是如此赞颂经书的梵文："书称天书，语为天语；文

1 欧阳修等：《新唐书》卷两百二十五，北京：中华书局，1995年，第6417页。
2 《高宗纯皇帝实录》卷十九，乾隆五十八年九月上，《清实录》第二十七册，北京：中华书局，2008年，第28220页。
3 《宣宗成皇帝实录》卷三，道光十年十一月下，《清实录》第三十五册，第37552页。
4 《宣宗成皇帝实录》卷六，道光二十二年七月上，《清实录》第三十八册，第40911页。

辞婉密，音韵循环；或一言贯多义，或一义综多言；声有抑扬，调裁清浊。"[1]这样的评价，与传统的"反舌"成见，相差何止千里。玄奘自己精通梵文，能在印度授课辩论著书，回国后译经千百卷，其对梵文的娴熟，后人难以望其项背。然而，玄奘并不是个孤例，在义净的《大唐西域求法高僧传》中记载的那些唐朝僧人，都以学习掌握梵文为弘法事业的基本条件。如他讲述的"沙门玄照法师者，……以贞观年中，乃于大兴善寺玄证师处初学梵语"[2]，表明当时在中国国内已有成熟的梵文教学，当然只限于伽蓝寺院。义净著录的那些高僧行状中，都有学习梵文的经历，或者是在中国，或者是在海外，然后再到印度完成他们的求法事业。可以说在那个时期有一批中国最优秀的学人，他们认可了一种和汉语一样高雅的语文，并尽力地去学习它，这在中国语言文化史上是史无前例的。

然而，这也是后无来者的，至少直到现代。可与印度佛教文明在华夏的传播相比拟的，是千年后基督教文明在明末传入中国的历程。同样是一个完全陌生的文明，同样是借助了宗教信仰的精神力量，同样是由非常杰出的博学人士传入的，同样为中国当时最优秀的学人所接受，但是结果颇为不同。拉丁语未必比梵文更难学，徐光启在才智上肯定不会比唐朝的那些僧人低，他对基督教义以及相关的西方文化的热忱也不可低估，然而他竟没有觉得有学习拉丁语的必要。他对西学的了解，全仰仗利玛窦等人的译作。在和利玛窦合作翻译《几何原本》时，也是请利玛窦"口传，自以笔受焉，反覆展转，求合本书之意，以中夏之文，重复订政，凡三易稿"[3]。不仅徐光启没有学习拉丁语，明末清初的那批和西方传教士密切来往的中国士子，不管是皈依基督教的还是只对西方学术感兴趣的，都没有像晋唐时的和尚那样努力学习载有新知的外来语文。理由当然有许多。利玛窦等欧洲传教士都已学好了汉语文，先替他们的中国对话者做好了语文转换工作，让人觉得学习拉丁文的功夫似乎是可以省去的。唐时流行于中国的佛教教义芜杂

1　释玄奘：《宋思溪藏本大唐西域记》第三册，北京：国家图书馆出版社，2017年，第152页。
2　义净：《大唐西域求法高僧传校注》，王邦维校注，北京：中华书局，1988年，第9页。
3　梁家勉原编，李天纲增补：《增补徐光启年谱》，上海：上海古籍出版社，2011年，第142页。

混乱，来华番僧良莠不齐，这促使玄奘等人决心去佛教的源头寻找真经；而传来基督教的利先生连李贽都觉得"尽能言我此间之言，作此间之文字，行此间之礼仪，是一极标致人也"[1]，他所言所书，当可令人完全信服，不必要到拉丁文的原著里辨出个是非。这些我们能想到的理由都存在。但是，更深层的原因或许还可探究。宋元以后，中国传统的文化意识更趋固化，哲思心灵那层通过吸收佛学禅理也已补上，严密稳定的科举制度使得以四书五经为核心的儒家经典文本占据了中国士子的全部思想，他们不觉得有越过语言界限去进入一个完全不同的意义世界的需要。中国文化的单语性在这个时代已经达到非常稳固的程度了。

当我们阐述中国文化的单语性并与西方文化的多语性比较时，我们还是要注意到，这两种文化并不是在语言构成方面一直保持着相反的特性的。正如前文所显示的，在晋唐时期，通过那些无畏的求法高僧，中国精英文化中曾经有过多语的因素，尽管只限于寺院的世界，也没有得到继承。在西方，我们同样能看到一个具有相当单语性的时代。在漫长的中世纪，拉丁文成了整个欧洲唯一的精神活动的载体，主要由修道院以及稍后的大学维持和发展的中世纪的精英文化完全围绕着拉丁文的文本在流布。地不分南北，人不分东西，欧洲中世纪的学者靠着拉丁文可以毫无障碍地互相交流，意大利学者撰写的神学论文，瑞典的教士们读来毫无困难，尽管他们各自的母语非常不同。西方中世纪流传至今的文献基本上都是拉丁文的，这和中国的文言起的作用颇为相似。在这个单一拉丁语的基础上，欧洲保持了近千年的思想上、文化上和制度上的统一和稳定。这种令人安心的单语状态从十三世纪开始就发生了分化。十四世纪初，但丁撰写了《论俗语》(*De vulgari eloquentia*)，他论述了欧洲各地语言的分布情况，赋予意大利方言以文学语言的地位。这部未完成的论著预示了即将到来的西方语言的巨大变化。但丁自己身体力行，开始以意大利文创作。意大利语、英语、德语、法语等原来只是方言的语言很快就进入了精英文化的殿堂，官方文书、高雅诗文、哲学讨论都开

1　李贽：《续焚书》，转引自《增补徐光启年谱》，第120页。

始使用各种近代欧洲语言来写作。印刷术的发明更加快了这个向多语演变的进程。1461年，第一本德语书籍出版；1462年，第一本捷克语书籍出版；1471年，第一本意大利语书籍出版；1474年，第一本英语书籍出版；1474年，第一本加泰罗尼亚语书籍出版；约1476年，第一本法语书籍出版；1477年，第一本佛兰德语书籍出版；1483年，第一本克罗地亚语书籍出版。[1] 欧洲的语言地图爆发式地进入了多语时代，欧洲文化也在这个时候爆发式地进入了一个伟大创新的时代，那就是欧洲的文艺复兴。文艺复兴是人类文明史上最值得关注的历史变化，做中西文化对比研究的学者喜欢讲"大分流"，在我看来，中西文化的真正大分流发生在文艺复兴时期。文艺复兴这样的巨大思想文化运动，其起源当然不是任何单一的原因所能解释的，中世纪晚期西方社会里酝酿涌动已久的各种动因风云际会，引发出了这场伟大的社会文化革新创造运动来。或许我们还难以证明是精英文化语言的多元化拓展了文艺复兴时代的思想地平线，还是中世纪思维的蜕变给各地的方言打开了发展的途径，何为因何为果并不容易确定，或许是互为因果的。所能确定的是这两个演进是同时发生的。在那几个世纪里，那些文艺复兴时代的巨人们越出了单一的拉丁文，先是以古典希腊文，随后以意大利语、德语、法语、英语等新兴的文化语言思考、创作和表达，在崭新的语言素料上织出了绚丽多彩的新文化，从而在根本上改塑了西方文化的面貌。然而，在西方已经重建了他们文化的多语化以后，当十七世纪耶稣会传教士到达中国的时候，中国最优秀的文化精英对汉语文言以外的语言文字完全失去了兴趣，没人觉得有必要去学习利玛窦他们带来的那些泰西新知的原文。如果说那时还有不少中国学者对这个陌生的文字感兴趣的话，也是因为拉丁字母能够被用来很方便地标示汉语的音韵结构。[2]

然而到了十九世纪，中西开始发生冲撞。船坚炮利的西方列强不仅打破了中国的海防国门，对整个中国政治思想文化体系都造成了巨大的震荡，所谓三千年

---

1 ［英］彼得·伯克：《语言的文化史》，李霄翔等译，北京：北京大学出版社，2007年，第1—9页。
2 参见方豪：《中西交通史》第四编第十一章，上海：上海人民出版社，2008年，第659—671页。

未有之大变局的一个后果是华夏文化的单语壁垒开始出现裂纹。张之洞算是位较温和的改革人士，在他的《劝学篇》中，提出了他的教育改革规划，其中有："中学堂各事，较小学堂加深，而益以习五经，习通鉴，习政治之学，习外国语言文字。"[1] 此时已近十九世纪末，离1818年马礼逊在马六甲开办"英华书院"教授华人英语，已经过了八十年，从华夏文明圈的边缘开始的外语教育，经过像郑观应这样的维新人物在《盛世危言》中的呼吁，终于为中土的精英人士普遍接受，主政的权臣在培养新的正统士人的计划中，破天荒地列入外国语文，这时汉语以外的外族语言已经被认为是未来士人应该具备的知识素养了。以胡适为代表的一代学者归国后开始执中国学界文坛的牛耳，实际上这是中国文化的一个相当根本性的范式转换。他们被称为新派学者，不仅是因为他们思想理念学术方法新，他们的学识背景与前人完全不同，其中相当重要的一点就是他们的学术视野是多语的，他们的学术世界里的精英文化语言是多元的，这是千百年来都没有过的，这是一个重大的范式转换。陈寅恪被认为是守旧的，且自许为"思想囿于咸丰、同治之世，议论近乎湘乡、南皮之间"，但他具备常为人称羡的相当广阔的语言背景，这是曾国藩、张之洞所没有的。他晚年专研钱谦益，表白其动机说："亦欲自验所学之深浅也，盖牧斋博通文史，旁涉梵夹道藏，寅恪平生才识学问固远不逮前贤，而研治领域则有约略近似之处。"[2] 然而陈寅恪懂梵文及其他多种相关语言，钱牧斋所学再精深，也没有外国语文，陈寅恪是在一个完全不同的知识范型里和钱谦益对话的。同样地，陈寅恪为清华入学考试所出的对对子题目，看似非常传统，好像村塾业师亦可为之，然而他对此举的思考如没有多种文化语言的背景则绝无可能。整体而言，十九、二十世纪交替时，中国学人所具备或被期望具备的语言能力从单一的汉语文言文扩展到英法德日多种语言，这个变化，与西方中世纪晚期欧洲学者的学术语言一下子从单一的拉丁文扩展到多种近代语

1　张之洞:《初学篇·设学第三》，清末民初文献丛刊，北京：朝华出版社，2017年，第96页。

2　陈寅恪:《柳如是别传》第一册，北京：生活·读书·新知三联书店，2015年，第3页。

言的变化庶几相近，这个变化给整个社会的精神生活带来的巨大变革也是类似的，值得我们深入探究。

文化依存于文化人，文化人的语言素养构成对文化的内涵和形态的演进到底是怎样产生影响的呢？换言之，建立在单一语言基础上的文化和生长在多种语言环境里的文化会各有什么不同的特质呢？这不是一个容易做出确切回答的问题，更难以下孰优孰劣的判断。若不揣浅陋试加辨识，则可说华夏文化与汉字几乎熔铸为一体，这给华夏文化带来一种非常恒定而纯一的面貌，自先秦至清末，华夏文化的承载者和实践者感受的是他们始终被笼罩在同一个文化的氛围之中，不管是儒法墨，还是儒道佛，他们共有的是同一个文化身份，都是"化内"之人，这个"化"，即是由汉语汉字明确划定的，由此而与"夷"区别。反观西方文化，其语言的多元性使得文化身份的认定具有相当的流动性，从古希腊文、拉丁文到文艺复兴时代开始蓬勃兴起的各种近现代语言，西方文化人很少有拒斥某种外族语言文字以保持自己的文化身份的反应，也很少执念于语言—族裔—文化—信仰这个连续线上。从另一角度来看，出入于各种不同语言的西方文化人拥有更加多样的语言观念资源，他们的思辨话语一直在吸收着来自不同语言的词语概念，从来自希腊语的eidos，nous，logos到来自法语的élan vital，differance，再到来自德语Ding an sich，Dasein等，多样化的语言源头一直在输入多样化的概念指陈；而在华夏文化的传统中，只有汉唐之际西来佛教给汉语的思辨话语增加了来自梵文的"般若""涅槃""禅"等外来新词，而且这些佛家语在华夏文化中还是比较边缘化，进不了科举卷题的正统话语中。两千多年以来，士人们的思辨始终围绕着来自上古汉语的那些基本概念来进行："道""仁""治""礼"等。从先秦诸子的论辩到明清大儒的心学、实学，就是一场几乎从没有中断的对话，今天读来，毫无隔绝之感。这是纯一语言给中国文化带来的令人惊叹的恒定同质性。然而，从另一个角度来看，敏锐的古代哲人所感叹的"书不尽言，言不尽意"（《周易·系辞上》）或许也可以以我们文化的单语特性来解释。我们能够就中西文化的语言背景问题从不同的角度来进行进一步的探讨，然而有一点是无可置疑的：

历史上华夏文化是织造在汉语文字上的，但是不管华夏文化今后会拥有什么样的前景，我们的文化再不会也不能只在单一文化语言的背景下发展了。关注世上其他的精英文化语言，和这些语言对话，吸收利用这些文化语言的资源，成了我们的文化未来发展的必要条件。

（文章发表于《北京大学学报（哲学社会科学版）》2018年第3期。本文系作者在联盟2017年年度论坛上的发言）

参考文献

王力:《汉语史稿》，北京：中华书局，1980年。

刘义庆:《世说新语笺疏》，北京：中华书局，2011年。

刘坚主编:《近代汉语语法资料汇编》，北京：商务印书馆，1995年。

史存直:《汉语史纲要》，北京：中华书局，2008年。

［美］巴克勒等:《西方社会史》，霍文利等译，桂林：广西师范大学出版社，2005年。

［日］市川勘、小松岚:《百年华语》，上海：上海教育出版社，2008年。

［英］伯克:《语言的文化史》，李霄翔、李鲁、杨豫译，北京：北京大学出版社，2007年。

柳诒徵:《中国文化史》，北京：中华书局，2015年。

［德］普法伊费尔:《古典学术史》，上、下卷，刘军、张弢译，北京：北京大学出版社，2015年。

［英］尼古拉斯·奥斯特勒:《语言帝国：世界语言史》，章璐、梵非译，上海：上海人民出版社，2011年。

颜之推:《颜氏家训》，诸子集成本，北京：中华书局，1954年。

［美］德克特·维克斯:《社会语言学导论：社会和身份》，何丽、宿宇瑾译，北京：中国书籍出版社，2015年。

Two Roads to a World Community:
Comparing Stoic and Confucian Cosmopolitanism

Yudan Chen*

In the recent four centuries since the signing of the Peace of Westphalia, an inter-state system, with national sovereignty as its fundamental principle, has spread from Europe into the entire world. While the nation-state has always been the core element in practice, reflections of cosmopolitanism which go beyond the nation-state have never disappeared from human thought, from the fields of serious philosophical works to romantic poems.[1] Since the discipline of international relations was established in early the twentieth century, however, most IR theorists have centered on the limited concept of "inter-national." They regard the existence of nation-states as a prerequisite of their analysis, showing little interest in cosmopolitanism.[2] At the same time, cosmopolitanism is still vivid in the disciplines of political science, sociology and philosophy. Ulrich Beck, Robert Fine, Martha Nussbaum and Thomas Pogge are only a few names among modern cosmopolitanism scholars, and

———————————

* Yudan Chen (陈玉聃) is Associate Professor in International Politics at Fudan University. His main interests are the history of international thought and the aesthetic turn in international political theory.

1 It is interesting that in the eighteenth and nineteenth centuries, when the institution of nation-states was fixed in Europe, great figures as Kant, Goethe and Schiller were keenly calling for an idea of "world citizenship." See for example: Kuno Francke, "Cosmopolitanism in German Romantic Thought," in *Proceedings of the American Philosophical Society*, Vol. 66, 1927, 183–190.

2 There are however some exceptions, see for example: Chris Brown, "Cosmopolitanism, world citizenship and global civil society," in *Critical Review of International Social and Political Philosophy*, Vol. 3, No. 1, 2000; Jens Bartelson, *Visions of World Community*, Cambridge: Cambridge University Press, 2009; Richard Beardsworth, *Cosmopolitanism and International Relations Theory*, Cambridge: Polity, 2011.

they do have their influence on IR studies, especially on normative theories. Many of them, in their discussions on cosmopolitanism, trace the cosmopolitan tradition back to Stoicism and even Cynicism.[1] The Stoic movement is indisputably the first among the "three major moments of cosmopolitan thought prior to recent and current re-engagement with its problematic and disposition."[2] Stoic cosmopolitanism provides modern cosmopolitan researchers with not only the notion of a "cosmos in which human kind might live together in harmony," but also, to some extent, the idea of "world citizenship."[3]

On the other side of the earth, since the mid-1990s, China has witnessed the rise of its own cosmopolitanism under the name of "Tianxia Zhuyi" (The doctrine of Tianxia).[4] Some scholars have tended to employ this conception which is generated from Chinese classical traditions to transcend the imported idea of nation-state. Li Shenzhi, one of the most prominent Chinese IR scholars of the last century and the former president of the Chinese Academy of Social Science,[5] declares in his 1994 article "Globalization and Chinese Culture" that "a vulgar nationalism, is totally against the trend and spirit of globalization as well as Chinese tradition ... The traditional Chinese idea is 'Tianxia Zhuyi' but not 'nationalism'."[6] Another important article which raised enthusiastic discussion and even disputes on Chinese cosmopolitanism was written by Sheng Hong, and published in 1996

---

1 It is noteworthy that Martha Nussbaum herself is a well-known classist.
2 Richard Beardsworth, *Cosmopolitanism and International Relations Theory*, 17.
3 David Held, "Principles of cosmopolitan order," in Gillian Brock and Harry Brighouse eds., *The Political Philosophy of Cosmopolitanism*, Cambridge: Cambridge University Press, 2005, 18; Jocelyne Couture and Kai Nielsen, "Cosmopolitanism and the compatriot priority principle," in Gillian Brock and Harry Brighouse eds., *The Political Philosophy of Cosmopolitanism*, 183.
4 "Tianxia" is a concept widely used in ancient China which means "the Universe," or "under the Heaven" literally. "Zhuyi" simply means "-ism," I will retain "Tianxia Zhuyi" if it is in a citation, but use "cosmopolitanism" otherwise for the reason of easy-reading.
5 Li participated in China's foreign affairs actively in 1950s with Premier Zhou Enlai and in late 1970s with Deng Xiaoping. He was also the founder of Institute of American Studies in Chinese Academy of Social Science in 1980s.
6 Li Shenzhi, "Globalization and Chinese Culture," in *Pacific Journal*, Vol. 2, 1994, 7–8.

in a leading Chinese social science journal under the title "From Nationalism to Tianxia Zhuyi." The author argues that "since China is the only civilization in human history that once ended a warring states period with the establishment of 'Tianxia Zhuyi' culture, its cultural tradition may become a spiritual resource for us to establish 'Tianxia Zhuyi' culture today."[1] From then on, quite a few Chinese scholars have tried to view the world from a traditional cosmopolitan perspective.[2] Like their Western counterparts, Chinese researchers often look back upon the Classical period, picking up phrases from Confucian classics two thousand years ago, which have been regarded as the main source of traditional cosmopolitanism. When China put forward the conception of a "harmonious world" in 2005, some scholars also tended to connect classical cosmopolitanism with the "harmonious world" idea, to prove that the latter is based on unique Chinese culture and may benefit from traditional cosmopolitanism.[3]

Since both modern Western and Chinese cosmopolitanisms appeal to a sense beyond the nation-state to some extent, it would be interesting and helpful to compare their respective ancestors, that is, Stoic cosmopolitanism and Confucian cosmopolitanism.[4] Are they essentially different and incommensurable? Or do they share some commonality that may even benefit contemporary reflections on a changing world? The comparison between these two cosmopolitanisms in this article includes two aspects: the political space for people in the world to dwell in, and the way they live harmoniously in such a space. The article then turns to modern theories in the conclusion, with a brief discussion based on the consideration of the two ancient thoughts.

---

1 Sheng Hong, "From Nationalism to Tianxia Zhuyi," in *Strategy and Management*, Vol. 1, 1996, 19.

2 The most influential figure is Zhao Tingyang, a professor in philosophy. He published the book *The Tianxia System: A Philosophy for the World Institution* in 2005, which has been widely spread among IR scholars in China.

3 There are numerous books, papers and articles on this topic, among which, I have to say, only a few are serious and profound academic works. See for example: Yang Faxi, *From "Universal Concord" to Constructing "Harmonious World,"* Beijing: Renmin Publish House, 2008.

4 While there existed diversity within both Stoicism and Confucianism, this article will take them as unified theories, or it would exceed the capacity of a single paper.

Cosmos and Tianxia: the Space to Dwell in

During the Classical period (fifth to fourth century B.C.), both political thought and political practice in Greece reached their climax within the form of polis (city-state). Beyond the level of polis, there were senses of ethnos and even "Greek identity," but the latter referred to common religion, culture and blood, not a political community.[1] However, the fourth century B.C. witnessed the conquest of the Greek poleis by Macedon, a peripheral kingdom, and it was Alexander the Great who led the Greeks to destroy the most typical barbarian figure in their minds: the Persian Empire.[2] The city-state system then began to collapse in political practice. Meanwhile, ideas beyond the city-state and even beyond the distinction between Greeks and barbarians appeared in political thought.

Diogenes, the renowned Cynic philosopher from the fourth century B.C., described as "a homeless exile, to his country dead," might be the earliest to put forward a cosmopolitan idea when he said, "I am a citizen of the world (cosmopolitēs)."[3] However, he has no surviving works today, and it is difficult to make clear the real meaning of his words. It might be "rather a rebellious reaction against every kind of coercion imposed by the

---

1 Recent studies in Classical Greek inter-state relations are contributed by both classists and political scientists. Cf., Paris Arnopoulos, *Exopolitics: Polis-Ethnos-Cosmos*, New York: Nova Science Publishers, 1999; Polly Low, *Interstate Relations in Classical Greece: Morality and Power*, New York: Cambridge University Press, 2007; Adalberto Giovannini, *Les relations entre États dans la Grèce antique du temps d'Homère à l'intervention romaine (ca. 700–200 av. J.-C.)*, Stuttgart: Franz Steiner Verlag, 2007.

2 We should keep in mind that the Macedonians were seen by the Greeks as semi-barbarians. Demosthenes in his famous *Philippic III* held Philip, the king of Macedon, in strong contempt: "not only is he no Hellene, not only has he no kinship with Hellenes, but he is not even a barbarian from a country that one could acknowledge with credit; he is a pestilent Macedonian, from whose country it used not to be possible to buy even a slave of any value." (Arthur Wallace Pickard, *The Public Orations of Demosthenes, Volume II*, Oxford: Clarendon, 1912, 31.)

3 Diogenes Laertios, *Lives of Eminent Philosophers*, translated by R. D. Hicks, Cambridge, Mass.: Harvard University Press, 1972, VI. 38, 63. See also VI.72 in the same work: "The only true commonwealth was, he said, that which is as wide as the universe." Both the Greek and English texts I cite here are from R. D. Hicks's text in Loeb Classical Library.

community upon the individual" than true "philosophic implications" of cosmopolitanism.[1]

The Stoic school created in the late fourth century B.C. is always viewed as the real origin of Western cosmopolitanism. The early development of the school was during the Hellenistic period, when Greek civilization spread into the non-Greek world. Zeno, the founder of Stoicism, was even not an authentic Greek. The center of Stoicism in the middle phase began to transit outside the Greek world, and the late Stoa finally established its headquarters in Rome. Therefore, Stoicism was born with the characteristics of universality and tolerance. We should not be surprised to read from the works of late Stoics, some of whom were Roman politicians, an ethical tendency of world citizenry.

Confucian cosmopolitanism, however, developed with a different background. It did not appear and develop by following the change of the world. On the contrary, it pursued an old universal world order against the emerging new system of independent states.[2] "Confucius," as Cho-yun Hsu noticed, "defined the idea of Confucian political culture through re-interpreting the Western Zhou order" in the era of "the collapse of rules of propriety," and modified the institution of Zhou "into the ideal political regime in Chinese culture."[3]

At first glance, the Stoics look forward in their political contemplation, while the Confucians look backward. However, they in fact share the same idea in different ways, that is, that the state system cannot comply with the development of the world, and there

---

1 Moses Hadas, "From Nationalism to Cosmopolitanism in the Greco-Roman World," in *Journal of the History of Ideas*, Vol. 4, No. 1, 1943, 108. For a brief but detailed discussion on Diogenes' cosmopolitanism and its relations with Stoic cosmopolitanism, see Malcolm Schofield, *The Stoic Idea of the City*, Cambridge: Cambridge University Press, 1991, 141–145.

2 The Western Zhou (1046–771 B.C.) was a united dynasty of feudality. The Eastern Zhou (771–256 B.C.) roughly covered two phases: the Spring and Autumn Period (770–476 B.C.) and the Warring States Period (475–221 B.C.). There are still disputes on the problem that to what extent the inter-state system from 771 to 221 B.C. is parallel to the modern nation-state society. But the states during the period were essentially independent, despite that there was still a nominal "common lord," Confucius was living during the end of the Spring and Autumn Period, and his school was booming in the Warring States Period.

3 Cho-yun Hsu, *We and the Other*, Beijing: SDX Joint Publishing Company, 2010, 14.

needs a superior political form to transcend the idea of independent states, whether the ideal pattern is new or old. Such a pattern is known as Cosmos for the Stoics, and Tianxia for the Confucians. Two questions, then, will be explored as follows.

First, what are the respective characteristics of Cosmos and Tianxia, as both are expected to be the higher political space beyond single states?

It is easy to find that Cosmos and Tianxia share the same essence: the largest space which includes all human beings. Zhao Tingyang, a leading Chinese philosopher who authored *The Tianxia System: A Philosophy for the World Institution*, defines Tianxia as "nothing outside."(无外) While recognizing it as a precise conclusion of Tianxia, I do not agree with his statement that "China has a world view totally different with Western world ... Only Chinese thought can reflect on harmony."[1] At least, the Stoic Cosmos is also of "nothing outside." Moreover, we should not forget that, in original Greek language, the word "cosmos" means "a harmonious system," although Chinese and Greeks might hold somewhat different perspectives on what "harmony" itself means.

There is no doubt that Tianxia excludes none in its political meaning. Examples may be easily found from Confucian classics, such as "Under the wide heaven, all is the King's land. Within the sea-boundaries of the land, all are the King's servants"; "[Y]ou obtained all within the four seas, and became sovereign of Tianxia." (*Shijing-Xiaoya-Beishan*; *Shangshu-Dayumo*)[2]

Nevertheless, one cannot simply conclude that there is no distinction between "the one" and "the other" from a Confucian perspective. One of the Confucian classics says that "the

---

1 Zhao Tingyang, *The Tianxia System: A Philosophy for the World Institution*, Nanjing: Jiangsu Education Press, 2005, 14–15.

2 The Confucian classics cited in this article include *Shijing* (*Classic of Poetry*), *Shangshu* (*Classic of History*), *Liji* (*Classic of Rites*), *Chunqiu* (*Spring and Autumn [Annals]*), *Lunyu* (*Confucian Analects*) and *Mengzi* (*The Works of Mencius*). The English text comes from the translation of James Legge, except for some slight changes when necessary. *The Sacred Books of China: The Texts of Confucianism*, translated by James Legge, Oxford: Clarendon Press, 1885; *The Chinese Classics* (in five volumes), translated by James Legge, Hong Kong: Hong Kong University Press, 1960.

barbarous tribes disturb our great bright land" (*Shangshu-Yaodian*), which may remind us of the ancient Greeks' view of barbarians. However, unlike the Greeks' conception, in the eyes of the Confucians, the barbarians are also covered by Tianxia. They are not, as Persians to Greeks, an absolute and external image of savages, but may be converted by, and integrated into, the central civilization through education. What is more, even Shun and King Wan, the two legendary ideal ancient rulers highly admired by the Confucians, were recognized as "Eastern barbarian" and "Western barbarian":

> Shun was born in Chû-fang, removed to Fû-hsiâ, and died in Ming-t'iâo;—a man near the wild tribes on the east. King Wan was born in Châu by mount Ch'î, and died in Pî-ying;—a man near the wild tribes on the west. Those regions were distant from one another by more than a thousand lî … But when they got their wish, and carried their principles into practice throughout the Middle Kingdom, it was like uniting the two halves of a seal. When we examine those sages, both the earlier and the later, their principles are found to be the same.

In other words, there is no definite distinction between barbarians and non-barbarians; what matters here is not kinship, but the "principles" one carries out. Such a special way is considered by Liang Qichao, an early twentieth century politician and scholar, as "a Chinese idea which was developed quite early, that the world (four seas) is a family and all men are equal."[1]

It was difficult for the Greeks in the Classical Period to imagine such a "nothing outside" world, since "the other" was essential for them to build the identity of "self".[2] However, a new thought appeared from the very beginning of Stoicism. According to Plutarch:

---

1 Liang Qichao, *History of Political Thoughts in Pre-Qin Period*, Changsha: Yuelu Publishing House, 2010, 51.

2 Cf., Edith Hall, *Inventing the Barbarian: Greek Self Definition through Tragedy*. Oxford: Oxford University Press, 1991; Thomas Harrison, ed., *Greeks and Barbarians*, London: Routledge, 2001; Paul Cartledge, *The Greeks: A Portrait of Self and Others*, Oxford: Oxford University Press, 2002.

... the much-admired *Republic* of Zeno, the founder of the Stoic sect, may be summed up in this one main principle: that all the inhabitants of this world of ours should not live differentiated by their respective rules of justice into separate cities and communities, but that we should consider all men to be of one community and one polity, and that we should have a common life and an order (cosmos) common to us all.[1]

Zeno's *Republic* does not survive today. But we may again see Marcus Aurelius, a representative of late Stoics, repeating and developing the view of Cosmos as an encompassing political space: "for what other single polity can the whole race of mankind be said to be fellow-members?"[2] Therefore, a Stoic, or a world citizen, will not see any man in the world as "the other" that is alien to "self." As Martha Nussbaum concludes, according to Stoicism, "we should think of nobody as a stranger, outside our sphere of concern and obligation."[3]

When we recognize the "nothing outside" characteristic of both Cosmos and Tianxia, another question follows to be explored in this part: what is the relationship between Cosmos / Tianxia and the individual states?

Cosmos and Tianxia, in their respective systems, obviously surpass the independent states. But it does not mean that the latter is simply removed from, or replaced by, the former. Neither Stoics nor Confucians exclude individual states, or other social or political organizations, from Cosmos / Tianxia. Hierocles, a Stoic whose life is little known now, provides a famous metaphor of concentric circles:

1 Plutarch, *Moralia(IV)*, translated by Frank Cole Babbitt, Massachusetts: Harvard University Press, 1936, 329A–B.

2 Marcus Aurelius, *The Communings with Himself of Marcus Aurelius Antoninus, Emperor of Rome: Together with His Speeches and Sayings*, translated by C. R. Haines, Massachusetts: Harvard University Press, 1930, IV. 4.

3 Martha Nussbaum, "Kant and Stoic Cosmopolitanism," in *The Journal of Political Philosophy*, Vol. 5, No. 1, 1997, 9.

... beginning with that representing our own body, then the circles representing our parents, siblings, spouse and children, and on to more remote relatives, and then to members of the same deme and tribe, to fellow citizens, to those who belong to the same people or ethnos, until we arrive at the widest circle, which is that of the entire human race.[1]

Confucians understand a similar illustration of circles which expand from self (body), to family, to state, and finally to Tianxia (*Liji-Daxue*). Both Stoics and Confucians thus admit that one may possess different identities, belonging to smaller units and to Cosmos / Tianxia at the same time.

Moreover, while international society is always regarded as opposing domestic society in modern IR theories, neither Cosmos nor Tianxia represents a field with principles that are totally different to those within a state. Cosmos / Tianxia is a magnified state. Marcus Aurelius argues repeatedly that "the Universe (cosmos) is as it were a state (polis)."[2] And the term "cosmopolitēs" (world citizen) frequently used by Stoics is itself a combination of "cosmos" and "politēs" (citizen of the city-state). Cosmos therefore is a larger and higher space for the accomplishment of the city-state's political ideas. Similarly, Confucians see Tianxia as rather an extension than an objection of state. A capable emperor, according to the Confucians, "regulated and polished the people of his domain," and in the same way "united and harmonized the myriad States of the empire," and what he brought about at last "was universal concord." (*Shangshu-Yaodian*)

However, a critical difference exists here between the Stoic and Confucian cosmopolitanisms. For the Stoics, Cosmos, although a magnified city-state, is superior and prior to the state,

---

1 Ilaria Ramelli, *Hierocles the Stoic: Elements of Ethics, Fragments, and Excerpts*, Atlanta: Society of Biblical Literature, 2009, lvi. Nussbaum also mentioned a similar illustration in Cicero's *De Officiis* (Martha Nussbaum, "Kant and Stoic Cosmopolitanism," 9).

2 See for example, Marcus Aurelius, *The Communings with Himself of Marcus Aurelius Antoninus, Emperor of Rome: Together with His Speeches and Sayings*, IV. 3–4.

and is the ultimate achievement embedded in all the lower political forms. Cosmos is "the highest state, of which all other states are but as households."[1] Similarly, Epictetus says to his readers, "Never in reply to the question, to what country you belong, say that you are an Athenian or a Corinthian, but that you are a citizen of the world"; since if one "has learned that the greatest and supreme and the most comprehensive community is that which is composed of men and God ... why should not such a man call himself a citizen of the world."[2] The most renowned statement is from Seneca:

Let us embrace with our minds two commonwealths (res publicae): one great and truly common—in which gods and men are contained, in which we look not to this or that corner, but measure the bounds of our state (civitas) with the sun; the other the one to which the particular circumstances of birth have assigned us.[3]

Briefly speaking, "the true city" for the Stoics "is the cosmic city."

Confucians, on the contrary, believe that the most private family ethics, which comprises the second-smallest concentric circle, is the fundamental political element. It is said in *Liji*, one of the Five Classics of Confucians, that "[t]he laying the foundation of (all) love in the love of parents teaches people concord ... Therefore he who is perfectly filial approximates to be king, and he who is perfectly fraternal approximates to being presiding chieftain," and this was the way the ancient kings "united and kept together the kingdom with its states and families." (*Liji-Jiyi*) A more popular version may be found from the doctrine of Mencius:

Treat with the reverence due to age the elders in your own family, so that the

---

1   Marcus Aurelius, *The Communings with Himself of Marcus Aurelius Antoninus, emperor of Rome: Together with His Speeches and Sayings*, III.11.
2   Epictetus, *The Discourses of Epictetus*, translated by George Long, London: George Bell and Sons, 1890, I.9.1–6.
3   Malcolm Schofield, *The Stoic Idea of the City*, 93.

elders in the families of others shall be similarly treated; treat with the kindness due to youth the young in your own family, so that the young in the families of others shall be similarly treated; ... do this, and the kingdom may be made to go round in your palm. (*Mengzi-Lianghuiwang I*)

Tianxia is just a larger form of state, but not a superior being. Both Tianxia and the state are natural extensions of the prime relationship: family.

We may conclude that Cosmos and Tianxia, as political spaces for people to dwell in, are similar. Both of the two concepts are a space of "nothing outside," which includes the whole of human beings and eliminates the distinction between "self" and "the other"; moreover, both of them cover, as well as magnify, the form of the state, rather than excluding the latter. The only difference is that Cosmos is ultimate and fundamental for Stoics, while for Confucians, family is the highest priority, with Tianxia as a copy or image of this.

Cosmos and Tianxia: the Way to Dwell in

Although both Stoics and Confucians advocate a "nothing outside" world community (Cosmos / Tianxia) surpassing the individual state for people to dwell in, this does not mean that members of the community (man, state and other organizations) are in natural harmony—even a domestic society with the highest authority is not bound to be harmonious. We thus need to continue to explore Stoic and Confucian cosmopolitanisms with the question of how Cosmos or Tianxia creates peace and harmony.

From the perspective of Stoics, a world community is not in a "state of nature" as introduced by modern political philosophers. In fact, the term "Cosmos" itself implies that such a community is of order and good. Yet why and how? There lies an explicit distinction between Stoics and most modern political scientists. Cosmos, as a political space, is not only political in essence. It is a synthesis of Nature (physis), logic (logos) and ethics, in which natural philosophy and political philosophy are not two separate fields. The general principle in Cosmos is logos, which has a rich meaning covering logic, speech, and, most importantly, reason. Since Cosmos is governed by universal reason, it is evidently harmonious and ordered. As Epictetus maintains, God has appointed "that there should be summer and winter, plenty and dearth, virtue and vice, and all such contrarieties, for the harmony of the whole."[1] Obviously, such an idea of universal concord under logos contains an embryo of "natural law" thought and reminds us of Spinoza's theory of harmony.[2]

The point here, however, is not that people, as well as other beings in Cosmos, need to do nothing but enjoy the existing harmony. On the contrary, individuals should "accord with Nature," since "Nature (God, pneuma, cause, logos or destiny) is a perfect being, and the value of anything else in the world depends upon its relationship to Nature."[3] Here lies the essence of Stoic (cosmopolitan) ethics. A "world citizen," as Epictetus argues, is one who is able "to understand the divine administration of the universe and to take into account what follows from it."[4]

Therefore, the harmony within Cosmos as a political community, the tie among individuals, or the basis of world order, is the universal reason shared by everyone:

If the intellectual capacity is common to us all, common too is the reason ... If so, we are fellow-members of an organised community. If so, the Universe is as it were a state.[5]

The common reason of human beings is granted by God:

---

1 Epictetus, *The Discourses of Epictetus*, I.12.16.

2 For more detailed discussions, see A. A. Long, *Hellenistic Philosophy*, London: Duckworth, 1986, 147–209; Marcia L. Colish, *The Stoic Tradition from Antiquity to the Early Middle Ages, I, Stoicism in Classical Latin Literature*, Leiden: E. J. Brill, 1985, 31–36.

3 A. A. Long, *Hellenistic Philosophy*, 179.

4 G. R. Stanton, "The Cosmopolitan Ideas of Epictetus and Marcus Aurelius," in *Phronesis*, Vol. 13, No. 2, 1968, 184.

5 Marcus Aurelius, *The Communings with Himself of Marcus Aurelius Antoninus, Emperor of Rome: Together with his Speeches and Sayings*, IV. 4.

... from God have descended the seeds ... to all beings ... and particularly to rational beings—for these only are by their nature formed to have communion with God, being by means of reason conjoined with him—why should not such a man call himself a citizen of the world, why not a son of God.[1]

Since each man is a son of God, sharing common reason, human beings may and should cooperate with each other, in equality and friendship, because "all that is rational is akin," and "it is in man's nature to care for all men"; because "rational creatures have been made for one another"; and because "the Nature of the Universe has fashioned rational creatures for the sake of one another with a view to mutual benefit based upon worth, but by no means for harm."[2] The good order of Stoic Cosmos is thus rooted in single individuals, in their abilities, as well as duties, to achieve their perfect personalities by following the direction of reason, which is the common logos of both Nature and human beings.

God or Heaven, in Confucianism, does not naturally guarantee an established harmony in Tianxia. However, just like the Stoics, the Confucians maintain that the order of the human community is not separate from Nature, that is to say, Heaven (Nature) stands as the fundamental ground and origin of human ethics in Tianxia (under Heaven) which may ensure harmony. One of the most remarkable Confucian classics tells us at the very beginning:

What Heaven has conferred is called The (human) Nature; an accordance with this nature is called The Path of duty ... This Equilibrium (of personality) is the great root from which grow all the human actings in the world, and this Harmony is the universal path which they all should pursue. (*Liji-Zhongyong*)

---

1 Epictetus, *The Discourses of Epictetus*, I.9.4–6.

2 Marcus Aurelius, *The Communings with Himself of Marcus Aurelius Antoninus, Emperor of Rome: Together with His Speeches and Sayings*, III. 4, IV. 3, IX. 1.

While both the Stoics and the Confucians emphasize the connection between ethical persons and Heaven or Nature to create a harmonious political space, the core concept which the Confucians focus on is not the Stoic individual "Reason," but "Ren" (roughly translated as benevolence or virtue), which is interpreted traditionally as "meeting of persons," whereby:

... the notion of "human" does not exist if each man is separated, which means that the so called "perfect personality" would never be found if there were only one person alone in the world.[1]

As mentioned above, the Confucians cherish family ethics as the fundamental value, which represents the essence of "Ren." Political principles in Tianxia are no more than a copy of relations between parents and children, and between siblings. The love and sympathy within family are the basis of social and political orders which is called "Li" (rules of propriety). Harmony in the world community, as well as in other organizations, is not only reconciliation or peace without justice. If one manifests harmony "without regulating it by the rules of propriety, this likewise is not done." (*Confucius-Xueer*)

Therefore, Confucian cosmopolitanism means to expand family love to the world community, from the elementary stage that "Every one loves (above all others) his own parents and cherishes (as) children (only) his own sons," to the ultimate stage that "men did not love their parents only, nor treat as children only their own sons," that "a public and common spirit ruled all under the sky (Tianxia)." (*Liji-Liyun*) Even then, Confucians reveal a "hierarchical" love for others as the basic characteristic of its cosmopolitanism, while the Stoics hold an "indiscriminative" love for all people in Cosmos since everyone is equally the son of God.

We may simply say that Stoic cosmopolitanism focuses on individual persons (or

---

1   Liang Qichao, *History of Political Thoughts in Pre-Qin Period*, 80.

even self), while Confucian cosmopolitanism on ethical relations between persons. At first glance, this is quite close to the conflict between liberalism and communitarianism in political philosophy, or between cosmopolitanism (in the modern sense) and communitarianism in normative IR theories.[1] Indeed, modern cosmopolitanism is always regarded as a successor of Stoicism and Kant, while Confucianism is sometimes criticized by liberalists as communitarianism.[2] Nevertheless, with more detailed research, we will find that, unlike liberalism / cosmopolitanism vs. communitarianism in the modern context, Stoic and Confucian Cosmopolitanisms are not in rivalry with each other. Although they begin from quite different starting points, the two ways have similar ends.

Stoic Cosmopolitanism does not seem to conform with Thomas Pogge's widely cited statement that individualism, universality and generality are the three elements "shared by all cosmopolitan positions."[3] Pogge's focus, I think, is universal individual rights. It is one of the main concerns of modern political philosophy, but not of classical Stoicism. The state, from the perspective of modern political thinkers, is chiefly an institution used to protect individual rights; while for the classical Greeks, the city-state is rather a space to perfect and display the virtue (aretē) of citizens through their participating in politics and taking responsibility for the community. When the Stoics say that Cosmos is like a city-state, they are not, as modern liberalists or cosmopolitans, calling for universal and general rights.

Marcus Aurelius tells us, as well as himself, "he that prizes a soul which is rational, universal, and civic ... keeps his own soul, in itself and in its activity, rational and social, and to this end works conjointly with all that is akin to him."[4] An "unencumbered self"[5]

---

1 Cf. Chris Brown, *International Relations Theory: New Normative Approaches*, New York: Columbia University Press, 1992, 12.

2 Cf. Lee Minghuei, *Political Thought in the Confucian Perspective*, Beijing: Peking University Press, 2005, 11–46.

3 Thomas Pogge, "Cosmopolitanism and Sovereignty," in *Ethics*, Vol. 103, No. 1, 1992, 48–49.

4 Marcus Aurelius, *The Communings with Himself of Marcus Aurelius Antoninus, Emperor of Rome: Together with His Speeches and Sayings*, VI. 14.

5 This is a term used by Michael Sandel to criticize liberalism. Michael J. Sandel, "The Procedural Republic and the Unencumbered Self," in *Political Theory*, Vol. 12, No. 1, 1984.

is not found in Stoic Cosmopolitanism. "Self" may only be defined and perfected through responsibility for the world community, which is also the way to realize one's reason and establish a well-ordered soul.[1] Colish correctly points out that:

> ... [t]he idea that all men share in the common possession of reason also means, for the Stoics, that all men by nature have moral obligations to each other. All men form a natural moral community of rational beings.[2]

On the other hand, although Confucian cosmopolitanism argues that the ethical relationship among people is the fundamental element, it does not, as some modern "collectivism" did, tend to dispel or oppress individuals. It is within communities, from family, state to the largest Tianxia, that individuals achieve self-fulfillment. That is why a noble man "cultivates himself so as to give rest to all the people," and it is through personal cultivation that Tianxia "is thereby tranquillized" (*Confucious-Xianwen*; *Mencius-Jinxin II*). The ultimate stage, where "a public and common spirit ruled all under the sky (Tianxia)" means that a great personality in the Universe is achieved.[3]

Chang Hao, a renowned scholar in Chinese philosophy and history, argues that Confucianism is a kind of "personalism," a third way beyond liberalism and communitarianism, which integrates collectivity and individuality.[4] Therefore, we may say that Confucian cosmopolitanism is not a version of communitarianism in normative IR theories, since what it pursues is harmony and mutual perfection between individuals and community in Tianxia. That is why Qian Mu, one of the most celebrated Chinese historians and Confucian scholars in the twentieth century, concludes that the idea of "family" has not constrained

---

1　Shi Minmin and Zhang Xuefu, *Stoicism II*, Beijing: China Social Science Press, 2009, 336.
2　Colish, *The Stoic Tradition from Antiquity to the Early Middle Ages*, I, *Stoicism in Classical Latin Literature*, 38.
3　Liang Qichao, *History of Political Thoughts in Pre-Qin Period*, 88.
4　Cf., Lee Minghuei, *Political Thought in the Confucian Perspective*, 21.

the minds of Chinese, on the contrary, it is in the inherent transition from such an idea to the notion of humanity that the Chinese are able to surpass beyond the narrow scopes of nation and of state.[1]

Starting from individual reason and personal relations respectively, Stoic and Confucian cosmopolitanisms thus lead to the same final purpose: realizing self being through practices and duties in a world community.

Conclusion

Both Stoic cosmopolitanism and Confucian cosmopolitanism propose a "nothing outside" world community which establishes none as "the other" opposing "self"; and their ways for people to dwell in the largest community are quite similar. There are, of course, a few differences between the two cosmopolitanisms. However, the two theories share some significant points and are not incommensurable. This historical comparison between the two political thoughts existing more than two thousand years ago, however, may shed some light on current reflections on international affairs.

First, it implies the possibility to communicate Western tradition and Chinese tradition in considering the world. As mentioned above, with the rise of China, some Chinese scholars intend to prove that Chinese culture (mainly the doctrine of peace and harmony in Confucianism) is a substitute for Western political thought for shaping a better world, since the latter focuses too much on individual national interests and struggles among nations.[2] It seems more like a passion to prove China's cultural superiority against the background of China's rise, than a serious and profound academic consideration. The study on Stoic and Confucian cosmopolitanisms, however, does not support such an arbitrary statement. I agree with Wang Dingding's expectation in his article "World Citizen and Tianxia Zhuyi"

---

1 Qian Mu, *Introduction to the History of Chinese Culture*, Beijing: The Commercial Press, 1994, 52.
2 Indeed, while the study on Western IR theories has already been an important subject in China, very few scholars are interested in cosmopolitanism.

that Stoic cosmopolitanism may act as a bridge for contemporary Chinese to understand our ancestors' vision of Tianxia, which many of us have forgotten for too long a time.[1] Yet, it is even more important to avoid artificially establishing the contrast between Chinese and Western traditions, which will only limit our minds in practice as well as in theory.

On the other hand, modern cosmopolitan political thought, which has by now been always rooted in the Western philosophical tradition, may also turn to Chinese traditions to draw some useful elements. A "fusion of horizons" (a term borrowed from Hans-Georg Gadamer) is necessary and helpful in constructing and promoting international political thought.

Second, the ideas shared by the two cosmopolitanisms are actually often ignored by mainstream IR theories. Obviously, they provide another vision of the world, which may enlighten our thoughts to escape the "Westphalian Straitjacket." Just as Jens Bartelson describes, many sources of visions of the world community "have traditionally attracted little or no interest from students of international political thought."[2] Furthermore, modern IR theories often focus on the themes of states, international organizations and transnational corporations, where "scientific" patterns exist, while living humans disappear. The two classical cosmopolitanisms, when emphasizing individual duties, provide us with a new perspective that includes everyone within the international arena.

We should not simply look forward to establishing a world "order" or "institution" with Stoic or Confucian characteristics. That might be the least we could benefit from them.[3] Conversely, we may recall Colish and Long's words on Stoic cosmopolitanism, which also

---

1 Wang Dingding, "World Citizen and Tianxia Zhuyi," in *IT Managers' World*, 2008, 103.

2 Jens Bartelson, *Visions of World Community*, ix.

3 For example, a Confucian Tianxia order would be much more awkward in the modern world, since no one can answer questions regarding which person or state should be the "sage king," what the status of females, how to distribute justice among sovereign states, etc. Yao Dali, a Chinese professor of history, pointed out that "[a]s for the political framework and institutional arrangement of national governance, Confucianism is no more than a low grade ore," Yao Dali, "Zhu Weizheng and His Style in Historical Studies," in *Wenhui Bao*, March 19, 2012.

fit Confucianism well: "In the ideal cosmopolis there are few institutions. They are not needed, for in this state men function in terms of their natural reason … The mutual natural obligations which constitute the ideal cosmopolis are also incumbent on the Stoic in this imperfect world … Stoic political theory is not a blue-print for reform but a paradigm of the world as it might be if men could be united not by artificial ties but by the recognition in each other of common values and common purposes."[1]

For the Stoics, every man is capable of sharing the common reason; for the Confucians, "[a]ll men may be Yaos and Shuns (the ideal sage kings) … The course of Yao and Shun was simply that of filial piety and fraternal duty." (*Mengzi-Gaozi II*) With embedding international affairs into general personal ethics, the two cosmopolitanisms may help us to reflect on the tendency of "dehumanization" in IR studies, and remind us that world politics cannot only be a realm with struggles for power and conflicts for interests among states and statesmen, but also one with the possibilities of perfecting personality and virtue through duties in every human's minds and practices.

Last but not least, the Stoic and Confucian cosmopolitanisms may also help us find a way out of the dilemma between cosmopolitanism and communitarianism in modern international political theories. On the basis of Martha Nussbaum's studies, Chris Brown offers "a sketch of one possible neo-Aristotelian resolution of the cosmopolitan-communitarian debate" in an article in 2000. With a special emphasis on "virtue ethics," Professor Brown makes an acute observation that:

… [w]hile the virtues will be shaped by and may only be exercised in an actual community—thus endorsing the central communitarian intuition—they are in some sense universals, reflecting common human responses to common human

---

1   A. A. Long, *Hellenistic Philosophy*, 205; Marcia L. Colish, *The Stoic Tradition from Antiquity to the Early Middle Ages, I, Stoicism in Classical Latin Literature*, 39.

experiences—and thus the central cosmopolitan intuition is also vindicated.[1]

The Stoic and Confucian cosmopolitanisms, with their similar focuses on virtue ethics, could be another, if not better, source to develop a solution for the "cosmopolitan-communitarian debate." As mentioned above, the two classical cosmopolitanisms reach the same end by different routes. Both of them intend to integrate individuality and collectivity in a universal "nothing outside" scope, through the practical virtues and duties of each person. There is still a long way to go before the classical theories may effectively inspire modern international political thought.

Yet, such an effort should not be inutile, as a Roman adage says, "Antiquitas est Nova."

(Acknowledgement: This chapter is a revised version of a paper first published in *Chinese Political Science Review*, Vol. 1, No. 2, 2016. The author thanks the journal for its kind permission to reprint. The article is a revision of the author's speech at the 2017 UKCHA Annual Forum.)

---

1   Chris Brown, "Towards a neo-Aristotelian resolution of the cosmopolitan-communitarian debate," in Maria Lensu and Jan-Stefan Fritz eds., *Value Pluralism, Normative Theory and International Relations*, Basingstoke: Palgrave Macmillan, 2000, 76–99.

文化交汇

Cultural Interplay

Mechanisms of Contact-Induced Linguistic Creations in Chinese Buddhist Translations

Juan Wu[*]

While commenting on the role of translation in the shaping of Chinese civilization, China's preeminent Indologist, the late Professor Ji Xianlin (季羨林, 1911–2009), notes:

> If compared to a river, the river of Chinese civilization has had its ebbs and flows, but it has never dried up, because there was fresh water flowing into it. There were many times when fresh water flowed into this river. The two largest inflows came separately from India and the West. Both inflows owed their success to translation. The *elixir vitae* that enables Chinese civilization to maintain perennial youth is translation. Translation is enormously useful! (Ji 1995, 3)[1]

This paper deals with one of the two largest foreign inflows mentioned above by Professor Ji, namely the project of translating Indian Buddhist scriptures into Chinese, which lasted from the mid-second century CE up to the 11th–12th centuries CE. In this paper I do not explore Chinese Buddhist translations from a religious studies perspective, that is to say, I do not use them as sources for understanding the Buddhism of India or China. Rather, I would like to approach them from a linguistic perspective, and hope to

---

* Juan Wu (吳娟) is a tenured associate professor of Buddhist Philology at the Department of Chinese Language and Literature, Tsinghua University, where she has worked since 2017. She has published on the scriptural traditions of Indian Buddhism, the history of Chinese and Tibetan translations of Indian Buddhist texts, Indian Buddhist monastic law codes, and the narrative literature of Buddhism and Jainism.

1 My translation.

demonstrate their value for elucidating the impact translation may have on language. More precisely, I seek to answer two questions. First, what are the major mechanisms of contact-induced creations that may be observed in Chinese Buddhist translations? Here, contact-induced creations refer to new language elements that were created due to the contact of Indian and Chinese languages during the translation process. Identifying the major mechanisms of contact-induced creations in Chinese Buddhist translations is essential for understanding both the temporary and lasting impacts of the translation of Indian Buddhist texts on the Chinese language. Second, what are the similarities and differences between the mechanisms of contact-induced creations in Chinese Buddhist translations and the mechanisms found in non-Sinitic language contacts? This question may help us determine to what extent Chinese Buddhist translations may be regarded as unique when compared with language contacts in other cultures.

With these questions in mind, I organise my discussion as follows. I will begin with some theoretical background concerning language contact through translation. Following this, I will examine various mechanisms of contact-induced creations in Chinese Buddhist translations. I will focus first on the lexical level, and then on the syntactic level. By presenting examples of contact-induced creations in Chinese Buddhist translations, I will correlate them with similar linguistic phenomena found in non-Sinitic language contacts. In the concluding section, I will summarize my results and consider what insights Chinese Buddhist translations may offer to the study of language contact through translation in general.

Language Contact Through Translation: Some Theoretical Background

Before looking at examples of contact-induced creations in Chinese Buddhist translations, let me briefly introduce two concepts. The first concept is language contact through translation. Language contact, in its simplest definition, refers to the kind of situation in which an individual or a group of people use "more than one language in the same place at the same time" (Thomason 2001, 1). Translation represents a particular kind of language contact. When a translator translates a text from a source language into a target language, by using his or her own bilingual skills, the translator brings source and target languages into contact. Such contact is called "language contact through translation" (see, for instance, Kranich, Becher and Höder 2011). The second concept is contact-induced language change. What kind of language change may be classified as contact-induced? According to Sarah Thomason, a leading expert on language contact, "any linguistic change that would have been less likely to occur outside a particular contact situation is due at least in part to language contact" (Thomason 2001, 62). Usually, contact-induced language change appears as a result of transferring certain linguistic elements or features from one language into another. In the case of language contact through translation, as some linguists put it, no matter how good or how bad a translation is, there is always a "shining-through" of source-language features in the translation text (Teich 2003, 145). Here, I give two examples, both concerning religious translations in premodern Europe, to show how this linguistic transfer works in language contact through translation.

The first example concerns idiomatic borrowing. As is well known, among English translations of the Bible, the King James Version (alias the King James Bible) has had the greatest influence on the English language. The King James Version was once read daily by millions of people in the English-speaking world; through this version of the Bible, many Hebrew and Greek idioms gained widespread currency and became part of everyday English conversation. Expressions such as "know for a certainty," "how are the mighty fallen," "to everything there is a season," "a thorn in the flesh," and "see through a glass, darkly," to mention but a few, were all imported from Hebrew or Greek into English through the King James Bible (see Crystal 2010, 263–291).

The second example relates to syntactic borrowing. In the late Middle Ages (c. 14th–16th century), when Latin religious texts were translated into Old Swedish, some Latin syntactic elements were consequently also imported into Old Swedish. For instance, Medieval Latin has a polymorphemic causal conjunction *pro eo quod* ("because"), which has no parallel in Old Swedish. By translating each of the three Latin morphemes into Old Swedish based on semantic equivalence (i.e., using Old Swedish *for* ["for"], *by* ["ablative / dative form of the demonstrative"] and *at* ["complementizer"] to render Latin *pro*, *eo* and *quod,* respectively), Latin–Swedish bilingual clerics created the new expression *for þy at* ("because"), which eventually became the standard causal conjunction in Old Swedish (see Kranich, Becher and Höder 2011, 19–26).

These are examples of contact-induced changes in Western languages. So far as I am aware, modern linguists working on language contact have not paid due attention to Chinese Buddhist translations, which in fact constitute an extremely valuable and rich source for understanding how translation may influence language. In what follows, I will provide some representative examples of contact-induced lexical and syntactic creations in Chinese Buddhist translations, with particular focus on the underlying mechanisms they reflect.

Mechanisms of Contact-Induced Lexical Creations in Chinese Buddhist Translations

The Chinese translation of Indian Buddhist scriptures, which lasted for nearly ten centuries, is one of the most spectacular, cross-cultural enterprises in human civilization. During this period, foreign missionaries from various regions including Western Central Asia, Eastern Central Asia, the Indian subcontinent and Southeast Asia, came to China and dedicated themselves to this enterprise for the sake of spreading Buddhism. Most (though not all) foreign Buddhist missionaries did not possess an excellent command of the Chinese literary language and tended to work closely with local Chinese assistants, who had almost never fully mastered any Indic language. As a result, the vast majority of Chinese Buddhist translations were products of collaboration, in which both foreign monks and Chinese assistants made indispensable endeavours. Besides foreign missionaries, there were also Chinese monk-translators, among whom the most famous were Faxian (法顯, c. 337–418), Xuanzang (玄奘, 600 / 602–664) and Yijing (義淨, 635–713).

Regarding the source languages of Chinese Buddhist translations (i.e., the languages of their Indic originals), scholars nowadays generally agree that many (though not all) Chinese Buddhist translations produced in the early centuries of the Common Era were translated from Indic texts, which were not composed in Classical Sanskrit, but in various Prākrits (of which the best known is Gāndhārī) or in various mixtures of Prākrit and Sanskrit.[1] After the 6th–7th centuries CE, as the tendency of Sanskritization gradually became dominant in India, the Indic texts from which Chinese Buddhist translations were made were generally highly Sanskritized, and only occasionally contained traces of the underlying Prākrits.[2]

Regarding the target language, some scholars call the language of Chinese Buddhist translations "Buddhist Scriptural Chinese" (Zürcher 2012 [1999], 11) or "Buddhist Chinese." (Zhu 2008) This is a peculiar type of Chinese literary language. It has two basic features. First, it contains numerous vernacular elements. These vernacularisms have been studied in detail by previous scholars (see for instance, Zürcher 1977, 1991, 1996; Karashima 1996a, 1996b, 1997). Second, it contains a large amount of contact-induced, new language elements. This second feature is the focus of the present paper. Let us now look at the major mechanisms of contact-induced creations in Chinese Buddhist translations. The examples given below are not meant to be exhaustive, and are only provided to illustrate the major mechanisms. I will first discuss lexical creations and then syntactic creations.

Phonemic Loan

In Chinese Buddhist translations, as in many other language-contact situations, the most noticeable type of lexical creation is a loanword, also called phonemic loan or

---

1   On Prākrit features of Indic originals of early Chinese Buddhist translations, see for instance, Karashima 1992, 262–275; 2006; 2007; 2013; Boucher 1998; Nattier 2008, 21–22.

2   Both von Hinüber (1989, 350) and Salomon (2001, 248) have convincingly argued that the Sanskritization of Buddhist literature already took place during the 2nd–3rd centuries CE under the Kuṣāṇas. von Hinüber (1989, 354) further noted that the Sarvāstivādins and Dharmaguptakas "seem to have followed the same pattern of development, which may have reached the final stage that is Sanskrit at about 500 AD." Professor Seishi Karashima kindly informed me, "the Mahāsāṃghika-Lokottaravādins used Buddhist Hybrid Sanskrit which became closer and closer to Classical Sanskrit, if we look at the Sanskrit manuscripts of the Mahāvastu of various periods." (email communication, February 1, 2019)

transliteration. A loanword maintains, either entirely or partially, the phonetic form (i.e. the sound) of its foreign origin. Loanwords are extremely common in language contact. English has many religious and non-religious loanwords borrowed from Latin (Durkin 2014, 105–119, 254–263). In Chinese Buddhist texts, most loanwords are transliterations of Indian Buddhist terminology, and only a small number of loanwords belong to non-religious vocabulary. The table below lists some representative examples of loanwords in Chinese Buddhist translations. Among them, *fó* 佛, *mílè* 彌勒, *chán* 禪, *tǎ* 塔, *mó* 魔, *bǐqiū* 比丘, *jiāshā* 袈裟 and *shělì* 舍利 are all Buddhist terms, whereas *chànà* 剎那, *pōlí* 頗梨, *nàluó* 那羅, *nàtóu* 那頭, *màn* 鬘 and *mòlì* 末利 are all non-religious words. While most loanwords listed below have Prākrit or Sanskrit origins, some (for instance, *fó* 佛 and *mílè* 彌勒) have Central Asian origins. Despite such differences, all loanwords preserve, to a greater or lesser extent, the sounds of their foreign origins.

Loan Translation

Loan translation, also called calque, is basically a morpheme-for-morpheme translation. For instance, the German word *Wolkenkratzer*, the French word *gratteciel* and the Spanish word *rascacielos* are all loan translations of the English word *skyscraper* (Haugen 1950, 214); the German term *Heilige Geist* and the English term *Holy Spirit* are loan translations of Latin's *Spiritus Sanctus* (Bynon 1977, 233). The difference between phonemic loans and loan translations is this: in the case of a phonemic loan, which is imported from a source language into a target language is the sound and meaning of a word, whereas in the case of a loan translation, what is imported is the lexical structure and meaning of a word.

There are mainly three types of loan translation in Chinese Buddhist texts. The first type comprises loan translations of Indic compounds or phrases. For instance, *shìjiè* 世界 is a word-for-word translation of the Sanskrit compound *lokadhātu* ("world system") or its Prākrit equivalents, with *shì* 世 and *jiè* 界 separately rendering *loka* ("world") and *dhātu* ("realm"). While both *shì* 世 and *jiè* 界 are indigenous Chinese elements, their combination

Table 1: Examples of Phonemic Loans in Chinese Buddhist Translations

Loanword	Reconstruction of Eastern Han Chinese (EHC)[1]	Reconstruction of Early Middle Chinese (EMC)[2]	Prākrit, Sanskrit or Central Asian Origin[3]
佛 ("buddha")	*bjət	*but	Central Asian *but[4]
彌勒 ("Maitreya")	*mjiei lək	*mjiǎ / mji lək	Tocharian Metrak, Maitrāk, or Bactrian Mētraga[5]
禪 ("meditation")	*dźjan	*dzian	Pkt. jhāna / jhāṇa (corresponding to Skt. dhyāna, "meditation")
塔 ("pagoda")	*thəp	*tʰap	Pkt. thupa / thuva (corresponding to Skt. stūpa, "pagoda")
魔 ("devil")	*ma	*ma	Skt. māra or Pkt. mara
比丘 ("monk")	*bjiəi khju	*pji kʰuw	Pkt. bhikkhu / bhikhu (corresponding to Skt. bhikṣu, "monk")
袈裟 ("monastic robe")	*kra sra	*kaɨ / kɛ: ʂaɨ / ʂɛ:	Skt. kaṣāya ("monastic robe")
舍利 ("bodily relics")	*śja- ljiəi-	*ɕia" liʰ	Skt. śarīra ("bodily relics")
剎那 ("instant")	*tshrat na	*tʂʰaɨt / tʂʰɛ:t naʰ	Skt. kṣaṇa ("instant, moment")
頗梨 (var. 玻璃, "glass")	*pha ljiəi	*pʰa li	Pkt. phalia (corresponding to Skt. sphaṭika, "crystal")
那羅 ("dancer")	*na la	*naʰ la	Pkt. naḷa / nala (corresponding to Skt. naṭa, "actor, dancer")
那頭 ("serpent")	*na dou	*naʰ dəw	Pkt. *nādo / *nā"o (corresponding to Skt. nāgo, "serpent")[6]
鬘 (var. 蔓, "garland")	*man / mjwɐn	*maɨn / mɛ:n	Skt. mālā ("garland")
末利 ("jasmine")	*mat ljiəi	*mat liʰ	Skt. mallikā ("jasmine")

Notes:

(1) Throughout this paper, the reconstructed pronunciations of Eastern Han (25–200 CE) Chinese are quoted from Coblin 1983.

(2) The reconstructed pronunciations of Early Middle Chinese are quoted from Pulleyblank 1991. The term "Early Middle Chinese" used by Pulleyblank refers to the language underlying the rhyme dictionary *Qieyun* 切韻 (601 CE), which represents the standard language "common to educated speakers from both north and south in the period of division that came to an end with the Sui reconquest of the south in 589." (Pulleyblank 1991, 2)

(3) In this paper I use Pkt. and Skt. to denote Prākrit and Sanskrit respectively. On the Prākrit origins of *bǐqiū* 比丘, *chán* 禪 and *tǎ* 塔, see Karashima 2010, 35, 57, 475; on the Prākrit origins of *nàluó* 那羅 and *bōli* 玻璃, see Karashima 2001, 187; 2014, 323.

(4) On the Central Asian (probably old Tocharian) origin *but* of *fó* 佛, see Bernhard 1970, 59; Ji 1992.

(5) See Bailey 1946, 780; Ji 1992, 29; 1998, 57–68; Karashima 2006, 356; 2010, 318.

(6) See Bailey 1946, 784; Karashima 1994, 17; 2006, 360–361.

is a contact-induced neologism. Likewise, *sì-shèngdì* 四聖諦 is a word-for-word translation of the compound *caturāryasatyāni* ("Four Noble Truths") or the synonymous phrase *catvāry āryasatyāni*, with *sì* 四, *shèng* 聖 and *dì* 諦 separately rendering *catur / catvāri* ("four"), *ārya* ("noble") and *satyāni* ("truths"). Similar instances include: *fǎlún* 法輪 (< Skt. *dharmacakra* ["Dharma-wheel"] or its Prākrit equivalents); *tiānyǎn* 天眼 (< Skt. *divyacakṣus* ["divine eye"] or its Prākrit equivalents); *ròuyǎn* 肉眼 (< Skt. *māṃsacakṣus* ["physical eye"] or its Prākrit equivalent); *lìgēn* 利根 (< Skt. *tīkṣṇendriya* ["of sharp faculties"] or its Prākrit equivalents); *tánzhǐ* 彈指 (< Skt. *acchaṭāsaṃghāta*, ["snap of fingers, i.e., a jiffy"] or its Prākrit equivalents); *zuòyì* 作意 (< Skt. *manasi-√kṛ* ["to reflect on"] or its Prākrit equivalents); and *zuòzhèng* 作證 (< Skt. *sākṣāt-√kṛ* ["to make visible before the eyes, i.e., to realize"] or its Prākrit equivalents). Loan translations of compounds or phrases are common in language contact. For instance, the German compound word *herunter-laden* was calqued from the English term *down-load*, the French word *presqu'île* from Latin's *paen-insula* (lit. "almost-island"), the English term *loan-word* from German's *Lehn-wort*, and the English phrase *marriage of convenience* from the French's *mariage de convenance* (Haspelmath and Tadmor 2009, 39).

The second type of loan translation comprises loan translations of Indic words containing prefixes or suffixes. Take, for example, Indic words with negative prefixes. Before the arrival of Buddhism, Archaic Chinese had verbs of negation and negative adverbs, but did not have negative prefixes. When Indian Buddhist texts were translated into Chinese through loan translation, some negative prefixes were introduced into the Chinese language (Zhu 2003, 14–18). For instance, *wèilái* 未 來 is a loan translation of Skt. *anāgata* ("not come, i.e., future") or its Prākrit equivalents, with *wèi* 未 and *lái* 來 separately rendering the negative prefix *an-* and the past participle *āgata* ("come, arrived"). Similar instances include: *wúshàng* 無上 (< Skt. *anuttara* ["without a superior, i.e., supreme"]); *wúlòu* 無漏 (< Skt. *anāsrava* ["without outflow"]); *wúmíng* 無明 (< Skt. *avidyā* ["ignorance, the state of being unwise"]); *wúxué* 無學 (< Skt. *aśaikṣa* ["one who no longer needs religious training, i.e., an *arhat*"]); *bùjiǔ* 不久 (< Skt. *acira* ["not long"]); *bùsīyì* 不思議 and *bùkěsīyì* 不可思議 (< Skt. *acintya* or Pkt. *acintiya* ["unconceivable"]);[1] *fēixiǎng* 非想 (< Skt. *asaṃjñā* ["non-conception, the state of being unconscious"]);[2] and *fēijiā* 非 家 (< Skt. *anagārikā*

---

1   For instance, Kumārajīva's fifth-century translation of the *Vimalakīrtinirdeśa* ("Exposition of Vimalakīrti") has the following sentence (T. 475 [xiv] 548b20–21): 舍利弗! 此室常現八未曾有難得之法。誰有見斯不思議事而復樂於聲聞法乎! ("Śāriputra! This room always manifests the eight unprecedentedly rare *dharmas*. Who could see these inconceivable things and still take pleasure in the *śrāvaka* Dharma!" [tr. quoted from McRae 2004, 130]) The Sanskrit parallel to the latter part of this Chinese sentence reads (Study Group on Buddhist Sanskrit Literature 2006, 72, folio 44a7): *ka imām acintyadharmatāṃ paśyañ śrāvakadharmatāyai spṛhayet* ("Who, seeing such inconceivable things, would desire for the *śrāvaka*-Dharma"), in which *acintya-* ("unconceivable") matches with the term 不思議 used by Kumārajīva. As for examples where 不可思議 corresponds to Skt. *acintya*, see Karashima 1998, 27–28; 2001, 25.

2   An example from Bodhiruci's sixth-century translation of the *Vajracchedikā Prajñāpāramitā* ("Perfection of Wisdom that Cuts like a Diamond") reads (T. 236 [viii] 759a19–20): 何以故? 我想、眾生想、壽者想、受者想, 即是非想 ("Why is that? The idea of self, the idea of living beings, the idea of a soul, and the idea of a recipient are all non-conceptions"), whose Sanskrit parallel reads (Harrison and Watanabe 2006, 125, §14c, folio 40v5–6): *tat kasya heto<ḥ> yāsāv ātmasaṃjñā saivāsaṃjñā <|> yā satvasaṃjñā jīvasaṃjñā pudgalasaṃjñā saivāsaṃjñā* ("Why is that? Any such conception of self is indeed non-conception. Any conception of a living being, any conception of a soul, any conception of a person, is indeed non-conception"), in which *asaṃjñā* ("non-conception") matches with the term 非想 used by Paramārtha.

["homeless life"]).[1]

Moreover, in Indic Buddhist texts, verbs with the gerundive suffix *-tavya* / *-anīya* / *-ya* were often (though not always) translated as "*yìng* 應 + Verb," including, for instance: *yìngzuò* 應作 (< *karaṇīya*, "to be done"); *yìngshuō* 應說 (< *vaktavya* ["to be said"] or *nirdeṣṭavya* ["to be expounded"]); *yìngjiàn* 應見 (< *draṣṭavya* ["to be seen"]); *yìngzhī* 應知 (< Skt. *jñātavya* ["to be known"]); and *yìng-gòngyǎng* 應供養 (< *vandanīya*, "to be venerated").[2] Loan translations of words with prefixes or suffixes may also be found in other language-

---

1 For instance, Xuanzang's seventh-century translation of the *Vimalakīrtinirdeśa* has the phrase 以清淨信, 棄捨家法, 趣於非家 (T. 476 [xiv] 587a16), whose Sanskrit parallel reads (Study Group on Buddhist Sanskrit Literature 2006, 121, folio 74b5): *śraddhayāgārād anagārikāṃ pravrajitaḥ* ("out of faith, gone from the household into homeless life"), in which *anagārikāṃ* ("homeless life") matches with the term 非家 used by Xuanzang.

2 The combination "*yìng* 應 + Verb" used to translate Sanskrit or Prākrit gerundives generally follows the syntactic rules of Chinese. For instance, Kumārajīva's translation of the *Vimalakīrtinirdeśa* contains the sentence (T. 475 [xiv] 553a9): 是應作, 是不應作 ("This should be done [and] this should not be done"). Its Sanskrit parallel reads (Study Group on Buddhist Sanskrit Literature 2006, 96, folio 58b1): *idaṃ karaṇīyam idam akaraṇīyam* ("This is to be done [and] this is not to be done"), in which *karaṇīya* ("to be done") and *akaraṇīya* ("not to be done") match respectively with 應作 and 不應作. Also in Kumārajīva's translation we find (T. 475 [xiv] 541c13): 唯羅睺羅! 不應說出家功德之利 ("O Rāhula! You should not expound the benefits of renunciation"). Its Sanskrit parallel reads (Study Group on Buddhist Sanskrit Literature 2006, 31, folio 18b6): *na bhadantarāhulaivaṃ pravrajyāyā guṇānuśaṃsā nirdeṣṭavyā yathā tvaṃ nirdiśasi* | ("Venerable Rāhula! The benefits and virtues of renunciation are not to be expounded in the same way that you expound"), in which *nirdeṣṭavya* ("to be expounded") matches with 應說. Bodhiruci's translation of the *Vajracchedikā Prajñāpāramitā* has the sentence (T. 236 [viii] 761b6): 由法應見佛 ("One should see a Buddha from the Dharma"). Its Sanskrit parallel reads (Schopen 1989, 105, folio 11a1): *draṣṭavyo dharmato buddho* ("A Buddha is to be seen from the Dharma"), in which *draṣṭavya* ("to be seen") matches with 應見. Also in Bodhiruci's translation we find (T. 236 [viii] 759c11–12): 一切世間天人阿脩羅等皆應供養 ("The whole world with its gods, humans and *asura*s should all worship [that piece of ground]"). Its Sanskrit parallel reads (Harrison and Watanabe 2006, 130, §15c, folio 45r5): *sadevamānuṣāsurasya lokasya vandanīyaḥ* ("It is to be venerated by the world with its gods, humans and *asura*s"), in which *vandanīya* ("to be venerated") matches with 應供養. In this regard I thank an anonymous reviewer for recommending Dr. Yezi Mu's PhD thesis *Tense and Aspect in Early Chinese Buddhist Texts: a Typological Approach*, which is, however, unfortunately inaccessible to me.

contact situations. For instance, the Middle English verbs *out-bake*, *out-dry*, *out-fight*, *out-hear*, *out-take* and *out-term* were calqued, respectively, from the Latin *excoquō* ("to boil"), *exsiccō* ("to dry up"), *expugnō* ("to overcome"), *exaudiō* ("to hear"), *ēripiō* ("to snatch away") and *exterminō* ("to banish"), with the English prefix *out-* rendering the Latin prefix *e-/ex-* (Schröder 2011, 126–127). The Latin terms *quālitās* ("quality") and *quantitās* ("quantity") were calqued separately from Greek ποιότης / *poiótēs* ("suchness") and ποσότης / *posótēs* ("muchness"), with the Latin suffix *-tās* (denoting abstractness) rendering the Greek suffix -της / *-tēs* ("-ness").

The third type of Chinese Buddhist loan translation may be called (folk-)etymological translation, since it is based on a particular tradition of Indian semantic analysis, known as *nirvacana*. As Max Deeg (2008, 97) has aptly put it, "A typical *nirvacana*-analysis breaks a word down into two (or more) verbal elements (roots)." For instance, *wénwù* 聞物 (lit. "hearing things"), is a pseudo-etymological translation of the city-name Śrāvastī (or its Prākrit forms), with *wén* 聞 ("to hear") and *wù* 物 ("thing") separately rendering *śrāv-* (< √*śru*, "to hear") and *-vastī* (correlated with *vastu*, "thing").[1] The name Śrāvastī does not really mean "hearing things." The breaking down of this name into two parts (*śrāv + [v] astī*) is the result of applying the *nirvacana* method of Indian semantic analysis. Likewise, the Indian master Paramārtha's (499–569) separate translation of the names Kāśyapa and Maudgalyāyana as, respectively, *yǐnguāng* 飲光 ("drinking light") and *shòu-húdòu* 受胡豆 ("receiving foreign beans [i.e., beans imported from the West]"), also resulted from applying the *nirvacana* method of Indian semantic analysis (see Funayama 2008, 155–156). *Yǐnguāng* 飲光 is based on an interpretation of Kāśyapa as being derived from √*pā* ("to drink") + √*kāś* ("to shine");[2] *shòu-húdòu* 受胡豆 is based on an interpretation of a

---

1 On *wénwù* 聞物, see Nattier 2008, 91. On the Tibetan etymological translation of Śrāvastī as *mnyan yod* (lit. "hearing existence"), which is based on the *nirvacana*-analysis of dividing Śrāvastī into two parts (*śrāv-* [< √*śru*, "to hear"] and *-asti* [< √*as*, "to exist"]), see Nattier 2008, 91 n. 216; Deeg 2008, 89.

2 Another rendering *hùguāng* 護光 ("guarding light") is based on the interpretation of Kāśyapa as derived

Prākrit form (*Mudgalāna or *Muggalāna?) of Maudgalyāyana as being derived from *mudga* ("mung bean") + √*lā* ("to receive"). Similar instances include: *chí-míngwén* 持名聞 ("bearing fame") as a translation of Yaśodharā, with *chí* 持 and *míngwén* 名聞 separately rendering -*dharā* (< √*dhṛ*, "to bear") and *yaśas* ("fame"); *néngrén* 能仁 (lit. "capable benefactor") as a translation of Śākyamuni, with *néng* 能 and *rén* 仁 separately rendering *śākya-* (< √*śak*, "to be capable") and -*muni* ("sage"); both *xīxīn* 息心 ("[one who] appeases his mind") and *jìzhì* 寂志 ("[one who] tranquilizes his mind") as translations of Pkt. *śamaṇa* or *samaṇa* (< Skt. *śramaṇa*, "monk"); *shìxīn* 逝心 ("[one, whose] gets rid of one's mind") and *fànzhì* 梵志 ("brahman") separately translating Skt. *brāhmaṇa* and Pkt. *braṃmaṇa* or *brammaṇa*.[1]

In terms of their lexical structure, many (though not all) such pseudo-etymological loan translations adopt the "Verb + Object" (VO) structure. That is to say, when applying the *nirvacana* analysis to an Indic word, breaking the word down into two components and rendering each component into Chinese, ancient translators appear to have tended to place the verbal component before the nominal component to form a Chinese translation, even when, in the original Indic word, the verbal component comes after the nominal component.[2]

Deeg (2008, 85) has already pointed out that such applications of etymological analysis are not unique to Chinese Buddhist translations, and are also found in European Biblical

---

from √*pā* ("to guard") + √*kāś* ("to shine"). On various renderings of the name Kāśyapa, see Brough 1975, 582.

1 On *chí-míngwén* 持名聞 and *néngrén* 能仁, see Karashima 1998b, 47, 301; Deeg 2008, 103. On *xīxīn* 息心 and *jìzhì* 寂志 based on an interpretation of Pkt. *samaṇa* / *śamaṇa* as < √*śam* ("to appease") + *maṇa* (< *manas*, "mind"), or as *śama(ṇa)* + *maṇa*, see Karashima 2016a, 112–113. On *shìxīn* 逝心 "probably based on an interpretation of *brāhmaṇa* as *bāhati*, *baheti* ("annihilates") or *bahi* ("outsides") + *maṇa* ("mind")" and *fànzhì* 梵志 probably based on an interpretation of Gāndhārī *braṃmaṇa* / *brammaṇa* as *braṃ-* / *bram-* + -*maṇa*, see Karashima 2016a, 107–108.

2 For instance, while Kāśyapa was interpreted as consisting of *kāśya-* (< √*kāś* ["to shine"]) and *pa-* (√*pā* ["to drink"]), it was translated not as *guāngyǐn* 光飲 but as *yǐnguāng* 飲光 ("drinking light"); while Yaśodharā was interpreted as consisting of *yaśas-* ("fame") and -*dharā* (< √*dhṛ*, "to bear"), it was translated not as *míngwén-chí* 名聞持 but as *chí-míngwén* 持名聞 ("bearing fame").

translations. In order to more concretely illustrate the similarity between Buddhist and non-Buddhist applications of this translation method, I offer several examples drawn from Notker Labeo's (c. 950–1022) translation of Boethius" early sixth-century *De Consolatione Philosophiae* ("The Consolation of Philosophy") from Latin into Old High German (OHG).[1] It has been noted that in translating Latin terminology, Notker sometimes "divides the Latin term with its complex of significations into its component parts and provides Old High German translations for each, thus rendering more clearly the varying semantic relationships within the complex" (Frakes 1988, 127). For instance, Notker coined the OHG term *hinafértig* as an etymological translation of the Latin *transitōriō* (dative singular of *transitōrius*, "transitory"), with *hina-* ("away from here") and *-fértig* ("finished," derived from OHG's *faran* ["to go"] = Modern German *fahren*) separately rendering *trans-* ("across, beyond") and *-itōriō* (correlated with Latin *eō* ["to go"]).[2] He coined the OHG term *gûotuuíllig* using the Latin model's *benevolus* ("benevolent"), with *gûot-* ("good") and *-uuíllig* ("willed") separately replacing *bene-* and *-volus* (derived from *volō* ["to wish, to be willing to"]).[3] He also coined the OHG term *uuídere zíhenta* as an etymological translation of Latin's *reclamantem* ("protesting," derived from *reclāmō* ["to protest"]), with *uuídere* ("against" = Modern German *wider*) and *zíhenta* (derived from OHG's *zīhan* ["to say"] = Modern German *zeihen*) separately rendering *re-* ("back") and *-clāmō* ("to shout"),[4] and the OHG term *úneruúlta* as an etymological translation of Latin's *inexpleta* (feminine form of *inexplētus*, "unfilled"), with *ún-, er-* and *-uúlta* (derived from OHG's *fullen* ["to fill"] =

---

1 Although Notker Labeo's translation of *De Consolatione Philosophiae* does not belong to the category of Biblical translations, it may still be used as a source to demonstrate the similarity between Buddhist and non-Buddhist (not particularly Biblical) applications of etymological analysis in translating foreign terminologies.

2 See Reinmuth 1937, 6; Tax 1990, 262, line 27. However, according to the *Oxford Latin Dictionary* (Glare 2012, 2166), *transitōrius* is actually derived from *transi-* (< *transeō*, "to cross over") + *-tōrius* (*-tōr* [a suffix denoting agent] + *-ivs*).

3 On OHG *gûotuuíllig* < Latin *benevolus*, see Reinmuth 1937, 6; Tax 1988, 151, line 15.

4 On OHG *uuídere zíhenta* < Latin *reclamantem*, see Reinmuth 1937, 13; Tax 1986, 15, line 22.

Modern German *füllen*) separately rendering *in-*, *ex-* and *-pleta* (derived from Latins *pleō* ["to fill"]).[1]

Hybrid Loan

The term "hybrid loan" is also called loan-blend, since it is a blend of transliteration and translation of a foreign word or phrase. Hybrid loans are common in language contact. For instance, German's *Grapefrucht* is a hybrid loan from the English word *Grapefruit*, Pennsylvania German's *Bockabuch* from the English term *pocketbook* (Haugen 1950, 219), Pennsylvania German's *was-ewe(r)* from the English term *whatever* (Weinreich 1953, 52), the Dutch term *software huis* from the English term *software house*, and so on. Hybrid loans are abundant in Chinese Buddhist translations. For instance, *fànxíng* 梵行 ("pure conduct, chastity") is a hybrid loan from Skt. *brahmacarya* (or its Prākrit equivalents), with *fàn* 梵 (EHC: *b(r)jam; EMC: *buam^h) transliterating *brahma-* (or rather, Pkt. *bram-* / *bram-*) and *xíng* 行 ("conduct") translating Skt. *-carya* or Pkt. *-cariya* / *-yirya* ("conduct");[2] *púsà-fǎ* 菩薩法 ("qualities of a bodhisattva") is a hybrid loan from Skt. *bodhisattvadharma* (or its Prākrit equivalents), with *púsà* 菩薩 (EHC: *bo sat; EMC: *bɔ sat) being an abbreviated transliteration of *bodhisattva* (or rather, Pkt. *bosisat[va]*) and *fǎ* 法 a translation of *dharma*;[3] *pút-sh* 菩提樹 ("tree of awakening") is a hybrid loan from Skt. *bodhivṛkṣa* (or its Prākrit equivalents), with *pút* 菩提 (EHC: *bo dei; EMC: * bɔ dɛj) transliterating *bodhi-* ("awakening") and *sh* 樹 translating *-vṛkṣa* ("tree"); *dà-bǐqiū-zhòng* 大比丘眾 ("big assembly of monks") is a hybrid loan from the Sanskrit phrase *mahat~ bhikṣusaṃgha~* (or its Prākrit equivalents), with *dà* 大 and *zhòng* 眾 separately translating *mahat* ("big") and *saṃgha* ("assembly"), and *bǐqiū* 比丘 (EHC: *bjiəi khju; EMC: *pji kʰuw) transliterating *bhikṣu* (or

---

1 On OHG *úneruúlta* < Latin *inexpleta*, Reinmuth 1937, 9; Tax 1986, 50, line 16.

2 On Gāndhārī *brama-* / *bramma-yirya* (corresponding to Skt. *brahmacarya*), see Brough 1962, 128, 129.

3 On *púsà* 菩薩 as a transliteration of Gāndhārī *bosisat(va)*, see Karashima 2010, 351. The term *púsà-fǎ* 菩薩法 does not always correspond to *bodhisattvadharma*. Sometimes it corresponds to *bodhisattvacaryā* ("conduct of a bodhisattva"; see Karashima 1998b, 313).

rather, Pkt. *bhikkhu* or *bhikhu*).[1]

Hybrid loans may contain redundant elements. Deeg (2008, 96) has rightly noted two types of the "redundant hybrid loanword" in Chinese Buddhist translations: in the first type, a hybrid loanword consists of a transliteration and its semantic synonym; in the second type, a hybrid loanword consists of a transliteration and a generic term. In some cases, the addition of a redundant element (either a semantic synonym or a generic term) serves a prosodic purpose, i.e., to turn a hybrid loanword into a disyllabic or polysyllabic form. Examples of the first type include, for instance: *jìsòng* 偈頌 (lit. "*gāthā*-hymn") as a rendering of Skt. *gāthā* ("verse"), with *jì* 偈 (EHC: *gjiat; EMC: *giaj^h) transliterating *gāthā* (or Gāndhārī *gadha*) and *sòng* 頌 being a redundant synonymous element;[2] *chándìng* 禪定 (lit. "*dhyāna*-concentration") as a rendering of Skt. *dhyāna* (or its Prākrit equivalents), with *chán* 禪 (EHC: *dźjan; EMC: *dzian) transliterating *dhyāna* (or rather, Pkt. *jhāna* / *jhāṇa*) and *dìng* 定 being a redundant synonym;[3] and *sānmèi-dìng* 三昧定 (lit. "*samādhi*-concentration") for Skt. *samādhi* (or its Prākrit equivalents), with *sānmèi* 三昧 (EHC: *səm mət; EMC: *sam məj^h) transliterating *samādhi* and *dìng* 定 being a redundant synonym.[4] Examples of the second type of redundant hybrid loanword include, for instance: *bùnàlì-huā* 不那利華 as a rendering of a Prākrit form (similar to *puṇari*) of Skt. *puṇḍarīka* ("white lotus"), with *bùnàlì* 不那利 (EHC: *pju na ljiəi; EMC: *put na li^h) transliterating the Prākrit form and *huā* 華 ("flower") being a redundant generic term;[5] and *píshěshě-guǐ* 毗舍闍鬼 as a rendering of Skt. *piśāca* ("a kind of fresh-eating demon"), with *píshěshě* 毗

1　On *dà-bǐqiū-zhòng* 大比丘眾 corresponding to *mahat~ bhikṣusaṃgha~*, see Karashima 2001, 47. On *bǐqiū* 比丘 as a transliteration of Pāli *bhikkhu* or Gāndhārī *bhikhu*, see Karashima 2010, 35.

2　The word 偈 may be read either as *jì* (EMC: *giajh [Pulleyblank 1991, 143]) or as *jié* (EMC: *giat / giat [Pulleyblank 1991, 154] or *giat / kiat [Schuessler 2009, 231]). Nattier (2004, 3) has pointed out that the reading *jié*, instead of the often-used reading *jì*, "would have led to the use of this character to transliterate Skt. *gāthā*."

3　On *chán* 禪 as a transliteration of Pkt. *jhāna / jhāṇa*, see Karashima 2010, 57.

4　On *sānmèi-dìng* 三昧定 for *samādhi*, see Karashima 1998b, 367.

5　On *bùnàlì-huā* 不那利華, see Karashima 2010, 51.

舍闍 (EHC: *bjiəi śja dźja; EMC: *bji ia^h dʑia) transliterating *piśāca* and *guǐ* 鬼 ("demon") being a redundant generic term.[1]

Redundant hybrid loans are also found in other language-contact situations. The Polish linguist Alicja Witalisz (2013, 331) has shown that in American Polish (i.e., the Polish used by the Polish diaspora in the United States) there are "redundant compounds," which "exhibit a hybrid nature, being composed of an English compound word and a Polish lexeme that is semantically equivalent to one of the constituents of the English compound," thus similar to the first type of redundant hybrid loanword in Chinese Buddhist translations discussed above. For instance, the American Polish term *downtown miasta* (lit. "downtown of town") is a redundant hybrid loan from the American English term *downtown*; the American Polish term *wieprzowy pork chop* (lit. "pork pork chop") from the American English term *pork chop*; and the American Polish term *knickers spodnie* (lit. "knickerbockers knickers") from the American English term *knickerbockers*.

Semantic Extension

According to the classic definition by Uriel Weinreich, semantic extension refers to "the extension of the use of an indigenous word of the influenced language in conformity with a foreign model" (Weinreich 1953, 48). The difference between phonemic loan, loan translation, and semantic extension is this: in the cases of phonemic loan and loan translation, a new word is imported into the target language, whereas in the case of semantic extension, a new meaning is imported into an existing word in the target language. An example used by Weinreich to illustrate semantic extension is the word *tahym* in the Yakut language: *tahym* originally signified "water level" but was later extended to signify "all

---

1 On *píshěshě-guǐ* 毘舍闍鬼, see Karashima 2001, 193. Yet another well-known example of this type is *qíshějué-shān* 耆闍崛山 for the mountain-name *Gṛdhrakūṭa* (see Deeg 2008, 96; Karashima 2010, 356).

levels," both concrete and abstract, as a result of modelling on the Russian term *уровень* that denotes "level" in any sense. Another example may be found with the Old English term *heofon*, which originally signified "sky, abode of deities," whereas the Medieval Latin term *caelum* possessed three meanings: "sky," "abode of deities," and Christian Heaven." When Latin Christian texts were translated into Old English, based on the equation of the first two meanings of *caelum* and *heofon*, translators consequently imported the third meaning ("Christian Heaven") into *heofon* (Hock 1991, 398).

The phenomena of semantic extension are ubiquitous in Chinese Buddhist translations. For instance, the term *zhōngguó* 中國 (lit. "middle country, central kingdom") was originally used to refer to the royal domain of the Western Zhou (1045–771 BCE).[1] During the Eastern Zhou period (770–256 BCE), this term came to refer to the "feudal states in the middle and lower reaches of the Yellow River," and was "also used in classics as a cultural concept to differentiate the Huaxia from the barbarians" (Wilkinson 2000, 132). From the Late Han onwards, ancient translators used *zhōngguó* 中國 to render Skt. *madhyadeśa* (or its Prākrit forms), whose literal meaning is also "middle country" but actually refers to the central part of north India. By doing so, the translators imported a new meaning ("central north India") into the term *zhōngguó* 中國 and thus expanded its semantic range.[2] Another example is the binome *shāshēng* 殺生, which originally only meant "to kill animals" in

---

1 For instance, in the hymn "Min Lao" 民勞 of the *Shījīng* 詩經 ("Classic of Poetry") we find: 惠此中國，以綏四方 ("be kind to this central kingdom, and so give peace to the [states of] the four quarters" [tr. quoted from Karlgren 1945, 75]), in which *zhōngguó* 中國 means the royal domain as opposed to the "four quarters" (i.e., the lands ruled by feudal lords).

2 An example from Lokakṣema's second-century translation of the *Aṣṭasāhasrikā Prajñāpāramitā* reads (T. 224 [viii] 455c17): 從欲處、色處、空處，從彼間來生中國 ("From the sphere of desire, the sphere of form and the sphere of emptiness, from there he came to be reborn in the middle country [i.e., Madhyadeśa, central north India]") (see Karashima 2010, 647); see also Kumārajīva's early fifth-century translation of the *Mahāprajñāpāramitopadeśa* (T. 1509 [xxv] 89c23–24): 唯中國迦毘羅婆淨飯王后能懷菩薩 ("Only the queen of King Śuddhodana of Kapilavastu in the middle country [i.e., Madhyadeśa] can conceive the bodhisattva"), in which *zhōngguó* 中國 clearly means central north India.

Archaic Chinese. When ancient translators used *shāshēng* 殺生 to render Skt. *prāṇātipāta* ("killing any living being, whether an animal or a human") based on their shared meaning of "killing animals," they consequently extended the semantic range of *shāshēng* 殺生 to denote the killing of any life-form. The semantic extension of *shāshēng* 殺生 is notably similar to the aforementioned example of *tahym* in Yakut given by Weinreich. Furthermore, in Archaic Chinese, the term *báiyī* 白衣 originally meant "white clothes" and "a white-clad person, i.e., a commoner (in contrast to an aristocrat)."[1] In Buddhist Sanskrit literature, the compound *avadātavasana* (or *avadātavastra*) may mean both "cleansed [and therefore white] clothes" and "a white-clad person, i.e., a Buddhist layperson," since Buddhist laypeople in ancient India were usually dressed in white, whereas Buddhist monks were dressed in reddish-brown robes. When ancient translators used *báiyī* 白衣 to render Skt. *avadātavasana* (or *avadātavastra*) based on the shared meaning of "white clothes," they consequently imported a new meaning ("Buddhist layperson") into *báiyī* 白衣, thus expanding its semantic range.[2]

---

1 For instance, in his *Records of the Great Historian* (*Shǐjì* 史記), Sima Qian (司馬遷, c. 145–86 BCE) writes: 公孙弘，以春秋，白衣为天子三公 ("Gongsun Hong who, because of his knowledge of the *Spring and Autumn Annals*, advanced from the rank of commoner to that of one of the three highest ministers in the government" [tr. quoted from Watson 1993, 358]), in which *báiyī* 白衣 (lit. "white-clad") means "commoner."

2 The term *báiyī* 白衣 occurs three times in Zhi Qian's (fl. 220–257) translation of the *Vimalakīrtinirdeśa*. In two of the three occurrences, it finds a parallel in the extant Sanskrit version of this text. The first sentence reads (T. 474 [xiv] 521a5): 雖為白衣，奉持沙門 ("Though being white-clad [i.e., being a Buddhist layman], he upheld [the precepts of] a *śramaṇa*"). Its Sanskrit counterpart reads (Study Group on Buddhist Sanskrit Literature 2006, 15, folio 9a4): *avadātavastradhārī śramaṇeryāpathasaṃpannaḥ* ("Wearing white clothes, perfect in the modes of behavior of a *śramaṇa*"), in which *avadātavastra* ("white clothes") corresponds to *báiyī* 白衣 used by Zhi Qian. The second sentence reads (T. 474 [xiv] 521c16): 賢者! 莫為居家白衣說法如賢者所說 ("Wise Man! Please do not preach the Dharma to white-clad householders [i.e., Buddhist laymen] in the same way as you do for a wise man"). Its Sanskrit counterpart reads (Study Group on Buddhist Sanskrit Literature 2006, 21, folio 12a6): *na bhadantamaudgalyāyana gṛhibhyo "vadātavasanebhya evaṃ dharmo deśayitavyo yathā bhadanto deśayati |* ("Venerable Maudgalyāyana! The Dharma should not be preached to white-clad

Double Translation

Double translation (also called "doublet," "double reading," "double rendering," "Doppelung" or "Doppelübersetzung" by Septuagint scholars) refers to the phenomenon that a word or an expression (or a part thereof) in the source language is translated twice in the target language.[1] Erik Zürcher was probably the first scholar to use the term "double translation" in the context of discussing Chinese Buddhist translations. Zürcher (1959, 336 n. 140) pointed out that *dùwújí* 度無極 (lit. "crossing [over into] infinitude"), a rendering of Skt. *pāramitā* (or its Prākrit equivalents), is a double translation, in which *dù* 度 (for 渡, "to cross") is a translation of *pāramitā* based on an etymological interpretation that takes this Indic term to be derived from *pāram* (accusative of *pāra* ["the other shore"]) plus *itā* ("gone"), and *wújí* 無極 is a retranslation of *amitā* ("unlimited") that forms the latter part of *pāramitā*.[2] Another prime example of double translation is the term *yuányījué* 緣一覺 (lit. "[one who is] awakened by a cause and by oneself").[3] Seishi Karashima has convincingly argued that the third-century translator Zhi Qian coined this term to render Gāndhārī *praceabudha*, a Prākrit form of Skt. *pratyekabuddha*, "of which *pracea* might have been understood by Zhi Qian as meaning both 'single, by oneself' (< *pratyeka*) and 'cause' (*pratyaya*); therefore, he rendered it as *yuanyijué* 緣一覺 ('one, who perceives

---

householders in the same way as one preaches [it] for a venerable man"), in which *avadātavasanebhya* ("for white-clad ones, i.e., for Buddhist laymen") corresponds to (為……) 白衣 used by Zhi Qian. The term *báiyī* 白衣 may also be a translation of *grhin* or *grhastha* meaning "householder" (see Karashima 1998b, 8–9; 2001, 10).

1 For various terms and definitions of this phenomenon that have been proposed by Septuagint scholars, see Vorm-Croughs 2014, 141–143.

2 Nattier (2004, 8–9) places *dùwújí* 度無極 in the category of "overlapping translation," and uses the term "double translation" to refer specifically to a type of translation "in which two quite different interpretations of a single term are given." In my discussion, I follow Zürcher in using the term "double translation" in a broader sense, encompassing the category of "overlapping translation" discussed by Nattier.

3 Norman (1997, 104) explains Pkt. *Pacceyabuddha* (equivalent of Skt. *Pratyayabuddha*) as "one who is awakened by a specific cause, a specific occurrence (not by a Buddha's teaching)."

causation and oneness') by mixing the two meanings together." (Karashima 2016b, 343)[1] Other instances of double translation that have been identified by previous scholars include, to mention but a few: *shì-zhī-míngfù* 世 之 明 父 ("wise father of the world"), with *míng* 明 ("wise") and *fù* 父 ("father") rendered from the same Prākrit word, which was first understood as *-*vidu* ("wise") and then as *-*pitu* ("father");[2] *huìshèng* 慧 乘 ("wisdom-cum-vehicle"), with *huì* 慧 and *shèng* 乘 rendered from the same Prākrit word (*jāna / *jāna*), which was first understood as corresponding to Skt. *jñāna* ("wisdom") and then as corresponding to Skt. *yāna* ("vehicle");[3] *guānshìyīn* 觀世音 (lit. "[one who] observes sounds of the world") for Skt. *avalokitasvara* ("[one who] observed sounds"), with *avalokita-* ("observed") first translated as *guān* 觀 and then its latter part *-lokita* retranslated as *shì* 世 (< Skt. *loka*, "world");[4] and *xìnjiě* 信 解 (lit. "faith and liberation") for Skt. *adhimukti* ("strong inclination towards"), with the entire term *adhimukti* first translated as *xìn* 信 and then its latter part *–mukti* ("liberation") retranslated as *jiě* 解.[5]

Double translation also appears in other religious translations. Scholars working on the Septuagint (which refers broadly to ancient Greek translations of the Hebrew Bible) have long devoted attention to this phenomenon (see Vorm-Croughs 2014, 141–143). In studying the Septuagint of Amos, for instance, W. Edward Glenny (2009, 68) has noted that the translator shows a clear predilection to use two Greek words to render one Hebrew word, "which could be motivated by a lack of understanding of the source text or a desire to convey completely what is in the source text." One of the examples used by Glenny (2009, 127) to illustrate this phenomenon is as follows: when translating the Hebrew expression בְּגָדִים חֲבֻלִים *begâdîm ḥaḇulîm* ("clothes taken in pledge") in Amos ii 8, the translator gives

---

1   The term *yuányījué* 緣一覺 also appears in Dharmarakṣa's translation of the *Lotus Sūtra*. For more detail, see Karashima 1998b, 566; Boucher 1998, 490–491.

2   See Karashima 1992, 119; Boucher 1998, 490; Nattier 2004, 8–9.

3   On the *yāna / jñāna* confusion in Buddhist texts (particularly in the *Lotus Sūtra*), see Karashima 2015. On the term *huìshèng* 慧乘, see Karashima 2015, 169–170.

4   On *guānshìyīn* 觀世音 (< *avalokitasvara*), see Karashima 2016a, 113.

5   On *xìnjiě* 信解 (< *adhimukti*), see Karashima and Nattier 2005, 370.

two Greek words δεσμεύοντες σχοινίοις / *desmeúontes schoiníois* ("binding together with cords") for the Hebrew word חֲבֻלִים *ḥabulîm* ("taken in pledge"). Glenny (2009, 127) explains, "both of these Greek words could be translations of Hebrew words with the same radicals as the Hebrew particle (חבל [*ḥbl*] meaning "to bind" or "chord [sic]")."[1] That is to say, the translator interpreted the Hebrew word חֲבֻלִים *ḥabulîm* twice, first in the sense of "binding" and then in the sense of "cord," thus resulting in a double Greek translation ("binding together with cords") for this Hebrew word.[2] This example is remarkably similar to *yuányìjué* 緣一覺, *míngfù* 明父, and *huìshèng* 慧乘, since they all show the same mechanism of giving two different interpretations of one single term in the source-text.

Disyllabification

Disyllabification represents a major change in the history of the Chinese language, which marks the transition from Archaic Chinese (c. 1250–200 BCE) to Early Middle Chinese (c. 1st century BCE–6th century CE).[3] In Archaic Chinese, the lexicon was primarily monosyllabic, but from the 2nd / 1st century BCE onwards, more words appeared. The tendency of disyllabification may be seen in almost all kinds of Chinese literary works produced in the early centuries of the Common Era.[4] Various theories have been proposed to account for the emergence of disyllabification at the end of the Late Archaic period.[5] During the medieval period, the Chinese translation of Indic Buddhist scriptures became

---

1 Square brackets are added by the present author.

2 I thank Professor Jonathan Silk and Professor Max Deeg respectively for correcting my romanization of Hebrew and Greek words.

3 On disyllabification as one of the most salient changes that mark the transition from Archaic Chinese to Medieval Chinese, see Meisterernst 2017, 500–502.

4 The disyllabification tendency is common to both Buddhist and non-Buddhist Chinese literature. For previous studies on the disyllabification process in non-Buddhist Late Archaic and Medieval Chinese literature, see for instance, Cheng 1992; Dong 2011, 48–285.

5 For an outline of these theories (of which the most influential theory explains disyllabification as making up for "the loss of consonant clusters, a phonological change from Archaic Chinese to Medieval Chinese"), see Feng 2017, 109–111.

an undeniable factor that accelerated the disyllabification process. The preference for four-character prosody that is often seen in Chinese Buddhist translations clearly contributed to the increase of disyllabic words.[1] Disyllabification, as such, is a complex phenomenon. While it is not possible to go into extensive detail within the scope of the present paper, I introduce here the three most prevalent methods of creating disyllabic words in Chinese Buddhist translations.

The first method combines a monosyllabic transliteration with a redundant monosyllabic synonym. For instance, *chàtǔ* 刹土 is formed by *chà* 刹 (EHC: *tshrat; EMC: *tʂʰait / tʂʰɛːt; transliteration of Skt. *kṣetra*, "land") and *tǔ* 土 (translation of *kṣetra*); *jìsòng* 偈頌 is formed by *jì* 偈 (EHC: *gjiat; EMC: *giajʰ; transliteration of Skt. *gāthā* or Pkt. *gadha*, "verse") and *sòng* 頌 (translation of *gāthā*); *tánshī* 檀施 is formed by *tán* 檀 (EHC: *dan; EMC: *dan; transliteration of Skt. *dāna* or Pkt. *dana*, "donation") and *shī* 施 (translation of *dāna / dana*); *sēngzhòng* 僧眾 is formed by *sēng* 僧 (EHC: *səng; EMC: *səŋ; transliteration of Skt. *saṃgha*, "assembly") and *zhòng* 眾 (translation of *saṃgha*); *móguǐ* 魔鬼 is formed by *mó* 魔 (EHC: *ma; EMC: *ma; transliteration of Skt. *māra* or Pkt. *mara*, "devil") and *guǐ* 鬼 (a redundant synonym to *mó* 魔).[2] This method of disyllabification represents a very special kind of process, which is different from the processes of disyllabification usually seen in indigenous Chinese literature.[3]

1　On the frequency of four-character prosody in some Chinese Buddhist translations, see for instance, Zürcher 1977, 178; 1991, 280–281, 284, 286, 290; 1996, 11–12. Nattier (2008, 18) observes that "four-character prosody" represents "a mark of literary rather than vernacular usage."

2　Disyllabic words created through the first method also belong to the first type of hybrid redundant loanword discussed above. However, the first type of hybrid redundant loanword contains not only disyllabic hybrids, but also polysyllabic hybrids (such as 三昧定 [lit. "*samādhi*-concentration] for Skt. *samādhi* ["concentration"], and 僧那鎧 [lit. "*saṃnāha*-armour"] for Skt. *saṃnāha* ["armour"]).

3　According to the detailed study by Dong (2011), within indigenous Chinese literature, there are three major ways in which disyllabic words emerged: first, "through the reinterpretation of phrases containing two mono-syllabic lexical words"; second, through the fossilization of "syntactic structures comprising a grammatical word and a lexical word"; and third, through the "reanalysis of non-constituent adjacent elements" (Dong 2011, 5–8).

The second method of disyllabification combines a monosyllabic translation with a redundant monosyllabic synonym or near-synonym. For instance, in the disyllabic translation *bìngyì* 病疫 for Skt. *vyādhi* ("disease"), both *bìng* 病 ("illness") and *yì* 疫 ("epidemic") are synonymous renderings of *vyādhi*, and thus, either may be deemed redundant; in the disyllabic translations *chíhù* 持護 and *hùchí* 護持 for derivatives of Skt. *(anu-)pari-√grah* ("to hold"), *chí* 持 ("to hold") is a translation of *(anu-)pari-√grah*, and *hù* 護 ("to guard") is a redundant near-synonym.[1]

The third method of disyllabification shortens a polysyllabic transliteration or translation into a disyllabic form. For instance, *tánhuā* 曇花 is a disyllabic abbreviation of *yōutánbō-huā* 優曇鉢華 (< Skt. *uḍumbarapuṣpa*, "flower of the fig tree"), in which 優曇鉢 (EHC: *²ju dam pat; EMC: *ʔuw dəm / dam pat) is a transliteration of *uḍumbara* and 華 ("flower") a translation of *puṣpa*; *mùlián* 目連 is a disyllabic abbreviation of 目犍連 or 目捷連 (EHC: *mjok kjan / gjan ljan; MC: *mjuk kjɛn / gjɛn ljän;[2] a transliteration of Maudgalyāyana or its Prākrit equivalents); *quánbiàn* 權便 is a disyllabic abbreviation of *shànquán-fāngbiàn* 善權方便 (a full translation of *upāyakauśalya*, "skill in expedients"). The interrogative *jiŭrú* 久如 (lit. "long like") is a disyllabic abbreviation of the phrase *jiŭjìn-rúhé* 久近如何 ("how long is the duration"), which, in turn, is a full translation of Skt. *kiyac ciram*, or *kiyac cireṇa* or *kiyac cira-* (all meaning "how long").[3]

Disyllabic words created through the first method belong to the category of redundant hybrid loanwords. As we saw above, this category is not unique to Chinese Buddhist translations, since similarly redundant hybrid forms also occur elsewhere (for instance, in American Polish). The second method is not unique to Chinese Buddhist translations either, and similar phenomena may be found, for instance, in the Septuagint. Glenny (2007) has noted that the translator of the Septuagint of Amos sometimes used two Greek near-

---

1 On *bìngyì* 病疫 (< *vyādhi*), *chíhù* 持護 and *hùchí* 護持 (< *[anu-]pari-√grah*), see Karashima 2010, 45, 79; Karashima 2001, 116–117.

2 Pulleyblank (1991) provides no phonological reconstruction for *jiàn* 犍 or *qián* 捷. The Middle Chinese (MC, around 600 CE) reconstructions given here are based on Schuessler 2009.

3 For discussion on the Indic origins of *jiŭrú* 久如, see Wu 2009.

synonyms to render one Hebrew term. In Amos iii 15, the translator rendered the Hebrew verb וְהִכֵּיתִי *wᵉhiketî* ("I will smite") into Greek συγχέω καί πατάσσω / *synchéō kai patássō* ("I will demolish and will smite"), in which πατάσσω / *patássō* ("smite") and συγχέω / *synchéō* ("demolish") separately convey the literal and contextual meanings of the same Hebrew verb. By adding the seemingly redundant Greek verb συγχέω / *synchéō*, "the translator takes precaution to communicate the full meaning of the Hebrew verb" (Glenny 2007, 532). The third method, disyllabic abbreviation, does not seem to be unique to Chinese Buddhist translations either. Although I have not found the same phenomena in Western religious translations, it is worth noting that abbreviated loanwords (either disyllabic or polysyllabic) are abundant in modern Japanese (for instance, *hōmu* for *platform*, *neru* for *flannel*, *biru* for *building*, *depāto* for *department*, *terebi* for *television*, etc.).

So far we have discussed six major mechanisms of contact-induced lexical creations in Chinese Buddhist translations: phonemic loan, loan translation, hybrid loan, semantic extension, double translation, and disyllabification.[1] None of these mechanisms is really unique to Chinese Buddhist translations, since almost all of them have parallels or partial parallels in other language-contact situations (either in modern language contacts or in premodern Western translations such as the Septuagint and Notker's translations). Unlike the five other mechanisms, disyllabification represents a full-scale development of the Chinese language as a whole that took place from the 2nd/1st century BCE onwards. Although this development initially occurred independently of language contact, it was subsequently greatly accelerated by the translation of Buddhist texts and thus particularly noticeable in Chinese Buddhist translations.[2] In terms of its widespread scale and long-term

---

1 My discussion above has not included erroneous translations that resulted from a translator's misreadings or misinterpretations of Prākrit originals. On such erroneous translations, see for instance, Boucher 1998, 458–476; Nattier 2004, 7; Karashima 2006, 362–363; 2016b, 344–349.

2 The strong tendency of disyllabification in Chinese Buddhist translations may also reflect a development in vernacular Chinese. On the vernacular features of Chinese Buddhist translations (particularly those produced before the sixth century), see Zürcher 1977, 1996; Zhu 1992, 101–122; Mair 1994; Karashima 1996a; Nattier 2008, 17–19.

impacts, disyllabification is a process indeed unique to the Chinese. However, the three basic methods of creating disyllabic words in Chinese Buddhist translations introduced above may certainly not be regarded as unique, since similar phenomena also appear in the Septuagint or in modern language contacts (for instance, American Polish and abbreviated Japanese loanwords). Furthermore, while the majority of the lexical creations discussed above were confined to Buddhist contexts, some neologisms gained wider currency and eventually entered the common lexicon of Chinese. These include, to list but a few: *tǎ* 塔 ("pagoda") and *mó* 魔 ("devil") from the category of Buddhist phonemic loans; *chànà* 刹那 ("instant"), *pōlí* 頗梨 or *bōli* 玻璃 ("crystal, glass"), *màn* 鬘 ("garland") and *mòlì* 末利 or 茉莉 ("jasmine") from the category of non-religious phonemic loans; *shìjiè* 世界 ("world-realm"), *ròuyǎn* 肉眼 ("physical eye"), *tánzhǐ* 彈指 ("snap of fingers") and *zuòzhèng* 作證 ("to realize, to testify") from the category of loan translations of Indic compounds (i.e., the first type of loan translation); *guòqù* 過去 ("past"), *xiànzài* 現在 ("present"), *wèilái* 未來 ("future"), *wúshàng* 無上 ("supreme"), *bùjiǔ* 不久 ("not long") and *bùkěsīyì* 不可思議 ("unconceivable") from the category of loan translations of Indic words containing prefixes (i.e., the second type of loan translation); the disyllabic *móguǐ* 魔鬼 and *hùchí* 護持 created by combining a monosyllabic transliteration or translation with a near synonym; and the disyllabic *quánbiàn* 權便 and *tánhuā* 曇花 created by abbreviating a polysyllabic translation or transliteration.[1] All these lexical creations have circulated beyond Buddhist contexts, and have finally become part of the common Chinese vocabulary still in use even today.

Mechanisms of Contact-Induced Syntactic Creations in Chinese Buddhist Translations

Over the past decades, scholars have identified a number of syntactic innovations in Chinese Buddhist translations, which are absent or rarely seen in Classical Chinese. Some

---

1 The binome *fāngbiàn* 方便, a standard translation of Skt. *upāya* ("stratagem, expedient"), also entered the common lexicon of Chinese.

of these innovations may be explained as contact-induced language changes, or more precisely, changes at least accelerated (or extended) by the contact between Chinese and Indic languages during the translation of Buddhist texts. In this section, I will discuss three examples: the indefinite use of the interrogative pronoun *hé* 何 ("what"); the aspect marker *yǐ* 已 signaling that the natural endpoint of a telic action had been reached; and the disposal structure "*chí* 持 ('to hold') + Object + Verb." I choose to focus on these examples because they represent three basic mechanisms of syntactic innovations in Chinese Buddhist translations. While discussing these examples, I will correlate them with similar (or partly similar) phenomena found in other language-contact situations.[1]

Importation of New Grammatical Function

The indefinite use of the interrogative pronoun *hé* 何 illustrates the mechanism of importing

---

1 For an overview of previous scholarship concerning the influence of language contact on the historical development of Chinese syntax, see Cao and Yu 2015. Recently Meisterernst (2018, 124–125) has aptly observed that in the current linguistic debate there are two different approaches to explaining syntactic innovations in Buddhist translations: the first approach focuses on external factors, i.e., attributing these innovations to the influence of "the syntax of the source languages from which the texts were translated," and the second approach focuses on internal factors, i.e., explaining these innovations as "native Chinese developments caused by changes in the Chinese language." It seems to me that these two approaches are not necessarily incompatible with each other. It is certainly possible that a syntactic innovation was triggered by some morphological change within the Chinese language, yet accelerated by the language contact of Chinese and Indic languages during the translation. In such a situation, a syntactic innovation was both internally triggered and externally accelerated. In fact, in my opinion, one cannot generalize the role (whether a trigger or an accelerator, or no role at all) played by language contact in studying syntactic innovations of Chinese Buddhist translations, because any evaluation of the role of language contact may only be made on a case-by-case basis after careful examination (which certainly involves a comparison of Chinese translations with their extant Sanskrit or Prākrit parallels). In this paper, I do not intend to claim that the three examples (namely the indefinite *hé* 何, the aspect marker *yǐ* 已 and the disposal 持OV) could not have appeared without language contact. Rather my purpose is to show how language contact may account for the frequent appearances of these syntactic elements or structures in Chinese Buddhist translations.

a new grammatical function from the source language (Sanskrit or Prākrit) into the target language (Chinese). In pre-Buddhist Archaic Chinese, *hé* 何 was most often used as an interrogative pronoun, adjective or adverb, meaning "what, which, why, how" (see Peyraube and Wu, 2005). Although the use of *hé* 何 as an indefinite pronoun is attested in indigenous Archaic Chinese literature, such usage is rare and much less common than the use of *hé* 何 as an interrogative.[1] In comparison, the indefinite use of *hé* 何 is far more common in Buddhist translations (especially those produced before the 7th–8th centuries).[2] For instance, in Kumārajīva's fifth-century Chinese translation of the *Saddharmapuṇḍarīkasūtra* ("Scripture of the Lotus of the True Dharma") we find:[3]

（１）其人雖不問、不信、不解是經，我得阿耨多羅三藐三菩提時，隨在何地，以神通力、智慧力引之，令得住是法中。(T. 262 [ix] 38c8–11 [*juan* 5])

Although these people do not inquire about this scripture, nor do they believe it, nor do they understand it, when I attain supreme perfect awakening, no matter in what place [one may be], I will guide him through my supernatural power and power of wisdom, and will make him abide in this teaching.[4]

In this sentence, the word *hé* 何 is not an interrogative, but an indefinite pronoun, just like English

---

1 For an in-depth analysis of *wh*-words used as indefinites in Archaic Chinese, see Aldridge 2010a, 25–27. Aldridge (2010a, 26) has found "twelve examples in archaic period texts of *wh*-words used as negative polarity items," which indicates the "relative paucity of negative polarity uses of *wh*-words" in the archaic period. Moreover, she has listed three examples of *shéi* 誰 ("who") and *shú* 孰 ("who") used as indefinites in archaic conditional clauses, without mentioning the similar use of *hé* 何 in conditional clauses. Overall, it would be safe to say that the indefinite use of *hé* 何 is attested but rare (or at least infrequently found) in Archaic Chinese.

2 For some other examples of the indefinite use of *hé* 何 in Buddhist texts, see Wu 2008, 142–151.

3 All translations of Chinese, Sanskrit and Gāndhārī textual quotations are mine, unless otherwise specified.

4 The counterpart in Dharmarakṣa's translation of the Lotus *Sūtra* does not contain any interrogative or indefinite pronoun (see T. 263 [ix] 109b12–15 [*juan* 7]).

"what" used in the indefinite sense. In a Sanskrit version of the *Saddharmapuṇḍarīka-sūtra*, we find the following counterpart to the Chinese sentence above:

kiṃ cāpy ete sattvā imaṃ dharmaparyāyaṃ nāvataranti na budhyante | api tu khalu punar aham etām anuttarāṃ samyaksambodhim abhisambudhya yo yasmin sthito bhaviṣyati taṃ tasminn eva ṛddhibalenāvarjayiṣyāmi pattīyāpayiṣyāmy avatārayiṣyāmi paripācayiṣyāmi | (Kern and Nanjio 1908–1912, 288, lines 3–6)

These beings do not at all penetrate or understand this Dharma-discourse. However, having attained the supreme perfect awakening, wherever one will be staying, I will convert exactly that one in that place through my supernatural power, and will make him believe and penetrate [this Dharma-discourse], and will bring him to spiritual maturity.

Although Kern–Nanjio's edition is based on Sanskrit manuscripts that considerably postdate Kumārajīva fifth-century Chinese translation, this edition may at least give us some clue about the syntactic structure of the Indic original underlying the Chinese sentence. The Sanskrit parallel to the Chinese phrase *suí-zài-hédì* 隨在何地 ("no matter in what place [one may be]") is *yo yasmin sthito bhaviṣyati* ("wherever one will be staying"). Due to the doubling of the relative, both *yaḥ* and *yasmin* acquire an indefinite meaning. The expression *zài-hédì* 在何地 ("in what place") corresponds to *yasmin* ("where, wherever," locative singular of *yad*), and *hé* 何 corresponds to the relative pronoun stem *yad* ("which, whichever") on the semantic level.[1]

The use of *hé* 何 as an indefinite pronoun is also seen in other Chinese Buddhist translations. Below are two examples drawn respectively from Kumārajīva's fifth-century translation

---

1   By saying that *hé* 何 corresponds to the Skt. relative pronoun, I do not mean to suggest that *hé* 何 obtains the full functions of a relative pronoun, but, rather, that *hé* 何 matches with the Skt. relative pronoun stem *yad* in terms of their shared lexical meaning, namely that both *hé* 何 and *yad* mean "which, whichever" in this context.

of the *Vimalakīrtinirdeśa* or "Teachings of Vimalakīrti" (T. 475) and Dharmaruci's sixth-century translation of the *Jñānālokālaṃkāra* or "Ornament of the Light of Knowledge." (T. 357) Each example is accompanied by its Sanskrit counterpart:

（2）隨諸眾生應以何國入佛智慧而取佛土。隨諸眾生應以何國起菩薩根而取佛土。(T. 475 [xiv] 538a23–25 [*juan shang*])

[A bodhisattva] seizes the buddha-lands according to what land sentient beings need to enter into the wisdom of a buddha. [A bodhisattva] seizes the buddha-lands according to what land sentient beings need to generate the roots [for becoming] bodhisattvas.[1]

yādṛśena buddhakṣetrāvatareṇa satvā buddhajñānam avataranti tādṛśaṃ buddhakṣetraṃ parigṛhṇāti | yādṛśena buddhakṣetrāvatareṇa satvānām āryākārāṇīndriyāṇy utpadyante tādṛśaṃ buddhakṣetraṃ parigṛhṇāti | (Study Group on Buddhist Sanskrit Literature 2006, 9, folio 5b2–3)

[A bodhisattva] seizes that kind of buddha-land, by entering into which buddha-land sentient beings enter into the wisdom of a buddha. [A bodhisattva] seizes that kind of buddha-land, by entering into which buddha-land sentient beings generate faculties with noble aspects.[2]

（3）如是依名說何等法，彼法非此處，不離此處。如是，文殊師利，如來如實知一切法本來不生、不起、不滅。(T. 357 [xii] 246b16–19 [*juan xia*])

---

1 The counterparts in Zhi Qian's and Xuanzang's translations of the *Vimalakīrtinirdeśa* do not contain any interrogative or indefinite pronoun (see T. 474 [xiv] 520a11–13 [*juan shang*]; T. 476 [xiv] 559a18–21 [*juan 1*]).

2 I translate *yādṛśena buddhakṣetrāvatareṇa* (lit. "through which sort of entrance into a buddha-land") loosely as "by entering into which buddha-land" to make my translation sound more like natural English.

Thus [if one] speaks of any *dharma* [i.e., any state of existence] by name, that *dharma* neither belongs to this place nor leaves this place. Thus, O Mañjuśrī, the Tathāgata knows, according to reality, that all *dharma*s are by nature unborn, non-arising and non-perishing.[1]

nāmnā yo dharmo 'bhilapyate so 'pi dharmo na deśastho na pradeśasthaḥ | evam ete mañjuśrīḥ sarvadharmās tathāgatena jñātā ādita evājātā anutpannā aniruddhāḥ | (Study Group on Buddhist Sanskrit Literature 2004, 118, folio 21b4–5)

Any *dharma* which is expressed by name, is neither situated in a region nor situated in a place. Thus, O Mañjuśrī, the Tathāgata knows from the very beginning that all *dharma*s are unborn, unoriginated and unobstructed.

In the example from Kumārajīva's translation of the *Vimalakīrtinirdeśa*, *yǐ-héguó* 以何國 (lit. "through which land") corresponds to *yādṛśena buddhakṣetrāvatareṇa* (lit. "through which sort of entrance into a buddha-land") in the Sanskrit version, with *hé* 何 matching with the relative *yādṛśa-* ("which kind of, whichever kind of") on the semantic level. In the example from Dharmaruci's translation of the *Jñānālokālaṃkāra*, *héděng-fǎ* 何等法 ("which *dharma*") corresponds to *yo dharmo* in the Sanskrit version, with *héděng* 何等 matching with the relative *yo* (*yaḥ*, "which, whichever") on the semantic level.

In all three examples above, *hé* 何 and *héděng* 何等 function as an indefinite pronoun, with no interrogative meaning. When the translators used *hé* 何 (or *héděng* 何等) to render the Sanskrit relative pronoun *yad* (or its derivatives) based on their semantic overlap (i.e., their shared meaning of "which, what"), they consequently imported the indefinite function of the Sanskrit relative pronoun into *hé* 何, as shown below in Figure 1.

---

1   The counterparts in two other Chinese translations of the *Jñānālokālaṃkāra*, separately made by Saṃghadeva (sixth century) and Fahu (early eleventh century), do not contain any interrogative or indefinite pronoun (see T. 358 [xii] 251b20–21; T. 359 [xii] 257b26–28 [*juan* 2]).

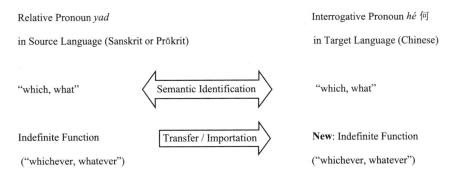

Figure 1: Indefinite use of *Hé* 何 as a result of contact-induced grammatical transfer

Now one may ask: could the development of an interrogative into an indefinite pronoun occur independently of language contact? In principle, the answer is yes. As Bernd Heine and Tania Kuteva (2002, 250–251) have shown, an interrogative may become an indefinite pronoun without any dependence on language contact, and there are indeed such cases in the world's languages. However, in the case of *hé* 何, its indefinite use is rare (though not absent) in Pre-Buddhist Archaic Chinese, and arguably uncommon in indigenous, non-Buddhist Chinese works composed in medieval times. In contrast, the indefinite use of *hé* 何 appears frequently in Buddhist translations. Such frequency was likely to have resulted from the influence exerted by the language of Indic source-texts during the translation process, or more precisely, by Sanskrit or Prākrit relative pronouns.[1]

---

1   An anonymous reviewer kindly suggests that the indefinite use of *hé* 何 in Buddhist translations does not have to be attributed to any Indian origin, since it may reflect a native syntactic development of Chinese, which was then employed to translate functional items in the source-texts. This is certainly possible. However, given the relative paucity of the indefinite use of *hé* 何 in Classical Chinese literature (see above n. 58), we must still explain why such usage occurs widely and frequently in Buddhist translations (for more examples of the indefinite *hé* 何in Buddhist texts, see Wu 2008, 142ff.). Of course, one may speculate that the indefinite *hé* 何already appeared with frequency in the vernacular language before entering into written texts. However, it is almost impossible to substantiate such a speculation, because apart from Chinese Buddhist texts we do not have any other corpus, which may provide us with "knowledge about any spoken variety of Chinese

A similar case occurs in the translation of Portuguese texts into Tariana (an Amazonian language used in northwestern Brazil) for Roman Catholic church services. The Portuguese word *que* ("what, which") may be used both as an interrogative pronoun and as a relative pronoun, whereas the Tariana word *kwana* is normally only used as an interrogative pronoun. According to Alexandra Aikhenvald's study, when translating the texts for Catholic church services from Portuguese into Tariana, young Tariana speakers used *kwana* to render Portuguese *que*, and consequently imported the relative-pronoun function into *kwana* (see Aikhenvald 2002, 183–184; Heine and Kuteva 2005, 251). The greatest difference between the change undergone by *kwana* and that undergone by *hé* 何 is this: unlike the Tariana interrogative *kwana*, the Chinese interrogative *hé* 何 did not develop into a relative pronoun during the translation process, but only acquired the indefinite function as a result of the contact-induced grammatical transfer.

Expansion of Existing Grammatical Function

The structure "Verb (+ Object) + *yǐ* 已" (hereafter "V(O)已"), in which *yǐ* 已 marks the completion of an action, appears widely and frequently in Chinese Buddhist translations.[1] There are two types of V(O)已 in Buddhist translations. In the first type, the verb used before *yǐ* 已 is atelic (for instance, *shíyǐ* 食已 ["after having eaten"]), and *yǐ* 已 serves as

---

in the first millennium of the Common Era" (Meisterernst 2018, 123–124). In my view, the frequent use of the indefinite *hé* 何 in Buddhist translations was due at least partly to the influence of the language of Indic source-texts. Since most foreign missionary translators did not attain excellent mastery of literary Chinese, it seems unlikely that they were familiar with the rare examples of the indefinite *hé* 何 in Classical Chinese literature. Thus, the likelihood that they directly adopted the indefinite *hé* 何 from Classical Chinese is low. Rather, it seems more likely to me that they were familiar with the interrogative *hé* 何, and used it to translate Indic relative pronouns based on their shared lexical meaning of "which, what," thus consequently importing the indefinite function of Indic relative pronouns into *hé* 何.

1   For previous studies on the structure V(O)已 in Buddhist translations, see, for instance, Karashima 1998a; 2010, 568–571, s.v. 已 (yǐ)(1); Mei 1999; Jiang 2007; Meisterernst 2011; Wei 2015; Aldridge and Meisterernst 2018.

an aspectual secondary predicate to supply an endpoint for the atelic event. Aldridge and Meisterernst (2018) have convincingly argued that this type of *yǐ* 已 grammaticalized from the verb *yǐ* 已 ("to end, to terminate"). The grammaticalization took place in Early Middle Chinese before the arrival of Buddhism, and was triggered by "the loss of derivational affixes distinguishing telic from atelic verbs" that occurred in Late Archaic Chinese.[1] In the second type of V(O)已, *yǐ* 已 follows a telic verb (for instance, *sǐyǐ* 死已 ["after having died"]), or follows a combination of an atelic verb with a definite quantified inner argument (for instance, *shuō-cǐjìyǐ* 說此偈已 ["after having recited this *gāthā*"]).[2] This type of *yǐ* 已 serves as an aspect marker to signal that the natural endpoint of a telic event has been reached. Two different opinions have been proposed regarding the origin of the second type of *yǐ* 已. One opinion holds that it was a syntactic innovation resulting from the contact between Chinese and Indic languages during the translation processes.[3] Another opinion holds that it was "a wholly indigenous Chinese development," a natural extension of the first type of *yǐ* 已 (i.e., the *yǐ* 已 occurring with atelic verbs and supplying an endpoint to atelic events).[4]

I take a middle way between the two opinions. Given that several examples of the second type of V(O)已 have recently been identified in Pre-Buddhist Chinese literature (Wei 2015, 224–225), there may be little doubt that this type of *yǐ* 已 emerged as a native development of Chinese. However, given the relative paucity of the second type of V(O)已

---

1   See Aldridge and Meisterernst 2018, 166–173.

2   Meisterernst (2011) suggests that the combination of an atelic verb (such as *shuō* 說 ["to say, to recite"]) with a definite inner argument (such as *cǐjì* 此偈 ["this *gāthā*"]) expresses a telic activity that has come to its natural endpoint, i.e., the endpoint of "one definite and quantifiable situation expressed by the predicate."

3   This opinion is represented by Jiang 2007, though in Jiang's analysis the second type of *yǐ* 已 occurs only with telic and punctual verbs, not with the combination of an atelic verb and a definite inner argument.

4   See Aldridge and Meisterernst 2018, 160. This opinion is represented by Aldridge and Meisterernst (2018), who have developed the proposals of Mei (1999) and Meisterernst (2011).

in Pre-Buddhist Chinese literature and its considerable frequency in Buddhist translations,[1] it seems likely to me that its frequency was due, at least partly, to the influence of the language of Indic source-texts. Thus, when explaining the frequency of the second type of V(O)已 in Buddhist translations, we should consider the influence of language contact. Karashima (2010, 568) has amply shown that in both types of V(O)已 found in Buddhist translations, *yǐ* 已 "generally correspond[s] to a gerund in Sanskrit texts." In Sanskrit, a gerund denotes an action that precedes the action expressed by the principal verb of the sentence. Below are two examples of V(O)已 quoted from Dharmarakṣa's third-century translation of the *Saddharmapuṇḍarīkasūtra* (T. 263). Each example is accompanied with its Sanskrit counterpart:

（4）佛告諸比丘: "於時, 五百百千億大梵天衆讚歎佛已, 啓勸令佛轉大法輪……" (T. 263 [ix] 91b20–21 [*juan* 4])

The Buddha told the monks: "At that time, five thousand trillion deities of the heaven of the great Brahmā, having praised the Buddha, implored and requested the Buddha to turn the great wheel of the Dharma…"

atha khalu bhikṣavas te mahābrahmāṇas taṃ bhagavantaṃ mahābhijñājñābhi-bhuvaṃ tathāgatam arhantaṃ samyaksaṃbuddhaṃ saṃmukham ābhiḥ sārūpyābhir gāthābhir abhiṣṭutya taṃ bhagavantam etad ūcuḥ | pravartayatu bhagavān dharmacakraṃ pravartayatu sugato dharmacakraṃ… (Kern and Nanjio 1908–1912, 178, lines 1–3)

[The Buddha said,] "Then, O Monks, the deities of the heaven of the great Brahmā, having praised the Blessed One, the Superior One with the Knowledge of the Great Supernatural Knowledges, the Tathāgata, the Arhat, the Perfectly-

---

1   The paucity of the second type of V(O)已 in Pre-Buddhist Chinese literature is noted by Wei (2015, 225).

Awakened one, in [his] personal presence, with suitable stanzas, said this to the Blessed One: "O Blessed One, please turn the wheel of the Dharma! O Sugata, please turn the wheel of the Dharma! …"

（5）適見佛已，尋時即往。(T. 263 [ix] 90b12–17 [*juan* 4])
Having just caught sight of the Buddha, they immediately approached [him].

dṛṣṭvā ca punar yena sa bhagavān mahābhijñājñānābhibhūs tathāgato "rhan samyaksaṃbuddhas tenopasaṃkrantā | (Kern and Nanjio 1908–1912, 169, lines 3–4)
Furthermore, having seen [the Blessed One], they approached the Blessed One, Tathāgata, Arhat, the Perfectly Awakened One, the Superior One with the Knowledge of the Great Supernatural Knowledges.

In Example (4), *zàntàn* 讚歎 ("to praise") is an atelic verb, and the phrase "讚歎……已" corresponds to the gerund *abhiṣṭutya* ("having praised"). In Example (5), *jiàn* 見 ("to see") is a telic verb, and the phrase "見……已" corresponds to the gerund *dṛṣṭvā* ("having seen"). In Pre-Buddhist literary Chinese, V(O)已 was first involved with atelic verbs, and later also with telic verbs (Aldridge and Meisterernst, 2018). Comparatively speaking, before the arrival of Buddhism, the first type of V(O)已 (V = an atelic verb) was more common, while the second type of V(O)已 (V = a telic verb) was relatively rare. Since most foreign missionary translators only had limited knowledge of literary Chinese, it is likely that they were more familiar with the first type of V(O)已, and that not all of them were aware of the existence of the second type of V(O)已 in Chinese. Translators who were aware of the existence of the second type of V(O)已 directly adopted it from literary Chinese. But for translators who were unaware of, or did not know of, the existence of the second type of V(O)已 in Chinese, they may well have devised the second type of V(O)已 by analogy with the first type of V(O)已. To be sure, for modern linguists, the categories of atelic and telic verbs are clear-cut and may be easily differentiated. However, in the eyes of foreign missionaries (especially those unaware of the existence of the second type of V(O)已 in Chinese), there may have appeared to be no fundamental difference between the first type of V(O)已 (V = an atelic verb) and the second type of V(O)已 (V = a telic verb). Given that all Indic (Sanskrit or Prākrit) verbs, whether telic or atelic, may form gerunds, when foreign missionaries translated the gerunds of Indic atelic verbs into the first type of V(O) 已, they would have likewise translated the gerunds of Indic telic verbs in a similar way and consequently introduced the second type of V(O)已 into translation texts. By doing so, foreign translators applied the aspect marker *yǐ* 已 to virtually any Chinese verb, whether telic or atelic, thus effectively expanding the usage of *yǐ* 已. This may account for the frequency of the second type of V(O)已 in Buddhist translations. The mechanism suggested above is illustrated below in Figure 2:

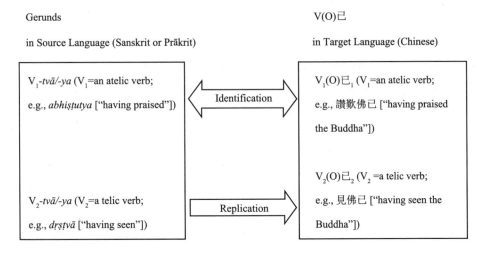

Figure 2: V(O) 已 as a result of contact-induced grammatical expansion

A partly similar case occurs in the language contact between Slovenian and German speakers in Trieste. According to Heine and Kuteva (2005, 52), the language contact in this region "had *inter alia* the effect that the Slovenian pattern of reflexive marking was replicated to some extent by German speakers." In Standard German, while a reflexive verb such as *waschen* ("to wash") takes a reflexive pronoun, a non-reflexive verb such as *lernen* ("to learn") does not take a reflexive pronoun. In Slovenian, both types of verbs may take the reflexive marker *se*. Following the model of the Slovenian reflexive marker *se*, the German speakers in Trieste likewise used the reflexive pronoun *sich* with non-reflexive verbs such as *lernen*, thus consequently expanding the usage of the reflexive pronoun *sich* by applying it to virtually all verbs (whether reflexive or not) and to all three persons (first, second and third).[1] Of course, this example does not involve any aspect marker and is thus not strictly parallel to the case of V(O)已 discussed above. Nevertheless, the expansion of the usage of the reflexive pronoun *sich* in the language of German speakers in Trieste does bear a similarity to the expansion of the usage of the aspect marker *yǐ* 已 in Chinese Buddhist translations, since both cases of expansion belong to contact-induced grammatical changes.

Replication of Syntactic Relation

The disposal structure "*chí* 持 + Object + Verb" (hereafter "持OV") frequently found in early Buddhist translations may illustrate the mechanism of transferring syntactic relation (or more precisely, the OV word order) from the source language (Sanskrit or Prākrit) into the target language (Chinese). In Classical Chinese, the predominant word order is "Subject + Verb + Object" (SVO).[2] In Sanskrit and Prākrit, the typical word order is "Subject + Object + Verb" (SOV), though there are many deviations from this typical word order.[3] Below I will argue that the frequent use of the disposal structure 持OV in early Buddhist

---

1   Heine and Kuteva (2005, 52) note that the reflexive pronoun *sich*, "which is restricted to third-person referents, was extended to second and first persons, e.g. *wir waschen sich*" by the German speakers in Trieste, as a result of replicating the Slovenian reflexive marker *se*.

2   On the basic SVO order of Classical Chinese, see Peyraube 1996, 165–168; 1997; Aldridge 2010b.

3   In fact, both verb-final and non-verb-final structures may be found in Sanskrit and Prākrit texts. On the free verb-final order (rather than rigid verb-final order) of Sanskrit and Prākrit, see Bubenik 1991; Hock 1997, 103–105.

translations was due, at least partly, to the influence of verb-final clauses or sentences in Indic source-texts. While *chí* 持 is often used in Classical Chinese as a verb meaning "to hold," it does not function as a verb in the structure 持 OV discussed here; rather, it is more like a preposition (similar to *yǐ* 以) used to bring the object to the front of the verb.[1] The disposal structure 持OV already occurs in Lokakṣema's second-century Chinese translation of the *Aṣṭasāhasrikā Prajñāpāramitā* or "Perfection of Wisdom in Eight Thousand Verses" (T. 224).[2] The following four sentences are quoted from T. 224, all containing the structure 持OV, along with their counterparts in a Sanskrit version of the *Aṣṭasāhasrikā Prajñāpāramitā*. The latter two sentences also have counterparts in a Gāndhārī *Prajñāpāramitā* manuscript that has been dated, "based on a C14 test, to 47~147 C.E., which means that this manuscript is probably contemporary with the original text of Lokakṣema's Chinese translation (translated in 179 C.E.)."[3]

（6）中又爲蛇所齧者，若男子、若女人持摩尼珠示之，見摩尼珠，毒即去。(T. 224 [viii] 436a6–8 [juan 2])[4]

As for someone among [them] who is bitten by a viper, if a man or a woman shows him the *maṇi* gem, as soon as he sees the *maṇi* gem, the poison will immediately go away.[5]

saced bhagavan strī vā puruṣo vā āśīviṣeṇa daṣṭo bhavet tasya tan maṇiratnaṃ da<r>śyeta | tasya saha daṃśanenaiva[6] maṇiratnasya tad viṣaṃ pratihanyeta vigacchet | (Mitra 1888, 97. 6–7 = Wogihara 1932–1935, 274. 25–28)

---

1 *Yǐ* 以 has been treated either as a light verb (Aldridge 2010b), or as a preposition / postposition (Peyraube 1997). On the relationship between *chí* 持 and *yǐ* 以, see discussion below.
2 For a detailed list of examples of such prepositional use of 持 in T. 224, see Karashima 2010, 70–74.
3 See Karashima 2010, 759–760.
4 See also a translation of this Chinese sentence and its Sanskrit parallel in Karashima 2011,105 n. 586.
5 All underlines in the sentences quoted here and below are added by the present author.
6 Emended to *darśanenaiva* (see Mitra 1888, 97 n.1; Wogihara 1932, 274).

O Blessed One, if a woman or a man were bitten by a viper, one should show him/her that gem. Exactly at the sight of that gem, the poison would be removed and would go away.

（7）正使菩薩摩訶薩持心了知，當作是學[1]知：“盡，無所有。”(T. 224 [viii] 438c5–6 [*juan* 3]) [2]

If a *bodhisattva-mahāsattva* comprehends the thought thoroughly, he shall perceive it as follows: "[The thought] is extinct, without existence."

sacet punar bodhisattvo mahāsattvo yac cittaṃ pariṇāmayati tac cittam evaṃ saṃjānīte evaṃ samanvāharati | tac cittaṃ samanvāhriyamāṇam eva kṣīṇaṃ kṣīṇam ity evaṃ saṃjānīte viruddhaṃ vigataṃ vipariṇatam ity evaṃ saṃjānīte... (Mitra 1888, 142.21–143.2 = Wogihara 1932–1935, 342.10–13)

Moreover, if a *bodhisattva-mahāsattva* perceives and concentrates in this way upon the thought which matures: he perceives the thought being concentrated upon as follows, "[It is] just extinct, extinct," [and] as follows, "It is stopped, departed, deteriorated" ...

（8）若善男子、善女人持般若波羅蜜經卷與他人，使書，若令學，若為說，及至阿惟越致菩薩書經卷，授與之……(T. 224 [viii] 437b18–20 [*juan* 3])[3]

If a good man or a good woman gives scriptural scrolls of the *Prajñāpāramitā* to other people, making them copy it, or making them study it, or explaining it for them, and even [goes so far as to] write its scriptural scrolls for non-retrogressing *bodhisattva*s and give them [the scrolls] ...

---

1 The variant reading 覺 should be adopted here (see Karashima 2011, 137).
2 See also a translation of this Chinese sentence and its Sanskrit parallel in Karashima 2011, 137 n. 67.
3 See also a translation of this Chinese sentence and its Sanskrit parallel in Karashima 2011, 121 n. 732.

yaś cānyaḥ kaścit kauśika kulaputro vā kuladuhitā vā teṣāṃ sarveṣām anuttarāyāṃ
samyaksaṃbodhau cittam utpādya tebhya imāṃ prajñāpāramitāṃ likhitvā dadyāt | yo vā
kauśika kulaputro vā kuladuhitā vā avinivartanīyāya bodhisattvāya mahāsattvāyaināṃ
prajñāpāramitāṃ likhitvā upanāmayed... (Mitra 1888, 128.18–129.1 = Wogihara,
1932–1935, 315.17–22)

O Kauśika, if someone else, either a son of good family or a daughter of good
family, having raised the thought of all these beings up to the supreme perfect
awakening, should give them this perfection of wisdom after having copied it, or,
O Kauśika, if someone, either a son of good family or a daughter of good family,
should present this perfection of wisdom to an irreversible *bodhisattva-mahāsattva*
after having copied it...

te (5-38:) + + + + + [.. saṃmasaṃbo] sae prathidaṇa
ima prañaparamida likhita dajati
yo ya aveva (5-39:) + + + +
.. sa imayeva prañaparamida likhita uvaṇamea (Gāndhārī parallel cited from Falk and
Karashima 2013, 146–148) [1]

"...their intent upon [...supreme awakening], should give this perfection of
wisdom after having copied it. If someone...should present exactly this perfection
of wisdom to an irreversible...after having copied it..."[2]

（9）從是輩中，若有一菩薩出，便作是言："我欲疾作佛。" 正使[3]欲疾作佛，

1　According to the conventions listed by Falk and Karashima (2013, 101), "(5-38:) + + + + +"
means that line 5-38 has lost the birch-bark needed for ca. 5 *akṣara*s up to the standard left-side
border; "(5-39:) + + + +" means that line 5-39 has lost the birch-bark needed for ca. 4 *akṣara*s
counting from a hypothetical right-side border; ".." denotes an illegible *akṣara*.

2　My translation.

3　On *zhèngshǐ* 正使 meaning "if, when" in the present context, see Karashima 2010, 632.

若有人持般若波羅蜜經卷書、授與者，其福轉倍多。(T.224 [viii] 437c16–19 [juan 3])[1]

Suppose that a *bodhisattva* emerges from them (i.e., from these irreversible *bodhisattvas*) and says, "I wish to become a *buddha* quickly." When [a *bodhisattva* thus] wishes to become a *buddha* quickly, if someone writes a scriptural scroll of the Prajñāpāramitā and gives [it to this bodhisattva], that person's merit would be much greater.

ataḥ khalu punaḥ sa kauśika kulaputro vā kuladuhitā vā bahutaraṃ puṇyaṃ prasaved yas teṣām avinivartanīyānāṃ bodhisattvānāṃ mahāsattvānāṃ kṣiprataraṃ anuttarāṃ samyaksambodhim abhisamboddhukāmebhya imāṃ prajñāpāramitāṃ pustakalikhitāṃ kṛtvā dadyād upanāmayet sārthāṃ savyañjanām upadiśet iha ca tān prajñāpāramitāyām avavaded anuśiṣyāt (Mitra 1888, 131.4–9 = Wogihara, 1932–1935, 319.4–10)

Furthermore, O Kauśika, a son of good family or a daughter of good family would acquire greater merit, if he or she, having written this perfection of wisdom down in a book, should give [and] present it to those who wish to attain more quickly the supreme perfect awakening among irreversible *bodhisattva-mahāsattva*s, if he or she should explain [this perfection of wisdom] with its meaning and with its letters, and if he or she should admonish and instruct [those irreversible *bodhisattva-mahāsattva*s] in regard to this perfection of wisdom.

teṣa sarveṣa avevaṭiaṇa (5-52:) + + + + + .. + .. + + + + + + [*ku*]*lap*(*u*)*tro va kuladhita vi* *ima prañaparamida likh*[*ita*] *uvaṇa*(*m*)*e*

---

1   See also a translation of this Chinese sentence and its Sanskrit parallel in Karashima 2011, 125 n. 759.

(5-53:) + + + + [ña]ṇa uvatidiśea (Gāndhārī parallel cited from Falk and Karashima 2013, 160) [1]

"Among all the irreversible...a son of good family or a daughter of good family...should present this perfection of wisdom after having copied it...should explain with its letters..."[2]

In all four examples, *chí* 持 is not used as a verb meaning "to hold" but instead serves as a disposal marker indicating the preverbal position of the object. In the Sanskrit and Gāndhārī parallels quoted above, we find no word meaning "to hold" that matches *chí* 持 in its literal sense. Let us look at these examples one by one.

In Example (6), the phrase 持摩尼珠示之 ("show him the *maṇi* gem") corresponds to the Sanskrit verb-final clause *tasya tan maṇiratnaṃ da<r>śyeta* ("one should show him that *maṇi* gem"), in which the noun *mónízhū* 摩尼珠 ("*maṇi* gem"), the verb *shì* 示 ("show") and the pronoun *zhī* 之 ("him") match respectively with *tan maṇiratnaṃ* ("that gem"), *da<r>śyeta* ("one should show") and *tasya* ("to him"), whereas *chí* 持 has no direct counterpart in the Sanskrit clause.

In Example (7), the phrase 持心了知 ("comprehend the thought thoroughly") corresponds to the Sanskrit verb-final clause *tac cittam evaṃ saṃjānīte evaṃ samanvāharati* ("[a bodhisattva] perceives and concentrates in this way upon the thought"), in which the noun *xīn* 心 ("thought") and the verb *liǎozhī* 了知 ("comprehend thoroughly") match respectively with *tac cittam* ("that thought") and *saṃjānīte samanvāharati* ("perceives and concentrates upon"), whereas *chí* 持 has no direct counterpart in the Sanskrit clause. The word *chí* 持 certainly does not mean "to hold" here, since it is impossible for anyone to hold an abstract object such as "thought."

---

1 According to Falk and Karashima (2012, 26), [a] denotes that letter "a" is only partially preserved; (b) denotes that letter "b" is not preserved but reconstructed. On the symbols "+" and "..", see above n. 85.

2 My translation.

In Example (8), the phrase 持般若波羅蜜經卷與他人 ("give scriptural scrolls of the *Prajñāpāramitā* to other people") corresponds to the Sanskrit verb-final clause *tebhya imāṃ prajñāpāramitāṃ likhitvā dadyāt* ("[if one] should give them this perfection of wisdom after having copied it"), in which 般若波羅蜜 (EHC: *pan nja: pa la mjiət ; EMC: *pan ɲiak pa la mjit; transliteration of Gāndhārī *praṇaparamida*, "perfection of wisdom"), the verb *yǔ* 與 ("give") and the pronoun *tārén* 他人 ("other people") match respectively with *imāṃ prajñāpāramitāṃ* ("that perfection of wisdom"), *dadyāt* ("one should give") and *tebhyaḥ* ("to them"), whereas *chí* 持 has no direct counterpart in the Sanskrit clause. The Gāndhārī parallel to this Chinese phrase reads *ima praṇaparamida likhita dajati* ("[if one] should give this perfection of wisdom after having copied it"), which contains nothing matching *chí* 持 either.

In Example (9), the clause 若有人持般若波羅蜜經卷書授與者 ("If someone writes a scriptural scroll of the *Prajñāpāramitā* and gives [it]") corresponds both to the Sanskrit verb-final clause *imāṃ prajñāpāramitāṃ pustakalikhitāṃ kṛtvā dadyād upanāmayet* ("[if one] should give [and] present this perfection of wisdom after having written it down in a book"), and to the Gāndhārī verb-final clause *ima praṇaparamida likh[ita] uvaṇa(m)e* ("[if one] should present this perfection of wisdom after having copied it"). In this Chinese clause, the noun 般若波羅蜜經卷 ("scriptural scroll of the perfection of wisdom") matches with the Sanskrit *imāṃ prajñāpāramitāṃ* ("this perfection of wisdom") and with the Gāndhārī *ima praṇaparamida* ("this perfection of wisdom"). The penultimate verb *shū* 書 ("to write") matches with the Sanskrit gerund phrase *pustakalikhitāṃ kṛtvā* (lit. "having made it written down in a book") and with the Gāndhārī gerund *likhita* (< Skt. *likhitvā*, "having copied").[1] The final verb *shòuyǔ* 授與 ("give") matches with the Sanskrit principal verbs *dadyād upanāmayet* ("one should give [and] present") and with the Gāndhārī principal verb *uvaṇa(m)e* ("one should present"). Neither the Sanskrit clause nor the Gāndhārī clause contains anything directly corresponding to the word *chí* 持. Since

---

1 On the Gāndhārī gerund (absolutive) ending -*ita* (=Skt. -*itvā*), see Salomon 2000, 89, 102.

the Gāndhārī manuscript has been dated back to "47~147 C.E." (Karashima 2010, 760), roughly contemporary with the Indic source-text used by Lokakṣema, it is likely that the Indic originals of the above-cited Chinese sentences had basically the same syntactic structures as those found in the Gāndhārī manuscript.[1]

In light of the Sanskrit and Gāndhārī parallels, we may suggest that in all four examples above, the word *chí* 持 was not translated from any Indic verb (or verbal derivative) meaning "to hold"; rather, the word *chí* 持 was added by Lokakṣema to shift the object to the preverbal position, presumably for the sake of replicating or imitating the OV word order in the Indic source-text he used. Here I do not mean to suggest that the structure 持OV originated from language contact. In fact, as some scholars have rightly argued, the disposal markers (*chí* 持, *jiāng* 將 and *bǎ* 把) may well have grammaticalized from verbs in serial verb constructions by analogy with the already existing *yǐ* 以 disposal structures.[2] Since both processes (grammaticalization and analogy) took place within Chinese independently of language contact, there may be little doubt that the disposal structure 持OV emerged as a native development of Chinese. Meanwhile, it should be noted that the theory of the native origin of 持OV does not suffice to account for the frequent appearance of 持OV in early Chinese Buddhist translations. We must still explain what motivated early translators (such as Lokakṣema) to frequently adopt the disposal structure 持OV instead of the regular VO structure.[3] In my opinion, Lokakṣema's preference for 持OV over the VO structure was motivated by his intent to align the word order of his translation with the OV word order of

---

1 As for its pedigree, the Gāndhārī manuscript "can be regarded as representing the forerunner to the one Lokakṣema knew" (Falk and Karashima 2012, 20).

2 On the theory that the *yǐ* 以 constructions in Archaic Chinese served as a model for the establishment of *chí* 持 / *jiāng* 將 / *bǎ* 把 disposals, see Mei 1990; Peyraube 1996, 170–174. The parallel between *chí* 持 and *yǐ* 以 is particularly notable in the examples (6) and (8), where *chí* 持 appears in combination with ditransitive verbs, with the direct object following *chí* 持 instead of the verb (I thank an anonymous reviewer for drawing my attention to this parallel). In the examples (7) and (9), *chí* 持 is used simply to mark the preverbal object.

3 For many more examples of the disposal structure 持OV in T. 224, see Karashima 2010, 70–74.

the Indic original. Thus, while the emergence of 持OV was indeed a native development, the frequent use of 持OV in early Chinese Buddhist translations may well have been a contact-induced phenomenon, as a result of the influence of the verb-final word order of the language of Indic source-texts.

A somewhat similar case occurs in the language contact between Latin and Old Swedish in the late Middle Ages. While in Classical Latin, the basic word order is verb-final (namely SOV), in Old Swedish, the dominant word order in main and subordinate clauses was normally verb-second. Höder and Zeevaert (2008, 170) have observed that from the fourteenth to the sixteenth century, the verb-late word order in Old Swedish subordinate clauses emerged as a "salient innovative pattern." This verb-late word order "is likely to be a contact-induced innovation," which arose "in the context of the adaptation of continental European—i.e. Latin-based—text types," or more precisely, in Old Swedish translations of Latin religious texts (Höder and Zeevaert 2008, 177–180). Such verb-late word order became even more frequently used in Late Old Swedish translations, probably because "later translators aim at producing texts in the vernacular that are formally equivalent to the foreign originals" (Höder and Zeevaert 2008, 177). The frequency of the verb-late word order in Old Swedish translations, and the frequency of the disposal structure 持OV in Lokakṣema's translation, may share a similar reason, since both frequencies were caused at least partly by language contact, precisely under the influence of the verb-final word order in source-texts.

Conclusion

This paper has discussed some major mechanisms of contact-induced innovations in Chinese Buddhist translations. Regarding lexical creations, there are six basic mechanisms: phonemic loan, loan translation, hybrid loan, semantic extension, double translation, and disyllabification. Regarding syntactic creations, there are at least three basic mechanisms: importation of new grammatical function (as illustrated by the indefinite use of the interrogative pronoun *hé* 何), expansion of existing grammatical function (as illustrated by the use of the aspect marker *yĭ* 已 with both atelic and telic verbs) and replication of syntactic word order (as illustrated by the frequent use of the disposal structure 持OV). The following conclusion may be drawn from the discussion above.

The six mechanisms of contact-induced lexical creations are not unique to Chinese Buddhist translations, since almost all of them have parallels or partial parallels in other language-contact situations (either in modern language contacts, or in premodern Western translations such as the Septuagint and Notker's corpus). Although disyllabification, a major development marking the transition from Archaic Chinese to Middle Chinese, is indeed unique to the Chinese language in terms of its widespread scale, the basic methods of creating disyllabic words in Chinese Buddhist translations (namely, the addition of a redundant element to a monosyllabic term, and the abbreviation of a polysyllabic term into disyllabic form) are nevertheless not unique and have parallels elsewhere (either in the Septuagint or in modern language contacts). Second, the three mechanisms of contact-induced syntactic creations are also not unique to Chinese Buddhist translations, since they all have parallels or partial parallels in other translation activities that took place in different cultural contexts (for instance, in the translation of Portuguese texts into Tariana for Roman Catholic church services in Brazil, in the language contact between Slovenian and German speakers in Trieste, and in the translation of Latin texts into Old Swedish in the Middle Ages). Taken as a whole, we may conclude that as far as the mechanisms of contact-induced linguistic creations are concerned, Chinese Buddhist translations and non-Sinitic language contacts show some striking similarities in the ways in which they brought about new lexical and syntactic elements.

(Acknowledgement: This chapter is a revised version of an article previously published in *Acta Orientalia Academiae Scientiarum Hungaricae*, Volume 73, Issue 3, 2020, 385–418. The article is reprinted here with minor alterations in wording and in the style of citation and referencing. An earlier draft of the present paper was presented at the workshop "Connections: China and the West in the Making of History" held at the University of Oxford China Centre on December 6, 2017. I thank participants for their helpful comments.

The paper was subsequently revised, with the financial support of the National Social Science Fund of China [Grant No. 2018VJX071]. My sincere thanks go to two anonymous reviewers for their constructive remarks. All remaining errors are mine alone. This article is a revision of the author's speech at the 2021 UKCHA Annual Forum.)

References

Aikhenvald, A. 2002. *Language Contact in Amazonia*. Oxford: Oxford University Press.

Aldridge, E. 2010a. Clause-internal *wh*-movement in Archaic Chinese. *Journal of East Asian Linguistics*, 19(1): 1–36.

——. 2010b. Focus and Archaic Chinese Word Order. In *Proceedings of the 22nd North American Conference on Chinese Linguistics (NACCL-22) and the 18th International Conference on Chinese Linguistics (IACL-18)*, edited by Lauren E. Clemens and Chi-Ming L. Liu, 84–101. Columbus, Ohio: NACCL Proceedings Online.

Aldridge, E. and Meisterernst, B. 2018. Resultative and termination: A unified analysis of Middle Chinese VP-YI. In *Topics in Theoretical Asian Linguistics: Studies in honor of John B. Whitman*, edited by K. Nishyama, H. Kishimoto and E. Aldridge, 157–179. Amsterdam: John Benjamins Publishing Company.

Bailey, H. W. 1946. "Gāndhārī." *Bulletin of the School of Oriental and African Studies*, 11(4): 764–797.

Bernhard, F. 1970. Gāndhārī and the Buddhist Mission in Central Asia. In *Añjali: Papers on Indology and Buddhism. A Felicitation Volume Presented to Olives Hector de Alevis Wijesekera on his 60th Birthday*, edited by J. Tilakasiri, 55–62. Peradeniya: University of Ceylon.

Boucher, D. 1998. "Gāndhārī and the Early Chinese Buddhist Translations Reconsidered: The Case of the *Saddharmapuṇḍarīkasūtra*." *Journal of the American Oriental Studies*, 118(4): 471–506.

Brough, J. 1975. "Buddhist Chinese Etymological Notes." *Bulletin of the School of Oriental and African Studies*, 38(3): 581–585.

——. 1962. *The Gāndhārī Dharmapada, Edited with an Introduction and Commentary*. London: Oxford University Press.

Bubenik, V. 1991. "Nominal and pronominal objects in Sanskrit and Prakrit." In *Studies in Sanskrit Syntax*, edited by H. H. Hock, 19–30. Delhi: Motilal Banarsidass.

Bynon, T. 1977. *Historical Linguistics*. Cambridge: Cambridge University Press.

Cao, Guangshun 曹廣順 and Yu, Hsiao-jung 遇笑容. 2015. "Language Contact and Its Influence on the Development of Chinese Syntax." In *The Oxford Handbook of Chinese Linguistics*, edited by William S-Y Wang and Chaofen Sun, 203–214. Oxford: Oxford University Press.

Cheng, Xiangqing 程湘清. 1992. "Lunheng fuyinci yanjiu《論衡》復音詞研究 [A study of disyllabic words in *Lunheng*]." In *Liang Han hanyu yanjiu* 兩 漢 漢 語 研 究 [Studies of Han Chinese], edited by Xiangqing Cheng, 262–240. Jinan: Shandong Education Press.

Coblin, W. S. 1983. *A Handbook of Eastern Han Sound Glosses*. Hong Kong: The Chinese University Press.

Crystal, D. 2010. *Begat: The King James Bible and the English Language*. Oxford: Oxford University Press.

Deeg, M., 2008. "Creating religious terminology: A comparative approach to early Chinese Buddhist translations." *Journal of the International Association of Buddhist Studies*, 31 (1–2): 83–118.

Dong, Xiufang 董秀芳. 2011. *Cihuihua: Hanyu shuangyinci de yansheng he fazhan* 詞彙化: 漢語雙音詞的衍生和發展 [Lexicalization: The Origin and Evolution of Chinese Disyllabic Words]. Revised edition. Beijing: The Commercial Press.

Durkin, P. 2014. *Borrowed Words: A History of Loanwords in English*. Oxford: Oxford University Press.

Falk, H. and Karashima, S. 2012. "A first-century *Prajāpāramitā* manuscript from Gandhāra – *parivarta* 1 (Texts from the Split Collection 1)." *Annual Report of the International Research Institute for Advanced Buddhology at Soka University*, 15: 19–61.

——. 2013. "A first-century *Prajāpāramitā* manuscript from Gandhāra – *parivarta* 5 (Texts from the Split Collection 2)." *Annual Report of the International Research Institute for Advanced Buddhology at Soka University*, 16: 97–169.

Feng, S. L. 2017. "Disyllabification." In *Encyclopedia of Chinese Language and Linguistics,* Vol. 2, edited by Rint Sybesma et al, 108–113. Leiden: Brill.

Frakes, J. 1988. *The Fate of Fortune in the Early Middle Ages: The Boethian Tradition*. Studien und Texte zur Geistesgeschichte des Mittelalters 23. Leiden: Brill.

Funayama, T. 2008. "The work of Paramārtha: An example of Sino-Indian cross-cultural exchange." *Journal of the International Association of Buddhist Studies*, 31(1–2): 141–183.

Glare, ed. 2012. *Oxford Latin Dictionary*. 7th edition. Oxford: Oxford University Press.

Glenny, W. E. 2007. "Hebrew Misreadings or Free Translation in the Septuagint of Amos?" *Vetus Testamentum*, 57(4): 524–547.

——. 2009. *Finding Meaning in the Texts: Translation Technique and Theology in the Septuagint of Amos*. Supplements to *Vetus Testamentum* 126. Leiden: Brill.

Harrison, P. and Watanabe, S. 2006. "Vajracchedikā Prajāpāramitā." In *Manuscript in the Schøyen Collection: Buddhist Manuscripts, Volume III*, edited by Jens Braarvig et al., 89–132. Oslo: Hermes Academic Publishing.

Haspelmath, M. and Uri, T. 2009. *Loanwords in the World's Languages: A Comparative Handbook*. Berlin: Mouton de Gruyter.

Haugen, E. 1950. "The Analysis of Linguistic Borrowing." *Language*, 26(2): 210–231.

Heine, B. and Kuteva, T. 2002. *World Lexicon of Grammaticalization*. Cambridge: Cambridge University Press.

——. 2005. *Language Contact and Grammatical Change*. Cambridge: Cambridge University Press.

von Hinüber, O. 1989. Origin and Varieties of Buddhist Sanskrit. In *Dialectes dans les littératures Indo-aryennes*, edited by C. Caillat, 341–367. Paris: Collège de France.

Hock, H. H. 1991. *Principles of Historical Linguistics*. 2nd edition. Berlin: Mouton de Gruyter.

——. 1997. "Chronology or Genre? Problems in Vedic Syntax." In *Inside the Texts, Beyond the Texts: New Approaches to the Study of the Vedas*, edited by M. Witzel, 103–126. Cambridge, MA: Department of Sanskrit and Indian Studies, Harvard University.

Höder, S. and Zeevaert, L. 2008. "Verb-late word order in Old Swedish subordinate clauses: Loan, Ausbau phenomenon, or both?" In *Language Contact and Contact Languages*, edited by Siemund and N. Kintana, 163–184. Amsterdam / Philadelphia: John Benjamins.

Ji, Xianlin 季羨林. 1992. "Zaitan futu yu fo." 再談「浮屠」與「佛」 [Another Discussion on Futu and Fo]. *Chung-Hwa Buddhist Journal* 中華佛學學報 [*Journal of Chinese Buddhist Studies*] 5: 19–30.

——. 1995. "Zhongguo fanyi cidian" xu《中國翻譯詞典》序 [Preface to *A Dictionary of Translations in China*]. *Zhongguo fanyi* 中國翻譯 6: 4–5.

——. 1998. "Tuhuoluowen milehuijianji yishi." 吐火羅文《彌勒會見記》譯釋 [Translation and Interpretation of the Tocharian *Maitreyasamiti-Nāṭaka*]. In *Ji Xianlin Wenji* 季羨林文集 [*Collected Papers of Ji Xianlin*]. Vol. 11. Nanchang: Jiangxi jiaoyu chubanshe.

Jiang, Shaoyu 蔣紹愚. 2007. "Yuyan jiechu de yige anli—zaitan 'V(O) *yi*'." 语言接触的一个案例——再谈 'V(O)已' [A case of language contact—another discussion of VO *yi*]. *Yuyanxue luncong* 語言學論叢 [*Essays on Linguistics*] 36: 268–285.

Karashima, S. 辛嶋静志. 1992. *The Textual Study of the Chinese Versions of the Saddharmapuṇḍarīkasūtra in the light of the Sanskrit and Tibetan Versions*. Bibliotheca Indologica et Buddhologica 3. Tokyo: The Sankibo Press.

——. 1996a. "Vernacularisms and Transcriptions in Early Chinese Buddhist Scriptures." *Sino-Platonic Papers*, 71: 32–42.

——. 1996b. "Kan'yaku butten no kango to onshago no mondai." 漢訳仏典の漢語と音写語の問題 [Problems in the Language and Transcriptions of the Chinese Buddhist Translations]. In *Higashi ajia shakai to bukkyō bunka* 東アジア社会と仏教文化 [East Asian Society and Buddhist Culture], edited by J. Takasaki and K. Kimura, 201–218. Tokyo: Shunshūkai.

——. 1997. "Hanyi fodian de yuyan yanjiu." 漢譯佛典的語言研究 [A Study of the Language of Chinese Buddhist Translations]. *Suyuyan yanjiu* 俗語言研究, 4: 29–49.

——. 1998a. "Hanyi fodian de yuyan yanjiu (2)." 漢譯佛典的語言研究(二) [A Study of the Language of Chinese Buddhist Translations (2)]. *Suyuyan yanjiu* 俗語言研究, 5: 47–57.

——. 1998b. *A Glossary of Dharmarakṣa's Translation of the Lotus Sutra*. Bibliotheca Philologica et Philosophica Buddhica I. Tokyo: The International Research Institute for Advanced Buddhology, Soka University.

——. 2001. *A Glossary of Kumārajīva's Translation of the Lotus Sutra*. Bibliotheca Philologica et Philosophica Buddhica IV. Tokyo: The International Research Institute for Advanced Buddhology, Soka University.

——. 2006. "Underlying Languages of Early Chinese Translations of Buddhist Scriptures." In *Studies in Chinese Language and Culture: Festschrift in Honour of Christoph Harbsmeier on the Occasion of his 60th Birthday*, edited by C. Anderl and H. Eifring, 355–366. Oslo: Hermes Academic Publishing.

——. 2010. *A Glossary of Lokakṣema's Translation of the Aṣṭasāhasrikā Prajāpāramitā*. Bibliotheca Philologica et Philosophica Buddhica XI. Tokyo: The International Research Institute for Advanced Buddhology, Soka University.

——. 2011. *A Critical Edition of Lokakṣema's Translation of the Aṣṭasāhasrikā Prajāpāramitā*. Bibliotheca Philologica et Philosophica Buddhica XII. Tokyo: The International Research Institute for Advanced Buddhology, Soka University.

——. 2013. "A Study of the Language of Early Chinese Buddhist Translations: A Comparison between the Translations by Lokakṣema and Zhi Qian." *Annual Report of the International Research Institute for Advanced Buddhology at Soka University*, 16: 273–288.

——. 2014. "Hanyi fodian yuyan yanjiu de yiyi ji fangfa."漢譯佛典語言研究的意義及方法 [Meaning and Method of Linguistic Research on Chinese Translations of Buddhist Scriptures]. *Guoji hanxue yanjiu tongxun* 國際漢學研究通訊 10: 322–342.

——. 2015. "Vehicle (*yāna*) and Wisdom (*jāna*) in the Lotus Sutra—the Origin of the Notion of *yāna* in Mahāyāna Buddhism." *Annual Report of the International Research Institute for Advanced Buddhology at Soka University*, 18: 163–196.

——. 2016a. "Indian Folk Etymologies and Their Reflections in Chinese Translations—*brāhmaṇa*, *śramaṇa* and *Vaiśramaṇa*." *Annual Report of the International Research Institute for Advanced Buddhology at Soka University*, 19: 101–123.

——. 2016b. "Yuimakitsu kyō no gengo no yōsō."『維摩詰経』の原語の様相 [Features of the Underlying Language of Zhi Qian's Chinese Translation of the *Vimalakīrtinirdeśa*]. In *Mitomo Kenyō Hakase Koki Kinen Ronbunshō* 三友健容博士古稀記念論文集 [*A Commemorative Volume in Honor of Prof. Dr. Kenyo Mitomo for His 70th Birthday*]. Tokyo: Sankibo Busshorin: 357–333 [sic].

Karashima, S. and Nattier, J. 2015. "Qiuluzi 秋露子, An Early Chinese Name for Śāriputra." *Annual Report of the International Research Institute for Advanced Buddhology at Soka University*, 8: 361–376.

Karlgren, B. 1945. "The Book of Odes: Ta Ya and Sung." *Bulletin of the Museum of Far Eastern Antiquities*, 17: 65–99.

Kern, H. and Nanjio, B. 1908–1912. *Saddharmapuṇḍarīka*. Bibliotheca Buddhica X. St. Pétersbourg: Commissionnaires de l Académie Impériale des Sciences.

Kranich, S., Becher, V. and Höder, S. 2011. "A tentative typology of translation-induced language change." In *Multilingual Discourse Production: Diachronic and Synchronic Perspectives*, edited by S. Kranich et al., 11–43. Amsterdam: John Benjamins Publishing.

Mair, V. H. 1994. "Buddhism and the Rise of the Written Vernacular in East Asia: The Making of National Languages." *The*

Journal of Asian Studies, 53(3): 707–751.

McRae, J. R. 2004. *The Vimalakīrti Sutra*, Translated from the Chinese (Taishō Volume 14, Number 475). Berkeley, CA: Numata Centre for Buddhist Translation and Research.

Mei, Tsu-lin 梅祖麟. 1990. "Tang-Song chuzhishi de laiyuan." 唐宋处置式的来源 [The origin of disposal constructions in Tang and Song Chinese]. *Zhongguo yuwen* 中国语文 [*Studies of the Chinese Language*] 3: 191–216.

——. 1999. "Xian Qin Liang Han de yizhong wancheng mao jushi."先秦两汉的一种完成貌句式 [One type of perfective aspect construction in the Pre-Qin and Han periods]. *Zhongguo yuwen* 中 国 语 文 [*Studies of the Chinese Language*] 4: 285–294.

Meisterernst, B. 2011. "Aspectual structures in Buddhist Chinese texts." In *Hanwen fodian yuyanxue* 漢文佛典言學. Taipei: Fagu Fojiao xueyuan, pp. 58–99.

——. 2017. "Warring States to Medieval Chinese." In *Encyclopedia of Chinese Language and Linguistics,* Vol. 4, edited by R. Sybesma et al., 498–508. Leiden: Brill.

——. 2018. "Buddhism and Chinese Linguistics." In *Buddhism and Linguistics: Theory and Philosophy*, edited by M. Herat, 123–148. Cham, Switzerland: Palgrave Macmillan.

Mitra, R. 1888. *Aṣṭasāhasrikā: A Collection of Discourses on the Metaphysics of the Mahāyāna School of the Buddhists.* Bibliotheca Indica 110. Calcutta: Asiatic Society of Bengal.

Nattier, J. 2004. "Beyond Translation and Transliteration: A New Look at Chinese Buddhist Terms." Paper presented at the annual meeting of the American Oriental Society (Western Branch) in Portland, Oregon in October 2004. Accessed March 4, 2019. https://berkeley.academia.edu/JanNattier.

Nattier, J. 2008. *A Guide to the Earliest Chinese Buddhist Translations: Texts from the Eastern Han* 東漢 *and Three Kingdoms* 三 國 *Period*. Bibliotheca Philologica et Philosophica Buddhica X. Tokyo: The International Research Institute for Advanced Buddhology, Soka University.

Peyraube, A. 1996. "Recent Issues in Chinese Historical Syntax." In *New Horizons in Chinese Linguistics*, edited by C.-T. James Huang and Y.-H. Audrey Li, 161–213. Dordrecht: Kluwer Academic Publishers.

——. 1997. "On Word Order in Archaic Chinese." *Cahiers de linguistique—Asie orientale* 26(1): 3–20.

Peyraube, A. and Wu, Fuxiang, 2005. "Origin and evolution of question-words in Archaic Chinese: A cognitive approach." *Cahiers de linguistique—Asie orientale* 34(1): 3–24.

Pulleyblank, E. G. 1991. *Lexicon of Reconstructed Pronunciation in Early Middle Chinese, Late Middle Chinese, and Early Mandarin*. Vancouver: UBC Press.

Reinmuth, H. G. 1937. *Abstract Terms in Notker's "Boethius": A Semantic and Etymological Study*. Ph.D. Diss., Northwestern University.

Salomon, R. 2000. *A Gāndhārī Version of the Rhinoceros Sūtra: British Library Kharoṣṭhī Fragment 5B*. Seattle and London:

University of Washington Press.

——. 2001. "Gāndhārī Hybrid Sanskrit: New Sources for the Study of the Sanskritization of Buddhist Literature." *Indo-Iranian Journal* 44(3): 214–252.

Schopen, G. 1989. "The Manuscript of the Vajracchedikā Found at Gilgit: An Annotated Transcription and Translation." In *Studies in the Literature of the Great Vehicle: Three Mahāyāna Buddhist Texts*, edited by L. O. Goméz and J. A. Silk, 89–139. Ann Arbor: Collegiate Institute for the Study of Buddhist Literature.

Schröder, A. 2011. *On the Productivity of Verbal Prefixation in English: Synchronic and Diachronic Perspectives*. Language in Performance 44. Tübingen: Narr Verlag.

Schuessler, A. 2009. *Minimal Old Chinese and Late Han Chinese. A Companion to Grammata Serica Recensa*. Honolulu: University of Hawai'i Press.

Study Group on Buddhist Sanskrit Literature. 2004. *Jñānālokālaṃkāra: Transliterated Sanskrit Text Collated with Tibetan and Chinese Translations*. Tokyo: Taisho University Press.

Study Group on Buddhist Sanskrit Literature. 2006. *Vimalakīrtinirdeśa: A Sanskrit Edition Based upon the Manuscript Newly Found at the Potala Palace*. Tokyo: Taisho University Press.

Tax, P. 1986. *Boethius, «De consolation philosophiae.»* Buch I / II. Die Werke Notkers des Deutschen. Neue Ausgabe Bd. 1. Tübingen: Niemeyer.

——. 1988. *Boethius, «De consolation philosophiae.»* Buch III. Die Werke Notkers des Deutschen. Neue Ausgabe Bd. 2. Tübingen: Niemeyer.

——. 1990. *Boethius, «De consolation Philosophiae.»* Buch IV / V. Die Werke Notkers des Deutschen. Neue Ausgabe Bd. 3. Tübingen: Niemeyer.

Teich, E. 2003. *Cross-linguistic Variation in System and Text: A Methodology for the Investigation of Translations and Comparable Texts*. Berlin: Mouton de Gruyter.

Thomason, S. G. 2001. *Language Contact: An Introduction*. Edinburgh: Edinburgh University Press.

van der Vorm-Croughs, M. 2014. *The Old Greek of Isaiah: An Analysis of Its Pluses and Minuses*. [Septuagint and Cognate Studies 61.] Atlanta: SBL Press.

Watson, B. 1993. *Records of the Grand Historian: Han Dynasty*. New York: Columbia University Press.

Wei, Peichüan 魏培泉. 2015. "Gu hanyu shiti biaoji de yuxu leixing yu yanbian." 古漢語時體標記的語序類型與演變 [Word order patterns of temporal and aspectual markers in Classical Chinese and their development]. *Language and Linguistics* 16(2): 213–247.

Weinreich, U. 1953. *Languages in Contact: Findings and Problems*. The Hague: Mouton.

Wilkinson, E. 2000. *Chinese History: A Manual, Revised and Enlarged*. Cambridge (Massachusetts) and London: Harvard University Press.

Witalisz, A. 2013. "English Linguistic Influence on Standard and American Varieties of Polish: A Comparative Study." *Studia Linguistica Universitatis Iagellonicae Cracoviensis* 130: 327–346.

Wogihara, U. 1932–1935. *Abhisamayālaṃkār" ālokā Prajñāpāramitāvyākhyā (Commentary on Aṣṭasāhasrikā-Prajāpāramitā) by Haribhadra.* Tokyo: The Toyo Bunko.

Wu, Juan 吴娟. 2008. "Hanyi fodian zhong yiwen daici 'hé' de renzhi yongfa." 漢譯佛典中疑問代詞「何」的任指用法 [The Indefinite Use of the Interrogative Pronoun *hé* in Chinese Buddhist Translations]. *Zhongwen xuekan* 中文學刊 [*Chinese Academic Journal*] 5: 141–157.

——. 2009. " 'Jiuru' tanyuan '久如' 探源 [An Investigation into the Origin of *Jiuru*]." *Hanyushi xuebao* 漢語史學報 [*Journal of Chinese Language History*] 8: 229–236.

Zhu, Qingzhi 朱慶之, 1992. "*Fodian yu zhonggu hanyu cihui yanjiu.*" 佛典與中古漢語詞彙研究 [*A Study of the Relationship Between Buddhist Scriptures and Vocabulary of Medieval Chinese*]. Taipei: Wenjin chubanshe.

——. 2003. "The Impact of Buddhism on the Development of Chinese Vocabulary (II)." *Pumen xuebao* 普門學報 [*Universal Gate Buddhist Journal*] 16: 1–35.

——. 2008. "On Some Basic Features of Buddhist Chinese." *Journal of the International Association of Buddhist Studies*, 31(1-2): 485–504.

Zürcher, E. 1959. *The Buddhist Conquest of China: The Spread and Adaptation of Buddhism in Early Medieval China.* Leiden: Brill.

——. 1977. "Late Han Vernacular Elements in the Earliest Buddhist Translations." *Journal of the Chinese Language Teachers Association*, 12(2): 177–203.

——. 1991. "A New Look at the Earliest Chinese Buddhist Texts." In *From Benares to Beijing: Essays on Buddhism and Chinese Religion in Honour of Prof. Jan Yün-Hua*, edited by K. Shinohara and G. Schopen, 227–304. Oakville: Mosaic Press.

——. 1996. "Vernacular Elements in Early Buddhist Texts: An attempt to define the optimal source materials." *Sino-Platonic Papers* 71: 1–31.

——. 2012. "Buddhism across Boundaries: The Foreign Input." In *Buddhism across Boundaries: The Interplay of Indian, Chinese, and Central Asian Source Materials,* edited by J. R. McRae and J. Nattier, 1–25. *Sino-Platonic Papers* 222. Philadelphia: Department of East Asian Languages and Civilization, University of Pennsylvania. [First published in 1999.]

汤姆斯译《花笺记》与19世纪早期欧洲的中国诗歌想象

余来明　严　欢*

　　汤姆斯（Peter Perring Thoms，1790—1855）是19世纪英国汉学草创期重要的中国文化翻译者和传播者。他率先译介到西方的"第八才子书"《花笺记》得到法国汉学家雷慕莎（Jean Pierre Abel Rémusat，1788—1832）和德国诗人歌德（Johann Wolfgang von Goethe，1749—1832）的高度评价，汤姆斯也因此被誉为英国历史上"第一个翻译中国叙事歌谣的人，第一个翻译中国方言作品的人，第一个翻译中国用韵文创作的爱情故事的人，第一个翻译中国女性诗作的人"[1]。在他之后，《花笺记》又陆续被译成俄语、德语、荷兰语、丹麦语、法语等六种语言，引起欧洲文坛广泛关注。20世纪以来，美国学者或以"信达雅"的翻译理论为标准，从汉学研究价值角度对汤译《花笺记》进行深入分析；或重点对汤译《花笺记》如何协调源语文化和目的语文化的关系，进行社会、文学与美学三个层面的研究。[2] 国内学者对汤译《花笺记》的关注，最初源于歌德"中国文学

---

* 余来明：武汉大学人文社会科学杰出青年学者、中国传统文化研究中心教授。研究领域为元明清文学、中国小说史、近代文学与文化。严欢：暨南大学中华文化港澳台及海外传承传播协同创新中心讲师、博士后。

1 Patricia Sieber, "Universal Brotherhood Revisited: Peter Perring Thoms (1790–1855), Artisan Practices, and the Genesis of a Chinacentric Sinology," *Representations* Vol. 130 (Spring 2015), p. 30.

2 K. C. Leung (梁启昌), "Chinese Courtship: The Hua jian ji in English Translation," *Chinoperl Papers* 20–22 (1997–1999)，汉译本题为《论木鱼书〈花笺记〉的英译》，《逸步追风：西方学者论中国文学》，北京：学苑出版社，2008年，第256—281页；Patricia Sieber, "Location, Location, Location: Peter

观"和"世界文学理念"的研究，近十年始有学者对其展开专门研究，主要分析了汤姆斯翻译《花笺记》的缘由，何以选择"以诗译诗"文体，以及汤译本在中西文化史上的价值。[1]本文在已有研究基础上，立足汤姆斯的生命成长，考察其工匠视野中的汉学审美，深入分析汤译《花笺记》的策略、目的及其对中国诗歌世界的构建，梳理中国诗歌西方之旅的历史进程，以考察汤译《花笺记》在这一过程中的意义和贡献。

一、诗意的诱惑：从印刷工到汉学家

汤姆斯从一名印刷工成长为汉学家，与汉学发展初期的开放性有一定关系，也离不开"双语"印刷工作给其学习汉语带来的压力与提供的方便，更是其自由汉学家身份及对中国通俗文学日益浓厚的兴趣使然。

法国大革命之后，欧洲工人阶级普遍接受过一定教育，开始觉醒，不再仅仅只是简单从事体力劳动。相反，他们对工人身份有着新的理解：能够在工作中找到价值，也能够为了自己的价值追求而不断学习。这一时期，很多欧洲工人去到不同的城市，甚至去国外工作，这些经历既增长见识，又精湛了手艺。在此背景下，汤姆斯开始了他的中国之行。

汤姆斯对自己印刷工人的身份有高度的认同感，印刷工对他来说不仅是简单的谋生手段，更是一种兼有技术和博学的社会身份。[2]因在新兴的多语印刷

Perring Thoms (1790–1855), Cantonese Localism, and the Genesis of Literary Translation from the Chinese," in Lawrence Wang-chi-Wong and Bernhard Fuehrer eds., *Asian Translation Traditions Series-2 (Sinologists as Translators in the Seventeenth to Nineteenth Centuries)*, 香港：香港中文大学出版社，2015年。中译本题为《汤姆斯、粤语地域主义与中国文学外译的肇始》，《翻译史研究》2016第6辑。

1　王燕：《〈花笺记〉：第一部中国"史诗"的西行之旅》，《文学遗产》2014年第5期；郑锦怀：《彼得·佩林·汤姆斯：由印刷工而汉学家——以〈中国求爱诗〉为中心的考察》，《国际汉学》2015年第4期。

2　Patricia Sieber, "Location, Location, Location: Peter Perring Thoms (1790–1855), Cantonese Localism, and the Genesis of Literary Translation from the Chinese," p. 28.

上不断追求精进，汤姆斯受到时任英国东印度公司图书管理员查尔斯·威尔金斯（Charles Wilkins）的赏识，在其推荐下，东印度公司于1814年雇佣其来华印刷马礼逊（Robert Morrison，1782—1834）的《华英字典》（*A Dictionary of the Chinese Language*）。作为最早来华的英国工人之一，这一旅途对汤姆斯来说注定意义非凡。

在中国的十一年间，汤姆斯发扬"工匠精神"，不仅克服了中国政府、英国东印度公司制造的种种麻烦，还攻克了印刷业上字母文字和汉字同时排版的历史性难题，圆满完成《华英字典》的印刷工作。虽没有受过正规的汉语教育，汤姆斯却凭着惊人的自学能力熟练掌握了汉语，在中国小说、诗歌、器物研究等方面都有一定造诣，曾被誉为"英国有史以来最好的汉学家"[1]。

在《华英字典》印刷期间，马礼逊经常不在澳门，因此汤姆斯要全权负责几乎所有的印刷工作，在《华英字典》"致辞"（Advertisement）中，马礼逊写道：

> 但是公允地说，在字典印刷期间的一段时间，作者远在印刷所九十英里之外。我们得注意到印刷者独自一人承担了排字工、印刷工、阅读者和校对者的所有职责，帮助他的惟有一些不懂英文的当地人。[2]

汤姆斯身兼排字工、印刷工、阅读者和校对者数职，不得不逼迫自己学习汉语。除求教于马礼逊外，最简单的方法是向每天与他一起干活的中国印刷工人请教。当时清政府禁止中国民众为外国人工作，亦不允许向外国人传授汉语知识，但汤姆斯非常清楚只有识字的中国人才最了解汉字的美感和中国文化的魅力，与他们合作，才可能高质量地完成《华英字典》的出版工作。于是他秘密招聘了一批

1　Patricia Sieber, "Universal Brotherhood Revisited: Peter Perring Thoms (1790–1855), Artisan Practices, and the Genesis of a Chinacentric Sinology," p. 28.

2　Robert Morrison, "Advertisement," in Robert Morrison ed., *A Dictionary of the Chinese Language*, 郑州：大象出版社，2008年，第1卷，第2页。

识字的中国工人协助印刷工作，视他们为朋友和汉语老师。汤姆斯同这些工人几乎吃住在一起，经常向他们虚心请教汉语和中国传统印刷等方面的知识，建立起了亲密友好的关系。由于相同的身份，汤姆斯对中国工人有着天然的同情、同理心，尊敬他们为"受过教育的当地人"[1]，而不像东印度公司其他精英或来华传教士一样，把他们当成剥削利用的对象或潜在的受感化者。

汤姆斯对中国工人的同情、同理心，还是传统的浪漫主义和激进主义共同作用的结果。在中国政府的法律暴力和英国东印度公司的经济剥削双重压迫下[2]，只有汤姆斯敢于挺身而出，不断寻求方法来保护中国工人的利益。在中国差役搜捕为外国人工作的中国工人时，他不顾个人安危，守住工厂的大门，与当地差役斡旋，为中国工人赢得了逃走的时间；还不惜冒着丢掉饭碗的危险，向东印度公司高层据理力争，帮助中国工人争得应有的待遇。汤姆斯的真心与尊重如春风化雨般温暖了中国印刷工人，他们对于汤姆斯的"求教"也知无不言，与汤姆斯分享许多流行于当地的文学。在与中国工人不断打交道的过程中，汤姆斯的汉语突飞猛进。1816年，因印刷工作量减少，东印度公司开除了全部的中国印刷工人[3]，他不得不独自带领葡萄牙印刷工人继续工作：

> 那时，我不得不自己写汉字，教葡萄牙工人切分汉字，还要负责排版和印刷工作。这也是为什么许多不甚精致的汉字出现在《中国大观》（*View of China*）及《字典》部首三十的篇末和正文的开篇。[4]

---

1 Peter Perring Thoms, "Preface," *A Dissertation on the Ancient Chinese Vases of the Shang Dynasty*, London: published by the Author, 12, Warwick-square, 1851, p. 8.

2 1817年，当地政府对东印度公司印刷所进行了突然袭击，以搜捕为印刷所工作的中国人。

3 当时东印度公司想要减少中国工人的数量，但是中国工人坚持"要留一起留，要走一起走"，这一谈判技巧在当时的伦敦印刷业很流行，因此有人认为，这些工人可能受到汤姆斯的指点。但不幸的是，最后公司决定开除所有的中国工人。

4 P. P. Thoms, "M. Klaproth's attack upon Mr. Morrison," *Asiatic Journal and Miscellaneous Monthly*, Vol. 2, 1830, p. 205.

在失去马礼逊和中国工人帮助的情况下，刚来华两年的汤姆斯能扛起所有的印刷工作，还能教葡萄牙工人汉语，可见其掌握汉语的速度之快之精。

1823年完成《华英字典》的印刷工作后，汤姆斯并未立即返回英国，而是不计报酬地继续逗留一年多，以完成自己未尽的中国文学翻译事业。英国早期汉学家主要关注政治、法律、宗教等，而汤姆斯却能够独闯文学领域，这与他由工匠成长起来的自由汉学家身份不无关系。反观早期来华的"英国汉学之父"小斯当东（Sir George Thomas Staunton，1781—1859）和英国新教来华第一人马礼逊的中西互译活动，则往往出于英国清晰的帝国主义计划，具有较强的"实用主义"倾向。小斯当东12岁便作为马嘎尔尼使团年龄最小的成员访华，亲身经历了使团访华任务失败的他，深知中国法律、外交政策等对英国在华扩张的重要意义。因此，他在选择翻译文本时，目的性非常强：必须有利于扩大英国在华影响，为英国获取更多的政治权益和商贸利益。为此，他先后翻译了《大清律例》《异域录》[1]，以便了解中国的法律、政治体系，以及中国对外政策和民族关系，为英政府和来华商人所用。马礼逊作为首位来华的英国传教士，在出行之前就收到伦敦传教会的指示：编撰一本汉英字典，并把《圣经》翻译成汉语。为此，他在英国就开始做准备：不仅着手学习汉语，还专门到伦敦博物馆手抄了一份之前由天主教传教士翻译成中文的《圣经》。来华后的马礼逊也时刻不忘将耶稣福音带到中国这个异教徒国家，在积极传教之余，翻译了《三字经》《大学》《三教源流搜神记》等经典作品，以期从中了解中国人长久以来形成的道德教化、宗教思想、礼仪习惯等，从而将基督教教义与中国经典进行很好的结合，便于传教；除《华英字典》外，马礼逊还编写了《通用汉言之法》（*A Grammar of the Chinese Language: Tung-yung han-yen chih fa*）、《中文会话及凡例》（*Dialogues and Detached*

---

1 《异域录》为1712—1715年间图理琛使团受康熙派遣出使土尔扈特部时，使团中的史官对出使历程的记述，包括出使经过、沿途的风物民俗和水文地理等，此外还收录了康熙帝给使团的谕旨，谕旨主要交代出使过程中使团成员与俄国人接触时可能出现的情况、应注意的事项等，因此被外国人视为了解清政府的对外政策和民族关系等非常重要的资料。

Sentences in the Chinese Language）等工具书，为之后到中国的传教士在语言等方面提供方便。作为虔诚的基督徒，马礼逊曾公开表示他对小说、说唱文学和其他虚构作品也有儒家式的疑虑[1]，因此很少从事纯文学的翻译。

小斯当东和马礼逊在华期间均担任东印度公司的翻译，小斯当东一度成为公司大班，马礼逊肩负着传教的重任，他们在华的翻译活动受制于机构的需求。与他们相比，汤姆斯无须代表英国在政治、商业或军事等方面的利益，也没有培训英国官员、东印度公司职员、传教士等学习中文的责任，更不用为了传教而埋头苦读中国经典。因此，他不必为了"实用"而强迫自己进行汉学研究，他的汉学活动更多是出自于个人早期的生活背景及在中国的生活工作环境塑造的独特个人审美兴趣。

汤姆斯对中国文学的兴趣萌生于印刷《华英字典》的每一个日夜。对印刷事业的精益求精，促使他主动学习汉语。汤姆斯阅读了大量马礼逊图书室的藏书，他"每天早8点到晚8点在印刷间工作，其余时间都沉浸在各种文学作品中"[2]，逐渐发自内心地喜爱上中国文学。为了检验汉语学习效果，同时把令自己痴迷的文学作品介绍给西方读者，让他们感受中国文学之美，从中了解中国人和中国文化，感受到中国人身上拥有的"同情、善良和爱这些更美好的道德情感"[3]，汤姆斯自发地开始翻译一些文学作品。他用富含情感的话写道："为了使用中国的诗意语言，我经常借助萤火虫的光学习，早上早得可以去驾驶阿波罗的战车。"[4]

19世纪初的英国同中国特别是广东等较开放地区在文化上有着一些共同的变化和趋势：这一时期的两国民谣兴起，浪漫主义复兴，地区文化和方言文化开始

---

1 Patricia Sieber, "Location, Location, Location: Peter Perring Thoms (1790–1855), Cantonese Localism, and the Genesis of Literary Translation from the Chinese," p. 137.

2 P. P. Thoms, *The Emperor of China v. The Queen of England*, London: Warwick-square, 1853, p. 29.

3 P. P. Thoms, "Preface," *The Affectionate Pair, or The History of Song-Kin*, London: Black, Kingsbury, Parbury, and Allen, 1820, p. iv.

4 P. P. Thoms, *The Emperor of China v. the Queen of England*, p. 28.

进入民族文学，古文物研究兴盛，女性文学开始复苏，等等。[1] 西方时代背景、整体文学氛围、同期读者口味等，直接影响着译者的审美趣味和文本选择，才子佳人类作品在这一时期中国文学西译中占有很大比重。对于真挚感情的向往，自然激起了汤姆斯对女性文学的兴趣。汤姆斯在华期间接触的大多是广东地区的印刷工人，必然会受到当时广东地区最为流行的民间娱乐形式木鱼歌的影响，而《花笺记》《背解红罗袄》《琵琶上路》《楼台会》等都是以才子佳人为主题的曲目，符合女性文学的审美旨趣。汤姆斯整日与中国工人生活在一起，最容易耳闻目见。其中最有名的"第八才子书"《花笺记》很自然就进入他的视野，并成为他翻译的对象了。

二、以《花笺记》想象的中国诗歌世界

《花笺记》属说唱文学——木鱼歌，融诗歌与小说于一体，有表演本、点评本等多种版本。有学者认为汤姆斯至少参照了其中两种以上的版本。[2] 汤译本后有两个附录和一则出书预告。附录一为32名中国古代女子的小传，其中31名来自《百美新咏》，最后一位邓皇后（Queen Tang）译自《后汉书·和熹邓皇后纪》。附录二为《中国税收》（On the Revenue of China），是关于一份中国政府税收的详细英译，有学者认为原稿由广西进士王贵兴（Wang-kwei-shing）编订。[3] 最后一页是一则关于《三国演义》出书预告，汤姆斯于1819—1821年在《亚洲杂志》上连载了《著名丞相董卓之死》（The Death of the Celebrated Minister Tung-cho），

1　Patricia Sieber, "Universal Brotherhood Revisited: Peter Perring Thoms (1790–1855), Artisan Practices, and the Genesis of a Chinacentric Sinology," p. 29.

2　参见徐巧越:《〈花笺记〉在英国的收藏与接受》,《图书馆论坛》2019年第4期; Patricia Sieber, "Location, Location, Location: Peter Perring Thoms (1790–1855), Cantonese Localism, and the Genesis of Literary Translation from the Chinese".

3　易永谊:《野蛮的修辞: 作为译者的汉学家汤姆斯》,《中国比较文学》2016年第2期。

该文译自《三国演义》第8—9回。虽然目前并未见汤姆斯《三国演义》的全译本，他关于此书的最终翻译进度也不为人知，但附于《花笺记》后的出书预告可以让读者看到汤姆斯对全译《三国演义》的满满雄心。

《花笺记》是汤姆斯的第三部中文译作，也是其文学翻译代表作，较之前两部译作受到的评价和关注更多，影响更大。在翻译中，汤姆斯大胆挑战"以诗译诗"，采取"异化"的翻译策略，力图保持原作风貌，向西方展示中国诗歌的精气神。众所周知，在中西翻译文学中，因为汉语表意文字体系与西方表音文字体系存在难以逾越的鸿沟，且诗歌中暗含的典故、意象、隐喻等，中国诗歌一直被认为是最难翻译的文体，以至西方长期盛行"诗不可译"的观点。虽然第一部诗歌总集《诗经》很早就受到西人关注，并在17世纪就已西传，但其最初并不是作为诗歌经典被欣赏，而是作为经书被传教士用于研究中国儒家传统，以了解中国的思想、礼仪和风俗，便于传教。因此，早期《诗经》的译文常因"散文"化而失去了"诗意"之美，且大多译者只敢尝试其中的个别篇章，导致汤氏之前，一直没有完整的《诗经》译本流行于西方，更少有人专门著文谈论中国诗歌。有鉴于此，中国诗歌的西传相对于小说与戏曲一直有所滞后。

《花笺记》体裁具有双重属性，既有诗歌的文体特点，讲究韵律和节奏，以七言为主，又仿效章回小说，以梁亦沧与杨瑶仙、刘玉卿的爱情故事贯穿全文，分为六十回（有的版本为五十九回），每回均以四字作目。清代评论家钟戴苍定义《花笺记》的体裁为"歌本小说"，兼顾了其融诗歌与小说于一体的属性。马礼逊也认为《花笺记》是一部用"诗体"创作的"中国小说"。[1]体裁的双重属性给《花笺记》译者提供了不同的翻译可能。汤姆斯将题目译为《中国式求爱，诗体》（*Chinese Courtship, in Verse*），以诗歌体进行翻译，而其后的包令（John Bowring）则将题目译为《花笺，一部中文小说》（*The Flowery Scroll, a Chinese*

1 Robert Morrison, *A Dictionary of the Chinese Language*, Vol. III. Part 1, London: Published and Sold by Kingsbury, Parbury, and Allen, Leadenhall Street. Macao, China; Printed at the Honorable East India Company's Press. By P. P. Thoms. 1823. p. 152.

Novel），以小说的形式进行翻译。

汤姆斯何以敢于选择被西方众人视为畏途的中国诗歌，并且是三万多字的长篇诗歌进行翻译，而且还敢于以难度最大的诗体进行翻译？这首先与其翻译《花笺记》的目的密不可分。汤姆斯在前言中写道：

> 虽然跟中国有关的书我们已经写了很多，但他们的诗歌一直几乎不被关注。这主要是汉语带来的困难，除了偶尔翻译的一个诗节或一些短的应景诗，汉语让所有人不敢再进一步尝试。我认为这些翻译都不足以让一个欧洲人形成关于中国诗歌的正确认识，所以我在此尝试把《花笺记》这部"中国第八才子书"译成英语。《花笺记》篇幅较长，因为大多数中国诗歌只有几行，他们大多是诗人为了抒发一时之情而创作。[1]

这段文字清楚表明汤姆斯翻译《花笺记》的初衷是做一个中国长篇诗歌西译的开创者，把中国长篇诗歌介绍到西方，以弥补欧洲人对中国诗歌了解的不足，矫正偏见。

当时西方社会更加欣赏鸿篇巨制的史诗，认为西方式的史诗在创作手法、意象使用、编排构思、造势铺陈等方面均优于中国的短篇诗歌，甚至有人断言中国没有值得翻译的诗歌，以致中国诗歌在西方长期受到忽视。汤姆斯对此有不同看法，他认为中国人在诗歌方面并不缺乏创造力和想象力，"诗艺"（art of poetry）在中国非常受重视，被认为是一种很高的修养，诗歌是科举考试的科目之一，几乎所有文人都沉湎于写诗，并且具有极高的创造力和想象力。针对西方对中国诗歌普遍较短的批评，他解释道"是因为被古代已有的诗歌创作定法所束缚了"[2]，并进一步指出根源在孔子整理编辑而成的《诗经》，因为"《诗经》通常篇幅较

---

1 P. P. Thoms, "Preface," *Chinese Courtship, in Verse*, Macao, China: Printed at the Honorable East India Company's Press. p. 3. 本文所引《花笺记》原文皆出自此版。

2 Ibid., p. iv.

短，一行只有四字，是中国古老的民族诗歌，对中国统治者、伟大的政治家以及其他事物的颂扬都深受尊崇"[1]。

汤姆斯虽然认为中国没有西方式的史诗，赞同大部分中国诗歌只有几行，是诗人的一时抒情之作，但他同时也注意到中国诗歌中叙事诗这一体例的独特之处，叙事诗的篇幅可以很长，为诗人展示才华提供更大的空间。[2]他认为中国诗歌中律诗最难驾驭，很多中国诗人也不擅长。《花笺记》不仅是长篇叙事诗，其中的若干诗歌还采用了律诗的形式，且并没有因为形式上的严苛而影响故事情节。因此，在汤姆斯看来，《花笺记》比《西厢记》更能体现中国诗歌的特点。[3]他在十分清楚同为爱情题材的《西厢记》，因天才般的文笔和更契合中国人情感的故事情节，在"才子书"中排名位于《花笺记》之前的情况下，仍然选择《花笺记》进行翻译。他坚信充满趣味且富有诗意的《花笺记》，一定会让那些对中国文学感兴趣的人，在细细品读的过程中感受到乐趣。[4]

为了尽可能保留《花笺记》这部东方文学作品的诗歌韵味和"原文精神"（the spirit of the original），汤姆斯最终选择了"以诗译诗"的文体来翻译《花笺记》，并开创性地采用每页上半部竖排中文，下半部横排英文，底部间夹注释说明的形式，以一句英文对应一句中文诗句逐行翻译。对于汤姆斯"双语"排版的创举，法国汉学家雷慕莎及后世学者给予了高度赞赏。

除了"双语"排版外，为了尽可能展现《花笺记》文本的诗歌性，汤姆斯还将中文原文竖行七字排列，对于字数较多的诗句，往往缩小最后的几个汉字，并将缩小的字两两并行排版，只占一个字的位置，这样编排使得版面十分规整，将诗歌的韵律性延伸到了视觉。

---

1 P. P. Thoms, "Preface," *Chinese Courtship, in Verse*, p. iv.

2 Ibid., p. v.

3 汤姆斯认为《西厢记》的行文风格颇为简单，类似于对话体形式，且每句中的字数从1—15不等，相差太多，因而不能很好地展示中国诗歌的特点。参见 P. P. Thoms, "Preface," *Chinese Courtship, in Verse*, p. vii。

4 Ibid., p. vi.

在翻译过程中，汤姆斯深知"以诗译诗"的难度，以及完全的直译存在使译文生硬、拗口，甚至不符合英文文法的弊端，也担心这样处理会损失很多原诗中的柔和之风和内容间的紧密联系。[1] 但同时他也明白，前人惯常的"以散文译诗"的方式，无法充分展示中国诗歌的韵律美，给中国诗歌在西方的形象带来了很多负面影响。杜赫德（Du Halde，1674—1743）的《中华帝国全志》（*Description De La Chine*，1735年）是欧洲汉学史上的奠基之作，影响深远。它最早为西方接受中国诗歌提供框架，但对于其中辑录的几个《诗经》篇章，汤姆斯批评其"文体过于散漫而不能反映原作的生机"[2]。法国耶稣会士钱德明（Jean Joseph-Marie Amiot，1718—1793）以散文体翻译的乾隆诗歌《御制盛京赋》（1770）被誉为"欧洲人拥有的最完美的中国诗歌译本"，但散文式的翻译仍然受到了小斯当东、汤姆斯等人的批评。[3]

为了弥补西方世界对中国诗歌了解的不足，并反驳其因"不了解"而形成的偏见，汤姆斯在前言、注释中试图建立对中国诗歌世界的整体认识。他不仅全译了朱熹的《诗集传序》，详细介绍了《诗经》的由来、思想，以及《风》《雅》《颂》的特点等，还翻译了《古唐诗合解》（*Tang-she-hǒ-keae*）序文中记录中国诗歌发展历程的一段文字，将中国诗歌从《典谟》到《诗经》，再到《离骚》以至三国时期诗人群起，陈、隋时诗歌衰落以及盛唐诗歌兴盛的历史路线展现给西方读者，使他们能够从宏观上认识中国诗歌的发展脉络。在此基础上，他进一步论述中国诗歌的基本特点，包括篇幅（四行或八行，每行五言或七言）、四声与平仄、押韵（隔行押韵或隔字押韵）、对仗等。"中国古典诗词格律有三大要素：平仄、押韵和对仗，基础是四声。"[4] 汤氏的论述围绕这四项展开，较准确把握了

1　P. P. Thoms, *Chinese Courtship, in Verse*, p. vi.

2　Ibid., pp. xii–xiii. 小斯当东批评阿米奥的译文"（以散文译诗）哪怕是在最有利的条件下，也会被认为极不恰当且不尽人意"。汤姆斯认为"不管翻译得再怎么准确，它没有保留原文的形式，可能会让欧洲读者产生中国诗歌结构不完善的看法"。

3　Ibid., p. xii.

4　王燕、房燕：《〈汉文诗解〉与中国古典诗歌的早期海外传播》，《文艺理论研究》2012年第3期，第45页。

中国诗歌的主要特征，对之后德庇时的《汉文诗解》（1829年）产生了一定影响。

在汤姆斯之前，很多西方汉学家认识到在中西翻译中，诗歌是最大的挑战，因此不轻易涉足。汤姆斯大胆挑战"以诗译诗"，除了尽可能地保持原诗的风貌外，一定程度上来说，也是为了突破前辈汉学家诗歌翻译的局限。他本人深知"诗体"翻译存在很多问题，但仍然迎难而上，这种勇往直前的精神值得钦佩。汤姆斯之后，理雅各、帕尔克、翟里斯等越来越多的西方汉学家开始以诗体翻译中国诗歌，发展到今日，"以诗译诗"早已成为诗歌翻译的主流，而作为首倡者的汤姆斯，虽受时代限制，翻译存在诸多问题和纰漏，但我们不能因为这些问题而忽视或贬低他在中英文化交流上的创举和贡献。

三、《花笺记》译本批评的知见与偏见

汤姆斯十分欣赏并着力翻译的《花笺记》，在中国文学史上虽被誉为"第八才子书"，却并非公认的杰出作品。尽管清代评论家钟戴苍将《花笺记》与《西厢记》相提并论，认为曲本有《西厢》，歌本有《花笺》，强调其文笔声调皆一样绝世。[1]郑振铎也只是认为《花笺记》在粤曲中算是很好的，颇脱出一般言情小说之窠臼。[2]虽然陈汝衡称赞《花笺记》"是说唱文学的一部佳作"[3]，现代学者对《花笺记》的评价却普遍不高，如陈铨认为《花笺记》不足以跻身"十才子书"之列，较《三国志演义》《水浒传》《西厢记》《琵琶记》相差太远[4]；王燕认为《花笺记》内容乏善可陈，近现代以来罕为人知，实属正常。[5]

1　[美]梁培炽：《〈花笺记〉会校会评本》，广州：暨南大学出版社，1998年，第67页。
2　郑振铎：《中国文学研究（下）》，北京：作家出版社，1957年，第1311页。
3　中国大百科全书总编辑委员会：《中国大百科全书·戏曲曲艺》，北京：中国大百科全书出版社，2002年，第128页。
4　陈铨：《中德文学研究》，北京：商务印书馆，1936年，第19—20页。
5　王燕：《〈花笺记〉：第一部中国"史诗"的西行之旅》，《文学评论》2014年第5期。

　　然而在西方汉学界，自汤姆斯将《花笺记》译介到欧洲后，引发了一个有趣的现象：欧洲文坛对《花笺记》文本给予很高评价，却对汤姆斯的翻译水平褒少贬多。歌德称《花笺记》为"一部伟大的诗篇"，由此奠定了其在世界文学中的地位。法国汉学家雷慕莎不仅对其高度赞赏，更在一场关于中国诗歌的报告中专门谈及汤姆斯翻译的《花笺记》。[1]但两位大学者的高度赞扬并未改变汤译《花笺记》在西方备受批评的命运，其中译本错误较多、缺乏诗意和韵律等受到指责最多。

　　英国《东方先驱》(*The Oriental Herald and Journal of General Literature*，1826年)虽然高度肯定《花笺记》的文学价值，将其与拜伦的《唐璜》相提并论，但对汤姆斯的翻译颇有微词，批评他的译本采用了最野蛮的用语，缺少美与柔和，并列出其中19个英语拼写和语法错误以质疑他的母语水平，认为汤姆斯中英双语均不过关，以至在很多方面都歪曲了原作，妨碍了《花笺记》本来可以在欧洲产生的影响。[2]《评论月刊》(*The Monthly Review*，1826年)同样对汤姆斯的英语水平提出了质疑，批评他长期生活在中国，似乎已经忘掉英语母语的语法结构和正字法。该文虽肯定汤姆斯以诗歌翻译《花笺记》的努力，认为这是一个逐字翻译的可读的 (literal and readable) 版本，但批评其译本虽有诗歌的形式，却没有体现原作诗歌上的优点，缺少生动的叙述，只能算一般的散文水平。[3]

　　较多的英语拼写和语法错误确实是汤译《花笺记》的一大硬伤。除《东方先驱》外，德庇时、旅美学者梁启昌先生等亦先后列出其中的一些错误。作为英国人，却在英语的使用上犯了如此多的低级错误，难怪《评论季刊》(*Quarterly Review*，1827年)愤怒地指出："汤姆斯所用的语言并不是英语，所有的语法规

1　雷慕沙将这场报告内容形成了一片关于中国诗歌的述评，收录于1826年的《学者学刊》(*Journal des Savans*)。

2　"Chinese Courtship," *The Oriental Herald and Journal of General Literature*, Vol. ix. April to June, 1826, pp. 17–25.

3　*The Monthly Review*, from January to April Inclusive.1826. Vol. 1. London: Printed for Hurst, Robinson, and Co. pp. 540–544.

则都被摒弃了，字都被他拼写错了。"[1] 人们往往对文人在语言上的错误忍受度较低，汤译《花笺记》中一眼可见的语言错误，当然会让西方读者先入为主地怀疑他的文化水平和翻译水准，带着审视的眼光进行阅读，批评自然也会毫不客气。比如，《评论月刊》在严厉批评完汤译本中的翻译问题后，又指责他将与《花笺记》毫无关系的中国税务资料附于最后不伦不类[2]，这就未免有"鸡蛋里挑骨头"之嫌。事实上，汤姆斯的这种安排在当时非常普遍：小斯当东翻译的《异域录》，其后就附有100多页内容迥异的其他中国作品的翻译，包括中国小说《玉娇梨》前四章的摘要、四部元曲的剧情简介[3]、中国植物学著作《群芳谱》的翻译，以及约40份清政府公文的翻译。

虽然汤姆斯在选词上尽量贴近原文，并且选择以较难的诗体进行翻译，是为了尽量保持原作的风貌，减少翻译的烙印。但讽刺的是，除语言错误外，他的译本受指责最多的就是表面上是诗，却用词野蛮，不讲究韵律之美。美国传教士卫三畏（Samuel Wells Williams，1812—1884）在其1883年再版的《中国总论》（*The Middle Kingdom*）中评论道："被译成英文的最长的（中文）诗歌是汤姆斯翻译的《花笺记》，该诗采用七步格的文体，译文相当乏味。"[4] "乏味"的翻译甚至影响了《花笺记》在西方的评价。如《亚洲杂志》（*The Asiatic Journal and Monthly Register*，1825年）批评《花笺记》缺少艺术性和趣味性，意象贫乏，所有的修饰比喻几乎都是桃树、柳树、花园、月亮，以及很少的神话和历史典故。[5] 该文对《花笺记》的批评建立在汤译本的基础上，并不能真实反映《花笺记》本身。因为汤姆斯对汉语中一些富有意象的特色词语理解不够透彻，经常只做字面

1　*Quarterly Review*, 36 June, 1827, pp. 504–505.

2　*The Monthly Review*, from January to April Inclusive. 1826, Vol. 1, p. 542.

3　四部元曲为《窦娥冤》《两军师隔江斗智》《王月英元夜留鞋记》《望江亭中秋切鲙》，皆取自《元人百种》。

4　Samuel Wells Williams, *The Middle Kingdom*. London: Wm. H. Allen. 1883. p. 704.

5　"Chinese Poetry-Hwa-tseen, or The Flower's Leaf," *The Asiatic Journal and Monthly Register*. London: Parbury & Allen, Leadenhall Street. January to June, 1825. pp. 402–408.

上的翻译，导致译作缺少意象美。这里可以举两个例子。

1. 得快乐时须快乐，何妨窃玉共偷香。（p. 1）

At seasons of joy and mirth, he should be sprightly and merry;

What should hinder his coveting a pearl, or robbing a flower of its fragrance?

这是原文第一页描写主人翁梁亦沧对爱情和美女渴望的内心。"香"在中国文学中经常作为"美女"的意象，这里的"偷香"一词表达了梁亦沧内心对美人的渴望。汤译文未做任何注解说明。

2. 山水无情能聚会，多情唔信肯相忘。（p. 2）

Though mountain springs are insensible of love, yet they revolve within themselves;

Why, when so much esteemed, should you believe you are forgotten?

"山""水"是中国诗歌中经常出现的意象。原诗用山水无情也能相聚，来反衬梁亦沧"我对美人多情，相信她一定不会相忘于我"的内心。汤姆斯将"山水"误译为"山上的泉水"，不仅理解错误，也使原诗的意象之美和韵味全无。

同时，汤姆斯对一些中国历史典故不甚了解，在翻译的过程中经常简单处理，导致有些历史典故并未显现出来。如下例：

1. 风流好似骑鲸客，雅致犹如跨凤郎。（p. 3）

As for vivacity and mirth, he greatly resembled ke-king,

While his decorous and genteel manners surpassed those of Fung-lang.

译文可以明显看出汤姆斯并不知晓"骑鲸客"和"跨凤郎"两个历史典故。

2. 瑶仙羞愧回言道，谁人肯学卓文君？［……］（p. 111）

Yaou-seen, confounded, blushing thus replied,

"Who is able to imitate the conduct of the prince Cho-wan? [...]".

这是《誓表真情》一回中，在面对梁亦沧"乞把团圆照学生"的进一步要求时，瑶仙的回答。这里汤姆斯对卓文君与人私订终身的典故一无所知，甚至不知道卓文君是位女性，以为这里的"君"是对"卓文"这个人的尊称，所以将其译为prince Cho-wan。

除以上例子以外，汤译《花笺记》中，还有很多原作的意象及典故没有表现出来。无怪乎给《亚洲杂志》评论员造成《花笺记》缺乏意象和历史典故的不好印象。

正是因为汤译本受到了如此多的关注和批评，包令（《花笺记》英译第二人）才萌生了重译《花笺记》的想法。他表示一个表达更自由，行文更流畅的版本可能对英国读者更有吸引力。[1]虽然没有直接批评汤姆斯的诗体译文，却以实际行动——以散文体重译《花笺记》——表明了自己的立场。

汤姆斯以从未接受过正规汉语教育的印刷工身份，却想染指高雅的文学，在有些人看来，颇有些自视过高，因此也招来一些非议。他在东印度公司的一些同事常常在私下和公开场合揶揄其在中国文学领域的学术抱负，尤其是德庇时，他的《汉文诗解》虽受惠于汤姆斯构建的中国诗歌基础，却从不提及。他们均与马礼逊交往密切，德庇时翻译的《三与楼》也由汤姆斯印刷，所以两人应该相识。但德庇时对汤姆斯那种激进的、在智识上的精进进行了毫不客气的批评：

---

1 Sir John Bowring, "Preface," *Hwa Tsien Ki-The Flowery Scroll, A Chinese Novel*, London: Wm. H. Allen & Co., 13, Waterloo Place, Pall Mall, S. W. 1868.

对于中国诗歌在英国读者中的声誉来说，遇到这样一位不称职的译者是相当不幸的；为了他（汤姆斯）本人的声誉着想，我们应当严肃地建议他放弃中文研究，至少等到他更好地掌握自己的语言之后再说。在那之前，我们劝他专心印刷，做好雕刻和排列字符的工作，安分守己，别再冒险从事翻译。尽管这样的建议可能被认为有悖于这个时代的自由精神，以及"向智慧进军"，即把我们的鞋匠和裁缝变成哲学家和政治家，但我们仍坚信这是能够提供给汤姆斯先生的最好建议。[1]

在西方，汤译《花笺记》虽然受到法国汉学家雷慕莎和德国诗人歌德的高度赞扬，但因汤姆斯未接受过正规的汉语教育，且译作中确实存在一些问题，以及印刷工身份带来的偏见，导致受到的批评远远多于褒扬。

反观国内学者对汤译《花笺记》的评价，整体显得比较包容，或淡化其不足，或找理由为其分辩。王燕在《〈花笺记〉：第一部中国"史诗"的西行之旅》一文中就指出了这一现象，认为国内学者对《花笺记》艺术成就的评价"不是引述郑振铎的赞词，就是借用歌德的嘉奖，对于该作在英语世界的真实处境，尤其是汤译本遭遇的种种尴尬，却始终没人提及"[2]。易永谊曾对《东方先驱》关于汤译《花笺记》"用词野蛮"的批评做出回应，在分析汤译《花笺记》原文一些句子的基础上，表明个人对汤姆斯翻译策略及其在英语世界中处境的理解。"事实上，汤姆斯之所以这样翻译，是为了既要传递诗歌的基本意思，又力求准确地传递中国人的特有审美特质。而对英国读者而言，这种异域的审美特质是陌生的，不符合英国文学的语言感知习惯与文学表现模式，所以被讽刺为'野蛮的修辞'在所难免。"[3]梁启昌先生在指出汤姆斯中国语言文化掌握得不够好，致使其译文

1　John Francis Davis, "Chinese Novels and Poetry," *Quarterly Review*, 36 June, 1827, p. 511.

2　王燕:《〈花笺记〉：第一部中国"史诗"的西行之旅》,《文学评论》2014年第5期。

3　易永谊:《野蛮的修辞：作为译者的汉学家汤姆斯》,《中国比较文学》2016年第2期。

有较多错误疏漏之处后，又表示对其汉语水平不高的理解，"虽然我花了不少篇幅讨论汤姆斯作为翻译者的弱点，但是我总觉得我们应该以他所处的那个时代的眼光去衡量他的译作"，并指出当时"中国官员有点怨恨外国人学习中文，并且将怨恨发泄在任何他们可以抓到的中国老师身上"。[1] 总结汤译本"虽然错误斑斑，整体而言成功地捕捉了一对年轻才子佳人相恋的浪漫情调。……这个故事的浪漫情调敲好正是《花笺记》原文的精髓"[2]。对梁启昌先生的观点，郑锦怀表示认同，并且补充了汤姆斯汉语水平不高的另一原因是要忙于印刷工作，"无时间和精力去提高自己对中国语言与文化的理解与把握"[3]。

虽然汤译《花笺记》在西方受到的批评多于褒扬，但如果将它与汤译的前两部译作进行对比，就会发现汤姆斯在汉学研究上的不断进步。首先在翻译对象的选择上，从《今古奇观》中的故事《宋金郎团圆破毡笠》到《三国演义》的八/九回，再到长篇诗歌《花笺记》，难度不断提高，对译者的汉语水平和中国文化素养要求也越来越高。《花笺记》中有非常多的文化特色词，汤姆斯显然没有完全洞察，而当时几乎没有任何汉学家可以完全避免这类错误。错误的出现并不能否认汤姆斯在翻译《花笺记》时对中国文化研究做过一番努力："萱堂""椿萱""金莲""《西厢记》""鸳鸯""才高八斗""巫山云雨""嫦娥""凤求凰""状元""牛郎织女""阎王""瓜田李下""媒人""俞伯牙"等文化词的正确解读，都显示了其丰厚的中国文化知识。其次，翻译《花笺记》时，汤姆斯不仅了一些关于中国诗歌的理论知识和见解，还能引经据典来论证自己的观点以达到说理目的，如引用了《诗集传序》《诗经》《古唐诗合解》等。不仅说明汤姆斯的中文水平和汉学修养越来越高，文学造诣也越来越成熟。

1　［美］梁启昌：《论木鱼书〈花笺记〉的英译》，第279页。

2　［美］梁启昌：《论木鱼书〈花笺记〉的英译》，第280页。

3　郑锦怀：《彼得·佩林·汤姆斯：由印刷工而汉学家——以〈中国求爱诗〉为中心的考察》，《国际汉学》2015年第4期。

四、《花笺记》与中国诗歌的西行之旅

"诗体小说"《花笺记》以梁亦沧与杨瑶仙的"才子佳人"爱情故事为载体，宣扬了中国的传统礼仪和美德，内含上的道德教化宗旨契合西方启蒙运动所宣扬的理性精神。男女主角之间"发乎情，止乎礼"的爱情蕴含的中国礼教传统以及原作华丽诗意和众多"中国式"的诗歌意象，是其长久不衰，被西方读者所认可的重要缘由。汤姆斯慧眼独具，跳出"官员汉学家"政治眼光和"传教士汉学家"宗教眼光，率先将目光放在文本的故事性和文学性上，从而较早进入文学领域的翻译，第一个将中国长篇诗歌译介到西方。汤姆斯翻译《花笺记》虽然存在很多问题，但若放在中国诗歌西传的历史长河中去考察，就能发现其重要意义。

中国诗歌和西方世界的第一次正式邂逅可以追溯到1589年英国作家兼批评家乔治·普腾汉（George Puttenham，1529—1590）的《英国诗歌艺术》（*The Arte of English Poesie*，现存最早版本为1869年重印本）。该书在第十一章介绍图形诗时，援引了两首鞑靼[1]诗歌译文。普腾汉没到过中国，也不会汉语，他从一位意大利人那得知中国有图形诗，在其帮助下逐字翻译了据说是中国皇帝和情人之间的两首菱形诗，并按原诗图形排列。虽然有所援引，但普腾汉认为这两首诗较"粗劣"，因而对中国诗歌的评价并不高。他在文中简单提及中国诗歌有一定的诗法和韵律，创作十分灵活，但不像西方人那样喜爱长篇大作；认为中国的图形诗是诗人有感而发按一定的韵脚创作，且以菱形等图形呈现的短诗，雕刻在金、银、象牙之上，或用一些彩色宝石组成汉字，镶在项链、腰带等配饰上，送给情人以作纪念。普腾汉对中国诗歌的发现带着偶然性，且只是作为例证服务于其对图形诗歌的论述，因此并没有引起很多关注。但他对中国诗歌简短而片面的论述不仅反映了西方世界最初对中国诗歌的印象，同时也因最早将这种"最初印象"形诸文字而为后来西方世界的中国诗歌形象打下了底色。加之较早传到西方且

1　鞑靼为早期西方对中国的称呼。

产生较大影响的《诗经》，篇幅较短，且长期被当作儒家经典解读，翻译也散文化，以至西方一直误以为中国只有短篇诗歌，且诗歌艺术不高，偏见由此产生。

早在1626年法国耶稣会士金尼阁就将《诗经》翻译成拉丁语并刊印，但此版未见流传。[1] 最先让《诗经》在西方社会产生影响的是1687年柏应理等耶稣会传教士在沈福宗[2]的帮助下编译的《中国哲学家孔子》。虽然该书主要为《大学》《中庸》《论语》的翻译，目的是向西方介绍孔子思想，沟通儒耶，然而其中孔子论述中散见的带有诗歌性的《诗经》片段却引起了后世学者对中国诗歌的关注。将近一个世纪后的1770年，英国东方学家威廉·琼斯（Sir William Jones）就是因为读到此书，深受孔子论述语言的哲理性和诗歌性感动，专门研读并翻译了《诗经》中的一些诗歌，并因此认识到"诗在任何民族、任何时代都被重视，而且在任何地域都采用同样的意象"[3]。

作为18世纪欧洲汉学中心，法国学术界早在1714年就注意到了中国诗歌，尼古拉·弗莱雷（Nicolas Fréret）这一年做了一场关于中国诗歌的报告，简单介绍了汉语的单音节特征和音乐性，并对《诗经》进行了一番论说，还用汉语和法语分别诵读、翻译了两首中国诗，其中一首来自黄嘉略[4]翻译的小说《玉娇梨》。弗莱雷的演说虽过于简略，且存在一些错误，但学术意义重大，首次让中国诗歌进入了法国学术界的视野。此后，杜赫德在巴黎出版的《中华帝国全志》（1735年）

---

1 西方公认的《诗经》最早西译本是法国传教士孙璋（Alexander dela Charme）1730年的拉丁文译本，但该译本直到1830年才被法国著名汉学家朱尔斯·莫尔发现并编辑出版，书名为《孔夫子的诗经》；1735年杜赫德《中国帝国全志》当作儒家经典辑录的十余篇《诗经》的散文体翻译与《中国哲学家孔子》中散见的《诗经》片段共同构建了早期西方世界的《诗经》形象，受其影响，西方世界长期只关注《诗经》中的道德教化和礼仪风俗，而忽略了其诗歌性。

2 华人传教士，1681年随柏应理到欧洲，随身携带中国儒家经典和诸子书籍40多部，所交多为欧洲宫廷皇室、社会名流，是目前所知早期到达欧洲并在中国文化西传上贡献最大的华人。

3 Garland Cannon ed., *The Collected Works of Sir William Jones*, New York University Press, 1993, Vol. 1, pp. 142—143. 转引自范存忠：《中国文化在启蒙时期的英国》，上海：上海外语教育出版社，1991年，第190—191页。

4 黄为最早旅居巴黎并在中法文化交流史做出巨大贡献的华人，是尼古拉·弗莱雷的中文老师。

中辑录的一些《诗经》篇章不仅为法国，更为欧洲接受中国诗歌提供了基础，如帕西在1761年整理编辑并出版詹姆斯·威尔金森翻译的《好逑传》时，增加的附录三《中国诗歌》（*Fragment of Chinese Poetry*）中的诗歌几乎都来自《中国帝国全志》。

除《诗经》外，钱德明为了歌颂路易十五和乾隆两位君主的友谊而翻译的《御制盛京赋》（1770年）是早期为数不多在欧洲广泛流行的非《诗经》诗歌，获得小斯当东等人的称誉。几年后，开始在法国刊行的百科全书《北京传教士回忆录》（1776年）收录约30首诗歌，除《诗经》外，也有几篇民间诗歌。

总而言之，19世纪前中国诗歌的西传以《诗经》为主，虽偶有其他诗歌被译介到西方，但尚未形成蓬勃发展的态势。这一时期，诗歌的翻译往往是为了其他目的，几乎都以散文体进行，很少有人从文学角度进行赏析。《诗经》的翻译尤其具有明显的导向性，有意无意地想要从中读出基督教真理，这与17—18世纪盛行于基督教内部的中国礼仪之争不无关系，耶稣会士们这么做的根本原因在于"说服欧洲人，孔夫子思想具有合法性，耶稣会士在中国传播福音的行为是合法的"[1]。

进入19世纪，随着东西方贸易的进一步加深，越来越多传教士以外的西方人士来到中国，加之礼仪之争的影响渐渐淡去，18世纪耶稣会士对中国典籍（包括《诗经》）"捕风捉影"的索引式翻译越来越受到批评，雷慕沙、儒莲、汤姆斯、德庇时等新一批汉学家努力摆脱耶稣会士影响，提倡翻译回归文学本身。此外，随着中西交流的加深，西人可以通过多种方式接触更多的文学作品，越来越多《诗经》以外的诗歌进入到他们的视野。

英国著名语言学家韦斯顿（Stephen Weston，1747—1830）虽不曾到过中国，但他通过时任英国皇家学会主席约瑟夫·班克斯爵士（Sir Joseph Banks）的妻子

---

1 ［法］包世潭：《涵化与本土化：18—19世纪法国文学界对中国诗歌艺术的诠释》，郭丽娜译注，《中山大学学报》2021年第6期。

班克斯夫人（Lady Dorothea Banks）接触到一批制作精美的中国瓷器，并分别于
19世纪初翻译了几首瓷器上的诗歌，其中最早的一首为1809年翻译的乾隆御题诗
《咏鸡缸杯》。[1] 乾隆皇帝因在位时间长、诗歌天赋和出身之谜在欧洲享有很高的
知名度[2]，韦斯顿因此对乾隆及其诗歌特别感兴趣。他翻译《咏鸡缸杯》的主要原
因就是该诗为乾隆帝所作，不仅如此，第二年（1810年）他又完成了一组乾隆晚
期征服苗疆时创作的诗歌。在1810年译本的序言中，他简短地介绍了汉语的四
声和平仄，以及诗歌中的平仄规则。擅长波斯语和阿拉伯语的韦斯顿，汉语水平
并不理想，但他却有着语言学家的自信，认为只要有勇气去攀爬上围绕汉语的高
墙，哪怕是没到过中国的欧洲人也能掌握汉语。他翻译的中国诗歌，一般附有原
文，且往往是边翻查字典，边揣摩语义整理笔记，试图弄清其中每一个字的读音
和意思。他总是将诗中汉字的拉丁文注音按照中文的书写习惯自上而下列出，并
相应列出每个字的英文意思，再给出字字对应的直译，最后再整理出相对顺畅的
意译本，形象展示了一个汉语初学者试图理解欣赏中国诗歌的整个过程。虽然有
着难能可贵的自信和勇气，韦斯顿翻译的结果却不尽如人意。译文中每个字对应
的英文意思都从字典而来，并未做进一步考察，因此错漏百出，且有些错误十分
离谱，充其量是个人在字典式阅读的基础上，通过灵活解释改写而来的诗歌，与
原文差别非常大。以《咏鸡缸杯》首句"李唐越器人间无"为例，韦斯顿将七字
读音竖行排列，右边对应英文解释：

1	Ly	Ly
2	Tang	Tang
3	Yue	said Ly Tang, idle and
4	Ky	tool

---

1 Stephen Weston, *Ly-Tang, an Imperial Poem, in Chinese, by Kien Lung*, London: printed and sold by C. and R. Baldwin, New Bridge-street, Black-friars, 1809.

2 Ibid., "Preface," p. 1.

5	jin	Man
6	hien	idle
7	vu	not

该句被译为"李唐，闲散无业，空虚无趣的时候，如是说："（Ly Tang, idle and unemployed, in a vacant and joyless hour, spake thus:）。韦斯顿不仅误将"李唐"当作人名，错把"间"认作"闲"字，还因"器"与他翻译的句子意思格格不入而略去。

韦斯顿的翻译虽不成功，却被几种重要的西方汉学书目汇编所收录[1]，这应与他的名人身份不无关系，同时也反映瓷器等物品很早就在中西文化交流中发生了作用。相比之下，汤姆斯翻译的《花笺记》无论翻译水准还是文学性均高于韦斯顿，却长期被西方主流汉学著作所忽视，这种学术上的"身份歧视"不得不令人慨叹、反思。

很少从事文学作品翻译的马礼逊其实也译介过一些诗歌，只不过他的关注点并不在诗歌本身，而是服务于其他目的。《华英字典》就散布着很多《诗经》中的诗句，它们的存在是为了更好地解释汉字意思，因而数量虽多，却没有一首完整的《诗经》篇章。此外他在《中文原文英译附注》（*Translations from the Original Chinese, with Notes*，1815年）中翻译了两首唐诗，分别为杜牧的《九日齐山登高》和许浑的《村舍》。《中文原文英译附注》主要是对嘉庆皇帝诏书的翻译，两首诗置于嘉庆《遇变罪己诏》之后，这是嘉庆为"癸酉之变"（嘉庆十八年九月十五日）而作的罪己诏书，据说当时因庆祝重阳节仪式，嘉庆回京的行程被推迟而幸免于祸乱。马礼逊因此事专门对中国九月初九的登高习俗予以介

1　如英国东方学家马斯登（William Marsden）的《东方学与哲学书目》（*Marsdeniana Bibliotheca, Philologica et Orientalis*，1827年）、法国著名汉学家考狄（Henri Cordier）的《中国学书目》（*Bibliotheca Sinica*，1904年）。

绍，并附上杜牧诗的英译和原文，以让读者进一步了解这一习俗。《村舍》紧随杜牧诗歌之后，除题目、诗人、译文外，没有其他任何说明。两首诗都采用直译的方式，译文与原作字句基本对应，虽存在一些典故和文化内涵上的误解，但基本达意。马礼逊进行以上翻译的目的并不是向西方介绍中国诗歌，也丝毫不关心其中的文学性，但译文还是引起了一些评论者从诗歌角度进行赏析。这是目前已知最早被译介到西方的唐诗，在中国诗歌的西传史上意义重大。

汤姆斯翻译《花笺记》的创举使其成为西方翻译中国长篇诗歌和女性诗歌的第一人，且翻译有着文学的自觉。他在前言中对中国诗歌的系统论述，尽管存在一些不足，但把握住了基本特征，且能引经据典，上承18世纪零星、片面的评论，下启雷慕莎、德庇时等专业的研究。正如前文所述，雷慕莎在汤译《花笺记》出版两年后，做了一场关于中国诗歌的报告；之后三年，德庇时的《汉文诗解》问世，随后被翻译成多种文字在西方广为流传。《汉文诗解》被认为是西方论述中国诗歌的第一本专著，为理雅各、翟里斯等将中国诗歌研究推向高潮打下了基础。

鸦片战争后，随着国门在坚船利炮中被打开，西方人士不断涌向中国，他们把西方文化和先进科技带来中国的同时，也为中国文学走出去打开了通道。中国人教外国人学习汉语不再犯法，外国人学习中文也不必再偷偷摸摸，各种文本的获得也较以前容易；印刷业的发展推动了报刊、杂志的出现和流行，为西人学习与交流中国文学作品提供了新的媒介；汉学教席在法国的率先设立，使得欧洲其他国家开始效仿，促进了欧洲汉学的学院化发展。多种助力下，中国文学作品包括诗歌迎来了西传的春天。

到19世纪末，《诗经》全译本已分别在德、法、英等国出现，且多次被重译出版。其中，理雅各1871年的英译本因有中国大翻译家王韬的参与，行文流畅而准确，因此影响最大，至今仍被使用。《离骚》先后被翻译成德、法、英等欧洲语言，《九歌》《天问》等屈原诗作也陆续被译介到欧洲。各种中国诗歌选集也开始涌现：法国有《唐诗选》（1862年）、《玉书》（1867年，后转译为德、英、葡萄牙等近十种语言）[1]、《14至19世纪中国诗》（1886年）[2]；英国有《中国抒情诗》（1872年，于1875年转译成德文）、《古今诗选》（1898年）；德国除转译其他国家翻译的中国诗集外，也翻译出版了《汉六朝中国诗精华》（1899年）。

　　西方世界与中国诗歌从16世纪末的偶然邂逅，到17、18世纪零散的《诗经》篇章和几个短诗形成的大致印象和偏见，再到19世纪初汤姆斯引入中国长诗和女性诗歌，初步从文学角度较系统的介绍中国诗歌，以至鸦片战争后中国诗歌西译的全面开花，这一过程，使得中国诗歌在西方的形象逐渐丰满多彩起来。为20世纪中国诗歌通过庞德等催生欧洲诗歌意象派，并推动欧美现代主义诗歌，特别是象征主义诗歌的发展奠定了基础。中国诗歌的西行之旅及其在西方世界产生的影响，很好地说明了其世界性意义。其间译者们通过翻译中国诗歌等文学作品来认识和建构西方视域下的中国社会文化的实践和努力，促进了中国文学在西方乃至世界的经典化进程。

　　（本文为教育部人文社会科学重点研究基地重大项目"中国学术话语古今演变研究"［22JJD750042］、国家社科基金人才项目"中国现代学术话语的生成与建构"［22VRC181］阶段性成果。本文系作者在联盟2022年年度论坛上的发言）

1　《玉书》近四分之一的内容来自1862年法译诗集《唐诗选》。
2　该诗歌集主要选译了明清两代历史和政治风云人物所作的诗歌21首。

《芬尼根的守灵夜》中乔伊斯的碎片化历史观

戴从容[*]

爱尔兰作家詹姆斯·乔伊斯（James Joyce）的最后一部作品《芬尼根的守灵夜》（*Finnegans Wake*，后文简称《芬尼根》）以其独特的用词方式，引发了从众多角度进行的不同解读，其中以乔伊斯的弟弟斯坦尼斯劳斯说的"夜晚"的语言[1]和德里达从书中的"He war"（他战争）两个词展开的解构主义分析[2]最为有名。乔伊斯本人在给赞助人韦弗女士的信中说他的创作目的是要写一部"世界史"[3]。英国学者芬·福特汉姆（Finn Fordham）在评论中即以该小说对中国的塑造为个案，分析世界史中普遍存在的种族主义倾向，提出"乔伊斯不是通过消解人物和叙述模式，而是通过让它们增殖来批判性地参与和反对世界史的结构模式，揭露这一体裁的缺陷"[4]。福特汉姆认为，小说戏剧性地夸大了东西方的二元对立，故而中国的象形文字和儒家文化在西方的现代技术文明的对照下被表现为原始落后的，但乔伊斯这样做其实是要通过"戏仿"西方世界史中的这类成见来"颠覆"

---

* 戴从容：南京大学全球人文研究院教授。研究领域：英国和爱尔兰文学、比较文学与世界文学、翻译研究。

1 Richard Ellmann, *James Joyce*, New York, Oxford: Oxford University Press, 1982, p. 579.

2 Jacques Derrida, "Two Words for Joyce," in *Post-Structuralist Joyce: Essays from the French*, eds.Attridge, Derek and Daniel Ferrer, Cambridge: Cambridge University Press, 1984, pp. 145–159.

3 Patricia Hutchins, *James Joyce's World*, London: Methuen, 1957, p. 140.

4 Finn Fordham, "'Until Hanandhunigan's Extermination': Joyce, China and Racialised World Histories," in *Modernism and Race*, Len Platt ed. Cambridge: Cambridge University Press, 2011, p. 174.

这种体裁。[1] 用戏仿来颠覆社会偏见确实是《芬尼根》的一个重要手法，但福特汉姆的分析只涉及了该小说的某些中国内容。如果全面审视小说对中国的呈现，就会发现乔伊斯的世界史构建要复杂得多。《芬尼根》不仅是一部颠覆的历史，更是一部建设的历史，只是这种建设采用了不同于传统世界史的书写方式。本文将以该小说中的中国形象塑造为例，分析乔伊斯这一具有启示性的历史叙述方式。

一、音乐剧中的中国

正如福特汉姆指出的那样，20世纪初，不少西方文献中的中国形象越来越趋于负面，从将中国与"软弱"和"卑贱"画上等号开始，最终发展为视中国为"黄祸"。例如，在文森特·乔伊斯（Vincent Joyce）于1903年出版的《天国之手》（The Celestial Hand: A Sensational Story）中，白人主人公之所以决定反抗入侵的中国人，原因即在于"与其一直被一大堆肮脏的中国人关着，最后总还会被杀死，那不如死在文明的绞刑架上"[2]。正因如此，很多研究都用"黄祸论"来概括那时的西方作品，称其中"'黄祸'叙述激增，将中国人妖魔化为一群低等人类组成的危险害虫"[3]。

但事实上，当时的中国经济和文明并非像这些文献中描写的那么落后。自1683年清政府取消贸易和旅行海禁后，中国商人就在海外尤其在亚洲积极拓展贸易。在东南亚历史上，1740至1840年这一百年甚至被称为"中国世纪"[4]。至1913

1　Finn Fordham, "'Until Hanandhunigan's Extermination': Joyce, China and Racialised world Histories," p. 186.

2　Vincent Joyce, *The Celestial Hand: A Sensational Story*, Sydney: J. C. MacCartie & Co. 1903, p. 234.

3　Adam Roberts, *The History of Science Fiction*, London: Palgrave Macmillan, 2016, p. 269.

4　Anthony Reid, "Chinese Trade and Economic Expansion in Southeast Asia in the Later Eighteenth and Early Nineteenth Centuries: An Overview," in *Water Frontier: Commerce and the Chinese in the Lower Mekong Region, 1750–1880*, Nola Cooke & Tana Li eds. Lanham: Rowman & Littlefield Publishers, 2004, pp. 21–34.

年，"中国在全球商品出口中所占的比重是日本的两倍，到1929年时又出现了
50%的增长"[1]。活跃的海外贸易，当然还有鸦片战争，促使原本遥远的中国进入
了普通西方人的视野，引起了西方人又羡又恨的复杂心态。值得注意的是，此时
西方对中国的心态并非只有黄祸论一种。虽然绝大多数西方人本质上很难逃脱萨
义德（Edward Said）所说的东方主义话语，但在程度和主观意图上依然有着千
差万别。[2]萨义德认为"既不愿意也没有能力考虑个体"[3]是造成东方主义偏见的
一个关键原因。乔伊斯所选择的那些描写中国的西方文本正反映了他"考虑个
体"的人文立场，其选择方式本身也是对当时甚嚣尘上的黄祸论的反驳。

19世纪末20世纪初，中国题材在英语音乐剧中一度泛滥，这对乔伊斯有非
常重要的影响，因为去剧院看剧是乔伊斯最喜欢的休闲方式，他尤其喜欢音乐剧
和歌剧。当时，无论音乐剧、歌剧还是话剧，都属于大众娱乐，就像当今社会的
电影那样，是知识传播的媒介。有次乔伊斯走在都柏林大街上，看见前面有个苏
格兰士兵穿着中式长袍去看戏，当时戏剧中的中国热[4]可见一斑。与"卑贱""软
弱"的中国相似，此时的爱尔兰正处在英国的殖民统治之下，而且因为19世纪
中叶的马铃薯饥荒，"贫穷和肮脏"[5]同样也成了爱尔兰人在世界上的标签。与此
同时，在叶芝（William Yeats）、帕内尔（Charles Parnell）、格里菲斯（Arthur
Griffith）、德·瓦勒拉（De Valera）等人的先后领导下，爱尔兰正致力于民族独

1　万志英：《剑桥中国经济史：古代到19世纪》，崔传刚译，北京：中国人民大学出版社，2018年，第
339页。

2　萨伊德在2003年为《东方学》再版添加的序言中自己也承认："出于理解、同情、仔细研究和分析这
些目的本身而得到的关于其他人和其他时代的知识，与另一方面作为一场自我肯定、对抗和公开战斗
的总体战役的一部分的知识——如果真是这样的话，这两种知识之间存在着不同。毕竟，意欲以共存
和人文视野的拓展为目的的理解与意欲以控制和外来统治为目的统治这两种意图之间有着根本的不
同。"Edward Said, *Orientalism*, London: Penguin Books, 2003, p. xiv.

3　Edward Said, *Orientalism*, p. 154.

4　Richard Ellmann, *James Joyce*, p. 548.

5　Thomas Bartlett ed., *The Cambridge History of Ireland, Volume IV: 1880 to the Present*, Cambridge: Cambridge
University Press, 2018, p. xxxiv.

立和文化独立，直至1937年爱尔兰共和国成立。乔伊斯创作《芬尼根》时，爱尔兰经历英爱战争和爱尔兰内战，正逐步走向共和，与反抗殖民统治、争取民族自强和独立的中国有众多的相似之处，这也让包括乔伊斯在内的不少爱尔兰人对中国有较多的认同和亲善。

在《芬尼根》中，乔伊斯直接或间接提到了三部与中国人有关的戏剧。除此之外，书中涉及中国题材的艺术作品还有庞德（Ezra Pound）的中国诗，"长着庞德的|思考的下颌说着中国的|唠叨的口音"[1]。庞德对中国的兴趣应该也是乔伊斯关注中国文化的一个重要原因，因为庞德可以说是乔伊斯的保护人，很早就公开宣称，"如果更多的人读乔伊斯先生的《一个青年艺术家的画像》（*A Portrait of the Artist as a Young Man*）和《都柏林人》（*Dubliners*）中的某些故事，今天爱尔兰的问题或许会少一些"[2]。

在小说中的三部涉及中国的戏剧中，第一个被提及的是1899年在伦敦上演的歌剧《桑多伊：或皇帝所爱》（*San Toy: The Emperor's Own*）。乔伊斯在《芬尼根》第三章写道："竞争者们|赞同者演着|玩着《桑多伊》|玩具|圣者像。"（58.32–33）这句话的上下文是有人指控主人公汉弗利·卿普顿·壹耳维蚵与"第一位女人"（58.29）偷情，因此桑多伊就是这"第一位女人"的一个化身。《桑多伊》的同名女主角桑多伊是一位中国贵族，她爱上了英国领事的儿子鲍勃·普莱斯顿，但却被皇帝看中，最终历经波折而与情人终成眷属。同时，她的贵族父亲虽然最后娶了皇帝的女官，但在情节发展过程中也一直追求着英国领馆的英国女仆。虽然《桑多伊》不无种族歧视，细节尽显西方人高中国人一等的意识，但剧中的中英联姻说明，在普通英国人的心中，中国并非洪水猛兽，而是一个可以让西方普通人满足贵族想象的异域空间。《桑多伊》的导演和作曲西德尼·琼斯在当时广受

1　James Joyce, *Finnegans Wake*, London: Faber and Faber, 1939, p. 89.24–25. 后面该书的引文页码都直接用括号放在引文后面，并沿用《芬尼根的守灵夜》的页码和行号这一传统引用方式。

2　此时乔伊斯还没有创作《尤利西斯》和《芬尼根的守灵夜》。Robert H. Deming ed., *James Joyce Critical Heritage*, London: Routledge, 1997, p. 83.

欢迎，他的另外一部音乐喜剧《艺妓：一个茶馆的故事》（*The Geisha: A Story of a Tea House*）同样也出现在了《芬尼根》中。[1] 当然，这两部音乐剧在当时的伦敦大受追捧，前者上演了768场，后者上演了760场。在美国的百老汇则一共上演了200多场。事实上，这两部剧中的中国角色都是由欧洲人扮演的，演员大多是业余演员，服装也是欧洲想象的中式服装，但这些丝毫没有影响观众们的热情，足以证明当时的英美观众对中国充满了好奇。

《艺妓》在《芬尼根》中以主导动机（leitmotif）的形式出现，即在书中不时出现的 "chinchin"，如 "chinchinjoss"（611.5）或 "Tsin tsin tsin tsin"（57.3）等变体。据乔伊斯本人讲述，这是因为一个中国学生给他看中国的 "山" 字，并告诉他读作 "chin"，乔伊斯觉得这正是一般人念 "Fin"（芬）的方式，所以 "chin" 在小说中也与作为主人公重要化身的爱尔兰巨人英雄芬·麦克尔、民谣人物芬尼根联系在了一起。[2] 但是，也有学者指出 "chin" 指代的是《艺妓》中的歌曲[3]，而《芬尼根》第304页该主导动机的一个展开 "Chinchin Childaman!"（亲亲中国人孩子!）也证明了该观点，因为《亲亲中国人》正是《艺妓》一剧中的中国人Wun-Hi的独唱歌曲。《艺妓》的故事其实发生在日本，讲的是英国皇家海军中尉雷吉·费尔法克在中国人Wun-Hi开的万乐茶楼发生的一系列爱情故事。Wun-Hi在剧中只是一个滑稽配角，他的独唱《亲亲中国人》也只是剧中的一个小插曲。Wun-Hi在歌中哀叹 "中国人赚不到钱"，各种生意都不好做，店铺只能关掉。他因欺骗被抓，被狠狠地又踢又打，就算找到了好地方卖茶，也总是饱受凌辱。[4] 乔伊斯却在该剧众多精彩的歌曲中选择了这首并不起眼的独唱，不排除是因为它少有地表现了中国商人海外行商的艰辛。

1　当然，琼斯真正感兴趣的并非中国，而是异域题材，比如他在这两部音乐剧之间推出的《希腊奴隶》讲的就是波斯女郎对家中希腊奴隶的爱情，只是这出音乐剧只上演了349场。

2　Stuart Gilbert ed., *Letters of James Joyce*, London: Faber and Faber, 1966, p. 250.

3　Matthew J. C. Hodgart & Ruth Bauerle, *Joyce's Grand Operoar: Opera in Finnegans Wake*, Urbana: University of Illinois Press, 1997, p. 168.

4　Sidney Jones, *The Geisha: A Story of a Tea House*, London: Hopewood & Crew, 1896, p. 149.

　　19世纪和20世纪之交的欧美音乐剧都是由西方人编导并上演的，而1934年熊式一根据中国戏曲中王宝钏故事改写并亲自导演的英语话剧《王宝钏》则是一部真正的中国剧。该剧在伦敦连续上演3年，共演出900多场，之后到百老汇上演时也同样引起了轰动。乔伊斯以非常隐晦的方式提及了这出真正的中国导演、中国题材、中国布景、中国演员的戏剧，只是在"上帝，我小伙子|夫人，蓝胡子配他，夫人|空虚|领导|丽达，宝川（plasheous stream）"（332.22-23）中暗指了该剧的名字。但由于这里的"宝川"首先指的是利菲河犹如珍宝，因此到底是中国文化本身吸引着乔伊斯，还是"precious stream"这个英文翻译唤起了乔伊斯对利菲河的联想，仍可商榷。

　　虽然在当时的社会文化背景下乔伊斯选取的这几出戏剧无法避免萨义德所说的"潜层的东方主义"[1]，但与诸如傅满洲小说与电影系列那些妖魔化中国人的作品相比，它们在总体上更愿意与中国或中国文化共存甚至联姻，全剧有别于《天国之手》里的你死我活或者福特汉姆所说的"直到汉匈尼根灭绝"。事实上，当时依然有不少西方人愿意向中国学习，比如当时英国报刊对《王宝钏》的评论中，就有人盛赞中国戏剧舞台布置简洁，称"这或许比几吨堆积的木制品和场与场中替换的服装更为有效"[2]，并认为"中国人更明白事理"[3]。可见，乔伊斯的选择可谓呈现了西方话语中的不同声音。

　　不过，如果研究者就此认为乔伊斯在选取西方艺术作品时有意避开了西方对中国的丑化，那也同样是对乔伊斯的误读。对乔伊斯来说，真实才是第一位的，无论是有意的歪曲还是刻意的纠偏，这些都不是他的世界史小说的目的。因为他的艺术理念是"我们必须按照我们看见的那个样子接受生活，男男女女就如

1　Edward Said, *Orientalism*, p. 206.

2　Ashley Thorpe, *Performing China on the London Stage: Chinese Opera and Global Power, 1759–2008*, London: Palgrave Macmillan, 2016, p. 106.

3　Ashley Thorpe, *Performing China on the London Stage: Chinese Opera and Global Power, 1759–2008*, p. 107.

现实中遇到的那样"[1]。他的世界史同样是按照现实的样子来呈现的：既有西方对中国的好奇和交流，同样也包含着对中国的批评乃至歪曲。比如，《芬尼根》中提到一个"磨坊主黄_{黄浦江划桨}"（297. 37），指的是英国作家哥尔德史密斯（Oliver Goldsmith）《世界公民》（*The Citizen of the World*）中一位既吝啬又贪财的中国磨坊主。哥尔德史密斯的《世界公民》其实是以中国来批判英国，书中的中国主人公和大多数中国人都是积极正面的，但磨坊主黄又的确是东方主义话语中典型的吝啬贪财且迷信的中国人。[2] 乔伊斯藏书中的《哥尔德史密斯全集》[3] 收有《世界公民》全文，但乔伊斯选取磨坊主黄却不选取更加正面的启蒙式主人公李安济，即表明他无意用正面形象为中国人申辩。但另一方面，磨坊主黄又像《艺妓》中的 Wun-Hi 一样是一个虽贪财但与人无害的角色，与阴险狡诈、为祸西方的傅满洲并不相同。显然，乔伊斯同样并不想丑化中国人。那么，乔伊斯要用中国材料实现什么目的呢？

二、中国碎片的杂糅与挪用

乔伊斯对中国实际上并无深入了解，而且似乎也无意去做深入的了解。他并没有来往密切的中国朋友，也曾经承认他认得的中文不比"月球人"[4] 认得的多。《芬尼根》中重要的"芬"与"山"的联系只是他从一个中国留学生那里偶然听来的，而且显然他跟这个中国学生不熟，所以没有机会对这个问题做进一步的辨析。乔伊斯的中国知识也常常似是而非。据艾尔曼（Richard Ellmann）记载，乔伊斯上课时讲过中国的飞将军李广的故事，但他说李广是在一棵树上吊死的。[5]

1　James Joyce, *The Critical Writing of James Joyce*, London: Faber and Faber, 1959, p. 45.

2　在哥尔德史密斯的书中，磨坊主黄是中国蒙书为了道德告诫而讲述的某则故事中的人物。

3　Richard Ellmann, *The Consciousness of Joyce*, London: Faber & Faber, 1977, p. 110.

4　Richard Ellmann, *James Joyce*, p. 511.

5　Richard Ellmann, *James Joyce*, p. 341.

乔伊斯的藏书目录中没有中国著作[1]，甚至连英译的也没有，这也说明乔伊斯感兴趣的并不是中国文化，而是中国的存在本身。他的大多数中国知识应该来自道听途说或者流行作品里的点滴片断，这使得《芬尼根》中出现的中国人和中国文化大多是流于表面的老生常谈，比如茶叶、中餐、蜜饯、尿壶等等："作为第一笔外快的祁门红茶、正山小种"（534.11），"国家需要熊掌做晚餐|要塞|叮叮|！"（110.2-3），"我们有蜜饯排骨、椅子、口香糖，水痘和中国尿壶"（45.33）。当然在这些西方异域想象中也少不了性感的中国女性："这两个中国|莫纳亨郡|修道院制度|小修女|一个仙女多么让人惊喜啊|按我的价格卖|！"（616.11-12）。而在"午餐|巨人和晚餐|中国正像|一起|她和我两个金发女郎伴着西格诺·弗利的男高音|锡工罗曼司|罗曼什语|混杂|人|麦克考麦克"（243.15-17）一句中，中国食品和中国女人甚至合为一体，都成为被吞食的对象；至于"在我的铁床|铁边界|铁路|裤脚带下硬硬地戳|枪柄，还有我那自称|蚕丝中国的|脊柱膝盖丰满面颊的侍女|室内配偶服务于夜晚的外国男人|邮件"（461.23-25），则更明确挑明了中国女性意象中包含的西方性想象。

乔伊斯同样注意到了西方人对汉语的单音节特征的歧视：中国"人人都长着茶眼睛|够了，女人和国家，闻着像|写成鱼。那是Ü"（299.34-35），说着"纯净的秦中蠢话|成语，任何情况下所有词都是一个音节|可解决的"（299.34）。这句话是看着两个哥哥做作业的妹妹在边上加的注释，是对正文"我们喜欢独白汉密尔顿|假笑阉羊追随|家伙金口|银调奥哈根"（299.22-23）的注释。正文中的汉密尔顿和奥哈根分别为18世纪和19世纪的爱尔兰政治家，随后的正文中对汉密尔顿的描绘也同样表明他的一个化身是中国人："他在屁股|技艺|r上翻滚，露出脚后跟的尺寸|他的时，全都太可爱了！就像一只有字缝词的羊羊狼|俚语|蛇。"（299.23-26）通过使用"tsifengtse"和"yangsheepslang"这样的中文（在《芬尼根》中。中文的呈现方式或为拼音，或为拼音与英文的混合体）以及妹妹的注释，乔伊斯暗示汉密尔顿有着中国化身。显然，乔伊斯把西方人对中国人的偏见用于描绘自己的爱尔兰族人，其目的

1　Richard Ellmann, *James Joyce*, p. 395.

不在于讽刺中国人，而是将爱尔兰和中国身份交织在一起，并对西方话语加以讽刺。

的确，在《芬尼根》中，中国和爱尔兰经常互为镜像，相互融合。科德尔·易（Cordell D. K. Yee）指出，在乔伊斯的时代，中国和爱尔兰这两个古老文化分别影响了各自的邻国日本和英国，却都正在被它们所影响的国家占领，这让乔伊斯对中国尤为认同。[1] 这也是为什么《芬尼根》中有不少中国与爱尔兰在地理空间上的融合。例如，在"当你那从中国塔拉|彩虹|茶来的乡下人|反对想要写字|纠正，这不是一个好迹象吗？"（490.28-29）这句话中，塔拉是古代爱尔兰凯尔特王国的都城，象征着爱尔兰文化的根，而用"中国的"来修饰塔拉，无疑表明对中国和爱尔兰的融合。此外，在"我们这些生活在天子脚下|天空之下的人，我们这些来自三叶草之国|花国的人，我们中国|罪中人常常仰望拱盖着|抵达大地的天空"（110.4-6）这部分中，三叶草是爱尔兰的国花，但在这里又与很多暗指中国的词语"天子脚下"和"中国"交织在一起，且其中的"花国"也指中国，因为乔伊斯阅读的《孔子的故事》（*Master Kung. The Story of Confucius*）的作者卡尔·克劳（Carl Crow）就在自己的另一部作品《花园里的洋鬼子》（*Foreign Devils in the Flowery Kingdom*）中把中国称为"Flowery Kingdom"。[2]

当然，即便乔伊斯将中国视为东方的爱尔兰，他也同样没有神话中国，反而毫不回避地使用了西方话语中那些可能带有种族歧视的东方碎片，因为这是他也是大多数普通西方人认识中国的主要知识来源。这种萨义德将之作为东方主义话语进行批判的"部分理论"[3]，即用可能导致以偏概全的知识片断取代对异文化全面深入认识的做法，对大多数人来说其实是无法避免的。但与东方主义话语不同，乔伊斯将这些知识片段彻底变成碎片并加以碎片式地使用，从而剥离了这些

---

1 Cordell D. K. Yee, "Metemsinopsychosis: Confucius and Ireland in 'Finnegans Wake'," in *Comparative Literature Studies*, 1983, Vol. 20, pp. 115-124.

2 Carl Crow, *Foreign Devils in the Flowery Kingdom*, Hong Kong: Earnshaw Books, Ltd., 1940.

3 Edward Said, *Orientalism*, p. 28.

文化碎片的东方主义语境。与此同时，他更将这些"他者"的碎片与"自我"的碎片交织在一起，甚至用于修饰自身，用文化碎片的杂糅和融合来化解他异性思维。这是乔伊斯超越原本必须依赖的西方话语中的陈词滥调，让相异的文化在《芬尼根》中组成一个大同世界的重要方式。

事实上，在《芬尼根》中并不只有中国和爱尔兰相互融合，因为该书的一个核心主题就是各民族、各文化的大融合：在"它的支那炒杂碎|家伙|糖|下巴|磕头[1]|牛奶咖啡|犒劳|耕牛法大量牛奶拿来面包师早餐|贝克兄弟公司|面包屑|麦片汤，煮茶里面有福州|未来茶叶"（608.19-21）中，早餐由中式饮食和文化与西式面包牛奶混合而成，这应该就是乔伊斯对未来人类文化交融的预想。这一人类文化大融合主题在《芬尼根》中最突出地体现在主人公的身份上。HCE即"Here Comes Everybody"（此即人人，32.18-19），不仅是20世纪都柏林的酒馆老板汉弗利·卿普顿·壹耳微蚵，也是基督教中的亚当、北欧的奥丁、埃及的奥西里斯、爱尔兰的芬·麦克尔、印度的湿婆、佛教的释迦牟尼、中国的孔子……他并不是具体的某个人，而是所有人的融合，象征着所有文化的融合。这种文化之间的包容共存是乔伊斯一贯的文化立场，尤其通过《芬尼根》中各种语言的交融混杂体现出来。因此，乔伊斯在《芬尼根》中追求的并不只是一个民族的独立，在他看来，"爱尔兰的民族主义不过是英国和罗马天主教的帝国主义的延续"[2]，他真正追求的是"疏通同胞们封闭的意识"[3]，让"世界大同主义胜过他的爱尔兰性"[4]。

乔伊斯的民族观是一种建立在对当时狭隘的民族主义的批判以及对新的民族良心的期待之上的"更清醒的民族主义立场"[5]，而文化碎片的杂糅和融合则是他探索出的一条建立在民族性之上的世界大同之路。正是出于这一立场，主人

1　此处原文为"chap sugay"，可以解读为"chop suey"，即炒杂碎，一道美式中国菜。

2　Emer Nolan, *James Joyce and Nationalism*, London & New York: Routledge, 1995, p. 18.

3　郭军：《乔伊斯：叙述他的民族——从〈都柏林人〉到〈尤利西斯〉》，北京：外语教学与研究出版社，2010年，第97页。

4　Emer Nolan, *James Joyce and Nationalism*, p. 3.

5　郭军：《乔伊斯：叙述他的民族——从〈都柏林人〉到〈尤利西斯〉》，第69页。

公HCE的爱尔兰身份也与中国身份交织在一起，正如在"同一个或类似的人将在快乐·奥图尔_{劳伦斯·奥图尔}与沮丧·两湖山谷（说丹麦话！）订婚的主教教区里友善地盯着，戴着中国面具_{主的晚餐}"（433.4–7）中，尽管劳伦斯·奥图尔是都柏林的主保圣人，两湖山谷是爱尔兰威克娄郡的修道院地区，但处身传统爱尔兰空间的人却"戴着中国面具"，或者说有着中国面孔，这显示出乔伊斯对"爱尔兰与中国身份的认同"[1]。所以HCE是一个有着"中国的_{唠叨的}口音"（89.24–25）的"中国人"（104.13），他的妻子则是"穿着唐人街_{瓷罐}外无人能比的_{矛盾地}最小号鞋子"（533.5–6）的"中国荡妇"（261.1）。

此外，HCE不只是人，他也象征着地理空间。在《芬尼根》中，每个人都有符号，HCE的符号就是中国"山"字的倒写，所以小说中才会有"当一个人的意思是一座山"（309.5）这种说法。HCE对应的中国山是泰山，"他那儒生头发上_{她在他上面}有最圆锥形的_{滑稽的}头巾_{裤子褶}_{灰浆桶}一片，他那曲曲阜[2]的寒暄_{秦朝}就像泰山泰土_{旧屋}_{泰国}_{塔斯马尼亚岛}附近的孔夫子_{节庆国王}_{袋鼠}"（131.33–35）。泰山不仅是中国的第一山，也与HCE的另一个化身孔子相呼应。因此，在HCE身上，爱尔兰的地理空间与中国的地理空间也是重合的，他"也许是爱尔兰的自由_{逃跑}港_{阴谋}，但一直_{夏娃时代}是皇城_{皇上}"（130.34–35）。

乔伊斯在《芬尼根》中用散落各处的中国地理碎片搭建起了一个中国地理空间，北方有位于陕西中部平原的古地秦中（chingchong 299.34），作为数代"皇城"（hwen ching hwan chang 322.6）的北京（spekin 533.6，peachskin 240.30，Pinkingtone 184.23）更被不断提及；中部有南京（nankeen 321.34）和殖民城市上海（shanghaied 485.24）；南方有福建（Fukien 468.3）；当然香港也被多次提及，例如"香江香港_{香肠}_唱"（119.25）和"在你我之间香港"（306.6–7）。第二个例子的上下文点出香港是书中两个儿子中的闪的化身，正如泰山是男主人公

---

1 Cordell D. K. Yee, "Metemsinopsychosis: Confucius and Ireland in 'Finnegans Wake'," p. 118.
2 在小说中，HCE的一个特征是口吃，原文以重复来表现他的这个特征，本文作者此处的翻译沿用了这个表现手法。

的一个化身。此外，其他国家的唐人街也出现在书中，如澳大利亚布里斯班市中心的中国城"阳关海岸"（264.23）和英国伦敦中国城附近的商业街"长亩街"（579.33）等。

《芬尼根》的女主人公ALP也同样拥有中国地理空间的化身——黄河，"直到在黄河黄河|钟|橙带党的单调歌唱|钟中快速尖叫|喘鸣的"（611.29-30），"黄河，我的悲伤"（213.6），"汉娜·丽维娅·妇鲁拉贝尔|全部重新美丽。……河黄！黄河！"（627.27-31）。在ALP身上，黄河也与利菲河融为一体，就像在HCE身上都柏林的霍斯山与中国的泰山融为一体一样。乔伊斯之所以选择黄河，应该不仅是因为它是中华文化的发源地，也因为黄河也是中国历史上"洪水"的主要造因，所以书中说"机会对中国洪水同样均等"（28.23-24）。乔伊斯对洪水的强调，应该是因为《芬尼根》的世界史是大洪水之后诺亚后代的人类史[1]，故而黄河与洪水的关系可以让中国的历史与《芬尼根》中的世界史同步共振。作为河流的化身，乔伊斯在书中著名的《汉娜·丽维娅·妇鲁拉贝尔》一章借助双关让世界各地的河流遍布全章，其中当然也流淌着众多的中国河流：楚河（choo 198.11）、衡水（hen 199.30）、汾河（femtyfyx 200.5）、嫩江（nen 203.14）、白河（peihos 205.32）、赤水（chichiu 209.23）、乌苏里江（O, susuria 209.35）、长江（yangsee 213.36）、黄浦江（Whangpoos 297.37），以及像黑龙江这样以"阿穆尔河"（Amoor 211.26）这个俄国名字出现的中国河流。乔伊斯让ALP的化身是河水，河水的流淌象征着时间的流淌，"她是循环的时间之河……在她的洪水里带着已逝文明的碎片，以及将要到来的庄稼和文化的种子"[2]。就这样，利菲河/黄河不仅是地理景观，它们也"让后人可以看见历史"[3]。由此，通过让HCE和

1　Congrong Dai, "The Original Sin in 'Finnegans Wake'," in *Neohelicon*, 2012, Volume 39, pp. 475–483.

2　Joseph Campbell & Henry M. Robinson, *A Skeleton Key to Finnegans Wake*, New York: Harcout, Brace and Cop., 1944, p. 10

3　［美］段义孚：《恋地情结》，志丞等译，北京：商务印书馆，2018年，第147页。

ALP分别化身为泰山和黄河，以及在文本中嵌入中国文化、历史和地理的其他碎片，乔伊斯不仅构建出了中国的三维地理空间，而且让这个空间有了历史。

当然，综观《芬尼根》，中国元素的占比相当有限，因此不应该过分夸大中国在乔伊斯心中的分量。但另一方面，乔伊斯把中国视为爱尔兰在亚洲的镜像，并没有像东方主义者那样有意识地歧视和丑化中国，他甚至用反讽的手法来讽刺西方文化对中国以及对爱尔兰的成见，这一点确实可以在《芬尼根》中看到。这表明乔伊斯以一种建设性的方式超越了东方主义话语，即通过把他者的碎片与自我的碎片、东方的碎片与西方的碎片杂糅起来，打破了作为东方主义话语基础的自我—他者对立。

三、辩证统一的中国史框架

在创作《芬尼根》时，乔伊斯事实上已经超越了自我—他者的对立，但同时也超越了对这种二元对立的对立。就像书中的男性妇人已经超越了男性与女性的对立，但书中又处处存在着男女两性的诱惑主题一样，乔伊斯在《芬尼根》中对二元对立的颠覆与对二元对立的使用同时存在，且不分轩轾。乔伊斯以"万花筒"（143.28）描述《芬尼根》的结构模式：万花筒由毫无规则的碎片组成，但碎片又交织叠加成对称的图案；万花筒的图案随意变化，但这些图案又建立在不变的规则之上。万花筒的这一矛盾统一的特点也是《芬尼根》中的世界史的特点：乔伊斯一方面用碎片来呈现驳杂的现实和现实的驳杂，另一方面又用深层的框架为表面的杂乱提供逻辑基础。这表明乔伊斯在坚信各民族历史的多样性的同时也坚信历史中暗含着某种基本规律。在《尤利西斯》中，这个深层框架是荷马史诗《奥德修纪》（Odýsseia）；在《芬尼根》中，这个框架则一般被认为是意大利哲学家维科（Giambattista Vico）的历史循环模式。但事实上，还有一个人在《芬尼根》中起着与维科同样重要的作用，那就是意大利哲学家布鲁诺（Giordano Bruno）。乔伊斯年轻时就倾心于布鲁诺，在文章中以布鲁诺的话作为开篇[1]；在《芬尼根》中，布鲁诺的名字更是频繁出现，他的对立统一的辩证法思想直接影响着《芬尼根》的历史观。[2] 从书中呈现的中国史断片看，乔伊斯的世界史的整体模式确实是维科式的历史循环，但各历史阶段的微观模式却呈现出布鲁诺式的辩证统一。

二元对立主题在《芬尼根》中主要由儿子闪与肖恩这一组人物来代表，但在碎片叙述中，时间与空间、山与水、树与石、拿破仑与惠灵顿、狐狸与葡萄、蚂蚁与蚱蜢等各种二元对立遍布全书，并组成了对立统一的辩证关系，就像书中说的，"他们的对立面偶然重新合并|重新出现到那个无法辨别者们的身份中"（49.36-50.1）。在乔伊斯看来，包括中国史在内的整个世界历史都是由对立抗争而又统一融合的二元关系模式构成的。在看似散乱的中国意象下面，在维科式的"中国循环|周年"（119.23）中，在中国古代、近代和现代这三个阶段（分别对应维科的神的时代、英雄时代、人民时代）里，每个阶段都聚焦于一组辩证统一的民族矛盾。

在书中最具表演性的酒吧一章中，都柏林裁缝柯西以中国皇帝的身份让中国古代史在酒吧舞台上隆重登场：在这段叙述中，柯西被描写成一个身着中式服装的中国北魏朝代的人，"小艾西[3]再次进来。一等一的北魏人|矮小，南京棉布马裤"（321.34）；之后，这段叙述又加入了"hwen ching hwan chang"（322.6）这几个词，可以理解为中文"换场"的拼音，即酒客们要求柯西下台，也可以理解为中文的"皇上"或"皇城"。也有研究者认为这是中文的"文昌"，指周文王，因为周文王姓姬名昌。无论选取哪种解释，这层含义都指向中国的帝王文化，表明

1　James Joyce, *The Critical Writing of James Joyce*, p. 69. 编辑在文章的注释中同样强调了布鲁诺在《芬尼根的守灵夜》中的频繁出现和重要性（p. 132）。

2　Ronald J. Koch, "Giordano Bruno and 'Finnegans Wake': A New Look at Shaun's Objection to the 'Nolanus Theory'," in *James Joyce Quarterly*, 1972, Vol. 9, pp. 237–249; see also Carla Baricz, "The *Finnegans Wake* Diagram and Giordano Bruno," in *Joyce Studies Annual*, 2008, pp. 235–242.

3　"艾西"即"柯西"，原文为"Ashe"（一个她）。乔伊斯在《芬尼根》中会不时变换人物的名字来加入不同的含义。柯西的名字在这句话中被写成了Ashe，让他同时也是一个女人，本文作者在翻译时就将其译为了"艾西"。

柯西的化身可能是中国帝王。其衣服的颜色似也可印证这一猜测："他有多么糟，红黄紫|皇子，他自己的爸爸|试衣裁缝|旅行用品商也认|鼻子不出他"（322.12-13），红黄紫在中国古代是帝王的专属颜色。与柯西的中国身份相应，下面的看客也变成了一群"老与少"（lao yiu shao，322.4），将此时的都柏林场景与中国场景叠加在了一起。

柯西之后，中国古代史中重要的二元对立随即进入读者的视野——"汉人|他再次|母鸡与匈奴人|她再次|母鸡依然经常四处出没来寻找他们的芬尼根|再次有|在里面|母鸡|往那边去"（332.4-5），由此展开了中国古代史的对立统一框架："汉人和匈奴人|他和她"（6.20）、"匈奴人|基纳汉|酒或汉人|酒店或神父"（108.17）。双方不仅对立，还会"重新合并"（49.36），因此匈奴人也不只是汉人的对立面，也与汉人一起融合进主人公HCE的身份之中，所以当主人公"站在那儿|它们的，一个出自天然的男人|哑的|小便"（251.4）时，旁边响起了呼声"匈人|她百！匈人！"（251.3）。而且HCE的后代也同样有匈奴人的化身，"他的那些匈奴儿子们|太阳们，他的那些鞑靼女儿们|投掷者，如今很多在这里"（135.23-24）。这也可以解释裁缝柯西为什么是北魏人。北魏是鲜卑人与汉人结合的王朝，虽然而鲜卑与匈奴并不是一个民族，且乔伊斯未必能区分二者，但它们同属北方"胡人"，鲜卑又长期依附于匈奴。因此，在乔伊斯笔下，汉人与匈奴人这种既对立又统一的二元辩证关系是他勾勒的古代中国的主要历史框架。

近代中国的二元对立是中国与西方的矛盾，作为起因的鸦片战争在第一卷狐狸与葡萄的故事中就已出现，侵入者狐狸与"鸦片之地|在这之后"（153.26）直接相连。而面对这场侵略战争，乔伊斯站在了被侵略被殖民的中国一边，提出了"谁会把鸦片之路|亚璧古道连根拔起|复活|罂粟？"（448.17-18）这个问题。同时，中西矛盾这一二元对立又在普通民众层面被刻画为中国义和团团民与西方传教士之间的对立。例如，在"穿过拳民舵手用金楼梯爬上房子"（105.5-6）中，Boxer（拳击手）与Rising可以合并在一起解释为"Boxer Rising"，即"义和团运动"；而在"保克斯起来，考克斯欺来|义和团起义"（Boxerising and coxerusing 347.29）中，"义和团"之意更加明显。而此句之后不久便出现的"对他们的中国传教|排尿欢欢欢

呼"（106.19）表明，乔伊斯显然知道在中国的近代史上义和团与西方传教士之间发生的冲突。在小说主人公的两个儿子中，闪的中国化身是香港，与之对立又统一的儿子肖恩则希望"成为一位福建传教使团的导师"（468.3）。肖恩的西方传教士化身也反映出乔伊斯对西方殖民侵略者的批判：闪是创作者（执笔者），肖恩只是传递者（邮差），两人做作业时是闪在教肖恩，可在争夺女性的竞争中闪却被肖恩取代，就像英国向爱尔兰学习却最终占据了爱尔兰一样，殖民者向中国学习却最终侵占了中国的香港。

中国与爱尔兰的融合在这里也同样得到了呈现：当肖恩的变体琼恩喊出"我不在乎一个同乡会的坦慕尼协会成员|毫无价值的东西"（442.2）时，中国民间组织同乡会也与在美国的爱尔兰团体坦慕尼协会交融在一起，并与代表着殖民力量的肖恩相对。这就可以解释为什么主人公HCE也有一个"绰号|堵住某人的嘴叫'麻利拳民|提词者'"（49.30），也同样解释了为什么HCE也是孙中山，领导了兴中会的民间团体领袖——"为什么是这个汉口糟糠|手绢，这个二口货|第二声调，孙逸仙|儿子却是太阳，从哪里来？他让他的拳民们|屠夫|盒子|裤子的磕头变成丢脸|剥去面皮"[1]（89.36-90.2）；以及为什么与肖恩相对的闪这个跟父亲HCE最像的儿子会因为"孙逸仙|害羞的年轻之物在支那|真宗从横滨|夜梦来穿过帝汶海"（231.9-10）而高兴得大叫。因为这不但是中国民间团体的反侵略斗争，也是爱尔兰民间团体的反殖民斗争。

到了现代部分，中国史中主要的二元对立无疑是中国与日本："在他们全部时代|监护整个中国独家报道|南斯拉夫国民议会的绝望喧闹背后，对日本的愤怒|金奴加裂隙|集合的|攻击"（343.15）。由于《芬尼根》对时间进行了模糊化处理，很难确认这里的报道是指1931年的"九一八事变"，还是1935年的"华北事变"，或是1937年的"卢沟桥事变"。不过，具体的时间应该并不重要，因为乔伊斯关注的是战争背后的逻辑，这也是为什么他甚至把中国和日本的二元对立与拿破仑和惠灵顿的二元对立融合在一起，"尼破仑|日本跟惠灵陶|卫灵咒干上了"（81.33-34），这里乔伊斯

1　在乔伊斯看来，孙中山用来自西方的"二口货"民主取代了中国封建等级制度下的"磕头"传统。

利用双关融入了日本和中国道教的"卫灵咒"。拿破仑与惠灵顿是《芬尼根》中重要的二元对立组合，他们之间著名的滑铁卢战役是小说的重要内容，乔伊斯将抗日战争与影响了整个欧洲历史进程的滑铁卢战役并置，显然表明他认为抗日战争也将影响亚洲的历史进程。而且，乔伊斯似乎也预见了中国将打败日本，"中国的龙猛咬|金鱼草日本|土卫八"（583.18），"在吟诵了你的诗歌|坐在夜壶上之后，你知道中国|脊柱|钟声推翻日本|衬裙时会发生什么"（435.26–27）。当时，日本军队正在中国耀武扬威，汪精卫也因认定中国政府不可能驱逐日本军队而卖国求荣，但乔伊斯却有如此远见，只可惜他并没有解释自己是如何得出这个看法的。

小说的这种辩证法的历史解读看似粗糙，但却像20世纪初的原型理论一样，出自对人类行为具有基本模式的坚信。意大利学者艾柯（Umberto Eco）就认为，中世纪对永恒真理的坚信使得乔伊斯同样试图在《芬尼根的守灵夜》中放入超越时间的永恒真理，而不是对历史瞬间的如实记录。[1] 不过，乔伊斯同样超越了这种中世纪的永恒真理式叙述，他将深层的不变规律与前文所强调的杂糅的碎片同时放入一部作品当中，从而让书中的历史呈现出既有序又杂乱的矛盾模式。这种矛盾而非均质的结构模式正是对东方主义的本质主义话语的最有力的破坏。

四、对孔子的深度解读

不能否认的是，虽然乔伊斯的种种叙述策略都在颠覆着东方主义话语，但因为他的解读依然主要建立在西方各类流行资料对中国的老生常谈和刻板印象之上，故而碎片中携带的种族主义态度在《芬尼根》中仍然有迹可循。在如何对待通俗文本的脸谱化问题上，《芬尼根》中的孔子叙述具有一定的启发性。

主人公HCE作为文化奠基者的原型，他的中国化身无疑是孔子，因此孔子

1　Umberto Eco, *The Aesthetics of Chaosmos: The Middle Ages of James Joyce*, Massachusetts: Harvard University Press, 1989, p. 81.

在《芬尼根》中主要是代表儒家文化来补足全书的世界文化大融合的图景。孔子、儒家、中庸这些词都出现在了书中，如"这里|地狱|是孔子|避身之处|混乱|和论语|自然元素"（485.35），孔子的嫡孙"子思子思|采采蝇"（423.4），而在"那是为什么疯狂的亚洲人|《传道书》|牧师|会众|和罪犯部长|总理|鼓吹他的早晨"（242.11）这句话中，与"亚洲人"相联系的"犯罪部长"也暗指孔子，因为孔子做过鲁国的大司寇。研究者认为，乔伊斯对孔子惺惺相惜，是因为孔子在去世之前并未得到世人的充分承认，而乔伊斯自己正在创作的《芬尼根》也遭到了评论界的冷遇，这让乔伊斯"很可能对这位中国哲学家倍感亲切"[1]。但应该指出的是，孔子的学说似乎也同样得到了乔伊斯的认同，他在《芬尼根》中将儒家的中庸和礼仪观视为对抗商业社会的一剂良方，"忧心忡忡的商人可能没有许多时间|动力|去掌握孔子的中庸学说或者伯鱼|果实|的礼仪法典|上帝的真理"（108.11–12）。在这句话中，叙述者告诫商人们要培养耐心，学习孔子的学说或者孔子儿子孔鲤的礼仪规则。[2] 除此之外，孔子的教诲似乎也同样被乔伊斯用来批评爱尔兰的社会弊病，正如有研究者指出的那样，"孔子告诫不要在言语和行为上过度铺排，可能让他［乔伊斯］想起了他自己对爱尔兰人的评论：'我们爱尔兰人……一事无成，但我们是自古希腊以来最夸夸其谈的人'"[3]。

据罗兰·麦克休（Roland McHugh）考证，乔伊斯对孔子的认识主要来自卡尔·克劳于1937年出版的《孔子的故事》[4]。《芬尼根》是1939年发表的，书中取自

---

1 Cordell D. K. Yee, "Metemsinopsychosis: Confucius and Ireland in 'Finnegans Wake'," p. 120.

2 这里应该是乔伊斯的误会。孔鲤对孔子思想的传播并无贡献，乔伊斯想说的可能是曾被视为《中庸》作者的孔子之孙子思。

3 Cordell D. K. Yee, "Metemsinopsychosis: Confucius and Ireland in 'Finnegans Wake'," p. 122.

4 Roland McHugh, "Confucius in Notebook VI.B.45," in *A Wake Newsletter: Studies in James Joyce's Finnegans Wake*, 1979, No. 16, pp. 83–88. 虽然卡尔·克劳只是一个新闻人和商人，但他于1911年从美国来到上海，在中国待了37年，对中国抱有好感，并深深地融入了当时的中国社会生活。在20世纪30和40年代，克劳出版了包括《孔子的故事》在内的13部有关中国的书籍，其中《四万万消费者》（*400 Million Customers*）还获得美国国家图书奖。克劳在中国的深度体验多多少少帮助乔伊斯深化了对中国的了解。

《孔子的故事》的片断大多是1938年间乔伊斯补充修改时添加进去的，这足以证明乔伊斯希望用更具体的知识来打破西方关于中国的老生常谈。

《芬尼根》中直接取自《孔子的故事》的故事主要有三处，此外还有一些句子也被认为化自《孔子的故事》，例如"展示祖先|之前姐妹的 精心制作的上楼|在那里礼仪"（109.18-19）这句话就被认为化自《孔子的故事》中对孔子制定复杂礼仪的描述。乔伊斯在增补修订小说时直接化用的三个历史故事都出现在小说第一卷第三章中对主人公HCE的审判部分。它们正是《芬尼根》突破老生常谈，进入到中国历史细微处的明证。第一个故事涉及鲁国季平子和郈昭伯斗鸡的故事，"但是在这一点上，虽然他的鸡距|自以为是的铁刺开始或许让我们做好准备，但是我们几乎被尾尖涂有芥末的尖钉|芥末瓶呛在那里|圣帕特里克"（50.2-4），这是《史记·孔子世家》中记载的公元前517年鲁国季平子与郈昭伯斗鸡一事，其中季平子在他的鸡翅膀上涂了芥末，郈昭伯则在他的鸡的爪子上装了铁爪。第二个历史事件是周幽王烽火戏诸侯，"只要玛丽·诺辛|空虚的无物 可能胀破|刷子她那嗜酒的意外收获|公山羊仙女，狼烟烽火|太阳神火仪式|巴尔 巴尔佛就会照亮最多足迹"（52.19-21）。第三个故事出现在叙述者对主人公的身份发出询问之时，"秦、秦、秦、秦！这个祖先|四个父亲与孟、齐和公孙|明、清和孙氏[1]在平躺之原争夺|民众|畅销书作家两只桃子[2]的奖赏"（57.3-5），"两只桃子"指的是春秋时期齐相晏子的"二桃杀三士"的故事。这三个故事表明，乔伊斯不再只是将孔子视为一般社会传说中超越了时间和空间的圣人，他对孔子的解读开始被放入具体的历史背景当中。而这段作为背景的历史是一段充满纷争、淫欲和诡计的历史，在这种历史背景下，孔子对礼仪和克制的强调变得更加具有深意。如果对照当时爱尔兰政党内部的明争暗斗、帕内尔因欧希夫人而失掉政治支持、以凤凰公园谋杀案为代表的一系列政治谋杀等这些爱尔兰政治事件

1　孟、齐和公孙指孔子所在的鲁国的三个大姓。

2　两个桃子也指书中的两个女子。

的话，读者就更能理解乔伊斯在书中对孔子的礼仪观的反复强调。这样的联想并非牵强附会，且不说中国与爱尔兰在书中互为镜像，仅书中"代替 |鲁|爱爱尔兰人 |圣帕特里克"（in Loo of Pat 51.24）这句话就非常清楚地表明乔伊斯相信可以用孔子的学说来解决爱尔兰的问题。此句中的"Loo"在读音上接近"Lu"（鲁），在句法上则应该解读为"lieu"，该词既有"代替"之含义，也可以翻译为"场所"，乔伊斯有意把它写成孔子的故乡鲁国，无疑暗示应该把爱尔兰人放到孔子的学说中来进行评判和改造，希望建设"爱尔兰人的鲁国"。在西方文本中提倡向中国学习已经颠覆了黄祸论的滥调，而赋予孔子具体的历史时空更是突破了东方主义的概括化（generalized）话语模式。因此虽然程度有限，《孔子的故事》至少使乔伊斯对中国的认识有了超越流行偏见的可能性。

早在1872年前理雅各就已经把包括《论语》在内的很多中国儒家经典译成了英文，如果乔伊斯真想深入了解中国文化，他应该阅读这些儒学译本。虽然卡尔·克劳在序言中说《孔子的故事》取材于司马迁的《史记·孔子世家》和理雅各的《中国经典》，但显然乔伊斯对克劳讲述孔子的方式更感兴趣。不同于中国作品中被神圣化了的孔子，克劳呈现的是一个郁郁不得志、临终都觉得自己一生失败的凡人孔子。克劳对孔子满怀敬意，说自己"衷心希望在把他塑造为一个普通人的同时，也同样能呈现出他人格的真正伟大之处，他的伟大从各个方面都印证了他的国人几千年来对他的推崇"[1]。而他之所以把孔子塑造成普通人，是因为他相信"孔子其人与圣化了的孔夫子是两种不同的存在，必须从不同的视角来审视"[2]。克劳看待历史的视角可以说与乔伊斯不谋而合。艾尔曼就指出，乔伊斯的一大贡献就在于他不仅大胆地描写"肮脏"的事物，还通过把人类行为中"高雅"与"卑俗"的因素交织在一起，向人们指出高雅正来自卑俗，二者间并不存在不可逾越的界限。

1　Carl Crow, *Master Kung. The Story of Confucius*, New York: Tudor Publishing Co., 1937, p. 16.

2　Carl Crow, *Master Kung. The Story of Confucius*, p. 15.

乔伊斯在《芬尼根的守灵夜》中呈现的世界史是一部英雄与凡俗、伟大与卑劣共存的世界史，他的中国史也是在日常生活映照下的普通中国社会史。换句话说，《芬尼根》的世界史并非伟大思想的历史和伟大人物的历史，而是崇高与卑贱混杂的日常世界史，是一个消除了等级结构这一东方主义话语根基的历史。正因为克劳笔下的孔子是崇高与卑贱的混杂，这一形象才吸引了乔伊斯，也帮助他找到了一个跟崇高与卑贱交织的主人公HCE若合符节的中国化身。因此在小说中，孔子说什么与怎么说孔子都是全书世界史中不可或缺的重要因素。就这样，通过《芬尼根》的独特历史叙述方式，中国不再只是欧洲文艺作品里的几个面孔，也不只是东方主义话语中的刻板形象，乔伊斯在书中用东方主义话语的碎片搭建起了一部具有空间的中国历史与一个拥有历史的中国空间。更重要的是，在这个过程中，乔伊斯通过杂糅和挪用日常话语中的中国文化碎片，改变了这些碎片的"态度与能指"[1]，并用看似杂乱的碎片与对立统一的框架，组成了既有序又无序、既崇高又卑俗、既对立又统一、既宏大又琐碎的复杂而立体的世界史模式，从而打破了传统世界史叙述中暗含的等级秩序，为各民族和文化的融合指出了可能的途径。

（文章发表于《外国文学评论》2022年第4期。本文系作者在联盟2022年年度论坛上的发言）

参考文献

［美］段义孚：《恋地情结》，志丞等译，北京：商务印书馆，2018年。

郭军：《乔伊斯：叙述他的民族——从〈都柏林人〉到〈尤利西斯〉》，北京：外语教学与研究出版社，2010年。

万志英：《剑桥中国经济史：古代到19世纪》，崔传刚译，北京：中国人民大学出版社，2018年。

1　Edward Said, *Culture and Imperialism*, New York: Alfred A. Knopt, 1993, p. 52.

Carla Baricz, "The Finnegans Wake Diagram and Giordano Bruno," in *Joyce Studies Annual*, 2008, pp. 235–242.

Thomas Bartlett, ed., *The Cambridge History of Ireland, Volume IV: 1880 to the Present*, Cambridge: Cambridge University Press, 2018.

Joseph Campbell & Henry M. Robinson, *A Skeleton Key to Finnegans Wake*, New York: Harcout, Brace and Cop., 1944.

Carl Crow, *Foreign Devils in the Flowery Kingdom*, Hong Kong: Earnshaw Books, Ltd, 1940.

Carl Crow, *Master Kung. The Story of Confucius*, New York: Tudor Publishing Co., 1937.

Congrong Dai, "The Original Sin in 'Finnegans Wake'," in *Neohelicon*, 2012, Volume 39, pp. 475–483.

Robert H. Deming, ed., *James Joyce Critical Heritage*, London: Routledge, 1997.

Jacques Derrida, "Two Words for Joyce," in *Post-Structuralist Joyce: Essays from the French*, eds. Attridge, Derek and Daniel Ferrer, Cambridge: Cambridge University Press, 1984, pp. 145–159.

Umberto Eco, *The Aesthetics of Chaosmos: The Middle Ages of James Joyce*, Massachusetts: Harvard University Press, 1989.

Richard Ellmann, *James Joyce*, New York, Oxfordo: Oxford University Press, 1982.

Richard Ellmann, *The Consciousness of Joyce*, London: Faber & Faber, 1977.

Finn Fordham, "'Until Hanandhunigan's Extermination': Joyce, China and Racialised World Histories," in *Modernism and Race*, Len Platt, ed. Cambridge: Cambridge University Press, 2011, pp. 173–191.

Stuart Gilbert, ed., *Letters of James Joyce*, London: Faber and Faber, 1966.

Matthew J. C. Hodgart & Ruth Bauerle, *Joyce's Grand Operoar: Opera in Finnegans Wake*, Urbana: University of Illinois Press, 1997.

Patricia Hutchins, *James Joyce's World*, London: Methuen, 1957.

Sidney Jones, *The Geisha: A Story of a Tea House*, London: Hopewood & Crew, 1896.

James Joyce, *Finnegans Wake*, London: Faber and Faber, 1939.

James Joyce, *The Critical Writing of James Joyce*, London: Faber and Faber, 1959.

Vincent Joyce, *The Celestial Hand: A Sensational Story*, Sydney: J. C. MacCartie & Co. 1903.

Ronald J. Koch, "Giordano Bruno and 'Finnegans Wake': A New Look at Shaun's Objection to the 'Nolanus Theory'," in *James Joyce Quarterly*, 1972, Vol. 9, pp. 237–249.

Roland McHugh, "Confucius in Notebook VI.B.45," in *A Wake Newslitter: Studies in James Joyce's Finnegans Wake*, 1979, No. 16, pp. 83–88.

Emer Nolan, *James Joyce and Nationalism*, London & New York: Routledge, 1995.

Anthony Reid, "Chinese Trade and Economic Expansion in Southeast Asia in the Later Eighteenth and Early Nineteenth Centuries: An Overview," in *Water Frontier: Commerce and the Chinese in the Lower Mekong Region, 1750–1880*, Nola Cooke & Tana Li, eds. Lanham: Rowman & Littlefield Publishers, 2004, pp. 21–34.

Adam Roberts, *The History of Science Fiction*, London: Palgrave Macmillan, 2016.

Edward Said, *Orientalism*, London: Penguin Books, 2003.

Edward Said, *Culture and Imperialism*, New York: Alfred A. Knopt, 1993.

Ashley Thorpe, *Performing China on the London Stage: Chinese Opera and Global Power, 1759–2008*, London: Palgrave Macmillan, 2016.

Cordell D. K. Yee, "Metemsinopsychosis: Confucius and Ireland in 'Finnegans Wake'," in *Comparative Literature Studie*s, 1983, Vol. 20, pp. 115–124.

Why did Milton Land in China Earlier than Shakespeare?

Tianhu Hao*

It is widely believed that in the history of English literature, Shakespeare occupies the center of the canon, and that Milton is usually considered second to none but Shakespeare. Shakespeare and Milton had their national poet status established in eighteenth-century England. The two often come to the fore together in the East Asian early reception of English literature. For example, according to Japanese scholars, in Japan, Shakespeare's and Milton's names were first introduced to the country in 1841, when the Japanese translation was made of a Dutch translation of Lindley Murray's *English Grammar* (Seto 2017, 3, 50–51, 274, 332; Miyanishi 1975, 5, 165). In China in 1839–40 (at approximately the same time yet slightly earlier than in Japan), Lin Zexu 林则徐 (1785–1850), one of the first Chinese intellectuals to open their eyes to the world, had a book translated and redacted as *Accounts of Four Continents* 四洲志, based on Hugh Murray's recent compilation *The Encyclopædia of Geography*. It is a miscellaneous work focusing on the history and geography of various countries of the world, the first of its kind in the late Qing with the conscious purpose to learn about the "barbarians" (*yi*, 夷) in order to cope with them. In the volume on England, Shakespeare and Milton are listed together as representatives of English literature:

兰顿建大书馆一所，博物馆一所；渥斯贺建大书馆一所，内贮古

---

* Tianhu Hao (郝田虎) is Qiushi Distinguished Professor, Zhejiang University. He has written extensively on early modern English literature, manuscript study, and comparative literature.

书十二万五千卷；在感弥利赤建书馆一所。有沙士比阿、弥尔顿、士达萨、特弥顿四人，工诗文，富著述。俗贪而悍，尚奢嗜酒，惟技艺灵巧。

A great library and a museum were built in London; a great library at Oxford, where 125,000 volumes of ancient books are stored; and a library at Cambridge. The four men of letters, Shakespeare, Milton, Spenser, and Dryden, are gifted in poetry and prose and profuse in writing. The people are avaricious and ferocious, worshiping luxury and indulging in alcohol, only they are adroit in mechanical arts. (Quoted in Hao 2012, 89)[1]

Hugh Murray's English original enumerates five literary masters: Shakespeare, Milton, Spenser, Dryden, and Pope. The fifth (Pope) is dropped in Lin's redaction, presumably out of the Chinese preference for the numeral four. Milton is hidden, or rather, obliterated, in the series of Buddhist-charm-like Chinese characters. It is not groundless to doubt whether the hitherto unexercised Chinese eye could, without punctuation,[2] pick out the name 弥尔顿 at all. Shakespeare's situation might be better, for 沙士比阿 or the mistaken 沙士比, being the first on the list, may be taken as *the* representative of English literature. This passage, broadcast far and wide via Wei Yuan's immensely popular and influential *Illustrated Accounts of the Countries Overseas* 海国图志, which incorporates the unprinted *Accounts of Four Continents* in its entirety, is currently regarded as the earliest appearance of Shakespeare's name in Chinese. However, this is not so for Milton. Milton made his debut in China even earlier.

---

1 The English translations in this essay are mine.

2 Before the Vernacular Movement, Chinese books were usually unpunctuated, and children had to learn how to punctuate as part of their schooling. For a convenient reference, see Han Yu's famous essay "On Teachers."

For his debut in China, Milton is indebted to Western Christian missionaries, who wrote in English and in Chinese concerning the epic poet. *The Chinese Repository* 中 国 丛 报, founded by American missionary Elijah Coleman Bridgman (1801–1861) in Canton in May 1832, is the first English journal that introduced China to the Western reader. In the November 1832 issue of *The Chinese Repository,* we read:

John Milton, the immortal poet. — "There are no songs comparable to the Songs of Zion, no orations equal to those of the Prophets, and no politics like those which the Scriptures teach." (Anon. 1832, 272–273)

Here, Milton is portrayed as a sacred immortal poet who highly praised the Holy Bible. The purpose of the quote is not to enhance the greatness of Milton as a poet, but to use Milton's greatness to strike home the necessity of printing the Bible in China, and thereby broadcasting the Word of Life. Milton's authority is exploited, along with others, including Bacon, Locke, and Sir William Jones. The sentence of three (the holy three) parallel parts is placed in quotation marks and presented as Milton's words. The thought contained is unmistakably Miltonic, yet not the wording. Actually, the sentence is a distillation of Milton's poetic lines. While, in the current schooled tradition, placing words around quotation marks signifies "that we have someone's exact written or spoken words and excludes the possibility that it might merely be a paraphrase, surmise or reinterpretation," in the early usage of quotation marks, what is placed in between could be a paraphrase as well as direct speech, for "what counts as 'quotation' and how it is treated and marked varies according to viewpoint, ideology, setting and interpretation" and people's practice across time, situation, and language is simply "heterogeneous" (Finnegan 2011, 102, 107).[1] The closest spot in Milton's oeuvre occurs in Book 4 of *Paradise Regained*, when the

---

1   For a later example of the paraphrase usage, see W. A. P. Martin, *A Cycle of Cathay*, 395, where the Empress's words cited in quotation marks are actually a summary of her edict.

Son eloquently refutes Satan against classical, pagan learning (lines 343–364) (Kerrigan, Rumrich, and Fallon 2012).[1] True wisdom is to be found only in God's words, while what those philosophers teach, Plato or Aristotle, cannot but be misleading, "Ignorant of themselves, of God much more." (*PR*, 4.310) Lacking "A spirit and judgment equal or superior," (4.324) the Greek philosophers are dismissed by the Son as mere "Children gathering pebbles on the shore." (4.330) The above citation was already current before the essay was published in 1832, e.g., in John B. Seely's *The Wonders of Elora* (1824), also ascribed to Milton (Seely 1824, 30), and the frequent appearance and sustained recycling of the quote in the nineteenth and twentieth centuries suggests the cultural authority the name of Milton carries, and the great importance missionaries and anthologists attach to the supposedly Miltonic aphorism. Therefore, the missionary appropriation of Milton occurred at the very moment of the poet's first introduction to China, when the missionary journal made what I call a "commonplace reading" of Milton (Hao 2014, Ch. 4). It is reasonable to attribute Milton's priority over Shakespeare partly to the biblical nature of Milton's poems, for the Bible contains the divine words and is the center of the missionaries' attention. *The Eastern Western Monthly Magazine* 东西洋考每月统记传, founded by German missionary Karl Friedrich August Gützlaff (1803–1851) in Canton in August 1833, is the first Chinese journal in China to introduce the West to the Chinese reader. An article entitled "Poetry" in the *Eastern Western Monthly Magazine* (1837) juxtaposes Homer and Milton:

诸诗之魁，为希腊国和马之诗词，并大英米里屯之诗。希腊诗翁推论列国，围征服城也，细讲性情之正曲、哀乐之原由，所以人事决下天道，和马可谓诗中之魁。此诗翁兴于周朝穆王年间。……夫米里屯当顺治年间兴其诗，说始祖之驻乐园，因罪而逐也。自诗者见其沉雄俊逸之樂，莫不景仰也。其词气壮，笔力绝不类，诗流转圜，美如弹丸。读之果可以使人兴

---

1 Thanks go to Professor John Rumrich for reminding me of the place (email correspondence, July 6 2019).

起其为善之心乎，果可以使人兴观其甚美矣，可以得其要妙也。其义奥而深于道者，其意度宏也。

The crown of poetry are works by Homer in Greece and Milton in England. The Greek master narrates how various states besiege and conquer a city and elaborates on the straightness and crookedness of emotions and temperaments, the causes and occasions of pleasures and sorrows. Thus human affairs harmonize with heavenly ways. Homer can be called the crown of poets, who flourished during the reign of King Mu of the Zhou Dynasty.... Milton published his poem in the reign of Shunzhi, telling the story of our first ancestors staying in the Garden of Bliss and being exiled for sin. From the poem we can see the poet's profound and powerful, graceful and superior spirit, to be adored by everyone. His style is imposing and majestic, his pen supreme and extraordinary, his lines flowing like the revolution of a round object, as beautiful as a ball [i.e. easy and smooth]. Its reading might arouse a kind heart into action, lead to the contemplation of the utmost beauty, and usher in the comprehension of significant and subtle points. Its meaning is deep and philosophical, its intention grand and magnanimous. (Quoted in Hao 2012, 86)

Both of these articles appear earlier than Imperial Commissioner Lin Zexu's compilation. In 1793, the Earl of Macartney (1737–1806), England's first envoy to China who met with the Qianlong Emperor, wondered in his diary over the Chinese crowd of "goodly creatures" as a "brave new world / That has such people in it" (Barrow 1807, 184), and his sentiment was just like Miranda's. Macartney came to China with his familiar knowledge of the Bard, as if with the ghost of Shakespeare, yet we cannot say that the Earl brought Shakespeare to China in 1793. We should discount English Sinologist Thomas Manning's (1772–1840) repeated requests in his personal letters to his friend Charles Lamb (1775–1834) for a copy of *Tales from Shakespeare* (1807) at the beginning of the nineteenth century (Dai 2019, 83–

97), for the Chinese people around Manning would have had no chance to read the English letters and whether the copy was sent to China or not is uncertain. Therefore, as far as we know, Milton landed in China (that is, his name or his work, not his physical body) earlier than Shakespeare. Milton was also translated into Chinese earlier than Shakespeare. Why so? Is it purely accidental?

To answer this question, we need to analyze closely the two Milton passages cited above. Both applaud Milton as a leading Christian poet, a poet outstanding enough to stand, beside Homer, for Western literature. Two observations are to be made here: first, the missionaries valued Milton as a religious poet; second, out of an intense anxiety for the miscalled barbarity, they are much concerned to convince the Chinese intellectuals that the West, like China, also has poetry. In the historical context of nineteenth-century colonialism and imperialism, the encounters between East and West show a salient tendency to strong mistrust and mutual contempt. The romance of Marco Polo (1254–1324) and the harmony of Matteo Ricci (1552–1610) had long gone. The Sino-Western interaction became hard as iron, cold as stone. The Westerners would view the worn empire of the Middle Kingdom as backward in technology, economy, and social development, therefore granting themselves the pompous *mission civilisatrice* towards the Far East; in the eyes of the Chinese, however, the Westerners were "foreign devils," ferocious and barbarous. Keenly aware of the Chinese cultural pride in their nation's long and glorious literary tradition and the corresponding contempt for the barbarity of Western countries, the Western missionaries in China were eager to defend their literate status and literary heritage. Without a positive image among the Chinese intelligentsia, the missionaries' Christian civilizing mission could hardly be accomplished. To achieve their purpose, the missionary author took particular care to adopt in the Chinese passage traditional critical jargons to cater to the tastes of feudal Chinese intellectuals, the intended readership of the missionary journal. The specific word choices indicate that the apt remarks on Milton's *Paradise Lost* are not only heavily embedded in the tradition of Western literary criticism, but the entire phraseology of the comments is borrowed from the body of classical Chinese literary criticism. The ready help provided by their Chinese assistants was inducible to the composition of such a splendid passage, which summarizes the plot of the poem, describes the poet's grand style, and commends the moral, aesthetic, and philosophical values of Milton's masterpiece. As producers of cross-cultural knowledge, the missionaries purposefully selected the medium of classical Chinese criticism and properly applied it to a Western poet.

While it would be difficult for the English journal to find any Chinese audience, the missionary accommodationism in the Chinese essay turned out to be a successful strategy. Many Chinese intellectuals at the time, such as Wei Yuan魏源 (1794–1857), Liang Tingnan 梁廷枏 (1796–1861), and Xu Jiyu徐继畬 (1795–1873), read the *Eastern Western Monthly Magazine* regularly and were influenced by it, for the journal opened a window for them to learn about the West. Textual evidence shows that Liang Tingnan was an ardent reader of the journal and the article cited above.[1]

The religious and moral values of Milton also make him translated into Chinese nearly half a century earlier than Shakespeare. In 1854, a wonderful verse translation of Milton's famous sonnet on his blindness was published in the missionary journal *Chinese Serial* 遐 迩 贯 珍 (Hao 2012, 92). This exquisite rendition, in the antique style of the *Book of Songs* with four-character rhyming lines, is surprisingly high in quality. Its authorship is uncertain, though. Since it is unsigned in the journal, Chinese and Japanese scholars debate the identity of its translator(s) fiercely. At least three conjectures have been suggested by Chinese and Japanese scholars: James Legge 理雅各 (1814–1897), Walter Henry Medhurst 麦都思 (1796–1857), and Joseph Edkins in collaboration with Jiang Dunfu. None of these is conclusive, and other possibilities still exist. Nevertheless, I am inclined to concur with Shen Guowei that the capable understanding must have come from a Westerner, and the stylistic expression was the work of a Chinese scholar. It is more likely than not that a missionary and a Chinese produced the marvelous translation collaboratively, though we are uncertain about their identity (C. Huang 2006, 51; Hao 2012, 93). In 1855, part

---

1 For a more detailed discussion of the Chinese passage, see Hao, 2012, 87–88.

of *Paradise Lost* (5.153–208) was translated in another missionary journal the *Chinese Western Almanac* 中西通书 edited by Joseph Edkins艾约瑟 (1823–1905) (Edkins 1855, 27–31).

Here a key issue emerges in the early Chinese translation of English poets, that is, the issue of the translator. In an age before the advent of machine translation, translations must be done by people. Evidence indicates that in the nineteenth century, both the Westerners and the Chinese possessed a clear interest in Shakespeare and Milton. But were there suitable translators? Who would be the willing and capable translator of the English literary masters? On the Chinese side, we know that Yung Wing (1828–1912) and Ku Hung-Ming (1857–1928) were early readers of Shakespeare and / or Milton. Yung Wing was the first Chinese that graduated from a first-class American college (Yale, 1854), while Ku Hung-Ming studied for an MA degree at the University of Edinburgh in 1873–1877. Ku could even recite Milton and Shakespeare (Hao 2005, 93–100). Unfortunately, neither Yung nor Ku was much interested in translating English literary works. Toward the end of the nineteenth century, Yan Fu (1854–1921)—who also studied in England—translated English books extensively into Chinese, which triggered a decisive intellectual revolution in the Chinese mind. It simply took time for the Chinese scholars to learn the foreign language well and for them to realize the significance of translating Western books. After a long preparation in the previous century, due to historical contingency, a translation boom arose in China in the early twentieth century. My recent research has uncovered Chinese translations of two Shakespearean dramatic excerpts in 1903, from *Hamlet* and *Twelfth Night* respectively (Hao 2019). Compared with what is already known among researchers, these two small fragments, done by Chinese translators, are noticeable in their traceable source in Shakespeare's original texts, rather than in the Lambs' adaptation of *Tales from Shakespeare*, which was rendered into classical Chinese as *Xiewai Qitan* 澥外奇谭 (1903) and *Yinbian Yanyu* 吟边燕语 (1904), the latter being most influential. The Japanese readers translated Shakespeare and Milton into Japanese much earlier than the Chinese. I think the rationale for the discrepancy lies not so much in the different levels of linguistic capability, but in the disparate attitudes toward Western culture: in the Meiji Restoration, the Japanese decided to "leave Asia and join Europe," embracing the West wholeheartedly as a welcome teacher; in contrast, the Chinese were reluctant to learn from the West, they must be forced to. As a result, in the nineteenth century, the worthy name of Shakespeare circulated in China as a symbol of Englishness, but no Chinese version of Shakespeare—either in translation or in performance—had ever appeared in the period, as far as we know (A. C. Y. Huang 2009, 18).

The missionaries possessed an excellent command of English, and they were interested in translating English literature. With the aid of Chinese assistants, they were able to do the job very well, as the 1854 Milton translation testifies. Actually, some missionaries were versed in Chinese as well as in English, with American Presbyterian missionary W. A. P. Martin (1827–1916) being one of them. In September 1888, *The North-China Daily News* and *The North-China Herald* reported, in English, that an imperial mandate instructed that Shakespeare be rendered into Chinese for the benefit of the young Manchu princes, and the writer speculates the best candidate for the task be Dr. W. A. P. Martin, President of the Tung-wên-kuan.[1] Obviously, the project was not carried out; in fact, the writer ridiculed the edict as a rumor. It turned out that Martin translated into Chinese, among other works, Henry Wheaton's (1785–1848) *Elements of International Law* and into English *Chinese Legends and Lyrics*, though not Shakespeare. The Bard was not on Martin's list of priorities. It seems that compared with the language qualification, the desire and motivation for translation was the more decisive factor in determining which authors were translated. The Christian missionaries cherished religious poet Milton's educational value; they were not so interested in literature *per se* or the entertainment value of Shakespeare or Shakespearean dramas.

The early Chinese reception of Milton was mixed, and the Chinese-educated audience

---

1 *The North-China Daily News,* 13 September 1888; *The North-China Herald,* 15 September 1888, "Shakespeare in Chinese."

seemed more captivated by the more secular and more spectacular Shakespeare. While some readers, such as Liang Tingnan, accepted Milton's *Paradise Lost* positively, and many people adored Milton's great accomplishments as a blind poet, others, such as Yang Xiangji 杨象济 (1825–1878), Liu Dashen 刘大绅, and Wu Quancui 伍铨萃 opposed the "foreign religion" almost instinctively. Even Liang Tingnan expresses the wishful thinking that someday the West will be assimilated by the Confucian "holy way." In his essay, Yang attacks the missionaries' religious propaganda with their own scientific knowledge by positing the contradiction between the two (Hao 2012, 88). Similarly, in their *The Biological Kingdom: Animals* (1908) Liu Dashen and Wu Quancui critique Milton's Bible-derived theory of the creation of the world in six days as outdated and untrustworthy; instead, the theory of evolution advocated by French naturalists Buffon (1707–1788) and Lamarck (1744–1829) are introduced to supplant Milton's popular but unscientific thinking (Hao 2018, 42–43). More sympathetic with the newly imported science, the Confucian scholars harbored an attitude of antipathy, resistance, and criticism toward the alien Christianity, which the missionaries overtly or covertly promoted. Milton the poet was favored by the missionaries for his religious subject matter, yet was challenged by the Confucians for the same thing. Among religion, poetry, science, and morality, religion met with the greatest resistance in its reception; the 1854 translation was effective for its sugar-coating of the divine God in poetry and morality. Later, Liang Qichao 梁启超 (1873–1929) held a high opinion of Milton for his having "supported Cromwell in the grand cause of the English revolution" and for his long narrative poems, which are rare in the Chinese literary tradition (Hao 2012, 95–96). Liang Qichao also lacked interest in religion, but he added politics to literature. For him, the political function of literature was of paramount importance and immediate urgency. Among English literary figures, Liang Qichao picked out Milton and Byron because they were both outstanding poets with lasting works and men of action involved in the fight for liberty. Lu Xun 鲁迅 (1881–1936) and his followers admired Satan's undaunted spirit, and their perverse but creative misreading of Milton's Satan as a fighter for freedom, and the benefactor of mankind, grew out of the national crisis China was placed in. For Liang Qichao and Lu Xun, literature is not pure belles lettres, but a political instrument to be made use of. Therefore, Milton, though adorable as a great poet, was sometimes resisted and often appropriated.

Shakespeare was more enjoyed as a storyteller and a dramatist. Unlike Milton, Shakespeare boasted the advantage of the stage. English publications in Shanghai, such as *The North-China Daily News* and *The Chinese Recorder*, actively promoted Shakespeare. The former contributed significantly to the establishment of the image of the Bard as a literary master by recording many readings, recitals, and stage performances of Shakespeare, as well as providing news reports concerning him, and the latter diffused various knowledge via and on Shakespeare: not only religious, but also literary and secular. On or about April 18, 1891, a theatrical company of 19 coming from Hong Kong, and led by Mr. Miln and Miss Louise Jordan, would open at the Lyceum Theatre in Shanghai with *Hamlet* (Mr. Miln as Hamlet and Miss Jordan as Ophelia); prior to that, a certain Mr. Fairclough had been in Shanghai acting Shakespeare.[1] On Wednesday, January 28, 1903, *The North-China Daily News* reported that the performances by the Janet Waldorf Company of *Twelfth Night* on the previous two nights in the Lyceum Theatre were not very successful, "if one is to take as a criterion of the local taste in drama the audiences present," for the stagings only drew a "well-nigh empty dress circle, and a somewhat unenthusiastic pit and stalls." However, the Company would continue with the performance of the romantic tragedy *Romeo and Juliet* on Wednesday night at the same theatre, starring Miss Janet Waldorf as the luckless heroine and Mr. Norval McGregor as Romeo.[2] In February 1904, Mrs. Hannibal Williams's "lively and dramatic" recital of *Much Ado about Nothing* at the Lyceum Theatre successfully attracted a large audience.[3] These performances and recitals were in English, yet in the same period, Shakespeare was also performed by

---

1   *The North-China Daily News*, March 26, 1891.

2   *The North-China Daily News*, January 28, 1903, two brief reports.

3   *The North-China Daily News*, February 11, 1904.

Chinese students in English, and a Chinese audience, present at the Lyceum Theatre, was possible. According to Zhong Xinzhi, the students of St. John's College / University performed in English scenes of Shakespearean plays regularly on the occasion of summer commencements:

July 18, 1896, from *The Merchant of Venice*

July 19, 1899, from *Julius Caesar*

July 19, 1901, from *Hamlet*

July 18, 1902, from *The Merchant of Venice*

July 21, 1904, from *Henry VIII*

July 6, 1906, from *As You Like It*

July 5, 1907, from *The Taming of the Shrew*

July 9, 1908, from *A Midsummer Night's Dream* (Zhong 2010, 18–26)

Comedies, tragedies, and histories were all acted, and the comedy of *The Merchant of Venice* was especially popular. The English media in Shanghai, such as *North China Herald* and *Shanghai Times*, highly praised these campus performances, and some pictures of the performances are still extant. Such campus events were well attended by society at large:

With the backing of an increasingly wealthy and influential body of alumni, this event received extensive coverage in the social pages of the Shanghai papers as well. Friends and families of students and alumni eagerly attended the performances, arriving in private chauffeured vehicles and dressed in fashionable clothing, each paying several *yuan* for admission and donation. (Yeh 1990, 73)

As a missionary university, St. John's offered a high level of English teaching and Shakespeare was eagerly sought after on campus. For example, in the first half of 1905, advocated by President Francis Lister Hawks Pott (1864–1947), the Shakespeare Club was founded at St. John's, consisting mainly of student members, who met every Saturday evening for the reading of Shakespeare's plays, the first play read being *Twelfth Night* (Zhong 2010, 20). With their fine command of English, the alumni of St. John's played a significant role in the spread of Shakespeare in early-twentieth-century China. For instance, Lin Shu's 林纾 collaborator Wei Yi 魏易 (1880–1933) in translating *Tales from Shakespeare* studied at the preparatory section of St. John's (1896–1900), and Wei Yi might have experienced the campus performance of Shakespeare (Zhong 2010, 25); among the Shakespeare books brought out by the Commercial Press in 1910–1911 (published in English, annotated in Chinese, advertised in *Shen-pao* and elsewhere many times)—*The Merchant of Venice*, *Macbeth*, and *Tales from Shakespeare*—a St. John's alum (or faculty member?) Sung Tsoo-zung annotated *Macbeth*. Not only St. John's male students took part in *huaju* productions of Shakespeare; students from girls' schools in Shanghai also performed Shakespeare. *The Chinese Recorder* (No. 10, 1918) publishes four pictures of the girl students of Eliza Yates Baptist School playing *As You Like It* (Shen 2011, 41–42). Shanghai Eastern Girls' High School's performance of *The Woman Lawyer* at the beginning of 1913, based on Bao Tianxiao's adaptation of *The Merchant of Venice*, is considered the first Chinese-language performance of Shakespeare (A. C. Y. Huang 2009, 241). Actually, Shanghai Eastern Girls' High School's students had already performed Shakespeare in May 1907, though we do not know whether this performance was in English or in Chinese.[1] Hong Kong was exposed to Shakespeare earlier than Shanghai. In 1867, Hong Kong Amateur Dramatic Club staged Francis Talfourd's *Shylock, or the Merchant of Venice Preserved*, revived in 1871 (A. C. Y. Huang 2009, 240). Besides Hong Kong, Shanghai is another important center for Shakespeare-related activities in late Qing and early Republican China. More than the foreign performances and recitals of the Bard in the Lyceum Theatre, the student amateurism in *huaju* productions of Shakespeare cultivated the first group of Chinese actors and audience, along with a local taste for *huaju*. Most of these student activities occurred

---

1 See the program in *Shen-pao*, May 2, 1907, No. 12222.

before 1907, the widely accepted year of the introduction of Western drama into China. If we still pinpoint 1907 as the starting date of Chinese *huaju* (which is controversial), then the student amateurism in Shanghai constitutes the pre-history of the birth of *huaju*, and Shakespeare's central role in this pre-history ought to be acknowledged and duly assessed, a task yet to be done systematically. In other words, Shakespeare's advantage of the stage makes him catch up with Milton quickly, and even outstrip his rival, in their respective visibility in China at the turn of the century.

This truth also applies to the domain of translation. Before 1900, Milton defeated Shakespeare with the translation of his famous sonnet, and Shakespeare was curiously silent; before 1920, many more translations of Shakespeare were published than of Milton. Shakespeare has his Lambs, and the Lambs have their Lin Shu, for popularization and wide circulation, whereas the difficulty of Milton deters him from easy cultural transfer and linguistic transplant. In the first two decades of the twentieth century, only a couple of scattered sentences of Milton were available in Chinese (Hao 2018, 45), yet Shakespeare's beloved tales were retold again and again, and Shakespeare's plays also began to be translated in dramatic form, e.g., *A Midsummer Night's Dream* (Yu 1911, 20–25).

Milton's attitude toward drama and theatre is a complex issue. When he was young, Milton loved watching plays, both Greek tragedies and modern dramas such as Ben Jonson and Shakespeare (*L'Allegro* and *Il Penseroso*). His first printed poem pays tribute to Shakespeare. Milton wrote the commissioned masque *Comus* and planned to compose *Adam Unparadis'd* in dramatic form. As the Puritan revolution developed and the theatre was closed (1642–1660), however, Milton's deep involvement in the anti-Royalist government and Charles II's ardent fervor for the theatre after the Restoration led to the epic poet's rejection of drama, especially the stage performance. Milton's Greek tragedy *Samson Agonistes*, published in his late years, is intended by the author as a closet drama rather than for staging. Moreover, the naked Adam and Eve in Eden are not suitable for stage or film productions. If Shakespeare is mainly a dramatic poet, then Milton's major accomplishments lie in epic poetry. Milton's achievements are not to be downplayed, yet

Shakespeare's advantage of the stage endows him with unparalleled impact in English literary history.

Why, then, did Milton land in China earlier than Shakespeare? A particular reason is that Milton's most successful character, Satan, lands in China even before Adam and Eve's exile from Eden (*Paradise Lost*, 3.437–39). As a latecomer, Milton knew China better than Shakespeare. Like Switzerland,[1] the Middle Kingdom received the epic poet earlier than the Bard largely for religious reasons.

(Acknowledgement: Supported by the National Humanities and Social Sciences Foundation, China (authorization: 19ZDA298). A condensed version of this article has been published in *Comparative Literature Studies*, 57.3 (2020): 497–508; reprinted here with permission by Penn State University Press. This article is a revision of the author's speech at the 2021 UKCHA Annual Forum.)

References

Anonymous. 1832. "Communications: Labors of the Missionaries." *Chinese Repository* 1(7): 268–273.

Barrow, J. 1807. *Some Account of the Public Life, and a Selection from the Unpublished Writings, of the Earl of Macartney*, Vol. II, *Journal of an Embassy from the King of Great Britain to the Emperor of China*. London.

Dai, Y. 2019. "'I Should Like to Have My Name Talked Of In China': Charles Lamb, China, and Shakespeare." *Multicultural Shakespeare* 20: 83–97.

Edkins, J., ed. 1855. "On *Paradise Lost*." *Chinese Western Almanac*. Shanghai: Mohai Shuguan, 27–31.

Finnegan, R. 2011. *Why Do We Quote?: The Culture and History of Quotation*. Cambridge, UK: Open Book Publishers.

Hao, T. 2005. "Ku Hung-Ming, an Early Chinese Reader of Milton." *Milton Quarterly* 39(2): 93–100.

——. 2012. "Milton in Late-Qing China (1837–1911) and the Production of Cross-Cultural Knowledge." *Milton Quarterly* 46(2): 86–105.

——. 2014. *Hesperides, or the Muses' Garden: A Study of an Early Modern English Commonplace Book*. Beijing: Peking University Press.

1 For early Shakespeare in Switzerland, see Balz Engler (email correspondence, 29 January 2020).

——. 2018. "John Milton and the Theory of Evolution, Self-Help, and the Formation of Modern Education in Early-20th-Century China." *Fudan Forum on Foreign Languages and Literature*, Vol. autumn: 42–48.

——. 2019. "Early Chinese Translations of Shakespeare," manuscript.

Huang, A. C. Y. 2009. *Chinese Shakespeares: Two Centuries of Cultural Exchange*. New York: Columbia University Press.

Huang, C. 2006. "See and Tell of Things 'Foreign' to 'Native' Sights: Chinese Translations / Rewritings of Milton and *Paradise Lost* in the Early Twentieth Century." Ph.D. diss., Taiwan University.

Kerrigan, W., Rumrich, J. and Fallon, S. M., eds. 2012. *Paradise Regained, Samson Agonistes, and the Complete Shorter Poems*. New York: Modern Library.

Martin, W. A. P. 1900. *A Cycle of Cathay*, 3rd ed. New York: Fleming H. Revell Company.

Miyanishi, M. 1975. *Milton in Japan, 1871–1971*. Tokyo: Kinseido.

The North-China Daily News. September 13, 1888.

The North-China Daily News. March 26, 1891.

The North-China Daily News. January 28, 1903, two brief reports.

The North-China Daily News. February 11, 1904.

The North-China Herald. September 15, 1888, "Shakespeare in Chinese."

Seely, J. B. 1824. *The Wonders of Elora; Or, The Narrative of a Journey to the Temples and Dwellings ... at Elora, in the East Indies ...* London.

Seto, H. 瀬户宏, 2017. *A History of Chinese Reception of Shakespeare*. Translated by Chen, L. Guangzhou: Guangdong People's Press.

Shen, H. 沈弘, 2011. "On the Origin and Early Development of Modern Drama in China." *Studies in Culture & Art* (4): 33–44.

Shen-pao. May 2, 1907, No. 12222, program.

Yeh, W. 1990. *The Alienated Academy: Culture and Politics in Republican China, 1919–1937*. Cambridge: Harvard University Press.

Yu, J. 俞惊坤, trans., 1911. *Good Night's Love Dream* 良宵情梦. *The Alumni Magazine of No. 1 Teachers' School of Zhejiang Province* (3): 20–25.

Zhong, X. 钟欣志, 2010. "The Campus Performance at St. John's University in Late Qing and its Significance for Modern Chinese Theater." *Theatre Arts* (3): 18–26.

中国传统礼制在近代的转变

杨　华　杨圣桑[*]

中国文明话语中的"礼"，可以译作Ritual、Rite、Ceremony、Etiqutte、Manner、Politeness、Custom、Courtesy、Propriety等等，但都不够准确，没有完整表达出"礼"的内涵。

以下，本文从日常生活的仪式、人际交往的原则、国家政治的法律这三个方面，来讨论中国传统之礼在近代社会的遭际，并试图从"礼"这个角度，阐释最近二百年来中国与西方外来文化之间的冲突和融合。

一、日常生活的仪式

近代中国，遭遇了"数千年来未有之变局"[1]，"西方化"是其中一个重要现象。从"文化"的四个层面——器用、行为、制度、思想——来观察，几乎每个层面，都带有西方文化的烙印。

在器用层面，西洋物品大量涌入，近代中国人的衣食住行都有其烙印。凡是来自西方的物品，都被冠以"洋"字。早在道光年间，当时人就有此类描述，凡是贵重的好物品，都称为"洋货"。陈作霖《炳烛里谈》谓：

---

* 杨华：武汉大学教授、教育部基地中国传统文化研究中心主任。研究领域为中国古代史（先秦秦汉史）、中国文化史、中国古代礼制研究。杨圣桑：荷兰格罗宁根大学硕士研究生。
1 赵尔巽等：《清史稿》卷411《李鸿章传》，北京：中华书局，1977年，第12017页。

> 道光年间，凡物之极贵重者，皆谓之洋。重楼曰洋楼，彩轿曰洋轿，衣有洋绉，帽有洋筒，挂灯名为洋灯，火锅名为洋锅。细而至于酱油之佳者，亦呼洋秋油；颜料之鲜明者，亦呼洋红、洋绿。大江南北，莫不以洋为尚。洋乎洋乎，岂非今日之先兆乎？[1]

近代以来，随着中国市场的被迫打开和民族工业的衰败，这种现象更加普遍了。洋车、洋布、洋油、洋火、洋场、洋行、洋钱、洋铁、洋装、洋瓷等等，类似名称不胜枚举。"（嘉道之际）中国，原已为洋人洋货倾销之市场矣"，"同光之际，洋货更尔充斥"。[2]

在行为方式层面亦复如此。由于传教士、西方商人和留西学生的引领，以及租界生活的展示，中国人看到了另一种全新的生活方式，并开始学习效慕。中国人用"文明"和"非文明"，即高级和低级，来区别西方生活方式和自己本土的生活方式。称放足为"文明脚"，称话剧为"文明戏"，称西式手杖为"文明棍"（实际上中国古代就有"鸠杖"）。晚清出现了一大批"文明常识"的普及工作。

在日常生活的细节方面，也变化多多。例如，中国人的相见礼在《仪礼·士相见》中专有记载，历代见面问候采取作揖和跪拜的方式。但是，来自西方的握手礼和鞠躬礼逐渐成为主流。众所周知，西方使节与中国皇帝的外交仪式，就是否应该跪拜而产生巨大争议。[3] 在民间，问候方式的变化也曾引起国人巨大争论。反对的声浪很高，例如康有为曾说："中国人不敬天，亦不敬教主，不知其留此膝以傲慢何为也？"[4] 叶德辉也曾说过："此言竟欲易中国拜跪之礼为西人鞠躬，居

---

1 陈作霖：《炳烛里谈·洋字先兆》，《金陵琐志九种》，南京：南京出版社，2008年，第307页。

2 陈登原：《国史旧闻》第4册《洋货》，北京：中华书局，2000年，第780—784页。

3 ［法］阿兰·佩雷菲特：《停滞的帝国：两个世界的撞击》，王国卿等译，北京：生活·读书·新知三联书店，1993年。王开玺：《清代外交礼仪的交涉与论争》，北京：人民出版社，2009年，第191—206、608—615页。

4 康有为：《以孔教为国教配天议》，汤志钧编：《康有为政论集》下册，北京：中华书局，1981年，第849页。

然请天子降尊，悖妄已极。"[1]但终究抵挡不住时代潮流，很多人认为，跪拜与奴性相联系，非废除不可。《箴奴隶》文说：

> 叩头也，请安也，长跪也，匍匐也，唱诺也，恳恩也，极人世可怜之状，不可告人之事，而吾各阶级社会中，居然行之大廷，视同典礼。[2]

废除跪拜、叩头，代之以点头、脱帽鞠躬、免冠、握手等西式礼仪，认为这是进化的表现。

对跪拜礼的废除，始于两方面的外因。一是欧美日各国与中国进行外交使聘时，强烈要求废除跪拜礼仪而改为鞠躬；二是传教士来到中国后，对西方礼仪的大力推广，他们带来欧美礼仪的书籍，诸如《西礼需知》《戎礼需知》之类。梁启超在1897年任教时务学堂之时，曾将废除跪拜与变法图强、维新救国联系起来："今日欲求变法，必自天子降尊始，不先变去拜跪之礼，上下仍习虚文，所以动为外国讪笑也。"[3]

到20世纪初，自两广总督岑春煊首倡，江苏、江西、湖北、河南等省政府纷纷下令，废除"屈膝请安俗仪"，下属见上级改为一揖，初见三揖。1912年2月12日，袁世凯内阁在养心殿向隆裕太后和宣统皇帝举行朝见仪式，首次摒弃跪拜礼，而改为三鞠躬礼。1912年3月，南京临时政府谕令各地，祭孔也可要用三鞠躬，不跪拜，着便服。[4]辛亥革命后，民国元年（1912）8月17日，北洋政府以大总统名义发布的《中华民国礼制》：

1 中国史学会编：《中国近代史资料丛刊》第二册《戊戌变法》，上海：神州国光社，1953年，第548页。
2 张枬、王忍之编：《辛亥革命前十年间时论选集》第一卷下册，北京：生活·读书·新知三联书店，1977年，第704—705页。
3 中国史学会编：《中国近代史资料丛刊》第二册《戊戌变法》，第548页。
4 王开玺：《试论中国跪拜礼仪的废除》，《史学集刊》2004年第2期，第18—21页。

第一章　男子礼

第一条，男子礼为脱帽鞠躬。

第二条，庆典、祀典、婚礼、丧礼、聘问，用脱帽三鞠躬礼。

第三条，公宴、公礼式，及寻常庆吊、交际、宴会，用脱帽一鞠躬礼。

第四条，寻常相见，用脱帽礼。

第五条，军人、警察有特别规定者，不适用本制。

第二章　女子礼

第六条，女子礼适用第二条、第三条之规定，但不脱帽。寻常相见，用一鞠躬礼。

第七条，本条自公布日施行。[1]

《时报》在1912年9月11日发表了一篇《规定书信后礼式》。这个礼式，呼吁将旧时代书信中常用的"顿首""百拜"等，改为"立正""脱帽""免冠""鞠躬""举手"，以趋新逐时。整个民国时期，类似的新式《书信必读》多不胜数，大多是对旧制的否定，对新制的提倡。

中国古代的礼仪，大致分为吉、嘉、军、宾、凶五种，经过宋代司马光、朱熹等人的改造，实际上对中国老百姓日常生活影响最深重的只是冠、婚、丧、祭四礼。在这四礼中，冠礼式微，丧祭之礼则非常稳定，近代受西方文化影响不大。西方化程度最高的，当属婚礼。下面以婚礼为例，说明西方文化对近代中国日常生活的影响。

中国传统婚礼有所谓"六礼"，即纳采、问名、纳吉、纳徵、请期、亲迎六道程序。虽然《朱子家礼》将其简化为议婚、纳采、纳徵、亲迎四个环节，但从

1　赵焕林主编，辽宁省档案馆编：《民国奉系军阀档案》（1912年卷），北京：线装书局，2016年，第128—129页。

根本上并未摆脱"无媒不婚"的传统模式。清朝国家颁布的《大清通礼》,甚至规定了不同等级的送礼数量、喜筵规格、订婚礼和结婚时的聘金数量、迎亲队伍的人数。按照人类学的理解,其实质在于,确立"接纳新媳妇的家庭和社会秩序准则,处理两家之间联系的规则和公开展示社会地位(和财富)"[1]。

近代以来,中国人的婚礼受到西方婚礼影响,不仅在程序上大大简化,而且通过自由恋爱、俭朴结婚,体现出一些价值观的变化。

中国人最早从传教士那里看到西式婚礼。咸丰九年三月二十八日(1859年4月30日),传教士理雅各(James Legge,1815—1897)的助手王韬(1828—1897)在上海虹口观摩并记载了一场西式婚礼:

> 前日为春甫婚期,行夷礼。至虹口神治文室,往观其合卺。西人来者甚众。神妇鼓琴讴歌,抑扬有节。其法:牧师衣冠北向立,其前高一几,几上置婚书、条约。新郎新妇南向立,将条约所载一一举问,傧相为之代答,然后仰空而拜。继乃夫妇交揖。礼成即退,殊为简略。[2]

他将西人结婚称为"行夷礼",明显仍戴着"华夷之辨"的有色眼镜。不过,经过近半个世纪的欧风美雨,这种文化自大的感觉在老百姓心中自然而然地减弱了。1914年6月20日,正在留学美国的胡适因为此前从未全面观察过西式婚礼,他的朋友维廉斯女士特地带他前往观礼。他说,西方人婚礼一般在男女父母家中举行,或者在牧师家中举行,或者在里正(Justice of the Peace)家中举行。这是一场教堂婚礼,来宾先入,婚嫁之家的近亲坐近礼坛,关系越疏远,距离越远。他看到有男傧四人、女傧四人(Bridesmaids),有荣誉女傧(Maid of honor),有执环童子(Ring bearer)。新娘由其父扶入,新郎与牧师从礼坛上的

---

1 [德]罗梅君:《北京的生育、婚姻和丧葬:十九世纪至当代民间文化和上层文化》,王燕生等译,北京:中华书局,2001年,第232—236页。

2 王韬:《王韬日记》,方行、汤志钧整理,北京:中华书局,1987年,第111页。

小门出来。接下来牧师问新郎、新娘，问新娘之父是否愿嫁此女，牧师为新娘戴婚戒（胡适此处可能为误记），牧师再引领新郎、新娘诵读誓辞（即 For better, for worse, for richer or for poorer, in sickness and in health, to love and to cherish, until death doth us part）。誓毕，牧师祈天降福于新婚夫妇及其家人。然后退出教堂，归女家赴婚筵，筵毕跳舞，跳舞未毕，新夫妇先告别归新居。[1] 这场婚礼的观察，可能对于胡适后来回国后设计自己的婚礼有重大影响。

受到这些西式婚礼影响，中国近代也开始流行新式婚礼，当时称之为"文明结婚"。文明结婚的实质，是提倡自由恋爱，反对"父母之命，媒妁之言"的旧式包办婚姻，反对索取聘礼（实际上这种现象并非始于近代，宋代大儒们对此已有种种批评），简化婚礼仪式。《清稗类抄》记载了当时"文明结婚"的大致程序：

> 文明结婚。亲迎之礼，晚近不用者多。光、宣之交，盛行文明结婚，倡于都会商埠，内地亦渐行之。礼堂所备证书（有新郎、新妇、证婚人、介绍人、主婚人姓名）。由证婚人宣读，介绍人（即媒妁）、证婚人、男女宾代表皆有颂词，亦有由主婚人宣读训词、来宾唱文明结婚歌者。
>
> 文明婚礼，实有三长。一，以父母之命，媒妁之言，而取男女之同意，以监督自由。其办理次序，先由男子陈志愿于父母，得父母允准，即延介绍人请愿于女子之父母，得其父母允准，再由介绍人约期订邀男女会晤，男女同意，婚约始定。二，定婚后，男女立约，先以求学自立为誓言。三，婚礼务求节俭，以挽回奢侈习俗，而免经济生活之障碍。
>
> 结婚之日，当由男女父母各给以金戒指一事，礼服一袭。婚礼未经制定，所习行者如下：

1　胡适：《胡适留学日记》，长沙：岳麓书社，2000年，第151—152页。

一、奏乐。

二、司仪人入席，面北立（以下皆由司仪人宣唱）。

三、男宾入席，面北立。

四、女宾人席，面北立。

五、男族主婚人入席，面南立。

六、女族主婚人入席。面南立。

七、男族全体入席，面西立。

八、女族全体入席，面东立。

九、证婚人入席，面南立。

十、介绍人入席，面南立。

十一、纠仪人入席，面北立。

十二、男女傧相引新郎新妇入席，面北立。

十三、男傧相入席，面北立。

十四、女傧相入席，面北立。

十五、奏乐。

十六、证婚人读证书。

十七、证婚人用印。

十八、介绍人用印。

十九、新郎新妇用印。

二十、证婚人为新郎新妇交换饰物。

二十一、新郎新妇行结婚礼，东西相向立，双鞠躬。

二十二、奏乐。

二十三、主婚人致训辞。

二十四、证婚人致箴辞。

二十五、新郎新妇谢证婚人，三鞠躬。

二十六、新郎新妇谢介绍人，三鞠躬。

二十七、男女宾代表致颂辞，赠花，双鞠躬。

二十八、奏乐。

二十九、新郎新妇致谢辞，双鞠躬。

三十、女宾代表唱文明结婚歌。

三十一、证婚人介绍人退。

三十二、男宾退。

三十三、女宾退。

三十四、新歟新妇行谒见男女主婚人及男女族全体礼。

三十五、奏乐。

三十六、男女主婚人及各尊长面南立，三鞠躬。

三十七、男女平辈面西立，男女晚辈面东立，双鞠躬。

三十八、男族女族全体行相见礼，东西相向立，双鞠躬。

三十九、男女傧相引新郎新妇退。

四十、男女两家主婚人及男族女族全体退。

四十一、纠仪人、司仪人退。

四十二、茶点。

四十三、筵宴。[1]

其大致程序是，男子先向父母禀告意愿，得允后，请介绍人向女子父母转达通婚意愿；得允后，再请介绍人约定时间男女双方会晤；若双方同意，即约定婚姻。婚礼不再在庙中举行，而多在礼堂或酒店举行。仪式中，有主婚人、证婚人、介绍人、男女傧相、双方亲属。由男女傧相引新郎新娘入席，证婚人宣布证书，证婚人、介绍人和新郎新娘依次用印，新郎新娘交换戒指，双方相对鞠躬。主婚人、证婚人、来宾代表致辞，新郎新娘鞠躬感谢证婚人、介绍人及来宾，并

1　徐珂：《清稗类钞》第五册《婚姻类·文明结婚》，北京：中华书局，2010年，第1987—1988页。

致答辞。有时，女宾代表还要唱文明结婚歌。客人退后，新人谒见双方主婚人及全体亲属，对尊长者三鞠躬，对平辈和晚辈双鞠躬。最后用茶点或开宴。[1]

概而言之，古代婚礼的六道程序，被简化为自由恋爱、订婚、行聘、迎娶四个主要环节，比上古"六礼"简化了很多。新娘乘马车出嫁，而不再用此前的轿子。废除了跪拜礼，改为鞠躬礼。对于重金聘礼、闹洞房等低俗行为也采取排斥态度，当然，这也是传统儒家婚礼所反对的。此外，还有赠送照片、西洋乐队等附带仪式。

婚礼中的演说，也是一个重要环节。民国时期很多文化名人，如梁启超、蔡元培、胡适、邹韬奋等，都是婚礼演说的提倡者和践行者，蔡元培就在自己的婚礼现场以演说替代闹洞房，并且大讲以演说代替婚礼的道理。后来，婚礼演说就演化成为主婚人讲训辞、证婚人讲祝辞、来宾讲贺词、新人讲答词的固定套路。[2]

留美回国的胡适，提倡新风气最力。根据新近公布的胡适《归娶记》，得以窥见他于1917年12月30日回绩溪老家迎娶江冬秀的婚礼细节。他对这场婚礼，非常认真，自己亲自做了具体设计。"所用婚礼，乃系新式"，有证婚人、主婚人、介绍人、司礼人。新郎新娘就礼案后，司礼人宣读结婚证书（用的是商务印书馆的活套）。"吾此次所定婚礼，乃斟酌现行各种礼式而成，斯于适用而已。此次所废旧礼之大者，如下：一、不择日子。是日为吾阴历生日，适为破日。二、不用花轿、凤帔、霞帔之类。三、不拜堂。以相见礼待之。四、不拜天地。五、不拜人。以相见礼待之。六、不用送房、传袋、撒帐诸项。七、不行拜跪礼。"接下来，举行如下仪式：

> 请新妇新郎用印。
> 请男家女家主婚人用印。
> 请证婚人用印。

---

1 严昌洪：《西俗东渐记：中国近代社会风俗的演变》，长沙：湖南出版社，1991年，第225—228页。
2 张涛：《近代婚礼改革中的演说》，《文汇报》2016年12月2日第25—26版。

请证婚人授婚约指环与主婚人。

请主婚人授婚约指环与新郎新妇。

新妇新郎行相见礼，一鞠躬。

新妇新郎谢证婚人，一鞠躬。

新妇新郎谢主婚人，一鞠躬。

新妇新郎见男女长亲，一鞠躬。

新妇新郎见来宾，一鞠躬。

新妇新郎受贺，贺者合一鞠躬，新妇新郎答一鞠躬。

接下来，进入演说环节。除了来宾演讲之外，胡适自己还大大地演讲了一番。在《归娶记》中，胡适说："吾初意本不拜祖先。后以吾母坚嘱不可废，吾重违其意，遂于三朝见庙，新夫妇步行入祠堂，三鞠躬而归，不用鼓乐。此次婚礼所改革者，其实皆系小节。吾国婚礼之坏，在于根本法之大谬。吾不能为根本的改革而但为末节之补救，心滋愧矣。"[1]他本来不准备行传统的庙见之礼，但拗不过母亲，还是在第三天带新妇去朝了祖庙，只不过三鞠躬而没有跪拜，也没有用乐。婚后七日，胡适与其小脚之妻江冬秀也曾有"回门"（"归宁"）之仪。

既然是自由恋爱而进行的文明结婚，新郎、新娘早就非常熟悉了，双方还需要什么"相见"？这当然是古代婚礼仪式的孑遗。在上古《仪礼·士昏礼》和中古《朱子家礼》中，都是到了亲迎环节，新郎、新娘才真正见面。在《朱子家礼》中把新娘迎娶回家后，就有"壻妇交拜"的仪式。《清稗类钞》中记载的"新郎新妇行结婚礼，东西相向立，双鞠躬"，与胡适设计的"新妇新郎行相见礼，一鞠躬"，都是这种礼俗的延续。

晚清以来的"文明结婚"，与传统婚礼仪式有诸多不同。第一，时间发生了

---

1 胡适：《归娶记》，《胡适留学日记手稿本》，上海：上海人民出版社影印，2015年，不分页。《东方早报》2014年6月22日B09—B10版。陈子善：《了不起的发现》，《北京青年报》2014年7月13日第15版。以上信息，承张涛教授相告，特此感谢！

变化，传统婚礼起源于"昏"，即在晚上举行，现代改为白天举行。而且，为了与工作节律相配合，结婚仪式大多选择在周末和节假日举行，传统的"请期"意义不大了。例如胡适的婚礼，就专门强调不择吉日。第二，地点发生了变化，不必再在庙中举行，多在酒店、礼堂、公园等公共场合，由"私礼"几乎转为"公礼"，以求见证人更多。第三，加进了鞠躬、演讲、用印、戴戒指等现代西方元素，结婚证书代替了传统的婚帖。这些环节的变化目的，旨在"见证求多"，由家族之间的婚姻协定，改为公众见证，就是为了加强婚约的合法性和婚姻的牢固性。第四，如上所说，仪式更加简化，由传统的"六礼"简化为自由恋爱、订婚、行聘、迎娶四个主要环节，有的更简化为恋爱、订婚、结婚这三道程序。最根本的变化，就是自由恋爱，取代了传统的"父母之合，媒妁之言"。

对传统丧礼的改变，亦是如此。相关内容，可参看胡适对自己母亲之丧的改革。例如，他改变了报丧讣闻的套话，改掉了丧仪中送祭、出殡、点主等细节，革新了丧服并实行短丧。总之，他主张丧礼易繁从简，"一方面把古丧礼遗下的种种虚伪仪式删除干净，一方面应该把后世加入的种种野蛮迷信的仪式删除干净"[1]。

二、人际交往的原则

在中国古代，关于如何处理人际关系，有一套基本的原则，那就是礼治秩序。"礼治"的核心，就是区分贵贱、尊卑、长幼、亲疏，要求人们的行为符合其相应的社会身份，不同的身份具有不同的行为规范，简而言之，就是男尊女卑、长尊幼卑、官尊民卑。

关于这些关系的原则，有多种说法。早在公元前7世纪的春秋时期，中国人将家庭内的关系概括为"五教"："父义、母慈、兄友、弟恭、子孝。"[2]后来，到公元前4世纪左右，中国人将这种家内人际关系的原则扩展到全部人际关系的原

1　胡适:《我对于丧礼的改革》,《新青年》第6卷第6号，1919年11月1日。
2　《左传·文公十八年》《国语·郑语》。

则，形成所谓"五伦"（five relationships），而在处理这"五伦"时，必须遵从"十义"。这见于《孟子》和《礼记》的总结：

> 父子有亲，君臣有义，夫妇有别，长幼有序，朋友有信。[1]
>
> 父慈，子孝；兄良，弟悌；夫义，妇听；长惠，幼顺；君仁，臣忠。[2]

可以看到，在上古中国，处理人际关系的原则（"十义"）是互为前提、互相尊重的，并非单向度的屈从和崇拜。

当儒学在西汉成为帝王之学，即国家意识形态之后，人际关系的原则被概括为"三纲六纪"。成书于东汉的儒家经学理论总集《白虎通义》，对其有一个整体概括：

> 三纲者何谓也？谓君臣、父子、夫妇也。六纪者，谓诸父、兄弟、族人、诸舅、师长、朋友也。故《含文嘉》曰："君为臣纲，父为子纲，夫为妻纲。"又曰："敬诸父兄，六纪道行。诸舅有义，族人有序，昆弟有亲，师长有尊，朋友有旧。"[3]

非常明显，"三纲"是单向度的人际关系原则，是一种差别伦理，强调下对上、妻对夫、子对父的绝对服从。此后两千多年，中国人大体遵循此一原则构建人际关系，没有平等意识。虽然其中一度有佛教的传入，"众生平等"观念曾经对中国文化产生过影响，但是终究被儒家正统诋斥为"无君无父"，而未深入到国人的内心。

宋代以来，司马光（《司马温公书仪》）、朱熹（《朱子家礼》）等人开始推行庶民通礼，即把上层社会和贵胄家族的礼制推行到民间基层。各地普遍制定家

---

1 《孟子·滕文公上》。
2 《礼记·礼运》。
3 陈立：《白虎通疏证》，吴则虞点校，北京：中华书局，1994年，第373—374页。

训、家礼和族规等平民礼制，乡间普遍制定有乡约、村规等地方性礼制，将民间基层社会的人际关系规定得非常细致。例如，北宋蓝田吕氏兄弟制定的《乡约》和《乡仪》规定了村民之间互相问候、揖拜、进退、迎劳、钱送、请召、相聚饮食、赠送物品、路途相遇时的种种细节，以及邻里之间的德业相劝、过失相规、患难相恤、乡村聚会的一些原则和礼仪，真正做到"非礼勿视，非礼勿听，非礼勿言，非礼勿动"[1]。这些礼仪影响了最近一千年来中国人的人际关系和乡村秩序。

但是近代以来，由于西方文化的进入，这些人际交往的规矩和秩序发生了巨变。近代工矿业的兴起，火车、轮船、汽车等新兴交通工具的兴起，导致人口移动范围扩大，族群的联系方式逐渐从血缘向地缘和业缘方式过渡。以乡村秩序为基础的人际交往模式受到冲击，而来自西方的人际交往方式却大受推崇。这从以下几方面得到说明：

第一，批判宗法制度，否定家庭和孝道。宗法制度是一种基于血缘关系的社会组织方式，儒家在处理人际关系时，完全认同并放大了这种制度，总是按照由己及人、由近及远的原则来处理亲疏、上下和尊卑关系。费孝通从社会学的角度，将其称为"差序格局"：

> 我们的格局不是一捆一捆扎清楚的柴（费氏对西洋格局的比喻——引注），而是好象把一块石头丢在水面上所发生的一圈圈推出去的波纹。每个人都是他社会影响所推出去的圈子的中心。[2]

在西方文化的影响下，近代产生了家庭革命。所谓家庭革命，即提倡用西方的小家庭结构来代替中国传统的大家族生活模式。激进的思想家号召人们投身政治革命，摆脱家庭的束缚，牺牲家庭利益，将国家和民族需求置于家庭利益之上。无政府主义者甚至提出"毁家"的主张。改良主义者康有为在《大同书》

---

1 《论语·颜渊》。

2 费孝通：《乡土中国》，北京：北京大学出版社，1998年，第26页。

中，构建了一种"无名、无分、无界、无限"的乌托邦，其中的男女关系以性关系为基础，而无须建立家庭。

儒家思想构建的差序格局的人际关系，主张家国同构（国家就是家庭和家族的放大），公私界限不清，给现代人际交往带来诸多负面影响。所以在近代尤其是"五四"新文化运动中，遭到强烈批判。吴虞喊出"打倒孔家店"的口号[1]，鲁迅也认为礼教"吃人"。"非礼"必然"非孝"，基于"家族本位"的孝道，受到的批判更是强烈，当时有学者甚至提出，"孝是一切罪恶的根源"[2]，"孝是生殖器崇拜"[3]。"非孝"在当时成为一时潮流。施存统、吴虞等人，都与父亲决裂，成为社会新闻。1919年11月，杭州第一师范学校学生施存统（后改名施复亮）发表《非"孝"》[4]，吴虞发表有《说孝》，鲁迅也发表有《我们现在怎样做父亲》[5]。走出家庭、背叛家庭，成为当时青年一大时尚，大量的文艺作品（如巴金的"激流三部曲"《家》《春》《秋》）控诉传统家庭礼教的残酷和黑暗，鼓励青年投身到反传统的革命洪流中去。

第二，提倡个人意志，追求平等和自由。毕业于英国皇家海军学校的严复（1854—1921）是中国近代传播西方思想最著名的思想家，他曾说："自由、平等、民主、人权、立宪、革命诸义，为我国六经历史之不言固也。"[6]这些概念均来自西方，它们对于推动中国最近二百年来的行为方式起到重要作用。

在中国传统文化系统中，虽然也存在"平等"和"自由"观念的思想资源，例如法家主张"法不阿贵"，墨家主张"兼爱""尚同"，佛教主张"众生平等"，

1　吴虞：《吃人与礼教》，《吴虞集》，田苗苗整理，北京：中华书局，2013年，第38—42页。

2　吴虞：《家族制度为专制主义之根据论》《说孝》，《吴虞集》，第7—12页。

3　周予同：《"孝"与"生殖器崇拜"》，朱维铮编：《周予同经学史论著选集》，上海：上海人民出版社，1983年，第70—91页，

4　施存统：《非"孝"》，《浙江新潮》（周报）第2期第1—2版，1919年11月8日。章果果、赵晓：《施存统〈非"孝"〉原文佚失百年后重现》，《金华日报》2022年3月15日A6版。田丹：《施存统〈非"孝"〉翻译》。《鲁迅研究月刊》2021年第8期，第82—86页。以上信息，承王川同学相告，特此感谢！

5　鲁迅：《我们现在怎样做父亲》，《鲁迅全集》第1卷，北京：人民文学出版社，2005年，第134—149页。

6　严复：《主客平议》，王栻主编：《严复集》（第一册），北京：中华书局，1986年，第118页。

老子主张"无忧"，庄子主张"逍遥"，但均不是中国文化的主流，而且与现代文明意义上的平等和自由均不能完全对应。儒家所主张的爱有差等才是主流。礼制的最大特点，也是等级制。[1]

来自西方的传教士、出使和留学西方的知识精英，将西方的自由和平等观念译介和引入中国。19世纪上半叶，传教士用"自主"或"自由"来对译"Freedom（Liberty）"。1868年，《中美续增条约》中首次在官方文件中将Freedom与"自由"对译。19世纪50年代以后，中外条约和教会文献更喜欢使用"自主"一词，有时也与Independence对译。经严复、黄遵宪等精英的写作和宣传，"自由"成为压倒性的概念。后来梁启超的文章风行一时，进一步奠定了"自由"话语在中国文化中的基本框架。[2]"自由"成为锐不可当的普遍性词汇，其观念也深入人心，"婚姻自由""不自由，毋宁死"等都成为一时口号。

1894年的中日甲午战争，中国败于日本这个"蕞尔小邦"，引起中国人真正的思想大触动，也成为西方思想在中国传播的一个里程碑。甲午战争前，传教士也宣传此理，但未得到国人的真切认同。以梁启超、唐才常、谭嗣同等人为代表，力倡平等观念。严复以其西学背景，论述最深刻。他将中西文化的观念冲突，加以列举描绘：

> 如中国最重三纲，而西人首明平等；中国亲亲，而西人尚贤；中国以孝治天下，而西人以公治天下；中国尊主，而西人隆民；中国贵一道而同风，而西人喜党居而州处；中国多忌讳，而西人众讥评。其于财用也，中国重节流，而西人重开源；中国追淳朴，而西人求欢虞。其接物也，中国美谦屈，而西人务发舒；中国尚节文，而西人乐简易。其于为学也，中国夸多识，而西人尊新知。其于祸灾也，中国委天数，而西人恃人力。[3]

1　杨华：《中国古代礼仪制度的几个特点》，《武汉大学学报》2015年第1期，第16—22页。

2　胡其柱：《晚清"自由"语词生成考略》，《中国文化研究》2008年夏之卷，第127—145页。

3　严复：《论世变之亟》，王栻主编：《严复集》（第一册），第3页。

类似的中西文化差异，在当时话语中不一而足。严复还说，西方文化重视平等和自由，必然导致"贵果信"；而中国文化重视纲常、孝道和尊亲。结果，尊亲之弊导致国人伪诈相欺，"忠孝之所存，转不若贵果信者之多矣"[1]。又如，谭嗣同《仁学》说：

> 五伦中于人生最无弊而有益，无纤毫之苦，有淡水之乐，其惟朋友乎！顾择交何如耳，所以者何？一曰"平等"，二曰"自由"，三曰"节宣惟意"。总括其义，曰不失自主之权而已矣。[2]

在这些思想先哲的启迪和推动之下，来源于西方罗马法、基督教和启蒙运动的自由、平等观念，在近代中国普遍流行开来。基于自由和平等观念，独立人格和契约精神也大受提倡。在20世纪对中国国民性进行批判的话语中，缺乏独立人格和契约精神都是非常负面的内容。显然，独立人格是对传统"三纲"伦理的严重否定。不仅人际交往中如此，20世纪的政治生活中，几乎所有政党和政府都把自由和平等作为重要政纲。今天，这两个概念已被确定为当代中国的核心价值观。

第三，提倡男女平等，推动妇女解放。在西方文化的影响下，男女平等观念普及开来，妇女受教育范围扩大，法律上追求平等权利。在传统中国，女子不能抛头露面，不能进祠堂祖庙，不能入族谱，这些规矩在近代均被渐次打破。女子的婚前贞操观和节烈观受到挑战，自由恋爱取代媒妁之言，一夫一妻制家庭普遍。各地都创办了"不缠足会"（如戒缠足会、天足会、放足会、卫足会）和识字会。挪威戏剧家亨利克·易卜生（Henrik Ibsen，1828—1906）的社会问题剧《玩偶之家》，在1907年被译介到中国之后，对中国的妇女解放起到极大推动作

1　严复：《原强修订稿》，王栻主编：《严复集》（第一册），第31页。
2　谭嗣同：《仁学》（下），《仁学：谭嗣同集》，加润国选注，沈阳：辽宁人民出版社，1994年，第86页。

用。萧红、丁玲等一大批女性用她们的人生和文学作品，见证了走出家庭，追求平等权利的历程。

总之，中国传统礼制注重等级差别、男女差别，完全是建立在"尊尊"和"亲亲"两大原则上的。随着西方文化的输入而产生的思想和观念变化，动摇了中国传统礼制的根基。它与西方礼制接轨，走向近代化也是不可避免的了。

三、传统礼制与现代法律的冲突

中国传统的礼制与法律之间从来就关系紧密。二者虽然分别由儒家和法家所主倡，但二者对于国家统治而言，实质相同。《礼记·乐记》说：

> 礼以道其志，乐以和其声，政以一其行，刑以防其奸。礼、乐、刑、政，其极一也，所以同民心而出治道也。

从汉代开始，古代朝廷制定法律时，就"援礼入法"，法律被儒家化了。换言之，法律条文反映了儒家的伦理规范，同罪异罚（"不同身份的人在法律上的待遇不同"）；反过来，法律又为维护儒家的伦理规范服务。瞿同祖先生认为这一过程发生在魏晋南北朝时期："〔元魏〕法律之儒家化彻底而有系统，非局部的，小规范的。疑中国法律之儒家化魏、晋已开始，但其完成则在北朝。""归纳言之，中国法律之儒家化可以说是始于魏、晋，成于北魏、北齐，隋、唐采用后便成为中国法律的正统。"[1]

其中最明显的是，中国古代的法律都以"五服制度"为基础。所谓"五服制度"，就是对直系和旁系亲属的服丧规制。亲属关系越近，服丧越重（丧服粗恶、服丧期长）；反之，关系越远，服丧也越轻。财产继承、法律义务等，也根

据这种丧服秩序来决定。在中国的历代法典中，都附有《服制图》。

到近代，这种礼法合一的法律体系受到挑战，出现转型。本来，乾隆五年（1740）制定有《钦定大清律例》，且一直在全社会实施。但晚清世风发生变化，国人已对外国法律有所了解。光绪二十四年（1898），晚清的改良派首领康有为在《上清帝第六书》中首次提出，仿效西方，设立法律局，制订民律民法。光绪二十八年（1902），清廷为了收回领事裁判权，正式下诏改革法律体系。在刘坤一、张之洞、袁世凯等人的联名保举下，沈家本、伍廷芳受命开馆修律。此次法律改革的指导思想，是折衷各国法规，兼采近世最新学说，且又兼顾中国历代沿袭的"礼教民情"。政府除了命令法律馆主持其事外，还命礼学馆共同参与其事。法律馆中，多是学习国外法律的新学人士；而礼学馆中，则是传统经学的饱学之士。这本身就说明，中国法律在向近代转型时，传统礼制是不可或缺的一部分。[1]在近代法律体制的形成过程中，礼法仍然是合一的。

在修律过程中，围绕着中国传统"礼教"与西方法律"法理"，两派产生了激烈争论，此即著名的"礼法论争"。礼教派以张之洞、劳乃宣等人为代表，法理派以沈家本、伍廷芳、杨度等人为代表。争论的焦点，主要是一些关于中国旧有纲常名教的法律条款，如"亲属相隐"、"干名犯义"、"存留养亲"、"亲属相奸"及"无夫奸"、"子孙违犯教令"等十几个问题。后来聚焦在"无夫奸"（无丈夫的女子与他人发生性关系）和"子孙违犯教令"（子孙卑幼"不听教令"）两条。沈家本等法理派主张废除此二刑，而劳乃宣等礼教派主张保存此二罪。[2]实质在于，新法是否应继续容纳传统"礼教"的内容，这反映了中国传统礼法结合的法律体系与近代西方法律文化之间的冲突。宣统元年正月二十七日（1909年2月17日），宣统皇帝下诏，说三纲五常是我国"相传数千年之国粹，立国之大

1 冉琰杰：《清末编修民律之争议》，《四川大学学报》（社会科学版）第42卷第3期（2015年5月），第149—156页。
2 李欣荣：《清末关于"无夫奸"的思想论争》，《中华文史论丛》总103期（2011年），第101—129页。

本"，要求"凡我旧律义关伦常诸条，不可率行变革，庶以维天理民彝于不敝"[1]。大臣刘廷琛在奏折中，对"子孙违犯教令""无夫奸"等行为之不加罪尤为愤慨，呼吁"礼教不可废则新律必不可行"[2]。

新律最初的执笔者伍廷芳（1842—1922），早年在伦敦大学学院攻读法学，是中国近代第一个法学博士，也是香港立法局第一位华人议员。曾作为清政府的法律顾问，参与多次外交谈判。1906年开始制定法律，由伍廷芳执笔草定的《大清刑事民事诉讼法》（5章206条），其仿照对象是英美之制，因遭到礼教派的抵制而未予公布。1907年，沈家本等修律大臣聘请的日本法学家制定了《大清新刑律草案》，这是一个当时全世界最新法律理论与中国礼教实情相结合的产物。这个草案，仍然受到张之洞、劳乃宣等人的抵制，认为它有悖君臣、父子、夫妇之伦，也违背男女有别、尊卑长幼之序。

后来又经修订，在修改稿中加上《附则五条》，规定："大清律中，十恶、亲属容隐、干名犯义、存留养亲，以及亲属相奸相盗相殴、并发冢犯奸各条，均有关于伦纪礼教，未便蔑弃。"死刑仍然执行斩刑，正当防卫之法不能适用于卑幼对尊亲。这个附则实际上部分地否定了正文，显示出传统礼教的强大。后来，《大清新刑律》与《附则》（《暂行章程》）一道提交审议。1911年1月25日，也就是清政府崩溃的前夕，中国第一部民法《大清新刑律》与《暂行章程》联同颁布了。

不过，也不可否认，这个充满矛盾和妥协的《新刑律》中，在罢除笞杖、停止刑讯、裁判独立、监狱改良等方面，已与西方法律体系趋同。另外，在婚姻制度、继承顺序、遗嘱制度等方面，也体现出相当明显的西方法律烙印。例如，《大清民律草案》第1335条明确规定："有配偶者，不得重婚。"有学者指出，这是从《日本民法典》中移植过来的。[3]但是，该《大清民律草案》中还遗存有大

---

1 爱新觉罗·溥仪：《凡旧律义关伦常诸条不可率行变革谕》，高汉成主编：《〈大清新刑律〉立法资料汇编》，北京：社会科学文献出版社，2013年，第469页。

2 刘廷深：《奏新刑律不合礼教条文请严饬删尽折》，高汉成主编：《〈大清新刑律〉立法资料汇编》，第789—790页。

3 李双元、温世扬：《比较民法学》，武汉：武汉大学出版社，2000年，第869页。

量的旧礼旧俗，例如，第1327条规定："家政统于家长。"又如，该法律中有嫡子、庶子的分别（第1380、1387条），显然也是中国古代多妻制和宗法制的遗留。第1338条规定："结婚须由父母允许。"这也是媒妁之言的遗痕。而第1341条又规定，"当事人无结婚之意思者"，婚姻无效。这又体现了对婚姻当事双方意愿的尊重。关于离婚，第1359条规定："夫妻不相和谐而两愿离婚者，得行离。"而第1360条又规定："前条之离婚，如男未及三十岁，或女未及二十五岁，须经父母允许。"也就是说，无论结婚还是离婚，父母的意志都相当重要。[1] 这里可看出，新旧伦理互相冲突，旧礼与新风互相杂糅。既有男女平等、自由契约的原则，又有宗法制度的遗迹。[2]

又以继承制度而言，《大清民律草案》虽然仍然肯定宗法承祧之制，即单系父系继承原则，但妻子、姊妹、女婿等也被列为继承人的范围。更重要的是，该法律肯定了遗嘱的作用，该法律设立专章分节对遗嘱设立之条件、方法、遗嘱的效力、遗嘱的执行、遗嘱的撤销等一一做了详细的规定。[3] 第1395条规定："以遗嘱择立嗣子者，从其遗嘱。"第1481条："所继人之遗嘱，定有分产之法或托他人代定者，须从其遗嘱。"所有这些，都体现出该部法律之"既中又西""亦中亦西""虽西还中"的矛盾特点。该法律部分地体现了平等、人权、契约、自由等立法原则。

值得注意的是，"礼教"和"法理"派双方在争论时都援引了西方法律原则。参与礼法之争的，除了中国的法学家、政治家之外，外国法律专家也分为两派。主张法理派的一方，以日本著名法学家冈田朝太郎（Okada Asataro，1868—1936）为主；而支持礼教派的另一方，也包括来自奥地利的赫善心（Harald Gutherz，1880—1912）。两者都是法学大师，但分别支持不同的阵营。冈田朝太郎援引法国启蒙思想家孟德斯鸠（Montesquieu，1689—1755）的法律进化论，

1 《大清民律草案·民国民律草案》，杨立新点校，吉林人民出版社，2002年，第171—175页。
2 陈宁英：《从〈大清民律草案〉"亲属""继承"两编的界定看我国法律文化的近代转型》，《中南民族大学学报》（人文社会科学版）第25卷第6期（2005年11月），第75—78页。
3 《大清民律草案·民国民律草案》，第178、190—197页。

认为中国的礼、法合一，与世界通例不合，显得落后：

> 礼之与法，不可混而一之物也。法者，以有民而立之者也；礼者，以为人而守之者也，而二者皆行谊之所必率也。……支那与斯巴达之法家，其不分法、礼、俗而一治之者。[1]

梁启超等学者也极力主张礼、法分离，推行法制主义。而赫善心则展现出日耳曼法学派的见解，强调法律必须与道德合一，法律必须与本国文化合一。

赫善心与冈田的分歧，加剧了晚清立法改革时的礼法之争，但此二人的争论，又恰好是他们本国法律文化在东方的折射。1907年日本颁布新刑法，1909年德国完成新刑法典草案，1907—1910年中国制定新刑法。一方面，他们用自己母国的知识和经验来协助中国制定新刑法；另一方面，二人在中国的经验和见解，又发回日本和欧洲，与其母国产生互动。这样，中国的礼、法之争，便与世界性法律史产生了有趣的连接。[2]

由上可见，在中国法律走向近代的转型过程中，以宗法制度为基础的传统礼制行为仍然具有强大的影响力，转型并非一帆风顺，一蹴而就的。

四、结语

中国的近代文化史，呈现出三重维度的冲突和融合，一是古老的华夏传统文明，二是西方文明，三是来自华夏汉族之外的满族文化。中国传统礼制向近代礼制的转变，也是在这三种因素的纠缠中进行的。

清朝前期的礼制冲突，集中在满族礼制与汉族礼制之间，例如，关于"雉

1　[法]孟德斯鸠：《孟德斯鸠法意》（上册），严复译，北京：商务印书馆，1981年，第409、418页。

2　陈新宇：《礼法论争中的冈田朝太郎与赫善心：全球史视野下的晚清修律》，《华东政法大学学报》2016年第4期，第66—76页。

发"的冲突，当时有"留发不留头，留头不留发"之说，关于跪拜与"请安"（北方民族单膝跪地而重视手上动作）的区别：

> 请安之礼，始于辽，历金、元皆然，明代犹未尽革。后则非独满、蒙二族有之，汉族亦有行此礼者，而尤盛于北方。《辽志》云："凡男女拜皆同。其一足跪，一足着地，以手动为节，数止于三、四。"彼言捏骨地者，跪也。夫一足跪一足着地，即一足立而着地，但屈彼一足也。以手动为节，即垂手近足跗之节也。但言数止三四，似犹有繁简之不同，固不仅如后之垂右手屈左膝之各仅一次也。惟妇女多请双安，则以两手抚两膝而同时屈之耳。光绪中，税务、邮政皆外人主持，自厘局、盐局亦归西人管辖，于是始与官场中人交涉。皖省有毛某者，首向办大通局之某西人行请安礼，闻者多非笑之。[1]

到了晚清时期，中国传统礼制与西方外来礼制的冲突则成为主流。这种冲突，在以费正清为代表的西方话语看来，就是"中国对西方的回应"，简言之，即"冲击-反应"模式。[2]但是，现在越来越多的学者（例如沟口雄三、狄百瑞、杨联陞、傅衣凌、杜维明、余英时等）相信，在中国文化内部，存在着自发转型的内在机理。例如，中国历史上并不缺乏契约和契约精神；在明清之际，顾炎武、黄宗羲、王夫之等人已开始反思专制集权的危害；明清以来各地已经开始探索地方自治之道，以限制君主制中央集权。这些文化因素，对于推动中国的近代化都不无价值。

就仪式本身而言，它随俗而变，并无所谓先进与落后之别，但仪式背后所反映的思想内涵和政治权力，则可清晰地体现出文化差异和时代变化。近二百年来，中国本土礼仪与西方礼仪之间，既有冲突，又有融合，但更多的是融合。传

1　徐珂：《清稗类钞》第二册《礼制类·请安》，第489—490页。

2　［美］费正清：《中国：传统与变迁》，张沛等译，长春：吉林出版集团有限责任公司，2008年，第229—257页。

统的五礼结构（吉、嘉、军、宾、凶）和四礼结构（冠、婚、丧、祭），在最近的二百年间，稳定和连续的内容很多，转型和新变的内容更多。例如，传统"天朝上国"格局的宾礼，转化为近现代平等的国际外交。今天，自由恋爱和自主婚姻已成为中国人的普遍婚礼样式，媒妁之言再也不是婚礼的必要条件；人们见面握手和拥抱，即使在正式场合，鞠躬也取代了叩首跪拜；"法律面前人人平等"早已成为司法共识，完全告别了宗法制度下的同罪异罚；契约精神深入人心，代替"三纲"中的人身依附式的愚忠愚孝；自由和平等、公正和法治都已成为中国的核心价值观。不能不承认，这都是近二百年来中西方文化融合的结果。

不过，进入新世纪以来，"礼"在中国的正面价值得到重新发现。第一，礼有助于"明刑弼教"，"德主刑辅"，维护社会稳定。用礼治的"自律"来辅助法治的"他律"，可以起到"软法"的作用。但是正如司马迁所说，"礼禁未然之前，法施已然之后。法之所为用者易见，而礼之所为禁者难知"[1]，人们容易忽视礼的价值。第二，礼有助于重建道德规范。近代以来的曲折历史，使得中国人的价值系统出现某些偏差或混乱，例如孝道一度被认为是负面价值，"五常"伦理与"三纲"一同遭到批判[2]，现在看来，都应当重新审视。第三，礼有助于提高公民素养。孔子说："道之以政，齐之以刑，民免而无耻。道之以德，齐之以礼，有耻且格。"[3]礼教的宗旨，就是培养君子人格。君子之风，彬彬有礼，在任何时代、任何地方都会受到尊重，它并不受民族、国家、年龄、身份的界限。小而言之，是个人风采的展现；大而言之，则是国家形象的展示。

（本文是国家社会科学基金重大项目"中国传统礼仪文化通史研究"［批号18ZDA021］的阶段性成果。本文系作者在联盟2017年年度论坛上的发言）

1　司马迁：《史记》卷130《太史公自序》，北京：中华书局，1959年，第3298页。

2　冯天瑜：《"五伦"、"三纲"分梳说》，《冯天瑜文集》，武汉：武汉大学出版社，2009年，第290—296页。

3　《论语·为政》。

参考文献

陈立：《白虎通疏证》，吴则虞点校，北京：中华书局，1994年。

《大清民律草案、民国民律草案》，杨立新点校，长春：吉林人民出版社，2002年。

徐珂：《清稗类钞》，北京：中华书局，2010年。

严复：《严复集》，北京：中华书局，1986年。

谭嗣同：《仁学：谭嗣同集》，加润国选注，沈阳：辽宁人民出版社，1994年。

胡适：《胡适留学日记》，长沙：岳麓书社，2000年。

吴虞：《吴虞集》，田苗苗整理，北京：中华书局，2013年。

张枬、王忍之编：《辛亥革命前十年间时论选集》，北京：生活·读书·新知三联书店，1977年。

赵焕林主编，辽宁省档案馆编：《民国奉系军阀档案》，北京：线装书局，2016年。

［德］罗梅君：《北京的生育、婚姻和丧葬：十九世纪至当代民间文化和上层文化》，王燕生等译，北京：中华书局，2001年。

康有为：《康有为政论集》，汤志钧编，北京：中华书局，1981年。

［法］阿兰·佩雷菲特：《停滞的帝国：两个世界的撞击》，王国卿等译，北京：生活·读书·新知三联书店，1993年。

王开玺：《清代外交礼仪的交涉与论争》，北京：人民出版社，2009年。

严昌洪：《西俗东渐记：中国近代社会风俗的演变》，长沙：湖南出版社，1991年。

张晋藩：《中国近代社会与法制文明》，北京：中国政法大学出版社，2003年。

瞿同祖：《中国法律与中国社会》，北京：中华书局，1981年。

费孝通：《乡土中国》，北京：北京大学出版社，1998年。

［美］费正清：《中国：传统与变迁》，张沛等译，长春：吉林出版集团有限责任公司，2008年。

鹿厅与中古时代的公共领域

——试析《贝奥武甫》对社会起源的文学再现

陈 雷*

　　《贝奥武甫》（*Beowulf*）以全书三分之二的篇幅讲述了同名主人公与怪物葛篓代母子间的一场殊死搏斗，这场斗争是围绕着一座名叫"鹿厅"（Heorot）的宏伟建筑展开的：鹿厅曾为希尔德族君臣共享盛宴和赐礼的欢乐之地，但因不断遭受葛篓代的袭扰而日渐衰落，正当丹麦人为此一筹莫展之际，高特武士贝奥武甫闻讯赶到，以一己之力杀死了作恶的母子，让鹿厅恢复了往日的生机。作为双方争斗的焦点，鹿厅在这部作品中显然占有一个极为重要的机枢地位：一方面，它是故事情节发生的主要场所，另一方面，这座建筑物本身的性质还在很大程度上决定了这场斗争的性质和意义。那么，鹿厅到底有何特别之处，以至于葛篓代竟会对它怀有如此强烈而持久的敌意呢？鹿厅之敌葛篓代究竟代表着什么？葛篓代与鹿厅的敌对关系以及贝奥武甫与葛篓代的敌对关系又反映出古盎格鲁撒克逊人对生活、世界和社会的怎样一种理解和感受？本文将尝试借鉴历史哲学和社会学理论中的一些思路来对上述问题做出回答，并期待以此跨学科视角来补充和丰富历来主要偏重于语文学分析的《贝奥武甫》研究。

---

* 陈雷：中国社会科学院外国文学研究所研究员。研究方向：英美文学。目前主要研究兴趣为早期现代英国文学、浪漫主义及思想史。

一、"厅中的欢乐"

历史学者一般认为，类似于鹿厅这样的大厅是北欧早期"部族公共生活中一个具有中心地位的场所"（the focus and center of people's communal being）[1]。在大厅里聚集的主要是国王和他的贵族武士，这些人之间存在着明确的封建等级关系，但通过在大厅里一起参与宴饮以及各种娱乐活动，君臣又表现出他们共同构成了一个"亲密友爱的群体"（intimate association）[2]。大厅作为一种社会机制源于何时现已无从考证，但至少生活在一世纪末的历史学家塔西佗就已经记录过日耳曼部族中类似的组织方式——他称之为comitatus，该词也经常被评论家借用来界定《贝奥武甫》中鹿厅里的社会形态[3]，也就是说，大厅与有案可查的北欧早期社会几乎一样古老。

在通过《贝奥武甫》这样的作品观察盎格鲁撒克逊早期社会时，现代读者最容易产生的一个认识误区就是不自觉地把我们现在所熟知的"社会"概念投射到我们所观察的那个陌生时代上去。对于现代人而言，社会是每个人自动身处其中的公共空间，是不由分说深深渗透进我们生活各个方面的一种体制，但这样一种状况却并非从来就有。根据哈贝马斯（J. Habermas）的社会学研究，我们今天所熟悉的作为公共领域的社会概念，也就是他所称的"自由公共领域"，实际上是近代以后随着市民社会兴起壮大以后才逐步形成的事物。在中世纪，公共领域则仅限于他所说的"代表型"（或"展示性"）公共领域："（各级）封建领主的宫廷是代表型公共领域的中心"[4]，"这种公共领域依附于领主，同时赋予其权威

---

1 Hugh Magennis, *Images of Community in Old English Poetry*, Cambridge: Cambridge University Press, 1996, p. 35.

2 Hugh Magennis, *Images of Community in Old English Poetry*, p. 12.

3 参见Tacitus, *Agricola and Germany*, trans. Anthony R. Birley, Oxford: Oxford University Press, 1999, pp. 44, 109。

4 [德] 哈贝马斯：《公共领域的结构转型》，曹卫东等译，上海：学林出版社，1999年，第9页。哈贝马斯在同书第7页曾明确说"封建主并非代表人民，而是在人民面前展现其封建主地位（They represented their lordship not for but 'before' the people）"，有鉴于此，"representative"更合适的译法或许应是"展示性"或"呈现性"。不过，本文仍从通译，采用"代表型"的说法。

以一种'神光灵气（aura）'"[1]。换句话说，站在今天的高度，我们知道文明/民政（civility）之光注定会照亮我们生活的每个角落，然而在最初阶段，它所能照亮的范围十分狭窄。在《贝奥武甫》中，这片被照亮的区域便是由"大厅"及其有限周边构成的贵族生活世界。《牛津英语词典》中society一词的最早义项是"association with one's fellow men, esp. in a friendly or intimate manner"。对应于历史现实，由于在"英雄时代"（维柯语）只有贵族武士之间才有这种"亲密友爱的伙伴关系（fellowship）"，因此，当把《贝奥武甫》还原到恩格斯所说的这个"野蛮时代的高级阶段"来审视时[2]，我们会发现，"社会"在此阶段仅仅存在于大厅这一贵族武士的聚义空间之内[3]——社会是在鹿厅这样的地方才第一次以一种可见的方式"展现"出它自己的，在史诗中，鹿厅实际上相当于希尔德部族层面上"公共领域"的全部。

一旦我们把大厅理解为最早的可见可触的社会，《贝奥武甫》开头罗瑟迦建造鹿厅的非凡意义便清晰地凸显了出来。鹿厅并非仅仅是一座冠绝各部族的辉煌建筑，它实际上是一个使不可见的社会变得可见的展示性场所——一个通过仪式性的宴饮娱乐和礼物互赠使参与者确认自身"社会性"（sociality）的公共空间。如果我们把"文明与礼仪"（它与"民政生活"实为同一个词，即civility）的确立看作"城邦"（city，civitas）建立大业的最后一个环节的话，那么鹿厅这块带有"神光灵气的公共领域"的出现便象征着这最后一环的最终完成。

城邦的建立绝非一件可以一蹴而就的工作，就《贝奥武甫》开头部分描写的

1　[德]哈贝马斯：《公共领域的结构转型》，第7页。

2　"野蛮时代的高级阶段"具体而言指的是这样一个阶段："高级阶段。从铁矿石的冶炼开始，并由于拼音文字的发明及其应用于文献记录而过渡到文明时代。这一阶段……生产的进步，要比过去一切阶段的总和还要来得丰富。英雄时代的希腊人、罗马建立前不久的各意大利部落、塔西佗时代的德意志人、海盗时代的诺曼人，都属于这个阶段。"参见恩格斯：《家庭、私有制和国家的起源》，中央编译局译，北京：人民出版社，1999年，第25页。本文讨论的丹麦人或早期盎格鲁撒克逊人即恩格斯所说的"海盗时代的诺曼人"。

3　"Society"一词后来也常指"上流社会"（如在巴尔扎克的《交际花盛衰记》中），可以说，这个词的词义中天生含有一种贵族性和宫廷性。

情况看，它是经过希尔德王朝四代国王的努力才宣告完成的。而且，它"产生于暴力，并且必须在一个暴力的世界中求生存"[1]，如果城邦本身可以比作一座建筑物，那么它深厚的根基部分便是残酷的战争。事实上，希尔德王朝四代国王最大的事业不外乎就是在四处征战中不断地击败其对手。关于这一王朝的创始人希尔德，诗中有这样的描写：

> 多少次，向敌军丛中
> "麦束之子"希尔德夺来酒宴的宝座，
> 威震众酋，他本是孤苦零丁
> 一个弃婴，自己赢来的后福。
> 飞云渺渺，他
> 一天天长大，受人敬重，
> 直至鲸鱼之路四邻的部族
> 纷纷向他俯首进贡：
> 好一个大王！（《贝奥武甫》4—11）[2]

"武心王"海勒摩覆亡之后，丹麦重新陷入无政府状态（这其实也是历史上一切"社会"诞生或重生的背景）。据诗中记载，当时"部落久无首领，（人民）屡遭灾祸"（14—16）；值此危难之际，希尔德脱颖而出，用武力逐步恢复了丹麦的秩序，成为新王朝的奠基者。他的王业后来由儿子贝乌继承；贝乌不负众望，也成为一位以武德闻名天下的国王：

1　Edward Keene, *International Political Thought: A Historical Introduction*, Malden: Polity Press, 2005, p. 117.

2　《贝奥武甫》，冯象译，北京：生活·读书·新知三联书店，1992年，第1—2页。除另有说明，本文所有出自《贝奥武甫》的引文（随文标出的数字为原文的行数）均采用冯象的译本，译文稍有修改。本文参照的古英语本为 Anon., *Beowulf*, ed. M. Alexander, Harmondsworth: Penguin Books Ltd., 1995。

接着，贝乌享用了丹麦人长久的拥护。

一座座城堡（on burgum），流传着他的业绩。（53—55）

这句描写中很值得注意的一个说法是"on burgum"。"burgum"的原形"burh"一般被解作"fortified place"，也就是我们常说的"军事要塞"或"堡垒"（德语中城堡仍为Burg），不过也有学者认为该词在此处应被理解为"城市"（city）或"市镇"（town）（英语中的borough仍保留着burh的痕迹），比如唐纳德森（E. Talbot Donaldson）在其著名的《贝奥武甫》现代英语散文译本中就把上面这句话译为"Then in the cities was Beow … long famous among nations"[1]。这两种理解何者为佳恐怕难有定论，但城市与堡垒在词源上的关联却反映出了历史上存在于此二者之间的一种真实联系，即，城市几乎总是在被称作堡垒的军事要塞旁发展起来的。城市是人的聚集之地，而人口之所以会不断向某一个地方归附，最重要的原因当然在于那里可以为他们提供有效的安全保障——尽管其代价是失去所有人身权利和劳动成果。在尚不知政府为何物的野蛮时代，能够为人们提供安全保障的只有那一个个在生存竞争中自发形成、各据一方且相互敌视的军事组织。这些军事组织是以强人为首的武士集团，按照意大利历史哲学家维柯的推测，他们的土地当时都位于"高山坡上"——"那里有形势险要的处所，是世界上最早的arces（堡寨）；后来又用军事建筑加以巩固"[2]。在战乱中被逼得走投无路的人逃到这些强人的势力范围内寻求庇护，便被安置在山下的平原上，构成了最古的城市中没有任何权利的平民阶层（亦即尚未被民政之光照亮的阶层）。[3]在拉丁文中这

---

1 Nicholas Howe, ed., *Beowulf* (Norton Critical Edition), trans. E. Talbot Donaldson, New York: W. W. Norton & Company, 2002, p. 4.

2 ［意］维柯:《新科学》，朱光潜译，北京：人民文学出版社，1997年，第252页。

3 蒙森关于罗马城形成史的下面这段文字可资参照："颇为相似的古代避难所至今在瑞士东部山地几个山峰上仍可看到。这种地方在意大利称为'高冈'（capitolium）……；它还不是一个城镇，而是一个未来城镇的基础，因为房舍自然聚集在城堡周围，以后又有围墙把它环绕起来。……意大利形成城镇前的政区组织法就以这些城堡为基础。"参见［德］蒙森:《罗马史》（第一卷），李稼年译，李澍泖校，北京：

一阶层被用"低暗地区"所指代，而山上堡寨内的贵族则被称为"高朗地区"的光明之子。[1]事实上，这些盘踞在堡垒中的军事组织最初与单纯的盗匪集团并无二致，但在巨大的生存压力的逼迫下——不久之后又有对权力和荣誉的渴望加入进来——这些盗匪集团逐步发展出了有利于最大限度发挥战斗力的严密而复杂的内部组织结构。通过竞争的严酷筛选，最有战斗力的集团存活了下来，这便是最早的封建主，而古代所谓的国王，比如上面所说的贝乌，实际上就是这些封建主中最强有力，并最终使所有其他封建主都俯首称臣的一个。

贝乌的事业接下来是由他的儿子"半丹麦人"海夫丹来继承的。诗中对海夫丹的描写甚为简略，但从他被形容为"gamol ond gúðréouw"（old and battle-fierce）（58）来看，他同样是一位以善战著称的国王。海夫丹共育有三子一女，王位最终由次子继承，此即后来建造了鹿厅从而引出贝奥武甫传奇的"光荣之矛"罗瑟迦。罗瑟迦是一位贤明的君主，在他早中期的文治武功之下，希尔德部族的威望与日俱增："胜利和光荣归了罗瑟迦，/他得到扈从们衷心的爱戴，/越来越多的年轻战士，从四面八方/投奔到他的帐下。"（64—67）到了暮年，眼看着希尔德王朝四代人努力的目标已接近完成，罗瑟迦心中遂萌发了建造一座最辉煌的大厅的念头：

……霸业既兴，

他于是萌发出一个心愿：

要丹麦拥有一座蜜酒大厅，

商务印书馆，2005年，第35页。中国古代乱世（相当于无政府的野蛮复归时代）中也有"坞聚"或"屯聚"的现象。陈寅恪在《桃花源记旁证》一文中曾写道："凡聚众据险者因欲久支岁月及给养能自足之故，必择险阻而又可以耕种及有水泉之地。其具备此二者之地必为山顶平原，及溪涧水源之地，此又自然之理也。"参见陈寅恪：《金明馆丛稿初编》，北京：生活·读书·新知三联书店，2001年，第192页。桃花源的故事中因而也包含着城邦源起的普遍规律。

1　[意]维柯：《新科学》，第252、273页。

> 一席让人的子孙永世不忘的庆筵
> 宝座前，他要向老将新兵
> 颁发上帝赐他的全部礼物，
> 除开部落的公地、人的生命。（67—73）

前面我们说过，城市是起源于堡垒，并在人口向堡垒周边聚集的过程中逐步形成的。然而单纯的堡垒势力的扩张还不足以使堡主的领地成为一个真正意义上的城邦，城邦的建立还需要有一种与城邦相匹配的道德原则获得最终确认才能算真正大功告成，而这一有待确立的道德原则便是前文所说的"文明与礼仪"。

在《仙后》第六卷"卡利多或守礼骑士（Knight of Courtesy）的传奇"中，埃德蒙·斯宾塞（Edmund Spenser）曾把civility描绘为美惠三女神（Graces）以自己手拉手的环舞向人类昭示的一种技艺（skill）："这三位女神用种种惠赠装点人类的身心，使他们的面貌焕然生辉；她们教给人美好得体的举止仪态、诚恳善意的交接技巧，以及各种具有凝聚力量的礼节规范，……这些技艺便是人们所说的'文明'。"[1] 斯宾塞把文明的起源追溯到美惠女神的默示的想法其实来自古罗马的塞涅卡（Seneca），在后者的《论恩惠》中，这位斯多葛派哲学家详细解释了美惠女神环舞的象征意义：

> 美惠女神为什么共有三个？……（因为）她们一个象征施惠，一个象征受惠，另一个象征回馈。为什么她们手拉手围成一圈翩翩起舞？因为善意从一个手里传到另一个手里，最终又一点不少地传回到第一个手中。如果中间有任何一个没能把善意传递下去，那么美妙的舞蹈就会被打乱。[2]

---

[1] Edmund Spenser, *The Faerie Queene*, ed. Thomas P. Roche, Harmondsworth: Penguin Books Ltd., 1978, p. 993.

[2] Seneca, *Moral and Political Essays*, ed. and trans. John M. Cooper, Cambridge: Cambridge University Press, 1995, p. 197.

文明生活的核心在于人与人之间的"善意"，而善意最直接的表达方式就是施惠与感恩（grace是"不求自来的礼物"，而从该词衍生出的gratitude则表示"感激"）。施惠者施惠应该是不求回报的，但如果受惠者知恩图报，那么单向的施惠就变为了双向的"互惠"，这就相当于美惠三女神"手拉手围成一圈翩翩起舞"。正如《仙后》中所描写的那样，这个环舞是可以不断扩大的，因为每个人都可以通过善意地施惠和感恩地受惠加入到互惠的行列中来。加入环舞的人越多意味着文明之光越强，若由近及远，这种互惠能够在所有人之间展开，那么不仅仅是某个共同体，甚至整个人类都将亲如兄弟，而爱的天堂就会在人间得到实现。

由此反观罗瑟迦的誓愿，我们不难看出，他希望通过建造一座大厅来确立的正是上述这样一种文明生活的原则。罗瑟迦的设想中包含了两个相互关联的重要理念，即互惠和共享。他所拥有的一切，除开那无法赠送的，他都打算与属下在鹿厅中共享，而分赐礼物，也就是施惠，将是达成共享的主要途径。受惠者从他手中接过贵重的礼物——不论是黄金、指环，还是战马或盔甲——其心中必会被激发出一种意欲回报的慷慨决心，这一决心虽不一定马上有机会转化为行动，但由于感恩本身就已经构成了对赠礼的一种回馈，因此罗瑟迦以自己的施惠行为所启动的实际上是一种可被称作"恩惠的往复"（reciprocity of benefit）的机制和过程——在此意义上他就好比一位领舞者。如果恩惠的往复，也就是互惠，能如他所愿在所有人之间展开，那么整个城邦就将变成一个建立在互爱基础上的"朋友共同体"（fellowship）。前文曾指出，城邦是起源于军事堡垒的。最初的人据险筑堡当然不是出于朋友间的互爱；借用霍布斯的说法，他们这样做的目的是为了在自然状态下的"每个人对每个人的永恒战争"中更好地保障自己的生命和财产安全，然而社会发展的奇妙规律是，从自利的堡垒中发展出来的城邦最终却会把自己的基础建立在互爱这一全新的原则之上。事实上，只要互惠共享的原则一天得不到确立，建立城邦的工作便一天不能说完成，这是因为，既然城邦是自然状态的对立面，那么它所奉行的原则也就必须与自然人所奉行的纯粹利己原则截然相反才行——否则人又何谈摆脱自然状态呢？城邦是始于战争的堡垒经由战友间的互助而成于以大厅为代表的文明的；只有当国王不再仅仅是令人生畏的最高主权者，而是同时又以楷模性的施惠者身份出现时[1]，只有当希尔德族人在鹿厅里第一次确认互惠共享原则并感受到由此带来的欢乐时，他们的"社会"生活才算真正开始。哈贝马斯虽然提出了"代表型公共领域"的概念，但并没有深入探究这种依附于封建主宫廷的公域是如何形成的，而《贝奥武甫》中对鹿厅建立的描写却以第一手材料为我们重现了这一过程。

在《贝奥武甫》中，大厅这一空间自始至终是与"欢乐"（joy）的情绪联系在一起的。这里有"日复一日的飨宴"、唱诗者悦耳的歌喉以及赏赐不尽的礼物——事实上国王在厅中的宝座就叫作"赠礼之椅"（gifstól，gift throne），而国王本人则为"赠金的朋友"（goldwine，gold friend）——武士们在此竟日纵酒作乐，"饭饱酒足，便坠入梦乡，无忧无虑"（88—120）。作为一个来自异邦的访客，鹿厅中的欢乐场景曾给贝奥武甫留下了格外深刻的印象，后来当他为罗瑟迦完成除妖大功回到自己的祖国时，他向国王赫依拉这样描述了他在鹿厅中看到的情形：

> 鹿厅欢笑了：
> 苍穹之下，我从未见过那样济济一堂，
> 开怀畅饮的场面。
> 那纺织和平的贵妇穿梭在大殿上
> 劝年轻战士进酒。入座之前
> 一次又一次，向客人分赐项圈。
> 同时，在将军们的上席，
> 罗瑟迦的公主手持银壶，
> 为他们一一注酒。（2014—2021）

1　这两个身份结合在一起才构成完整的王权。"鹿厅"（Heorot）得名于"鹿"，而雄鹿（"heorot"即"hart"）在古盎格鲁撒克逊文化中象征着神圣君权（sacral kingship），参见William A. Chaney, *The Cult of Kingship in Anglo-Saxon England*, Manchester: Manchester University Press, 1970, p. 130。

作为人的理性与自我保存本能合力造就的产物，社会最大的功能就是为人提供安全保障和生活的便利。在现代人看来，安全与便利恐怕是最为普通的两样东西了，然而假如社会确实是有一个起点的话，那么这就意味着，在社会被创造出来以前——亦即在自然状态之下——最初的人所过的必然是一种既没有安全也没有便利的生活。安全与便利是一切幸福的前提条件；没有前者，由后者生发出来的欢乐自然也就无从谈起了。换句话说，在最初阶段，社会本身就是欢乐的直接源泉。

有别于个体的愉悦（delight或pleasure），欢乐本质上是一种集体性和社会性的情绪。它伴随着人的聚集而产生，并给个体带来一种超越自身、成为更大整体一部分的陶醉。席勒（F. Schiller）的《欢乐颂》中欢乐与人类大同的关联就清楚地展现出了该词的这一内涵。涂尔干（E. Durkheim）认为，对于个人来说，社会具有一种明显的"赋予力量和生气的作用（dynamogenic effect）"："在共同的激情的鼓舞下，我们在集会上变得易于冲动，情绪激昂，……感到体内充溢和泛滥着一种异常的力量并且试图奔涌而出。"这种力量往往具有激发道德感的效果："一个恪尽责守的人，面对他的同伴所表现出来的种种赞赏、敬重和倾慕，会感到一种平常没有体会过的舒畅。"[1] 欢乐是生气与力量的激荡所引发的感受。最具"赋予生气和力量作用"的群体莫过于士气高涨的军事组织了。在最古老的法语史诗《罗兰之歌》中，法兰克军队统帅查理曼大帝的佩剑就叫作"Joyeuse"（欢乐），而其麾下战士们的战吼（battle cry）则叫"Mountjoy"。[2] 前文说过，城邦发源于军事组织，互惠共享原则的基石实际上是武士间在战斗中形成的互助和友爱。鹿厅之所以具有"神光灵气"，正在于"伙伴们"的聚集使它散发出一种赋予生气的能量。由此而言，下面这一猜想或许并不像初看起来那么虚诞，即，欢乐最早是在大厅中被发现和领悟的，而罗瑟迦的武士们在鹿厅中纵情作乐的场景为我们真实地还原了人类历史上对欢乐最早的感受。

---

1 ［法］涂尔干：《宗教生活的基本形式》，渠东、汲喆译，上海：上海人民出版社，1999年，第280—282页。

2 Anon., *Song of Roland*, trans. D. L. Sayers, New York: Penguin Books, 1957, p. 147.

在《贝奥武甫》的社会语境下，鹿厅的欢乐是与"朋友"息息相关的。维柯曾注意到"朋友"与"部落"在词源上的关联："在爱奥尼亚地区的希腊文里philios就是'朋友'，经过一个字母的音变，它就变成了希腊词phylē，亦即'部落'。"[1] 维柯此处所举虽然仅是个别语言中的现象，但从这一个例子中我们却可以窥见一个也许具有普遍意义的认知模式：通过把"朋友"延伸为"部落"，社会生活带来的幸福便呈现为朋友–部落给人带来的欢乐，而与朋友在一起则成了幸福的不二保证——有时候，甚至"朋友"本身就变成了"幸福"。《贝奥武甫》中最常用的表达这两个意思的词分别是wine和wynn，二者同出一源，均可追溯至原始印欧语中表达"爱与欲望"的词根的*wenhx-。[2] 古英语所表征的精神世界里"朋友"与"欢乐"的联系之深，由此也可见一斑了（中国读者或许可以从

1 ［意］维柯:《新科学》，第271页。

2 J. P. Mallory and D. Q. Adams, *Oxford Introduction to Proto-Indo-European and the Proto-Indo-European World*, Oxford: Oxford University Press, 2006, p. 341. 值得注意的是，美神维纳斯的名字（Venus）也源于该词。美与欢乐是两种具有天然紧密关联的孪生事物，美总能让人身心愉悦，而给人带来欢乐的东西也很少有不让人产生美感的。说到美，一般人想到的首先是自然的美，其次是品德的美——前者是人用感官所能领会的部分与整体之间的和谐，后者是美好的德行给人带来的愉悦——但维柯却认为人最初感受到的美应该是民政之美，亦即把人领出黑暗、使他们第一次沐浴在民政生活之光里的英雄的高贵之美；维纳斯这一神祇的产生便反映和记录了古人在这方面的感受：

　　　　另一个在这些最古老的人类制度中诞生的神就是维纳斯，一个代表民政美的诗性人物性格，因此 honestas 就有高贵、美和德行这些意思。这三个观念想必就是依这样的次第诞生的。首先是"高贵"，它应被理解为特属于英雄们的民政的美。其次是自然的美，这是人用感官来领会的，……最后是品德的美，这只有哲学家才能理解。因此，美（最初）必然是阿波罗、巴克斯、伽倪墨德、柏勒罗丰以及忒修斯之类英雄所具有的民政的或文明的美。（《新科学》，280—281）

值得注意的是，与欢乐一样，美也经历了一个对社会或共同体的感受从其内涵中渐次撤离的过程，它逐步蜕变为带有个人主观性的审美判断力的观照对象。这一点或许可以从侧面为我们对欢乐含义的变化所做的分析提供一个印证。

"民政之美"类似于本尼迪克特·安德森所说的"自然共同体之美"（the beauty of Gemeinschaft），这种美感是从人与人之间的"自然连带关系"中自然发生的（［美］安德森:《想象的共同体》，吴叡人译，上海：上海人民出版社，2011年，第138页）。

"有朋自远方来不亦乐乎"这句话中去体味两者间的关联）。既然朋友的聚合能给人带来欢乐，那么设想最大数量的朋友以最集中可见的方式聚合在一起，如此造成的欢乐显然就应该是最大最强烈的欢乐了。在《贝奥武甫》所描写的早期社会中，大厅起到的作用便是把人在社会关系层面上的聚合——这悄无声息地发生于城邦形成的缓慢过程中——转化成了一个可感知和可把握的具体现实。

在一个社会才刚刚诞生不久的时代，人们生活中被民政之光照亮的那个区域必定是十分狭窄的。如果我们把"朋友"这个称呼所适用的范围界定为"社会"延及的领地，那么社会这种东西此时还仅仅存在于大厅这一有限的空间之内，而这也就让欢乐这种社会性情感与大厅的空间紧密地联系在了一起。这是一种会让现代人感到颇为陌生的生活–世界感受，在《贝奥武甫》中，它最清晰地表现在了一段常被称作"最后幸存者的叹息"的著名诗章里——死亡逐一夺走了"一支高贵部落"所有成员的生命，当最后一名幸存者感到自己也来日无多时，便独自一人将部落世代敛聚的财富搬运到海边一座新筑的墓冢里埋藏，同时发出了一段关于人生欢乐短暂和尘世功名徒劳的感叹；这段感叹的开头几句是这样的：

> 大地啊，既然人无法再享用这尊贵的宝藏，那就请你来收留它吧！它本就由英雄从你的怀抱中获得。而今战争的屠戮掠走了我族所有的战士，他们离生命而去（þis life ofgeaf; gave up this life），从此再不知宴饮厅中的欢乐（gesawon sele-dreamas; had seen joy in the hall）。……（2247—2252）[1]

现代读者看到这里的"sele-dream"（hall-joy）一词时心中恐怕多少都会生出一些疑惑：什么是厅中的欢乐？欢乐为何还有厅内厅外之分？"离开生命而去"意味着被剥夺世间所有的欢乐，但诗人在此为何却只强调"厅中的欢乐"？难道在

1　此处采用了李赋宁的译文，参见李赋宁：《英国中古时期文学史》，北京：外语教学与研究出版社，2005年，第46页。

一个走到生命尽头的人的最后回望中，大厅之外就只剩下一片凄冷和灰暗？[1]不难看出，这些困惑之所以会产生，关键原因还是在于，对于现代人而言，欢乐与社会生活空间是没有任何必然联系的。颇具权威性的《韦氏字典》给"joy"所下的定义是"the emotion evoked by well-being, success, or good fortune or by the prospect of possessing what one desires"。如果此定义能够被看作对今人观念的一个忠实反映的话，那么很显然，在现代人的观念中，欢乐非但不涉及任何具体的社会生活空间，它甚至与抽象意义上的"社会"也保持了相当的距离——除了"成功"，上述定义里提到的"安康""好运"及"欲望的满足"均可毫无争议地划入私域范围。当然，正如前文分析所指出的，这种变化之所以出现并非因为社会对于现代人不再重要，而是因为公共领域已经从最初的大厅延伸到了我们生活的各个角落，并在这一过程中逐步失去了它在空间上的特异性。在最早的时候，由于只有大厅中才有欢乐，"厅中的欢乐"实际上就等同于"欢乐"本身，但随着社会的扩张，厅外也渐渐有了光明和温暖，大厅不再是公共生活的中心场所[2]，欢乐也不再必然地与大厅相连，"厅中欢乐"的说法自然也就慢慢失去了它原有的清晰内涵。

二、厅中的"噩梦"

弄清了鹿厅的来龙去脉，鹿厅之敌葛婪代代表着什么也就不难回答了。

欢乐总是与忧惧相伴随的。鹿厅的欢乐使人第一次感受到了社会生活的光明和温暖，但它同时也把自然状态下——也就是社会生活的对立面——的无欢乐

---

1 该词显然对译者也构成了一个问题，在冯象译本中，"大厅"索性被完全虚化了，取而代之的是更为人们所熟知的"宴席"意象——"战争的屠戮，捕走了我们一族，/截断了他们的生命，/他们最后的宴席"。

2 Magennis认为大厅在盎格鲁撒克逊社会中的中心作用从十二世纪开始削弱，其背景为封建制的高度等级化以及城镇和教堂的影响力的与日俱增，参见Magennis, *Images of Community in Old English Poetry*, pp. 12, 36。

性（joylessness）充分凸显了出来；这一无欢状态此刻不仅在时间上距离人们尚不遥远，它在地理位置上也十分迫近：被民政之光照亮的只是鹿厅及其周边这片有限的空间，而由此向外不远处就是那由"茫茫荒原"和"戚戚沼泽"构成的阴冷黑暗的世界，这里在民政生活开始前就是人们避之唯恐不及的地方，而今在鹿厅的光明和温暖的映衬下，这些地方更是显得比以往任何时候都还要阴冷和黑暗。在这一意义上，我们可以说鹿厅的建立实际上同时创造出了两个互相敌对的世界：它不仅赋予"此地"的社会生活以具体可感的形态，它还以否定的方式赋予"彼地"的野蛮状态以一种具体可感的形态。人们长期以来一直在文明和野蛮的边界"无意识"地往返游走，直到此刻光明的决定性的确立彻底区分开光明自身与异己的黑暗，人们这才第一次清晰而强烈地"意识"到了前者的美好和后者的恐怖。早期人类的生活-世界感受总是以具体形象呈现出来的，当上述这种因衬托而加强了的恐惧感也需要有一个活生生的对象来承载时，狰狞的怪物葛娄代便呼之欲出了。

社会初生，在人们的意识里，光明和黑暗这两个世界是随大厅的建立"同时"出现的；在《贝奥武甫》的故事层面上，这一"同时性"则以一种隐喻的方式体现在了这样一个特别的情节安排中，即，鹿厅甫一落成便开始遭受葛娄代的袭扰，而在此之前，这怪物虽据说一直都栖居在附近的荒沼中，但我们却从未听到任何关于他攻击人类的报道：

> 这时，一头逡巡在黑暗之中的恶魔
> 再也按捺不住了。他无法忍受
> 鹿厅内日复一日的缛宴，
> 悦耳的竖琴，嘹亮的歌喉……。
> 夜幕降临时分，他从荒原走来，
> 挨近巍峨的大厅，窥视
> 佩戴金环的丹麦人，宴会结束如何安顿。（86—117）

葛婪代攻击对象的单一性也从另一个角度表明了他所表征的那种忧惧与鹿厅所代表的欢乐之间的共生关系：葛婪代的破坏力虽然堪称巨大，但他似乎只知在鹿厅以内展开其无理由的屠戮，要躲开他的魔爪，人们根本不必四散奔逃，他们只需"挑个偏僻的角落或靠近外间的卧房休息"便可保证性命无虞（139—140）；同样，若想与葛婪代决一雌雄，勇敢的武士也不必费心去野外寻找他的藏身之所，他们只需在鹿厅里静候，深夜时分怪物定然会如期前来造访。鉴于其愤怒和暴行仅仅针对鹿厅，葛婪代在很大程度上可以说是被兴建鹿厅这一人类行为召唤出来的一个怪物。"欢乐"在古英语中的对应词是dream，这个词经过演化后来变成了现代英语中的"梦"，如果我们据此把"厅中的欢乐"理解为"厅中的美梦"的话，那么葛婪代就恰好相当于厅中的一个挥之不去的"噩梦"了。[1]

　　除了上述行为方面的特征，葛婪代的家系族谱也可进一步证明他与野蛮状态之间的关系；关于这怪物的来历，诗里是这样描写的：

> 这恶魔名叫葛婪代，
> 茫茫荒原，全归他独占，
> 戚戚沼泽，是他的要塞。
> 他借了怪物的巢穴潜伏多年，
> 从来不知道人世的欢乐——
> 造物主严惩了他那一族，
> 该隐的苗裔（因那第一桩血债，
> 永恒的主施加的报复）：亚伯的凶手，
> 亲弟弟的屠夫，被上帝远远逐出了人群。
> 从该隐孳生出一切精灵魍魉，

1　参见 Alvin A. Lee, *Gold-Hall and Earth-dragon: Beowulf as Metaphor*, Toronto: Toronto University Press, 1998, p. 243。

借尸还魂的厉鬼；还有巨人，

他们与上帝抗争了许久，

上帝给了他们应得的报偿。（102—114）

这段描写中最值得注意的地方是它把葛婪代与该隐联系在了一起。前文说过，社会的实质就是在人与人之间建立起一种互惠的纽带，互惠的对立面是互相伤害，而在互伤的行为中，由杀人所引发的血仇（faéhð，feud）——其实质是与恩惠的往复截然相反的"仇恨的往复"（reciprocity of hatred）——无疑又是最具破坏性，因而也最具反社会倾向的一种。在洛克看来，民政社会建立起来的最大标志就是人们把自然状态下掌握在每个人手中的惩罚凶手的权力转移给了社会[1]，换个角度，这一观点也可以被理解为，社会的出现终止和废除了血仇制度以及由这一制度所体现的"仇恨往复"原则。上帝因该隐杀人而对他做出的惩罚是将他"远远逐出人群"。人群亦即社会，在社会尚未出现的时代，以"逐出人群"作为惩罚当然不会有任何意义；要让远离人群的生活成为一种悲惨可怕的境遇从而使这一惩罚具有强大的震慑力，社会作为黑暗世界中唯一一座光明和温暖的堡垒必须首先被牢固地建立起来。从这一意义上来说，《旧约·创世记》中的上帝其实是新生的民政秩序为声张自己的意志而创造出来的一个代言人，他对该隐的放逐看似发生在遥远的过去，但这一处罚反映出来的实际上却是新起的文明社会对野蛮状态遗留下来的人类行为方式的全面否定和摈弃。除了是最早的杀人者以外，该隐据传说还是历史上第一个建造城市的人。[2]最早的城市居然是由一个杀人犯所建，这初听起来似乎颇为悖谬，但细想一下我们却不难发现这一传说背后的深意。城市的前身堡垒是在自然状态下的永恒战争中修筑起来的，由于战争的本质就是通过消灭敌人来保存自己，因此说最早的城市由该隐这样的嗜血凶人所建很可能也

1　［英］洛克：《政府论》（下册），叶启芳、瞿菊农译，北京：商务印书馆，2003年，第53页。

2　John Byron, *Cain and Abel in Text and Tradition*, Leiden: Brill, 2011, p. 124.

确实反映了这一历史阶段的某些真实面貌。然而城市最终是要以自然状态的否定形式来确立自身的，否定自然状态意味着自然状态下的行为方式也将被谴责和摈弃，如此一来，即便在奠定民政秩序的过程中杀人之事不可避免——甚至更进一步，即便说自然状态下本无善恶可言，善恶的区分只是民政生活后天教会给人的一种知识——该隐作为杀人者的代表也难逃被自己建立起来的城邦永远放逐的命运了。对于北欧人来说，该隐是一个来自异族的神话人物，成书于基督教影响在盎格鲁撒克逊人中间日益增长时期的《贝奥武甫》把他和葛婪代放进同一份族谱，足以见出该书作者对差异背后的共性有一种非凡的直觉把握能力。这两个人物都是以反社会行为而被逐出社会之外的反社会象征，二者间的区别仅仅在于，由于长期放逐于荒原沼泽之中，葛婪代已经失去了大部分人类面目，变得和魑魅魍魉没什么两样了。

作为葛婪代和他母亲的领地，"茫茫荒原"和"戚戚沼泽"在书中构成了一个与鹿厅内的光明空间截然相反的阴暗世界。这个阴暗世界的核心部分是葛婪代母子的老巢，一座四周麇集着各种妖魔鬼怪的水下宫殿。为了彻底铲除妖孽，贝奥武甫只身一人勇闯这座从未有人和动物敢于接近的洞窟；关于他在水底看到的诡异情形，书中有下面一段生动的描写：

> ……此刻不管他如何英勇，
> 也无济于事，因为无数海怪
> 已将他团团围住，一齐进攻，
> 獠牙顶着盔甲。他抽不出宝剑，
> 也动不了四肢。
> 接着勇士发现，
> 已经进入一个洞穴，一间不祥的
> 大厅。潭水不见了，
> 石洞的拱顶挡住了怒涛。

只见一处耀眼的火光

明晃晃地照着。(1508—1517)

中译本此处的"不祥的大厅"在原文中实为 nîðsele，意即 hall of hatred，而两行之后所谓"石洞的拱顶"同样也是对"大厅的拱顶"(hrófsele，hall-roof)的意译，再联系下文描写与妖母的决斗时作者把贝奥武甫称作"大厅的客人"(selegyst，hall-guest)(1545)，以及贝奥武甫回到故乡向赫依拉讲述自己在丹麦的战斗时把葛婪代母子的水下宫殿称作"战厅"(guðsele，war-hall)(2139)，我们不难看出作者的意图实际上是要在罗瑟迦的鹿厅和葛婪代母子的妖窟之间建立起一种对称的关系，换句话说，这座妖窟实际上是鹿厅的一个"反讽性对应物"(ironic counterpart)[1]，它与鹿厅隐约互为镜像，但两者却建立在完全相反的原则之上：鹿厅里充盈的是善意和互惠精神，而这座水下大厅正如其名 nîðsele 所示却是一座弥漫着仇恨的大厅；这里同样也有礼物的施与和回赠，但这礼物不是金环或盔甲，而是殊死搏斗中招招致命的你来我往——"那女怪马上回报了他(andlean forgeald，repaid him his gift)，狠毒的魔爪将他死死掐住"(1541—1542)。结合前文的分析我们现已不难看出，妖窟和鹿厅的对称其实只是作品中一个贯穿始终的巨大主题对称中的必要一环：如果葛婪代母子确如上文所言是被社会放逐出去的人类野蛮生存状态的象征的话，那么让他们以这样一座颠倒过来的大厅为巢穴应该说是再合适不过的安排了。"光明的城市"(byrhtan byrig，bright city)(1199)存在于大厅之中，它的黑暗敌人理所当然就应该盘踞在一座建立在仇恨原则之上的"反大厅"(anti-hall)里。[2]

经过一番激烈搏斗，贝奥武甫最终将葛婪代母子全部杀死，从而彻底消除了十余年来不断困扰鹿厅的来自怪物的威胁。在一场盛大的欢庆之后，贝奥武甫及

---

1 Hugh Magennis, *Images of Community in Old English Poetry*, p. 61.

2 Fabienne L. Michelet, *Creation, Migration, and Conquest: Geographical Imagination and Sense of Space in Old English Poetry*, Oxford: Oxford University Press, 2006, p. 84.

其随从满载着罗瑟迦赠送的厚礼跨海回到了自己的祖国，史诗中与鹿厅相关的情节至此也告一段落。不过，虽然逃过了葛蒌代母子这一劫，鹿厅本身的曲折故事却还远远没有结束，关于这个故事的最终结局书中虽未做直接描述，却也在多个地方给出了明确的铺垫和预言——事实上，早在对鹿厅刚刚建成后的盛况所做的描写中，作者就清清楚楚地告诉了读者，鹿厅最终将在战火中被焚毁：

> ……大厅高高耸立，
> 张开宽阔的山墙，它在等待
> 战争的火焰，恐怖的焚烧；
> 时间尚未到来，当利剑在罗瑟迦翁婿之间
> 挑起血仇，布下无情的屠宰。（81—85）

也就是说，鹿厅接下来还将迎来一个更大更恐怖的葛蒌代，但届时却不会再有另一个贝奥武甫能挺身而出来拯救它于水火之中了。由于这带来毁灭的危机源于"罗瑟迦翁婿之间的血仇"，新葛蒌代显然并非来自社会外部。前文说过，栖居在荒沼中的老葛蒌代实际上是新生的社会人对鹿厅之外的野蛮状态的恐惧的一种投射，不过，空间位置并非决定人是否处于野蛮状态的关键因素，"野蛮"毋宁说是对内心状态以及由此产生的行为方式的一种描述，而这就意味着，人即便身处大厅的光明之中，只要他的贪婪、野心、嫉妒以及复仇欲等激情没有得到有效遏制，野蛮状态还是会趁着由这些激情所引发的灾难随时降临到社会上来的。关于罗瑟迦翁婿之间的战争书中虽未做实写，但通过贝奥武甫凭经验想象出来的一系列场景，我们却也能对其前因后果略窥一二。

希尔德族第三代国王海夫丹在战场上被髯族王费洛德击杀，后者不久又死于海夫丹之子罗瑟迦之手，希、髯两族从此结下血仇。按照当时的习俗，部族之间的矛盾经常是通过和亲方式解决的，为了消弭与髯族的宿怨，罗瑟迦也早早把自己的女儿弗莱娃许配给了费洛德之子英叶德作王后。贝奥武甫访问丹麦宫廷时弗

莱娃尚未出嫁，在除妖成功后为他举办的庆筵上，莆莱娃穿梭于席间为勇士们一一注酒，贝奥武甫看在眼里，心中却对她未来的命运产生了一种不祥的预感，因为他深知，"倒下一位国王，/复仇的长矛便不肯有一刻太平，/哪怕娶进再好的新娘"（2029—2031）。基于这一预感，贝奥武甫进一步想象出了几年后莆莱娃出嫁来到髯族大厅时将要发生的事情。按照礼俗，新娘和她的扈从将在髯族大厅受到英叶德的盛情款待，宾主双方将在那里济济一堂，共享酒宴以及各种"厅中的欢乐"，然而危机的暗流却也将在这一派祥和底下不安地涌动。在场的髯族勇士中肯定有人曾亲历过当年与希尔德族的战争，而惨败留下的阴影肯定还在他们心中挥之不去，这些老战士中的一个发现新娘的侍卫中竟有人佩戴着当年从髯族战士身上缴获的战利品，痛苦的回忆瞬间点燃了他胸中压抑已久的怒火：

> 于是酒宴上，一位年迈的武士忍不住了。
> 熟悉的金环在眼前晃动，心头一幕幕浮起
> 当年长矛的宰杀——他的心沉下去了！
> 他开始恨恨地试探某个年轻战士，
> 向他表露心底的想法，
> 唤醒他对厮杀的渴望：
> "朋友，你不认识那支剑吧？
> 那是你父亲最后一次戴上面盔出征，
> 手里拿着的宝剑哪！
> 丹麦人杀了他，做了战场的主人，
> 而威折将军和英雄们一同倒下，
> 再没有起来，好狠的丹麦人！
> 现在，那帮凶手中某个人的儿子
> 得意洋洋，在大厅里走来走去，
> 披着那一身珠宝，吹嘘那一场屠杀，

> 佩挂着那支理应归你的宝剑。"
> 就这样一次次，他用恶毒的话语
> 催促、挑拨，直到时机成熟，
> 公主的侍臣为他父亲的旧债
> 倒在血泊中，被利刃夺去了生命。（2041—2061）

就这样，厅中的欢乐转眼间变成了厅中的屠戮，两族间艰难建立起来的和平轻易就化为了乌有，受局势的裹挟和部下的挑唆，英叶德的心灵也将被复仇的欲望所占领，"旧恨新仇之中，他将淡忘新婚的妻子"（2065—2066），越来越多的人将加入到仇恨的环舞中来，起于髯族大厅的屠戮将很快延烧至鹿厅，象征着友爱和互惠的鹿厅最终将在新葛婪代带来的血仇烈焰中彻底陷落。

那些曾沉浸在大厅的欢乐中的早期社会人——不管他所属的是鹿厅还是髯族大厅抑或是其他部族的任何大厅——对这样一种结局当然不会是毫无心理准备的，事实上，正是这种忧惧和不祥的预感在他们的头脑中召唤出了葛婪代这样一个怪物的狰狞形象；然而需要注意的一点是，对葛婪代的恐惧反过来也会进一步凸显厅中欢乐的美好与可贵，这实际上是一个双向加强的过程：一方面，厅内的光明让人们发现了厅外的黑暗，另一方面，对黑暗的意识强化了人们对欢乐的感受——这一感受在忧惧的映衬下是如此刻骨铭心，以至于当"最后的幸存者"即将离开人世时，他心中唯一留存的美好事物就是对"厅中欢乐"的记忆。

三、大厅的卫士

英雄是由他所完成的事业来定义的，如果葛婪代确如前文所说是一切对"文明与礼仪"造成威胁的力量的代表的话，那么贝奥武甫担当起来的显然就应该是捍卫文明与礼仪的重任了。在此意义上，我们不妨把贝奥武甫看作《仙后》第六卷的主人公"守礼骑士"卡利多的一个早期原型，而卡利多所追逐并最终战胜的"喧嚣之兽"（Blatant Beast），亦即礼节之敌,则相当于葛婪代的一个衍生或变体。[1]从词源关系上看,"礼节"（courtesy）最早是出现在"宫廷"（court）里的[2]，由于罗瑟迦的鹿厅实际上就是丹麦最早的宫廷，我们在这里应该也能够发现丹麦人礼仪的最早萌芽。最初的礼仪必定是十分粗简的，但原始的礼仪由于没有繁文缛节的干扰反而更有助于我们把握礼仪的真谛。礼仪的本质同我们前面谈到过的社会的本质其实是完全一样的，它归根结底就是一种善意的回馈：当一个人对另一个人施与的惠赠心存感激并在合适的时机给予报答时，最早的"知礼行为"（act of courtesy）便诞生了。作为文明的捍卫者，贝奥武甫首先应当是一个礼仪的践行者，而从他除妖义举背后的动机看，他也确实是担得起"守礼骑士"这一光荣名号的。

贝奥武甫甘愿冒巨大的风险去为一个异邦的人民剪除凶患，其动力首先当然来自他的荣誉感和好胜心——葛婪代已为祸丹麦十二载，谁要是能除掉这个妖孽谁就能赢得世人最高的赞誉，这对于一个勇力过人的年轻武士来说当然是个不容错过的成名机会——但除此之外另一层原因也不应被我们忽视，那就是，贝奥武甫很可能也想借此行动来报答多年前罗瑟迦对他父亲的一个恩情。前一个原因是大家都能猜到的，而后者则只有罗瑟迦一人知道；在鹿厅接见远道而来的贝奥武甫一行时，老国王亲口向众人道出了这段往事：

> 罗瑟迦，希尔德子孙的护主道：
> "贝奥武甫我的朋友，出于仁慈
> 不忘旧谊，你特来丹麦援助。

1　参见Alvin A. Lee, *Gold-Hall and Earth-dragon: Beowulf as Metaphor*, p. 206。根据《仙后》第6卷第5章第13—14节，"喧嚣之兽"代表着"恶意"（Despetto）、"欺骗"（Decetto）和"侵犯"（Defetto）。很显然，这三个词几乎囊括了一切有可能对友爱与和平也就是"大厅"构成威胁的因素。

2　《仙后》第6卷第1章的第一句话就是"Of Court it seems, men Courtesie doe call"。"礼"是文明生活的精髓，"礼"源出于宫廷这一事实可进一步佐证"社会成于大厅"这一命题。从《礼记·曲礼》中我们也得知，礼最初是"不下及庶人"的，也就是说，不出于"宫廷"之外。

想当年，你父亲手起刀落，

杀了狼子族的何锁拉，

惹出一桩大仇。风族的人

因惧怕战争报复，不敢再将他

收留。于是他越过汹涌的波涛

投奔到光荣的希尔德子孙中间。

那时，我刚刚开始统治丹麦，

风华少年，拥有这辽阔的国度。

……我用赎金了结了这场仇隙，

跨过大海的背脊，给狼子族送去

古代的珍宝。你的父亲艾奇瑟

则向我起了重誓。"（456—472）

贝奥武甫来到丹麦时罗瑟迦已为王五十载，上述情况如果确实发生在他即位之初，那么这至少也应该是四十多年前的往事了。一个人因为另一个人在四十多年前有恩于自己的父亲（当时他自己肯定还未出生）就甘愿为他赴汤蹈火，这无论如何都足以说明此人是个知恩重义的好汉。换言之，贝奥武甫不仅武功过人，在立身处世方面他也同样卓越超群，堪称他所处时代和社会在道德上的一个典范。

贝奥武甫的到来令罗瑟迦大喜过望，这一方面固然是因为年轻战士的神武再次燃起了人们对消灭葛婪代的希望，另一方面，贝奥武甫在危难之际前来襄助也以生动的实例向罗瑟迦证明了他长期信奉并亲身实践的一条为君之道的正确性，即，为君者应该不吝财宝，"赏赐大方"：

年轻王子侍奉君父左右，

就应当品行端正、赏赐大方，

以便老来他有部下追随，

战火临头，扈从与首领同在。

通过行动赢取美名，这样的人

无论在哪里都能成就一番伟业！（20—25）

赏赐大方作为一条为君之道对于现代人来说之所以不言而喻，是因为有恩必报作为一个道德原则早已内化人们心中，但文明人所熟知的一切道德原则以及在背后支撑着这些原则的道德情感却都不是天生就有的；事实上，如果我们能返回到过去某个时刻去观察生活在文明与野蛮交界线上的人们的道德状况的话，我们会发现统治他们中间绝大多数人的心灵的仍然只是各种简单直接的欲望以及诸如畏惧、欢喜、忧愁和愤怒之类最原始粗糙的激情。这些激情和欲望是后来发展出来的道德情感的原材料，然而此时它们还都只是无形式的物质，"从这些物质中抽绎出形式"的工作在拉丁文中叫作educere，这便是我们现在称为"教育"的过程。按照维柯的推测，最早的教育是从英雄时代开始的，这也是人类在英雄的规训和庇佑下初沐民政之光的时代，这一时期流传下来的神话把依旧生活在自然状态下的野蛮人称作"巨人"（《奥德修纪》第九卷中有关于巨人的描述，《贝奥武甫》第112行则把巨人与葛蝼代归为同类），而所谓教育就是"以某种方式使原先完全淹没在巨人们的庞大身躯里的人类灵魂的形式呈现出来，同时也使人体本身具有恰当身材的形式，从原先不平衡不匀称的巨人身躯中呈现出来"[1]。

不过，要把道德情感从这一片欲望与激情的海洋中抽绎出来，人类最早的教化者应该从何处着手开始他的工作呢？或者说，当俄耳甫斯（Orpheus）的琴声使猛兽纷纷俯首时——俄耳甫斯的故事是英雄时代神话中另一个和教育有关的隐喻[2]——最初响起的究竟是怎样一种奇妙的和弦？这一和弦又是在猛兽心灵中

1　[意]维柯：《新科学》，第248页。

2　类似于舜的治理致使"百兽相率而舞"，从舜的身份可以推想出俄耳甫斯的真实身份。

的哪一根"心弦"上激发出共鸣，以至于原本凶猛的野兽竟顿时变得驯服起来了呢？这是一个颇难回答且永远无法得到实证的问题，然而如果我们相信古代神话中确实包含着关于古代历史的真相的话，那么前面提到的有关美惠三女神教给人类以文明的技艺的传说倒是为上述问题提供了一个合理的回答。

道德情感想必是伴随着社会的出现而产生的。达尔文认为，"人的社会本能中包含着道德感最初的基石和起源"[1]。这一假说若能成立，那么人类心灵中最初产生的道德情感就应该是与促使分散的个体凝聚为社会的心灵活动密切关联的，而按照美惠女神的神话，社会是肇始于恩惠的施受的，恩惠施受的核心是"善意"的来回往复，如此说来，简单纯粹的"善意"就应该是原始教化者从人类灵魂的原始海洋中抽绎出来的第一缕有形式的细丝了。兽人心中潜藏的善意只能通过包含着善意的行动来激发，或者说，原始人的心灵就像一个封闭的城门，只能用善意的不断撞击来攻破。包含着善意的行动就是恩惠的施与，这也是俄耳甫斯竖琴奏出的第一声和弦，而对恩惠的感激则为这一和弦在兽人心灵中引发的第一声共鸣和回响。施惠并不是必然能激发出感恩之情的，原始教化者想来应该是经历过无数次试错和挫折之后才把野兽般的巨人训练为人的，不过正如拥有优势基因的个体更有机会存活并把其基因传给下一代一样，通过实践获得友爱美德的人群也更有希望在战争状态中幸存壮大并把这一社会美德的基因不断传播开去。从这个角度再回看罗瑟迦与贝奥武甫之间的互动，这一互动背后包含着的道德意义便清晰地显现出来了：赏赐大方的罗瑟迦继承的实际上是原始教化者的衣钵和余绪，而贝奥武甫以报恩之举展现出的则是原始教化者最希望在其教化对象身上看到，同时也是最有利于社会形成和稳固的一种美德，"知礼"。在史诗的故事层面上贝奥武甫打败葛娄代靠的是一双铁掌的千钧之力，在隐喻意义上，他的胜利其实是心灵中发生的知礼对野蛮征服。

一个既知礼又拥有勇力和智慧的骑士是最适合当国王的。随着贝奥武甫连除

1　Philip Appleman, *Darwin* (Norton Critical Edition), New York: W. W. Norton & Company, 2001, p. 248.

二凶，人们越来越清楚地看到了这位年轻豪杰的远大前景。在送别贝奥武甫的宴会上，罗瑟迦预言他将来一定会成为"人民持久的支柱，战士的靠山"（1707—1709），为此，他特地以海勒摩为反面典型对这位未来的王者做了一番郑重的告诫。海勒摩年轻时受到奥丁的眷顾，拥有超凡的勇力和胆略，一度曾被百姓寄予莫大的希望，然而这样一个威加四方的英雄在登上权力顶峰后却迅速堕落为一个嗜血的暴君，致使人民的生活再次陷入水深火热之中：

> 相反，海勒摩却成了
> 艾戟威拉的后代、光荣的丹麦人的祸害。
> 他的王业带来的不是幸福，而是屠杀。
> 他动辄迁怒于同桌的伙伴，拿亲信开刀，
> 直至他，孤家寡人，一时的暴君，
> 被永远地逐出了人们的欢乐。
> 虽然全能的上帝曾满足他勇力的富足，
> 置他于万人之上，号令四方，
> 然而他心中滋长出越来越残忍的恶念，
> 根本不顾名誉，断绝了丹麦人
> 金环的赐礼。他被幸福所抛，
> 因倒行逆施和对人民的蹂躏，
> 而久久不得解脱煎熬。
> 记住这个教训，勿忘慷慨的美德。（1709—1722）

作者此处用在海勒摩身上的描写如"被永远逐出了人们的欢乐""被幸福所抛"等让人不由得会联想起诗中其他地方对葛蒌代的描写（如"从来不知道人世的欢乐"［105］、"断绝了希望和幸福"［1275］，当然，葛蒌代的先祖该隐也因杀害亲弟而"远远离开了人的欢乐"［1264］）。另一方面，海勒摩在大厅中的所作所

为也与葛娄代颇有可比之处：两者都是厅中武士的屠夫，都给丹麦人带来了无尽的灾难。作为国王，海勒摩最初也曾是大厅的创立者，但到最后他却成了自己建造的大厅中令人胆寒的葛娄代，这样一种戏剧性的角色反转之所以会出现，归根到底还是因为他忘记了施惠的重要性，"断绝了丹麦人金环的赐礼"。大厅本应是互惠发生的欢乐之地，但当恩惠之舞的领舞者自己抽身离开了这个环舞时，互惠的链条也就被彻底打破了。互惠之链被打破意味着社会的基础不复存在，而海勒摩的暴虐统治最终也确实导致了丹麦社会的分崩离析。"勿忘慷慨的美德"是一条看似十分简单的箴言，但它实际上却凝结着前人的惨痛教训以及希尔德王朝几代人的政治经验。罗瑟迦把它作为临别忠告赠给了未来的高特国王贝奥武甫，对于我们而言，它也以一种高度概括的方式回答了本文最初提出的问题，即，若一个君主因骄傲和残忍而"断绝了金环的赐礼"，那么他本人就会成为大厅最危险的敌人。

处于"野蛮时代高级阶段"的丹麦人尚无抽象意义上的"社会"概念，但从《贝奥武甫》对大厅及其种种敌人的描写看，他们显然已经能够用形象思维和神话语言来把握"社会"这一事物的基本内涵了。

（文章发表于《上海交通大学学报（哲学社会科学版）》2019年第4期。本文系作者在联盟2019年年度论坛上的发言）

历史记忆

Historical Memories

For the Greater Good: English COVID-19 Poems and a Sense of Community

Jian Zhang[*]

Introduction: Two Paradigms

The COVID-19 pandemic has brought up memories of similar plagues which broke out in the past, as well as memories of literary works which reflect those plagues. From Boccaccio's *Decameron* to Daniel Defoe's *A Journal of the Plague Year*, literary works describe those plagues which devastated Europe, from time to time, between the fourteenth and seventeenth century. These plagues have appeared in one way or another in the works of British writers from Chaucer onwards. The Pardoner's Tale from *The Canterbury Tales* mentions a plague which struck London in 1348. Thomas Nashe's *Summer's Last Will and Testament* has a character dying of a plague in 1592, who sings the now familiar song "A Litany in the Time of Plague." Shakespeare lost several loved ones, including sister and brother, to the plague which struck London in 1603 and which reportedly took 30000 lives. Thomas Dekker shifted his writing from drama to pamphlets because a plague caused the closure of theatres (Dekker 1925). Ben Jonson's *Alchemist* is set in the plague year of 1610.

The most serious plague which struck Britain was certainly the Great Plague of London in 1665, the story of which is told in Defoe's *A Journal of the Plague Year*, first published in 1722. The narrator is a Londoner named "H. F." (Henry Foe) who allegedly lived through the devastating effects of the pestilence and produced this eye witness account of

---

* Jian Zhang (张剑) is professor of English Literature at Beijing Foreign Studies University, Beijing, China, specializing in Modernism, Romanticism and China-West literary relations. He has written on T. S. Eliot's tradition, Ecological awareness of the Romantic poets, and the China Works of W. H. Auden, William Empson, Allen Ginsberg and Gary Snyder.

that terrible year. Henry Foe claims that the plague was brought into England by active commerce with mainland Europe. Despite the different measures taken by the health authorities, it spreads like wildfire among the city's population. The narrator reports black "tokens" on the bodies of a great number of victims and the consequent mass burials (Defoe 1992). In the end, the pestilence left tens of thousands of Londoners dead.

In British poems of the time, plagues are treated in two different ways. First, plagues are viewed as punishment, due to the anger of God, who uses pestilence to punish sinners. Second, plagues are viewed as a reminder that humanity is an interconnected whole and all lives are integrated. The first viewpoint is a religious interpretation of the plague, and dates back to ancient Greek drama and the Homeric epic poems. However, it is mainly in the Christian era that plagues acquired more moral, political and religious meanings. As Susan Sontag wrote in her *Illness as Metaphor*, diseases are traditionally interpreted metaphorically, because the nature of the disease is not understood, and therefore, is likely to arouse wild imagination concerning its purpose and motive. Sontag has listed the pestilence in *Oedipus Rex* as an example of divine punishment, and later on in Christian writings, this kind of interpretation is even more common (Sontag 1978). Plagues are widely utilized to enhance moral teaching, to condemn evil, and to promote good and benevolent behavior.

Thomas Nashe's "A Litany in Time of Plague" is a metaphorical interpretation of the plague, as well as a poetic preaching against the vanity of human wishes: "trust not in wealth / Gold cannot buy you health" (Nashe 1964, 130). Indulgence in earthly pleasures, carnal joys, material wealth, physical beauty, physical strength, eloquence, and wit, is regarded as the probable cause of the speaker's impending death. Alternatively, the impending death is regarded as the probable result of sinning or indulging in such earthly bliss. As the time of death approaches, the speaker comes to the realization that a sinful life is punished with plague and immature death: "Heaven is our heritage / Earth but a player's stage" (Nashe 1964, 130). In other words, the plague is used as a tool to preach virtuous life, and to warn people away from earthly pleasures.

Apart from this interpretation of the plague, another interpretation can be found among poets of the time. About 30 years after Thomas Nashe, John Donne wrote another response to a plague which took place in the early seventeenth century. Originally, "No Man Is an Island" was not a poem; it was part of a sermon, preached to the author's congregation and collected under the title of "Devotions upon Emergent Occasions." It has acquired fame and circularity following Earnest Hemingway's use of it as the title of his novel. Lifted out of its context, it looks much more like a poem than a sermon, and displays all the characteristics of a metaphysical poem. The centerpiece of the poem, if interpreted as a poem, is a conceit that regards humanity as a continent and the individual as an island, an extended metaphor which suggests that no human can exist separately like an island and that, taken altogether, all human life is like a continent (Donne 2001).

The emphasis here is on unity and community: when we face the threat of a horrible disease, we need to strengthen ourselves by belonging to a larger whole, by thinking that human nature unites us all. In other words, just as we are all an integral whole, in the same way, one human's death is not his / her death alone, it is the partial death of all of us. "any man's death diminishes me," Donne says, "because I am involved in mankind." (2001, 446) Considered in this way, the poem suggests that we live each other's life, and we die each other's death. At a time when death occurs as a daily phenomenon and consolation is hard to achieve, Donne's emphasis on the unity of mankind is obviously a comfort to those who have lost their loved ones. Therefore, Donne says, "never send to know for whom the bell tolls, it tolls for thee." (2001, 446) In other words, it tolls not just for the dead, but it tolls for all of us.

It seems that these two interpretations of the seventeenth century plague are the major paradigms which, in our time, poets draw from to interpret the COVID-19 pandemic. The COVID-19 poems, which this essay discusses, include those published in magazines and newspapers and those published on the internet, as posts on web pages and as global online writing projects organized by famous poets and editors. The poems, written by professional poets as well as teachers, students, doctors, drivers, barbers, etc.; by poets from English-speaking countries, as well as from India, Malaysia, the Philippines, and other parts of the Third World, represent a variety of responses to the pandemic. In other words, the poems come from all those who have a word to say about the pandemic and they represent a medley of voices and a display of democracy.

"14 Classic Must-Read Poems on Plague and Pestilence" comes from the Interesting Literature website; "Parody: Writer in Lockdown" comes from *ALSo*, a publication of Alliance of Literary Societies; "WRITE where we are NOW" comes from a global writing project organized by poet laureate Carol Ann Duffy; another global writing project was organized by Indian editor R. S. Regin Silvest, who published the poems in the five-volume collection, *Covid-19 Pandemic Poems*. Alice Quinn, former poetry editor of the *New Yorker*, collected nearly 100 poems and published them as *Together in a Sudden Strangeness: America's Poets Respond to the Pandemic*. A look through the titles will show that the poems fall mostly into the two categories demonstrated above regarding the pandemic's metaphorical use: for the purpose of moral teaching and for the purpose of community building.

Moral Teaching: Sin and Punishment

The idea of retribution persists in the modern understanding of the plague, despite the decline of religion and faith. Just like those in the seventeenth century, the present pandemic led some people to believe that moral depravity causes God's anger and results in God's punishment. As can be seen in the title "Perhaps You Are a Trojan Horse," the poem regards the virus as "God's agent" that is secretly administering an "invisible justice." The virus is said to be placed "on the doorstep of the world" to teach a lesson to the "worshipers of black magic" in America, Europe, and other parts of the world; a lesson to "the stony-hearted people" who do not notice or do not care about the sufferings and pains of the Third World; a lesson to the "worshippers of power" and "global arms dealers and warmongers," forcing them to obey the Veda principle of nonviolence. This is an exact interpretation of the pandemic as Susan Sontag's formula describes it: "disease as a tool of divine retribution" (Silvest et al. II 2020, 17).

The Trojan horse in Homer's *The Iliad*, as we all know, is a trick or ruse used by the Greek army to break into the stronghold of the city of Troy which had persisted, unfallen, for ten years, despite the attack of the Greek forces. If COVID-19 is a trick or a ruse in the great drama of sin and punishment, then it has indeed broken the battlement of humanity's defense and has brought a huge disaster to this world, killing thousands of the human population. Yet, on the other hand, it has also brought positive changes: leveling society, decentralizing powers, making "houses into homes and crowds into families" again. As such, there is reason for the poet to exclaim, "Oh, coronavirus, you conquered humanities' vices" (Silvest et al. II 2020, 18).

Another poem, entitled "Pan[dem]ic Realities," is also based on the idea of divine retribution, assigning the virus the role of helping to correct human depravity and cleanse human vices, including arrogance, self-inflation, hatred, avarice, dishonor, and violence. Mother Earth's anger is set on fire and she hurls the Porcupinean COVID-19 to besiege the world (Silvest et al. I 2020, 51). The environmental dimension of the retribution is especially and clearly directed against humanity's arrogance and avarice in its attitude towards nature: to be more specific, against its "conquer nature" ideology. The moral teaching in this instance is obviously to curb humans' selfish exploitation of natural resources and massive destruction of natural ecology.

"The Wrath of the Crown" views the pandemic as having jammed on the brake of modern, fast-paced life because, in the eyes of God and nature, all the ways of humans are at fault. The pandemic is an ultimatum issued to humans "for returning back to the flock / for a healing to happen before the clock / for there is much poison deeply rooted down in the decayed hearts" (Silvest et al. II 2020, 22). Obviously, the coronavirus is seen as God or nature's punishment of humankind. Just as Craig Santos Perez says in the poem "Contact Tracing," what we need is not inoculation against the virus, but a "vaccine for virulent outbreaks of human greed and violence" (Perez, 2020, 139).

Fatal epidemics, as shown by past and present experiences, are usually caused by viruses which, previously parasites on animals, have escaped from their host. These epidemics can also be said to "come from our chronically exploitative relationship with animal—animals we exploit for entertainment and, most dangerously, for food" (Estok 2021, 438). If animals have a voice, they will surely point their finger on humans for causing their distress. The poem "Distress of the Earth" presents exactly an animal's complaint regarding their conquest by humans. "We are suffocated with toxic / our feet were torn from our hair / Why you make cruelty on us?" (Silvest et al. I 2020, 48) Now, with the COVID-19 pandemic, animals have an opportunity for revenge, armed with an unexpected weapon which they may use' to destroy their destroyer. This is a typical example of what Sontag calls a metaphorical use of illness, attributing to the virus a moral function for teaching humans to behave and to curb their avarice.

Another interesting poem in this category is Mitch Siskind's "The Coronavirus Holds a Press Conference." The virus is presented as "nature's agent," coming to us with a "message": "the universe is always sending / coded messages;" but "you people need to be aware of them and understand / them." In this melodramatic setting, many problems from American politics are addressed. First of all, the virus cites Dostoyvski's *The Possessed* to say that he is here to "make a mess of life," to make "as big a mess of it as possible." (Sisskind 2020) Followingly, he claims to have not read Susan Sontag's *Metaphor of Illness*, yet he still attributes his destructive action against the University of Chicago to a racist remark made by a professor from its Department of Political Science. When questioned on his view of President Trump, he answers, "Trump is not important, the important thing is how you, you and you respond to him." (Sisskind 2020) He goes on to compare Trump to the Pharaohs of ancient Egypt and to Lindsey Graham, the segregationist of the American Civil War period. Lindsay Graham reminds him of the Graham crackers, and of one of *cracker*'s meanings as "bigoted white man." Metaphorically, the virus wants his audience to understand that its purpose in coming here is to fight racism.

Indeed, many of these poems' disease narratives do not concern the disease itself, but the social problems which are highlighted by the disease. As Wald says, "it is possible to revise the outbreak narratives, to tell the story of the disease emergence and human connection in the language of social justice rather than of susceptibility" (Wald 2008, cited in Estok 2021, 346). The social problems often discussed in English COVID-19 poems include racial discrimination, police violence, poor-rich disparity, inequality in the distribution of wealth, and medical resources. Although COVID-19 is often seen as a "leveler," because it attacks all equally, irrespective of race, class, or gender, ultimately this cannot cover up the injustices and inequalities which adamantly persist in western society and which are intensified and enlarged by the pandemic into even more violent forms. The "Black Lives Matter" protests reveal not just police violence, but also the existential condition of the blacks, and the unfair treatment they received during the pandemic. Their rates of poverty and death are higher, and their rates of inoculation and hospitalization lower, than the average of the whites and other minority groups. Just as Estok says, "The truly radical idea here is that it is not the germ, but more importantly, social conditions that give rise to many varieties of disease" (Estok 2021, 346).

A Sense of Community: Fighting a Common Enemy

Any society, east or west, will consist of separate individuals with a diversity of interests and pursuits. Since the Enlightenment, the idea of the "sovereign individual" encourages the individual to assert rights and to realize their potential. A society is designed to protect the interests and welfare of the individual against infringement from collective power. However, in a crisis like the COVID-19 pandemic, the society needs to be united in action and a sense of community becomes the prominent need. For the society to persist, the variety of interests and right claims must not clash with each other but reach or negotiate some kind of balance or equilibrium. Imagine what will happen when a nation faces an invasion from a foreign power: the common threat will unite the nation into greater solidarity. The previous differences and conflicts are temporarily forgotten or laid aside. This is exactly what we see in the many English COVID-19 poems, which perceive the virus as an invisible and deadly enemy, and the fight against it as a war.

John P. Read's "Keep Safe" warns people against the act of the handshake, because such an innocent and simple gesture will pass on the deadly virus. "It contaminates and does us harm / By the simple touch of our hands." In his view, "Our world is now at war / With an enemy that's unseen." He pleads with people to wash their hands because "hygiene is our only shield." (Read 2020) The war metaphor here is used to show the fierceness of the pandemic, and plead for a united effort in order to prevail. Elizabeth Mitchell's "Apocalypse" shows a doctor preparing herself for the war against the horrible disease. She ties the yellow gown behind her back, and ties her hair into a bouffant. Like a warrior going to a final and decisive battle against a monster, she goes to her position in the hospital, armored with shields to protect her mouth, nose and eyes (Mitchell 2020). The Armageddon metaphor is used to compare the virus with Satan, the arch enemy and the deadly opponent who, in the form of invisible droplets, lurks on the handle or in the sink, trying to "find their way into our trusting hands or mouths or eyes."

If COVID-19 is an equalizer which erases differences of race, class, sex, or age and attacks all humanity, then we humans are facing a common threat and for our common survival we should face it together, because COVID-19 will not disappear until the last patient is cured, and no country will be safe until all countries are safe. Therefore, it is a battle between humanity and a common enemy. This is the sense of community that the COVID-19 pandemic arouses in the people who wrote these poems.

Marsha Warren Mittman in "The Almost Apocalypse" says that COVID-19 should close gaps and narrow differences. It enables people to rise above the bickering and nagging of blind politics and release from the heart "a groundswell of compassion," a new spirit of cooperation, aid, and love. "People themselves took wing," she says, "they rose as one to help / each other and set examples / to raise spirit and offer hope" (Silvest et al. III 2020, 1). The poem sees in the pandemic not so much a catastrophe as a call upon "the good inherent in each of us" to effect a change in the world so huge that the poem describes it as an "almost apocalypse." According to the poem, instead of "tearing us apart" or "destroying the planet," the pandemic will actually unite us and bring us together.

This call for unity, though badly needed in the fight against COVID-19, is paradoxically so difficult to realize in the context of widespread contagion. People are advised to stay home and keep socially distanced; one of the most serious problems that the pandemic posed to people's life may be said to relate to sequestration during quarantine. When socialization is suddenly halted, people begin to realize how important society or community is for them. In his poem "Sequestration," Billy Collins compares human hearts to "pilot lights" to warn people not to approach (in Quinn, 33). Hearts which previously yearned for privacy and love must now resist temptation.

Jessica Salfia's poem "The First Lines of Emails Received While Quarantining" collects many different people's emails to show that "people are struggling." (Salfia 2020) Though the title suggests the poem to be a "found" poem, with a collage of disparate sentences written by different people in their emails, it is in fact a well-organized piece of writing presenting the life of people living through the pandemic. Some features of this life include distance learning, food shortage, and cabin fever. This last one suggests that, while privacy is previously highly valued, isolation and lockdown are felt to be more unbearable. While people must become used to this "new normal," they also yearn for the time when they were able to go out or socialize again.

Charles Bernstein's "Covidity" writes about the pains of isolation. With an oversize mask, the speaker of the poem obeys the rules of social distancing. He "feels like the Lone Ranger / Just before he gets the clap." What other people call social distancing, is to him a "pain in the soul"—it is "too heavy a load" (Bernstein 2021, 82). "Covidity" in the title means a state of existence disrupted by the COVID-19 pandemic, and the most painful feature of this existence is isolation. The speaker, in a state of lonely helplessness, tries to contact "you" on the telephone. The "you" seems his last resort, his last hope in this terrible crisis, but "you" is not available.

The "Lone Ranger" metaphor transforms the speaker into a fugitive, who is being pursued by the bad guys. He hides from them, "buried under covers, sheltered in halls," for fear that they will find him where he is. The terror of being found out and being killed is a haunting fear in the poem: "The covid gonna get me / if not now, soon" and it forms the greatest psychological pressure for the speaker. If the lonely speaker has someone there to support him, he will probably have the strength and the courage to resist the fear. As we can see, community is not always an infringement on the individual's rights; sometimes it provides support, aid, and hope.

Death, a more than common occurrence during the pandemic, is a more painful experience of separation than social distancing, because it realizes permanent distance and permanent separation. In his poem "Time of Death: 7:19 pm," Craig Spencer records a lonely death in hospital, unaccompanied by relatives or friends. This experience of death must be devastating because there is no companionship, no comforting company of family. The only people present are the doctors and nurses who are busy trying to save other patients. However, as they "stop the drips and turn off the ventilator," they automatically stand around the dying. A nurse cannot help sobbing, and someone begins to say a prayer. Although "This isn't what we do," he says, the doctors and nurses are not family members. Still, they do this out of compassion, "You stand by. You wait." (Spencer 2020) This also reminds us of John Donne's famous dictum that one human's death diminishes us all and the bell tolls not just for the dying, but for all of us.

Compromising Egotism: For a Greater Good

Traditional pandemic narratives show that quarantine, travel bans, and social distancing are usually not welcome. Such policies caused riots in the 1665 plague: towards London's lockdown on the infected families, the city government was resisted with swearing, violence, and even murderous actions. Plague and protest often go hand in hand. In the 1830 cholera epidemic, the Russian government's "compulsory treatment" policy caused the angry people to storm into hospitals to release patients who were locked in against their wishes (McMillen 2016, 65). In a society which highly values personal freedom, the right to free movement is considered inalienable.

This is perhaps why, in the present COVID-19 pandemic, segregation, the mask mandate, and compulsory vaccination have met with various extents of resistance and are considered an infringement of personal freedom and personal choice. Under the condition of quarantine, people's yearning for freedom is understandable. "Joy" is an important phenomenon in traditional pandemic narratives and it is as contagious as the disease. "People usually seek comfort from worldly pleasures, abstract thinking, and indulgence in glorious past" (Zhang Xiuli 2021, 37). Indeed, pleasure and humor are the best means with which to deal with fear. John Keats, author of the famous "Ode to the Nightingale," was a victim of tuberculosis and knew well the suffering caused by the terrible disease. In Duncan Wu's parody "The Sharp-Nosed Frog (written while self-isolating in Rome)," the dream to escape to a painless fairyland is still there, but the nightingale is transformed into a "sharp-nosed frog" (Wu 2020, 8). In the dream, the frog has a wonderful time drinking and reveling in this fairyland, surrounded by Libyan Maenads, fairy Songstress, and Venusian hippies, until the dream ends, and he is back again in the cold and swampy reality.

The conflict between lockdown and joy is in fact a conflict between personal freedom and social responsibility. Gerard Manley Hopkins had cloistered as a Catholic priest for many years in a monastery and knew loneliness and segregation. In the monastery, he wrote the famous poem "The Windhover," concerning an eagle that flies high up in the air, and is therefore a symbol of the freedom he yearned for. In Hoon Manley's parody "Tandem Liberi," freedom is also an important theme. People pour out of their houses, when the pandemic eases temporarily, and swarm into pubs and restaurants. "Let hostelries be full again, swift half or cheeky sesh!" But the author warns that, if we do not restrain ourselves, the pandemic will be back again. "Overhead / threat hangs by a thread" (Manley 2020, 12).

However, the question we face is: are quarantine policies justified for the purpose of controlling the epidemic? Should personal freedom not be balanced by social responsibility? In the poem earlier cited, "Contact Tracing," Craig Santos Perez expresses much impatience for those who, during the pandemic, still want to go and suntan themselves on the beach, or go out and drink in the pub, or travel to all kinds of places in the world to enjoy themselves. He laments for the people who came in large groups to

Hawaii in grand cruise ships, which have turned out to be super spreaders of the virus or a "reservoir of disease." "It seems not even a pandemic," he says, "can cancel paradise" (Perez 2020, 139).

Personal freedom is indeed an inalienable right; however, the problem is that people are not even willing to compromise such a right for a limited period of time for the greater good of community health. This cannot but be seen as a distortion of the idea of personal freedom. It cannot but be seen as extreme selfishness or egotism. In "Thirteen Ways of Looking at the Virus," Perez again confronts "the covidiots of America" with questions like "Why do you travel for spring break? Don't you see how virus / Transmit from the mouths / Of the asymptomatic?" (Perez 2021, 2) The indignation contains not just a condemnation of the violation of the quarantine rules, but also a call for the traditional and noble spirit of altruism and self-control.

In his poem "Lockdown," Simon Armitage tells the story of a far-away village in England during the great plague of 1665. Like the present pandemic, the plague created panic among the villagers of Eyam, some of whom intended to escape north but were stopped by the village priest, who said we should not pass on the virus, we should pass on kindness. Led by the priest, the village implemented self-quarantine, the so-called "lockdown" which stopped the village's mobility and cut its commerce with the outside world. This action of self-isolation successfully contained the plague within the village and prevented it from spreading to other areas of Britain. The cost was more than 300 villagers' lives lost.

This story, now a legend in the history of the British fight against plagues, is told as an example of altruism and self-sacrifice. The moving story of the lovers, separated by quarantine until the girl's death, highlights the great sufferings that the villagers underwent and the tragic consequence of the plague on individuals (Armitage 2020). Yet it is also a great action of self-sacrifice for the sake of the community, a noble action worthy of praise and remembrance, which transcends self-interest. The poem is obviously not written as an anecdote of history to satisfy curiosity. The title of the poem "lockdown," designated by many countries as "the word of the year" in 2020, is specially chosen to suggest that the poem is a comment on the present pandemic. The plague has indeed adversely affected individuals' lives, but to conquer the plague will need communal and consorted effort. It suggests that when people go to the streets to protest against lockdown policies and assert their individual rights, they should also look at history and learn from the examples. Though of course not a direct comment, the poem's point is quite clear.

Pubs, restaurants, and grocers have become so integral a part of life that people have taken them for granted and do not usually notice their existence. It is only during a crisis like the COVID-19 pandemic that people realize the value of the services they previously received and therein attributed no special significance. In "Garden," Raymond Antrobus pays tributes to the teachers, the dentists, the psychiatrists, the cleaners, the construction workers, the plumbers, and the barbers because their work enables people to have a normal life (Antrobus 2020). Indeed, the awareness that our life depends on each other's services increases a sense of community.

Hilton Obenzinger's "Flatten the Curve" does not just reflect the anxiety and fear of the people during the rise of the COVID-19 curve, but also expresses a confidence that humanity will, in the end, win this war against the virus. The curve will only be brought down or "flattened" with the consorted or united efforts of all the people fighting the virus and all the people cooperating with the fight, including doctors, nurses, salesmen, cashiers, bus drivers, deliverers, and other ordinary workers (Obenzinger 2020). In the poet's view, although we use many words of praise for them, such as hero, courage, bravery, resilience, professional, noble, and moving, words compared with action are weak or mean nothing. Only by our collective actions, may we hope to flatten the curve and win the final victory.

Conclusion: "Community Thinking"

The traditional Western philosophical discussion of "community" often opposes community with the individual. We see it discussed in the work of such philosophers as Tonnis, Marx, Anderson, Williams, Bataille, Nancy, Blanchot, and discussed in various contexts associated with race, class, nation, self, and other. "Community" is often seen as a totalization which erases singularity, angularity, and individuality. It acquires a negative sense because it implies collectivism and an infringement on individual rights. In Freud, even civilization is considered as a repressive force which curbs the individual's instincts and represses his wishes. In Foucault, the individual is often the victim of disciplining forces from such social institutions as prison, hospital, mental asylum, school, and church. Of course, the individual's rights ought to be respected, and in the time of a pandemic, this is especially so, and Western thinkers are worried that special circumstances will allow the pendulum to be swung to the other end (Žižek 2021).

While it is admitted that individual differences are infinite and that totalization means violence, it is probably also to be admitted that for society to persist, some kind of management or government is required. Though government is considered repressive, it is also often considered a "necessary evil," an institution which we cannot do without. Philosophically or metaphysically speaking, community is indeed opposed to the protection of individuality, yet in reality, community also strengthens the individual's power and extends its potential. EU, formerly European Economic Community, was formed because a Union of sovereign states enhances the power of all the states. Even philosophers Nancy and Blanchot are not totally opposed to the idea of community, though they would qualify the concept to avoid misunderstanding. For them, community (la communaute) is not exactly totalization, but dis-con-junction, or communism without community (Nancy 2007, 111). A passage between self and other is always kept open, though one's alterity always stands inviolable and not to be compromised. An emphasis is laid on the "interdependence between communism and individualism" (Blanchot 2016, 6), not the opposition.

Community is not just a social or political entity; it is also a way of thinking. In China, we say he-er-bu-tong, the differences do not obstruct the individuals from coming together, because we emphasize the similarity (Zhang Jian 2021). Community means a desire to belong to a larger whole. It is to regard other humans as part of us. Therefore, you do not regard other people as threats, but as friends. "Community thinking," if we may so call it, is a way of thinking which promotes harmony and unites the world. It may be seen in the poems of John Donne in the seventeenth century, and in the COVID-19 poems by Simon Armitage, Charles Bernstein and many other poets in the twenty-first century. Promoted by China, "community thinking" is different from the "antagonistic thinking" which is common in Western geo-politics and parliamentarian politics, which valorizes differences and polarizes the world. In a sense, community thinking is not only needed when we face a huge pandemic like COVID-19; it is needed all the time in the world we live in.

(Acknowledgement: This article is a revision of the author's speech at the 2021 UKCHA Annual Forum.)

References

Antrobus, Raymond. 2020. "Garden." In *WRITE where we are NOW*, edited by Carol Ann Duffy. Manchester Metropolitan University website. Available at: http://www.mmu.edu.cn//write/. [Accessed February 7, 2022]

Armitage, Simon. 2020. "Lockdown." *The Guardian*, March 21, 2020.

Available at: https://www.theguardian.com/books/2020/mar/21/lockdown-simon-armitage-writes-poem-about-coronavirus-outbreak. [Accessed March 4, 2021]

Bernstein, Charles. 2021. "Covidity." *Critical Inquiry* 47, No. S2 (Winter): 82–84. https://www.journals.uchicago.edu/doi/10.1086/711443. [Accessed February 11, 2021]

Collins, Billy. 2020. "Sequestration." In *Together in a Sudden Strangeness: America's Poets Respond to the Pandemic*, edited by Alice Quinn. New York: Alfred A. Knopf.

Cooke, Jennifer. 2009. *Legacies of Plague in Literature, Theory and Film*. Houndmills, Basingstoke: Palgrave Macmillan.

Dekker, Thomas. 1925. *The Plague Pamphlets of Thomas Dekker*. Edited by F. P. Wilson. Oxford: Clarendon Press.

Defoe, Daniel. 1992. *A Journal of the Plague Year*. Norton Critical Edition. Edited by Paula R. Bckscheider. New York & London: W. W. Norton.

Donne, John. 2001. *The Complete Poetry and Selected Prose*. Edited by Charles M. Coffin. New York: Modern Library (Random House).

Estok, Simon C. 2021. "Introduction to the Special Cluster 'Never Really Far From Us—Epidemic and Plagues in Literature.'" *Neohelicon* 48: 435–442.

McMillen, W. Christian. 2016. *Pandemics: A Very Short Introduction*. New York: Oxford UP.

Manley, Hoon. 2020. "Tandem Liberi." In "Parody: Writer in Lockdown." *ALSo*… 15 (2021): 1–34.

Mitchell, Elizabeth. 2020. "Apocaplypse." In *New York Times* website. Available at: https://www.nytimes.com/2020/03/24/us/coronavirus-doctor-poetry-boston.html. [Accessed April 15, 2020]

Nashe, Thomas. 1965. *Selected Works*. Edited by Stanley Wells. Cambridge, Mass.: Harvard UP.

Obenzinger, Hilton, 2020. "Flatten the Curve." In Best American Poetry website. Available at: https://blog.bestamericanpoetry.com/the_best_american_poetry/2020/03/flatten-the-curve-a-plague-poem-by-hilton-obenzinger.html. [Accessed on February 7, 2022]

Perez, Craig Santos. 2020. "Contact Tracing." *Oceania* 90, Suppl. 1: 139–140.

——. 2021. "Thirteen Ways of Looking at the Virus." *Kenyon Review* 43 (Mar/Apr): 2.

Read, John P. 2020. "Keep Safe." In Family and Friends Poems website. Available at: https://www.familyfriendspoems.com. [Accessed on January 5, 2021]

Salfia, Jessica, 2020. "The First Lines of Emails Received While Quarantining." In *The Guardian*, April 12, 2020. Available at: https://www.theguardian.com/books/2020/apr/12/poem-constructed-from-emails-during-quarantine-goes-viral. [Accessed on January 1, 2021]

Silvest, R. S. Regin et al., eds. 2020. *Covid-19 Pandemic Poems*. Vols. I–V. Kanyakumari, Tamilnadu. India: Cape Comoin Publisher.

Sisskind, Mitch. 2020. "The Corona Virus Holds a Press Conference." In Best American Poetry website. Available at: https://blog.bestamericanpoetry.com/the_best_american_poetry/2020/03/the-corona-virus-holds-a-press-conference-by-mitch-sisskind.html. [Accessed on February 7, 2022]

Sontag, Susan. 1978. *Illness as Metaphor*. New York: Farrar, Straus and Giroux.

Spencer, Craig. 2020. "Time of Death: 7:19 pm." In NBC 4 New York website. Available at: https://www.nbcnewyork.com/news/local/time-of-death-719-a-somber-poem-of-the-coronavirus-as-death-toll-rises/2358051/. [Accessed on May 7, 2023]

Stannard, Martin. 2020. "An English Plague Poem." In Best American Poetry website. Available at: https://blog.bestamericanpoetry.com/the_best_american_poetry/2020/03/an-english-plague-poem-by-martin-stannard.html. [Accessed on February 7, 2022]

Wald, Priscilla. 2008. *Contagious Cultures, Carriers, and the Outbreak Narrative*. Durham and London: Duke UP.

Wu, Duncan. 2020. "The Sharp-Nosed Frog." In "Parody: Writer in Lockdown." *ALSo*…15 (2021): 1–34.

Žižek, Slavoj 2021. "Is Barbarism with a Human Face Our Fate?" *Critical Inquiry* 47, No. S2 (Winter): 4–8.

莫里斯·布朗肖 2016.《不可言明的共通体》，夏可君、尉光吉译. 重庆：重庆大学出版社。

[Blanchot, Maurice. 2016. *The Unavowable Community*. Translated by Xia Kejun & Wei Guangji. Chongqing: Chongqing UP.]

让-吕克·南希 2007.《解构的共通体》，夏可君等译. 上海：世纪出版集团。

[Nancy Jean-Luc. 2007. *The Inoperative Community*. Translated by Xia Kejun et al. Shanghai: Century Publishing Group.]

王松林 2021.《人类命运共同体视域下的英美诗歌瘟疫书写》,《外国文学动态研究》第2期, 第17—28页。

[Wang Songlin, 2021. "English and American Poems' Pandemic Narratives through the Perspective of Human Community of Shared Future." *New Perspective on World Literature*, No. 2:17–28.]

张剑 2021.《没有人是一座孤岛: 疫情中的英美诗歌》,《光明日报》8月12日。

[Zhang Jian, 2021. "No Man Is An Island: English Poems during Pandemics." *Guangming Daily*, August 12.]

张秀丽 2021.《道德教诲、娱乐与欢笑》,《外国语言与文化》第4期, 第36—45页。

[Zhang Xiuli, 2021. "Moral Teaching, Joy and Laugh." *Foreign Languages and Cultures*, No. 4:36–45.]

Measuring non-Han Bodies: Anthropometry and Biopower in China's South-Western Borderland in the 1930s and 1940s

Jing Zhu[*]

Introduction

The history of Chinese anthropology, frontier regimes, and the construction of nations during the Second Sino-Japanese War (1937–1945) are intimately interconnected (Yen 2017). During the 1930s and 1940s, particularly during the war, Chinese anthropologists switched the focus of their research from the Han Chinese community, located near the east coast, to the ethnic minority groups of the south-western borderlands (Guldin 1993, 57; Hu 2006, 78–90; Wang 1997, 229–243). Soon after the clash at the Marco Polo Bridge and the occupation of large areas by the Japanese army in 1937, the Chinese government announced the removal of its capital to Chongqing in Sichuan. Government agencies established temporary offices in Wuhan in Hubei, while people, schools, and factories relocated from coastal areas to the interior and the frontier (van de Ven and Drea 2011). Chinese anthropologists believed that anthropology was a useful tool for governing the

* Jing Zhu (朱敬), Xi'an Jiaotong-Liverpool University, Department of China Studies, Humanities and Social Sciences Building, Suzhou, Jiangsu 215123, China. Jing Zhu received her PhD in history from the University of Edinburgh. Before joining XJTLU as an assistant professor, she held postdoctoral fellowships at the University of Warwick, Humboldt University in Berlin, and the Science Museum in London. Jing is interested in the history of images and material cultures, and her interdisciplinary research explores the intersections of histories of empire, visuality, frontier studies, gender history, anthropology, and the history of science. This features in her monograph *Visualising Ethnicity in the Southwest Borderlands: Gender and Representation in Late Imperial and Republican China* (Brill, 2020).

frontiers (Ma 1947, 10). They measured and studied the bodies of non-Han peoples in the south-western frontier and undertook anthropological research into their clans, religions, customs, marriage, family, economy, social structure, and languages. This article explores the biopolitics of ethnographic bodies in the frontier regimes during the 1930s and 1940s by focusing on anthropological research conducted on the bodies of non-Han peoples by Han Chinese scholars. It reveals the political adoption of Western anthropometry in China in the process of nation-building.

The article's discussion of the measurement of non-Han bodies is located within a broader debate relating to the history of the human sciences in modern China, particularly the biopolitics of population management. In several important works edited by Howard Chiang, scholars have examined the sciences of social organization and human experience in China and the reciprocal influence of politics and human science disciplines (Chiang 2015, 2019). Several works addressing health, nutrition, and genetics in modern East Asian history have demonstrated how biological and behavioural norms have been determined by the state and the agents of the state through coercion, regulation, or interpellation (Leung and Caldwell 2019; Leung and Nakayama 2017; Nakajima 2018; Schneider 2003, 19–114). In her study of mass immunization in modern China, Mary Brazelton (2019, 1–14) emphasizes the political control of biopower. In his study on the history of anatomy in Republican China, David Luesink (2017) highlights the use of anatomy as a political tool. He highlights how state control and discipline were exerted through human dissection law and the biological knowledge of the population. Likewise, Jia-chen Fu has examined the intimate relationship between body measurement and public health and dietary intervention in Republican China (Fu 2016).

Frank Dikötter, in his analysis of the discourse of race in modern China, argues that race was understood in the Republican period in terms of biological species. This reflected the anthropological and archaeological research that took place between 1915 and 1950 into skin colour, hair, brain size, and odour. Science was used to rationalize race structures (Dikotter 1992, 126–164). In his studies of racial classifications, Thomas Mullaney

(2004, 2011) has shown how ethnic taxonomization in modern China has been envisaged and structured through linguistic tools. The following discussion develops the existing scholarship of biopower in East Asia to include the government of the non-Han population in the south-western borderlands of Republican China. As a case study examining how Republican archaeologists assembled an array of physical traits representing the non-Han, it enriches our understanding of biopolitics and frontier regimes.

The concepts of biopower and biopolitics interrogate an underlying relationship between politics and everyday life. Crucially, they relate to the governmentality of species and populations (Cisney and Morar 2016, 5–7). As Paul Rabinow and Nikolas Rose put it:

We can use the term biopolitics to embrace all the specific strategies and contestations over problematizations of collective human vitality, morbidity and mortality; over the forms of knowledge, regimes of authority and practices of intervention that are desirable, legitimate and efficacious. (Rabinow and Rose 2006, 197)

In race studies with political rationality, biopower is a very useful analytical tool that frequently draws on the biological understanding of racial differences (Rabinow and Rose 2006, 205–208). Indeed, in her analysis of Michel Foucault's *History of Sexuality*, Ann Laura Stoler underscores the intimate relationship between biopower, bourgeois sexuality, and racisms of the state (Stoler 1995, 1–19). As regards Republican China, the body traits of non-Han populations were extracted from anthropological studies of individual bodies, while the scientific identification of non-Han bodies contributed to the political interpretations of nation and the justification of frontier cultivation. The introduction of Western anthropometry in China offers a significant non-European case study for examining and complicating our understanding of the transnational practice of biopolitics.

Elise Burton (2012) has examined the practices of genetic anthropology and science in the Middle East. She argues biology was interpreted within the contexts of Jewish and

444

Persian nationalism among elite Israeli and Iranian scientists from the mid-1950s to the late 1970s (Burton 2018a). In Burton's study of national-level projects throughout the Middle East to decode the Arab, Turkish, and Iranian genomes, she reveals nationally framed narratives of genomic diversity, as well as the influence of local histories and politics on the interpretation of genetic sciences of racial diversity (Burton 2018b, 762–768). Hidefumi Nishiyama (2015) examines the biopolitics of Japanese fingerprint anthropology. Although situated in an earlier historical period, the Chinese experience of adopting Western anthropology and science for interpreting national ethnicity and diversity shares several similar trajectories with Burton's studies of the Middle East experiences. This article thus also argues the importance of nationalism, politics, and local agency in narrating racial diversity in China.

In historical studies of European anthropology, scholars have identified a close relationship with colonialism and imperialism (Asad 1973; Conklin 2013; Tilley and Gordon 2007). Likewise, in the Chinese empire, the Qing dynasty (1644–1911) adopted a similar anthropological approach to the colonial regimes of the borderlands (Hostetler 2001). In the Republican period, Chinese scholars harnessed Western anthropology to study the frontiers, particularly as a means of assisting with the ruling and cultivation of the south-western borderlands. However, the study of non-Han body measurements must be considered in the context of its mutual associations with anthropology, colonial regimes, and body sciences. Hsiao-pei Yen (2012, 2019) has revealed the colonial and national uses of anthropology in the borderlands of China through case studies of several Republican anthropologists. As she puts it, Chinese wartime frontier anthropology not only supported the Nationalist colonization of the southwestern frontier but also facilitated the naturalization of the colonial practices under the banner of Han-centric nationalism (Yen 2017, 160). The investigation of non-Han bodies that this article considers further enriches our understanding of the colonial practices of frontier rule through anthropology and body sciences.

This discussion draws on research reports, proposals, photographs, travel accounts, diaries, and memoirs, all of which relate to body measurements taken by Chinese anthropologists. These sources yield rich evidence on the political uses of anthropology in China. The article is divided into three principal sections. The first part discusses the introduction of physical anthropology to China and the major research projects on the body measurements of non-Han peoples. The second analyses the physical attributes of the non-Han body through data and statistics calculated from body measurements and how it responded to the Western racial categorization of the Mongolian / Yellow race. The final section examines the political use of non-Han body traits as a means of rationalizing the improvement of malnourished non-Han bodies, the military defence of the frontiers, the assimilation of non-Han peoples, and the construction of a unified China.

Measuring non-Han Bodies: Physical Anthropology in Republican China

At the turn of the twentieth century, physical anthropology, or anthropometry (*tizhi renlei xue*), and the methodology of body measurement (*renti celiang*) were introduced to China from Europe and America (Du 2013; Wang 1996; 1997, 243–250). Originating in Europe, anthropometry was the art and science of measuring the bodies of individuals to obtain a scientific understanding of the physical variations within a demographic context. Its principal use was the ethnographic study of indigenous colonial subjects, as anthropologists endeavoured to construct a science of man on the basis of a comparative study of racial traits. Anthropometry was also used to study the bodies of criminals and psychopaths and, in late nineteenth- and early twentieth-century Europe, as a way of selecting soldiers (Hrdlička 1920, 7–9; Garson and Read 1892, 8–15). Living bodies as well as skulls were measured (see Poskett 2019, 19–50). Elise Smith's (2020) research on anthropometry in late nineteenth-century Britain also suggests British anthropologists, such as Francis Galton (1822–1911), promoted body measurement as a means of examining public health, heredity, and fitness.

As briefly mentioned in the Introduction, the research on bodies of non-Han peoples in the south-west was inextricably linked with the Second Sino-Japanese War. When it moved the capital to the west of China, the Republican state sought to further a nation-state project in the south-western borderland, devising a series of frontier construction plans that encompassed economic and cultural transformations in the region. Chinese anthropologists and politicians believed that anthropology was an essential tool for colonial regimes (Ma 1947, 10; Yang 1948). This is best exemplified in the widespread use of the term frontier administration (*bianzheng*) in several scholars' discussions (Wang 2014, 1–18). The leading Republican anthropologist Wu Wenzao (1901–1985) used the term studies of frontier administration (*bianzheng xue*) when discussing the growing importance of studying the frontier for political purposes (Wu 1942, 2). Several anthropologists whose previous research had focused principally on Han Chinese communities thus began to turn their attention to the ethnic minority groups in the south-west of China (Lin 1999, 57). The measurement of non-Han bodies became part of the research of Chinese anthropologists in the south-western borderlands. This anthropometric research noticeably increased during the Second Sino-Japanese War but came to an end when the war ended in 1945 (Chen 2013).

Body measurement in the first half of the twentieth century was used to conduct research into ethnic minority groups. In fact, it was regarded as a means of producing the most reliable racial classifications in China. The body (*tizhi*) assumed significance in discussions relating to the scientific methodology of racial categorization. Indeed, results generated from the analysis of body measurements were regarded as the most reliable (Ma 1936, 185). Dai Yixuan (1908–1988), a Republican historian and ethnologist, claimed that racial classifications generated from body measurements provided the most scientific and objective methodology in the study of races within China (Dai 1938, 32). Liu Xian (1902–?), who had graduated in anthropology from the University of Oxford, argued publicly in 1928 that the body represented an important criterion of racial classification, helping to produce reliable racial taxonomy in China (Liu 1929, 92). By contrast, anthropometry was a contested science in the West, and measurements were not necessarily accepted as the best means of understanding humanity (Smith 2020). However, it seems that most Chinese anthropologists and ethnologists during the Republican era chose to stress the reliability of anthropometry and its contribution to racial classification. Fei Xiaotong (1910–2005), one of the most influential sociologists in twentieth-century China (see Hamilton and Wang 1992), studied physical anthropology at Tsinghua University with Sergei Mikhailovich Shirokogoroff (1887–1939), a Russian anthropologist who worked and taught for many years in China (Fei 1994). Fei asserted that anthropometric research was undertaken for the purpose of racial classification. He claimed that from the index numbers calculated from the length and size of each body part [an anthropologist] could decide which racial type this person belongs to (Fei 1935, 37). He went on:

If we could study all the people in our country, and if the survey were complete, we could clearly understand the structure of the Chinese people. Within this structure, we could then understand all sorts of issues of ethnicity. (Fei 1935, 39)

The exploration of structure, meaning, and the constituent parts of the *Zhonghua minzu* (Chinese ethnicity) was of great interest to Chinese anthropologists and intellectuals in the 1930s and 1940s. The constitution of the *Zhonghua minzu* was one of the principal concerns of Chinese intellectuals during the Republican period. Chinese anthropologists, by means of anthropometry, sought new evidence to demonstrate a politically defined concept of Chinese ethnicity. The interpretation of data that had been extrapolated from body measurements was linked with the constitution of the *Zhonghua minzu*, which will be discussed further below. Fei did not specify the issues among different ethnic groups in China, but he believed that anthropometry could help researchers understand all sorts of current issues relating to ethnicity (*minzu wenti*). Anthropometry was expected to be useful for the politics of ethnicity.

Racial classification and research into the origins of *Homo sapiens* was an international endeavour. Western anthropologists, as well as physicians and missionaries, undertook anthropometric research in China. These included Paul Huston Stevenson (1890–1971), an American physician who had worked at the Peking Union Medical College between the 1920s and the 1940s (Stevenson 1940). Members of the anatomy department at the Medical College worked closely with Chinese colleagues who excavated human remains in Beijing in the 1920s. Measurements of skulls and living bodies enabled them to explore the origins of the human species (Schmalzer 2008, 33–53). William Reginald Morse (1874–1939), a Canadian medical missionary in western China and the founder of the West China Union University, measured the bodies of various ethnic minority groups in the south-western borderland, including Tibetans (Morse 1937). Sergei Mikhailovich Shirokogoroff studied the bodies of the Tongus and Manchu in northern China (Shirokogoroff 1923). Frequently working closely with Chinese colleagues, Western anthropologists expected to achieve an understanding of human diversity and racial taxonomy worldwide; the disciplines of archaeology, anthropology, and anatomy often intersected.

Body measurements in Republican China were taken in order to create a body profile for every province in China. Li Ji (1896–1979) undertook anthropological research at Harvard that provided scope for provincial differentiation (Li 1928). When he returned to China, Li conducted body measurements in Hubei, where he analysed physical differences between those living in the south-east and the north-west of the province (Li 2006 [1924]). Wu Jingding (1901–1948), a student of Li, measured the bodies of people in Shandong, publishing a monograph on body traits within that province (Wu 1931). Research into body measurements in Republican China also sought to enhance the Chinese physique (Fu 2016). Writing to the director of the Academia Sinica, the leading research centre for anthropological research in China, Chiang Kai-shek demanded that the Academia undertake research to improve the quality of the Chinese physique. The Academia Sinica responded with research plans that included the heredity of the Chinese body, the brain of the Chinese people, and the bodies of Chinese young people. Echoing Chiang's political appeals for research-led improvements of the bodies of the Chinese populace, Wu Dingliang (1894–1969) proposed the establishment of the Preparatory Office of the Department of

Anthropometry (*Tizhi renleixue choubei-chu*; Du 2011). For the purpose of scientific racial classification, ethnographic research, and eugenics, body measurement was promoted in Republican China, which included the measuring of non-Han bodies in south-western China.

Anthropometry pertained to the science and art of body measurement, and measurement was a key constitutive practice of anthropometry. The monograph Anthropometry by Ale Hrdlička (1869–1943), the leading Czech / American physical anthropologist, offered detailed instructions on body measurement. Various parts of the body, including the height and breadth of the nose, ear, mouth, face, and head, were measured with tools including spreading calipers, sliding compasses, tapes, standard meters, standard blocks, dynamometers, and weighing scales, while skin, eye, and hair colour were recorded using standard shades. Tables were designed to facilitate the careful recording of the measurements, before the statistics were compiled into indices, such as the Nasal Index, Ear Index, Chest Index, and Facial Index. Based on these data and indices, anthropologists hoped to analyse body characteristics and racial taxonomies. This methodology was expected to determine the body's identifying features and to capture the structure of human variation (Hrdlička 1920, 52–88). Chinese scholars trained abroad played significant roles in the introduction of anthropometric research in China. Wu Dingliang considered Hrdlička and Rudolf Martin (1864–1925) two of the greatest physical anthropologists in the world (Wu 1948). Martin, a Swiss-German anthropologist, made significant contributions to the standardization of anthropometric research in the early twentieth century (Morris-Reich 2013). The anthropometric research of the Academia Sinica followed the guidelines of Martin's *Lehrbuch der Anthropologie in systematischer Darstellung* (Textbook of Anthropology in Systematic Representation; Martin 1928; Rui 1954, 278–279).

Extensive research on non-Han bodies in south-western China took place during the Second Sino-Japanese War. From the late 1920s to the mid-1940s, the Academia Sinica was the leading research institution on ethnic minority groups; its population studies included those of the Hezhe in the north-east, the Miao in western Hunan, the She in Zhejiang, and the Qiang in Sichuan, as well as various ethnic minority groups in Yunnan and Guizhou. Wu Dingliang, who joined the Academia Sinica in 1935, strengthened its studies on bodies in China. Wu had studied anthropology at Columbia University and University College London, where his supervisor was Ronald Aylmer Fisher (1890–1962), a well-known British statistician and geneticist, and had worked at the Galton Laboratory, which specialized in eugenics research (Owen 1962). In the course of his studies in the UK and Europe, Wu researched statistical models for calculating facial traits and measuring skulls, including Egyptian and newly excavated Chinese skulls from the Shang dynasty (1600 BCE–1046 BCE; Du 2011, 96–97). After returning to China in 1935, Wu worked at the Academia Sinica, where he studied skulls recovered from archaeological excavations in Anyang, as well as the living bodies of the Han Chinese and ethnic minority groups in the south-west of China (Du 2011, 97).

In an article introducing this research methodology in the borderland, Wu presented a tool of his own design, the Form and Table for Anthropological Research (*Renleixue diaocha biaoge*; Figure 1; Wu 1944, 6–20). We see on the lower part of the form bodily measurement, observation, and experiment [diaoliang guancha yu shengli shiyan], divided into 32 sections. Eye colour is listed alongside the dimensions of the head, nose, ear, mouth, and forehead. Blood group is also included. The work of Martin Rudolf was Wu's primary reference (Wu 1944, 13). Compared to Rudolf's table of measurements, appended to the end of his book that introduced the methodology of anthropometry (Martin 1928), Wu's table contains less in terms of the measurement of contents. According to Rui (1954, 279), the Academia Sinica specified two distinct tables for body measurements: one for laboratory measurements, the other for field work. Owing to various difficulties when undertaking field work, the table for body measurements collated in the field was more simplified than the one used in the laboratory.

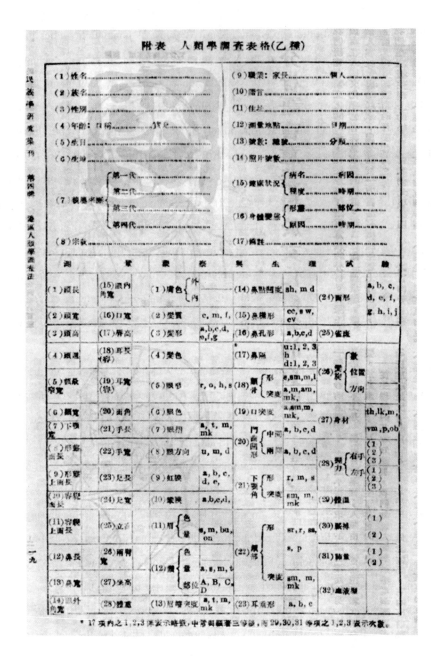

Figure 1: Wu Dingliang, Form and Table for Anthropological Research, 1944 (Wu 1944, 19).
Digital Collection of Shanghai Library.

Having undertaken research in over 60 villages in Guizhou, a research team led by Wu Dingliang and Wu Rukang (1916–2006) collected around 2000 samples of body measurements and more than 1000 samples of fingerprints and blood from members of ethnic minority groups in 1941 (Wu 2014, 668–674).

According to an annual research report by the Academia Sinica in 1945, the majority of anthropometric research projects were related to the borderlands. These included studies of the body traits of the Xiao Huamiao people in West Guizhou, the Shuixi Miao in West Guizhou, the Lolo in Guizhou, and the Lisu. They also included studies of the blood pressure of children in southern Sichuan and the distribution of blood types among the people of southern Sichuan (Academia Sinica 1947).

Non-Han bodies were also measured in other forms of social and cultural anthropological research. Tao Yunkui (1904–1944) was another physical anthropologist who had trained abroad. He received his doctoral degree in anthropology from Berlin University in the 1930s, under the supervision of Eugen Fischer (1874–1967), a German professor of medicine, anthropology, and eugenics. Tao's thesis, which was later published in Chinese, sought to demonstrate the law of Mendelian inheritance, by exploring the genealogy and heredity of the bodies of a hybrid Chinese and European couple; he measured and analysed the skin, heads, faces, hair, and bodies of several Chinese and Europe families (Tao 1940a). After returning to China, he joined the Academia Sinica and studied the non-Han peoples in Yunnan during the course of several research trips (Li 2012, 1–20). Although Tao's major publication veered towards social and cultural anthropology, his travel diary reveals that he measured the bodies of several ethnic groups in western Yunnan during his research trip (Tao 1942).

Under the influence of Tao, Chinese anthropologists recognized the body as an essential dimension of research in the borderlands. Lin Yaohua (1910–2000), whose earlier research had centred on rural families in southern China, studied anthropology with Wu Wenzao at Yenching University. Later, he attended Harvard University, where, as a doctoral research student, he studied physical anthropology, linguistic anthropology, archaeology, and cultural anthropology (Lin 1999, 59).

His thesis related to the history of the documentation of the Miao in Guizhou during the Qing dynasty (Lin 1941). After returning to China in 1941, he worked at Yunnan University. In 1943, after he had received funds from the Society Opposing Japan and Frontier Cultivation (Kangjian Kenzhishe), the Rockefeller Foundation, and the Harvard-Yenching Society, he attended the Liangshan, where he studied local ethnic minority groups (Lin 1947b, 2). As part of his research, he measured the bodies of the Lolo in the Cold Mountain areas (Lin 1947b, 1). In Lin Yaohua's travel account of research on the Sichuan frontier, he mentions how his party met a staff member and two students from the medical school of Tongji University, who were also measuring the bodies of the Lolo in villages in the county of Leibo in 1943 (Lin 1947b, 121).

The anthropometric research undertaken by Chinese scholars during the Republican era was conducted principally by those who had studied abroad, their students, and their assistants. Their training backgrounds, which included placements in leading anthropological departments in the UK, the US, Germany, and France, were diverse. It seems that European anthropologists argued endlessly among themselves about their research techniques, measurements, approaches, perspectives, methodologies, and instruments. However, Chinese anthropologists, despite their different backgrounds, were less inclined to dispute underlying matters. In his study of the history of anthropology in China in the first half of the twentieth century, Wang Jianmin contends that Chinese anthropologists may have placed different emphases on research methodology and theory. Indeed, scholars based in the northern parts of China tended to lean more towards functionalism, while those in the south were shaped by the French historical tradition. In comparison to the debates of different anthropological schools in Europe and America, however, the conflicts among Chinese scholars were minor (Wang 1997, 156). As regards physical anthropology in Republican China, it appears that Chinese anthropologists were less interested in debating the conflicts of methodologies and theories among different schools. Rather, through the lens of anthropometry in wartime, they focused on the projection of racial classifications, the constitution of the Chinese nation, and administration in the frontiers, all of which will be examined further in the following sections.

Body Traits of non-Han Populations and a Response to the Mongolian / Yellow Race: The Cases of the Miao in Guizhou, the Yao in Guangdong, and the Luohei in Yunnan

As discussed in the previous section, research reports, summaries, diaries, and memoirs of Chinese anthropologists provide evidence that anthropometric research was conducted on the non-Han peoples in south-western China. However, research that was produced and published with an analysis of data is relatively limited. The journal *Collected Papers on Anthropology* (*Renleixue jikan*) of the Academia Sinica, which was devoted to physical anthropology, contains articles on Han Chinese bodies but few relating to the non-Han peoples in the south-west. This may be attributable to difficulties in measuring non-Han bodies. It was very hard to persuade non-Han people to agree to have body measurements taken. As Lin Yaohua writes,

non-Han people were extremely suspicious of measuring tools, believing that they would steal their souls and that death would follow. Often, however, anthropologists were allowed to measure their bodies through the help of influential local residents and the exchange of gifts, which included needle and thread. (Lin 1947a, 129)

Similar examples can be found in Yang Chengzhi's account of his anthropometric research in Guangdong, where he found the Yao people afraid of measuring tools, such as tapes and calipers. Music from a gramophone, followed by gifts of cigarettes and needles, persuaded some Yao men to allow themselves to be measured (Yang 1937, 16).

Lin Yaohua, in his field research report, *The Lolo in Cold Mountain* (*Liangshan Yijia*), discussed the geography, clans, family, marriage, economy, class, conflicts, and witchcraft of the Lolo in the cold mountains, but not specifically their bodies, although he had undertaken anthropometric research. The introduction of *Liangshan Yijia* described how it had taken a long time to clarify and analyse body measurement data; his description of the bodies of the Lolo, he added, would be given in another article (Lin 1947b, 1). In a later memoir describing his research in Liangshan, Lin said that the body measurement material was lost while he was travelling across China during the war (Lin 1999, 57). Likewise, Fei Xiaoton attributes the loss of his data on the bodies of the Yao people in Guangxi in 1936 to upheavals in the first half of the twentieth century (Fei 1994, 21). Nevertheless, three articles on the body measurements of the Miao in Guizhou survive (the Miao by Wu Dingliang, the Yao in Guangdong by Yang Chengzhi, and the Luohei in Yunnan by Rui Yifu), which contain highly detailed analyses of body measurements. These may still provide rich material on how body characteristics of the whole group were constituted through the methodology of anthropometry and how the racial type of each group was determined.

It is important to acknowledge that the idea of representing the non-Han body was not new in Republican China. In fact, Chinese anthropologists were revisiting an area that had already received attention from imperial ethnographers, continuing to use the medium of the body as a way of creating or reconfirming a neocolonial order of human variation. Miao albums, a genre of ethnographic illustrations depicting the bodies, culture, and environment of ethnic minority groups in southern China in the late imperial period, were representative of typical ethnographic material that depicted non-Han people. Generally, each album consisted of several alum leaves, each page representing one ethnic group (Hostetler 2001; Zhu 2020). Skin colour, hairstyle, customs, religion, and clothing colour were all considered elements of differentiation. The bodies of non-Han people were depicted in a set of visual grammar. Indeed, specific aspects of physiognomy were assigned to non-Han people, including deep-set and yellow eyes, high or hooked noses, red hair, and white teeth (Zhu 2019, 169–198). The Miao albums highlight ethnic minority women's feet as both large and exposed, contrasting with the bound feet prevalent among upper-class Han Chinese.

Naked female bodies became standardized as a visual code in the depiction of some ethnic groups in Yunnan and Guizhou (Zhu 2019, 169–198). In her studies of the Miao albums of Taiwan, Emma Teng (2004, 172) observes that the indigenous Taiwanese were depicted with savage bodies that featured nakedness, tattoos, piercings, bulging muscles, and belligerent postures. Although referring to a much earlier period, Marc Abramson has also demonstrated the power associated with the bodies of northern non-Han subjects (Abramson 2008). He observes that deep eyes and high noses was the most common phrase used to describe non-Han physiognomy in the Tang era.

A curly or thick beard was another feature associated with barbarian men. Hairstyle was also a significant marker of the barbarian figure (Abramson 2003). The body was manipulated to conform to a binary coding of the superior and inferior, weaving a narrative web of human variation in imperial China. Bodies throughout history have been important indicators of ethnic differences through intersections with culture, gender, and sexuality norms. In Republican China, Chinese scholars utilized imported Western physical anthropology to produce collective body traits in their representations of the non-Han population. Although anthropologists employed new scientific methodology and rhetoric to observe and represent non-Han bodies, the body provided a useful tool and medium for conveying racial differences; it enabled them to circulate imperial ideas of a hierarchical racial order in both the late imperial and the modern period.

Yang's anthropometric research adopted the guidelines of Rudolf Martin's 1928 version of the *Lehrbuch der Anthropologie* (Martin 1928). Yang measured the bodies, heads, faces, and noses of 48 Yao people. He reached a conclusion on the collective body characteristics of the Yao. He claimed that the average height of a Yao person was 157.75 cm, which suggested the Yao were small. Their average head index was 82.22%, suggesting medium-sized heads; their face index was 77.56%, indicating broad faces. A nose index of 81.74 meant that the Yao had medium-high noses (Yang 1937, 31). On the basis of morphological observation, Yang suggested that the hair of the Yao was typically thick, straight, and black. Their body hair was sparse, as were their beards. Their head shape was between medium and short. Their medium-size noses were convex and concave. Their skin colour was yellow and black. Their lower jaws neither protruded forwards nor receded backwards. As regards height, some were very tall and others small, but their average height was short. Their eyes were Mongoloid and folded; their eye colour was black and white. Their mouths were very wide and their lips extremely thick. Their cheekbones were high (Yang 1937, 31–32). Yang claimed the bodies of the Yao belonged to Menggu Zhong (the Mongolian race) and Huang Zhong (the Yellow race; Yang 1937, 33). Yang described the bodies of the Yao in Western anthropometric language; numerical precision was important. The use of expressions such as medium-sized or short type suggests that he defined the bodies of the Yao by following the international criteria on body types that had been produced by physical anthropologists.

Menggu Zhong and *Huang Zhong* were European categorizations of various peoples in Asia from the end of the eighteenth century. The concept of Asia as the Mongolian / Yellow race was circulated among the general public during the Republican period. The physical body of *Huang Zhong* was generally believed to be of short stature and to have black hair, sparse body hair, and a light brown skin colour (Lin 1932; Ye 1931). Michael Keevak's (2011, 1–21) work examines how East Asians became the "Yellow" or "Mongol" race in Western scientific discourse during the nineteenth century. Keevak argues that the work of Peter Simon Pallas had the most profound influence on the use of the word Mongolian in describing all the peoples of East Asia (Keevak 2011, 74). Johann Friedrich Blumenbach's classification of five major races of the world in the late eighteenth century (the Caucasian race, the Mongolian race, the Aethiopian race, the American race, and the Malayan race) largely shaped racial science and classification in later centuries. Since the early twentieth century, the Mongolian race has variously been described as brownish red and yellowish, yellow and olive, brownish yellow, and the Yellow race (Keevak 2011, 97–98). The constitution of the Mongolian / Yellow race was dependent on numerous historical, scientific, and cultural contingencies that had little to do with the "real Far East" (Keevak 2011, 128). Although the Chinese people had never previously associated themselves with a "Yellow" race, Republican Chinese anthropologists began to adopt an artificial European racial-scientific structuring of the peoples of the world, demonstrating that the nations of China belonged to that Yellow category.

To counter this European conflation of the Japanese, Chinese, and Koreans into a larger "Mongolian" racial category, anthropometric research was also conducted by Japanese researchers in Japan, Korea, and China in the first half of the twentieth century. The efforts of anatomists and anthropologists to differentiate the modern Japanese from the Ainu, Korean, and Chinese led to increasingly precise measurements of human anatomy and physiology (Low 2012). Different uses of anthropometry in Japan and China are evident. When science and technology spread across different regions and countries, it was frequently adopted and driven by local social and political desires. Echoing Yang Chengzhi in his travel account of the Sichuan frontier, Lin Yaohua also claimed that the Lolo belonged to the *Mongolian* race. As he put it,

We carried measuring tools to the mountain areas, where we collected rich source material on the body measurements of ethnic minorities; the data is in the process of analysis. According to measuring and observation, we know that the non-Han peoples absolutely belong to the Mongolian race. (Lin 1944, 64)

Analysis of anthropometric research in China thus manifested a localization of global ideas on racial classification and the reinvention of regional identity through Western racial structures.

Based on his research in Yunnan in 1935 and 1936, Rui Yifu (1898–1991) wrote an article on the bodies of the Luohei in Yunnan under the supervision of Wu Dingliang, but it was not immediately published owing to the outbreak of the Sino-Japanese War in 1937. Having moved to Taiwan with the Kuomintang, who had lost the civil war of 1945 to 1949, Rui published a revised version of the article in the journal of the Academia Sinica in Taiwan in 1954 (Rui 1954). Rui's research concluded that the Luohei often had the Mongolian folded eye; the upper part of their teeth was concave, and they had high cheekbones. They had the most typical characteristics of the Yellow race (*huangzhong ren*). The skin of the majority was dark yellow (*an huangse*), their eye colour dark brown (*an hese*), which was similar to that of the Kala (another ethnic group in Yunnan). Their bodies were short, their noses long, and their jaws narrow. Their noses were classed as medium-size. Their bodies most resembled those of the Kala; the similarities to neighbouring ethnic groups were determined by the geographic distances rather than languages (Rui 1954, 322–323). Rui compared the bodies of the Luohei with those of several other ethnic groups nearby. His principal conclusion was that the Luohei belonged to the Yellow race. The Mongolian folded eye, cheekbone, jaw, skin colour, eye colour, nose, and body size represented the major features that defined the Yellow type. It seems Chinese scholars working on anthropometric research all tried to respond to the European grouping of the Mongolian/Yellow type. After measuring 302 men and 100 women from the Pa Miao of central Guizhou, Wu Dingliang defined their body characteristics as follows:

> The skin colour of the inner surface of the upper arm ranges from pale yellow, which is most common, to a tawny yellow. Their hair is almost invariably black and straight, and sparse on the body. The prevailing eye colour is medium brown and lighter than that of most southern Chinese. The epicanthic fold is less marked than among the Chinese, being absent in about 30 percent of cases and most commonly recorded as only a trace. Moderated development of the supraorbital ridge is most common, and the root of the nose is less depressed than among the Chinese and Lolo. Most of the people are of lank or medium body build. These qualitative characters show that the Pa Miao people resemble the Chinese closely, though they have somewhat "diluted" Mongolian characteristics. (Wu 1942, 53)

Wu clearly paid considerable attention to colour, not just of the skin but of other regions of the body, including the hair and eyes. In the first half of the twentieth century, colour appears to have been an important criterion in research into the bodies of Asian people. This was indistinguishable from the European construction of the Yellow race in the nineteenth century. Wu also suggested that the bodies of the Pa Miao had Mongolian characteristics. The work of Yang, Rui, Wu, and Lin all suggested that the Yao, Miao, Luohei, and Lolo belonged to the Mongolian / Yellow race. The Western invention of the Mongolian / Yellow race was received in China and reaffirmed by Chinese scholars through the medium of anthropometric research. The physical traits of ethnic minority bodies, in terms of individual body components, resulted from the Western methodology of anthropometry.

At the end of his article, Wu appended four photographs of the Miao in Guizhou, which included men, women, and children (Figure 2). Portrait D, which shows a young Miao man in half-length, is a highly representative image showing the facial and body traits of the Miao.

Figure 2: Wu Dingliang, photographs of the Miao in Guizhou, 1942 (Wu 1942, 20).

The bodies of non-Han people were visually organized and represented through data and images; images of individuals were used to represent the body traits of the whole group.

In late nineteenth- and twentieth-century Europe, photography was utilized in scientific and anthropological research (Edwards 1992; Pinney 2011; Poskett 2019, 193–240). Anthropometric-style photography was standardized as a means of offering useful anthropological information (Morris-Reich, 2013). When photography was introduced to China, it became a leading visual medium in the representation of ethnic minority bodies in south-western China in the 1930s and 1940s (Zhu 2020, 180–189). A number of anthropometric-style photographs that showed the front, profile, and rear side of the non-Han body were produced and preserved in the archives of the Academia Sinica. Yang, writing about the body traits of the Yao, used photographs to create a generic visual representation of the Yao (Figure 3). The nose, eyes, lips, and cheeks of the portraits shown in Figure 3 are consistent with Yang's textual description of the body traits of the Yao, effected through anthropometry. Anthropometric-style photographs representing non-Han bodies were produced by Chinese anthropologists and also circulated in popular Republican periodicals (Zhu 2020, 180–195). Through text, data, and images, Chinese anthropologists constructed the bodies of non-Han groups, as particular types, and circulated them among professionals and the urban public.

When statistics from more than one ethnic group were made available, scholars were able not only to analyse the collective traits of each group but also to compare them with other groups. In the course of several research trips to Yunnan from the 1910s to the 1930s, Ding Wenjiang (1887–1936), one of the leading scientists of the Republican era, as well as an important political figure, measured the bodies of various ethnic groups in Yunnan and Guizhou (Ding 1933, 17; 1935, 14). In total, Ding collected 65 groups of data on non-Han bodies in the south-west as well as Han bodies in several provinces. For comparative purposes, he planned to write about "the body and classification of the Chinese people" [Zhongguo ren tizhi zhi fenlei]. Unfortunately, his article remained unfinished at the time of his death as a result of an accident during a research trip in Hunan (Wu 1936). Ding also assisted other scholars' anthropometric research in China. With his assistance, the Science Society sponsored the anthropometric research of Li Ji in Hubei as soon as Li returned to China (Li 2006 [1924], 420). In more ambitious plans, anthropometry in China was conducted to produce a racial taxonomy that included the body traits of every ethnic group in China.

Although anthropometry was used to develop racial classifications in Republican China, it is important to appreciate that anthropometry was not imported automatically to China; its introduction was a selective process. For example, when Wu Dingliang studied statistics at University College London under the supervision of Karl Pearson (1857–1936), a well-known mathematician and biostatistician, his research and publications focused principally on the biometric study of human bodies, bones, and skulls (Wu 2014, 668–74). He worked closely with the Galton Laboratory, the work of which centred mainly on biological evolution and eugenics through statistical science. Wu's research interests turned to the non-Han peoples after he returned to China; several of his studies were interpreted within the context of nation-building, which will be considered in more detail in the following section. Wu did not simply adopt what he learned in the West before shifting it to China; rather, he transferred it to the Chinese context in a unique way.

Biopolitics of non-Han Bodies: The Configuration of the *Zhonghua minzu* and Frontier Regimes

Apart from responses to the Western taxonomy of the Mongolian / Yellow race, interpretation of the non-Han body was largely influenced by and used for frontier ruling and nation-building. Chinese anthropologists stressed that the bodies of the Han Chinese and ethnic minority groups were similar in terms of the Mongolian / Yellow type. Focusing on the application of body measurement to non-Han peoples in the borderlands, this section explores the role of biopower in envisioning racial categorization, frontier administration, and the constitution of the *Zhonghua minzu*. In his article on the bodies of the Yao, Yang argued:

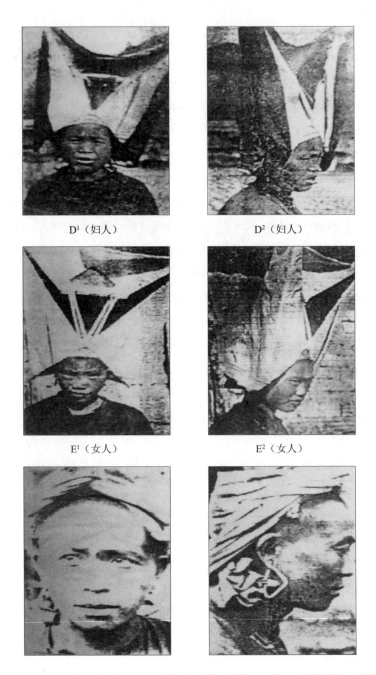

D¹（妇人）　　　　　D²（妇人）

E¹（女人）　　　　　E²（女人）

Figure 3: Yang Chengzhi, photographs of Yao bodies in Guangdong, 1937 (Yang 2004, 107).

The Yao body, no matter whether subjected to the methodology of bodily measurement or morphological observation, does not exceed the range of the yellow races. In particular, it is quite similar to the Han Chinese one pivotal component of *Zhonghua minzu* [Chinese]. We cannot really draw an obvious line which on the face of it would distinguish Yao bodies from Han bodies. (Yang 1937, 33)

Yang argued, using anthropometric and morphological research, that Yao and Han bodies were very similar. Rather than racial differences, Yang emphasized similarities between Yao and Han bodies. Yao body characteristics, as discussed in the previous section, suggested that they were of small stature, with medium-size heads, broad faces, and medium-high noses, which demonstrated that the Yao belonged to the Yellow race. In fact, at the very beginning of Yang's article, he set out the basis for his research. As Yang put it:

The Yao are members of the Mongolian race, and belong to one of the [peoples], [tribes] or [groups] of the *Zhonghua minzu*. This is the premise of this article. Now I will analyse and demonstrate this through the facts generated by anthropometry. (Yang 1937, 15)

Yang claimed his anthropometric enquiry was intended to demonstrate that the Yao people were an essential part of the *Zhonghua minzu*. The quality of information in Yang's account is extremely rich; it evidences the use of terminology including *Zhonghua minzu*, *Hanzu*, *Menggu Zhong*, and *Huang Zhong*. All these terms refer to racial types established, domestically and globally, in the first half of the twentieth century. Racial categorization in China was a changing historical process, constructed and determined for political regimes. Over the past two decades, scholars have examined how China became a multinational state of 56 officially recognized ethnic groups (Huang and Shi 2005; Mullaney 2011). Focusing on individual ethnic groups in the People's Republic of China, including the

Hui, Yi, Ge, Miao, Yao, Dulong, and Mongols, anthropologists have demonstrated that classifications were not a given but that state intervention and politics played a significant role in their formation (Cheung 1996; Gladney 1991; Gros 2004; Harrell 1995; Khan 1996; Litzinger 2000). The political use of science has also been addressed in studies that have drawn on the *minzu* identification (*minzu shibie*) project in Yunnan in the 1950s. During this project, scientists were sent by the state to rural areas to investigate and classify local non-Han populations (Yang 1999). Focusing on the remarkable role of language criteria in modern racial categorization, Thomas Mullaney has made use of linguistic tools to reveal the grouping of the non-Han peoples in Yunnan (Mullaney 2004).

The term *Zhonghua minzu*, which appeared in the early twentieth century, was used by late Qing reformers, including Liang Qichao (Huang 2017, 149–154). In the first half of the twentieth century, the discourse of *Zhonghua minzu* underwent a process of development throughout the establishment of Republican China, embracing the May Fourth Movement, the Nanjing decades of Republican government, and later the Sino-Japanese War (Huang 2017, 132–216). Initially, it referred only to the Han Chinese but later, between the 1910s and the 1930s, incorporated the concept of the five major races: the Manchu, Han, Mongolian, Tibetan, and Muslim. In the 1930s and 1940s, Chinese intellectuals introduced the ethnic minority groups of the south-west of China (the Miaoyi) into the debate about the definition of *Zhonghua minzu* (Huang 2017, 258–564).

Yang's claim that the Yao were a part of the *Zhonghua minzu* clearly demonstrates how the meaning of *Zhonghua minzu* extended beyond the Han Chinese or the five major races. Moreover, Yang considered the Han Chinese the most significant component of the *Zhonghua minzu*. The concept of the Han Chinese as a biracial category of Chinese people had existed as a modern construction since the late Qing dynasty (Leibold 2012; Mullaney 2012, 1–12). The discourse of the *Zhonghua minzu* was thus conceptualized in the 1930s and 1940s during debates centred on the concepts of the Han Chinese and ethnic minority groups. In his studies of the constitution of Turkish identity, Murat Ergin (2017, 99–162) observes that early Republican Turkey made intense efforts to erase and downplay physical differences between ethnic groups in order to support assimilation policies in the 1930s. Similarly, Chinese anthropologists constructed racial sameness to construct a unified China that included both the Han and non-Han peoples.

Ralph Litzinger argues that the discourse of race is (like all discourses) full of ambivalence and contradictions and always deployed selectively in any specific context (Litzinger 1995). Similarly, in his study of three Republican intellectuals travelling to the north-west in the 1930s, Jonathan Lipman (2002, 113–130) finds that the concept of *minzu* remained among the core concerns of the researchers but that their interpretations of racial difference differed radically. This section demonstrates that the concept of *minzu* in Republican China was a dynamic concept and needs to be examined within a specific context. China was in the process of constructing a modern nation-state. The meanings of *Zhonghua minzu* evolved and were constituted by political events, wars, government, and public intellectuals. The categorization of race had to be examined cautiously and in context.

Significantly, Wu, in his article published in English in the Journal of the Royal Anthropological Institute of Great Britain and Ireland in 1942, compared body differences among the Miao, Lolo, and Han groups but eschewed norms like the *Zhonghua minzu* (Woo 1942). The article in the English journal was aimed primarily at European audiences who had anthropological interests. However, Yang's article on the Yao in Canton was published in *Folklore* (*Minsu*), a journal based at Sun Yat-sen University, which promoted research into Chinese folklore, including Chinese songs, stories, legends, religion, and customs, for both academic and public audiences. Terms like *Zhonghua minzu* were also noticeably absent in Rui's 1954 article on the bodies of the Luohei (Rui 1954). The meanings of *Zhonghua minzu* were constructed within specific contexts and for specific audiences. The interpretation of human variation was dictated by audiences, reflecting the social and political adoption of racial science. However, the uses of anthropometric research for the construction of the *Zhonghua minzu* appeared in Wu's other article, which introduced the methodology of frontier anthropology to a Chinese readership (Wu 1944, 6–7).

Wu listed four reasons justifying the practical use of frontier anthropology in colonial rule. He claimed that because people in the frontier regions were impoverished, their economy was backwards. They suffered from everyday malnutrition. Because they lacked any knowledge of hygiene, the growth and development of their bodies were seriously impaired. Therefore, if the poorly developed bodies of the non-Han peoples were to improve, they needed to be measured and studied. Second, the Americans during the First World War had selected their soldiers through general anthropometric examination. Likewise, if the frontier peoples were to contribute to the war effort in the borderlands, anthropometry could assist with the selection of soldiers with strong bodies. Third, the bodies of those belonging to the *Zhonghua minzu* differed only slightly. Through anthropometric research, Wu claimed, one could demonstrate the correlations among the *minzu* within China, in order to avoid misunderstandings and discriminations among the different nations. Finally, scientific proof of similarities between the bodies of those who were part of the *Zhonghua minzu* could help to promote marriage among different groups, thus assimilating ethnic minority groups (Wu 1944, 6–7).

The first of these reasons reflects a national appeal to improve the bodies of Chinese people through scientific research, in which non-Han bodies were also included. The bodies of non-Han groups were, however, conceived of as weak and maldeveloped owing to their impoverished environment, poor economy, and bad sanitation. In his discussion of nation-building in modern China, Magnus Fiskesjo (2006) suggests that the new Chinese state is a resurrection of the old idea of China as a civilizing imperial centre. In terms of understanding race, Chinese scholars during the Republican period also inherited imperial legacies. The non-Han populations continued to be conceived of as impoverished, peripheral people who needed to be enlightened.

China has a long tradition of documenting ethnic others: their locations, costumes, local products, food, religion, and customs. Wang Mingming suggests that the history of anthropology can be traced back to ancient China. One of the most important aspects of Chinese anthropology is its conjunction with ideas of *tianxia* (all under heaven).

Hierarchy was the defining characteristic of the Sino-centric world system of *tianxia*, which represented ethnicity by means of a civilizing line starting from a central zone (of civilization) and extending into the zones of savages (Wang 2012, 359–365). When Western anthropology was introduced to China, the idea of seeing the frontier as a periphery did not change; nor did the justification for political rule through anthropological observation and documentation.

Wu's third point, that those belonging to the *Zhonghua minzu* differed among themselves only slightly, mirrors Yang's account of the bodies of the Yao and Han. Indeed, Lin Yaohua described the bodies of the Lolo as follows: The black Lolo may have one or two body traits, slightly different from the Han Chinese, such as average height, hooked nose and black skin. Yet for all other traits, the Lolo body is the same as the Han Body (Lin 1944, 64). Chinese anthropologists like Yang, Wu, and Lin seem to have been consistent in their accounts of bodily differences between the Han Chinese and ethnic minority groups. Moreover, Wu suggested a demonstration of bodily similarities between the Chinese races as the aim of anthropometric development, advocating its political use within a specific historical context.

These aims—of selecting soldiers to guard the frontier, avoiding misunderstandings and discrimination among different ethnic groups, and assimilating distinct groups— all suggest the use of academic and scientific endeavour in the service of frontier management in Republican China. The goal of assimilating the non-Han peoples was also a reflection of national policy. David Deal (1979) has revealed how the Republican government designed and carried out several national minority policies through administration, economic policy, and education, aiming to assimilate and dominate non-Han groups in the south-west. All four of Wu's justifications indicate the political uses of anthropology in the borderland.

Wu's account coincided with several other anthropologists' appeals for academic research to be pressed into service in frontier regimes, echoing earlier discussions on frontier administration (*bianzheng*). Similarly, the colonial study of borderland populations along India's North-West Frontier in the mid-nineteenth century also demonstrates the intimate connection between state power and knowledge production (Zak 2016). The entangled history of anthropology and colonial regimes in the south-west during the Second Sino-Japanese War is evident in the sponsorship of research. Several research projects were sponsored by societies promoting the frontiers. For example, research on the Lolo in Liangshan, including the anthropometric measurement of their bodies by Lin Yaohua, was sponsored partly by the Society Opposing Japan and Frontier Cultivation (Lin 1947b, 2). The establishment in the 1940s of the Nankai University Research Centre for Frontier Humanity (Nankai Daxue Wenke Yanjiusuo Bianjiang Renwen Keyanshi) was intended to further railway construction across Yunnan's non-Han regions. Tao Yunkui, the physical anthropologist who had trained in Germany, was the director of this research centre (Nie and Zhu 2013). Tao offered suggestions on how to govern the frontier through anthropology (Tao 1940b). Chinese anthropologists in Republican China valued the practical uses of anthropology and sought to develop it as a useful discipline for ruling the frontiers.

Notwithstanding Tao's contribution to the idea of ruling the frontier through anthropology, it is evident that anthropometry was his principal area of expertise when he studied in Berlin. However, it seems that his anthropological research interests shifted away from body measurement when he returned to China. Tao studied eugenics under the influence of Eugen Fischer; his PhD thesis, which focused on the eugenics of a hybrid Chinese and European couple, drew on rich statistics relating to body measurements (Tao 1940a). Few of his publications after his return to China appear to have related to anthropometry. In his eulogy of Tao, the historian and sociologist Qu Tongzu (1910–2008) described how he had invited Tao to teach anthropometry at Yunnan University. Tao had refused, however, saying he was tired of the subject and unwilling to reprise old material. In the event, he had taught a course on the society of the south-western borderlands (Qu 1944). It appears that Tao was not willing to promote anthropometric research in China. While is difficult to find any further factual evidence supporting his refusal to teach anthropometry in China, this example appears to illustrate the different attitudes towards anthropometry prevalent among Chinese scholars. As noted earlier, Chinese anthropologists did not argue much among themselves as regards the methodologies and theories of different anthropological schools, but the example of Tao in some ways suggests different attitudes towards the transfer of anthropometry to China.

Stephen Jay Gould (1996, 351–365) has revealed how the obtaining of anthropometric data and its interpretation were skewed towards a desired end. The anthropometric research into the bodies of non-Han peoples in the south-west shared similarities with Gould's observations. It also echoes Charles Keyes's (2002) suggestion regarding the political adoption of racial science in Asian countries. James Poskett (2017) has found intimate connections between phrenology and political concerns in nineteenth-century Britain, ranging from the abolition of slavery to the reform of prison discipline. In recent decades, racial typologies have been reimagined through the lens of emerging genetic findings; genome research has also often operated alongside other factors, including politics and commerce. Anthropometry in Republican China was another instance that shows the political use of the sciences. An intertwined history of politics and science shares similar trajectories with Elise Burton's analysis of anthropology and genetics in the Middle East, which was referred to in the introduction (Burton 2018a; 2018b, 762–768).

In her study of body measurement in China, Jia-chen Fu observes how the bodies of the Han Chinese were measured by anthropologists and physicians in China. Fu argues that body measurement provided evidence demonstrating Chinese deficiencies; as a form of technology, it enabled Chinese scientists to justify the development and imposition of public health and dietary interventions to improve the bodies of the Chinese race and nation (Fu 2016). In his discussion of racial anatomy in modern China, David Luesink reflects on the intertwined histories of racial anatomy and anthropometry. Chinese physicians conducted measurements on hundreds of live participants, usually students, soldiers, and hospital residents, in an attempt to accumulate scientific evidence about the Chinese population and its many regional and class-based variations (Luesink 2017, 1027–1028). One of the shared aims of body measurement, across disciplines and regions, was to generate body characteristics for specific populations. The research was driven by political desires and its results often used to justify political and social regimes.

Through the measurement of individual bodies, statistics were calculated and scaled up to create a generic body-character for an entire ethnic group. This was then used to justify state rule in the borderland; the implication was that these non-Han bodies were simply waiting to be improved by the state. The conclusions drawn from detecting bodily similarities between the Han and ethnic minority groups in the south-west of China helped to justify political appeals for unity within the *Zhonghua minzu*.

Although anthropometry provided a useful tool for constituting the idea of the nation in the 1930s and 1940s, anthropometric research, particularly in relation to non-Han peoples, was largely scaled down after the Second Sino-Japanese War. The Preparatory Office of the Department of Anthropometry at the Academia Sinica was closed in 1946 (Du 2011). Chinese anthropology was not reinvigorated until the 1980s (Braybrooke 1980; Wang 2005). Although non-Han peoples were examined as part of a project of racial recognition instigated by the state in the 1950s and 1960s, anthropometry was barely used as a means of racial categorization. Anthropometry was redeveloped in several Chinese academic institutions but used mainly for paleoanthropological research (Liu 2020). This indicates the complexity and dynamics of racial classification in modern China.

Conclusion

This article has examined the introduction and adoption of Western anthropometry in the study and identification of the bodies of non-Han peoples in the south-west of China in the 1930s and 1940s. It has highlighted the role of biopower in frontier rule and population management, by revealing how Republican-era scholars projected their preconceptions and theories of the *Zhonghua minzu* onto anthropometric research. The bodies of several non-Han groups, including the Miao, Yao, Lolo, and Luohei, were presented as examples of the Mongolian / Yellow race. Western racial taxonomy was locally received in China and reconfirmed through Chinese anthropologists' analyses of body measurements. The accumulation of detailed statistics on body measurements generated collective knowledge of the non-Han population, which enabled state interventions in the governance of frontier peoples through body politics. The body was an extremely useful medium for exhibiting and conveying the existence of racial difference and hierarchy throughout Chinese history, while Republican scholars represented the bodies of non-Han people through scientific tools.

This article enriches our understanding of the intersections of anthropology, racial science, and frontier rule. Anthropology was regarded by Chinese anthropologists as an important ingredient of colonial regimes; the practical uses of anthropology were valued by frontier administrations. Through the practice of body measurement, the organization of this data, and its interpretation, Republican scholars sought to identify the physical traits of the non-Han population and to develop racial categories, including the *Zhonghua minzu* and the Han, Miao, Lolo, and Yao peoples. The political use of the body measurements of non-Han people promoted the construction of a unifying *Zhonghua minzu* that included both the Han Chinese and frontier ethnic minority groups. This article has also emphasized the internal dynamics of the use of anthropometric research by Chinese scholars and how they drew on Western knowledge selectively. It has also examined the global transmission of Western racial taxonomy of human variation, as well as the response of Republican anthropologists to the concept of the Mongolian / Yellow race. Analysis of anthropometric research in China manifested a localization of global racial classifications and the reinvention of regional identity through Western racial structures. In the context of strengthening nationhood and the solidarity of nations, similarities between Han and ethnic minority bodies were exaggerated by Chinese anthropologists. Race was a dynamic concept and must be understood within a specific context. Western anthropology in Republican China demonstrates the dynamism and complexity of biopower, in particular when the human sciences intersect with Chinese colonial regimes.

ORCID iD

Jing Zhu ⓘ https://orcid.org/0000-0002-2705-766X

Notes

I would like to thank the CCKF for International Scholarly Exchange for funding my postdoctoral fellowship. Sincere thanks are due to Francesca Bray, Mary Brazelton, Anne Gerritsen, and James Poskett for reading drafts of this article and offering sustained guidance. I am also grateful to the anonymous reviewers and editors for their incisive comments, and to Alastair Learmont for his proofreading help.

China is a multi-ethnic nation-state comprising one major ethnic group (the Han Chinese) plus 55 other ethnic minority groups. Non-Han refers to any of the ethnic minority groups in China. For ethnic classification in modern China, see Mullaney (2011).

One of these works, the book *The Making of the Human Sciences in China* (Chiang, 2019), explores the human sciences of technology, ethnography, anthropology, sociology, political sciences, ethnicity, race, and anatomy. Another, a special issue of *History of Science* edited by Chiang with his introduction (Chiang, 2015), covers the topics of psychiatry, human fossils, physiology, love, and scientific study.

Kangjian Kenzhishe was a society established in Chongqing in 1939 for the purpose of cultivating and managing resources in the south-western regions during the Second Sino-Japanese War.

The Lolo have been recategorized and renamed as the Yi minority group in contemporary China. For the history of the Yi, see Harrell (1995, 2001).

For the history and constitution of the Yao, see Litzinger (2000).

All translations of Chinese quotations and titles into English are my own.

The Luohei have been officially recognized and renamed as the Lahu in contemporary China.

For the history of the Miao and the construction of the Miao group, see Diamond (1995).

(Acknowledgement: This article is a revision of the author's speech at the 2019 UKCHA Annual Forum.)

References

Abramson, M. S. 2003. "Deep Eyes and High Noses: Physiognomy and the Depiction of Barbarians in Tang China." In *Political Frontiers, Ethnic Boundaries, and Human Geographies in Chinese History*, edited by N. Cosmo and D. Wyatt, 119–159. London: Routledge.

———. 2008. *Ethnic Identity in Tang China*. Philadelphia, PA: University of Pennsylvania Press.

Academia Sinica. 1947. "Zhongyang yanjiuyuan sanshisi niandu gongzuo jianbao" [Brief Report of Academia Sinica in 1945]. *Kexue* 29(1): 30.

Asad, T., ed. 1973. *Anthropology & the Colonial Encounter*. London: Humanities Press.

Braybrooke, G. 1980. "Ethnology in China." *Current Anthropology* 21(2): 264–266.

Brazelton, M. A. 2019. *Mass Vaccination: Citizens' Bodies and State Power in Modern China*. Ithaca, NY: Cornell University Press.

Burton, E. K. 2018a. "'Essential Collaborators': Locating Middle Eastern Geneticists in the Global Scientific Infrastructure, 1950s–1970s." *Comparative Studies of Society and History* 60(1): 119–149.

———. 2018b. "Narrating Ethnicity and Diversity in Middle Eastern National Genome Projects." *Social Studies of Science* 48(5): 762–786.

———. 2021. *Genetic Crossroads: The Middle East and the Science of Human Heredity*. Stanford, CA: Stanford University Press.

Chen, H. 2013. "Zhongguo tizhi renleixue bainian huigu" [Review of Chinese Anthropometry in the Past 100 Years]. *Xiandai Renleixue* 1(2): 5–9.

Cheung, S. W. 1996. "Representation and Negotiation of Ge Identities in Southeast Guizhou." In *Negotiating Ethnicities in China and Taiwan*, edited by M. Brown, 240–273. Berkeley, CA: Institute for Asian Studies.

Chiang, H. 2015. "Ordering the Social: History of the Human Sciences in Modern China." *History of Science* 53(1): 4–8.

Chiang, H., ed. 2019. *The Making of the Human Sciences in China: Historical and Conceptual Foundations*. Leiden: Brill.

Cisney, V. W. and Morar, N. 2016. "Introduction: Why Biopower? Why Now?" In *Biopower: Foucault and Beyond*, edited by V. Cisney and N. Morar, 1–25. Chicago, IL: University of Chicago Press.

Conklin, A. L. 2013. *In the Museum of Man: Race, Anthropology, and Empire in France, 1850–1950*. Ithaca, NY: Cornell University Press.

Dai, Y. X. 1938. "Zhongguo minzu shishang zhi zhongzu fenlei wenti jiqi fangfa" [The Problem of Ethnic Classification in Chinese Ethnographical History and Its Methodology]. *Minzu Wenhua* 1(2): 26–33.

Deal, D. 1979. "Policy Towards Ethnic Minorities in Southwest China, 1927–1965." In *Nationalism and the Crisis of Ethnic Minorities in Asia*, edited by T. Kang, 33–40. London: Greenwood Press.

Diamond, N. 1995. "Defining the Miao: Ming, Qing, and Contemporary Views." In *Cultural Encounters on China's Ethnic Frontiers*, edited by S. Harrell, 92–116. Seattle, WA: University of Washington Press.

Dikötter, F. 1992. *The Discourse of Race in Modern China*. London: Hurst.

Ding, W. J. 1933. "Manyou sanji (shisan): Yunnan de tuzhu renzhong" [Accounts of Roaming (Thirteen): The Tribal of Yunnan]. *Duli Pinglun* 34: 13–19.

——. 1935. "Cunwen congke zixu" [Preface for the Scripts of Ethnic Minorities]. *Dili Xuebao* 2: 9–21.

Du, J. 2011. "Zhongyang Yanjiuyuan 'Yanjiu tigao minzu suzhi'an' zhi shimo-jianshu Zhongyang yanjiuyuan tizhi renleixue yanjiusuo choubei zhi liuchan" [The Complete Process of "Case of Research on Improving the National Body" by Academia Sinica and the Failure of the Department of Anthropometry of Academia Sinica]. *Ziran Kexueshi Yanjiu* 30(1): 91–107.

Du, J. 2013. *Zhongguo tizhi renleixue shi yanjiu* [Research on the History of Chinese Anthropometry]. Beijing: Beijing Chanquan Chubanshe.

Edwards, E., ed. 1992. *Anthropology and Photography, 1860–1920*. London: Yale University Press in association with the Royal Anthropological Institute.

Ergin, M. 2017. *"Is the Turk a White Man?": Race and Modernity in the Making of Turkish Identity*. Leiden: Brill.

Fei, X. T. 1935. "Fenxi Zhonghua minzu renzhong chengfeng de fangfa he changshi" [The Methodology and Attempt to Analyse the Component of *Zhonghua minzu*]. *Shehui Yanjiu* 56: 37–39.

——. 1994. "Cong Shi Luguo Laoshi xuexi tizhi renleixue" [Learning Physical Anthropology from Professor Shirokogoroff]. *Beijing Daxue Xuebao* 5: 13–22.

Fiskesjo, M. 2006. "Rescuing the Empire: Chinese Nation-Building in the Twentieth Century." *European Journal of East Asian Studies* 5(1): 15–44.

Fu, J. C. 2016. "Measuring Up: Anthropometrics and the Chinese Body in Republican Period China." *Bulletin of the History of Medicine* 90(4): 643–671.

Garson, J. G. and Read, C. H. 1892. *Notes and Queries on Anthropology*. 2nd ed. London: Anthropological Institute.

Gladney, D. C. 1991. *Muslim Chinese: Ethnic Nationalism in the People's Republic*. Cambridge, MA: Harvard University Press.

Gould, S. J. 1996. *The Mismeasure of Man*. New York, NY: W. W. Norton.

Gros, S. 2004. "The Politics of Names: The Identification of the Dulong (Drung) of Northwest Yunnan." *China Information* 18(2): 275–302.

Guldin, G. E. 1993. *The Saga of Anthropology in China: From Malinowski to Moscow to Mao*. London: Routledge.

Hamilton, G. G. and Wang, Z. 1992. "Introduction: Fei Xiaotong and the Beginnings of a Chinese Sociology." In *From the Soil, the Foundations of Chinese Society: A Translation of Fei Xiaotong's Xiangtu Zhongguo*, edited by G. G. Hamilton and

476

Z. Wang, 1–16. Berkeley, CA: University of California Press.

Harrell, S. 1995. "The History of the History of the Yi." In *Cultural Encounters on China's Ethnic Frontiers*, edited by S. Harrell, 63–91. Seattle, WA: University of Washington Press.

——. 2001. *Perspectives on the Yi of Southwest China.* Berkeley, CA: University of California Press.

Hostetler, L. 2001. *Qing Colonial Enterprise: Ethnography and Cartography in Early Modern China.* Chicago, IL: University of Chicago Press.

Hrdlička, A. 1920. *Anthropometry.* Philadelphia, PA: Wistar Institute of Anatomy and Biology.

Hu, H. B. 2006. *Zhongguo renleixue shi* [History of Chinese Anthropology]. Beijing: Zhongguo Renmin Daxue Chubanshe.

Huang, G. X. and Shi, L. Z., eds. 2005. *Zhongguo de minzu shibie: 56 ge minzu de Laili* [Ethnic Classification in China: The Origins of the 56 Ethnic Groups]. Beijing: Minzu Chubanshe.

Huang, X. T. 2017. *Chongshu Zhonghua: Jindai Zhongguo "Zhonghua Minzu" guainian yanjiu* [Reconstructing China: Research on the Concept of "Zhonghua minzu"]. Beijing: Beijing Shifan Daxue Chubanshe.

Keevak, M. 2011. *Becoming the Yellow: A Short History of Racial Thinking.* Princeton, NJ: Princeton University Press.

Keyes, C. 2002. "Presidential Address: 'The Peoples of Asia'—Science and Politics in the Classification of Ethnic Groups in Thailand, China, and Vietnam." *Journal of Asian Studies* 61(4): 1163–1203.

Khan, A. 1996. "Who Are the Mongols? State, Ethnicity, and the Politics of Representation in the PRC." In *Negotiating Ethnicities in China and Taiwan*, edited by M. Brown, 125–159. Berkeley, CA: Institute for Asian Studies.

Leibold, J. 2012. "Searching for Han: Early Twentieth-Century Narratives of Chinese Origins and Development." In *Critical Han Studies: The History, Representation, and Identity of China's Majority*, edited by T. Mullaney and J. Leibold, 210–233. London: University of California Press.

Leung, A. K. C. and Caldwell, M. L., eds. 2019. *Moral Foods: The Construction of Nutrition and Health in Modern Asia.* Honolulu, HA: University of Hawaii Press.

Leung, A. K. C. and Nakayama, I., eds. 2017. *Gender, Health, and History in Modern East Asia.* Hong Kong: Hong Kong University Press.

Li, J. 1928. *The Formation of the Chinese People: An Anthropological Inquiry.* Cambridge, MA: Harvard University Press.

——. 2006 [1924]. "Hubei renzhong celiang zhi jieguo" [Results of the Anthropometry Research in Hubei]. In *Li Ji Wenji*, Vol. 5 [*Anthology of Li Ji*, Vol. 5], edited by G. Z. Zhang, 420–423. Shanghai: Shanghai Renmin Chubanshe,

Li, D. Y. 2012. "Daodu: xunzhao shiqu de qinghuai" [Introduction: Looking for the Lost Feeling]. In *Tao Yunkui minzu yanjiu wenji* [Anthology of Ethnographic Research of Tao Yunkui], edited by Y. K. Tao, 1–20. Beijing: Minzu Chubanshe.

Lin, H. X. 1932. *Shijie renzhongzhi* [Races of the World]. Beijing: Shangwu Yinshuguan.

Lin, Y. H. 1941. "The Miao-Man Peoples of Kweichow." *Harvard Journal of Asiatic Studies* 5(3–4): 261–345.

——. 1944. "Daxiao Liangshan kaochaji" [Research Trip in Big and Small Cold Mountain]. *Bianzheng Gonglun* 6: 61–64.

——. 1947a. "Chuanbian kaocha Jicing" [Research and Travel in the Frontier of Sichuan], in *Liangshan Yijia* [The Lolo in Cold Mountain]. Beijing: Shangwu Yinshiguan, 115–133.

——. 1947b. *Liangshan Yijia* [The Lolo in Cold Mountain]. Beijing: Shangwu Yinshiguan. Lin, Y. H. 1999. "*Liangshan Yijia yu shaoshu minzu kaocha*" [The Cold Mountain Yi and the Survey of Ethnic Minorities]. In *Lin Yaohua xueshu* [Anthology of Lin Yaohua], edited by Y. H. Lin, 57–96. Hangzhou: Zhejiang Renmin Chubanshe.

Lipman, J. 2002. "How Many Minzu in a Nation? Modern Travelers Meet China's Frontier Peoples." *Inner Asia* 4(1): 113–130.

Litzinger, R. A. 1995. "Review of the book The Discourse of Race in Modern China by F. Dikötter." H-World, H-Net Reviews, available at: https://www.h-net.org/reviews/showrev. php?id=135.

——A. 2000. *Other Chinas: The Yao and the Politics of National Belonging*. Durham, NC: Duke University Press.

Liu, W. 2020. "Tizhi renleixue jinnian zai Zhongguo de kuaisu fazhan" [The Quick Development of Anthropometry in China in Recent Years]. *Acta Anthropologica Sinica* 39(4): 509–510.

Liu, X. 1929. "Renzhong fenlei biaozhun gaishuo" [A Review of Criteria for Ethnic Classification]. *Liuying Xuebao* 4: 87–92.

Low, M. 2012. "Physical Anthropology in Japan: The Ainu and the Search for the Origins of the Japanese." *Current Anthropology* 53(5): 57–68.

Luesink, D. 2017. "Anatomy and the Reconfiguration of Life and Death in Republican China." *Journal of Asian Studies* 76(4): 1009–1034.

Ma, C. S. 1936. "Zhongguo xinan minzu fenlei" [The Ethnic Classification in the Southwest of China]. *Minzuxue Yanjiu Jikan* 1: 177–196.

——. 1947. "Renlei xue zai woguo bianzheng shang de yingyong" [The Uses of Anthropology for our Frontier Administration]. *Minzhu Luntan* 1(4): 9–13.

Martin, R. 1928. *Lehrbuch der Anthropologie in systematischer Darstellung: Mit besonderer Berücksichtigung der anthropologischen Methoden; für Studierende, Ärzte und Forschungsreisende* [Textbook of Anthropology in Systematic Representation: With Special Consideration of Anthropological Methods; for Students, Doctors, and Explorers]. Jena: Gustav Fischer.

Morris-Reich, A. 2013. "Anthropology, Standardization and Measurement: Rudolf Martin and Anthropometric Photography." *British Journal for the History of Science* 46(3): 487–516.

Morse, W. 1937. *Schedule of Physical Anthropological Measurements and Observations on Ten Ethnic Groups of Szechuan Province, West China*. Chengdu: West China Border Research Society.

Mullaney, T. 2004. "Ethnic Classification Writ Large: The 1954 Yunnan Province Ethnic Classification Project and Its Foundations in Republican-Era Taxonomic Thought." *China Information* 18(2): 207–241.

——. 2011. *Coming to Terms With the Nation: Ethnic Classification in Modern China*. Berkeley, CA: University of California Press.

——. 2012. "Critical Han Studies: Introduction and Prolegomenon." In *Critical Han Studies: The History, Representation, and Identity of China's Majority,* edited by T. Mullaney and J. Leibold, 1–22. London: University of California Press.

Nakajima, C. 2018. *Body, Society, and Nation: The Creation of Public Health and Urban Culture in Shanghai.* Cambridge, MA: Harvard University Press.

Nie, P. S. and Zhu, C. 2013. "Kangzhan shiqi Tao Yunkui zai Yunnan de tianye diaocha shuping" [Review on the Research of Tao Yunkui in Yunnan during the Second Sino-Japanese War]. *Minzu Luntan* 5: 25–29.

Nishiyama, H. 2015. "Towards a Global Genealogy of Biopolitics: Race, Colonialism, and Biometrics Beyond Europe." *Environment and Planning D: Society and Space* 33(2): 331–346.

Owen, A. R. G. 1962. "An Appreciation of the Life and Work of Sir Ronald Aylmer Fisher: F. R. S., F. S. S. Sc.D." *Journal of the Royal Statistical Society* 12(4): 313–319.

Pinney, C. 2011. *Photography and Anthropology.* London: Reaktion.

Poskett, J. 2017. "Phrenology, Correspondence, and the Global Politics of Reform, 1815–1848." *Historical Journal* 60: 409–442.

——. 2019. *Materials of the Mind: Phrenology, Race, and the Global History of Science, 1851–1020.* Chicago, IL: University of Chicago Press.

Qu, T. Z. 1944. "Dao Yunkui" [Mourning Yunkui]. *Bianzheng Gonglun* 9(3): 9–10.

Rabinow, P. and Rose, N. 2006. "Biopower Today." *Biosocieties* 1(2): 195–217.

Rui, Y. F. 1954. "Yunnan Luohei tizhi zhi yanjiu" [Research on the Bodies of Luohei in Yunnan]. *Zhongyang Yanjiuyuan Lishi Yuyan Yanjiusuo Jikan* 43(6): 269–325.

Schmalzer, S. 2008. *The People's Peking Man: Popular Science and Human Identity in Twentieth-Century China.* Chicago, IL: University of Chicago Press.

Schneider, L. 2003. *Biology and Revolution in Twentieth-Century China.* Lanham, MD: Rowman & Littlefield.

Shirokogoroff, S. 1923. *Anthropology of Northern China.* Shanghai: Royal Asiatic Society North China Branch.

Smith, E. 2020. " 'Why Do We Measure Mankind?' Marketing Anthropometry in Late-Victorian Britain." *History of Science* 58(2): 142–165.

Stevenson, P. 1940. *Detailed Anthropometric Measurements of the Chinese of the North China Plain.* Shanghai: Commercial Press.

Stoler, A. L. 1995. *Race and the Education of Desire: Foucault's History of Sexuality and the Colonial Order of Things.* Durham, NC: Duke University Press.

Tao, Y. K. 1940a. "Hua'ou Hunxuezhong: Yige renlei yichuanxue de yanjiu" [The Hybrid of Chinese and European: A Study on Heredity]. *Minzuxue Yanjiu Jikan* 2: 69–103.

——. 1940b. "Kaihua bianmin wenti" [Problem of Cultivating the Frontier People]. *Xinan Bianjiang* 10: 1–17.

——. 1942. "Qiujiang jicheng" [Travel Records in Qiujiang]. *Xinan Bianjiang* 14: 32–36.

Teng, E. 2004. *Taiwan's Imagined Geography: Chinese Colonial Travel Writing and Pictures, 1683–1895*. Cambridge, MA: Harvard University Press.

Tilley, H. and Gordon, R., eds. 2007. *Ordering Africa: Anthropology, European Imperialism and the Politics of Knowledge*. Manchester: Manchester University Press.

Ven, H. van de and Drea, E. 2011. "Chronology of the Sino-Japanese War, 1937–1945." In *The Battle for China: Essays on the Military History of the Sino-Japanese War of 1937–1945*, edited by M. Peattie, 7–26. Stanford, CA: Stanford University Press.

Wang, H. L. 2014. *Minguo shiqi de bianzheng yu bianzhengxue (1931–1948)* [Frontier Administration and the Studies of Frontier Administration (1931–1948)]. Beijing: Renmin Chubanshe.

Wang, J. M. 1996. "Ershi shiji qianbanqi Zhongguo tizhi renleixue fazhan gaishu" [Review of the Development of Chinese Anthropometry in the First Half of the Twentieth Century]. In *Zhongguo renleixue de fazhan* [The Development of Chinese Anthropology], edited by G. Q. Chen and J. H. Lin, 142–150. Shanghai: Shanghai Sanlian Shudian.

——. 1997. *Zhongguo minzuxue shi, 1903–1949* [The History of Ethnology in China, 1903–1949]. Kunming: Yunnan Jiaoyu Chubanshe.

Wang, M. M. 2005. "Ershiwu nian lai Zhongguo de renleixue yanjiu: chengjiu yu wenti" [Anthropological Research in China in the Past Twenty-Five Years: Achievements and Problems]. *Jiangsi Shehui Kexue* 12: 7–13.

——. 2012. "All Under Heaven (Tianxia): Cosmological Perspectives and Political Ontologies in Premodern China." *Hau: Journal of Ethnographic Theory* 2(1): 337–383.

Woo, T. L. (Wu, D. L.) 1942. "The Physical Characters of the Pa Miao People of Kweichow and Other Peoples of South China." *Journal of the Royal Anthropological Institute of Great Britain and Ireland* 72(1/2): 45–53.

Wu, D. L. 1936. "Ding Zaijun zai renleixue de gongxian" [The Contribution of Ding Wenjiang in Anthropology]. *Duli Pinglun* 188: 27–29.

——. 1944. "Bianqu renleixue diaochafa" [Research Methodologies of Anthropology in the Frontier]. *Minzuxue Yanjiu Jikan* 4: 6–20.

——. 1948. "Haiteliexijia zhu Shiyong Renti Celiangxue" [Aleš Hrdlička: Practical Anthropometry]. *Zhejiang Xuebao* 2(2): 141.

——. 2014. *Wu Dingliang yuanshi wenji (1894–1969)* [Collected Works of Wu Dingliang]. Beijing: Zhishi Chanquan Chubanshe.

Wu, J. D. 1931. *Shandong ren tizhi zhi yanjiu* [Research on the Bodies of People in Shandong]. Nanjing: Zhongyanyuan.

Wu, W. Z. 1942. "Bianzheng xue fafan" [The Development of Frontier Administration]. *Bianzheng Gonglun* 1(5–6): 1–11.

Yang, B. 1999. "Central State, Local Governments, Ethnic Groups and the Minzu Identification in Yunnan (1950s–1980s)."

Modern Asian Studies 43(3): 741–775.

Yang, C. Z. 1937. "Guangdong Beijiang Yaoren de wenhua xianxiang yu tizhixing" [The Yao Cultural Phenomenon and Body Type on the North River in Guangdong]. *Minsu* 1(3): 1–36.

——. 2004. *Yang Chengzhi wenji* [Anthology of Yang Chengzhi]. Guangzhou: Zhongshan Daxue Chubanshe.

Yang, X. M. 1948. "Bianjiang xingzheng yu yingyong renleixue" [Frontier Administration and Applied Anthropology]. *Bianzheng Gonglun* 3(7): 62–65.

Ye, C. F. 1931. "Shijie renzhong fenleifa he fenbu gaiyao" [The Classification and Distribution of Races of the World]. *Xiaoshi Xuesheng* 3: 1–6.

Yen, H. P. 2012. "Li Anzhai and Frontier Anthropology: Tibet, Discourse of the Frontier and the Making of Chinese Applied Anthropology During World War II, 1937–1945." In *Sociology and Anthropology in Twentieth-Century China: Between Universalism and Indigenism*, edited by A. Dirlik, G. Li, and H. P. Yen, 139–160. Hong Kong: Chinese University of Hong Kong Press.

——. 2017. "Frontier Anthropology and Chinese Colonialism in the Southwestern Frontier During the Second Sino-Japanese War." *Boundary 2* 44(2): 157–186.

——. 2019. "Anthropology." In *The Making of the Human Sciences in China: Historical and Conceptual Foundations*, edited by H. Chiang, 354–373. Leiden: Brill.

Zak, L. 2016. "Colonial Ethnography on India's North-West Frontier, 1850–1910." *Historical Journal* 59(1): 175–196.

Zhu, J. 2019. "Visualising Human Differences in Late Imperial China: Body, Nakedness and Sexuality." *Ming Qing Studies* 23(1): 169–198.

——. 2020. *Visualising Ethnicity in the Southwest Borderlands: Gender and Representation in Late Imperial and Republican China*. Leiden: Brill.

Friend or Foe? British Interpretations of China before the Opium War

Hao Gao*

Sino–British encounters occurring before the Opium War (or the First Anglo–Chinese War, 1840–42), have received less scholarly attention compared to those which follow the conflict. The existing literature and academic debates principally focus on two areas: first, the two British royal embassies to China—the Macartney embassy of 1793 and the Amherst embassy of 1816—and second, the opium trade which triggered the war. Hence, this scholarship largely (yet not exclusively) concerns diplomatic and commercial histories, with "embassy" and "opium" as its keywords. Various historians have studied the Macartney and the Amherst embassies, including aspects of the kowtow controversy,[1] British presents to the Qianlong emperor, as well as the Qing court's attitudes towards

---

* Dr Hao Gao (高昊) is Senior Lecturer in Imperial and Global History at the University of Exeter. He is a historian of British imperialism in Asia, particularly the encounters between the British and the Chinese empires in the eighteenth and nineteenth centuries. Dr Gao is the author of *Creating the Opium War* (MUP, 2020) and various research articles in both English and Chinese journals. He currently serves as the University's Academic Director for the UK–China Humanities Alliance (UKCHA), with Exeter as the Lead Institution for the UK universities.

1 See, for example: Bickers, Robert A. ed. 1993. *Ritual and Diplomacy: The Macartney Mission to China, 1792–1794*. London; Hevia, James L. 1995. *Cherishing Men from Afar: Qing Guest Ritual and the Macartney Embassy of 1793*. Durham, NC; Esherick, Joseph W. 1998. "Cherishing Sources from Afar." *Modern China* 24(2): 135–161; Kitson, Peter J. and Markley, Robert. eds. *Writing China: Essays on the Amherst Embassy (1816) and Sino–British Cultural Relations*. Woodbridge; and Gao, Hao, 2016. "The Inner Kowtow Controversy During the Amherst Embassy to China, 1816–1817." *Diplomacy and Statecraft* 27(4): 595–614.

Britain and western technology.[1] Others have focused on the trade in opium, examining not only how this caused conflicts between Britain and China,[2] but also the ways in which it influenced the Chinese people's social lives and the Qing government's suppression of the drug.[3] A second area of interest, independent from the embassy-/opium-/war-related historiography, are those cultural investigations which explore the place of China in the literature of Britain and Europe. David Porter (2010) and Elizabeth Hope Chang (2010), for example, have researched the cultural understanding of China in eighteenth- and nineteenth-century England/Britain.[4] Robert Markley (2009) and Peter J. Kitson (2013) have provided surveys on the English/British imagination of China from the seventeenth to the early eighteenth century and during the Romantic period.[5] For those scholars whose research concerns the wider European contexts, the majority of their works dwell on

---

1 See, for example, Berg, Maxine. 2006. "Britain, Industry and Perceptions of China: Matthew Boulton, 'Useful Knowledge' and the Macartney Embassy to China, 1792–94." *Journal of Global History* 1(2): 269–288. Harrison, Henrietta. 2017. "The Qianlong Emperor's Letter to George III and the Early-Twentieth-Century Origins of the Ideas about Traditional China's Foreign Relations." *American Historical Review* 122(3): 680–701; Waley-Cohen, Joanna. 1993. "China and Western Technology in the Late Eighteenth Century." *American Historical Review* 98(5): 1525–1544; and Mosca, Matthew W. 2013. *From Frontier Policy to Foreign Policy: The Question of India and the Transformation of Geopolitics in Qing China*. Stanford, 163–198.

2 See, for example, Hanes III, W. Travis, and Sanello, Frank. 2002. *The Opium Wars: the Addiction of One Empire and the Corruption of Another*. Naperville, IL; Melancon, Glenn. 2003. *Britain's China Policy and the Opium Crisis: Balancing Drugs, Violence and National Honour, 1833–1840*. Aldershot; and Gelber, Harry G. 2004. *Opium, Soldiers and Evangelicals: Britain's 1840–42 War with China, and its Aftermath*. New York.

3 See, for example, Zheng, Yangwen. 2005. *The Social Life of Opium in China*. Cambridge; Bello, David Anthony, 2005. *Opium and the Limits of Empire: Drug Prohibition in the Chinese Interior, 1729–1850*. Cambridge, MA; and Derks, Hans. 2012. *History of the Opium Problem: The Assault on the East, Ca. 1600–1950*. Leiden and Boston.

4 Porter, David. 2010. *The Chinese Taste in Eighteenth-Century England*. Cambridge; Chang, Elizabeth Hope, 2010. *Britain's Chinese Eye: Literature, Empire and Aesthetics in Nineteenth-Century Britain*. Stanford, CA.

5 Markley, Robert. 2009. *The Far East and the English Imagination, 1600–1730*. Cambridge; Kitson, Peter J. 2013. *Forging Romantic China: Sino–British Cultural Exchange 1760–1840*. Cambridge.

Catholic missionaries' accounts of China, or how key intellectuals such as Leibniz, Voltaire and Quesnay represented the Chinese civilisation to cloak their attacks on obscurantism and misgovernment in Enlightenment Europe.[1]

This article seeks to make a connection between the two largely separate bodies of literature, to explore the interplay between cultural representations of, and policy towards, China, as a way of understanding pre-Opium War Sino–British relations. The task to scrutinise how British merchants interpreted China, moreover, is different from an investigation into the views of China presented by Catholic missionaries, influential European intellectuals, or the British embassies. These interest-oriented men were not as well-educated as the missionaries who travelled to the hinterland of China and immersed themselves in Chinese culture. Nor could they be compared with the Enlightenment philosophers or the British missions in terms of challenging authorities in Europe or shaping the country's diplomacy with China. The primary concern for these British mercantile communities was to benefit from the lucrative China trade. Ulrike Hillemann (2009) has made some fruitful attempts to know more about these groups, particularly in relation to how new knowledge of China and India was produced in the process of Britain's imperial expansion.[2] She touches lightly, however, on the first few years of the 1830s and the extent to which this period influenced Britain's trade and diplomacy with China.[3]

The early 1830s were significant because they were the last few years of the British East India Company's monopoly of Britain's China trade. Since the early nineteenth century, the EIC had been placed in an awkward position as theories of free trade became increasingly popular in Britain and across its imperial world. Although the East India Company Act of

---

1 See, for example, Mackerras, Colin. 1989. *Western Images of China*. Oxford; Kiernan, V. G. 1995. *The Lords of Human Kind: European Attitudes towards the Outside World in the Imperial Age*. London; and Spence, Jonathan D. 2000. *The Chan's Great Continent: China in the Western Minds*. London.

2 Hillemann, Ulrike. 2009. *Asian Empire and British Knowledge: China and the Networks of British Imperial Expansion*. Basingstoke.

3 Ibid., 87–91.

1813 renewed the Company's charter for twenty years, its monopoly in India was abolished, with the exception of the tea trade and trade with China. This partial opening of the Indian trade initiated significant changes in the structure of Britain's trade with Asia by allowing British private merchants to establish themselves in India. Unprecedentedly close to the Chinese market, many of them were keen to have access to trading with China. Although, in theory, non-EIC merchants were still prohibited from trading with the Chinese, a lot of them had succeeded in approaching the Chinese market by different means. Claiming themselves to be "free traders," these British men either purchased an expensive license from the EIC to conduct the so-called "country trade,"[1] or they bypassed the Company's control by forging commercial links with foreign companies.

The relationship between the EIC and the "free traders" was complicated. In the beginning, the private merchants were unable to seriously challenge the EIC at Canton. Nevertheless, the rapid growth of their trade changed the situation. In parallel with the Company's commerce with the Qing-government-authorised Hong merchants, these British "free traders" developed a lucrative trade with unlicensed Chinese dealers, mainly in opium. Instead of using the term "illegal trade," they often referred to it as the "unauthorised trade." From the EIC's point of view, this trade was a mixed blessing, because, on the one hand, these EIC's representatives knew that the Qing court would be unhappy with the private merchants' trade if it continued to develop. On the other hand, the EIC needed the trade in opium. For decades, the Company had been struggling to find a market for British goods in China to pay for its import of Chinese tea. It was opium that offered a solution to this long-lasting problem. Although the EIC kept their hands clean from the opium trade in Canton, it developed opium production on a huge scale in its colony in Bengal. The private merchants bought the company's opium on credit, sold it to the Chinese, and then paid the EIC's representatives in Canton, who used the money to purchase tea. From the perspective of the "free traders," they had many reasons to dislike the EIC's monopoly. Since their trade

---

1 The "country trade" began in the late eighteenth century, yet significantly expanded following the East India Company Act of 1813.

was not safeguarded by the government on either side, nor by the EIC's representatives at Canton, their position in China was never secure. Although very few of them were entirely pro-free-trade, these newcomers to the Asian markets believed that the EIC's monopoly had posed significant obstacles to the extension of their trade. It had been their desire that the British government could remove these constraints for them.

In the early 1830s, a prime opportunity to terminate the EIC's monopoly presented itself, as the Company's charter was at the point of expiring again. The private merchants, along with their supporters back home—including merchants and industrialists in Liverpool, Glasgow, Manchester and other provincial cities—as well as their allies in London, not only petitioned parliament for full commercial freedom with China, but waged a pamphlet war against the EIC. This debate on the EIC's monopoly and Britain's China policy went hand-in-hand with a controversy over the images of China. To defend their respective standpoints, the campaigners for the EIC and those for its critics constructed vastly different images of the China trade, the Chinese government and its people. Although historians have studied the termination of the EIC's monopoly in great detail,[1] this underlying debate regarding China's image remains little researched.

The EIC's Views

It should be noted first that the EIC and its supporters were not a homogenous group. In the early 1830s, some London East India agency houses began to perceive advantages in the opening of the China trade, as they developed links with manufacturers in British industrial cities. The emergence of these interest groups means that there was no complete unity within the EIC's leadership in London. Also, the Company's select committee at Canton

---

1 See, for example, Morse, Hosea Ballou. 1926. *The Chronicles of the East India Company Trading to China 1635–1834*. 5 vols. Oxford. IV; Greenberg, Michael, 1951. *British Trade and the Opening of China 1800–42*. Cambridge; Philips, C. H. 1961. *The East India Company 1784–1834*. Manchester; Webster, Anthony. 2009. *The Twilight of the East India Company: The Evolution of Anglo-Asian Commerce and Politics, 1790–1860*. Woodbridge; and Kumagai, Yukihisa. 2012. *Breaking into the Monopoly: Provincial Merchants and Manufacturers' Campaigns for Access to the Asian Market, 1790–1833*. Leiden.

did not always abide by the instructions given by the court of directors, partly due to the long time needed for information to travel between China and Britain (usually four to five months). There were officials of the EIC who became "free traders." A prominent example is Hugh Hamilton Lindsay, who challenged the Company's China policies and later set up his own business.[1] There were also those who were outside the Company such as R. Montgomery Martin, an Irishman who later became the Colonial Treasurer of Hong Kong (from 1844 to 1845); there were others again, such as Thomas Fisher, who had not worked in China, yet were in favour of the continuance of the EIC's monopoly. Therefore, in this article, "the EIC and its supporters" may only be understood in general terms. This does not mean that the Company produced only one voice regarding China and the China trade. It is the *general* attitude that these campaigners held to defend the EIC's monopoly in China that this article concentrates on.

According to Webster, the "defenders of the Company's privileges did little or nothing to lobby in their defence."[2] Philips has also maintained that the directors of the EIC "made no effort ... to controvert the arguments of the merchants of the outports" and "[t]he Court of Proprietors sleepily, unquestionably awaited its fate."[3] A wider reading of historical sources, however, shows that although the Company's leadership did not do much to defend the EIC's position in China, a lot of the Company's supporters did campaign for the continuance of the EIC's monopoly. First and foremost, they endeavoured to justify the economic importance of its monopoly. According to the EIC's critics, since the India trade had opened in 1813 based on the principle of free trade, it was unreasonable to preserve the Company's trading privileges in China. Opposed to this argument, the pro-monopoly

---

1 Hugh Hamilton Lindsay (1802–1881) began working for the EIC in 1821. He left the Company in 1833 and founded his own company, Lindsay & Co., in Canton in 1836. For more of Lindsay's activities and views, see Bickers, Robert. 2012. "The Challenger: Hugh Hamilton Lindsay and the rise of British Asia, 1832–1865." *Transactions of the Royal Historical Society* 6(22): 141–169.

2 Webster. 2009. *The Twilight of the East India Company: The Evolution of Anglo-Asian Commerce and Politics, 1790–1860*, 100.

3 Philips. 1961. *The East India Company 1784–1834*. Manchester 291.

commentators' main justification was that however compelling this theory sounded in principle, "the peculiar circumstances" of the China trade rendered the principles of international commerce inapplicable to the case of China. To support this claim, they pointed out that it was unrealistic to expect that the opening of China trade from the British side alone could produce any material effect, because, as long as the Chinese monopoly remained, no significant change could occur. In this respect, Henry Ellis, who served in the civil service of the EIC for six years and was the third commissioner of the Amherst mission, maintained that:

> The peculiar circumstances under which the trade of foreigners is placed by the laws of China, ... have led me to reject, as fallacious, the anticipations of those who consider the surprising effects produced in India by unrestricted intercourse, as indicative of equal results in China.[1]

For this reason, Ellis believed that, under the present circumstances, it would be wrong to open the China trade only from the British side. "Until some change takes place in both these respects," he wrote, "the extension of the British trade contemplated by the merchants and manufacturers who have petitioned parliament on the subject, is hopeless."[2]

Based on this assertion, others in favour of maintaining the EIC's trading privileges, such as Martin, asserted that since, under the current system, the China trade was carried on with profit and a certain degree of security, there was an "absolute necessity for an undisturbed continuance of the Company's factory at Canton."[3] Staunton added that, through its

---

1   Ellis, Henry, 1830. *A Series of Letters on the East India Question, addressed to the Members of the Two Houses of Parliament*. London, 60. This view was backed up by George Thomas Staunton, the second commissioner of the Amherst mission. See Staunton, George T. 1829. "Considerations on the China Trade." *The Asiatic Journal* 28: 684–685.

2   Ibid., 37–38.

3   Martin, R. Montgomery. 1832. *The Past and Present State of the Tea Trade of England, and of the Continents of Europe and America*. London, 131.

lawful and extensive commercial activities, the EIC had, over the decades, developed a wholesome system that "diffuses the profits and advantages of a great and well-regulated commerce, in equitable proportions, directly or indirectly, over the whole of the British community."[1] Because of their long-lasting commercial relations with the Hong merchants, the Company's representatives were said to have developed considerable power in Canton. An anonymous writer in *The Asiatic Journal* stressed that "by the extent of their dealings, the unerring regularity of their transactions, their proverbial probity, and the duration of their connections with China," the EIC's representatives gained a high character and an augmented influence in the minds of the Chinese.[2] Moreover, according to the "Report of the Select Committee of the House of Commons in 1831," all forms of foreign trade had more or less benefited from this positive influence of the British EIC. Even the private merchants' trade was not an exception, because "by the influence of the Company, searches of country ships had been prevented, and difficulties in the prosecution of their transactions removed."[3]

In addition to these statements, the Company's supporters emphasised that the EIC was the only party that could guarantee the present prosperity and comparative security of the China trade. In opposition to the view that it was now time to throw open the door to the China trade, Staunton insisted that, given the uniqueness of this trade, nothing could prevent "the exercise of arbitrary and dictatorial powers over the trade, on the part of the Chinese merchants, but the present system."[4] To prove this, Ellis created a fearful image that the whole international trade in China would be in danger if the EIC system ceased to operate:

---

1 Staunton. 1829. "Considerations on the China Trade," 690–691.

2 Anon. 1829. "The American Commerce with China." *The Asiatic Journal* 27: 2.

3 Report of the Select Committee of the House of Commons on the Affairs of the East India Company: China Trade (1830), cited in Martin. 1832. *The Past and Present State of the Tea Trade of England, and of the Continents of Europe and America*, 132.

4 Staunton. 1829. "Considerations on the China Trade," 686.

There can be no doubt that ... the announcement that the East India Company were no longer the representatives of the British nation ... would shake the confidence of the Chinese; and that no consul ... could establish for himself the confidence and influence now attached to the Company's factory. All that might be lost in these respects ... would be turned to the advantage of the local government and of the Hong merchants, and consequently to the injury of the foreign trade in general.[1]

Martin, who visited India in the 1820s and later became an India expert, added that the termination of the EIC's China monopoly might cause even greater detrimental effects across the British empire, including:

... ruin to the Indian, as well as to the English, Chinese commerce ... with a diminishing government revenue, increasing public burthens, a possibility of general war, and a variety of taxes pressing on the industry and comfort of the people.[2]

Nevertheless, in an era when criticism of the EIC's administration in India (and its negative impact on the economy) was considerable, the Company's supporters knew that their arguments in favour of the monopoly would sound more convincing with the "local inside knowledge" of China possessed by the EIC's employees. To win support from parliament as well as the British public, they highlighted that China was a culturally "peculiar" nation. Since China's commercial and political culture was so different, it would be wrong to assume that the doctrine of free trade could be applied in China.

---

1 Ellis. 1830. *A Series of Letters on the East India Question, addressed to the Members of the Two Houses of Parliament*, 43.

2 Martin. 1832. *The Past and Present State of the Tea Trade of England, and of the Continents of Europe and America*, 4.

These key differences, or "peculiarities," first include the long history of China's self-contained economy, which had led the Chinese to believe that they stood in no need of trade with other countries. Hence, the Chinese did not value external trade as much as the Europeans did. Since the Chinese government had, from the earliest ages, directed its attention to render the intercourse between the different provinces of the empire easy and secure, China had long been "enjoying within its own territories all the necessaries and conveniences, and most of the luxuries of life."[1] As a result, throughout Chinese history, neither the necessities of the people nor the policy of the government had looked to foreign trade as a principal source of individual wealth or of imperial revenue.

Second, China's unique history and its geographical position had resulted in the country's political isolation, as well as the government's suspicious attitude towards foreigners. Fisher, for example, claimed that since "the Chinese had acquired the art of living in a state of high mental cultivation and social enjoyment … long before they could have the remote idea of intercourse" with foreign nations, their government had proclaimed its independence from every nation in the world during much of its history.[2] For this reason, the benefits of international communication had never been cultivated in China. On the contrary, the Chinese authorities believed that the safety of the state rested upon insulating the nation from outside influences. In this context, Ellis pointed out that in China, unlike in European countries, having contact with foreigners was considered as "having a positive tendency to corrupt the morals and derange the harmony of those institutions, political and domestic."[3] To restrict contact with foreigners hence quite naturally became the maxim of state policy in China.

Furthermore, because the culture of China was so different from that of Britain, the British were unable to appreciate some of the Chinese institutions. British observers, for

---

1 Martin. 1832. *The Past and Present State of the Tea Trade of England, and of the Continents of Europe and America*, 6.

2 Fisher, Thomas. 1833. "Statistical Notices of China." *The Gentleman's Magazine* 103(April): 296.

3 Ellis. 1830. *A Series of Letters on the East India Question, addressed to the Members of the Two Houses of Parliament*, 28.

example, had often regarded the principle of strict control and subordination in the Chinese government as signs of China's backwardness. In opposition to this view, Staunton pointed out that, "however despotic and oppressive the operation of this principle may appear in our eyes, in those of the Chinese it has invariably been considered as one of the first requisites of a good government, and one of the surest tests of a civilised people."[1] Speaking from his long experience of living in China, Staunton explained that the principle pervaded not only the government of China, but the domestic lives of the Chinese people: "In the same manner as the magistrate controls and is responsible for the conduct of the inhabitants of his district," he wrote, "the master of each family is supposed to control, and [is] required to be responsible for, his relations, connections, and dependents."[2] By pointing out these facts concerning the Chinese context, it seems that Staunton, as someone who had considerable first-hand knowledge of China, was suggesting that it was China's cultural *difference*, rather than its backwardness, that distinguished the Chinese from the British. The British criticism of Chinese institutions hence deserved reconsideration.

The EIC's campaigners stressed the cultural difference or "peculiarity" of China because, compared to the private merchants, they had advocated a higher degree of reverence towards Chinese laws and usages. Instead of promoting a rather barbaric image of the Chinese, some pro-monopoly commentators tended to view the Chinese as "highly civilised,"[3] or "semi-civilised,"[4] people who had a right to regulate their own affairs. The EIC's court of directors also clearly stated that:

We cannot, in fairness, deny to China the right which our own nation exercises as she sees fit … China must be considered free in the exercise of her

---

1   Staunton. 1829. "Considerations on the China Trade," 678.

2   Ibid.

3   Fisher, 1833. "Statistical Notices of China." *The Gentleman's Magazine* 103 (May): 392.

4   Martin. 1832. *The Past and Present State of the Tea Trade of England, and of the Continents of Europe and America*, 128.

affairs, without being accountable to any other nation.[1]

In terms of the application of the so-called "natural" law of free trade to China, the EIC and its supporters stressed that no one had the right to demand China that it must open its markets. Martin, for example, claimed that the principle of free trade should depend on "the disposition, wants, or reciprocal feelings of a separate, and perhaps, rival or hostile state."[2] Moreover, "freedom in *politics*, and freedom in *commerce*, are two distinct things; that they are not ... at every period called for by all countries."[3]

In line with these principles, campaigners for the EIC's China monopoly proclaimed that Britain should not employ a coercive line of action in its future relations with China. To justify this view, Fisher maintained that "any attempts to force upon this singular people an unacceptable intercourse with us, by outraging their laws or institutions, would ... only render profitable intercourse with them more difficult."[4] Furthermore, the Chinese should be regarded as a reasonable people. He stated, "the educational bias of the Chinese disposes them on all occasions to appeal to reason," hence the Chinese developed a disposition towards "mildness and urbanity, with a wish to show that their conduct is reasonable, and generally a willingness to yield to what appears to be so."[5] Even the government of China, which was often believed to be arbitrary and despotic, was keen "to make it appear to the people that its conduct is reasonable and benevolent on all occasions."[6] This interpretation of the Chinese people's natural willingness to appeal to reason gave the EIC's court of directors another reason to contend that Britain's commercial intercourse with the Chinese

---

1 Letter from the court of directors to the select committee, 13 January 1832, in Martin. 1832. *The Past and Present State of the Tea Trade of England, and of the Continents of Europe and America*, 214.
2 Martin. 1832. *The Past and Present State of the Tea Trade of England, and of the Continents of Europe and America*, 5.
3 Ibid., 9. Italics in the original.
4 Fisher, 1833. "Statistical Notices of China." 103(May), 392.
5 Ibid., 389.
6 Ibid.

could be improved only "by evincing a disposition to respect their regulations"[1] rather than by challenging that authority.

As defenders of the Company's privileges were presenting these seemingly objective observations of China, they were also suggesting that the cultural difference of China was beyond the comprehension of anyone else except the EIC's representatives. An anonymous writer summarised the attitudes of the EIC as:

> We [The Company] alone are acquainted with the Chinese people; We alone have established any relations with the Chinese government. That people is incomprehensible by any but our servants; that government hates and despises all foreigners, except only our supercargoes of the factory at Canton.[2]

This statement clearly shows that the EIC and its campaigners were attempting to portray the Company as the exclusive authority in understanding China and in dealing with Britain's relations with that country. In sum, in the debate on the EIC's China monopoly, the Company's supporters endeavour to promote a two-fold image of China. First, in spite of its various differences from Britain, China was by no means too depraved to be respected. Second, China's "peculiarities" were not inexplicable if one had a deep understanding of Chinese history and culture. For these reasons, commercial and diplomatic relations with China must be conducted by professionals who are equipped with profound local experience. Since the EIC had accumulated such abundant knowledge of this unique nation and had established positive relations with the local authorities in Canton, it would be most unwise to abolish such advantages that had proved "so safe and so efficacious."[3]

---

1 Letter from the court of directors, in Martin. 1832. *The Past and Present State of the Tea Trade of England, and of the Continents of Europe and America*, 214.

2 Anon. 1832. *The Foreign Trade of China Divested of Monopoly, Restriction, and Hazard by Means of Insular Commercial Stations*. London, 8–9.

3 Staunton. 1829. "Considerations on the China Trade," 684.

Views of the "Free Traders"

While the EIC and its campaigners were sparing no effort to justify its trade monopoly in China, the private merchants' call for its removal grew even stronger. These so-called "free traders," together with their friends in both provincial Britain and London, launched an anti-EIC campaign aiming to abolish the Company's privileges in China. They claimed that the removal of the EIC's monopoly, according to an anonymous author, "would be an undoubted advantage to the commerce and manufactures of Britain" (Anon. 1830, 116).[1] To strengthen this opinion, some British merchants in Calcutta employed John Crawfurd, one of Britain's leading "oriental" experts at this time, to write articles to support their disputes with the EIC. Crawfurd, a Scot and a life-time free trade advocate, had paid multiple visits to Southeast Asia, yet had never been to China. To form his ideas concerning Chinese affairs, Crawfurd relied on interviews with, and reports from, those who traded with the Chinese. The fact that he was regarded as a specialist on China also shows that, at this point, the British did not make too much effort to understand the "Orient" —few of them even bothered to distinguish China from the rest of Asia. Webster has stated that:

in many ways Crawfurd epitomised Said's notion of the influence of the orientalist intellectual. Not only did his writings … shape western thinking about India, south-east Asia and China, but he was also an active political campaigner on a range of issues related to Britain's Asian empire.[2]

Since, in the campaign of the early 1830s, Crawfurd used his reputation and knowledge of the East to promote the notion that Britain should free up the China trade, he proved vital to the victory of the "free traders."

---

1 Anon. 1830. "The East-India Question." *The Asiatic Journal* 1: 116.
2 Webster. 2009. *The Twilight of the East India Company: The Evolution of Anglo-Asian Commerce and Politics, 1790–1860*, 98–99.

To challenge the EIC's views, Crawfurd first accused the Company and its supporters of misleading the public by presenting untruthful views of the China trade. Against the EIC's statements regarding its positive impacts on the China trade, Crawfurd produced a number of works to argue that the Company's actual records, "so far from showing what they assert, show the very reverse of it."[1] In addition, he criticised the EIC for exaggerating the problems caused by the Chinese monopoly, in order to show that free trade was unrealistic in China. From interviews he conducted with the private merchants, Crawfurd concluded that the so-called "restrictions" set by the Qing government were actually not that significant. Although the private traders' commerce was not sanctioned by the Chinese authorities, in practice the "unauthorised trade" had been openly conducted to such an extent that a substantially "free" trade on the Chinese side had already been established. In contrast to the images of the Chinese monopoly presented by the pro-EIC commentators, Crawfurd's interviewees denied that the Canton system posed an insurmountable obstacle. For example, one of them pointed out:

Individuals are ... at perfect liberty to deal with any Hong merchant ... or with any *outside merchant*, that is, with any Chinese merchant not belonging to the Hong ... though there are only eight or ten Hong merchants at Canton, there is, notwithstanding, quite as extensive a choice of merchants with whom to deal in that city as in Liverpool or New York. (Interviewee 1831, quoted in Crawfurd 1831a)[2]

Apart from this considerable freedom in trading with the Chinese, Crawfurd discovered that the scale of the "unauthorised trade" had greatly exceeded that of the EIC's regular

---

1   [Crawfurd, John]. 1834a. "Voyage of Ship Amherst." *The Westminster Review* 20: 45.

2   [Crawfurd, John], 1831a. *Observations on the Influence of the East India Company's Monopoly on the Price and Supply of Tea; and on the Commerce with India, China, etc.* London, 26. Italics in the original.

trade. According to his statistics, its total volume in the early 1830s reached nearly three times that of the Company's trade.[1] In this regard, an anonymous writer also condemned the EIC's attempts to fix public attention on the Company's trade. Once the importance of the "unauthorised trade" was communicated to the public, the writer believed, "the Company's monopoly of the British market would be considered doubly unjust and injurious to the nation."[2]

Furthermore, against the EIC's contention that the private merchants' lack of understanding of China or experience trading with the Chinese was likely to cause disputes between the two countries, Crawfurd asserted that this claim was utterly "futile and visionary."[3] Using words of his interviewees, Crawfurd stressed that the "unauthorised trade" had actually been operating with great order and mutual confidence for a long time. American merchant Joshua Bates even told him that the facilities and efficiency that Canton provided foreign traders were "decidedly superior in both these respects to London."[4] Moreover, Crawfurd learned that in the past few decades, the British private merchants had not experienced any inconvenience when contacting the Chinese. Nor had other western traders, such as the Americans and the Dutch who were already "free traders," ever met "any interruption or obstacle of any sort"[5] when they traded with the Chinese. This information allowed Crawfurd to demonstrate that the EIC's campaigners had exaggerated the difficulties on the Chinese side. He made a rather convincing case that the company was attempting to hide certain "truths" about the China trade. The EIC's monopoly, rather than the Canton system, hence seemed more likely to be the primary constraint on the application of free trade principles in China.

---

1 [Crawfurd], 1834a. "Voyage of Ship Amherst," 45.

2 Anon. 1832. *The Foreign Trade of China*, 41.

3 [Crawfurd, John], 1831b. "East India Company—China Question" *The Edinburgh Review* 104: 306.

4 [Crawfurd], *Observations on the Influence*, 20. More about Bates and his impact may be found in Webster. 2009. *The Twilight of the East India Company: The Evolution of Anglo-Asian Commerce and Politics, 1790–1860*, 97–98.

5 [Crawfurd], "East India Company—China Question," 294.

Advocates of "free trade" in China also challenged other images of China presented by the Company, especially regarding China's cultural "peculiarity" and the need to respect the Chinese government and its laws. A notable source of information came from a clandestine reconnaissance of the southern and eastern ports of China in 1832. This was led by Hugh Hamilton Lindsay, who, at this point, was still an EIC employee, yet managed to persuade the select committee in Canton to dispatch the voyage in defiance of the Chinese prohibition and the instructions of the Company's leadership in London. Perhaps having formed the idea of trading on his own account in the presumably forthcoming "free trade" era, Lindsay took this initiative to scout out business opportunities beyond Canton, especially in the ports of Xiamen, Fuzhou, Ningbo and Shanghai—all of which later became the "treaty ports" according to the *Treaty of Nanjing*, 1842. This voyage also provided the "free trade" advocates an opportunity to gather so-called "first-hand" knowledge about China, so that they could contest the EIC's claim that only its servants in Canton knew the real state of the country. The "free trade" advocates, it should be noted, were an amorphous group. They were not necessarily the private merchants who had been conducting the "unauthorised trade." Lindsay, although still not a "free trader," clearly agreed with the private merchants regarding the need to challenge the existing system of the China trade. Another key figure, Karl Gützlaff, who served as the interpreter and physician during the voyage of 1832, was neither British nor a merchant. A Lutheran missionary from Prussia, Gützlaff was keen to spread the word of God among the Chinese. Hence, he shared the same interests with the British private merchants in "opening" China. Often referring to the British as "us" in his writings, Gützlaff played an important role in Britain's intercourse with China in the 1830s and 1840s. He commanded good knowledge of the Chinese language, which allowed him to interpret for Jardine, Matheson & Co. during its smuggling of opium and to assist in the Sino–British negotiations during the Opium War.[1] Both Gützlaff and Lindsay published

---

1 For more information about Gützlaff, see Lutz, Jessie Gregory. 2008. *Opening China: Karl F. A. Gützlaff and Sino-Western Relations, 1827–1852*. Grand Rapids, MI.

their reports of the reconnaissance shortly after the voyage. Together with articles written by Crawfurd and others, these publications, which were arguably results of a first-hand investigation, greatly challenged the EIC's assertion that China was so culturally different that the free trade principle was inapplicable there. This point of view was bolstered by the following claims.

First, the Chinese were "*a highly commercial people*"[1] just as the British were. According to Crawfurd, the ordinary Chinese people were not only "able and willing to trade," but "desirous of an extended intercourse with foreigners."[2] During the voyage up the China coast, Gützlaff accumulated much evidence showing that the natives whom he met appeared "anxious to gain a livelihood and accumulate riches"[3] and sometimes "complained bitterly of the system of exclusion."[4] In addition, even some of the government officials, who were supposed to suppress contacts between foreigners and the Chinese, had acknowledged in private that vast advantage could be drawn from international trade. In this respect, Gützlaff noted a remarkable case occurred in the vicinity of Xiamen, where the admiral of a local station asked to purchase opium. When he was told that no opium was carried on board the ships, the admiral appeared "much disappointed when we [the British] had none to sell."[5] Reports on such first-hand experiences in China enabled Crawfurd to claim with confidence that:

It appears quite certain that the Chinese, a money-making and money-loving people, are as much addicted to trade, and as anxious as any nation on earth to

---

1   [Crawfurd], *Observations on the Influence*, 14. Italics in the original.

2   [Crawfurd], 1834a. "Voyage of Ship Amherst," 37–38.

3   Gützlaff, Karl. 1834. *Journal of Three Voyages along the Coast of China, in 1831, 1832, & 1833*. London, 136.

4   Ibid., 172.

5   Gützlaff's Report, 1833. *Report of Proceedings on a Voyage to the Northern Ports of China, in the Ship Lord Amherst: extracted from papers, printed by order of the House of Commons, relating to the trade with China*. London, 278.

court a commercial intercourse with strangers. The government and its officers perhaps not less anxious for foreign commerce than the people themselves, could they see their way to admit it without danger.[1]

Second, the Chinese were a friendly and "kind-hearted race of people"[2] who were keen to have free intercourse with foreigners. In his journal of the voyage, Gützlaff carefully recorded the kindness with which the common Chinese people received him. For example, he wrote, although some natives lived "in the most wretched hovels imaginable," their hospitality "formed a striking contrast to their extreme poverty."[3] They not only invited Gützlaff and other foreign visitors into their houses, but shared with them their scanty meal. Particularly, as one of the few quotations cited from conversations with the Chinese, the following statement was minutely noted down by the Prussian missionary: "How gladly … would we, if permitted, [have] cultivated amicable intercourse with you! But we are always forbidden to obey the impulse of our hearts!" (Anon. quoted in Gützlaff 1834)[4] With the assistance of these vivid images, Gützlaff concluded that "the Chinese character in its true light" was "that of friendliness and kindness towards foreigners."[5] This opinion confirmed Crawfurd's belief that "Whatever peculiarities may attach to the Chinese … an antipathy to strangers is not one of them."[6]

Third, the Chinese held an open attitude towards knowledge about the external world. In particular, they were eager to possess information regarding Christianity and the character of the English people. This impression was formed mainly because, during the voyage, Lindsay and Gützlaff took opportunities to distribute a number of Chinese-language

1 [Crawford, John]. 1834b. "Chinese Empire and Trade." *The Westminster Review* 21: 254.
2 A correspondent in China. 1834. "Intercourse with China." *The Asiatic Journal* 13: 104.
3 Gützlaff. 1834. *Journal of Three Voyages along the Coast of China, in 1831, 1832, & 1833*, 211.
4 Ibid., 172.
5 Ibid., 301.
6 [Crawfurd]. *Observations on the Influence*, 26.

pamphlets, which they believed could disseminate favourable images of the British among the natives and help convert them to Christianity.[1] These books were described as eagerly sought after whenever they were distributed. Without attempting to ascertain how many Chinese were able to read these pamphlets (literacy rate was very low in China at this time), advocates of "free trade," such as "a correspondent in China," interpreted the phenomenon as a sign that "there exists among the people of China an unquenchable thirst after knowledge."[2] To Gützlaff, the demand for the religious tracts he circulated not only afforded an inviting filed, but suggested that the Chinese people wished to read the Gospels. These interpretations led Gützlaff to represent the Chinese as victims who were in need of moral reformation. "It is truly distressing," Gützlaff lamented, "that this people is anxious for the word of eternal life, but unable to obtain it."[3]

While holding that the Chinese people had no antipathy to commerce, foreigners or external knowledge, the "free trade" advocates maintained that the Chinese government did not deserve respect. They claimed that the current Qing government did not express the opinions or promote the interests of the Chinese people. An anonymous writer, for example, described the ruling Manchus as barbarians and conquerors as "disliked by the people, and living in constant fear of rebellion which may drive them out of China."[4] In December 1830, a group of private merchants presented a petition to parliament. In this document, they stated: "so many millions of comparatively civilised human beings were subdued by its bitterest enemies, and yielded implicit obedience to a tribe of rude and ignorant barbarians."[5] Similarly, Lindsay claimed that "the mere will of a despot ... for the

---

1   Details about the distributed pamphlets may be found in Lindsay's Report, 1833. *Report of Proceedings*, 44.

2   A correspondent in China, 104.

3   Gützlaff. 1834. *Journal of Three Voyages along the Coast of China, in 1831, 1832, & 1833*, 155.

4   Anon. 1832. *The Foreign Trade of China*, 15.

5   *Petition to the House of Commons from British Subjects Residing in China* (also known as "Canton Petition"), December 24, 1830, in Le Pichon, Alain. ed. 2006. *China Trade and Empire: Jardine, Matheson & Co. and the Origins of British Rule in Hong Kong 1827–1843*. Oxford, 555.

last century ... separate near 400000000 of human beings from all communication with their species."[1] On the basis of these images, the private merchants and their supporters condemned the way the present government of China treated foreigners with constant suspicion, and made every effort to prevent foreigners from contacting the Chinese people. They believed that, in areas where the country's external trade was conducted, the government promoted mutual antipathy between its subjects and foreign merchants. On the one hand, it gave foreigners "the worst ideas of the stupid and treacherous natives,"[2] on the other, the government endeavoured to prepossess its people, particularly in Canton, against foreigners by "representing them ... as a barbarous, ignorant, and depraved race, everyway inferior to themselves, thereby exciting the lower orders to treat them with habitual insolence."[3] To account for the belief that the contempt of foreigners in Canton was more the result of the government's policy than the natural disposition of the people, Lindsay noted that, outside the province of Guangdong, "we had met with nothing but expressions of friendship and good will."[4] He found that, in general, "foreigners in China were better liked the less they were known."[5] Such first-hand evidence strengthened Crawfurd's idea that the current situation in China was a "government of the few" against "the interests of the many"[6] According to this view, the Qing government, instead of being a respectable institution as the EIC claimed, was but a detestable obstacle which stood between foreigners and the vast majority of the Chinese people, both of whom desired free communications.

In addition, the "free trade" advocates attempted to present the laws of China as equally unworthy of respect. With regard to the Chinese laws of limiting the intercourse between

---

1 Lindsay's Report, 211.

2 Gützlaff. 1834. *Journal of Three Voyages along the Coast of China, in 1831, 1832, & 1833*, 231.

3 "Canton Petition," 556–557.

4 Lindsay's Report, 10.

5 Ibid., 33.

6 [Crawfurd], "Chinese Empire and Trade," 256.

foreigners and the Chinese, Gützlaff wrote that, "it was not our wish to oppose the laws of the empire, but we could not believe that there were any laws *compelling* to such misanthropy."[1] In a similar tone, Gützlaff created an impression that the "unnatural" laws of China were in conflict with the divine law of the God. He contended that:

All mankind are created and upheld by the same God ... therefore have a natural right to claim fellowship. The refusal of it is a transgression of the divine law of benevolence, which is equally binding upon all the nations of the earth.[2]

On this ground, Gützlaff believed the Chinese people were under "the thraldom of Satan"[3] and in need of rescue. These images complemented the intentions of other observers to attribute all signs of underdevelopment in China to the harmful effects of the Chinese laws. Charles Marjoribanks, who served as the head of the select committee at Canton and later an MP from 1832 to 1833, believed that the laws brought "ruin and impoverishment"[4] to the Chinese nation. "A correspondent in China" wrote in *The Asiatic Journal* that because of the negative influence of the Chinese laws, the people in China had been reduced to "nothing more than semi-barbarians."[5]

Demonstrating that it was unnecessary to respect the Qing government and its laws, "free trade" advocates then had further reason to disagree with the EIC's campaigners regarding the need to follow a conciliatory policy towards Chinese authorities. Since no government had a right to exclude its subjects from peaceful intercourse with foreigners, it

---

1 Gützlaff. 1834. *Journal of Three Voyages along the Coast of China, in 1831, 1832, & 1833*, 253. Italics in the original.

2 Ibid., 1–2.

3 Ibid., 124.

4 Marjoribanks, Charles. 1833. *Letter to the Right Hon. Charles Grant, President of the Board of Control, on the Present State of British Intercourse with China*. London, 27.

5 A correspondent in China, 105.

was legitimate to challenge the Qing government for the benefit of both the British and the Chinese people. Notably, unlike some of the EIC's supporters, such as Fisher, who asserted that the Chinese had a natural disposition to appeal to reason, Lindsay asserted that "much more may be gained by an appeal to their fears."[1] The anonymous author of *The Foreign Trade of China* agreed with this view. He claimed that, as in the cases of the Macartney and the Amherst embassies, "those objects which foreigners have sought by means of reason and persuasion, and especially by a show of respect, have scarcely ever been attained," while recent experience had shown that "a tone of defiance, more particularly when backed by any display of physical force, has nearly always proved successful."[2] The voyage of 1832, once again, proved useful to show that the Chinese authorities indeed respected firmness more than conciliation. Gützlaff noted, for example, "even the least thing was refused when we humbly asked for it"[3] yet "as soon as the mandarins perceived that we were firm and reasonable in our demands, they became polite, and yielded."[4] Such first-hand findings made it easier for the private merchants and their campaigners to argue that a submissive approach could not improve Britain's relations with China, while a firmer attitude would help.

In August 1833, the British government decided to abolish the EIC's monopoly of China trade. Trade with China was finally opened to British private merchants. Webster's and Kumagai's analyses have presented a range of factors regarding the government's decision, neither of which favoured the EIC. Economically, since the opening of the India trade to private merchants in 1813, the EIC's trade with India declined rapidly. The Company's financial status deteriorated throughout the 1820s. Britain also faced increasing competition from American companies in the Chinese market. The threat fuelled the anti-monopoly campaigners' argument that, unless trade with China was thrown open, the British

---

1 Lindsay's Report, 57.
2 Anon. 1832. *The Foreign Trade of China*, 14–15.
3 Gützlaff's Report. 1833, 289.
4 Gützlaff. 1834. *Journal of Three Voyages along the Coast of China, in 1831, 1832, & 1833*, 284–285.

merchants would be unable to compete with their American counterparts. Politically, the early 1830s was a time of turmoil. The question of parliamentary reform was the British governments' main concern. Many of the landed elite feared that a revolution might occur in Britain. Such a political climate might have made it easier for politicians to listen to the voices outside the government calling for reform and to compromise if necessary. These underlying trends went hand in hand with the formidable campaign created by the opponents of the Company's privileges. According to Webster:

a decisive factor ... had been the development since 1813 of new political and commercial links between those private trading organisations ... the London East India agency houses, and the emergent industrial interests of provincial Britain.[1]

Kumagai's research has concentrated on the role that the provincial interests, especially the East India Associations of Glasgow and Liverpool, played in the abolition. Kumagai has shown how these pressure groups initiated and orchestrated the campaign. They not only rallied wide support in their own localities, bombarded parliament and government with petitions, but used their connections with MPs, senior politicians, London-based merchants and those with knowledge of Asia to strengthen the impact of the movement. The end of the EIC's China monopoly could not have been possible without the strenuous and tactical efforts made by these provincial interests to influence the opinions of policymakers as well as the public.[2]

It should be noted, however, that although the anti-monopoly campaigners won the debate with the EIC, this did not necessarily mean that the images of China presented

---

1   Webster. 2009. *The Twilight of the East India Company: The Evolution of Anglo-Asian Commerce and Politics, 1790–1860*, 102.

2   Kumagai. 2012. *Breaking into the Monopoly: Provincial Merchants and Manufacturers' Campaigns for Access to the Asian Market, 1790–1833*, 179–189.

by them were incontestable. At least, their contentions deserve consideration from the following perspectives.

First, although it seems that some of the critical opinions concerning China were derived from first-hand discoveries of the voyage, it is difficult to determine whether they were genuine "discoveries" independent from any predispositions. Since the late 1820s, the Chinese government had been heavily criticised by foreign traders in Canton. As mentioned earlier, in 1830, a group of British merchants in China even petitioned parliament for the British state's direct intervention in Chinese affairs partly based on the claim that China had an extremely corrupt government that was liked neither by its people nor the foreign traders. Since they did not receive any positive response, the petitioners, as well as other "free trade" advocates, were keen to gather more convincing arguments, or "evidence," regarding the characters of the Chinese government and people, to continue to lobby the British government to take action. In this context, the two central figures of the voyage, namely Lindsay and Gützlaff, had been inclined to agree with such views of China before they started their journey.

Second, although evidence obtained on the voyage had helped the "free trade" advocates to claim that the Chinese were naturally friendly to foreigners and that they were keen to understand Christianity, these images could well be representations based on the personal prejudices of the travellers. Gützlaff, for instance, made every effort to record how much his religious tracts were welcomed in China and how hospitable the Chinese became when they lived beyond the reach of the government. He took it for granted that these signs represented the Chinese people's genuine dispositions, yet never really questioned whether they had other motives, especially their hope of gaining something from the foreign visitors. Lindsay suggested that it might be the free medical services that Gützlaff provided for the natives that gave rise to the "the extraordinary degree of respect and friendship shown to us by all classes of Chinese."[1] Even Gützlaff himself recorded some occurrences

---

1 Lindsay's Report, 87.

which might have challenged his conclusions, however the Prussian missionary made no attempt to explain these phenomena. He once noted that:

> We had had a long conversation with the owner of a house, who had posted himself right in the way to prevent our entering his dwelling. I now thought it high time to make them a present of some books. When they found that I really intended to *give* these to them, they changed their tone, became friendly and hospitable.[1]

Such an encounter may well indicate that the claimed friendliness or hospitality of the Chinese did not necessarily represent their real feelings. When Gützlaff came to present the "genuine" character of the Chinese nation, however, he simply ignored these occurrences.

Third, despite the fact that the "free trade" campaigners were aware that some duplicity was innate to the Chinese character, they tended to fix this trait on government officials rather than the common people. To justify his view that the Qing authorities did not represent their subjects, Lindsay maintained that, although there was a friendly disposition on the part of the people, the Chinese mandarins had a "lying spirit."[2] Even when the officials treated him in the same favourable manner as some ordinary Chinese people did, Lindsay never forgot to point out that "there was more of policy than sincerity" in the officials' "*professions* of friendship."[3] This charge of duplicity, however, was never employed by Lindsay in his portrayal of the hospitality of the common people. Furthermore, when he and other "free trade" supporters were satisfied with the comments of some Chinese officials, they never bothered to understand why they spoke in this way. For example, according to the orders of the emperor, mandarins from various places were

---

1 Gützlaff. 1834. *Journal of Three Voyages along the Coast of China, in 1831, 1832, & 1833*, 418. Italics in the original.
2 Lindsay's Report, 78.
3 Ibid., 111. Italics added.

anxious to drive foreigners out of their districts. Under such circumstances, and perhaps to avoid an open conflict, some officials conceded that international trade was beneficial. "[A]s the laws of the Celestial Empire prohibited trade with foreigners," they expressed their wish for the foreign visitors to leave their districts without delay, even though "for themselves, they would be highly desirous that the trade was opened."[1] In these cases, the mandarins' favourable remarks on foreign trade, no matter whether they were sincere, were taken out of context and were treated as further evidence of China's general eagerness for external trade—even government officials were not opposed to it.

Fourth, in a similar way, the "free trade" campaigners attempted to hide certain important contexts when they were endeavouring to convince the British public that the Chinese government was extremely suspicious of foreigners. In particular, a few months before the voyage, a serious quarrel broke out between the EIC's factory at Canton and the local authorities. As a result, a rumour spread among the Chinese that the EIC had demanded assistance from India. Instead of referring to this background situation, Gützlaff, Lindsay and others insisted that the Chinese mandarins were "always suspicious that we [the British] design to attack them,"[2] as if this fear were totally unreasonable. During the voyage of 1832, the travellers disguised their connection with the EIC. Since, unlike most non-EIC British merchants, they carried no opium for sale, Chinese officials were given ample reason to suspect the real intention of these visitors. These aspects of the voyage might not overthrow the claim that China possessed a suspicious government, yet they at least suggest that the anxiety exhibited by the Chinese authorities was not entirely unwarranted.

Last, with regard to the "free trade" advocates' contention that the Chinese were a

---

1 Gützlaff's Report, 1833, 282–283. This was sometimes accompanied with a promise that they would turn a blind eye to the happenings beyond their region, see Lindsay's Report, 211; and Marjoribanks. 1833. *Letter to the Right Hon. Charles Grant*, 23.

2 Gützlaff. 1834. *Journal of Three Voyages along the Coast of China, in 1831, 1832, & 1833*, 268. Similar views may also be found in Lindsay's Report, 10, 93; and Marjoribanks. 1833. *Letter to the Right Hon. Charles Grant*, 23–24.

commercially minded nation, since foreigners had very limited contact with the Chinese people (with the exception of the coastal trading communities), it was unfair to assess the "national" character of China based on meeting only a small proportion of such a vast nation. Furthermore, influential opinion-formers such as Crawfurd sometimes even drew their conclusions from information regarding those who lived outside Chinese territory. Discoveries concerning the Chinese diaspora in Southeast Asia (people who lived thousands of miles away from China) were often seen as being representative of the character of all Chinese. For instance, in the writings of Crawfurd and others, the following conjectures were quoted:

> Mr John Deans, ... who resided twenty years in the Eastern archipelago ... [claimed:] "The Chinese of the Archipelago, who, I *believe*, do not differ from the Chinese in their native country, are very sensible of the importance of commerce, and are, as I have already observed, the keenest speculators perhaps in the country." [1]

Robert Rickards, Esq. [claimed:]

> I *believe* that the Chinese are a perfectly commercial people. Wherever the Chinese have been established in Singapore, in Java, in Borneo, ... they are found to be the principal traders, ... I therefore take the Chinese, generally speaking, to be a perfectly commercial people. [2]

From such comments, it may be seen that these "beliefs" were purely personal opinions

---

1 [Crawfurd]. *Observations on the Influence*, 300–301. Italics added.
2 Anon. 1832. *The Foreign Trade of China*, 36. Italics added. Similar examples may be found in the same book that different individuals interpreted the general commercial spirit of the Chinese from their experience in Batavia, Cochin China, Java, Penang and Singapore. See ibid., 24–38.

regarding the character of the Chinese. Some of these commentators had never visited China; however, simply because they had some experience of Asia, and their opinions supported the private merchants' arguments, their personal interpretations were propagated as proven facts in the anti-monopoly campaign. This vital difference between opinions and facts could have had an important impact in misleading the British government and concerned public, regarding the perception of the Chinese people's character, and to what extent they needed international trade.

(Acknowledgement: This article first appeared as Gao, Hao, 2019. "Understanding the Chinese: British Merchants on the China Trade in the Early 1830s." *Britain and the World* 12(3): 151–171, and is reused here with kind permission. This article is a revision of the author's speech at the 2019 UKCHA Annual.)

灾难记忆与新冠疫情纪念空间构建理路

肖　波　黄晶莹[*]

　　新冠疫情是百年来全球发生的最严重的传染病大流行，是中华人民共和国成立以来我国遭遇的传播速度最快、感染范围最广、防控难度最大的重大突发公共卫生事件。[1]面对全球复杂严峻的疫情形势，我国为抗击疫情做出了巨大牺牲和不懈努力。在党中央的坚强领导下，14亿中国人民无私奉献、团结协作、坚韧不拔，构筑起同心战疫的坚固防线，彰显了人民的伟大力量。经过三个多月的艰苦抗疫，取得了武汉保卫战、湖北保卫战的决定性成果，国内疫情基本得到有效控制，疫情防控进入常态化阶段，社会经济秩序有序恢复。在战"疫"中涌现出的感人壮举、英雄人物、抗争精神，令人动容，其间有很多历史见证物。恩格斯说："一个聪明的民族，从灾难和错误中学到的东西比平时要多得多。"[2]灾难不应该被忘记，只有铭记历史，补齐发展过程中的问题短板，才能继续砥砺前行。新冠灾难为何要被纪念？疫后如何保存集体记忆并纪念这一世纪灾难？如何构建新冠疫情纪念空间，让后人知悉、铭记和反思这场灾难，化灾难为前行的力量？这是本文探讨的中心问题。

---

[*]　肖波：武汉大学国家文化发展研究院教授。研究领域为文化遗产、文化产业、民间文学。黄晶莹：工作单位，成都高新技术产业开发区管理委员会。
　　文章发表于《东南文化》2021年第2期。

[1]　习近平：《在全国抗击新冠肺炎疫情表彰大会上的讲话》，《人民日报》2020年9月9日第002版。

[2]　［德］马克思、恩格斯：《马克思恩格斯全集》第39卷上册，中共中央马克思恩格斯列宁斯大林著作编译局译，北京：人民出版社，1974年，第149页。

一、灾难记忆：为何要纪念新冠疫情

社会集体记忆是民族认同或国家认同的重要资源。美国学者本尼迪克特·安德森（Benedict Anderson）提出近代国家是"想象的共同体"，它建立在人们共有记忆的基础上[1]，集体记忆成为国家形成的前提。以色列复国、苏联解体等史实证明，如何对待灾难所产生的集体记忆在某种程度上决定了国家的前途。一个民族共同经历的灾难能够将民族命运紧密地联系在一起，构建起深刻的集体记忆。延续灾难的集体记忆，后人可以对自我身份进行构建，总结出前人面对灾难的经验教训，凝练出独特的精神气质和精神品格，进而认同、弘扬国家文化和民族精神。新冠疫情是一场突如其来的空前灾难，给民众、国家和世界留下了不可磨灭的集体记忆。这些灾难记忆是疫后构建国家认同、增强民族自信、实现中华民族永续发展的重要记忆资源。

一方面，新冠疫情留下了不能忘却的集体记忆。对个体而言，个人记忆是学习、进步的基础；对国家、民族而言，集体记忆是建构国家认同、推动社会改革进步的根基，在某种程度上，集体记忆建构了国家的民族性格和民族精神。"集体记忆"与"个人记忆"相对，源于法国社会学家埃米尔·涂尔干（Émile Durkheim），他认为共同回忆创造了一种凝聚感，形成"集体意识"，能为共同体找到一种方式描述他们自己的事实。[2]法国学者莫里斯·哈布瓦赫（Maurice Halbwachs）在此基础上提出"集体记忆"（又称"社会记忆"，Collective Memory），即："一个特定社会群体之成员共享往事的过程和结果，保证集体记忆传承的条件是社会交往及群体意识需要提取该记忆的延续性。"[3]集体记忆包括集体共享的知识体系，社会群体的形象、叙述、价值观和观念，以及事

1　［美］安德森：《想象的共同体——民族主义的起源与散布》，吴睿人译，上海：上海人民出版社，2003年，第12页。

2　［法］埃米尔·涂尔干：《社会分工论》，渠东译，北京：生活·读书·新知三联书店，2000年，第240页。

3　［法］莫里斯·哈布瓦赫：《论集体记忆》，毕然、郭金华译，上海：上海人民出版社，2002年，第335页。

件的集体记忆发生变化的连续过程。集体行动的过程会沉淀为集体记忆，集体行动越是艰苦卓绝，集体记忆就越刻骨铭心。新冠疫情袭来，大到国家，小到个人，都在用行动抗击疫情，留下了刻骨铭心的民族集体记忆。党中央立即做出重要部署，成立中央应对疫情工作领导小组，组织力量建设火神山、雷神山等重症救治医院和方舱医院，派遣医疗队和医护人员进行对口支援；全国各类企业、社会机构、民间组织和个人倾囊相助，抗疫英雄冲锋在前，专家、医务人员、军人、民警、基层干部、志愿者等用行动筑牢抗疫防线；新闻媒体在第一时间高效、精准报道疫情进展；数亿普通中国人听从国家指挥，居家隔离。全国上下开展了一场艰苦卓绝的抗疫斗争，汇聚成举国空前的集体行动。在抗疫中，民众的恐惧、焦虑、痛心与崇敬、感恩、关爱等情绪交织，混合成为"社会黏合剂"，将所有人的命运联系在一起，固化沉淀成为民族深层次的集体记忆。中国抗疫充分体现了以人为本、关爱生命的人文情怀，彰显了社会主义制度的优越性，焕发出患难与共、血浓于水的民族精神。抗疫过程更是一段用鲜血和汗水、智慧和毅力书写的历史，不能被时间忘记。作为灾难的亲历者，我们有责任把抗疫历程记录下来、保存下去，这样集体记忆才能得以延续，历史教训才能得到铭记。

另一方面，新冠疫情是值得纪念的空前灾难。黑格尔说："人类从历史中获取的最大教训就是，从来不从历史中吸取教训。"[1]历史总在不断地告诫后人，但人类对于历史的记忆又常常健忘，以致灾难重蹈覆辙。对于灾难的记忆，往往囿于个体记忆之中，个体一旦消逝，记忆便不复存在。只有通过某种载体，对灾难进行纪念，让集体记忆固化下来，才能让人类的历史记忆得到延续。[2]纪念灾难具有特殊的社会意义：一是纪念灾难，凭吊逝者。对灾难的纪念，能够唤醒公众对灾难的感知和记忆，唤起生者对生命的敬畏与思索，是凭吊逝者、抚慰伤痛、纪念英雄、保存灾难记忆的有效途径，修建纪念空间和举办纪念活动均是为了纪

---

1 ［德］黑格尔：《法哲学原理》，杨东柱、尹建军、王哲译，北京：北京出版社，2007年，第51页。

2 刘迪：《灾难博物馆与灾难教育》，《城市与减灾》2013年第4期。

念灾难。二是铭记历史，警示后人。灾难留下的遗址和物件，是通往灾难集体记忆的桥梁。以多种方式记录、讲述灾难的历史过程，将灾难的惨烈和痛苦表象化，以警示幸存者和后世，铭记先烈和历史。三是引导研究，普及科学。纪念灾难是为了反思灾难，从灾难中获得教训和启示，促进对灾难知识的普及和培训，帮助公众树立正确的灾难观，如1995年日本阪神大地震后，日本社会在纪念灾难的同时强调对未来同类灾难的防范，增强全社会的防震减灾意识，以更加理性地应对灾害。

灾难是对能够给人类和人类赖以生存的环境造成破坏性影响的事物总称，又称为灾害、灾祸、祸患、浩劫等。灾难可分两大类：人为灾难和自然灾难。因人为因素导致的灾难称为人为灾难，如战争、恐怖事件、核事故、工业灾难等。"二战"后，以战争为主题的灾难纪念空间蓬勃发展，在战争废墟上修建较为恢宏的纪念空间，主要发挥表达国家意志、凝聚民族团结、珍惜和平的作用。因自然因素导致的灾难称为自然灾难，地震、火灾、海啸、恐怖袭击等自然灾难是灾难纪念的重要主题，其纪念空间多位于城市内，目的在于缅怀逝者和教育后代。[1] 此次新冠源于自然，但又区别于一般的自然灾难，人类在其传播过程中充当着重要媒介，疫情的人为防控效果直接与灾难受损程度相关联，防控不力将导致更为严重的人为灾难，叠加为"双重灾难"。为重大瘟疫事件成立专门博物馆，世界上已经有先例，如瑞士日内瓦国际红十字与红新月博物馆（Musée international de la Croix-Rouge et du Croissant-Rouge）、澳大利亚新南威尔士州人类疾病博物馆（Museum of Human Disease）、英国德比郡亚姆村瘟疫博物馆（Eyam Museum）等，都为人类抗疫提供了科学价值和精神典范。迄今为止，我国鲜有与瘟疫相关的纪念空间。以此次抗疫为契机，构建新冠疫情的纪念空间，是传承抗疫文化的重要依托。

纪念灾难是强化集体记忆、凝聚民族精神的重要方式。自近代民族国家出

1　牛景龙：《城市重大灾难型纪念空间周边环境圈层规划》，华南理工大学硕士学位论文，2016年。

现以来，世界各国普遍建立了国家性纪念空间，以镌刻灾难记忆和展现抗灾壮举。德国柏林的欧洲被害犹太人纪念碑（Denkmal für die ermordeten Juden Europas）、中国各地的抗战纪念馆、美国的越南退伍军人纪念碑（Vietnam Veterans Memorial）、爱尔兰的大饥荒博物馆（The Jeanie Johnston Tall Ship and Famine Museum）等，都是对灾难记忆的空间表达，旨在以表象物来强化民族或国家的集体记忆。新冠疫情是近百年来最严重的全球公共卫生突发事件，是全人类共同的集体记忆，无论是被病毒无情带走生命的人们，还是默默战斗在抗疫前线的医护人员和始终坚守岗位的工作者，他们的名字和故事应当被铭记。纪念疫情不仅要反思灾难原因，警示后人，更要传承中华民族的抗疫精神，总结抗疫经验，为我国常态化防控疫情、为世界抗击疫情凝聚中国力量，贡献中国智慧。

二、空间表达：人类如何展示灾难记忆

灾难记忆既存储于人心与文献，又外化和再现为纪念空间。记忆主体在空间和时间上进行记忆重构而形成了纪念，纪念需要记忆的表象物来承载。莫里斯·哈布瓦赫指出，集体记忆必须依赖于某种集体场所和公众论坛，大至社会、宗教活动，小至家庭团聚、朋友聚会，都是记忆的公众场所。[1] 皮埃尔·诺拉（Pierre Nora）认为，人们在特定的纪念时间和空间里举行神圣的纪念仪式，就会形成以这个时间和空间为节点的"记忆之场"，它具有"物质性""功能性"和"象征性"，分别指依托灾难遗址建立的纪念空间或场所、在场所内举行纪念仪式或活动、人们的灾难集体记忆。物化的"记忆之场"即为纪念空间，能唤醒个人、民族及国家的历史记忆，是社会集体记忆中的标志性元素。[2] 纪念空间一

1　［法］莫里斯·哈布瓦赫：《论集体记忆》，第335页。
2　［法］皮埃尔·诺拉：《记忆之场：法国国民意识的文化社会史》，黄艳红等译，南京：南京大学出版社，2017年，第3页。

般由纪念物及历史环境所构成，其最重要的特质是空间性和纪念性，通过建筑、雕塑、碑等元素来进行空间的限定和形象的塑造，运用隐喻、暗示等环境手段来引导人们思考，从而表达出空间的纪念性。[1] 纪念空间是近代以来世界各国普遍接受和广泛采用的保存集体记忆的方式，其具体形态丰富而多元。

　　灾难型纪念空间作为纪念空间的一种，能够激发人们对灾难的情感共鸣和对民族的文化认同，进而实现哀悼、教育、鼓舞等作用，从社会学的角度来讲具有存在的必要性与合理性。[2] 灾难博物馆或纪念馆是灾难纪念空间的重要表达实体。刘迪认为，灾难博物馆是以灾难为主题，多数依托于灾难原址兴建，通过呈现人类群体性灾难，供社会进行反思的综合性博物馆空间。[3] 罗梦豪将灾难型纪念馆界定为：为纪念某次重大灾难或灾难中的遇难者，多数依托灾难原址或发生地而建立的，同时以展示灾难及相关题材，供社会纪念与反思为主要目的纪念馆。[4] 黄凡认为记忆需要地点并趋向于空间化，灾害记忆的空间表象体现为记事碑、纪念碑等"纪念物"的构筑。[5] 李佳宁提出纪念景观是通过情感传递创造的精神场所，是反映情感、精神和社会功能的场所，是纪念、哀悼、沉思和集会的场所。[6] 随着网络技术的发展，灾难纪念空间的内涵进一步拓展，虚拟的灾难纪念空间被广泛应用，如奥斯威辛集中营（Konzentrationslager Auschwitz）毒气室的虚拟探访，是在网络空间中创造和重现过去的创伤。[7] 笔者认为，灾难型纪念空间（Disaster-type Memorial Space）是灾难记忆的空间表达，是为纪念某次灾难，依托原址建立纪念馆、纪念碑、纪念广场等实体场所或依托互联网建立的虚

1　陈蕴茜：《纪念空间与社会记忆》，《学术月刊》2012年第7期。

2　范可：《灾难的仪式意义与历史记忆》，《中国农业大学学报（社会科学版）》2011年第1期。

3　刘迪：《灾难博物馆定位问题初探》，《中国博物馆》2013年第1期。

4　罗梦豪：《灾难纪念馆空间体验设计研究》，华南理工大学硕士学位论文，2014年。

5　黄凡：《灾害记忆空间的建构——以通海大地震中的记事碑为例》，中国民俗学会2016年年会论文。

6　李佳宁、林旭东：《遗址纪念景观空间初步研究》，《美术教育研究》2018年第23期。

7　Lutz Kaelber, "A Memorial as Virtual Traumascape: Darkest Tourism in 3D and Cyber-Space to the Gas Chambers of Auschwitz, Ertr," e Review of Tourism Research, 2007: 24–33.

拟场所，是人类用于记录、缅怀、反思灾难的文化空间。一方面，灾难型纪念空间是灾难过程的物质载体，凝聚着集体记忆的历史遗存和文化地标，灾难中的故事赋予灾难纪念空间以灵魂[1]，让灾难记忆与有形空间结合起来，帮助民族、集体、个人共同铭记灾难历程。另一方面，人们对灾难的恐惧、对亲人的哀思、对抗灾英雄的崇敬以及对援灾者的感恩，构成了人类对灾难、对社会、对个人的情感联系，形成了复杂的情感网络。灾难纪念空间有助于引发公众的情感共鸣，实现情感寄托的社会功能。

灾难型纪念空间的命名可体现灾难的发生时间、原因或位置，纪念空间应主要围绕人、物、事三要素展开。纪念行为源于人类本能的情感需求，一切纪念都与"人"密切相关，纪念灾难性事件应遵循以人为本原则，其空间设计宜以人的感知体验为出发点，引导参观者的情感定位、共鸣和升华。客观事物作为"纪念"表达的物质载体，更能引起纪念主体的共鸣，纪念灾难最好的方式是让遗址说话，用真实、客观的遗址最大限度地保存灾难记忆，实现纪念意义的最大化。事件本身是"纪念"的重要内容，准确完整的叙述更能揭示事件真相，引发人们的思考，在纪念灾难事件时坚持叙事完整性原则，将灾难的起因、过程和结果完整地记录和呈现出来，既能让参观者清晰地认识和反思灾难，也是对受难者及其亲属的一种尊重和抚慰。

灾难型纪念空间可划分为不同的表达形态，如灾难发生地或相关地建馆[2]，或依据事件表达手法分为直接依附于景观元素或以空间变化传达纪念情感两种类型。[3] 近几十年来，灾难纪念建筑逐渐从单一纪念碑式向多空间组合式转变，更多使用象征主义元素来唤醒精神上的反思，用整体景观而不是单一纪念物进行呈现，来表达纪念场所的历史感和空间感。[4] 作为对灾难记忆的空间表达，往往通

1　肖波、陈泥：《从抗疫故事、情感主题到场景再现：瘟疫遗产地构建的欧洲经验和模式》，《深圳大学学报（人文社会科学版）》2021年第1期。

2　刘迪：《灾难博物馆定位问题初探》，《中国博物馆》2013年第1期。

3　温昕、张磊：《人为事件型灾难纪念空间的主题表达手法探讨》，《美术教育研究》2018年第22期。

4　王丹：《基于环境认知的灾难纪念型景观设计研究》，重庆大学硕士学位论文，2014年。

过功能记忆和存储记忆的模式[1]，将记忆存储、延伸和提炼。再现灾难记忆的形式通常有三种：一是存储记忆，纪念馆与灾难遗址结合，形成灾难遗址型纪念空间；二是延伸记忆，纪念馆与城市公园结合，形成主题公园型纪念空间；三是提炼记忆，纪念碑与纪念广场结合，形成文化广场型纪念空间。这三类空间表达方式在国内外都有先例。

记忆存储型空间表达方式，如四川省汶川特大地震纪念园。为纪念2008年5月12日发生的汶川特大地震，地方政府在震中映秀镇修建了地震纪念园，由漩口中学遗址（图一）[2]、映秀震中纪念馆（图二）[3]、纪念陵园构成。漩口中学遗址保留了大量地震后歪斜、坍塌的教学楼和宿舍楼，教学楼前是地震纪念组雕和汉白玉雕塑《汶川时刻》；映秀震中纪念馆包括以流水、地殇、崛起、希望为主题的四个庭院，分别通过水、石、树、光等要素营造场所精神[4]，客观展示灾难现场，叙述抗震救灾和灾后重建的历程；纪念陵园由遇难同胞纪念墙、抗震救灾叙事墙和纪念碑组成。整个纪念园将空间序列的组织、场所精神的营造与展览的主题内容形成密切关联，成为人们缅怀、纪念汶川大地震的第一现场和精神家园。

记忆延伸型空间表达方式，如美国"9·11"纪念博物馆（The 9/11 Memorial & Museum）。[5]为纪念2001年发生的"9·11"恐怖袭击事件，"9·11"纪念博物馆在世贸中心（World Trade Center）遗址落成，主要由博物馆、纪念馆（含纪念广场）两部分构成。[6]博物馆内，由近3000名不同性别、肤色、年龄和表情的罹

1　[德]阿莱达·阿斯曼：《回忆空间：文化记忆的形式和变迁》，潘璐译，北京：北京大学出版社，2016年，第146页。

2　湖北省地震局官网：《探访映秀漩口中学地震遗址　全国网媒向遇难同胞献花祭奠》，[EB/OL] [2018-05-07][2021-03-13]http://www.eqhb.gov.cn/info/1494/14212.htm。

3　5·12汶川特大地震纪念馆官网，[EB/OL][2021-03-13]http://www.512dzjng.com/content/column/4726101?pageIndex=1.

4　何镜堂、郑少鹏、郭卫宏：《大地的纪念 映秀·汶川大地震震中纪念地》，《时代建筑》2012年第2期。

5　The 9/11 Memorial & Museum-Visit, [EB/OL] [2021-03-13]https://www.911memorial.org/learn.

6　蔡琦：《试论作为黑色旅游目的地的纪念馆设计——以美国9/11纪念博物馆为例》，《中国博物馆》2020年第3期。

图一　汶川漩口中学遗址　　　　图二　"5·12"汶川特大地震映秀震中纪念馆

难者肖像形成的面孔墙（图三）[1]，表达对遇难者的缅怀和遇难者家属的追思。纪念馆是世贸双子塔纪念广场的重要组成部分和唯一建筑[2]，其入口处保留了两根顶端呈三叉戟形状的巨型钢柱，是双子塔建筑结构中的一部分，震撼至极。纪念馆外的纪念广场上，双子塔遗址赫然在目，在此基础上修建了两个凹入地下的正方形瀑布池（图四）[3]，水池外围的青铜墙上刻着2983名遇难者的名字，将亲人、同事、朋友的名字刻在一起，在闹市中形成了一片宁静、美丽、和谐的纪念空间，让人既能充分感受到双塔的存在，又能获得深度的纪念性体验。

图三　"9·11"博物馆面孔墙　　　　图四　"9·11"纪念馆和瀑布池

1　The 9/11 Memorial & Museum-Visit: In Memoriam, [EB/OL][2021-03-13]https://www.911memorial.org/visit/museum/exhibitions.

2　周婧景：《具身认知理论：深化博物馆展览阐释的新探索——以美国9·11国家纪念博物馆为例》，《东南文化》2017年第2期。

3　The 9/11 Memorial & Museum-Visit: The Memorial-Tribute in Light, [EB/OL][2021-03-13]https://www.911memorial.org/visit/memorial.

记忆提炼型空间表达方式，如黑龙江省哈尔滨防洪纪念塔广场（图五）。[1] 为纪念哈尔滨人民战胜1957年特大洪水，防洪纪念塔广场于1958年在松花江畔建成。广场由纪念塔、喷泉、围廊和广场四部分组成。纪念塔下部是人民战胜洪水的群像浮雕；中部浮雕讲述防洪筑堤的艰险过程；顶部由工农兵和知识分子的圆雕组成，凸显抗洪抢险的英雄形象。纪念塔外面环立的20根科林斯圆柱构成罗马式半圆围廊，形成和谐统一的文化广场景观。防洪纪念塔广场既表达了对抗洪英雄的尊重和感恩，又展现了历史文化名城的特色风貌，成为哈尔滨市的重要文化符号，并入选第二批中国20世纪建筑遗产名单。

为存储记忆而建设灾难遗址型纪念空间，为延伸记忆而建设主题公园型纪念空间，为提炼记忆而建设文化广场型纪念空间，上述经典案例为灾难记忆的空间表达进行了有益尝试和可贵探索。基于纪念灾难的共识，灾难纪念空间的表达方式是多元和立体的，

图五　哈尔滨防洪纪念塔广场

通过多维组合共同营造有意义的文化空间，以表达对灾难的纪念、对灾难记忆的存储和再现。这些宝贵经验对新冠疫情纪念空间的构建不无启发。

三、记忆再现：新冠疫情纪念空间构建理路

新冠疫情在短短几个月内迅速蔓延到多个国家和地区，引起全球性灾难。随着国内疫情得到缓解，在严防输入的同时，应及时对抗疫工作进行总结和反思，

1　搜狐网：《畅游东北 感受我国大东北的独特风情！》，[EB/OL][2018-08-28][2021-03-09]https://www.sohu.com/a/250580760_356022。

疫后有必要在疫情"震中"武汉市修建系列纪念物，以纪念被病毒夺去的生命，弘扬抗疫过程中涌现出的先进典型、英雄人物和感人事迹，铭记战"疫"的经验教训，进而反思灾难和凝聚民族认同。抗疫纪念物的本质是以空间表达的方式，对灾难记忆进行存储和再现。

一个民族共同经历的痛苦和灾难成为刻骨铭心的集体记忆。新冠疫情给人民、国家和世界带来了不可磨灭的伤痛，抗击疫情成为全民族重要的集体记忆。灾难不应该被忘记，疫后应保存集体记忆、纪念这场灾难，科学布局文化空间，让后人知悉、铭记、反思这场灾难，化灾难为前行的力量。考虑到灾难记忆的特点和空间表达的方式，宜在我国疫情"震中"武汉市选址，规划建设系列文化纪念物；宜聚焦人、物、事三要素，用多元方式表达对灾难记忆的储存、延伸、提炼和镌刻，让抗疫故事深刻留存并立体呈现。可综合考虑以下四种路径。

其一，储存灾难记忆，用博物馆再现抗疫篇章。抗疫过程中的文献、实物和口述资料，具有重要的收藏、纪念和研究价值。"为了未来，收藏教训，为了安宁，收藏灾难。"[1]通过博物馆收藏灾难逝者或亲历者的私人物品，如照片、日记、衣物等，展示抗疫过程、个例和细节，是保存个体记忆的必要手段。疫后可考虑将原废弃仓库改造的方舱医院作为馆舍，建设集科普、公共卫生、生物、爱国主义教育于一体的综合性抗疫博物馆。博物馆外观可突出抗疫特色，如放大的病毒模型、逆行者大鹏展翅形象等，馆内定期举办纪念仪式和活动，使之成为个体记忆与集体记忆有机融合的载体。

其二，延伸灾难记忆，用文化空间再造抗疫地标。将纪念空间巧妙融入城市生活空间，让部分停用的抗疫场所浴火重生，蜕变成为新的城市地标。可利用完成使命后不再使用的部分抗疫场所，打造抗疫主题的纪念公园、纪念广场或文化街区等开放型文化空间，注重空间的情感表达。一方面为缅怀逝者、致敬英雄、

1　师永刚、刘琼雄:《国人到此低头致敬：中国建川博物馆聚落》，北京：新星出版社，2008年，第9页。

教育反思而营造不同空间氛围；另一方面站在"人类命运共同体"的高度，展现人类共同抗击疫情的时间轴和典型事迹，以开放的姿态接纳世界不同受众，展现人性光辉。

其三，提炼灾难记忆，用文化符号铭记援助恩情。文化符号折射出一个国家或民族的内在气质和社会共识。抗疫充分展现了中华民族独特的内在气质，凝聚了社会力量，发挥了社会主义制度的优越性。参与抗疫的英雄个体和群体应该被历史铭记。疫后可在抗疫重点医院如金银潭医院、火神山医院设立纪念雕塑，在定点医院设计小的纪念牌或纪念砖，铭记给予援助的医疗单位和医护人员；在大型公共空间树立抗疫英雄纪念碑和雕像群等标志性文化符号，以弘扬抗疫精神，表达感恩之情。

其四，镌刻灾难记忆，用名录表达对生命的敬重。灾难过后，不少幸存者面临亲人逝去的痛苦，灾难纪念空间成为缅怀逝者、重塑生者希望的重要场所。对生命的尊重与敬畏是世人的共识，每一个不幸因疫情夺去生命的人都应该被记录。疫后可择址建造名录墙或面孔墙，为生者提供一个哭泣疗伤的精神之墙，以文明祭奠亲人、寄托哀思，安放个人记忆，同时，疫情名录墙也可成为珍惜生命、携手应对困难的希望之墙。

上述四种方式不是彼此孤立的，而是多元组合、有机融合的，共同作为构建新冠疫情纪念空间的方法和模式。当前全球疫情形势依然十分严峻，全球抗疫是当代社会不可磨灭的集体记忆。疫后应及时反思灾难、纪念灾难，把握灾难背后的精神财富和珍贵契机。作为疫情初期的"震中"，湖北武汉宜以新的城市面貌展现英雄城市文化和抗疫精神。建设系列文化纪念物、构建灾难纪念空间是实现这一目标的有效路径。灾难纪念空间在内容表达上可把握缅怀、纪念、反思的主旨，突出以人为本的原则；在表现形式上组合利用多种纪念物，整体表现文化景观，突出抗疫精神；在功能上将纪念功能和教育功能相结合，为缅怀逝者、纪念英雄、教育后代提供精神文化场所。总之，借鉴国内外灾难型纪念空间的建设思路和经验，在疫情初期"震中"和中国抗疫决胜之地武汉市选址构建新冠疫情纪念空间，可实现对灾难记忆的储存与再现，帮助我们化悲痛为力量，以更加从容自信的姿态迎接未来挑战。

（本文原载《东南文化》2021年第2期。基金项目：武汉大学"抗击新冠肺炎疫情人文社会科学应急研究"专项课题《后疫情时代的文化纪念研究》[2020YJ062]，得到"中央高校基本科研业务费专项资金"资助。本文系作者在联盟2022年年度论坛上的发言）

方兴未艾

Looking Forward

英国和中国史学的新趋势

——民族史与世界史的对立和破局

向　荣[*]

很久以来，历史就被划分为两大类：民族史和世界史。世界史最初指外国的历史，但到20世纪八九十年代，世界史更多指跨文化交流的历史、全球史。本文认为，世界史应该既包括前者，也涵盖后者。

一、英国和中国的新趋势

在晚近世界史或全球史的写作和研究过程中，美国人最为积极，从威廉·麦克尼尔的《西方的兴起》、斯塔夫里阿诺斯的《全球通史》，到杰里·本特利的《新全球史》，一直引领时代潮流。相对来说，英国和中国的反应是比较慢的。于尔根·奥斯特哈默在《牛津历史写作史》"世界史"条目中写到，世界史和全球史的兴起是20世纪80年代的新现象，90年代才开始引人注目地发展起来。世界史的兴起、发展和专业化最初主要在美国，直到作者撰写该条目，即2010年时才有少数国家开始赶上。[1]麦克·本特利在回顾英国当代历史写作时说，我们正处在一个全球化的时代，环境的变化使我们需要"世界史"，需要关于全球环境、食物、服装等方面的历史。我们需要进入这块条件与限制并存、近乎混乱的研究

---

[*] 向荣：复旦大学历史学系教授。主要从事近代早期欧洲史、英国史研究。

[1] Jürgen Osterhammel, "World History," in Axel Schneider and Daniel Woolf eds., *The Oxford History of Historical Writing*, Vol. 5, Oxford: Oxford University Press, 2011, p. 108.

领域，并充分意识到将不列颠同美国或欧洲的发展孤立开来会越来越困难。[1]

但近年无论英国还是中国，变化都很大。伯明翰大学历史系从事中国史研究的娜奥米·斯坦登教授说，直到2000年，英国高校历史系几乎还没有专门从事中国史研究的教师，中国史只是以文学为主的传统汉学的一部分，但到2013年英国已经有20多所高校的历史系设立了中国史的教职。[2]英国华威大学、牛津大学在2007年和2011年相继成立全球史研究中心。英国学者迅速将全球史研究的理论和方法付诸实践，2013年华威大学的乔治·列洛教授推出了《棉：创造现代世界的织物》，2015年牛津大学的彼得·弗兰克潘教授出版了《丝绸之路：一部新世界史》。[3]

中国的情况与英国有所不同。直到20世纪80年代末，中国从事世界史研究的大学教师为数不少，吴于廑先生还在80年代初提出了"整体世界史观"，即在关注人类历史由低级社会形态向高级社会形态更迭发展的同时，也要重视人类历史从分散到整体的发展。整体世界史是对传统世界史即外国史的补充，而非替代。但是，从20世纪90年代到21世纪头十年，中国的世界史教学和研究出现了一个低谷。直到2012年世界史成为新的一级学科之后，世界史学科才迎来了一个迅速发展的时期。我国的全球史研究起步相对较早，早在2004年首都师范大学就成立了全球史研究中心，2014年北京外国语大学也成立了全球史研究院。

二、民族史和普世史的对立

那么，我们需要探讨，为什么英国和中国对20世纪八九十年代兴起的世界史和全球史反应比较慢，而最近又跟进较快呢？我觉得其中的原因可能有相似之

1　Michael Bentley, "British Historical Writing," in Schneider and Woolf eds., *The Oxford History of Historical Writing*, Vol. 5, p. 291.

2　Naomi Standen:《历史学而非汉学——二战后英国的中国史研究沿革》，仁可编译，《中国社会科学报》2011年8月25日。

3　Giorgio Riello, *Cotton: The Fabric that Made the Modern World*, Cambridge: Cambridge University Press, 2013; Peter Frankopan, *The Silk Roads: A New History of the World*, London: Bloomsbury, 2015.

处，最主要的原因是，这两个国家都存在着普世史和民族史的对立。

英国的普世史深受启蒙运动的影响。启蒙思想家认为人类有共同的理性，人类历史发展有着共同的规律，通过历史研究人们可以发现这些规律，休谟、吉本等人是这种传统的代表。后来从德国引进的历史主义，一方面表现为民族史学，另一方面表现为严格的史料考据。但是英国人最开始接受德国的史学思想就是一分为二的，以阿克顿勋爵为例，他认为在方法方面必须坚守德国式的史料考据，但作为一个著名的自由主义者，他又认为在历史的本质方面不能像德国人一样，将历史简单地等同于过去，历史学家应该有价值判断和现实关怀。到后来，英国的普世史和民族史交替上升，比如说20世纪上半叶的汤因比、巴勒克拉夫等人，他们延续了英国普世史的研究路径。剧烈冲突发生在20世纪60年代，牛津大学著名历史学教授H. R.特雷弗-罗珀对汤因比进行了系统的批判，认为尽管汤因比的《历史研究》很畅销，但对于专业历史学家来说，它是"不真实、不合理、教条式的"[1]。从他开始到G. R.埃尔顿，实证学派逐渐占了上风，事实上埃尔顿比兰克还要兰克。在这个时候谁提倡世界史和全球史都会遭到怀疑或批判，因为历史研究要立足于原始材料，否则就没有发言权。

中国也存在类似的冲突。中国的世界史是从苏联引入的，受苏联教条式"马克思主义"史学，特别是"五种生产方式"的影响，史学家的任务是探讨人类历史发展的普遍规律，因此要研究外国的历史。正因如此，从新中国成立到20世纪80年代末，中国对世界史是比较受重视的。奥斯特哈默甚至认为，除了美国之外，最大的世界史工作者群体可能在日本和中国。[2]中国的民族史传统也来自德国。受德国历史主义影响的历史学家如傅斯年认为，中国历史学家应致力于中国史研究，因为中国有丰富的历史材料和史料批判的历史传统。在他们看来，在中国做世界史研究几乎是不可能的，资料条件是不够的。有学者将中国近百年的史

1　H. R. Trevor-Roper, "Arnold Toynbee's Millennium," *Encounter*, Vol. 8, No. 6 (1957), pp. 14–28.

2　Jürgen Osterhammel, "World History," in Schneider and Woolf eds., *The Oxford History of Historical Writing*, p. 108.

学争论归结为史观派和史料派之争，从新中国成立初直到20世纪80年代末，史观派是占支配地位的，八九十年代则是史料派复兴并大有一统天下之势。王学典先生说："进入1990年代后，史观派的学术史地位就越发无足轻重，乃至可有可无了。"[1] 事实上，世界史研究工作者大多属于史观派，这可以部分解释为什么中国的世界史在世纪之交的前后10年步入低谷。

但现在这个情况发生了很大变化。首先，从20世纪90年代以来，全球化的趋势变得越来越明显。在全球化的时代不可能不研究世界史，因为世界史是促进不同民族、不同文明之间相互理解、相互沟通的重要工具。如果说民族史的功能是培养民族认同和爱国主义的话，世界史则是一种"国际教育"，两种缺一不可。其次，西方学界对历史的认知也发生了很大的变化。在兰克史学占支配地位的过去，人们认为历史只是以研究过去为目的，但现在大多数学者认为历史学还具有道德教育的功能，它应当关注当下。从《棉：创造现代世界的织物》和《丝绸之路：一部新世界史》中，可以明显感到两位作者正力图摆脱欧洲中心论的影响，关注被历史所遗忘的人群和地区，探讨历史与当下的关联。尽管两位作者大量依赖甚至主要依赖二手文献，但丝毫不影响其著作在学界内外获得如潮好评。当人们不再只是从方法或技术的层面去评判历史研究的高下时，心胸就会变得开阔一些，不再像过去那样狭隘极端。再次是资料条件的改善。过去由于受资料条件的限制，中国的世界史研究常不得不借助二手资料，因而从专业研究的角度很难达到原创水平。但是现在不一样了，很多资料网上都可以找到并下载，现在的问题恐怕是下工夫读的人还不多。

三、世界史研究破局之探讨

民族史与普世史的长期对立是我国世界史研究发展的重要障碍，那么该如何

1　王学典：《近五十年的中国历史学》，《历史研究》2004年第1期，第165—190页；王学典、陈峰：《二十世纪中国历史学》，《引言》，北京：北京大学出版社，2009年，第1—14页。

破局？这是我们目前真正需要关心的问题。现在西方学者中不少人提出普世史复兴，对此我深表疑虑。如果直到今天我们还把历史当成哲学来做的话，世界史将永远被人看不起。严格意义上的历史学，不管是世界史还是民族史，都应该从原始材料做起。

如何破局？首先，要从努力提高我们自身的专业研究水平开始。我个人倾向于将世界史分为两类：一类是传统意义上的世界史，即外国史，另一类是晚近出现的"新世界史"，即以跨文化交流为中心的全球史。前者应更重视具体问题研究和实证研究，虽然全球史可以更多地利用综合，但也需要有所取舍，尽可能将全球视野与具体问题研究相结合。同美国全景式的全球史相比，英国全球史研究的对象更具体，问题意识更明确，这一方面反映了英国经验主义史学传统的影响，另一方面也是全球史研究进一步走向深入的表现。我国世界史学界的全球史研究起步并不算晚，但到目前似乎还停留在全球史的内涵、意义和可行性争论上，这些争论既反映了一部分学者对学理问题的偏好，也反映了一部分学者对宏大叙事的不信任。[1] 我个人认为，吴于廑先生20世纪80年代的整体世界史研究值得借鉴。他不仅提出了整体世界史观，而且围绕整体世界史中的几个重大问题进行了深入具体的探讨，比如前资本主义时代游牧世界与农耕世界的矛盾与交往，15、16世纪整体世界史的初步形成及其动因等。[2] 从某种意义上，笔者认为，吴于廑先生的整体世界史就是一种具有中国特色的全球史。[3]

其次，将个人的学术专攻放入世界历史的大背景之中，进行历史比较研究。R.I.穆尔是英国著名的中世纪欧洲文明史专家，也是一位世界史学家，麦克·本

1　刘新成教授对我国世界史学界关于全球史的观点和争论有系统的梳理和点评。刘新成：《全球史观在中国》，《历史研究》2011年第6期。

2　吴于廑：《世界历史》《世界历史上的游牧世界与农耕世界》《世界历史上的农本与重商》等，收入氏著《吴于廑文选》，武汉：武汉大学出版社，2007年。

3　1989年丹麦历史学家李来福（Leif Littrup）在丹麦《文化与历史》杂志上以"具有中国特色的世界史"为题，介绍了吴于廑先生的整体世界史观。[丹]李来福：《具有中国特色的世界史》，李荣建译，《武汉大学学报》1993年第4期。

特利主编的《史学史指南》中"世界历史"条目就是由他撰写的。[1] 他认为，从世界历史发展的全局来看，中世纪是欧亚文明大发展、大转型、大分流的时期。从公元1000年左右开始，欧亚大陆的农业不仅空间范围扩大，而且生产和经营更为集约，从而为以城市为基本特征的文明扩张奠定了基础。但是，经济集约化和社会复杂化也对古代社会遗留下来的价值体系提出了挑战，使得作为传统价值体系守护者的文化精英面临危机。在应对危机的过程中，东西方文化精英以不同的程度、不同的方式对古代典籍进行了再诠释，从而创造出适应各自环境的新的价值体系。在他看来，12世纪是欧亚大陆前近代传统确立的时期，是人类文明经历的第一次"大分流"。[2] 布鲁斯·M. S. 坎贝尔是著名的中世纪英国农业史专家，不久前转向研究中世纪晚期英国生态环境的变化。他将自己新的研究成果置于同一时期欧亚大陆的大环境中思考，于2016年推出了《大转变：中世纪晚期世界的气候、疾病和社会》。在他看来，13世纪后期开始的气候变冷、大瘟疫给亚欧大陆带来了普遍的危机，尤其是人口锐减和经济萧条，迫使亚欧大陆各地区做出相应的结构调整。以英国和荷兰为代表的西北欧地区由于种种主客观原因，如混合农业容易适应气候变化的影响，在农产品价格下跌时发展手工业，发展波罗的海、北海和大西洋贸易等，最终成功地完成了大转型。因此，在他看来，彭慕兰所说的"大分流"根源于中世纪晚期的大转变。从这点看，民族史与世界史并非截然对立，而是可以相互补充的。[3]

再次，加强学术交流与合作，建设世界史学术共同体。传统的史学研究是个性化的，一个人、一支笔足矣，但当今的世界史，尤其是全球史研究仅凭个人之

---

1 R. I. Moore. "World History," in Michael Bentley ed., *Companion to Historiography*, London: Routledge, 1997, pp. 918–936.

2 R. I. Moore, "The Eleventh Century in Eurasian History: A Comparative Approach to the Convergence and Divergence of Medieval Civilizations," *Journal of Medieval and Early Modern Studies*, Vol. 33, No. 1 (2003), pp. 1–21; "Medieval Europe in World History," in Carol Lansing and Edward D. English eds., *A Companion to the Medieval World*, Oxford: Willey-Blackwell, 2009, pp. 563–580.

3 Bruce M. S. Campbell, *The Great Transition: Climate, Disease and Society in the Late-Medieval World*, Cambridge: Cambridge University Press, 2016.

力已远远不够，需要更多发挥学术共同体的作用。列洛教授在《棉：创造现代世界的织物》的"引言"中坦陈："尽管有可能获取大量的信息、解释和史学文献，全球史仍难免经常出现偏见。欧洲（西方语言）的学术和档案资料是问题的核心。本书依赖英语（和一定程度少量的其他欧洲语言），这是一开始就要交代清楚的。我也许可以通过指出当材料如此丰富，梳理不同语言的史学之困难来为自己辩解，不过我只想说由于缺乏语言技能，并易于获得熟悉的资料，造成了从初始就有偏见的结果。"[1] 列洛教授遇到的问题是几乎所有从事世界史，尤其是全球史研究的人都有可能遇到的。文化上的隔膜、学术背景不一致、语言的多样性等使得世界史研究异常艰难，除了个人的努力之外，团队合作也是消除上述障碍的重要途径。20世纪80年代初吴于廑先生在武汉大学成立十五、十六世纪世界史研究室，研究室成员包括从事西欧、日本和中国史研究的专家学者，目的就是希望研究不同地区或国别、具有不同语言技能的学人通力合作，优势互补，以便写出真正具有整体性的世界史。今天国内外学术交流与合作的条件比过去好多了，而且随着中国国际地位的提高，越来越多西方国家的高校希望同我国建立学术交流与合作关系。事实上，在诸如棉的全球史、丝绸之路世界史研究方面，我们中国学者拥有不少相关资料，完全可以和外国学者开展对话与合作研究。

总之，由于历史上民族史与普世史的长期对立，英国和中国的世界史都发展缓慢。但进入21世纪以来，受全球化局势和史学自身变化的影响，两国的世界史都进入快速发展时期。但是，要消解民族史与普世史对立的影响，使我国的世界史成熟发展并得到学界的普遍认可，还有大量工作要做，包括重视具体问题研究和实证研究，努力提高自身专业研究水平；将个人的具体研究放入世界历史大背景中，开展历史比较研究；加强学术交流与合作，建设世界史学术共同体等。

（文章曾刊于《探索与争鸣》2018年第5期。本文系作者在联盟2017年年度论坛上的发言）

1　Giorgio Riello, *Cotton: The Fabric that Made the Modern World*, Cambridge: Cambridge University Press, 2013, p. 12.

Thriving in the New Normal for Language Learning: Challenges, Needs and Opportunities of International Universities

Li Li*

Introduction

Technology-enhanced language learning has become increasingly popular since 2000. Much research has evidenced the benefits of technology in developing language knowledge and skills (Li 2017a; see a review by Macaro et al. 2012). However, the research also evidenced the slow uptake of technology in language education across cultures until early 2020, when a global pandemic necessitated the educational community to adapt to online education completely (Li & Morris 2021). Since then, various technological tools, platforms, and apps have been fully integrated into learning activities, and numerous studies have investigated the effectiveness of online teaching and technology-enhanced language learning (Hodges et al. 2020; Murphy 2020). One of the underlying assumptions is that gaining insights into educational values and pedagogies regarding online provision is essential for stakeholders such as policymakers, material designers, and teachers (Bernard et al., 2004). As such, many studies have investigated the effectiveness and efficiency of online and blended learning during this period (e.g., Al-Fraihat et al. 2020; Korkealehto & Leier 2021; Zou et al. 2021). Among these studies, quite a number focused on students' perception of online learning (e.g., Hani & Saleh 2020), whereas limited research was conducted to shed light on teachers' experiences (Wu et al. 2020). Research comparing teachers' and students' views is scarce. Zou et al. (2021) is one of the few studies that compare the experiences of students and teachers. They claim teachers could deliver more

* Li Li (李利), Professor in the School of Education, and Associate Pro-Vice-Chancellor for the Faculty of Humanities, Arts and Social Sciences, University of Exeter.

effective online teaching and learning with more training, skills, and confidence.

Gaining insights into teachers' and students' experiences is critical. First, there is increasing awareness that effective pedagogy must consider teachers' knowledge and students' experiences. Teachers must be upskilled when innovations are introduced to embrace the changes (Evers et al. 2016; Li 2017a), but these innovations must be context-specific, and consider students' needs and experiences. Second, teachers, as agents for change, require an in-depth understanding of the needs, challenges, and opportunities for their students and themselves in each context. Without such understanding, teachers will struggle to use their knowledge and expertise to create opportunities for learners or exercise agency (Li 2020). Third, insufficient attention has been given to the gap between teachers and learners regarding technology-enhanced teaching and learning (Li 2017a; Zou et al. 2021). In addition, there have been so many valuable experiences and knowledge when teaching and learning were switched to online platforms, and it will be beneficial to capture this knowledge and experiences to influence policy-making, future directions of technology-enhanced language learning, e-material development, and teacher learning. It is even more important to gain insights into the two groups in different cultural settings.

In light of these issues, this study considers the cross-culture analysis of stakeholders' experiences in three universities to address the challenges, professional needs, and perceived opportunities enabled by online learning.

Technology-enhanced language education

Technology-enhanced language learning has been an influential research agenda in language education since 2000 (Chapelle 2003; Li 2017b; Tu et al. 2020). And there have been numerous research studies investigating the impact of technology on second language learning. Golonka et al. (2014) summarised the effect of technology on (1) improving language learners' learning motivation, efficiency, and communication frequency, (2) developing learners' language knowledge and skills (e.g., speaking, listening, vocabulary, grammar), as well as metacognitive and metalinguistic knowledge,

(3) enriching input resources, and (4) encouraging peer feedback. Similarly, Li (2017b) discussed the "value and usability" of technology in language learning (Chapelle 2003, 67) and proposed six benefits of technology in language learning, claiming that technology can (1) enrich authentic input and provide a context for the language use, primarily through the use of web 2.0 technologies, (2) increase linguistic knowledge through multimedia technologies, (3) enhance shared understanding and facilitate mediation, (4) provide an environment for interaction, (5) offer individualised feedback and (6) enhance motivation and autonomy. Elsewhere, Hubbard (2019) suggested that technology can positively influence learning efficiency, learning effectiveness, access, convenience, motivation, teaching efficiency, and teaching effectiveness.

Regarding online and distance learning, using a virtual learning environment or synchronous conferencing techniques has been perceived as a critical part of effective learning (Michel & Cappellini 2019). In particular, online technological tools, such as videos and social media, can offer efficient and convenient ways to achieve learning goals (Pineda et al. 2021). Effective technology-enhanced language teaching requires teachers to have an integrated knowledge of CALL because teachers act as change agents and must be prepared to incorporate technology into teaching. For example, research suggests that students can use computers or electronic devices to access learning resources without the restriction of time and location (Salama et al. 2020); however, to realise the potential, teachers need to be able to evaluate what materials are compatible with the mobile devices and how to ensure flexibility and accessibility.

New learning environment

When universities closed their campuses in early 2020, teaching and learning had to be completely switched to online. Teachers adopted synchronous teaching modes to offer online classes by learning how to apply videoconferencing tools, such as Teams and Zoom (Li & Morris 2021; Rha 2022). Despite the challenges that teachers faced, this type of lesson offered advantages such as a high level of interaction through technology (Chesla

2022), convenience and flexibility (Li & Morris 2021), and multimodality in learning materials (Jebbour 2022). However, the new mode of teaching and learning also put both teaching and administrative staff in a challenging situation. Technology competence has been highlighted as one of the most challenging issues (Li & Morris 2021; Peachey 2017; Rehn et al. 2018). Teaching online or synchronously also requires different communication skills, as participants are not in the same physical space, and it is hard to "see" each other, especially when students choose / are required to turn off their video cameras. These challenges in online teaching are evidenced in research. For example, Moorhouse (2020) describes it as a "bumpy" experience as teaching is pretty much teacher-centered and challenging to enhance learner-centredness. The classroom interaction featured long silences and limited student participation, and teachers experienced black screens. Payne (2020) echoed this view and pointed out a practical problem, arguing that "it is difficult to have an interactive L2 conversation with more than about four to six individuals" and "conversational turn-taking in a video conference is challenging enough when everyone is speaking their first language (L1), let alone a L2" (Payne 2020, 246).

This new learning environment requires teachers and students to adapt and fundamentally change their views of teaching and learning and the competencies required. At the technical level, teachers must tackle technological problems they face when delivering teaching, for example, connectivity and technical glitches. Active participation from students has also been an issue. On the latter, scholars have proposed the utilisation of breakout rooms, which has similarities to group work in a face-to-face setting (González-Lloret 2020). Equally, teachers must change how they present their materials at the pedagogical level and manage interactions and assessments (Li & Morris 2021). However, it is difficult for teachers to make the transition without sufficient training (Li 2023). When it comes to teacher training and development, research suggests that a positive learning culture is critical, where teachers feel that they are well supported by their colleagues and the management team, provided with time and space to learn from each other, and equipped with resources (Hargreaves & O'Connor 2017; Li 2017a; 2020; Li & Morris 2021).

Therefore, understanding teachers' challenges and professional needs becomes critical in supporting teachers to adapt to the new environment, and improve effectiveness (Li, 2023).

The Study

This section outlines the context for the study and introduces the mechanism for data collection and analysis.

The Context

The data reported here are from an extensive survey investigating the online experiences of staff and students in international universities.

University A is a university in the UK with a significant portion of its students being international. The university's internationalisation strategy stipulates that increasing international students and staff is critical for the university, and improving students' international experience lies at the heart of the university's education policy. There were very active student exchange programmes for their undergraduate students who majored in foreign language students pre-covid, and the university provided sufficient support to enable students to take advantage of those opportunities. During Covid, the programmes explored virtual exchanges to compensate for losing study abroad opportunities.

University B is a Sino-British university located in a developed area in China. It attracts high-quality Chinese students, most of whom choose to transfer to UK universities at a later stage of their degrees. The university follows a UK curriculum and instruction. In the language departments, few local teachers take the teaching responsibilities, and most of the teaching staff are native speakers of the target language. Students always have natural exposure to the language in class, and there are ample opportunities to interact socially with foreign staff and students.

University C is a typical Chinese university in a Tier 2 city. Pre-covid, most of the teaching was done in a physical environment, with teachers delivering the lectures to a large cohort (n=80+). Fixed textbooks were used, and students were learning a few core modules on language skills (e.g., listening, speaking, extensive reading, intensive reading, and writing) and linguistic knowledge (e.g., vocabulary, phonology, and pronunciation, grammar). There were limited opportunities to practice the target language in real-life situations.

The three universities are similar and different in many ways. First, these three universities responded quickly to the Covid-19 situation, switching to online teaching and implementing a series of schemes to support the transition. Second, these three universities provide successful foreign language programmes with innovative practices (e.g., offering students opportunities to engage with the target language and culture) and have bespoke teacher development programmes.

The participants were recruited through a combination of convenience and snowball sampling strategies. In total, 367 participants were recruited for this survey, including 283 students, 35 administrative and technical staff, and 49 teachers. Due to the space constraints, only results from students and teachers are reported in this paper. Table 1 provides demographic information about the participants. Ethical considerations were adhered to through institutional stipulations and BERA ethical guidelines (2018) to ensure anonymity, confidentially, and participants' well-being.

Table 1: Participants

Universities	A	B	C
Teachers	5	32	17
Students	22	101	130

Data and Analysis

Two different questionnaires were used to collect data. The student questionnaire was built upon previous studies and the literature (e.g., Li 2008; Li & Morris 2021). It focused on students' online perceptions and experiences to allow the participants to conduct reflection and self-evaluation. The questionnaire consists of five main sections, covering participants' biographic data, technology-enhanced language learning (TELL) knowledge and skills, and online experiences with particular attention to challenges, learning needs, and opportunities (open-ended questions). A Cronbach's alpha internal consistency reliability was calculated, and an acceptable Cronbach value was achieved for online experience and needs sections ($\alpha = 0.737$ and $\alpha = 0.781$). The open-ended question required students to provide free-style answers.

The questions from the teacher questionnaire were formed as a way for teachers to engage in a reflection, focusing on:

Their online experience and feelings, including challenges and needs.

Their understanding of opportunities that are facilitated by technological tools.

Any insights and examples they could offer.

The questionnaire was designed in English, with Chinese translation. The participants were asked to use the language they felt comfortable with to answer the questions. The online questionnaire was distributed to teachers, and they were encouraged to pass the link to their fellow teachers and students. Information about the project was offered at the beginning of the survey, and consent was sought before they completed the questionnaire. Participants were explicitly reminded of the right to withdraw from the study and how their data would be stored, used, and destroyed. The student questionnaire data was populated to SPSS 28 and analysed using descriptive statistics. The teacher questionnaire and the open-ended question from the student questionnaire were processed with content thematic analysis to reveal insights into challenges, needs, and opportunities.

Findings

Challenges

Despite the success of moving classes online swiftly, both teachers and students experienced challenges in various aspects.

Teachers' views

The most salient themes from the teachers' questionnaire are insufficient technical knowledge and skills, lack of confidence in delivering effective teaching, and incompetence in creating materials.

· Technology challenge

As noted by teachers, many different platforms were utilised in the initial phase of online teaching; thus, various technical issues also emerged. One area highlighted by teacher participants is tackling technical problems with technical glitches and connectivity. One teacher offered an example of spending a considerable amount of class time dealing with students' technical issues resulting in being unable to finish the planned lesson. Various setups were required because students used different technological tools, such as mobiles, laptops, iPads, and touch pads. Some teachers were frustrated by the complexities, as they hadn't received any technology training before starting to teach online to help resolve students' technical problems. Another area concerning technical challenges was the lack of technical support. No teachers commented on receiving technical support from their universities, and the following extracts illustrate typical reflections among teachers:

We have only one technician who usually does the maintenance of our machines, for example, installing software required for our research, and the central team is not accessible. The support they could offer will not be in time anyway, as we have to register the issue and wait for an answer. (University A)

Technical support was never offered, but we tend to resolve the problems ourselves, sometimes involving students too. (University B)

I am struggling with technology, and technical training and support must be provided. (University C)

Insufficient support for tackling technical issues has been widely reported as one barrier for teachers to integrate technology into teaching (Pelgrum 2001). Li (2008; 2014; 2017b) pointed out that technology competence and confidence are essential factors in technology integration. Teachers are only prepared to integrate technology into their teaching if they feel confident and competent in using technology. It is interesting to note that teachers self-assessed as competent for technology for social purposes but considered technical challenges as their primary concern for teaching, suggesting the different expectations for professional needs and personal use.

· Pedagogical knowledge

Developing pedagogical principles for effective technology-enhanced pedagogy is the second area that teachers identified. It was impossible for most of the teachers to make the transition, as teaching online and face-to-face are quite different. When integrating technologies into teaching in a face-to-face environment, Li (2017b, 99) argued that "teachers adapt technology to fit current teaching patterns rather than making modifications to their instructional ways." However, when teaching is moved online, teachers face entirely different challenges. When examining effective teaching, they struggled to see how they made an appropriate pedagogical design because they could not visualise what pedagogy looked like in an online environment, and there was no pre-existing experience. Of course, we know that teachers' conception of effective teaching is heavily shaped by social, cultural, and educational contexts. Therefore, what counts as effective teaching will change subsequently when the teaching context changes. Nevertheless, the most common concern is developing online interactive and collaborative activities to enable students to use and practice the language. Generally, teachers felt they were limited in creating opportunities for student-student interaction.

There is minimal interaction in my class, as I don't know how to effectively design an activity suitable for online teaching to involve students (University A)

I deliver teaching online the same way without group work, which is very challenging, as I never know whether my students are with me. (University B)

I lecture most of the time, and all students have their cameras off due to network issues. I know this is ineffective, as I don't know whether my students are asleep, playing games, or listening to me. Because of the bandwidth, I always ask students to turn off their cameras. I don't see them, but a black screen. (University C)

· Designing appropriate materials

Designing appropriate materials or evaluating digital materials is another challenge identified by teachers, which is also evidenced in previous studies (e.g., Li 2014; 2023). Concerning technology-assisted language learning, Chapelle and Hegelheimer (2004) argue that almost "all teachers need to know how to use the Web as a resource for current authentic language materials in written, audio, and visual formats." (305) However, this study suggests that teachers were not equipped with the skills and found it challenging to select appropriate materials for the task. Reflections from the questionnaire are an illustration of such a view.

I uploaded the same PowerPoint presentation to our virtual learning platform, as I do not know what else I can do. I also recorded my lectures to upload them online. (University A)

I don't have much freedom in designing materials, but I use the designated materials and activities. They are ineffective, but I am unsure if I could improve them. (University B)

We all share the materials, designed by a particular unit, as usual. Most of us find it challenging to make new materials as we have no training in this area. (University C)

Students' views

It is worth noting that students reflected on somewhat different challenges from the teachers. The top three challenges are lack of social interaction, insufficient knowledge about self-directed learning, and lack of motivation.

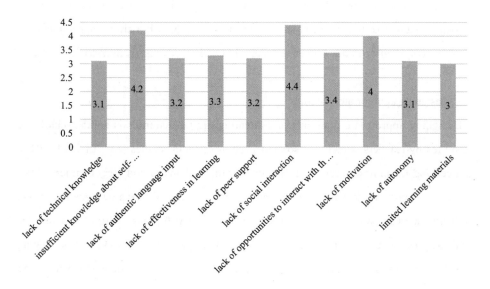

Figure 1: Challenges for students

Most students (n=205, accounting for 81.0%) have agreed or strongly agreed that they needed more opportunities for social interaction in the university setting. When comparing the different cultural contexts, it is interesting that all University A students strongly agreed that there was no opportunity to interact with their classmates, despite being friends on Facebook or Instagram. For students in University B and C, the view was mixed. Still, many students agreed or strongly agreed that they needed more opportunities to interact with each other. However, it is worth noting that they also have a WeChat group for their class, yet the view was that there were not enough opportunities to socialise.

Interestingly, many students (n=197, accounting for 77.9%) believed that one of their most challenging areas was to need more self-directed learning skills. Somehow, the online learning experience made students think they were conducting self-directed learning.

Despite the different cultural and educational settings, no differences were observed between the three universities.

The third area worth commenting on is the lack of motivation. Students in this study strongly believed they lacked the motivation to learn the language when teaching was moved online. There might be two reasons for that. First, students might need to see the immediate relevance of learning a language because they did not have opportunities to use it in real-life situations. Second, a lack of social interaction with the target language communities impeded students' interest in learning.

Needs

Teachers' perspectives

Understanding teachers' professional needs is critical in successfully integrating technology into teaching. This study has identified the top four areas for teachers' needs, despite their different social, cultural, and educational contexts.

· Access to more appropriate materials

Access to technology and resources was identified as a critical factor for effective technology integration (Li 2008; 2014; Pelgrum 2001). The teachers overwhelmingly reported the desire for more appropriate digital resources, which include electronic materials and online language activities. The responses revealed insights into this issue.

Not having free access to some materials restricts how I teach, but more importantly, students should have access to online resources so that they can practice the language without paying extra money. (University A)

We are constrained by what we can use. On the one hand, we don't have enough digital resources; on the other, we don't have the skills or knowledge to design such materials. (University B)

> We need more electronic resources that are matched with the textbook. (University C)

Of course, there are subtle differences between teachers' views about materials. The UK university placed more importance on accessibility for students, addressing students' power in managing and regulating their studies. In China, teachers, despite their nationalities, all wanted more appropriate materials closely linked to their textbooks or pedagogical goals.

· Technology training to build competence and confidence

Teachers all require a degree of training in technology use. The desire to learn different tools was apparent. Although accessibility is still important, we can see that teachers' needs have switched to technology training (Li 2023). Technology training is not restricted to teachers; five teachers mentioned that their students also need to be trained to use technology for learning.

> Not sure how much training others have, but I don't have any, and I desperately need some so that I am confident in dealing with technical issues when I teach. (University A)
>
> We all need some training, including students and administrative staff, as we all need to tackle the uncertainty brought by online activities. (University B)
>
> I have never had a technical lesson. I only know the basics, so I will need systematic training in using technology to support teaching, perhaps starting with some technical features of the platform we are using. (University C)

· Pedagogical training

The desire for further pedagogical training in designing online tasks or technology-enhanced pedagogy is closely related to technology training. The need for technological pedagogical content knowledge (TPACK) (Mishra & Koehler 2006) is beyond whether teachers know about or believe in the advantages of new technology. Teachers across the board felt they were out of depth, and they described their teaching as merely innovative but transferred the slides to the platform with more detailed instructions for students. Such desire resulted from the realisation of differences between online and face-to-face teaching. Because there were "no actual classroom settings" (University A), teachers felt less confident in managing a class. Specifically, the lack of confidence in transforming their education lies in three areas: motivating students to participate in online activities actively (e.g., making more contributions to online discussion), addressing different learning styles, and designing innovative group work by using collaborative tools.

· Assessment

Another significant area for further training from teachers' perspective is online assessment. With teaching and assessment having to move online, it is understandable that teachers would feel that additional training in evaluation would have been beneficial. This result also aligns with previous research (Li 2023; Li & Morris 2021). For teachers, how to assess students' language proficiency becomes an essential question as it is not viable for them to implement tests online. Interestingly, although all teachers were concerned about various assessment methods, only the teachers from University C raised the need to develop an online testing platform to implement tests. Teachers from the other two universities were more concerned about alternative ways to assess students, besides asking students to write a short essay or record a speech for the oral test.

Students' perspectives

As indicated in Figure 2, the results suggest four critical areas where students' needs must be addressed, namely opportunities for practicing the target language, well-being support, peer interaction and guidance in managing one's study.

Clearly, for language students, having the opportunity to practice the target language is

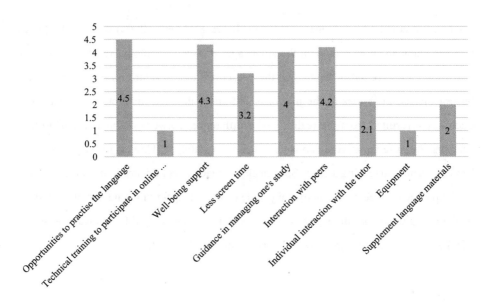

Figure 2: Students' needs

critical. Learning online has seen a loss of learning for many students during the pandemic, especially in literacy (Howard et al. 2021). Due to the border closure, students could not take advantage of the study abroad programmes or be exposed to the target language environment, which resulted in losing vital opportunities to use the language in real-life situations. In addition, not having opportunities to practice the language with their peers in a social environment is also viewed as a barrier to language learning. Despite the challenges that the pandemic brought to teaching and learning, innovative ways must be found to address students' needs.

In addition to the learning needs, students also placed the need to address well-being matters as a critical area of need. It is widely believed that many students experienced loneliness, especially those admitted to the university in the autumn of 2019 and 2020. The well-being issue concerns depression, anxiety, lack of interest, and boredom. When looking at the different groups, University A scored higher than University B and C. This might be due to several reasons:

1. Most Universities B and C students managed to go home and live with their parents.

2. Universities B and C had WeChat groups for each class, and students were required to participate in WeChat discussions.

3. University A had more training for students regarding addressing their well-being needs and seeking help when necessary.

Peer learning and support are critical elements in learning. There was a strong desire for all students to interact with their peers. To some extent, online education during the pandemic constrained students to develop friendships and peer support. Despite the WeChat groups established by the tutors in University B and C, students in those universities showed no differences from their counterparts in University A. Another area worth commenting on regarding students' needs is the demand for guidance on their studies. Most students (n=198) desired to receive advice to help them navigate the materials and tasks, and manage their studies. Again, this might be because the students lack in-person interaction with the tutors and peers.

Opportunities

Challenges and opportunities go hand in hand. The final part of the survey asked teachers and students to identify opportunities that emerged from online learning. Again, teachers and students identified different areas.

Teachers' perception

· Virtual exchanges

The virtual exchange was a novel idea before Covid, although some form of virtual exchange was researched pre-2000 (e.g., Warschauer 1995). However, due to travel constraints, teachers started to explore virtual internships and exchange opportunities for students.

We started talking to our European colleagues to see how we might get students together for virtual exchange, given that the technology can facilitate that. (University A)

We would consider exchange online as an alternative, if there is no way to resume the regular international programmes. (University B)

· Integrating Social networks into language learning

Implementing Social networks is another innovative practice to support online learning. For universities B and C, WeChat was already implemented in teaching pre-covid. However, the pandemic allowed the tutors to fully realise the potential of WeChat. For example, it was organised by students themselves pre-covid in some language classes in University B. However, during the pandemic, it was accepted by more tutors as a core tool to engage students, make announcements and build a community. Despite the value of social networks, the teachers at University A were keen to leave that to the students. Different social expectations and educational values can be observed here between teachers. In China, where teachers play a central role in managing learning, it is expected that all activities concerning learning will be organised by the teacher. On the contrary, learning is perceived as a more individual act in the West, and students should be responsible for their learning activities and take charge of how they want to engage in informal learning.

Students' perception

Two salient areas merged from students' responses: autonomy, convenience and flexibility in learning.

· Autonomy

Many students (n=73) mentioned that online learning enabled them to become more autonomous as they needed to monitor and regulate their education. For some students, this means employing different learning strategies compared to when they are in a face-to-face environment, and for others, this means they become more independent. In addition, they could conduct self-evaluation consciously to meet the module requirements.

· Convenience and flexibility in learning

It is noted that students welcomed the convenience and flexibility of learning online. Specifically, many students reflected that the online components made it "more convenient to review course content" and that they could "learn anytime and anywhere." The boundary of the classroom no longer exists, and students can take control of their studies and use the learning materials accruing to their needs.

Discussion

This study revealed teachers' and students' challenges, needs, and opportunities when engaging in online teaching and learning. Insights into these issues offer researchers, policymakers, and practitioners valuable knowledge.

Challenges for teachers and their professional needs

This study has identified challenges teachers face when teaching online, particularly around technology, pedagogy, and material design, as shown in Figure 3. Most teachers faced challenges in the pedagogical transition due to a lack of relevant knowledge. As such, they followed the traditional way of using technology to support teaching, i.e., addressing the presentational needs (Li 2008; Macaro et al. 2012). Lack of technology and pedagogical knowledge put these teachers in a difficult position as they struggle to achieve effectiveness in teaching. These areas are closely related to teachers' TPACK, which emphasises (1) the dynamic relationships between content, pedagogy, and technology for teachers, and (2) successful technology integration in teaching and in developing their knowledge and competence in the technology integration (Koehler et al. 2007; Mishra & Koehler 2006). When it comes to delivering a lesson online, the core part is to know about integrating appropriate pedagogy and technological tools into language learning activities and appropriately assessing materials.

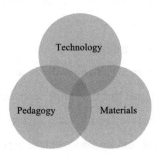

Figure 3: Critical challenges for language teachers

Research suggests that technology can provide authentic input and create a context for language learning, for example, through blogs and videos (e.g., Arndt & Woore 2018). However, it does require teachers to use them to address their pedagogical purposes (Li 2017b). The result suggests that teachers are not equipped with the needed skills and find it challenging to select appropriate materials for the task. It is apparent to provide teachers with the relevant knowledge and skills to evaluate and adapt materials. In evaluating materials, teachers need to engage in a process to judge the appropriateness of the material for a given language learning setting, identify ways to effectively implement the materials / tasks in that setting, assess its degree of success, and make a recommendation for future use (Hubbard 2006). It is noted that teachers in this study do not process these skills but demonstrate awareness of needing them. This might be because teachers are novice technology users, and no prior training is provided to prepare them (Li 2017b; 2021). For future teacher education or development programmes, therefore, it is vital to consider the three critical elements in Figure 3 to ensure teachers understand their interrelatedness for effective online delivery.

Considering the challenges that teachers face in online teaching, it is understandable that they also identified these areas as their professional needs. Li (2023) stresses the importance of examining teachers' professional needs in understanding the scope and focus of professional development for teachers, individually and collectively. The current study identifies four teacher education and development areas concerning technology-enhanced language teaching, including technology training, pedagogical knowledge regarding using technology, material development and evaluation, and assessment. These four areas represent the critical components of the teaching cycle, as seen in Figure 4. These elements are closely linked and significantly influence each other. For example, We have a teacher who does not possess sufficient technology knowledge. In that case, they might not be able to locate or assess digital materials appropriately, and they will be likely to stick to the traditional way of using technology to assist teaching and less likely to adopt innovative approaches in assessment. On the other hand, if a teacher is competent in evaluating materials, they might feel more confident and competent in using technology to deliver a lesson using appropriate and effective pedagogy. As such, they are more likely to adopt a different way to assess students as the aim of teaching and learning will have multiple layers. Therefore, teacher education and development become more significant when teachers face unique challenges when using technology, and the focus of teacher learning, thus, should be directed "to keep the teacher up-to-date with the continuously changing practices and student needs" (Badri et al. 2016, 1). Without training, teachers tend to teach online courses the way they would in traditional classrooms (Kreber & Kanuka 2013), with cosmetic changes to how they deliver the lessons (Li 2014). There is an urge to develop teachers' knowledge and skills in using technology appropriately and effectively (e.g., Liu & Kleinsasser 2015; Hubbard 2008; Li 2017b; Sert & Li 2017). Therefore, TPACK must be fully incorporated into teacher education and development programmes. One way forward for future teacher education programmes is to embed reflective teaching in the curriculum. As Chen (2022) argues, such approaches might facilitate teachers to maximise digital affordances and enhance teacher agency. Research also notes that teachers prefer engaging in collaborative endeavours (Karlberg & Bezzina 2020; Li 2017a; 2020). Thus, teachers need to be provided with opportunities to share practical ideas, collectively build a repertoire of teaching resources, understand the process and critical elements of student learning, engage in some deliberate practice in assessment and feedback, and address pedagogic challenges and demands (Cooper et al. 2020; Mansfield 2019).

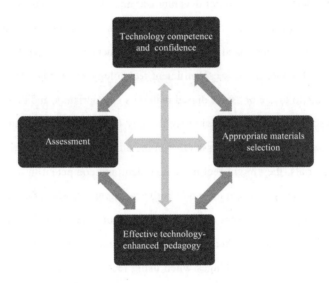

Figure 4: Teachers' professional needs

Challenges for students and their needs

For students, challenges can be categorised into psychological, cognitive, and social aspects (Figure 5). Motivation is a determining factor for successful language learning (Bradford 2007; Dörnyei 2001; Engin 2009), and evidence suggests that technology motivates students to learn a language (Stockwell 2012). What this study reveals, however, is that online learning can be lonely, boring, and disengaging. Therefore, further work needs to be carried out to see how to engage and motivate learners in an online environment. One might argue that there is a loss of live feedback in online teaching, for example, there is no body language, gestures, and verbal cues, resulting in a lack of student engagement in sessions. Nevertheless, other methods might be introduced to give the power to students in class through using breakout rooms (Moorhouse et al. 2021) and using online collaborative tools, such as Google Docs or OneNote (e.g., Alsubaie & Ashuraidah, 2017; Li & Mak 2022). Regarding students' cognitive challenges, the research suggests that online learning has the feature of self-directed learning, where individuals are in charge of planning, implementing, and assessing one's learning process (Bonk 2020; Loyens et al. 2008). Self-directed learning is a critical ability for individuals to engage in a digital or hybrid learning environment, such as online learning, to manage their study at their pace. One crucial element is time management, and the other is monitoring, such as reflecting on their progress, understanding their competence, asking relevant questions to themselves, and identifying the learning gaps and strategies to deal with the gap. This relates to metacognitive awareness of various dimensions of self, task, and context (Azevedo et al. 2004). This awareness of multiple dimensions is influenced by five variables: "judgment of learning, the feeling of knowing, self-questioning, content evaluation, and identifying the adequacy of information available" (Azevedo et al. 2004, 104). What is clear then, apart from giving students technology training (according to some teacher participants), it is more important to enhance students' metacognitive awareness and strategies to become more competent in self-directed learning.

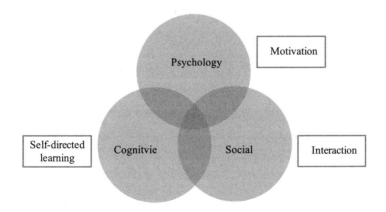

Figure 5: Critical challenges for students

Concerning students' needs, three areas are identified: opportunities for language practice, social interaction with peers, and student welfare. To some extent, these three areas also map the areas where students face challenges, particularly in psychological and social aspects. However, instead of focusing on life-long learning skills, such as self-directed learning, students focus more on immediate gains and opportunities in language learning, such as exposure to the target language and culture. Equally, instead of stressing the importance of motivation, students pay more attention to broader well-being issues, such as coping with loneliness, depression, anxiety, etc. Nevertheless, social interaction (particularly with peers) appears to be a crucial aspect of learning, which often is overlooked by programmes, as it might be perceived as peripheral to learning. I argue that online learning should not just focus on the subject matter but also create social opportunities so that students learn in a well-supported community.

Opportunities facilitated by online learning

Various opportunities are identified by teachers and students in this study, linking to the affordances of technology or online learning.

Teachers have realised the affordances of technology in developing virtual exchange programmes. As evidenced in the study and the literature, digital platforms are now available for developing virtual exchanges, which can be considered an integral part of teaching languages (Dooly & O'Dowd 2018; Godwin-Jones 2019). It is possible that studying abroad will resume in the post-covid times, but further considerations need to be given to virtual exchanges or collaborative online international learning (COIL) where students from different countries and cultures can study together. It is possible that such learning experiences not only provide students who cannot afford to study abroad with an opportunity to gain valuable multicultural learning experiences but also offer teachers an international collaborative space in search of effective pedagogy and innovation because such courses require carefully designed tasks and activities that must be *collaboratively* designed and implemented between more than one teacher.

This study suggests that social networking could be integrated into online learning to create a new mode of learning in which material accessibility, social interaction, and learning support are different from previous computer-mediated learning environments. Effective use of social networking provides extraordinary opportunities for course designers and learners to engage with each other in real-time with emotional connections (e.g., using emojis and animations) (Özyurt & Özyurt 2015; Tsai et al. 2016). Traditionally, social networking sites have been widely used by people for social purposes. However, given the significance of a solid relationship between peers for successful learning, it is necessary to find innovative ways to integrate social networks into teaching. Research also suggests that social networks create a constructivist learning environment that allows learners to construct interpretations and meanings of their individual life experiences while working in a collaborative team (Ou-Yang &Wu 2016; Wang & Du 2014). Therefore, it enhances the learner's agency in learning and develops their skills in managing and monitoring their learning. In addition, the learning communities that students and the teacher jointly create give participants a sense of belonging (Qian et al. 2018; Watson et al. 2016). It is important to note that Chinese universities have adopted this approach, which could be valuable to other institutions worldwide. However, cautions must be made regarding the appropriateness of how to utlise social networks in each context.

As recognised in this study, technology has advantages in accessibility and flexibility; for example, students can use computers or electronic devices to acquire learning resources instantly without restricting location and time (Hillmayr et al. 2020; Salama et al. 2020). Furthermore, students can learn at their pace and convenience (Kent et al. 2016; Lander 2015). However, effective integration of social networking sites into online learning requires two conditions: first, the teacher is fully aware of the advantages and disadvantages of technological tools and platforms and can address their pedagogical goals; second, learners need to be able to regulate their learning, manage the learning pace and monitor the progress effectively.

Conclusion

This study examines and compares online experiences and perceptions of university language teachers and their students across three different social and educational settings. The study highlights the differences between teachers and students in the challenges and professional needs and identifies online learning opportunities. Specifically, teachers are more concerned about the critical elements for effective online teaching, for example, technology competence, pedagogical knowledge, material evaluation, and assessment. In contrast, students are more concerned with learning activities' social and psychological aspects. Peer interaction is a significant element for successful online learning, which merits further investigation, particularly regarding the impact of social interaction on learning achievements. Despite the differences in the views of students and teachers regarding opportunities or affordances of online learning, key themes such as virtual exchanges, the importance of social networking, and convenience and flexibility emerge. It further indicates that ongoing professional education through collaborative work or reflective teaching for teachers or specific training on self-directed learning for students would have differential influences on effective online teaching and learning. The findings support more significant attention to discipline-specific professional training in technology and pedagogy for teachers, understanding their professional needs, developing competence in material evaluation and assessment, and maximising the benefits of online teaching. Equally, addressing students' psychological, cognitive, linguistic, and social needs will enable them to regulate and monitor their learning and achieve effectiveness.

Despite the study's new insights into the field, the study has a few limitations. First, this study cannot be deemed exclusive or exhaustive as it only offers insights into particular groups, and the participants were recruited through a convenient snowball sampling strategy. Therefore, the participant size is relatively small, and the result might not be generalised to broader contexts. It would have been more informative if the sample sizes from different settings were comparable. Considering the differences in the culture of learning, further research and analysis are required to examine where there are significant differences between different cultures. Second, this study offers a snapshot of the views and experiences of students and teachers. A longitudinal study would capture the potential changes or developments over time. Thus, future research might consider a longitudinal design to offer further insights.

Notably, while this study is based on three universities, further work in this area with similar results may help generalise the findings revealed here to a wide range of learning contexts. Future research might explore the cultural differences when approaching online teaching and learning, preferably with a mixed method. Researchers might also target how to address the challenges identified in this study, taking an experimental approach.

(Acknowledgement: This article is a revision of the author's speech at the 2022 UKCHA Annual Forum.)

References

Al-Fraihat, D., Joy, M., Masa'deh, R., & Sinclair, J. 2020. Evaluating E-learning systems success: An empirical study. *Computers in Human Behavior*, 102, 67–86. https://doi.org/10.1016/j.chb.2019.08.004.

Alsubaie, J. & Ashuraidah, A. 2017. Exploring writing individually and collaboratively using Google Docs in EFL contexts. English Language Teaching, 10 (10), 10–30, https://doi.org/10.5539/elt.v10n10p10.

Arndt, H. L., & Woore, R. 2018. Vocabulary learning from watching YouTube videos and reading blog posts. *Language Learning & Technology*, 22(3), 124–142. https://doi.org/10125/44660.

Azevedo, R., Guthrie, J. T., & Seibert, D. 2004. The role of self-regulated learning in fostering students' conceptual understanding of complex systems with hypermedia. *Journal of Educational Computing Research*, 30(1–2), 87–111. https://doi.org/10.2190/DVWX-GM1T-6THQ-5W.

Badri, M., Alnuaimi, A., Mohaidat, J., Yang, G., & Al-Rashedi, A. 2016. Perception of teachers' professional development needs, impacts, and barriers: the Abu Dhabi case. *SAGE Open*. https://doi.org/10.1177/2158244016662901.

Bernard, R. M., Abrami, P. C., Lou, Y., Borokhovski, E., Wade, A., Wozney, L., Wallet, P. A., Fiset, M., & Huang, B. 2004. How does distance education compare with classroom instruction? A meta-analysis of the empirical literature. *Review of Educational Research*, 74(3), 379–439. https://doi.org/10.3102/00346543074003379.

Bonk, C. J. 2020. Pandemic ponderings, 30 years to today: Synchronous signals, saviors, or survivors? *Distance Education*, 41(4), 589–599. https://doi.org/10.1080/01587919.2020.1821610.

Bradford, A. 2007. Motivational orientations in under-researched FLL contexts: Findings from Indonesia. *RELC Journal*, 38(3), 302–323. https://doi.org/10.1177/0033688207085849.

Chapelle, C. A. 2003. *English language learning and technology: lectures on applied linguistics in the age of Information and Communication Technology*. Amsterdam: John Benjamins Publishing.

Chapelle, C. A. & Hegelheimer, V. 2004. The language teacher in the 21st century. In S. Fotos & C. M. Browne (Eds.), *New perspectives on CALL for second language classrooms* (pp. 299–316). Mahwah, NJ: Lawrence Erlbaum.

Chesla, A. L. 2020. Technology as a mediating tool: Videoconferencing, L2 learning, and learner autonomy. *Computer Assisted Language Learning*, 33(5–6), 483–509. https://doi.org/10.1080/09588221.2019.1572018.

Chen, M. 2022. Digital affordances and teacher agency in the context of teaching Chinese as a second language during COVID-19. *System*, 105. https://doi.org/10.1016/j.system.2021.102710.

Cooper, R., Fitzgerald, A., Loughran, J., Phillips, M., & Smith. K. 2020. Understanding teachers' professional learning needs: what does it mean to teachers and how can it be supported? *Teachers and Teaching*, 26(7–8), 558–576. https://doi.org/10.1080/13540602.2021.1900810.

Dooly, M., & O'Dowd, R. 2018. Telecollaboration in the foreign language classroom: A review of its origins and its application to language teaching practices. In M. Dooly & R. O'Dowd (Eds.), *In this together: Teachers' experiences with transnational, telecollaborative language learning projects* (pp. 11–34). New York, NY / Bern, Switzerland: Peter Lang.

Dörnyei, Z. 2001. *Motivational strategies in the language classroom*: Cambridge University Press Cambridge.

Engin, A. O. 2009. Second language learning success and motivation. *Social Behavior and Personality*, 37(8), 1035–1041.

Evers, A., Van der Heijden, B., & Kreijns, K. 2016. Organisational and task factors influencing teachers' professional development at work. *European Journal of Training and Development*, 40, 36–55. https://doi.org/10.1177/1534484310397852.

Godwin-Jones, R. 2019. Telecollaboration as an approach to developing intercultural communication competence. *Language Learning & Technology*, 23(3), 8–28. http://hdl.handle.net/10125/44691.

Golonka, E. M., Bowles, A. R., Frank, V. M., Richardson, D. L., & Freynik, S. 2014. Technologies for foreign language learning: A review of technology types and their effectiveness. *Computer Assisted Language Learning*, 27(1), 70–105. https://doi.org/10.1080/09588221.2012.700315.

González-Lloret, M. 2020. Collaborative tasks for online language teaching. *Foreign Language Annals*, 53(2), 260–269. https://doi.org/10.1111/flan.12466.

Hani, A., & Saleh, A. 2020. Study on students' experiences about online teaching during COVID-19 Outbreak. *Technium Social Sciences Journal*, 8(1), 102–116. https://doi.org/10.1016/j.stueduc.2022.101182.

Hargreaves, A. & O'Connor, M.T. 2017. Cultures of professional collaboration: their origins and opponents. *Journal of*

Professional Capital and Community, 2(2), 74–85. https://doi.org/10.1108/JPCC-02-2017-0004.

Hillmayr, D., Ziernwald, L., Reinhold, F., Hofer, S. I., & Reiss, K. M. 2020. The potential of digital tools to enhance mathematics and science learning in secondary schools: A context-specific meta-analysis. *Computers & Education, 153*. https://doi.org/10.1016/j.compedu.2020.103897.

Hodges, C., Moore, S., Lockee, B., Trust, T., & Bond, A. 2020. The difference between emergency remote teaching and online learning. *Educause Review*, 27, March. Available at https://er.educause.edu/articles/2020/3/the-difference-between-emergency-remote-teaching-and-online-learning.

Howard, E., Khan, A., & Lockyer, C. 2021. Learning during the pandemic: review of research from England. Ofqual's Strategy, Risk, and Research Directorate.

Hubbard, P. 2006. Evaluating CALL software. In L. Ducate & N. Arnold (Eds.), *Calling on CALL: from theory and research to new directions in foreign language teaching*. San Marcos: CALICO.

Hubbard, P. 2008. CALL and the future of language teacher education. *CALICO Journal, 25(2)*, 175–188. https://www.jstor.org/stable/calicojournal.25.2.175.

Hubbard, P. 2019. Five keys from the past to the future of CALL. *International Journal of Computer-Assisted Language Learning and Teaching*, 9(3), 1–13. http://dx.doi.org/10.4018/IJCALLT.2019070101.

Jebbour M. 2022 The unexpected transition to distance learning at Moroccan universities amid COVID-19: A qualitative study on faculty experience. *Social Sciences & Humanities Open*, 5(1), 100253. https://doi.org/10.1016/j.ssaho.2022.100253.

Karlberg, M. & Bezzina, C. 2020. The professional development needs of beginning and experienced teachers in four municipalities in Sweden. *Professional Development in Education*, 1–18. https://doi.org/10.1080/19415257.2020.1712451.

Kent, C., Laslo, E., & Rafaeli, S. 2016. Interactivity in online discussions and learning outcomes. *Computers and Education*, 97, 116–128. https://doi.org/10.1016/j.compedu.2016.03.002.

Koehler, M. J., Mishra, P., & Yahya, K. 2007. Tracing the development of teacher knowledge in a design seminar: Integrating content, pedagogy and technology. *Computers & Education*, 49, 740–762. https://doi.org/10.1016/j.compedu.2005.11.012.

Korkealehto, K., & Leier, V. 2021. Facebook for engagement: Telecollaboration in German language learning between Finland and New Zealand. *International Journal of Computer-Assisted Language Learning and Teaching*, 11(1), 1–20.

Kreber, C., & Kanuka, H. 2013. The scholarship of teaching and learning and the online classroom. *Canadian Journal of University Continuing Education*, 32(2), 109–131. https://doi.org/10.21225/D5P30B.

Lander, B. 2015. Lesson study at the foreign language university level in Japan: Blended learning, raising awareness of technology in the classroom. *International Journal for Lesson and Learning Studies*, 4(4), 362–382. Retrieved from. https://doi.org/10.1108/IJLLS-02-2015-0007.

Li, J., & Mak, L. 2022. The effects of using an online collaboration tool on college students' learning of academic writing skills. *System*, 105. https://doi.org/10.1016/j.system.2021.102712.

Li, L. 2008. *EFL teachers' beliefs about ICT integration in Chinese secondary schools*. [Unpublished PhD Thesis, Queen's University Belfast].

Li, L. 2014. Understanding language teachers' practice with educational technology: a case from China. *System*, 46, 105–119. https://doi.org/10.1016/j.system.2014.07.016.

Li, L. 2017a. *New Technology and Language Learning*. Basingstoke: Palgrave Macmillan.

Li, L. 2017b. *Social interaction and teacher cognition*. Edinburgh: Edinburgh University Press.

Li, L. 2020. *Language teacher cognition: A sociocultural perspective*. London: Palgrave Macmillan.

Li, L. 2021. Learning Together Online: Insights into Knowledge Construction of Language Teachers in a CSCL Environment. *Iranian Journal of Language Teaching Research*, 9(3 (Special Issue)), 39–62. doi: 10.30466/ijltr.2021.121075.

Li, L. 2023. Technology + Pedagogy in EFL Virtual Classrooms: University Teachers' Professional Needs on Technology-Enhanced Pedagogy. In K. Sadeghi & M. Thomas (Eds) *Second Language Teacher Professional Development* (pp. 169–190). Palgrave.

Li, L., & Morris, G. 2021. Thriving in the New Normal: In-Service Professional Development Needs and Experiences. In C. Xiang (Ed.) *Trends and Developments for the Future of Language Education in Higher Education* (pp. 253–271). IGI Global.

Liu, M-H., & Kleinsasser, R. C. 2015. Exploring EFL teachers' CALL knowledge and competencies: in-service program perspectives. *Language Learning & Technology*, 19(1), 119–138. http://dx.doi.org/10125/44405.

Loyens, S. M., Magda, J., & Rikers, R. M. 2008. Self-directed learning in problem-based learning and its relationships with self-regulated learning. *Educational Psychology Review*, 20(4), 411–427. https://doi.org/10.1007/s10648-008-9082-7.

Macaro, E., Handley, Z. & Walter, C. 2012. A systematic review of CALL in English as a second language: focus on primary and secondary education. *Language Teaching*, 45(1), 1–43. https://doi.org/10.1017/S0261444811000395.

Mansfield, J. 2019. *Pedagogical equilibrium: the development of teachers' professional knowledge* (1st ed.). Routledge. https://doi.org/10.4324/9780429053573.

Michel, M., & Cappellini, M. 2019. Alignment during synchronous video versus written chat L2 interactions: A methodological exploration. *Annual Review of Applied Linguistics*, 39, 189–216. https://doi.org/10.1017/S0267190519000072.

Mishra, P., & Koehler, M. J. 2006. Technological pedagogical content knowledge: A new framework for teacher knowledge. *Teachers College Record*, 108(6), 1017–1054. https://doi.org/10.1111/j.1467-9620.2006.00684.x.

Moorhouse, B. L. 2020. Adaptations to a face-to-face initial teacher education course "forced" online due to the COVID-19 pandemic. *Journal of Education for Teaching*, 46(4), 609–611. https://doi.org/10.1080/02607476.2020.1755205.

Murphy, M. P. A. 2020. COVID-19 and emergency eLearning: Consequences of the securitisation of higher education for post-pandemic pedagogy. *Contemporary Security Policy*, 41(3), 492–505. https://doi.org/10.1080/13523260.2020.1761749.

Ou-Yang, F. C., & Wu, W.-C. V. 2016. Using mixed-modality vocabulary learning on mobile devices: Design and evaluation.

Journal of Educational Computing, 54(8), 1043–1069. https://doi.org/10.1177/0735633116648170.

Özyurt, O., & Özyurt, H. 2015. Learning style based individualized adaptive e-learning environments: Content analysis of the articles published from 2005 to 2014. *Computers in Human Behavior*, 52, 349–358. https://doi.org/10.1016/j.chb.2015.06.020.

Payne, J. S. 2020. Developing L2 productive language skills online and the strategic use of instructional tools. *Foreign Language Annals*, 53(2), 243–249. https://doi.org/10.1111/flan.12457.

Pelgrum, W. 2001. Obstacles to the integration of ICT in education: results from a worldwide educational assessment. *Computers & Education*, 37, 163–178. https://doi.org/10.1016/S0360-1315(01)00045-8.

Peachey, N. 2017. Synchronous online teaching. In, M. Carrier, R. M. Damerow, and K. M. Bailey (Eds.), *Digital Language Learning and Teaching: Research, Theory, and Practice* (pp.153–155). Routledge.

Pineda, E. J., Tamayo Cano, L. H., & Peralta, A. M. 2021. An inquiry-based framework for teaching English in synchronous environments: Perceptions from teachers and learners learning. *International Journal of Computer-Assisted Language Learning and Teaching*, 11(1), 38–58. DOI: 10.4018/IJCALLT.2021010103.

Qian, K., Owen, N., & Bax, S. 2018. Researching mobile-assisted Chinese-character learning strategies among adult distance learners. *Innovation in Language Learning and Teaching*, 12(1), 56–71. Retrieved from. https://doi.org/10.1080/17501229.2018.1418633.

Rha, K-H. 2022. Exploring English teachers' attitudes and perceptions of online classes: Based on the teachers' experiences. *Studies in Linguistics*, 64, 143–168.

Rehn, N., Maor, D. & McConney, A. 2018. The specific skills required of teachers who deliver K–12 distance education courses by synchronous videoconference: Implications for training and professional development. *Technology, Pedagogy, and Education*, 27(4), 417–429. https://doi.org/10.1080/1475939X.2018.1483265.

Salama, R., Uzunboylu, H., & Alkaddah, B. 2020. Distance learning system, learning programming languages by using mobile applications. *New Trends and Issues Proceedings on Humanities and Social Sciences*, 7(2), 23–47. https://doi.org/10.18844/prosoc.v7i2.5015.

Sert, O., & Li, L. 2017. A qualitative study on CALL knowledge and materials design: Insights from pre-service EFL teachers. *International Journal of Computer-Assisted Language Learning and Teaching*, 7(3), 73–86. https://doi/org/10.4018/IJCALLT.2017070105.

Stockwell G. 2012. *Computer Assisted Language Learning: Diversity in Research & Practice*. New York: Cambridge University Press.

Tsai, C. H., Cheng, C. H., Yeh, D. Y., & Lin, S. Y. 2016. Can learning motivation predict learning achievement? A case study of a mobile game-based English learning approach. *Education and Information Technology*, 22(5), 2159–2173. https://doi.org/10.1007/s10639-016-9542-5.

Tu, Y., Zou, D. & Zhang, R. 2020. A Comprehensive Framework for Designing and Evaluating Vocabulary Learning App. *International Journal of Mobile Learning and Organisation*, 14(3), 370–397. https://doi.org/10.1504/IJMLO.2020.108199.

Wang, R. B., & Du, C. T. 2014. Mobile social network sites as innovative pedagogical tools: Factors and mechanism affecting students' continuance intention on use. *Journal of Computer and Education*, 1(4), 353–370. https://doi.org/10.1007/s40692-014-0015-9.

Warschauer, M. 1995. Virtual connections: Online activities and projects for networking language learners. Honolulu, HI: University of Hawaii Second Language Teaching and Curriculum Center.

Watson, W. R., Kim, W., & Watson, S. L. 2016. Learning outcomes of a MOOC designed for attitudinal change: A case study of an animal behavior and welfare MOOC. *Computers and Education*, 96, 83–93. https://doi.org/10.1016/j.compedu.2016.01.013.

Wu, W., Yao, R., & Xie, Z. 2020. A study on the differences of college teachers' online teaching satisfaction between regions and universities. *Open Education Research*, 26(3), 71–79.

Zou, B., Huang, L., Ma, W., & Qiu, Y. 2021. Evaluation of the effectiveness of EFL online teaching during the COVID-19 pandemic. *SAGE Open*. https://doi.org/10.1177/21582440211054491.

Rethinking Foreign Language Education in China's Universities: A Humanistic Approach

Li Jin*

Introduction

In recent years, many people have been calling for a humanistic return to China's the higher education. Applying a humanistic approach to the foreign language education in China's universities, we need to reflect on the foreign language teaching in China today, have a clear understanding of the real objects of our foreign language teaching, and seek measures to ensure the integration of humanistic spirit and foreign language learning, in order to train high quality foreign language majors for them to serve our country better, and contribute to a well-constructed, value-oriented society. In sum, the cultivation of humanistic spirit should be an integral part of current higher education and plays an extremely important role in promoting students' all-round development.

Current Situation of Foreign Language Education in China's Universities

We are living in an age of globalization and are witnessing the rapid development of economy and information technology. With the advent of globalization, our society has put forward higher requirements for the quality and ability of college students and high-qualitied foreign language talents are in great demand. Therefore, education, especially higher education, shoulders the responsibility of training talented people to promote our country's economic development. However, along with the development of the economy, comes the latent threat to the healthy development of higher education, which is now

---

* Li Jin (金莉), Professor, School of English, Beijing Foreign Studies University, Beijing, China.

becoming highly commercialized and marketized. Since the reform and opening up, China's economic growth has made remarkable progress, but our country is still lagging behind the western countries in this respect and is in great need of catching up. In the process, the utilitarian value of foreign language education is overstressed, and consequently it has oriented towards a kind of vocational education. This educational philosophy has resulted in the qualitative decline of the humanities and the neglect of the real goals of foreign language higher education. The desire for individual well-being makes many people ignore the existence of moral values. These problems interfere with effective foreign language learning, and enthusiasm for the humanistic impulse of self-edification is hampered. As a result, it leads to the narrowness of students' range of knowledge, the weakness of their cultural deposits of both Chinese and western cultures, and the lack of the ability to think independently and make correct moral judgements.

Former vice premier Liu Yandong emphasizes the importance of teaching and learning foreign languages. She maintains that we should realize that learning and using foreign languages should be encouraged and supported because it is to meet the needs of expanding, opening up and strengthening our contact and intercourse with the world; learning advanced science and technology and absorbing the achievements of human civilization are also important (Wang and Wang 2011, 10). Wang Shouren and Wang Haixiao argue that foreign languages should play a very important role in the cultivation of college students' humanist spirit. In their report on the findings of a survey on college English teaching in 530 Chinese universities conducted by the National Foreign Languages Teaching Advisory Board under the Ministry of Education in 2009–2010, they point out that we should strengthen foreign language teaching for general education in order for students to have a better understanding of western civilization, its way of thinking, and way of life, to look at western culture and its core values with critical eyes, and to familiarize themselves with the similarities and differences of Chinese and foreign cultures (Wang and Wang 2011, 11).

Although the cultivation of the humanistic spirit in foreign language teaching is drawing more and more attention, and has been agreed upon by most college educators, how to achieve such a goal is still an issue that universities must constantly explore. As many universities, especially those universities of science and technology, still pay too much attention to the function of foreign language for its practicability and instrumentality and ignore its humanistic nature, this paper argues for the priority of humanistic education in Chinese universities in this era of advanced science and technology, and offers some suggestions for promoting humanistic education in foreign language teaching.

Objectives of Foreign Language Education in China's Universities

The core task of foreign language teaching is to teach learners to use a foreign language as a language resource and tool to know, criticize, and change the world, and promoting humanistic quality will reduce the instrumentality of foreign language teaching. Humanistic quality itself is not the ultimate goal of education, and it is an important means of achieving the ultimate goal of education. (Anonymous 2020, 211)

To fulfill the goal of foreign language teaching, we should take the following factors into consideration.

Understanding China, Understanding the World

As everyone knows, the aim of foreign language teaching is to "introduce the world to China," which means FLT (foreign language teaching) should enable students to learn, to understand, and to absorb the culture of a foreign country. China's College English Curriculum Teaching Requirement puts forward that the target of college teaching is to cultivate students' comprehensive ability of English in order to meet the requirement of our country's development and international communication.

President Xi Jinping has recently called for the building of a community with a shared future for humankind. To achieve this goal, it is natural that foreign language majors should strive to understand both China and the world. Moreover, besides teaching a foreign language, the foreign language educators should include the expansion of cognitive and analytical abilities of students, and the cultivation of the humanistic spirit in our students, in regard to understanding and respecting other cultures and the members of other communities.

Letting Other Societies Learn about China in Foreign Languages

Humanistic knowledge plays an important role in communication across cultures. Besides allowing students to use English (or other foreign languages) to introduce China to the world, we also need to stress the importance of the mutual learning of civilizations. To fulfill our country's strategic goal of "Culture going global," we need to train high-quality foreign language talents. We should train students to understand themselves, our society and country, and our civilization. We should also let students understand other cultures and the world. In the process of learning about foreign civilizations, let them deepen their knowledge of our own civilization (Li 2020, 41). On the one hand, we teach foreign languages to give play to their function of instrumentality, and allow students to own the knowledge and ability to serve our society; on the other hand, we should always be aware of our goals, that is, to cultivate students' ability to absorb the quintessence of foreign cultures, and develop our own culture, and ultimately adapt themselves to the requirements of our country's foreign language talents. More importantly, in their study of foreign languages, students may discern the differences between Chinese culture and foreign culture, and realize the goal of promoting their humanistic quality in their study and thinking. In sum, students should have global vision, gain a fairly thorough understanding of Chinese and foreign cultures, and be able to conduct effective cross-cultural communication, thereby ultimately becoming bridges between Chinese culture and foreign cultures.

Learning to Become a Socially Responsible Person

The mission of universities is to train young talents, whose quality is directly related to the destiny of a nation (Li 2020, 39). The most successful all-round personality development of foreign language majors occurs in conditions of using the humanistic pedagogical techniques of foreign language teaching. According to the UNESCO report of the International Commission on Education for the Twenty-first Century, education should contribute to the total development of the whole person (UNESCO 2002, 24). Accordingly, higher education should be oriented towards complete human growth in which students' learning initiative should be brought into full play, rather than simply the training of skills or cultivation of competence and transmission. The lack of a humanistic quality is harmful to students' all-round development, serving as an obstacle to their growth as an individual and a member of society.

College students should not only develop the skills they will need later in life, but also form positive attitudes and empathy (Arifi 2017, 194). Therefore, "the receiver in education is considered first a human being, and then considered a learner" (Khatib 2013, 45). Moskowitz argues that humanistic education is related to the concern for personal development, self-acceptance, and acceptance by others, that is, to make students more humane (1978, 12). Furthermore, she states that humanistic education should bring out the uniqueness of each individual. To be self-actualizing is to "function to one's fullest capacity." (12)

The humanistic approach has the eligibility to be practiced in foreign language teaching and contributes to the all-round development of foreign language learners—to encourage and facilitate the growth of students' inner selves, to cultivate their humanistic feelings and attitude, and to enlighten them to the value of life and the true meaning of life. Humanistic education in foreign language teaching is an important way for students to form the correct life outlook, world view, and values, to help students on their way in pursuing truth, goodness and beauty, and to better understand the world by using a foreign language as a window to the world.

Forming socially acceptable attitudes and developing empathy are extremely important if the goal of education is to enable students to become "a whole person." Our education should help students develop the skills and knowledge they need to participate actively and responsibly in a constantly changing world. This means that students should be trained to be independent, to recognize connections between school subjects and the world surrounding them, and to use knowledge, to rely on experience, and to think critically when solving life's problems. They should learn to acquire the right attitudes, interests, and social values, to learn to interact with other people in society, and to live more enriched and worthwhile life. Thus, they could contribute to the ethical progress of all humankind, and be a person full of principles, ideals, and moral values and apply them in their personal and professional life. In short, humanistic education should engage the whole person, and foreign language teaching should orient towards training students' personal growth in humane relations among all the participants of this educational process as they grow up and prepare to enter professional life.

Measures to Integrate Humanistic Spirit into Foreign Language Teaching

"The characteristics of humanistic education lie in their 'non-utilitarianism' and 'invisible and formative influence'." (Zhao 2019, 134) Students should both learn "ji" (skills) and "dao" (natural rules, law). "Ji" refers to instrumentality and applicability, while "dao" refers to educability and humanism (Wang 2018, 15). Teaching a foreign language allows students to not only master the language skills and enhance their cognitive and analytical abilities, but also nurture their humanistic spirit. To ensure the humanization of the educational process in the educational institutions, foreign language classes need to be made as relevant as possible to the present and future needs of students. Acknowledgement of the students' inner motivation is an important means in the educational process's stimulation, and the shaping of college students' personality and morality should be prioritized. Instrumentality and humanism will be used complementarily as a whole in the teaching of a foreign language.

Strengthening the Training of Students' Critical Thinking

"Modern pedagogics is oriented to the development of students' creative thinking and the formational of the collective and individual skills." (Shakirova and Valeeva 2016, 151) We need to cultivate the innovative thinking of students through the change of their self-perception, the acceptance of new social and cultural behaviors, and understanding the members of other communities (Arifi 2017, 195). We should actively involve students in the whole educational process, emphasize development and self-development of the students' abilities, and cultivate students' critical and independent thinking, and by doing this, expand their horizon, and fully open up their creative potential.

Foreign language learning is not a cultural vacuum. It cannot be denied that western culture nowadays has a great impact on young students, especially on foreign language students. As foreign language majors, students are so immersed in a foreign language and culture, that they tend to possess a kind of blindness and extremity in their absorption of a foreign culture, and neglect their own cultural tradition, moral values and social responsibilities. As a result, they are inclined to be indifferent to our own country but worship foreign things. Under such circumstances, the improvement of their cultural literacy should be stressed. It is important that we should guide students to gain critical awareness of the ideological environment, to introduce to them various world cultures and viewpoints, as well as pressing issues facing them as global citizens. By learning a foreign language, students will be able to learn to form their own thinking, raise meaningful questions and make correct judgements.

Balancing the Relations between Mother Tongue and a Foreign Language

It is regrettable that, nowadays, many people (including the foreign language teachers) believe that the task of FLT only concerns the teaching of a foreign language, and our own language and culture can be ignored. As a consequence, our foreign language majors know very little about our own language, history and culture, even though they are fluent in speaking or writing a foreign language. However, we have to realize that even though our main task is to introduce foreign cultures to China, the completion of this task should be based on the understanding of our own culture. Language is an important component of civilization. We need to add more Chinese language courses to our curricula to allow our students a better command of the Chinese language. For one thing, only those people with a good command of Chinese can really learn a foreign language well; for the other, the purpose of learning a foreign language is to communicate with foreigners. If their knowledge of Chinese language and culture is very limited, how can they effectively communicate with people of other countries and become real cultural ambassadors of our country in their communication with the outside world?

In the 1990s, the world-renowned Chinese scholar Fei Xiaotong put forward the idea of "cultural awareness," which should be regarded as an essential concept for the discipline of foreign languages. We can only build the human civilization together with others when we grasp the essence of our own cultural tradition and ascertain our own cultural values. In this respect, implementing humanistic education in foreign language teaching is essential.

What we need to do now is to enhance the cultural awareness of our students. A closer connection between the discipline of foreign languages and that of the Chinese language should be built. More courses and content on the Chinese language and culture are of high necessity now. Our students should have a global vision, but at the same time, a better understanding of our own cultural tradition is essential. As China is connecting with the world, the task "to introduce China to the world" has also become important for our foreign language students.

Balancing the Relations between Command of Language Skills and Study of Culture

Another pair of relations in FLT is the balance between the command of language skills and the study of culture. Language cannot be separated from culture, and culture is reflected through language. For many years, FLT in China has attached too much importance to the mastery of language skills and cognitive capabilities, and many class hours have been spent on grammar exercises and pattern drills instead of reading. Imitation is stressed rather than thinking. As a consequence, our students have a very shallow understanding of a foreign country's culture, education, economy, history, etc. Furthermore, compared with students of other disciplines in humanities and social sciences, foreign language majors show apparent deficiency in the depth of thoughts, knowledge structure, and analytical ability.

We need to realize that language is not pure word symbol; learning a foreign language actually means much more than simply mastering the language skills, and the system of rules and grammar of a given language. Language is the carrier of culture, whereas culture is the content of language. To learn and use a foreign language cannot be separated from the way of thinking in it, so students should learn and grasp the culture behind the language at the same time. A better balance is needed between the acquisition of language skills and cultural knowledge, so students may move, step by step, from the learning of language skills to the learning of culture and training of critical thinking. "Language acquisition is determined by interaction among a number of student-related and contextual factors, and using of humanistic method of teaching can increase students' motivation and class sociability." (Khatib 2013, 48) As educators, we will make efforts to teach students to respect cultural diversity, and to cultivate their ability in cross-cultural awareness. Eventually, language may become the tool of the language learners for pursuing knowledge in literature, history, culture, etc. and in their critical thinking.

When the foreign language department of Tsinghua University was founded in 1926, it set up its educational goal as training "scholars of profound knowledge," which means that students should "read the classics of the western literature," "understand the spirit of the western civilization," and "connect and communicate with each other its spiritual thoughts." The two well-known Chinese scholars who graduated from Tsinghua and later came to teach at Beijing Foreign Studies University also argued for the learning of culture through language. Prof. Wang Zuoliang once said that "a language studied through culture will be mastered in a better way," and Prof. Xu Guozhang believed that "the goal of English education is to use English to learn a culture, to know the world, and to cultivate the intelligence" (quoted in Youzhong 2017, 865).

This, of course, does not mean that language skills are not important for foreign language majors, or foreign language teachers do not need a firm command of the language being taught or proper training in language teaching pedagogy. A higher goal should be set for teachers to better balance the teaching of language skills and culture. Whereas the teaching of language skills is stressed, the reading (especially the reading of classics) should not be ignored. Furthermore, professors should themselves be familiar with the cultural subjects they are teaching; therefore, the improvement of professors' humanistic quality is extremely important. Only in this way may they help students view culture in language phenomena, use culture to direct their language learning, cultivate their cultural consciousness, and increase their sensibility and tolerance in cultural differences.

Adding Weight to the Reading of Literature

Language is the carrier of literature, and literature is the best means to study language. Studying a foreign language is not only for the improvement of students' communicative competence in language, but also for their construction of morality and value ideas. In the process of humanistic education, and especially in foreign language teaching, we should emphasize the importance of reading literature in original, which could improve their cultural attainments, and enlighten them to the value of life and the true meaning of existence. Literature can affect a person's life, it reveals truth, kindness and beauty, and revokes the dark sides of society and individuals. In literature we see how mammonism and utilitarianism are assailed. Literature courses are of great significance in one's studies and should be an indispensable part of university curricula. Universities should set up more compulsory and selective literature courses, hold lectures on literature, and organize more activities related to Chinese and foreign literatures. More time should be allotted for students to read literature independently, to train themselves to appreciate the literary works in their original languages, to experience literary works and contexts, and finally for them to become a mature person.

In addition, our curricula should also include courses on Chinese literature. The purposes are: on the one hand, to enable students to become more familiar with both our own literature and culture, and foreign literature and culture; and on the other hand, to give students a comparative perspective, for them to appreciate the different cultures in comparison, and to propagate and disseminate fine traditional Chinese culture.

In short, reading literature is not only beneficial for improving the language ability of students: more importantly, it teaches students to understand the differences and similarities between different cultures, and further arouses their deep thinking on human nature and values.

Improving the Humanistic Quality of College Teachers

Obviously, Universities should continue to encourage teachers to improve their qualifications. "Foreign language teachers are not only the implementers of the cultivation of the humanistic spirit, but also the practitioners of the humanistic spirit" (Ren 2017, 285). The foreign language teachers shoulder the responsibility of introducing the western culture to the students and carrying forward the fine Chinese cultural tradition. To accomplish such a task, they should be rich in humanistic knowledge in order to stimulate students' motivation and interest in learning both Chinese language and culture and a foreign language and its culture. In their teachings, teachers may improve students' humanistic quality while, at the same time, allowing them to acquire language knowledge and skills.

For better fitting the current needs of humanistic college education, college teachers should pursue a Ph.D. degree, either in linguistics and literature or in other disciplines, such as a foreign country's history, education, foreign policy, etc. The knowledge of a teacher includes both the depth and width of their command of foreign language studies, their familiarity with our history and culture, as well as their grasp of the tendency of social development. Teachers should think of themselves as facilitators responsible for stimulating students' interest in studies and encouraging students to acquire the quintessence of a foreign culture.

As college teachers are people who are directly responsible for cultivating students and transmitting wisdom, they should try advanced educational ideas and explore optimized teaching strategies. Teachers' humanistic vision and perspectives directly influence students. Naturally, teachers should expand their range of knowledge, broaden their horizon, accumulate knowledge in related areas, and be well cultured in literature and raise their ethical attainments. Only through integrating the knowledge of Chinese and western cultures in their teaching, may they carry their humanistic education forward.

Humanistic cultivation is the result of accumulation and internalization of humanistic knowledge. It is important for teachers to exert an invisible, formative influence on the students, and create a favorable environment for them to absorb cultural elements. College foreign language teachers should not only disseminate knowledge, but also create new knowledge; they should, through their teaching, let students learn and experience different cultures.

Apart from imparting knowledge in class, colleges should open the school doors for students to be in touch with their society, to experience what they cannot learn from books, to help them face difficulties in life directly, and to find and solve problems.

Using New Media to Integrate Humanistic Spirit into Foreign Language Teaching

We need to build up efficient humanistic educational technologies for teaching foreign languages. A reform of the teaching system and curricula is needed in humanistic education, and more humanistic courses should be set up. Teachers are the key to deepening teaching reform and integrating foreign language teaching into humanistic education; they should constantly improve teaching methods and implement effective teaching monitoring by adopting new practices.

Teachers should take advantage of new media, and substantiate the efficiency of its usage. The use of new media in the learning of a foreign language is a valid approach to helping build a learning community. New media can create a realistic context, environment, and platform for the interaction of foreign language teaching and studying; thus, effective foreign language teaching is achieved. The internet, QQ, WeChat, microblogging, etc. can enrich the resources needed in the teaching and learning process, stimulate students' curiosity and initiative, and encourage students' self-learning ability and collective learning. Moreover, with the use of new media, students may have more time for their own exploration and reading, and do more independent study.

Conclusion

As China enters the global community, the demand for foreign language talents becomes more urgent, and the importance of college foreign language teaching is increasingly highlighted. Obviously, humanistic education has brought about significant changes in recent years in the field of language education. However, only when we reach a consensus on the goals of foreign language teaching in China and persist in retaining the humanities as the core of foreign language teaching, may we enhance students' foreign language proficiency through cultural and humanistic knowledge teaching, and cultivate the high qualitied, foreign language talents. Furthermore, we may only achieve this by developing strategies on an all-round improvement in educational objectives, curricula, teaching methods as well as teacher development.

(Acknowledgement: This article is a revision of the author's speech at the 2018 UKCHA Annual Forum.)

References

Anonymous. 2020. "Foreign Language Major Education." In *Research Report on China's Language Policy*.

Arifi, Qatip. 2017. "Humanistic Approach in Teaching Foreign Language." In *European Scientific Journal* 13 (35): 194–205.

Jiang, Hongxin. 2010. "The Education of Humanities and Development of English Major in Chinese University." In *Foreign Languages in China* 7, No. 3: 10–13, 18.

Khatib, Mohammad. 2013. "Humanistic Education: Concerns, Implications and Applications," in *Journal of Language*

Teaching and Research 4, No. 1: 45–51.

Li, Silong. 2020. "The Theory and Practice of Cross-Disciplinary Humanistic Education." In *Chinese College Teaching* 4: 39–45.

Moskowitz, Gertrude. 1978. *Caring and Sharing in the Foreign Language Class: A Sourcebook on Humanistic Techniques.* Rowley, MA: Newbury House.

Ren, Ling. 2017. "Reflection on the Significance of the Integration of Humanistic Education into College English Teaching." In *The 4th International Conference on Social Science.*

Shakirova, Aliya A. and Valeeva, Roza A. 2016. "Humanistic Educational Technologies of Teaching Foreign Languages." In *Mathematics Education* 11, No. 1: 151–64.

Sun, Youzhong. 2017. "On Liberal English Education." In *Foreign Language Teaching and Research* 49, No. 6: 859–870.

UNESCO. 2002. *Learning to Be.—A Holistic and Integrated Approach to Values Education for Human Development,* Thailand: UNESCO Asia and Pacific Regional Bureau for Education.

Wang, Shouren and Wang, Haixiao. 2011."On the State of College English Teaching in China and Its Future Development." In *Foreign Languages in China* 8, No. 5: 4–11, 17.

Wang, Wenbin. 2018. "On Foreign Language Teaching and Foreign Language Education, Instrumentality and Humanism." In *Foreign Languages in China* 15, No. 2: 11–16.

Zhao, Dinggui. 2019. "Humanistic Education and Measures in the New Epoch." In *Sichuan University of Arts and Science Journal* 29, No. 3: 133–139.

UK–China Academic Relations in a World of Strategic Rivalry

Tim Summers[*]

This chapter examines recent trends in relations between the United Kingdom (UK) and China, and British policy towards China, with a particular focus on academic and research ties. It focuses primarily on the UK's political debates and perspectives, approaching the topic by combining policy research and foreign policy analysis, with a view to assessing the state of, and prospects for, UK–China academic collaboration in a world of strategic rivalry.

Over the last decade, UK–China relations have been through a number of changes and have attracted growing analytical and political interest in both policy and academic worlds. Much of the focus of analysis has been on the overall approach of the UK to China and specific issues, such as the role of Chinese telecommunications company Huawei in the UK or contention over developments in Hong Kong or Xinjiang, and British reactions to them (Summers 2022a, 2021a). There has been limited consolidated analysis on academic and research ties between the two countries, and this chapter begins to address this gap. The first part of the chapter sets the scene by examining UK–China relations over recent years. Shifts in those relations, and in particular the growing securitisation—understood as

---

* Tim Summers (夏添恩) is Assistant Professor at the Centre for China Studies, The Chinese University of Hong Kong. His research covers the international relations and political economy of contemporary China. Recent publications include *China's Hong Kong: the politics of a global city* (second edition, 2021), *China's Regions in an Era of Globalization* (Routledge, 2018) and journal articles on the Belt and Road Initiative, China's maritime disputes, UK–China relations and Hong Kong.

a "speech act that raises a concern to the level of a threat by giving it the name 'security'" (Reeves 2014, 145)—of ties in the UK's approach to China, is an important context for the second part of the chapter, which examines academic and research links. This section covers a number of issues: collaboration in science and technology, rising Chinese student numbers in the UK, the growing state regulation of research partnerships in the UK, and the securitisation of academic ties alongside concerns regarding "dependence" which have emerged recently in the UK political and media debate regarding academic collaboration with China.

While the gradual creep of deteriorating ties and a more "hawkish" British approach to China has begun to infect academic and research relations, these relations were previously seen in "win-win" terms as delivering mutual benefit for the UK and China. In the process, both bilateral opportunities and an objective assessment of China's growing strength in research and innovation have been marginalised in the UK's policy making. The chapter identifies several emerging concerns in the UK's policy debate around education and research ties to China: concern that scientific links could have negative implications for national security, especially in relation to "dual use" technologies; concern over political "interference" and academic freedom in universities in the UK; and concern regarding unhealthy dependence on Chinese funding, especially student fee income.

Overall, these concerns are based on an emerging assessment that China poses some sort of "threat" to the UK, rather than an opportunity, to use the conceptual foreign policy analysis framework explored by Scott Brown (2018) in an examination of European approaches to China. The third part of the chapter takes issue with this view, by dissecting one recent statement of the thesis that "China is a threat." Reevaluating this creates space for a different approach to education and research ties, one which draws on opportunities and acknowledges China's growing strengths in these areas. The chapter concludes by sketching out what this might look like as an alternative to the current trajectory of British policy.

UK–China Relations: London "Toughens Up"

Recent years have seen significant changes in UK–China relations, accompanied by a growth in scholarship examining ties between the two countries. The peak of bilateral engagement was marked by the state visit to the UK by Chinese President Xi Jinping in October 2015, and the declaration of a "comprehensive global strategic partnership for the twenty-first century," commonly referred to as expectation of a "golden era" in UK–China relations. Since then, the trajectory has been one of gradually cooling ties. The UK's decision in 2016 to leave the European Union ("Brexit") led to a change of prime minister and a gradual re-evaluation of British foreign policy, including towards China. Over subsequent years, ideas that China offered an opportunity to the UK, primarily in the economic sphere, weakened in the policy discussions, to be replaced by assertions that China posed some sort of security or normative threat to the UK (Summers 2021a).

The ongoing sense of flux in the UK's China policy, and the UK's wider approach to international affairs, may be evaluated by looking at two key policy documents: the British government's Integrated Review of Security, Defence, Development and Foreign Policy, published in March 2021, and a "Refreshed" version of the Integrated Review, released two years later in March 2023. While the broad context for these position papers was the UK's global positioning after Brexit, the specific context for China policy was one of growing political interest, involving a greater politicisation of many aspects of ties which had previously been taken for granted. This manifested itself, for example, in growing parliamentary and media scrutiny of China policy, including Chinese investments in the UK. In particular, the pressure from critics regarding engagement with China continued to grow during this period, boosted by largely negative media reporting of developments in China and some pressure from the US on London to take a "tougher" line against China (Summers 2023).

The original Integrated Review of 2021 (HM Government 2021) suggested a policy of balancing different elements of relations with China. It described China as a "strategic challenge" for the UK, whilst emphasising the need for engagement in economic areas and global governance, such as climate change. This reflected the range of British interests in relation to China, yet was criticised by those calling for a tougher China policy. This revealed one feature of the UK's China policy debate, which has been ongoing since the late 2010s: the role of lobby groups pushing for a "tougher" policy approach to China. Particularly prominent have been the Conservative Party's China Research Group of MPs (CRG), set up in 2020; the London-based Inter-Parliamentary Alliance on China (IPAC), also set up in 2020; Hong Kong Watch (HKW), which was established in 2017 and intervenes in China-related policy issues beyond Hong Kong; and the neoconservative Henry Jackson Society. The House of Commons Foreign Affairs Committee (FAC), under chairs Tom Tugendhat (2017–2022) and Alicia Kearns (from 2022), has also been vocal in calling for a tougher China policy. The growing level of political interest can also be seen in the establishment of a dedicated newsletter on UK–China relations, *Beijing to Britain*, targeted primarily at government, parliament and others interested in China policy.[1]

One strand of this pressure involves calls for the government to publish a consolidated "China strategy," and criticism of the 2021 Integrated Review for being unclear or too soft in its approach to China. Responding to some of these calls—for example, from MPs in the CRG or FAC—the government stated that it did have an internal China strategy, yet was not minded to make a detailed version public (Doherty 2022; Ahmad 2022). However, the government's intention to "refresh" the Integrated Review was maintained after Rishi Sunak became prime minister in October 2022, and expectations grew that the revised document would say more about China than its predecessor. The 60-page "Integrated Review Refresh 2023" was launched in March 2023 (HM Government 2023), amidst substantial ongoing domestic challenges for the UK and a turbulent international backdrop, especially due to the conflict in Ukraine. It coincided as a major statement in British foreign and security policy with Prime Minister Rishi Sunak appearing alongside US President Biden and Australian Prime Minister Albanese at an American submarine base to reiterate their commitment to the controversial trilateral "AUKUS" deal to sell nuclear-powered submarines to Australia.

---

1   This is now a paid subscription newsletter, available at https://beijingtobritain.substack.com/.

Given the conflict in Ukraine, it is perhaps not surprising that security concerns dominated the "refreshed" Integrated Review of Security, Defence, Development and Foreign Policy, which said much more about security and defence policy than development or diplomacy. In a tilt to "guns over butter," the government announced that defence spending would rise to 2.5% of GDP.[1] The refreshed Review also highlighted institutional changes in the security realm, from a "new strategic affairs specialism" in British diplomacy to developing the intelligence agencies further, building a new "open-source intelligence" hub, and a reiterated commitment to a new College for National Security. The government has also put additional funding into "information operations" over recent years. A major message of the "refresh" was that the UK's priorities lie in the "Euro-Atlantic," which was highlighted by the symbolism of Sunak standing alongside Biden on his visit to the US. The primary alignment it envisages is with the US, not the post-Brexit European Union or the emerging powers of Asia or the Global South. The document does not contain any critical reflection on the state of the United States or its foreign and security policy, exactly two decades after Britain followed Washington into Iraq.

This "security first" approach is also reflected in the refreshed approach to China policy. The 2023 document departs from the 2021 Integrated Review by including a two-page standalone statement on China policy, with China being the only country to receive this treatment. This provides more (in terms of a consolidated public statement) than the previous integrated review, and may be seen as a response to political pressure over the last few years—mainly from more hawkish Conservative parliamentarians—for a public "China strategy." In his foreword (HM Government 2023, 2–4), Sunak says:

China poses an epoch-defining challenge to the type of international order we want to see, both in terms of security and values—and so our approach must

---

1 It might be worth noting that ADS (the trade association for the UK's aerospace, defence, security, and space industries), suggested that the IR update (the "refresh") provides an "ideal opportunity to accelerate delivery of underpinning strategies." Foreign Affairs Committee (2022, 6).

evolve. We will work with our partners to engage with Beijing on issues such as climate change. But where there are attempts by the Chinese Communist Party to coerce or create dependencies, we will work closely with others to push back against them. And we are taking new action to protect ourselves, our democracy and our economy at home.

He also says that China is willing to "use all the levers of state power to achieve a dominant role in global affairs" and refers to "China's more aggressive stance in the South China Sea and the Taiwan Strait." The more detailed two-page statement on China policy begins by framing China as "an epoch-defining and systemic challenge with implications for almost every area of government policy and the everyday lives of British people" (HM Government 2023, 30). This phrase should be read against the background of political debates, since at least summer 2022, over whether Sunak's government would call China a "threat," as his short-lived predecessor Liz Truss (prime minister for 49 days from September to October 2022) had said she would. Sunak had earlier suggested he would follow suit, yet after taking office he talked of China as a "systemic challenge" instead. The message of the "refresh" is that Sunak's government would not categorise China formally as a "threat," though its framing of China treats it as a threat in all but name.

The "refreshed" policy framework set out to deal with China is based around three keywords: "protect, align and engage." Among the three, the emphasis is clearly on "protect," reflecting the *de facto* framing of China as a threat and the security focus outlined in the previous paragraphs. The idea behind "align" could open up a number of partners, though the reaffirmation of AUKUS, as well as previous comments by Sunak, suggest that the US is clearly number one, and that Australia and Japan are ahead of the UK's European neighbours as partners for "alignment" on China policy.[1] "Engagement" with China

---

1   For example, Sunak highlighted alignment with the US, Japan and Australia when speaking to the Foreign Affairs Committee in December 2022; available at: https://twitter.com/ChinaResearchGp/status/1605223782918258689?s=20&t=sBMr5kl7w5R79JqShjqEZQ.

comes a grudging third, and the detailed language on "engagement" is heavy on the need for "protection," which is effectively a securitisation of engagement through which the potential or perceived risks of engagement are emphasised, while upsides are marginalised. Indeed, there is little evidence of acknowledgement of potential opportunities in dealing with China, which is not just a large economy but an increasingly vibrant and innovative one. The "refresh" further securitises economic relations with a prominent reference to "avoiding dependencies in our critical supply chains and protecting our national security" and only a brief note that a "positive trade and investment relationship can benefit both the UK and China" (HM Government 2023, 31). Initial political and media responses to the "refresh" in the UK were generally positive (Beijing to Britain 2023).

Nonetheless, there are some nuances and ambiguities. The use of "engage" may have been surprising to some given that criticism of "engagement" with China has grown in the UK as well as in the US, where the idea of the "failure of engagement" has become a mainstream feature of China policy debates (Johnston 2019). This language suggests that while the UK has shifted substantially towards Washington's language and approach to China, especially in comparison with the mid-2010s, it has not (yet) gone wholesale down the American route. Some of the government spin around the "refresh" was more nuanced, seeking to highlight space for engaging China and suggesting some hedging ahead. In the run-up to a high-profile speech in late April 2023, the foreign minister, James Cleverly, commented that the UK should not "pull the shutters down" on China (*The Guardian* 2023a). His speech elaborated on the three-point framework of the refreshed *Integrated Review* (Cleverly 2023); it offered more nuance than hoped for by those seeking an unambiguous critical stance, yet still showed the extent to which British policy has shifted over the years, with prominent criticisms of China's approach to Xinjiang and Taiwan in particular. The idea of a "threat" from China is not far below the surface. Looking forward, the domestic politics mitigate against nuance, and the political pressure remains for a further shift to a more hawkish approach to China.

In sum, security is in command as the UK's move to reduce engagement with China continues. All of this is key background and context for the ways in which the British policy debate has been developing in the securitisation of multiple sectors. The central element to note is the growing dominance of the idea that China constitutes a "threat" (whether explicitly stated or not), with little attention being paid to potential "opportunities." I will return to a critical discussion of this framing later in this chapter, after discussing bilateral academic and research relations.

Academic and Research Relations: From Win–Win to Securitisation

These developments in the UK's China policy provide important background for the consideration of recent developments in education and research relations between the two countries. This section begins by mapping the development of education and research ties. It then discusses some of the policy shifts based on parliamentary reports and debates and media coverage, as well as government responses and positions.

Academic and research links between the UK and China have grown substantially since the 1990s. Three areas are particularly noteworthy. First, the number of Chinese students studying in the UK has grown rapidly, though it should be noted that this has not been matched by a similar increase in British students studying in China. Second, there has been a substantial increase in research and innovation partnerships, particularly in science subjects, with this going beyond universities to include corporations, public bodies and other actors. Third, there have been a number of institutions established in each country, with several British universities setting up "joint venture" campuses in China, and a significant number of Chinese Confucius Institutes and Confucius Classrooms set up in the UK.

The first area concerns Chinese students in the UK. By the early 2000s, it was already becoming evident that Chinese students would become a more important part of the student body in British universities. For most of this period, that was generally accepted in the UK as a positive development. British education was seen as an important part of the country's soft power, a generator of significant economic activity and employment, and a platform to support wider economic and technological development. The number of international students grew substantially over this period, not just from China, in the context of declining public (i.e., government) funding for British universities, and the introduction of, and increases in, tuition fees for domestic students. Chinese students have been an important part of this growth, especially in the 2010s as the country's economic status and wealth have grown. In 2020–2021, there were 216000 Chinese students in the UK (Erudera College News 2021), over twice the number for the 2014–2015 academic year. Numbers have continued to rise, and it should be noted that after Brexit, the number of EU applicants dropped by half (by 54% to 23160) between 2019 and 2022, and there were more Chinese than EU applicants in 2021 (Kothia 2021). In autumn 2022 the number of Chinese applicants to UK universities reached a new record high. There has been relatively little research into the economic benefits of this for the UK, with the notable exception of a report published by the China–Britain Business Council (CBBC) in February 2021. CBBC found that around 3600 full-time equivalent jobs in London were supported by expenditure by Chinese students, the largest of any region, while the equivalent numbers in the North West and Yorkshire and the Humber regions were around 2000 each in 2018–2019 (China–Britain Business Council 2021).

The second area of rapid growth in academic ties has been in research and innovation collaboration. The first two decades of the twenty-first century saw a substantial deepening and broadening of science and innovation collaboration between the UK and China. Much of this was led by individual researchers and institutes, supported by both governments and other bodies, such as the UK's scientific research councils. From the British perspective, such collaboration has offered an opportunity to tap into a large and rapidly growing research community: for example, in 2017, expenditure in China on R&D (research and development) was close to £200 billion, accounting for over 2% of its GDP, compared to 1.67% in the UK in 2016. China's expenditure has since risen further as a proportion of GDP and is roughly on a par with that in the US. China has around 25% of the global R&D workforce, is the second-largest producer of scientific articles, and is home to over

1500 foreign-run R&D centres. Innovation (broadly conceived) is a central principle in the country's social and economic development plans, with the vast majority of R&D spending directed towards development and commercialisation rather than basic research (UK Science and Innovation Network 2018). The private sector has accounted for around three quarters of the total spend, in particular in provinces such as Guangdong, which is home to some of the best-known innovative Chinese corporations. In 2017, the British and Chinese governments signed a Joint Strategy for Science, Technology and Innovation Cooperation (HM Government 2017), and as of late 2019, the UK Research and Innovation China office—supported by the UK's research councils—had brokered £360 billion in joint partnerships, with 363 projects involving over 350 academic institutions and businesses (UK Research and Innovation 2019). Examples of projects cited here included: new materials that convert surplus renewable energy into domestic heating; treatment to neutralise drug-resistant bacteria; a robot to assist the elderly; virtual reality technology that preserves community heritage; and new methods to help protect species threatened by climate change. As well as delivering research outcomes, collaboration has also facilitated new exports from the UK, reaching £69 million in 2017, and investment into the UK of £3.3 million as of 2017 (UK Science and Innovation Network 2018).

The third area of expansion in academic ties has been the establishment of British and Chinese educational institutions in each other's countries. From China to the UK, more than 30 Confucius Institutes have been opened in the UK since the beginning of this scheme, which is substantially more than in any other European country. As a result, before Brexit, the UK accounted for one quarter of the Confucius Institutes in the European Union (Summers 2017). There are also many Confucius Classrooms in the UK (over 100 at the end of 2016, and more since then). This was generally seen as an example of beneficial educational exchange which could deepen mutual understanding, and help young people in the UK to learn Chinese language and engage with the emerging China. In the other direction, several British universities have set up joint venture campuses in China, including Nottingham–Ningbo and Xi'an Jiaotong–Liverpool.

Much of this activity was supported proactively by successive British governments. Funding for education and research ties has constituted a significant part of what London has categorised as "development assistance" or aid over the 2010s, contributing towards government targets to spend a certain proportion of GDP on overseas development. This included direct government funding to support research and innovation collaboration, as well as scholarships and other activities, including the UK government's flagship Chevening Scholarship programme and support for the British Council in China. UK-based institutions, rather than Chinese counterparts, have tended to receive most of the government money spent on research and academia. For example, funding under the Newton Fund—a total of £33 million in 2019—and the Global Challenges Research Fund primarily went to British universities to support collaboration in research with Chinese counterparts. Both funds have since been discontinued (Loft and Brien 2023).

In all of these areas, education and research ties between the UK and China were viewed positively for many years. This was in the context of a broadly benign geopolitical environment (for China and the West at least), and an intensifying economic globalisation. The dominant mindset was one of promoting exchanges, or viewing engagement with China as more of an opportunity than a threat. However, as noted above, this geopolitical context began to shift in the mid-2010s, and entered a new phase in 2017 and 2018 with the Trump administration's turn to strategic rivalry with China. Vice President Mike Pence's October 2018 speech was a clear marker of this shift, and its blanket criticism of China's approach in a number of areas included education, with Pence accusing China of using funding to influence American universities to avoid discussion of issues which the CCP might deem sensitive (Pence 2018). Controversy in the US over science collaboration grew, with a particular focus on Chinese scientists working in the US who had some links with Chinese institutions or had participated in Chinese government funded programmes (Zweig and Kang 2020; Mervis 2023).

This turn in US policy was not felt immediately in the UK, where policy towards China was still shaped by the idea of engagement, even though the shine of the "golden era" announced in 2015 had already begun to come off. During 2018 and into 2019, however, there was a growing shift in the UK's China policy, following the US lead. Issues at the forefront of this were Huawei and 5G, and the response to developments in Hong Kong in 2019. Other matters have since been added to the list of British complaints, as those pushing for a more hawkish British policy towards China shift their lobbying from one issue to another.

In terms of education and research ties, the political mood changed more slowly than in other areas, with the shift only really beginning around late 2019 or 2020. In an early sign of what was to come, in a November 2019 report, the House of Commons Foreign Affairs Committee—chaired by Tom Tugendhat MP—expressed concern that UK universities were vulnerable to "influence by autocracies," and that the Foreign and Commonwealth Office (FCO, as it was then called) and universities "should develop together a strategy to address the challenges posed by autocracies to UK universities" (Foreign Affairs Committee 2019). The few examples given in the report relate to political issues, rather than science and innovation, and in its reply to the committee, the FCO noted the availability of "Trusted Research guidance" and advice for universities from the FCO Chief Scientific Adviser and Centre for the Protection of National Infrastructure.

The issue was subsequently picked up by the China Research Group, formed by Conservative Party MPs in 2020, also chaired by Tugendhat. In a CRG webinar in October 2020, Tugendhat hosted an online panel discussion which largely characterised China as a risk or a threat to UK universities (China Research Group 2020). Panellists spoke of what they described as "Chinese interference" with academic freedom, especially after the Hong Kong National Security Law was passed in June 2020 (Steve Tsang), and of the risk that UK universities would be too "dependent" on overseas fee income, especially from China (Will Tanner). While there were some balancing points in the discussion (Cindy Yu), the overall tone of the event was that "China" posed a threat to British academia. In a later report on the United Front, the CRG argued that Chinese students in the UK were being mobilised as part of Chinese influence campaigns (China Research Group 2022a).

Over the last two years, the discussion of similar themes by lobby groups and the media has grown. There are several main strands to the arguments made. First, there has been a growing discussion of the idea that UK universities are overdependent on Chinese students for fee income, in particular for some universities. One data point suggests that the elite Russell Group of universities together depend on Chinese students for more than 20% of revenue. In July 2022, the incoming head of Universities UK, Vivienne Stern, warned universities to prepare for a scenario in which relations with China broke down (Yeomans 2022). Others, such as former universities minister Jo Johnson, advised universities to seek more students from other markets, for example India. A few years back, Chinese student numbers were over twice those from India, in second place, and seven times Nigeria, in third, though the number of Indian students has grown significantly since then and more student visas were issued to Indian than Chinese students for the first time in 2022 (Financial Times 2023). This issue has become part of a wider emergence of a meme of unhealthy British "dependence" on China (Summers 2022b).

Second, there has been a growing political focus on science and research collaborations. This has particularly been targeted at scientific (STEM) areas where it is argued that there may be dual civil and military uses for research. For example, prominent China commentator Charles Parton wrote in *The Times* in February 2022 that UK scientists were "working closely with Chinese scientists from institutes intimately associated with weapons development," such as in railguns, cryptography and helicopter technology (Parton 2022). The way this is written insinuates that the joint research was related to weapons development, though it is not clear that this was the case. A subsequent report by Civitas (Clark 2022) claimed to have found "at least 60 Chinese nationals employed at universities" who have had "connections" with "PLA-linked universities." This phrase also disguises significant ambiguity, as the list of such universities—drawn up by the controversial Australian Strategic Policy Institute—lumps together all sorts of Chinese institutions whose work covers all areas of academia. Other examples of media stories show problems with the ways that these collaborations have been presented. In some cases, the government has since intervened to stop research collaborations, such as the July 2022 Order to University of Manchester and Beijing Infinite Vision Tech Company Ltd, which had a licence agreement to use IP related to vision sensing technology (Department for Business, Energy and Industrial Strategy 2022). Talk emerged of greater government monitoring and tighter visa regimes, as well as new requirements to declare research collaborations above a relatively low threshold of £50000.

Meanwhile, other universities have been criticised for offering training to Chinese officials. In an earlier period, this would have been seen as an opportunity for the UK to influence Chinese thinking, and an expression of British soft power. However, in the new securitised environment, these are turned around in public discourse to become apparent examples of Chinese infiltration or influence on British institutions. A notable case has been criticism of Jesus College, Cambridge (*The Spectator* 2022), while other reports have targeted Cambridge for its research collaborations with Chinese partners, in a way that is highly problematic (see Summers 2021b for a rebuttal). In the public debate, there has occasionally been more balanced commentary; for example, a recent report by RAND Europe (2022) for the British Embassy in Beijing recognised that the UK and Chinese research ecosystems have become increasingly integrated since the early 2000s, and set out possible good practices for knowledge sharing and risk mitigation whilst enabling connections.

Third, political discussions regarding Confucius Institutes in the UK have taken hold. As noted above, for a long time, there was little discussion of these; however, there has since been something of a coordinated campaign. A report by the Henry Jackson Society in September 2022 and a shorter note from the China Research Group (2022b) both argued that some practices of CIs were inappropriate—not just where these lobby groups have identified examples of non-educational activities, but, for example, suggesting that "Most scholars and academic associations tend to agree that CIs should not be involved in the core functions of a university—knowledge production and undergraduate teaching" (Henry Jackson Society 2022, 8).

This issue also featured in the 2022 political campaigns for the position of prime minister and the chair of the FAC. In a bid to close off a potentially weak flank against Liz Truss in the contest for Conservative Party leader in summer 2022, Rishi Sunak described China as a "threat" and promised to:

> ... involve MI5 with British businesses and universities to counter Chinese influence ... legislate the Higher Education Bill which would force universities to declare foreign funding partnerships above £50k ... review all UK–China partnerships relating to technology and military ... and ban Confucius Institutes ... (Beijing to Britain 2022a)

The issue also featured in the subsequent campaign to select a new chair of the FAC after Truss made Tom Tugendhat a government minister. Sam Hogg, the author of *Beijing to Britain*, commented in his briefing note on this contest that Alicia Kearns—who won the race—"is perhaps most renowned in UK–China circles for leading the successful Confucius Institutes campaign to the Higher Education Bill" (Beijing to Britain 2022b); Kearns has since said that the UK should look to Taiwan to provide Chinese language training as an alternative to Confucius Institutes or partners from mainland China. Interestingly, though, there has not been a clear consensus on how to handle Confucius Institutes among those who have lobbied for a more hawkish British approach to China, with Charles Parton, for example, suggesting they should be regulated more tightly, rather than banned.

The government has so far responded slowly to some of this pressure. Its main response has been the drafting of a new Higher Education Bill,[1] though this does not solely deal with China-related issues. Writing to the House of Lords Committee on International Relations and Defence in February 2022, Foreign, Commonwealth and Development Minister of State (i.e., equivalent to a deputy minister), Amanda Milling said:

---

1 The Bill may be accessed at: https://bills.parliament.uk/bills/2862.

The Government has made it clear that views can be expressed and challenged, but any improper attempts to limit freedom of speech or academic freedom, whatever their origin, will not be tolerated. All academics, students and visiting speakers must be empowered to challenge ideas and discuss controversial subjects without fear of negative repercussions. That is why we are strengthening protective measures through the Higher Education (Freedom of Speech) Bill, which will ensure that lawful freedom of speech is supported to the fullest extent by strengthening existing freedom of speech duties and directly addressing gaps within the existing law, including the current lack of clear enforcement routes.

In October 2022, in answer to a parliamentary question, a government minister said that the government was:

... committed to supporting UK businesses and academia to engage with China in a way that reflects the UK's values and takes account of national security concerns. The UK is a world-leading destination for international students and we have robust procedures in place to protect against any undue foreign influence. (Norman 2022)

Subsequently, a further parliamentary question in the House of Lords asked the government what steps it had taken to close Confucius Institutes following remarks by the newly-promoted Security Minister, Tom Tugendhat, that they "pose[d] a threat to civil liberties in many universities in the [UK]." At the time Tugendhat made those comments, it was not clear that they represented government policy, an impression confirmed by the ministerial response to the parliamentary question, which began with general points on the UK's policy towards China, and continued as follows:

The Higher Education (Freedom of Speech) Bill will require and empower registered higher education (HE) providers in England to push back on freedom of speech related threats from overseas. It will also require the Office for Students (OfS) to monitor the overseas funding of registered HE providers and their constituent institutions, in order to assess the extent to which it presents a risk to freedom of speech and academic freedom in HE. This includes the reporting of educational or commercial partnerships, and therefore includes arrangements with Confucius Institutes. The Bill will allow the OfS to take appropriate action, including issuing penalties, if there is evidence that an HE provider has breached its freedom of speech duties.

Like all similar bodies, Confucius Institutes should operate transparently and with a full commitment to our values of openness and freedom of expression. Universities have a responsibility to ensure that any partnership with a Confucius Institute is managed appropriately, and the right due diligence is in place. The department would encourage any providers with concerns to contact the government. (Barran 2022)

In other words, as of early 2023, it appears as though Confucius Institutes will continue to operate, albeit with a greater degree of scrutiny regarding their operations and wider academic and research partnerships with China, and reduced government support (see also *The Guardian* 2023b). However, this is a securitisation of this aspect of bilateral interactions, which are no longer seen simply as offering "win–win" mutual benefit.

Is China a Threat to the UK?

Overall, the concerns which emerged in the UK regarding education and research ties to China are based on a broader strategic assessment that China poses some sort of "threat" to the UK, rather than an opportunity. The question of whether China constitutes a threat to the UK appeared on the agenda in the summer 2022 contest between Liz Truss and Rishi Sunak for leadership of the governing Conservative Party and position of prime minister. Truss stated that, if selected, she would officially declare China a threat, though there was insufficient time in her short-lived premiership to determine whether she would have followed through. Sunak's campaign material implied that he would do the same, yet he ultimately described China as a "systemic competitor" and challenger once he had taken office. As noted above, the March 2023 "refresh" of the 2021 Integrated Review of Security, Defense, Development and Foreign Policy effectively treats China as a threat, though without saying so explicitly, describing it as "an epoch-defining and systemic challenge with implications for almost every area of government policy and the everyday lives of British people."

There is relatively little in the Integrated Review in terms of a justification for this framing, beyond the familiar (yet rather vague and rarely evidenced) phrase that China has become more "aggressive" overseas (in some cases, "aggressive" is replaced by "assertive," which has rather different connotations, though the two are often used interchangeably) and more "authoritarian" at home. I have addressed some of the problems with such language elsewhere (Summers 2020). Beyond the Integrated Review, there is limited public analysis which addresses directly whether China is a threat to the UK. Increasingly, many in parliament and the media appear to assume it is without offering supporting arguments or evidence. US rhetoric regarding "threats" from China is echoed frequently, and the media paints a consistently negative picture of China, though these do not themselves make China a threat to the UK.

One recent attempt to argue that China is a "threat" comes in a pair of short reports by Charles Parton, published by a relatively new think tank, the Council on Geostrategy, in March 2023, shortly after the "refresh" appeared (Parton 2023a, 2023b). Parton's conclusion is clear: "The PRC *is* a threat." (Parton 2023a, 1) However, he comments that the government should avoid *calling* China a threat in order to be able to cooperate when needed. A critical examination of Parton's arguments may contribute to discussion of whether China today is indeed a "threat" to the UK, an important question in evaluating the trends in academic and research relations between the two countries.

The first question one might ask is, "a threat to whom?" The argument in this section is that even on the basis of the evidence presented by Parton, China is clearly *not* a threat to the UK. Threats need to have objects to be meaningful, and whether deliberately or not, the vast majority of Parton's references are to the PRC (or sometimes the CCP) as a "threat" without specifying an object of that threat. At no point in either paper does Parton explicitly say that the PRC (rather than the CCP) is a threat "to the UK," though by starting his analysis with discussion of Sunak's position and the Integrated Review "refresh" he creates the impression that the threat from the PRC includes one to the UK. Parton comes closest to naming who might be threatened by China when he describes the CCP (rather than PRC) as a "systemic" threat "to free and open countries," with the following reasoning:

The realisation of the CCP's aims would undermine the three pillars upholding the democratic way of life: national security, including democratic and political institutions; long-term economic prosperity (ultimately indivisible from national security); and values. The CCP is also using data from free and open countries—the "new oil"—against them, while destroying the privacy of their citizens. (Parton 2023a, 2)

These initial statements by Parton are highly questionable. Taking the first of the "three pillars," in the absence of evidence, the idea that the CCP aims to undermine other countries' national security is a circular argument. If China is a threat to the UK, then the UK's national security would be challenged—by definition. This is just another way of saying the PRC is a threat, rather than an argument to support that assertion. Parton's second pillar of "long-term economic prosperity" may well be indivisible from national security, though this comment begs the question as to what Parton means by national security in the first place. However, the gap here is the failure to consider the possibility that China—or more specifically the UK's engagement with China in various ways—

might actually *enhance* the UK's long-term economic prosperity, rather than threaten it. For there to be a threat to "values," the third pillar, there would have to be some evidence that the Chinese government is trying to impose its values on the UK. On the contrary, China has made no effort to suggest that the UK should not be a democracy or that its political or social values should be altered in any way, and its stated position is that it does *not* seek to impose its values or political system on other countries. What it has done— and we return to this below—is to reject the idea that the West (including the UK) should impose its values on China. If there is a threat here, it is from the West to China, not the other way around.

The bulk of Parton's first report is structured around discussion of Chinese "hostility, intent and capability" (though the distinction between an attitude of "hostility" and the nature of "intent" is not made clear). Parton introduces these three ideas with an overview of his argument:

> Being a threat presupposes hostility, intent and capability (*sic*). Hostility to the US and its allies is the basic building block of the CCP's foreign relations. The intent is to replace the US as the world's preeminent power and to remould global governance, systems and values. Building the capability to do so is work in progress, but the methodology being employed is already clear. (Parton 2023a, 2)

These points are highly questionable. First, at least since the early 1970s, PRC foreign policy has *not* been based on hostility to the US or its allies, but on engagement. However, especially since around 2017, US administrations (both Trump and Biden) have adopted a policy towards China which could well be described as "hostile"—if anything, it is striking how Beijing's response has been reactive and delayed, even making concessions in order to try to avoid the relationship deteriorating, such as the "phase one" trade deal negotiated near the end of Trump's presidency, in which almost all the concessions were on the Chinese side. This is not to say that the blame lies entirely with Washington, but to suggest that to argue PRC policy is one of hostility without considering the historical trajectory of US policy towards China is at best highly deficient analysis. From a British perspective, it should be noted that Beijing has not adopted the same policy towards London as towards Washington. Compare, for example, the Chinese readouts or commentaries on Chinese diplomats' discussions with American or British counterparts. It is clear that Beijing seeks to differentiate its policies (partly to encourage London and other European governments not to follow Washington), in the process not engaging in a policy of hostility to the UK, though this is a difficult balancing act for the Chinese government.

In further discussion of Chinese "hostility and struggle," Parton goes on to cite the discussion of "cooperation and conflict," yet only draws conclusions from the "conflict" part of this statement (Parton 2023a, 2–3). He cites "Document No. 9," which is not a statement of a hostile foreign policy towards the West but a reflection of a desire to prevent "Western anti-China forces" from "splitting" China or inducing "colour revolution." Chinese fears of this may or may not be overstated (they are not unreasonable given the anti-China rhetoric from Washington), however, if there is hostility involved here it is from the West towards China. Beijing is in defensive mode, not proactively pushing a hostile foreign policy. Parton continues by citing what he calls "obvious examples" of hostility, including China's actions in the South China Sea, against Taiwan, and "bullying" smaller countries such as Australia or Lithuania. Once again, though, there is no awareness of the relational dynamic at play, from US warships sailing through the South China Sea to American politicians departing from the US's long-standing Taiwan policy. Moreover, none of these examples constitute a foreign policy which threatens the UK.

Parton begins his discussion of Chinese "intent" with a standard statement of the Chinese centenary goal for 2049, that China should become a "strong, democratic, civilised, harmonious, and modern socialist country" (Parton 2023a, 4). It is most natural to interpret this as being a statement regarding the nature of Chinese society, an improved life for Chinese people, economic prosperity, and peaceful external relations. Yet without explaining why or how, Parton adopts the Orientalist mantel of interpreter of what he calls "partyspeak" into "plain English," suggesting that what this goal really represents is a desire to "become the top superpower," following which "the US will be pushed into second position, and global governance, systems and values will be so ordered as better to suit CCP interests" (Parton 2023a, 4).

To try to adduce further evidence for this, Parton cites a number of official Chinese references to the need to "struggle" with the US. Yet there is no reason why such a "struggle" must be interpreted as a Chinese desire for dominance. In fact, as commented above, given the hostile turn in US policy towards China, struggle is being brought to China. A defensive struggle for survival does not mean a desire to be global hegemon or to threaten the UK. Nor would such a policy be a rational one (Kirshner 2010). In the absence of evidence, it is misleading to assume Chinese intentions are simply malign, especially when Chinese statements point to a different conclusion.

Parton's arguments that Chinese capability constitutes a threat are more detailed, and he includes short discussions of military, economic, propaganda and united front, global governance, science and technology, and data capabilities. However, the evidence he cites actually suggests serious limitations to Chinese capabilities, and is more consistent with an argument that China is *not* a threat than with an argument that it is a threat.

This is clear from the discussion of China's military capability. Parton says China is "not yet a fearsome force" nor "logistically capable of projecting meaningful military power beyond its immediate region" (Parton 2023a, 6). That will require "at least a decade" (during which one assumes other countries will not stand still) and be dependent on continued economic growth, about which Parton is doubtful. He himself describes the Chinese military as possessing "more bark than bite," and while its capabilities are clearly increasing, there is nothing here to suggest that China's military is targeted at the UK or constitutes a threat to it; neither is any evidence presented of Chinese intent to use military force against the UK. There is a more complex debate regarding whether China's military poses a threat to US dominance in the Indo-Pacific, though from Parton's "bark-bite" comment, it seems he may well be doubtful of that too.

Regarding the economy, Parton says that "neither the benefits nor the downsides [of Chinese economic sticks and carrots] are as great as the CCP tries to promote" and that "those who end up in the diplomatic doghouse" do not "suffer to any great degree" (Parton 2023a, 7). On the basis of these points, it is hard to see where any meaningful threat to the UK might lie. And as noted above, Parton does not even begin to discuss whether China's large and increasingly sophisticated economy might actually offer opportunities to the UK, rather than threats.

Neither is there any evidence that Chinese "foreign propaganda" constitutes a threat. Parton says that the Chinese authorities have made much effort, yet "for many developed countries the propaganda is not persuasive" and "CCP attempts to sell its line do not convince" (Parton 2023a, 8). Presumably Parton realises that this includes the UK, where the trend is actually the opposite—thanks partly to Parton and other lobbyists, negative and critical views of China have strengthened over recent years to the point where it is hard to find anything positive concerning China in the mainstream British media (Summers et al. 2022). It is a similar story with the united front, which Parton has long argued lies behind CCP efforts to "interfere" in the UK. However, while he cites efforts to "control the narrative," he gives no evidence of success in the UK. Again, this cannot seriously be taken as a threat to the UK, unless British political institutions are so flimsy that they will collapse at the merest hint of Chinese wooing.

In relation to global governance, Parton argues that Chinese goals are to "align international organisations with its interests and values" (Parton 2023a, 9). China would not be alone in this, and if it is to be sustainable, global governance and its institutions should reflect more than one voice and more than one set of interests and values. The issue here does not really concern China, but the diminishing global influence of the West in persuading others that institutions historically set up on the basis of Western power are fit for purpose in a twenty-first century where the global distribution of power is changing rapidly.

Parton's next two points relate to science and technology and link back to the earlier part of this chapter. It is certainly the case that Chinese goals are ambitious, and—as with other countries or global corporations—both fair and foul means may well be used. Yet is this a threat to the UK, which prides itself on being a global leader in some aspects of research, innovation and science? I suggest that the problem for the UK comes not from increased capability elsewhere, including China, but from cutting itself off from the best work done elsewhere—the best research and innovation is based on global networks—or allowing its own institutions to wither. As with economic areas, there is plenty of potential here for the UK to strengthen its own capabilities by cooperating with those elsewhere, including in China. Parton then discusses "data and dependencies," where it is certainly the case that Chinese companies are disrupting and challenging American or European dominance (mainly American, though the issue of 5G was an exception to this). The response from the US, and increasingly from the UK, is to shut those companies out of their markets and protect their own or other Western industries (as it happens, American companies in particular stand to benefit from this). In the short term, Chinese companies are suffering most, as American policy sometimes threatens their ability to survive.[1] There is no obvious threat to the UK here, unless the furtherance of American corporate interests is itself assumed to be a net negative for the UK.

In conclusion, although Parton argues that the PRC *is* a threat, this is not even borne out by the evidence he himself adduces, which suggests that China is not a military, economic, propaganda, or technological threat to the UK. Might things change? Here Parton appears to be conflicted—he states that the "threat is likely to be even greater by 2049," yet also that we are now seeing "plateau China" (Parton 2023a, 11). Reflecting a typical feature of

---

1   In his discussion of this issue, Parton makes a point which will probably play well politically yet reflects an odd understanding of China. He says that "As anyone with experience in the PRC knows, if the CCP says 'jump,' the only answer is 'how high?'" I would argue that plenty of people with experience in the PRC will disagree with this, and there is extensive academic literature which says something quite different, highlighting the major and long-term challenges the central authorities have had with policy implementation in China. A pithy Chinese saying sums up the reality rather well: 上有政策 下有对策 ("policies from the top are met by counter-measures from below"; author's translation).

current Western debates concerning China, Parton cannot make up his mind whether China is going to grow more powerful or wither. Either way, his claim that the PRC *is* a threat is not backed up by evidence.

An Alternative Approach to Education and Research Ties

What does all this amount to? If China is not a threat to the UK, then we should reevaluate recent discussions regarding academic ties. Rather than a response to an objective "threat assessment," the securitising of these ties should be seen as a political move which is a response to political pressure (from the US and within British politics) to reduce engagement with China as part of an effort to restrict China's development space, or a result of fear that the UK will not be able to control its engagement with China.

Earlier arguments that both the UK and China benefited from research and academic ties still hold given the nature of research and innovation. A shift to a less open approach from the UK will help neither China nor the UK. The best research and innovation is globally networked, done through transnational partnerships which tap into global expertise and expertise, wherever it is found (Kwok et al. 2018). A shift in British policy will have costs for both the UK itself and global issues where international cooperation is beneficial. The critics of engagement will argue that there are costs to working with China, as we have seen. At the very least, though, a serious cost-benefit analysis—rather than political posturing—should accompany policy recommendations to close off avenues for collaboration.

That cost-benefit analysis should be fundamentally altered by the realisation that many of the arguments that China constitutes a threat are built on very shaky foundations. For the UK, to say China is not a threat is not to say there are no risks in individual cases. For example, intellectual property should be protected when dealing with China in the same way that it would with other research collaborations. Yet this suggests a case-by-case approach to managing risk, not blanket policies which stigmatise any interaction with Chinese institutions.

Other aspects of UK education policy may require examination too. As Ivan Franceschini and Nicholas Loubere (2022) have argued in their stimulating recent book, *Global China as Method*, many of the concerns regarding Western universities' relations with China may primarily be a consequence of the "neoliberal" university model, by which universities rely on fee income and research partnerships as state funding is reduced. It certainly seems that if politicians or the government want to have less international involvement in the UK university sector, they will have to pay for it. They will also have to absorb the wider costs of reducing institutional autonomy and access to the best global research. While, clearly, potential risks to national security should be managed, retaining institutional autonomy and access to the best global research are also essential to the UK's globally competitive university sector and broader economic success.

A rebalance in the debate regarding education ties with China would help to achieve that objective. Alternatives do exist. Perhaps there is also a role for the humanities, which explore aspects of China which are less politically sensitive in the UK. In that context, the UK–China Humanities Alliance is more important than ever.

(Acknowledgement: An earlier version of this paper was presented at a panel on "Universities in a post-pandemic world" at the UK-China Humanities Alliance annual conference, hosted online by Fudan University in December 2022. I am grateful to participants in that conference for their feedback and comments. I am also grateful to Zhang Chong for research assistance on trends in Chinese student numbers in the UK. This article is a revision of the author's speech at the 2022 UKCHA Annual Forum.)

References

Ahmad, Lord. 2022. "Ministerial Response to Parliamentary Question in the House of Lords UIN HL4192, Tabled on 9 Dec. 2022." Available at: https://questions-statements.parliament.uk/written-questions/detail/2022-12-09/HL4192. [Accessed April 25, 2023]

Barran, Baroness. 2022. "Ministerial Response to Parliamentary Question in the House of Lords UIN HL4955, Tabled on

23 Jan. 2023." Available at: https://questions-statements.parliament.uk/written-questions/detail/2023-01-23/HL4955. [Accessed April 25, 2023]

Beijing to Britain. 2022a. "Rishi Sunak's China Strategy." Available at: https://beijingtobritain.substack.com/p/new-rishi-sunaks-china-strategy. [Accessed April 25, 2023]

——. 2022b. "Parliament's Critical Leadership Race." Available at: https://beijingtobritain.substack.com/p/parliaments-critical-leadership-race. [Accessed April 25, 2023]

——. 2023. "Integrated Review Refresh and AUKUS Reaction." Available at: https://beijingtobritain.substack.com/p/integrated-review-refresh-and-aukus. [Accessed April 25, 2023]

Kothia, K. 2021. "Chinese Applicants Overtake EU as Brexit Raises U.K. Student Fees." Bloomberg, Aug 3. Available at: https://www.bloomberg.com/news/articles/2021-08-03/china-ousts-eu-as-brexit-sparks-fee-changes-at-u-k-universities#xj4y7vzkg. [Accessed April 25, 2023]

Brown, S. A. W. 2018. *Power, Perception and Foreign Policy Making*. London and New York: Routledge.

China–Britain Business Council. 2021. *UK Jobs Dependent on Links to China*. Available at: https://www.camecon.com/wp-content/uploads/2021/06/CBBC-Phase-2.pdf. [Accessed April 25, 2023]

China Research Group. 2020. "UK and China Relations: Higher Education." Online webinar panel discussion, posted October 27. Available at: https://youtu.be/6dQYTe8wERw. [Accessed April 25, 2023]

——. 2022a. *Explainer: United Front in the UK*. Available at: https://chinaresearchgroup.org/research/explainer-united-front-1. [Accessed April 25, 2023]

——. 2022b. *Confucius Institutes in the UK*. Available at: https://chinaresearchgroup.org/research/confucius-institutes-in-the-uk. [Accessed April 25, 2023]

Clark, R. 2022. *Inadvertently Arming China? One Year On: The Chinese Military Complex and its Exploitation of Scientific Research at UK Universities*. Civitas. Available at: https://www.civitas.org.uk/content/files/One-Year-On-FINAL.pdf. [Accessed April 25, 2023]

Cleverly, J. 2023. "Our Position on China: Foreign Secretary's 2023 Mansion House Speech." Available at: https://www.gov.uk/government/speeches/our-position-on-china-speech-by-the-foreign-secretary. [Accessed April 27, 2023]

Department for Business, Energy and Industrial Strategy. 2022. "Acquisition of Know-How Related to SCAMP-5 and SCAMP-7 Vision Sensing Technology: Notices of Final Order and Variation of Final Order." Available at: https://www.gov.uk/government/publications/acquisition-of-know-how-related-to-scamp-5-and-scamp-7-vision-sensing-technology-notice-of-final-order. [Accessed April 25, 2023]

Doherty, L. 2022. "Ministerial Response to Parliamentary Question in the House of Commons UIN 71124, Tabled on 25 Oct. 2022." Available at: https://questions-statements.parliament.uk/written-questions/detail/2022-10-25/71124. [Accessed April 25, 2023]

Erudera College News. 2021. "216,000 Chinese Students Choose UK for Higher Education Due to Visa Restrictions in US."
   May 21. Available at: https://erudera.com/news/216000-chinese-students-choose-uk-for-higher-education-due-to-visa-
   restrictions-in-us/. [Accessed April 25, 2023]

Financial Times. 2023. "UK Universities Target Overseas Students From Outside China." Jan 19. Available at: https://www.
   ft.com/content/84f3ecaf-00e9-4961-991c-4f4ca23d8d8d.

Foreign Affairs Committee. 2019. "A Cautious Embrace: Defending Democracy in an Age of Autocracies." Available at:
   https://publications.parliament.uk/pa/cm201919/cmselect/cmfaff/109/109.pdf. [Accessed April 25, 2023]

——. 2022. "Refreshing Our Approach? Updating the Integrated Review." Available at: https://publications.parliament.uk/pa/
   cm5803/cmselect/cmfaff/882/report.html. [Accessed April 25, 2023]

Franceschini, I. and Loubere, N. 2022. *Global China as Method*. Cambridge: Cambridge University Press.

The Guardian. 2023a. "UK Should Not 'Pull the Shutters Down' on China, Says James Cleverly." April 18. Available at:
   https://www.theguardian.com/politics/2023/apr/18/uk-should-not-pull-the-shutters-down-on-china-says-james-cleverly.
   [Accessed April 25, 2023]

——. 2023b. "UK Expected to Stop Funding Chinese State-Linked Mandarin Teaching Schools." April 24. Available at:
   https://www.theguardian.com/world/2023/apr/24/uk-stop-funding-chinese-confucius-institute-mandarin-teaching-schools.
   [Accessed April 25, 2023]

Henry Jackson Society. 2022. *An Investigation of China's Confucius Institutes in the UK*. By Sam Dunning and Anson Kwong.
   Available at: https://henryjacksonsociety.org/publications/an-investigation-of-chinas-confucius-institutes-in-the-uk/.
   [Accessed April 25, 2023]

HM Government. 2017. *UK–China Joint Strategy for Science, Technology and Innovation Cooperation*. Available at: https://
   assets.publishing.service.gov.uk/government/uploads/system/uploads/attachment_data/file/665199/uk-china-strategy-
   science-technology-innovation-cooperation.pdf. [Accessed April 25, 2023]

——. 2021. *Global Britain in a Competitive Age, the Integrated Review of Security, Defence, Development and Foreign Policy*.
   Available at: https://www.gov.uk/government/collections/the-integrated-review-2021. [Accessed April 25, 2023]

——. 2023. *Integrated Review Refresh 2023: Responding to a More Contested and Volatile World*. Available at: https://www.
   gov.uk/government/publications/integrated-review-refresh-2023-responding-to-a-more-contested-and-volatile-world.
   [Accessed April 25, 2023]

Johnston, A.I. 2019. "The Failures of the 'Failure of Engagement' with China." *The Washington Quarterly* 42(2): 99–114.

Kirshner, J. 2010. "The Tragedy of Offensive Realism: Classical Realism and the Rise of China." *European Journal of
   International Relations* 18(1): 53–75.

Kwok, K. C., Lau, L. J. and Summers, T. 2018. *EU-China Innovation Relations: From Zero Sum to Global Networks*. Chatham
   House Research Paper. Available at: https://www.chathamhouse.org/sites/default/files/publications/research/2018-05-25-

eu-china-innovation-relations-summers-kwok-lau.pdf. [Accessed April 25, 2023]

Loft, P. and Brien, P. 2023. *UK Aid and China. House of Commons Library Research Briefing No. 9762.* Available at: https://commonslibrary.parliament.uk/research-briefings/cbp-9762/. [Accessed 25 April 2023]

Mervis, J. 2023. "Pall of Suspicion." *Science.* Available at: https://www.science.org/content/article/pall-suspicion-nihs-secretive-china-initiative-destroyed-scores-academic-careers. [Accessed April 25, 2023]

Milling, A. 2022. Letter to Rt Hon Baroness Anelay of St Johns, posted on Twitter by Beijing to Britain.

Norman, J. 2022. "China: Higher Education. Ministerial Response to Parliamentary Question UIN 62024, Tabled on 12 Oct. 2022." Available at: https://questions-statements.parliament.uk/written-questions/detail/2022-10-12/62024. [Accessed April 25, 2023]

Parker, C. and Ellery, B. 2021. "Students Tell Exeter to Cut Ties with Chinese University." *The Times*, Nov 16. Available at: https://www.thetimes.co.uk/article/students-tell-exeter-to-cut-ties-with-chinese-university-q2j5zj0nq. [Accessed April 25, 2023]

Parton, C. 2022. "Is Getting into Bed with President Xi for Science … or Just Sleazy?" *The Times*, Feb 5.

——. 2023a. *Is China a Threat?* Council on Geostrategy, Explainer GPE13. Available at: https://www.geostrategy.org.uk/research/is-china-a-threat/. [Accessed April 25, 2023]

——. 2023b. *The "10 Be Clears": Clarifying Relations with China.* Council on Geostrategy, Primer GPP04. Available at: https://www.geostrategy.org.uk/research/the-10-be-clears-clarifying-relations-with-china/. [Accessed April 25, 2023]

Pence, M. 2018. "Vice President Mike Pence's Remarks on the Administration's Policy Towards China." Available at: https://www.hudson.org/events/1610-vice-president-mike-pence-s-remarks-on-the-administration-s-policy-towards-china102018. [Accessed April 25, 2023]

RAND Europe. 2022. "Exploring the Opportunities and Challenges of Research Engagement with China." *Research Brief.*

Reeves, J. 2014. "Structural Power, the Copenhagen School and Threats to Chinese Security." *The China Quarterly* 217: 140–161.

The Spectator. 2022. "The CCP Training Programme at the Heart of Cambridge." Feb 5.

Summers, T. 2017. *Brexit: Implications for EU-China Relations.* Chatham House research paper. Available at: https://www.chathamhouse.org/sites/default/files/publications/research/2017-05-11-brexit-eu-china-summers-final.pdf. [Accessed April 25, 2023]

——. 2020. "Why the UK Needs to Work with China." Working paper. Available at: https://www.researchgate.net/publication/341732404_Why_the_UK_needs_to_work_with_China_policy_working_paper. [Accessed April 25, 2023]

——. 2021a. "Imagining Brexit: The UK's China Policy after the Referendum." In *A New Beginning or More of the Same: The European Union and East Asia after Brexit*, edited by Michael Reilly and Chun-yi Lee, 101–134. Singapore: Palgrave Macmillan.

——. 2021b. "Did China Buy Cambridge?" *Pearls and Irritations*, July 16. Available at: https://johnmenadue.com/did-china-buy-cambridge/. [Accessed April 25, 2023]

——. 2022a. "Britain and Hong Kong: The 2019 Protests and their Aftermath." *Asian Education and Development Studies* 11(2): 276–286.

——. 2022b. "UK: Vulnerability or Politics? 'Strategic Dependence' and the China Debate." In *Dependence in Europe's Relations with China: Weighing Perceptions and Reality*, European Think-Tank Network on China. Available at: etnc.info.

——. 2023. "The UK's Approach to China." In *From a China strategy to no strategy at all: Exploring the diversity of European approaches*, European think-tank network on China. Available at: etnc.info.

Summers, T., Chan, H. M., Gries, P. and Turcsanyi, R. 2022. "Worsening British Views of China in 2020: Evidence from Public Opinion, Parliament and the Media." *Asia Europe Journal* 20: 173–194.

UK Research and Innovation. 2019. Twitter feed, Nov 22. 2019. Available at: https://twitter.com/UKRI_China/status/119775355 58004690944?s=20. [Accessed April 25, 2023]

UK Science and Innovation Network. 2018. *China Country Snapshot*. Available at: https://assets.publishing.service.gov.uk/government/uploads/system/uploads/attachment_data/file/757150/China_Snapshot_2018.pdf. [Accessed April 25, 2023]

Yeomans, E. 2022. "Beware China 'Catastrophe,' UK University Campuses Told." *The Times*, July 11. Available at: https://www.thetimes.co.uk/article/beware-china-catastrophe-uk-university-campuses-told-szcfv90gc#:~:text=British%20universities%20must%20prepare%20for,an%20education%20leader%20has%20warned. [Accessed April 25, 2023]

Zweig, D. and Kang, S. 2020. *America Challenges China's National Talent Programmes*. CSIS Report. Available at: https://www.csis.org/analysis/america-challenges-chinas-national-talent-programs. [Accessed April 25, 2023]

新时代发展区域国别研究学科的意义

——以上海外国语大学为例

———————

李岩松[*]

女士们、先生们、朋友们：

　　大家好！十二月的香港，依然温暖宜人。非常高兴来到这次"中英高等教育人文联盟峰会"，与来自中英高校的专家学者们在人文学术和教育领域开展跨文化、跨民族的对话交流。接下来，我将以上海外国语大学为例，与各位分享新时代发展区域国别研究这一学科的重要意义。

　　区域国别研究，是针对特定国家或者区域的人文、地理、政治、经济、社会、军事等进行的全面深入研究。了解外部世界一直是中国历史发展的重要的组成部分，而在新中国成立之后，我们也曾对以苏联及相关地区为代表的国家、地区，展开过较为深入的研究。改革开放之后，中国的外国研究范围更广，也更重视对美、欧、日等国家的研究。可以说，区域国别研究一直深受时代和环境影响，而这一特点随着我国经济与社会的迅速发展而表现得更加突出，也更加迫切地召唤着我们的学者"扎根中国大地"，在深入了解中国自身的同时，积极地去认识和研究世界。可以说，在新时代背景下，更深入、准确地理解世界，意义重大。服务城市建设与国家发展，服务构建人类命运共同体，是国别和区域研究在新时代的核心任务。

*　李岩松：上海外国语大学党委副书记、校长。研究领域为高等教育管理、国际政治与国际组织等。

为更好地承载这一使命，上海外国语大学确立了建成国别区域全球知识领域特色鲜明的世界一流外国语大学的发展目标，深化学科建设、加强人才培养，为打造人类命运共同体贡献上外力量。

一、以建成国别区域全球知识领域特色鲜明的世界一流外国语大学为愿景，为全球知识体系建构提供中国视角

上海外国语大学创建于1949年12月，是一所与新中国同龄的、以外语教育与国际研究为特色的中国重点大学。从成立初期的华东人民革命大学附设上海俄文学校，到多语种多学科的上海外国语学院，再到现在向国际化高水平大学迈进的上海外国语大学，上外 的成长一直与中国与世界的发展息息相关。迈入新时代，上外秉承"格高志远、学贯中外"的校训精神，以"服务国家发展、服务人的全面成长、服务社会进步、服务中外人文交流"为办学使命，致力于建成国别区域全球知识领域特色鲜明的世界一流外国语大学。

Interpret the World, Translate the Future——诠释世界、成就未来。在这一办学理念的指引下，上海外国语大学立足多语种、跨学科、跨文化的综合优势，不断传承和彰显外国语言文学的传统特色，汇聚中外高端研究团队，协同创新打造高校学术智库群，致力在语言文学、国际关系和国别区域研究领域打造"上外品牌"。近年来，学校积极对接国家人文交流和"一带一路"战略，以"多语种+"卓越国际化人才培养、构建多语种全球知识体系和区域国别研究为特色的新型智库为导向，搭建高水平国际合作平台，深化、创新与"一带一路"与沿线国家的教育合作与人文交流，促进对沿线国家和地区历史、哲学、政治、经济、文化等各方面的研究，从而为全球知识体系和话语体系的构建提供独特的中国视角，成为全球治理中国方案的重要思想依据，为世界发展和地区繁荣做出应有的贡献。

二、以构建国际学术共同体为特色，
打造政产学研用紧密结合的知识聚合

面对全新的世界，中国政府倡导人类命运共同体的理念，提出了解决世界问题的中国策略与中国方案。发展国别区域研究学科，既能让中国更深入地了解世界，也能让世界更深入地了解中国，大大有利于"一带一路"建设和全球治理的开放发展大局。因此，上外大力推进"战略语言"建设，为国家和地方发展提供最急需的关键人才储备。同时，学校建有70余个研究机构和学术团体，以语言政策规划、国际外交战略、涉外舆情研究为核心，构建成果应用渠道，为国家部委和地方政府制订和实施相关政策提供智力支持。

1. 成立上海全球治理与区域国别研究院

2018年9月，在教育部和上海市人民政府支持下，学校充分发挥区域国别研究综合优势，成立上海全球治理与区域国别研究院。研究院以"立足本土，放眼全球"（Global at Home）为建设理念，着力打造全球治理与区域国别研究高端智库，建设高端人才培养储备基地与国际研究大数据中心，是一所集"资政、咨商、启民、育人"多功能为一体的国内、国际学术共同体。就在一周前，"2018联通世界与未来"国际研讨会刚刚召开，包括吉尔吉斯斯坦前总理卓奥玛尔特·奥托尔巴耶夫、尼泊尔前总理马达夫·库马尔·内帕尔、联合国教科文组织前总干事伊琳娜·博科娃在内的来自全球各地七十多位知名政要和学者围绕"转折中的世界与全球秩序""一带一路倡议与沿线各国""中国特色大国外交与新型国际关系""全球治理与人类命运共同体"等重要议题展开探讨。2017年，研究院已被列入"上海服务国家'一带一路'建设，发挥桥头堡作用行动方案"专项行动。未来，研究院还将继续聚焦中国参与全球治理的重大理论问题与现实问题，服务上海卓越全球城市、"五个中心"和"四大品牌"建设战略与实际需求。

2. 建立中阿改革发展研究中心

为落实习主席访问阿盟成果，经中央领导批准，中阿改革发展研究中心于2017年4月正式成立，由外交部、教育部、上海市政府共同主办，上海外国语大学承办具体运营。截至2018年11月，中心已经成功举办了五期阿拉伯国家官员研修班，137名阿拉伯国家中高级官员、知名学者参与其中。研修班采用专家讲座、现场教学、参观考察等形式，围绕中国基本国情和治国理政新方略、中国政治制度与决策过程、中国经济改革与开发区建设、中国教育发展规划及改革实践、上海城市发展回顾与展望等专题展开研修。中心的设立对于推进中阿共建"一带一路"，增进中阿间的正向认知，促进中阿民心相通具有重要意义。

3. 推动国别区域研究一流智库建设

上海外国语大学努力推进区域国别研究平台网络建设，区域国别研究智库群已初具规模。目前，学校拥有教育部人文社会科学重点研究基地中东研究所、外交部共建基地中日韩合作研究中心、教育部国际合作与交流司区域与国别研究培育基地、教育部教育管理信息中心共建教育信息化国际比较研究中心、上海高校人文社会科学重点研究基地G20研究中心、上海市社会科学创新研究基地"中外文化软实力比较研究中心"等多个国际科研合作平台，以及10多个校级国别区域研究中心。学校中东研究智库入选"中国智库综合评价核心智库榜单"，在国家信息中心发布的《"一带一路"大数据报告2018》中位列第五，丝路战略研究所智库则在《中国高校"一带一路"智库2018年度影响力报告》中位居全国第四。

三、以语言互通和民心相通为重点，
培养"多语种+"卓越国际化人才

语言互通是实现民心相通的首要条件。在《上海外国语大学本科人才培养发展规划（2016—2020）》中，学校提出大力发展非通用语种专业，重点增设服务

"一带一路"倡议和社会经济发展急需的非通用语种专业。近三年，学校成立了俄罗斯东欧与中亚学院，新开设了匈牙利语、波兰语等"一带一路"沿线国家非通用语种专业，陆续开设了乌尔都语等多门非通用语种课程，并邀请校内专家教授联合开设了《中东国别史》等国别区域研究入门课程，积极探索有上外特色的战略性语言人才培养模式培养后备人才。

2015年，上海外国语大学卓越学院正式成立，创新"多语种+"人才培养模式，开展荣誉教育，设立"多语种高级翻译人才实验班""多语种国别区域人才实验班""多语种国际组织人才实验班""多语种外交外事人才实验班"等拔尖创新人才实验班。2018年起，学校又设立了"欧亚文明研究特色研究生班"，开设"全球文明史研究""文明互鉴与融通""欧洲一体化研究""区域国别研究方法"等方向，加强全球治理与区域国别研究研究生的跨校培养。

上外高级翻译学院是国际高校翻译学院联合会（CIUTI）亚太工作组所在地，英汉语对排名全球第一。近年来，学院积极开拓国际组织人才培养新模式、新渠道，获得国家留学基金委、上海市教委等多个立项，共派出84人次至联合国、欧盟等国际组织实习。学校还派出师生赴纽约联合国总部旁听联合国秘书长发言人每日简报新闻发布会，进行实地参访。

此外，学校主动对接国家人文交流机制，积极参与人文交流活动，大力推动中外青年外事外交，促进国际理解与民心相通。青年学子参与中国—中东欧青年研修交流营、中国—中东欧青年学者论坛等活动，组织"一带一路青年观察团"赴哈萨克斯坦、乌兹别克斯坦、波兰、匈牙利开展田野调查。2019年上半年，"上海外国语大学全球重大事件多语种全媒体报道团"将来到阿根廷，对G20峰会以及阿根廷的政治、经济、文化和社会等方面进行实地观察、采访和报道。

当今世界正在发生极为深刻而又根本的变化，政治多级化、经济全球化、社会信息化、文化多元化日益明显。世界向何处去？未来从何处来？符合各国利益的全球政治发展模式与经济治理模式究竟应该是怎样的？这是当今世界无法回避的理论问题，更是一个迫在眉睫的实践问题。因此，积极深入开展区域国别研究，有助于丰富相关国家的细节认知和全面认识，更有针对性地开展人文交流和公共外交，掌握国际交往枢纽的发展动向，为全球治理和合作共赢的新型国际关系贡献力量。

面对日益变化的世界，我们坚信，世界格局的变化中同样孕育着合理的变革与积极的希望。因此，上海外国语大学愿与国内外高校和科研机构携手同行，整合国际、国内优质资源，坚持协同创新、开放流动的发展理念，凝聚集体智慧，聚焦区域国别研究，构筑学术研究平台，服务国家发展，为打造人类命运共同体贡献上外力量。

（本文系作者在联盟2022年年度论坛上的发言）

编者后记

———

在各承办高校的努力下，中英高等教育人文联盟的每一次活动都相当精彩，成果丰硕。每次会后，大家都认为应当将讨论的成果出版面世。此项工作，最早由武汉大学的杨华教授承担，他于2022年6月编成了一个目录初稿。当时由于疫情影响，交流不畅，进展缓慢。2023年，该项工作迎来了加速度。在清华大学颜海平教授的推动下，上海交通大学的何伟文教授、中国社会科学院外国文学研究所的陈雷研究员、复旦大学的陶友兰教授、中国传媒大学的金海娜教授、英国埃克塞特大学的李利教授分别加入进来。

在清华大学燕勇老师的联络下，我们开设了一个微信群组，并与商务印书馆上海分馆的总编辑鲍静静和编辑张鹏两位形成了良性互动。在这个微信群中，我们几乎每周都在讨论出版流程中遇到的各种细节。大家共同筛选稿件，分头约稿和审稿，进展相当顺利。在这个过程中，商务印书馆两位编辑的高效给人留下特别深刻的印象。

在此，我要特别感谢清华大学世界文学与文化研究院及埃克塞特大学的全力支持，感谢在历届论坛上发言的中方和英方学者，感谢本辑的各位作者。感谢颜海平教授和各位编辑的无私奉献，感谢商务印书馆编辑的辛勤工作。人文关怀、学术发展和中外交流，是中英人文学者共同的理念。在此共同理念之下，大家获得并分享共同的喜悦。

本辑的出版，只是中英人文学术交流活动的一个小结、一个纪念。唯愿我们的工作成果为今后各辑的出版开一个好头，祝愿中英人文交流事业永远蓬勃发展！

王淑英

中英高等教育人文联盟出版委员会

Postscript

With the relentless support from all of our participating universities, every event hosted by the UK–China Humanities Alliance has been incredibly impressive, filled with intellectual excitement and creative excellence. After each meeting, we all thought that we should publish the results of our discussions, which were full of vigorous exchange of ideas and insights. This task was first undertaken by Professor YANG Hua from Wuhan University, who compiled the table of contents in June 2022. Impacted by the pandemic, communication and progress were slowed during that period. Then the task gained momentum in 2023. It was further driven by the support of Professor YAN Haiping from Tsinghua University, and we have since welcomed Professor HE Weiwen from Shanghai Jiao Tong University, CHEN Lei, Research Fellow from the Institute of Foreign Literature, Chinese Academy of Social Sciences, Professor TAO Youlan from Fudan University, Professor JIN Haina from Communication University of China, and Professor LI Li from University of Exeter.

With the support and coordination of Mr. YAN Yong from Tsinghua University, we have created a WeChat group, and have had many cordial exchanges with editor-in-chief BAO Jingjing and editor ZHANG Peng from The Commercial Press (Shanghai). We discussed various details and possible elaborations encountered in the publication process in the WeChat group almost every week. We jointly screened the manuscripts, and assigned writing tasks and reviews, with great progress made. Their efficiency has indeed been remarkable.

I would also like to take this opportunity to express my deepest gratitude to the Institute for World Literatures and Cultures of Tsinghua University and Exeter University for their unwavering support, without which the publication endeavour would not have been as smooth. My great appreciation and admiration also go to all scholars from China and the UK who have spoken at the forums over the years, as well as all authors of the present collection. My heartfelt thanks to Professor YAN Haiping and each editor, for their selfless dedication, and to our two editors from The Commercial Press, for their excellent hard work. Care for the humanities, academic development, as well as cross-cultural and international exchange are common values shared by scholars from China and the UK alike. We all find and share in great joy under these shared values.

The publication of this volume represents a milestone to mark our commitment—let this accomplishment be the beginning of many more volumes to come, and of an ever-growing partnership between China and the UK, in our concerted collaboration to further the development of the humanities!

Wong Suk Ying

UK–China Humanities Alliance Publication Committee